STUDY GUIDE

COLLEGE PHYSICS 7TH EDITION

SEARS / ZEMANSKY / YOUNG

STUDY GUIDE

COLLEGE PHYSICS 7THEDITION

SEARS / ZEMANSKY / YOUNG

Barney Sandler
Daria Bouadana

New York Technical College of the City University of New York

Addison-Wesley Publishing Company
Reading, Massachusetts • Menlo Park, California • New York
Don Mills, Ontario • Wokingham, England • Amsterdam • Bonn
Sydney • Singapore • Tokyo • Madrid • San Juan

ISBN 0-201-51246-7

4 5 6 7 8 9 10 BA 959493

Preface

The purpose of the study guide is to make your studying more efficient. As you probably have noticed, the text contains a tremendous amount of valuable information. The study guide applies itself only to the basic facts, concepts, principles, and problem solving strategies. Furthermore, to make you aware of what you know and what you may only think you know, there are numerous self-tests in a programmed format. This type of format enables you to know instantly whether you have the right answer to a question or solution to a problem. Since not only the answers but also the solutions to the problems are presented, you can resolve your difficulties immediately before going any further. Also, this constant drill will be an invaluable asset in preparing you to take classroom examinations.

How should you use this study guide? After you have read a particular chapter in the text, go on to the study guide. The study guide follows the text chapter by chapter. In addition, the spiral approach is often used: A particular concept is repeated, and each time it is explained differently. Each chapter has the following sections:

1 Chapter Summary The organization of the chapter as well as the main areas covered are presented.

2 Basic Terms In this section the most important terms of the chapter are listed, but you must write out the definitions or meanings. To help you, the appropriate textbook section numbers are given in parentheses. For future reference, all the terms together with their definitions or meanings should be written in your notebook as a glossary of terms.

3 Programmed Quiz Here you have questions designed to measure how much information you have gleaned from reading the chapter. Remember, check each answer as you go along.

4 Main Ideas Various techniques and mathematical methods are explained in great detail in this section, especially those that are prerequisites for solving the problems.

5 Programmed Quiz The above concepts are tested. The goal is to be able to do each question/problem without looking at the answer until the end.

6 Step-by-Step Solutions of Problems Various problems are solved here including problems similar to the illustrative examples in the text as well as the ones in back of the chapter.

7 Programmed Test Since complete mastery of a topic means that you are able to solve the problems, the final test in each chapter is designed to measure your problem solving ability.

A note about the programmed quizzes and tests. All the answers are given next to each question/problem for immediate feedback. Try not to look at the answers before attempting the exercises. A convenient way of doing this is to cover the answer column with a narrow piece of paper, which you move downward from frame to frame as you complete the exercises. However, if you get stuck, look at the solution and try to determine what difficulty you are encountering. Then try to solve the exercise again. Remember, you have not mastered the material until you have answered each question and solved each problem completely by yourself — no peeking. At the end of each chapter ask yourself the following question: Am I familiar with the definitions, equations, units, fundamental principles, and the problem solving techniques associated with the chapter?

There have been many individuals who have helped us with the revision of this study guide. In particular we express our gratitude to our colleagues in the Physics and General Science Department, New York City Technical College, for their support and encouragement. We wish to thank Daniel Bouadana, Irene Czajkowskyj and Miriam Sandler for their cooperation and patience during the writing of the manuscript.

Contents

1 UNITS, PHYSICAL QUANTITIES, AND VECTORS   1

2 MOTION ALONG A STRAIGHT LINE   27

3 MOTION IN A PLANE   47

4 NEWTON'S LAWS OF MOTION   75

5 APPLICATIONS OF NEWTON'S LAWS—I   93

6 APPLICATIONS OF NEWTON'S LAWS—II   129

7 WORK AND ENERGY   155

8 IMPULSE AND MOMENTUM   175

9 ROTATIONAL MOTION   195

10 EQUILIBRIUM OF A RIGID BODY   213

11 PERIODIC MOTION   227

12 ELASTICITY   245

13 FLUID MECHANICS   259

14 TEMPERATURE AND EXPANSION   279

15 QUANTITY OF HEAT   289

16 HEAT TRANSFER   299

17 THERMAL PROPERTIES OF MATTER   307

18 THE FIRST LAW OF THERMODYNAMICS   319

19 THE SECOND LAW OF THERMODYNAMICS   335

20 MOLECULAR PROPERTIES OF MATTER   349

21 MECHANICAL WAVES   361

22 REFLECTIONS AND NORMAL MODES   369

23 SOUND   381

24 COULOMB'S LAW   395

25 THE ELECTRIC FIELD   409

26 ELECTRICAL POTENTIAL   429

27 CAPACITANCE AND DIELECTRICS   447

28 CURRENT, RESISTANCE AND ELECTROMOTIVE FORCE   463

29 DIRECT-CURRENT CIRCUITS   477

30 THE MAGNETIC FIELD AND MAGNETIC FORCES   495

31 SOURCES OF MAGNETIC FIELD   513

32 ELECTROMAGNETIC INDUCTION   533

33 INDUCTANCE   547

34 ALTERNATING CURRENTS   561

35 ELECTROMAGNETIC WAVES   579

36 THE NATURE AND PROPAGATION OF LIGHT   591

37 IMAGES FORMED BY A SINGLE SURFACE   613

38 LENSES AND OPTICAL INSTRUMENTS   629

39 INTERFERENCE AND DIFFRACTION   647

40 RELATIVISTIC MECHANICS   661

41 PROTONS, ELECTRONS, AND ATOMS   675

42 QUANTUM MECHANICS   687

43 ATOMS, MOLECULES, AND SOLIDS   701

44 NUCLEAR AND HIGH-ENERGY PHYSICS   713

1

Units, Physical Quantities, and Vectors

CHAPTER SUMMARY

Physics is a study based on observation and experience; therefore any physical theory can be validated by observing and measuring physical phenomena. The chapter includes a discussion of measurement, the Système Internationale (used predominantly in this text), fundamental quantities, units, significant figures, scientific notation, estimates, orders of magnitude and dimensional consistency. The main topic of the chapter, however, deals with physical quantities. Some quantities, such as displacement, force, and velocity, can be described by vectors. The mathematical method of vector addition by means of component vectors is presented.

BASIC TERMS — *Give definitions or meanings for the following:*

fundamental quantity (1-1)
model (1-2)
physical quantity (1-3)
unit (1-3)
Système Internationale (SI) (1-3)
meter (1-3)
kilogram (1-3)
second (1-3)
operational definition (1-3)
prefix (1-3)
factor-label method (1-3)
scientific notation (1-4)

dimensional consistency (1-4)
significant figures (1-5)
order of magnitude estimate (1-6)
vector sum (1-7)
magnitude (1-7)
direction (1-7)
scalar (1-7)
vector (1-7)
displacement (1-7)
resultant (1-7)
component vectors (1-8)
rectangular component vectors (1-8)

PROGRAMMED QUIZ

1 What are the three fundamental quantities in mechanics?

1 Length, mass, and time.

2 What are the fundamental quantities in other areas of physics?

2 Temperature, electric charge, and luminous intensity.

3 What are the units of length, mass, and time in the Système Internationale (SI)?

3 Length — meter
mass — kilogram
time — second

---

4 What are the meanings and abbreviations of the following prefixes?
- centi
- milli
- kilo
- micro
- mega
- nano

4

Prefix	Meaning	Abbreviation
centi	$0.01 = 10^{-2}$	c
milli	$0.001 = 10^{-3}$	m
kilo	$1000 = 10^{3}$	k
micro	$0.000001 = 10^{-6}$	μ
mega	$1,000,000 = 10^{6}$	M
nano	$0.000000001 = 10^{-9}$	n

---

5 A derived unit is formed by multiplying and/or dividing fundamental units. Give examples of the following:
- area
- volume
- density
- velocity

5

Area	m^2
Volume	m^3
Density	$kg \cdot m^{-3}$
Velocity	$m \cdot s^{-1}$

---

6 Express 479,000,000 in scientific notation.

6 4.79×10^8

---

7 If 1 in = 2.54 cm, compute the number of inches in 80.3 cm.

7

$$\left(80.3 \text{ cm} \right) \left(\frac{1 \text{ in}}{2.54 \text{ cm}} \right) = 31.6 \text{ in}$$

---

8 What is the volume of a sphere if its diameter is 0.614 m? In accordance with the convention of the text, what is the correct answer?

8

$$V = \frac{4}{3}\pi r^3 = \frac{\pi d^3}{6} = \frac{\pi(0.614 \text{ m})^3}{6}$$

$$= 0.1212003 \text{ m}^3 \text{ (by calculator)}$$
$$= 0.121 \text{ m}^3$$

(three significant figures)

---

9 Define a scalar and give an example.

9 A scalar is a quantity that has magnitude only; length, mass, time, speed.

---

10 Define a vector and give an example.

10 A vector is a quantity that has magnitude and direction; displacement, force, velocity.

---

11 What is the distinction between speed and velocity?

11 Speed is a scalar quantity (magnitude only). Velocity is a vector quantity (magnitude and direction).

---

12 A definition in terms of a procedure for measuring a defined quantity is called _____ .

12 An operational definition.

---

13 How many nanoseconds are there in 1 gigasecond?

$1 \text{ Gs} = 10^9 \text{ s}, 1 \text{ ns} = 10^{-9} \text{ s}$

13

$$1 \text{ Gs} = 10^9 \text{ s} \left(\frac{1 \text{ ns}}{10^{-9} \text{ s}} \right) = 10^{18} \text{ ns}.$$

---

14 In 1791, the meter was defined as 1/10,000,000th of a quadrant of the Earth's surface. Compute the polar diameter (km) of the Earth to three significant figures.

14 Since the circumference is equal to 4 × quadrant length, the circumference of the Earth is 40,000,000 m.

$$4 \times 10^7 \text{ m} = 4 \times 10^7 \text{ m} \left(\frac{1 \text{ km}}{10^3 \text{ m}} \right) = 4 \times 10^4 \text{ km}$$

Circumference $= \pi$ diameter

$$C = \pi d$$

$$d = \frac{4 \times 10^4 \text{ km}}{\pi} = 1.27 \times 10^4 \text{ km}$$

---

15 What is the percent error of the approximation $\pi = \sqrt{10}$?

15

$\sqrt{10} = 3.16$

% error

$$= \frac{|\text{experimental value} - \text{standard value}|}{\text{standard value}} \times 100$$

$$= \frac{|3.16 - 3.14|}{3.14} \times 100$$

$$= 0.6\%$$

---

16 How are vectors represented? Illustrate.

16 Vectors can be represented by arrows drawn to scale. Direction must be indicated.

1cm = 5 N

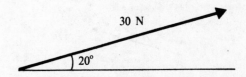

---

17 Construct the sum of vectors **A** and **B** by the graphical method (tail to head).

17

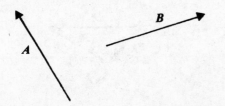

18 Construct the sum $B + A$.

18

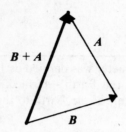

---

19 What statement can you make about vectors $A + B$ and $B + A$? What mathematical relationship does this illustrate?

19 $A + B = B + A$
This illustrates the commutative law of addition.

---

20 A and B are referred to as the _____ of $A + B$.

20 Components.

---

21 Determine, by the graphical method, the sum of vectors A, B, and C. How many possible sketches can be drawn? What are they?

21 Six sketches
$A + B + C$
$A + C + B$
$B + A + C$
$B + C + A$
$C + A + B$
$C + B + A$

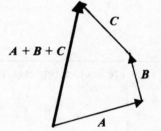

---

22 Given vector A, draw vector $-A$.

22

---

23 Given vectors A and B, draw $A + (-B)$.

23

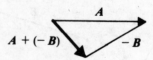

---

24 Replace vector *A* by its rectangular components (show graphically). | **24**

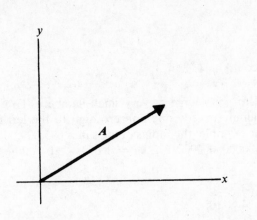 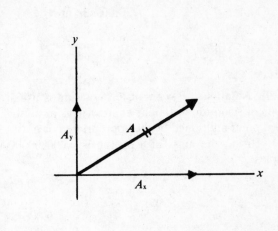

MAIN IDEAS

Physics is an empirical study. In order to understand the behavior of physical phenomena we use a procedure known as the scientific method. The basic steps of the scientific method are: observation of the phenomena of nature, the formation of a hypothesis, and the testing of the hypothesis through measurement.

The fundamental quantities of mechanics are length, mass, and time. In other areas of physics the fundamental quantities of temperature, electric charge, and luminous intensity are introduced. Combinations of fundamental quantities (formed by multiplication and/or division of fundamental units) are referred to as derived units. For example, m^2 = unit of area, m^3 = unit of volume, $m \cdot s^{-1}$ = unit of velocity, $m \cdot s^{-2}$ = unit of acceleration, $kg \cdot m^{-3}$ = unit of density, etc. Some combinations are given special names. For example, $1 \, kg \cdot m \cdot s^{-2} = 1 \, N$ = unit of force, $1 \, N \cdot m = 1 \, J$ = unit of work, $1 \, N \cdot m^{-2} = 1 \, Pa$ = unit of pressure. (Note: N = newton, J = joule, and Pa = pascal.)

Dimensional Consistency. In any equation expressing physical relationships, after the mathematical procedures of addition, subtraction, multiplication, division, and cancellation have been performed, the units on one side of the equation must equal the units on the other side. Units should be carried through all calculations as this provides a useful check.

Precision. In the measurement 8.436 ± 0.005 kg, the precision is 0.005 kg. This means that if the measurement were to be repeated under conditions as close as possible to the original, the difference between the two measurements would probably not be more than 0.005 kg.

Percent Error. Percent error indicates the precision of a measurement. In the measurement 8.436 ± 0.005 kg, the percent error is 0.005 kg/8.436 kg = 0.00059 = 0.059%. In the laboratory we often compare the experimental value with the standard value using the formula

$$\% \text{ error} = \frac{|\text{experimental value} - \text{standard value}|}{\text{standard value}} \times 100.$$

Note that the percent error is an absolute value.

Number of Significant Figures. Significant figures are the meaningful digits in a number. A numerical result cannot have a greater number of significant figures than the value from which it was calculated; i.e., it cannot be more precise. For example, the values 42.08 cm and 21.46 cm each have four significant figures. If we divide these and find that the ratio is 1.960857409, only the first four digits in the answer are meaningful. Other examples:

Number	Number of Significant Figures
2.06 kg	3
0.000438 m	3
6.0×10^4 s	2
200 m^3	uncertain, could be 1, 2 or 3

Scientific Notation.   Powers-of-ten notation is usually used for very large or very small numbers. To write a number in scientific notation, express it as a number containing exactly one nonzero digit to the left of the decimal point multiplied by the appropriate power of ten. For example: the radius of the sun is 695,000,000 m = 6.95×10^8 m; the mass of a proton is 0.00000000000000000000000000001673 kg = 1.673×10^{-28} kg. Other examples:

$$56,800,000 = 5.68 \times 10^7$$
$$224,000 = 2.24 \times 10^5$$
$$0.000431 = 4.31 \times 10^{-4}$$
$$0.0000000729 = 7.29 \times 10^{-8}$$

Conversion.   To illustrate the technique of converting from one unit system to another, we will present a problem: Convert 80 km $\cdot$ h^{-1} to m $\cdot$ s^{-1}. First determine the relationship between kilometers and meters (1000 m = 1 km) and hours and seconds (1 h = 3600 s). It is immediately apparent that these relationships can be expressed as $\dfrac{1000 \text{ m}}{1 \text{ km}} = 1$ and $\dfrac{1 \text{ h}}{3600 \text{ s}} = 1$. (We shall refer to these ratios as conversion factors.) Since multiplying or dividing by 1 does not affect the value of any quantity, we can multiply $80 \dfrac{\text{km}}{\text{h}}$ by $\dfrac{1000 \text{ m}}{1 \text{ km}}$ and by $\dfrac{1 \text{ h}}{3600 \text{ s}}$.

Hence we have $80 \dfrac{\text{km}}{\text{h}} = 80 \dfrac{\text{km}}{\text{h}} \left(\dfrac{1000 \text{ m}}{1 \text{ km}} \right) \left(\dfrac{1 \text{ h}}{3600 \text{ s}} \right)$ which is actually $80 \dfrac{\text{km}}{\text{h}} (1)(1)$. Cancellation of units results in $\left(\dfrac{80 \text{ km}}{\text{h}} \right) \left(\dfrac{1000 \text{ m}}{1 \text{ km}} \right) \left(\dfrac{1 \text{ h}}{3600 \text{ s}} \right) = 22.2 \dfrac{\text{m}}{\text{s}}$ or 22.2 m $\cdot$ s^{-1}. This procedure is known as the factor-label method. In essence, we are following three rules: 1) Any quantity divided by itself or its equivalent is equal to 1 (exception — division by zero is not permitted). 2) Multiplying or dividing any quantity by 1 does not affect its value. 3) Units may be treated as any algebraic quantity and thus may be cancelled.

Vectors.   Regardless where they are located in space, two vector quantities are equal if they have the same magnitude (length) and direction. Thus vector **A** is equal to vector **B**. Even though they have the same magnitude, vector **C** is not equal to vector **A** because its direction is opposite to that of **A**.

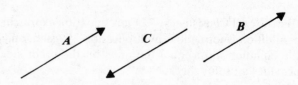

Vector **C** is the negative of vector **A**. The negative of a vector quantity is defined as a vector quantity having the same magnitude but opposite direction to that of the original vector. The negative of **A** is denoted −**A** (note boldface minus sign).

Boldface Notation.   It should be emphasized that in the relationship **A** = **B**, the boldface equals sign denotes the equality of two vector quantities (same magnitude and direction). A boldface negative sign denotes that two vectors have opposite directions. Magnitude of **A** = A.

The vector sum (resultant of two vectors).   Consider the following problem. A particle P undergoes a displacement from point (1) to point (2). At point (2) it undergoes a second displacement, which moves it to point (3). What is the *total effect*? It is immediately apparent that the particle could have undergone a single displacement from (1) to (3). Identifying displacement (1) to (2) as **A**, (2) to (3) as **B**, and (1) to (3) as **C**, **C** is defined as the vector sum of **A** and **B** and can be expressed as **C** = **A** + **B**.

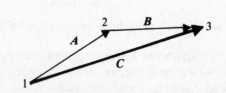

Commutative Property of Vectors. $A + B = B + A$. This means that vectors can be added in any order.

Transitive Property of Vectors. If $A = C$ and $B = C$, then $A = B$.

Addition of two or more vectors by the polygon method. First choose a suitable scale. Lay off the first vector to scale in its proper direction (use a protractor). Then lay off the second vector by beginning at the arrowhead of the first vector. In a similar manner the third vector is laid from the arrowhead of the second vector. Thus, we draw the given vectors in succession, with the tail of each at the arrowhead of the one preceding it, and complete the polygon by drawing the sum, which is the vector drawn from the beginning point of the first vector to the arrowhead of the last vector as illustrated.

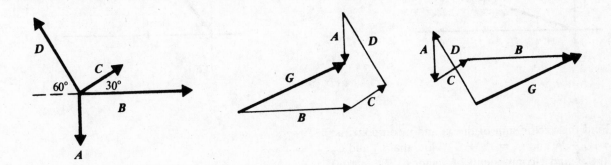

In addition to the cases cited in the text, $A + B + C + D$ and $A + C + D + B$, we have drawn $B + C + D + A$ and $D + A + C + B$; you may wish to try other possibilities that will result in the vector sum G. *Note: The order in which the vectors are drawn makes no difference!*

Rectangular Component Vectors The rectangular components of vector A are A_x and A_y. In order to indicate that A_x and A_y replace the original A, two short lines are drawn through A.

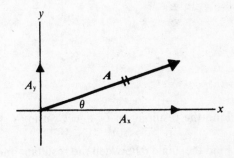

$$\frac{A_x}{A} = \cos \theta \qquad\qquad \frac{A_y}{A} = \sin \theta$$

$$A_x = A \cos \theta \qquad\qquad A_y = A \sin \theta$$

$$\frac{A_y}{A_x} = \tan \theta \qquad\qquad A = \sqrt{A_x^2 + A_y^2}$$

$$\theta = \arctan \frac{A_y}{A_x} = \tan^{-1} \frac{A_y}{A_x}$$

Resultant of Two or More Vectors. The procedure can be outlined as follows:

1 Find the x- and y-components of vectors **A** and **B**.

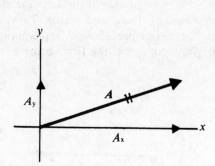 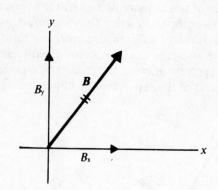

2 Find the vector sum of the x- and y-components: $C_x = A_x + B_x$ and $C_y = A_y + B_y$. Note that C_x and C_y are the x- and y-components of vector **C**.

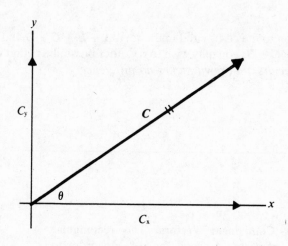

3 Find the resultant of C_x and C_y using $C = \sqrt{C_x{}^2 + C_y{}^2}$. Thus C is the magnitude of vector **C**.

4 Find the angle θ between the resultant and the x-axis using $\dfrac{C_y}{C_x} = \tan\theta$; $\theta = \arctan\dfrac{C_y}{C_x}$. The same analysis can be used for forces, velocities, accelerations, etc., since any vector can be replaced by its rectangular components acting at the same point.

In order to find the x- and y-components of a vector, the student has two choices.

Choice 1

Use angle θ as indicated below and the appropriate sign (+ or −) of the trigonometric functions. If angle θ is measured counterclockwise from the positive x-axis, then it is considered to be a positive angle (negative if measured clockwise).

QUADRANT

	I	II	III	IV
$\sin\theta$	+	+	−	−
$\cos\theta$	+	−	−	+
$\tan\theta$	+	−	+	−

In the first quadrant A_x is positive and A_y is positive.

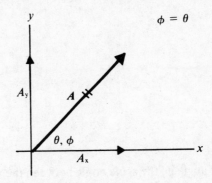

In the second quadrant B_x is negative and B_y is positive.

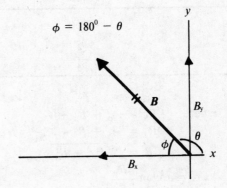

In the third quadrant C_x is negative and C_y is negative.

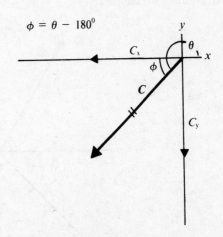

In the fourth quadrant D_x is positive and D_y is negative.

$$\phi = 360^0 - \theta$$

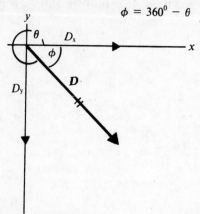

Choice 2 Use angle ϕ, the acute angle between the vector and the x-axis, and the signs ($+$ or $-$) of the components as determined by the direction of the coordinate axis as indicated in the illustration of Choice 1.

To find the vector difference $A - B = A + (-B)$, first determine the x- and y-components of vectors A and B, then find the vector difference of the x- and y-components $C_x = A_x - B_x$ and $C_y = A_y - B_y$. Note that C_x and C_y are the components of the resultant vector C, which can be determined by the method illustrated previously in the section on finding the resultant of two or more vectors.

Tabular Form for Solving a Vector Problem (for any number of vectors). Let R be the vector sum of A, B, C, D, ... The components of all the vectors and the calculations can be arranged systematically as follows:

Vector	Angle	x-components	y-components
A	ϕ_1	A_x	A_y
B	ϕ_2	B_x	B_y
C	ϕ_3	C_x	C_y
		R_x	R_y

where
$$R_x = A_x + B_x + C_x$$
$$R_y = A_y + B_y + C_y$$
$$R = \sqrt{R_x^2 + R_y^2}$$

$$\tan \alpha = \frac{|R_y|}{|R_x|}, \quad \alpha = \arctan \frac{|R_y|}{|R_x|}$$

Angle α is located between the resultant and the x-axis. The vertical lines on either side of R_y and R_x are the symbols for absolute values; i.e., only the positive values are used. This means, for example, that $|-10\,\text{N}| = + 10\,\text{N}$. After finding α, always check to see in which quadrant your resultant is located.

We shall illustrate the two choices:

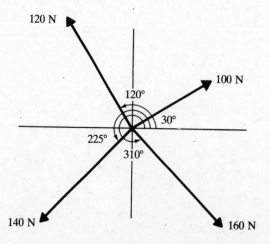

Choice 1

Force	Angle	x-component	y-component
100 N	30°	100 N cos 30° = + 86.6 N	100 N sin 30° = + 50.0 N
120 N	120°	120 N cos 120° = − 60.0 N	120 N sin 120° = + 104 N
140 N	225°	140 N cos 225° = − 99.0 N	140 N sin 225° = − 99.0 N
160 N	310°	160 N cos 310° = + 103 N	160 N sin 310° = − 123 N
		$\Sigma F_x = R_x = + 30.6$ N,	$\Sigma F_y = R_y = − 68.0$ N

$$R = \sqrt{R_x^2 + R_y^2}$$
$$= \sqrt{(30.6 \text{ N})^2 + (− 68.0 \text{ N})^2}$$
$$= 74.6 \text{ N}$$

$$\tan \alpha = \frac{R_y}{R_x} = \frac{− 68.0 \text{ N}}{+ 30.6 \text{ N}} = − 2.22$$
$$\alpha = − 65.8° \quad \text{by calculator}$$
$$\text{or } 294.2°$$

However, if α is in the second quadrant, tan α will be negative also. To determine the quadrant, we must look at the individual components. In this example, R_x was positive and R_y was negative. Therefore, R must be in the fourth quadrant.

Choice 2

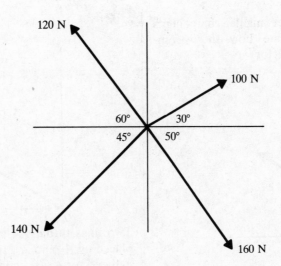

Force	Angle	x-component	y-component
100 N	30°	$+ 100 \text{ N} \cos 30° = + 86.6 \text{ N}$	$+ 100 \text{ N} \sin 30° = + 50.0 \text{ N}$
120 N	60°	$- 120 \text{ N} \cos 60° = - 60.0 \text{ N}$	$+ 120 \text{ N} \sin 60° = + 104 \text{ N}$
140 N	45°	$- 140 \text{ N} \cos 45° = - 99.0 \text{ N}$	$- 140 \text{ N} \sin 45° = - 99.0 \text{ N}$
160 N	50°	$+ 160 \text{ N} \cos 50° = + 103 \text{ N}$	$- 160 \text{ N} \sin 50° = - 123 \text{ N}$
		$\Sigma F_x = R_x = + 30.6 \text{ N},$	$\Sigma F_y = R_y = - 68.0 \text{ N}$

$$R = \sqrt{R_x{}^2 + R_y{}^2}$$
$$= 74.6 \text{ N}$$

$$\tan \alpha = \frac{|R_y|}{|R_x|} = \frac{|-68.0 \text{ N}|}{|+30.6 \text{ N}|} = 2.22$$
$$\alpha = 65.8°$$

This is the acute angle between the resultant and the x-axis. To determine the quadrant, draw a sketch.

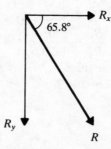

A force can be defined operationally by means of a spring balance, calibrated as follows. A 1N weight is suspended, and the position of the balance is noted. An additional 1N weight is now added, and the position of the pointer is noted. This process is continued until a sufficient number of points have been noted on the scale to give the desired range. Then the magnitude of an unknown is measured. Note that no assumption or demand is made that the extension on the spring be proportional to the applied weight. A force can be represented by a vector. Investigation shows that if two or more forces are applied simultaneously at the same point of a body, these can be replaced by a single force called the resultant. This single force is the vector sum of all the other forces.

PROGRAMMED QUIZ

1 Resolve vector A into its rectangular components (x-and y-components). Indicate how these components replace the original vector.

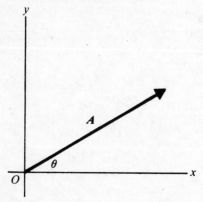

1

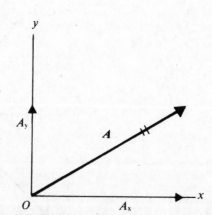

Two lines through A symbolize that A has been replaced by A_x and A_y. It should be stressed that originally vector A was acting at point O. Now that vector A has been replaced by A_x and A_y, there are two vectors acting at O.

2 Resolve the following four displacement vectors into their corresponding x- and y-components.

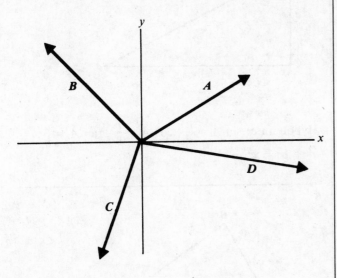

2

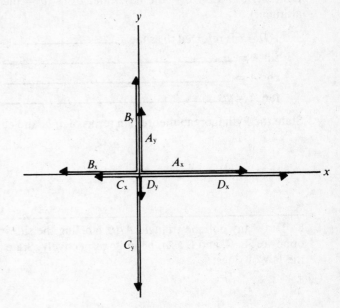

3 Find the vector sum of the x- and y-components respectively.

$$R_x = A_x + B_x + C_x + D_x$$
$$R_y = A_y + B_y + C_y + D_y.$$

3

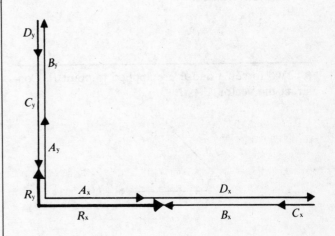

4 Since R_x and R_y represent the components of R, draw R.

4

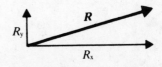

5 Let us have a brief review of basic trigonometric concepts. Draw right triangle ABC. (C represents the right angle, $AC = b =$ the base, and $BC = a =$ the altitude.)

$AB = c$ is referred to as the _____.

$\sin A =$ _____

$\cos A =$ _____

$\tan A =$ _____

State the Pythagorean theorem in terms of a, b, and c.

5

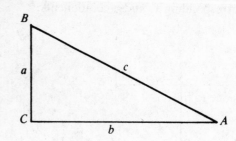

Hypotenuse; $\sin A = \dfrac{a}{c}$, $\cos A = \dfrac{b}{c}$, $\tan A = \dfrac{a}{b}$; $a^2 + b^2 = c^2$

---

6 Draw any oblique triangle ABC labeling the sides opposite A, B, and C as a, b, and c respectively. State the law of sines.

6

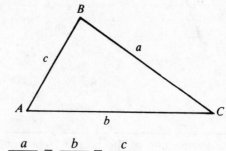

$$\frac{a}{\sin A} = \frac{b}{\sin B} = \frac{c}{\sin C}$$

---

7 State the cosine law.

7 $a^2 = b^2 + c^2 - 2bc \cos A$
$b^2 = a^2 + c^2 - 2ac \cos B$
$c^2 = a^2 + b^2 - 2ab \cos C$

---

8 Two forces A and B are applied to point P. Construct the vector $A + B$.

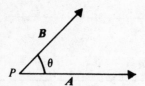

8

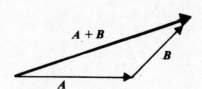

---

9 If the angle between A and B is θ, what is the angle opposite $A + B$?

9 $(180 - \theta)$

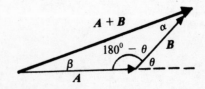

10 Apply the cosine law to obtain the magnitude of $A + B$.

10
$$A + B = \sqrt{A^2 + B^2 + 2AB \cos \theta}$$
Note: $\cos(180 - \theta) = -\cos \theta$

---

11 In reference to the answer in frame 9, find angles α and β by the law of sines.

11
$$\frac{\sin \alpha}{A} = \frac{\sin(180 - \theta)}{A + B}$$
Since $\sin(180 - \theta) = \sin \theta$,
$$\sin \alpha = \frac{A \sin \theta}{A + B}$$
$$\sin \beta = \frac{b \sin \theta}{A + B}$$

---

12 What should be the value of the force applied to P in frame 8 so that it balances A and B?

12 $-(A + B)$
Note: Equilibrium of a particle is the subject of Chapter 4.

---

13 How many cm^3 are there in 1 in^3?

13
$$1 \text{ in} = 2.54 \text{ cm}$$
cube each side
$$(1 \text{ in})^3 = (2.54 \text{ cm})^3$$
$$1 \text{ in}^3 = 16.39 \text{ cm}^3$$

---

14 Convert $60 \text{ mi} \cdot \text{hr}^{-1}$ to $\text{ft} \cdot \text{s}^{-1}$.

14
$$60 \frac{\text{mi}}{\text{hr}} = \left(\frac{60 \text{ mi}}{\text{hr}} \right) \left(\frac{5280 \text{ ft}}{1 \text{ mi}} \right) \left(\frac{1 \text{ hr}}{60 \text{ min}} \right) \left(\frac{1 \text{ min}}{60 \text{ s}} \right)$$
$$= 88 \text{ ft} \cdot \text{s}^{-1}$$
Note that $\frac{5280 \text{ ft}}{1 \text{ mi}} = 1, \frac{1 \text{ hr}}{60 \text{ min}} = 1, \frac{1 \text{ min}}{60 \text{ s}} = 1.$

Multiplication by 1 does not change the value of $60 \text{ mi} \cdot \text{hr}^{-1}$. The fractions are set up with the idea of cancellation in mind.

---

15 If the radius of the earth is 6.38×10^6 m, what is its volume (m^3)?

15
$$V = \frac{4}{3} \pi r^3$$
$$= \frac{4}{3} \pi (6.38 \times 10^6 \text{ m})^3$$
$$= 1.09 \times 10^{12} \text{ m}^3$$

16 The density of most rocks near the earth's surface, such as granite, is about $3 \text{ g} \cdot \text{cm}^{-3} = 3000 \text{ kg} \cdot \text{m}^{-3}$. The density of the interior is higher. If the density of the earth is estimated to be $5.5 \text{ g} \cdot \text{cm}^{-3} = 5500 \text{ kg} \cdot \text{m}^{-3}$, what is the mass of the earth in kilograms?

16

$$\text{density} = \frac{\text{mass}}{\text{volume}}$$

$$m = \rho V = \frac{5500 \text{ kg}}{\text{m}^3} (1.09 \times 10^{21} \text{ m}^3)$$
$$= 6.00 \times 10^{24} \text{ kg}$$

---

17 How many people holding outstretched hands are required to form a human chain around the equator? (Assume that they could stand on water.) The radius of the earth $= 6.38 \times 10^6$ m.

17 Circumference of the earth $= 2\pi r$
$$= 2\pi (6.38 \times 10^6 \text{ m})$$
$$= 4.01 \times 10^7 \text{ m}$$
We estimate the length of one person's outstretched arms to be 2 m.

$$\text{number of people} = \frac{4.01 \times 10^7 \text{ m}}{2 \text{ m/person}}$$
$$\approx 2 \times 10^7 \text{ persons}$$
$$\approx 20{,}000{,}000 \text{ persons}$$

STEP BY STEP SOLUTIONS OF PROBLEMS

Problem 1 Compute the number of seconds in 10 minutes.

1 First determine the relationship between minutes and seconds.

1 60 s = 1 min

---

2 Express this as a conversion factor.

2

$$\frac{60 \text{ s}}{1 \text{ min}} = 1$$

---

3 Multiply 10 minutes by this conversion factor.

3

$$10 \text{ min} = (10 \text{ min}) \frac{(60 \text{ s})}{(1 \text{ min})}$$

which is in essence (10 min) (1).

---

4 Cancel units and multiply.

4

$$(10 \text{ min}) \frac{(60 \text{ s})}{(1 \text{ min})} = 600 \text{ s}$$

Problem 2 An acre is equal to 160 square rods, where 1 rod = 5.50 yards. How many square meters are there in an acre?

5 How many square rods are there in 1 square yard?

5

$$1 \text{ rod} = 5.50 \text{ yd}$$
$$1 \text{ rod}^2 = 30.25 \text{ yd}^2$$

---

6 How many square yards are there in 1 square meter?

6

$$1 \text{ m} = 1.0936 \text{ yd}$$
$$1 \text{ m}^2 = 1.1960 \text{ yd}^2$$

---

7 Express these as conversion factors. Multiply 1 acre = 160 rod² by these conversion factors.

7

$$1 \text{ acre} = (160 \text{ rod}^2)\left(\frac{30.25 \text{ yd}^2}{1 \text{ rod}^2}\right)\left(\frac{1 \text{ m}^2}{1.1960 \text{ yd}^2}\right)$$

---

8 Cancel units and multiply.

8

$$1 \text{ acre} = (160 \cancel{\text{rod}^2})\left(\frac{30.25 \cancel{\text{yd}^2}}{1 \cancel{\text{rod}^2}}\right)\left(\frac{1 \text{ m}^2}{1.1960 \cancel{\text{yd}^2}}\right)$$
$$= 4047 \text{ m}^2$$

Problem 3 A particle undergoes four successive displacements as indicated in the figure. How far and in what direction is the particle from the starting point?

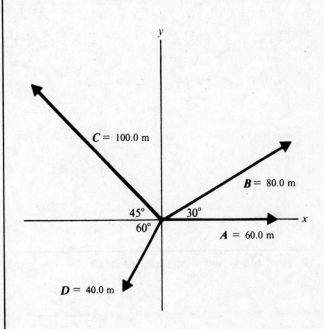

---

9 Tabulate what is given and what must be found.

9 Given
A = 60.0 m at 0°
B = 80.0 m at 30°
C = 100.0 m at 45°
D = 40.0 m at 60°
Find
R (Resultant)
(magnitude and direction)

10 Find the *x*- and *y*-components of **A**.

10

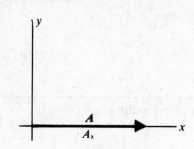

$A_x = A \cos \theta$　　　　$A_y = A \sin \theta$
$\quad = 60.0 \text{ m} \cos 0°$　　$\quad = 60.0 \text{ m} \sin 0^0$
$\quad = 60.0 \text{ m} (1.000)$　$\quad = 60.0 \text{ m} (0)$
$\quad = 60.0 \text{ m}$　　　　$\quad = 0$

---

11 Find the *x*- and *y*-components of **B**.

11

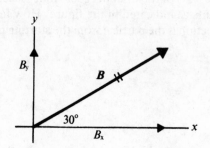

$B_x = B \cos \theta$　　　　$B_y = B \sin \theta$
$\quad = 80.0 \text{ m} \cos 30°$　$\quad = 80.0 \text{ m} \sin 30°$
$\quad = 80.0 \text{ m} (0.866)$　$\quad = 80.0 \text{ m} (0.500)$
$\quad = 69.3 \text{ m}$　　　　$\quad = 40.0 \text{ m}$

---

12 Find the *x*- and *y*-components of **C**.

12

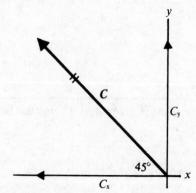

$C_x = C \cos \theta$　　　　$C_y = C \sin \theta$
$\quad = -100 \text{ m} \cos 45°$　$\quad = 100 \text{ m} \sin 45°$
$\quad = -100 \text{ m} (0.707)$　$\quad = 100 \text{ m} (0.707)$
$\quad = -70.7 \text{ m}$　　　$\quad = 70.7 \text{ m}$

---

13 Find the x- and y-components of D.

$D_x = -40m \cos 60° =$
$D_y = -40m \sin 60° =$

13

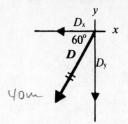

$$D_x = D \cos \theta \qquad D_y = D \sin \theta$$
$$= -40.0 \text{ m} \cos 60° \qquad = -40.0 \text{ m} \sin 60°$$
$$= -40.0 \text{ m} (0.500) \qquad = -40.0 \text{ m} (0.866)$$
$$= -20.0 \text{ m} \qquad = -34.6 \text{ m}$$

---

14 Summarize in tabular form.

14

Distance	Angle	x-component	y-component
$A = 60.0$ m	0°	$+ 60.0$ m	0
$B = 80.0$ m	30°	$+ 69.3$ m	$+ 40.0$ m
$C = 100.0$ m	45°	$- 70.7$ m	$+ 70.7$ m
$D = 40.0$ m	60°	$- 20.0$ m	$- 34.6$ m

---

15 Add the x-components

15

$$R_x = A_x + B_x + C_x + D_x$$
$$= 60.0 \text{ m} + 69.3 \text{ m} - 70.7 \text{ m} - 20.0 \text{ m}$$
$$= 38.6 \text{ m}$$

---

16 Add the y-components

16

$$R_y = A_y + B_y + C_y + D_y$$
$$= 0 + 40.0 \text{ m} + 70.7 \text{ m} - 34.6 \text{ m}$$
$$= + 76.1 \text{ m}$$

---

17 Find the magnitude of the resultant by the Pythagorean theorem.

17

$$R = \sqrt{R_x^2 + R_y^2}$$
$$= \sqrt{(38.6 \text{ m})^2 + (76.1 \text{ m})^2}$$
$$= 85.3 \text{ m}$$

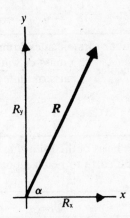

18 Find the direction of the resultant by
$$\tan \alpha = \frac{|R_y|}{|R_x|}.$$

18
$$\alpha = \arctan \frac{|R_y|}{|R_x|}$$
$$= \arctan \frac{76.1 \text{ m}}{38.6 \text{ m}} = \arctan 1.97$$
$$= 63.1°$$

---

19 Check by solving the problem graphically.

19

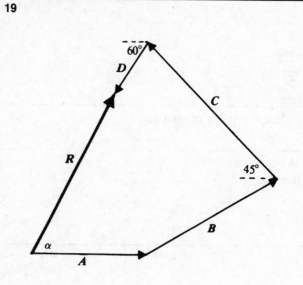

Problem 4 How many molecules are there in a glass of water?

20 What does a molecule of water consist of?

20 Two hydrogen atoms and one oxygen atom (H_2O).

---

21 What is the mass of a water molecule?
mass of hydrogen atom = 1.67×10^{-27} kg
mass of oxygen atom = 26.6×10^{-27} kg

21 Mass of water molecule
$$= 2(1.67 \times 10^{-27} \text{ kg}) + 26.6 \times 10^{-27} \text{ kg}$$
$$= 29.9 \times 10^{-27} \text{ kg}$$

---

22 Estimate the mass of a glass of water.

22 Since four glasses = 1 q t $\approx$ 1 liter, the mass of a glass of water $\approx$ 0.25 kg.

---

23 Obtain the number of molecules from
$$\text{number of molecules} = \frac{\text{mass of water}}{\text{mass of molecule}}$$

23
$$n = \frac{0.25 \text{ kg}}{29.9 \times 10^{-27} \text{ kg/molecule}}$$
$$= 8.34 \times 10^{24} \text{ molecules}$$

Problem 5 On the basis of the following population table, estimate the number of years that it would take for the population of the earth to reach a point where each inhabitant would occupy 1 m^2 of the earth's surface.

Year	1950	1980	2000	2025	2050	2100
Population (millions)	2,504	4,435	6,147	8,298	9,780	10,870

From "The Population Problem — Time Bomb or Myth?" study undertaken by the World Bank, Robert S. McNamara.

24 What is the surface area of the earth?

24 If the radius of the earth is 6.38×10^6 m,
$$A = 4\pi r^2$$
$$= 4\pi (6.38 \times 10^6 \text{ m})^2$$
$$= 5.11 \times 10^{14} \text{ m}^2$$

---

25 Estimate the land mass of the earth. Assume that 70% of the earth's surface is covered by water.

25 The area of "solid earth" is 30% of 5.11×10^{14} m^2
$$= 0.30 (5.11 \times 10^{14} \text{ m}^2)$$
$$= 1.53 \times 10^{14} \text{ m}^2$$

---

26 How many people can occupy this land mass if each person occupies 1 m^2?

26 1.53×10^{14} people

---

27 Using the period from 1950 to 2050, estimate the rate of increase in population per year.

27 Since the table indicates an increase of 7.276 billion people in 100 years, we estimate an increase of 0.075 billion people per year.

---

28 How many years will it take for the earth to reach this crisis?

28

$$\text{number of years} = \frac{\text{increase in population}}{\text{increase/year}}$$
$$= \frac{1.53 \times 10^{14} \text{ people}}{7.5 \times 10^7 \text{ people/year}}$$
$$= 0.2 \times 10^7 \text{ years}$$
$$= 2 \times 10^6 \text{ years}$$
$$= 2 \text{ million years}$$

PROGRAMMED TEST

1 *Problem 1* Find graphically the resultant (magnitude and direction) of the three forces acting on a particle at point P.

1

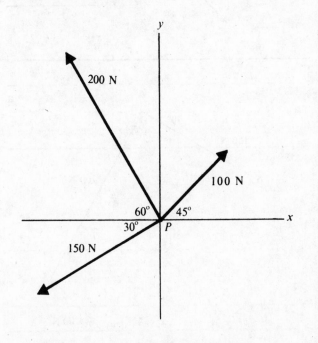

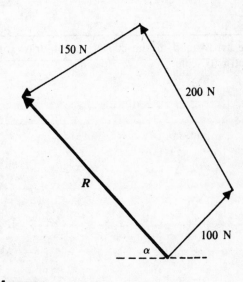

Answer
232 N, 46.7°

If you solved this problem correctly, go to frame 6. If you could not solve this problem, go through frames 2–5.

Since there are three vectors, there are (3) (2) = 6 combinations of adding the vectors.

(100 N + 200 N + 150 N)   (100 N + 150 N + 200 N)

(200 N + 100 N + 150 N)   (200 N + 150 N + 100 N)

(150 N + 100 N + 200 N)   (150 N + 200 N + 100 N)

We will demonstrate the first combination.

2 Draw the 100 N vector to scale.

2 1 cm = 40 N

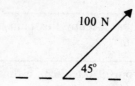

3 At the arrowhead of the 100 N vector draw the 200 N vector to scale.

3

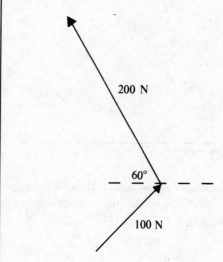

4 At the arrowhead of the 200 N vector draw the 150 N vector to scale.

4

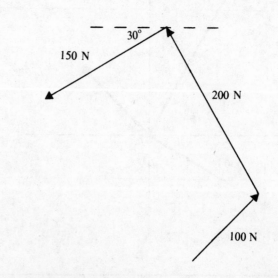

5 Draw the resultant, i.e., the vector from the starting point of the 100 N vector to the arrowhead of the 150 N vector.

5 $R = 232$ N

$\alpha = 46.7°$

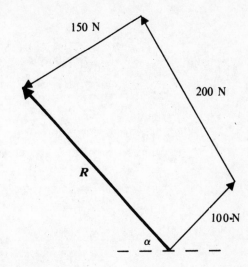

---

6 Solve problem 1 by the method of x- and y-components.

6 *Answer*

232 N, 46.7°

If you solved this problem correctly, go to frame 12. If you could not solve this problem, go through frame 7–11.

7 Find the x- and y-components.

7

Force	Angle (with x-axis)	x-components	y-components
100 N	45°	+ 70.7 N	+ 70.7 N
200 N	60°	− 100 N	+ 173 N
150 N	30°	− 130 N	− 75 N

8 Find R_x.

8

$$R_x = \Sigma F_x = 70.7 \text{ N} - 100 \text{ N} - 130 \text{ N} = -159 \text{ N}$$

9 Find R_y.

9

$$R_y = \Sigma F_y = 70.7 \text{ N} + 173 \text{ N} - 75 \text{ N} = 169 \text{ N}$$

10 Find the magnitude of the resultant.

10

$$R = \sqrt{R_x^2 + R_y^2}$$
$$= \sqrt{(-159 \text{ N})^2 + (169 \text{ N})^2} = 232 \text{ N}$$

11 Find the direction of the resultant and indicate by a sketch.

11

$$\tan \alpha = \frac{|R_y|}{|R_x|} = 1.06$$
$$\alpha = 46.7°$$

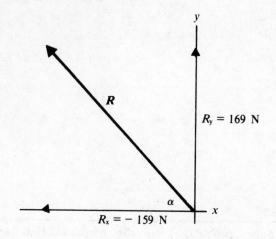

$R_y = 169$ N

$R_x = -159$ N

12 ***Problem 2*** Find the magnitude and direction of the resultant of the four forces 100 N, 150 N, 200 N and 250 N which make angles of 40°, 100°, 230° and 340° respectively with the positive x-axis.

12
Answer
159 N, 9.48°

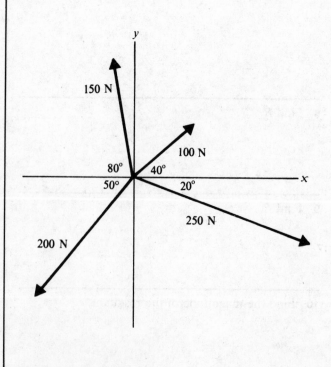

If you solved this problem correctly, go to frame 16. If you could not solve this problem, go through frames 13–15

13 Tabulate the *x*- and *y*-components. We are using the acute angle the vector makes with the *x*-axis.

13

Force	Angle	*x*-components	*y*-components
100 N	40°	+ 100 N cos 40° = + 76.6 N	+ 100 N sin 40° = + 64.3 N
150 N	80°	− 150 N cos 80° = − 26.0 N	+ 150 N sin 80° = + 148 N
200 N	50°	− 200 N cos 50° = − 129 N	− 200 N sin 50° = − 153 N
250 N	20°	+ 250 N cos 20° = + 235 N	− 250 N sin 20° = − 85.5 N

---

14 Find R_x and R_y. Use the Pythagorean theorem to find R.

14

$$R_x = \Sigma F_x = + 76.6 \text{ N} - 26 \text{ N} - 129 \text{ N} + 235 \text{ N}$$
$$= 157 \text{ N}$$
$$R_y = \Sigma F_y = + 64.3 \text{ N} + 148 \text{ N} - 153 \text{ N} - 85.5 \text{ N}$$
$$= - 26.2 \text{ N}$$
$$R = \sqrt{(157 \text{ N})^2 + (- 26.2 \text{ N})^2} = 159 \text{ N}$$

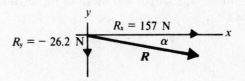

---

15 Find the angle.

15

$$\tan \alpha = \frac{|R_y|}{|R_x|} = \frac{|-26.2 \text{ N}|}{|157 \text{ N}|} = 0.167$$
$$\alpha = 9.48°$$

---

16 **Problem 3** The density of water is $1 \text{ g} \cdot \text{cm}^{-3}$. What is this value in $\text{kg} \cdot \text{m}^{-3}$?

16 **Answer** $10^3 \text{ kg} \cdot \text{m}^{-3}$

If you solved this problem correctly, go to frame 22. If you could not solve this problem, go through frames 17–21.

---

17 What is the relationship between centimeters and meters?

17 1 m = 100 cm

---

18 Cube both sides.

18 $1 \text{ m}^3 = 10^6 \text{ cm}^3$

---

19 What is the relationship between grams and kilograms?

19 $1 \text{ kg} = 10^3 \text{ g}$

---

20 Express the relationships of frames 18 and 19 as conversion factors. Multiply $\dfrac{1\text{g}}{\text{cm}^3}$ by these.

20

$$\frac{1\text{ g}}{\text{cm}^3} = \left(\frac{1\text{ g}}{\text{cm}^3}\right)\left(\frac{10^6\text{ cm}^3}{1\text{ m}^3}\right)\left(\frac{1\text{ kg}}{10^3\text{ g}}\right)$$

---

21 Cancel units and multiply.

21

$$\frac{1\text{ g}}{\text{cm}^3} = 10^3\,\frac{\text{kg}}{\text{m}^3}$$

We did not form $\dfrac{1\text{ m}^3}{10^6\text{ cm}^3}$ and $\dfrac{10^3\text{ g}}{1\text{ kg}}$ even though the conversion factors are each equal to 1. Why? Because we would not be in the position to cancel units.

---

22 **Problem 4** How many pennies are needed to pave a four-lane transcontinental highway from New York City to San Francisco?

22 **Answer** 5×10^{11} pennies

If you could not solve this problem, go through frames 23–26.

23 Estimate the length and width of this highway in meters.

23 The distance from New York City to San Francisco is approximately 3000 miles. If 1 mile = 1.6 km, then the estimated length of this highway is 5000 km or 5×10^6 m. The width is about 40 m.

---

24 What is the area of this highway?

24

$$\begin{aligned}
\text{Area} &= \text{length} \times \text{width}\\
&= (5 \times 10^6\text{ m})\,(40\text{ m})\\
&= 2 \times 10^8\text{ m}^2
\end{aligned}$$

---

25 What area would a penny cover?

25 Although each penny is a circle, the area it would cover would be a square.

$$\begin{aligned}
A &= l^2\\
&= 0.02\text{ m}^2\\
&= 4 \times 10^{-4}\text{ m}^2
\end{aligned}$$

---

26 How many pennies would be required to pave this highway?

26

$$\begin{aligned}
\text{number of pennies} &= \frac{\text{area of highway}}{\text{area/penny}}\\
&= \frac{2 \times 10^8\text{ m}^2}{4 \times 10^{-4}\text{ m}^2/\text{penny}}\\
&= 5 \times 10^{11}\text{ pennies}
\end{aligned}$$

2

Motion Along A Straight Line

CHAPTER SUMMARY

In this chapter, we are introduced to kinematics, in particular, motion in a straight line with constant acceleration. To facilitate the mathematical description of the motion of a given body such as a car or a falling stone, we assume that it is a point moving in a straight line along a coordinate axis. In the case of a car, this would be the x-axis; for a falling stone it is the y-axis. The average and instantaneous velocities and the average and instantaneous accelerations are defined, and formulas relating velocity, acceleration, distance and time are presented. Special emphasis is placed on freely falling bodies and relative velocity.

BASIC TERMS — *Give definitions or meanings for the following:*

kinematics (2-I)
model (2-I)
coordinate axis(2-I)
coordinate (2-I)
average velocity (2-1)
instantaneous velocity (2-2)

speed (2-2)
average acceleration (2-3)
instantaneous acceleration (2-3)
acceleration due to gravity (2-5)
freely falling bodies (2-5)
relative velocity (2-6)

PROGRAMMED QUIZ

1 A particle goes from the 2 m to the 8 m mark and back to the 2 m mark in 3 seconds. Determine its average speed.

1

$$\text{Average speed} = \frac{\text{total distance traveled}}{\text{elapsed time}}$$
$$= \frac{2\,(6\ \text{m})}{3\ \text{s}}$$
$$= 4\ \text{m} \cdot \text{s}^{-1}$$

2 Determine its average velocity.

2 Zero, since the displacement is 0.

27

3 Sketch a graph of distance vs. time for frames 3–5. Constant positive velocity.

3

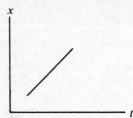

---

4 Constant negative velocity.

4

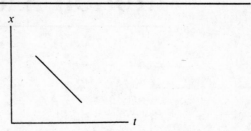

---

5 Zero velocity.

5

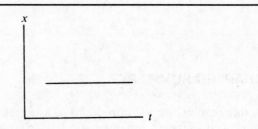

---

6 How would the average acceleration between t_1 and t_2 be represented on this graph?

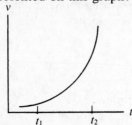

6

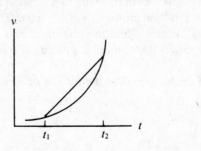

---

7 How would the instantaneous acceleration at t_2 be represented on the same graph?

7

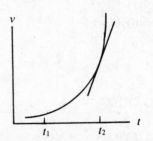

---

8 When will the average acceleration equal the instantaneous acceleration?

8 When the acceleration is constant.

---

9 Is the acceleration of a ball thrown into the air greater when it is going up or when it is coming down?

9 Same; always equal to $-g$.

---

10 If the velocity is constant, the acceleration must be _____.

10 Zero.

---

11 A car traveling at 30 km · hr^{-1} north turns west without a change in speed. Is the car accelerating?

11 Yes, a change in the direction constitutes a change in velocity; therefore the car is accelerating.

---

12 Give SI units for the following:
speed
average velocity
average acceleration
instantaneous acceleration
distance
time

12

Speed	m · s^{-1}
average velocity	m · s^{-1}
average acceleration	m · s^{-2}
instantaneous acceleration	m · s^{-2}
distance	m
time	s

---

13 Describe a situation where an object is accelerating but not changing speed.

13 When the direction changes while the speed is constant.

---

14 On the moon, a feather and a hammer will fall to the ground at the same time if they are released simultaneously. Will the results be the same if the experiment is performed on the earth?

14 Due to air resistance, the time of fall for the hammer will be less than the time of descent of the feather.

---

15 In a free fall problem, the initial speed with which an object is thrown upward equals the final speed with which it falls to earth. Are the initial and final velocities equal also?

15 No, initial velocity is upward, final velocity is downward although both have the same magnitude.

---

16 When would a car have a great acceleration but a small velocity?

16 At the start from rest.

---

17 What is the difference between a velocity of 4 m · s^{-1} and an acceleration of 4 m · s^{-2}?

17 A velocity of 4 m · s^{-1} means that with each second the position is changing by 4 m; an acceleration of 4 m · s^{-2} means that with each second the velocity is changing by 4 m · s^{-1}.

---

18 An object is thrown upward from the roof of a building. At its highest point, the velocity is ___ and the acceleration is _____ .

18 Zero; − 9.8 m · s^{-2}

---

19 When will a falling object have an acceleration of magnitude less than g?

19 When the shape is such that air resistance impedes its descent.

---

20 Is it ever possible for an object to fall with an acceleration of magnitude greater than g?

20 No.

MAIN IDEAS

This chapter will be devoted to the motion of a particle along one of the coordinates axes. The following symbols will be used:

x = distance from the origin along the x-axis.
y = distance from the origin along the y-axis.
t = time.
$x_2 - x_1 = \Delta x$ = change in x.
$y_2 - y_1 = \Delta y$ = change in y.
$t_2 - t_1 = \Delta t$ = change in t.

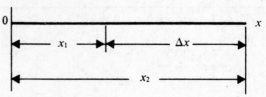

$$v_{av} = \frac{\Delta x}{\Delta t} \quad \text{or } v_{av} = \frac{\Delta y}{\Delta t} = \text{average velocity.}$$

$$v = \lim_{\Delta t \to 0} \frac{\Delta x}{\Delta t}, \, v = \lim_{\Delta t \to 0} \frac{\Delta y}{\Delta t} = \text{instantaneous velocity.}$$

$$a_{av} = \frac{\Delta v}{\Delta t} = \text{average acceleration.}$$

$$a = \lim_{\Delta t \to 0} \frac{\Delta v}{\Delta t} = \text{instantaneous acceleration.}$$

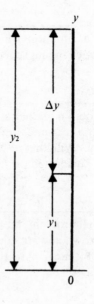

Motion with constant acceleration (the case where the average acceleration equals the instantaneous acceleration) along one of the coordinate axes can be described by the following relationships:

$$v_{av} = \frac{v_0 + v}{2}$$

$$x - x_0 = v_{av} t$$

$$v = v_0 + at$$

$$x - x_0 = v_0 t + \frac{at^2}{2}$$

$$v^2 = v_0^2 + 2a(x - x_0)$$

At $t = 0$:
x_0 = initial position,
v_0 = initial velocity.
At elapsed time t:
x = final position,
v = final velocity
Throughout the motion,
a = constant acceleration.

(Similar equations can also be written in terms of y.)

The constant acceleration of a freely falling body is referred to as the acceleration due to gravity, and its magnitude is denoted by g. Note that g is the symbol for a positive number.

$$g = 9.8 \text{ m} \cdot \text{s}^{-2} = 980 \text{ cm} \cdot \text{s}^{-2} = 32 \text{ ft} \cdot \text{s}^{-2}.$$

In free fall, the acceleration is downward. If the upward direction is considered to be positive, then the acceleration (in the negative y-direction) is

$$a = -g = -9.8 \text{ m} \cdot \text{s}^{-2} = -980 \text{ cm} \cdot \text{s}^{-2} = -32 \text{ ft} \cdot \text{s}^{-2}.$$

Steps to follow in the solution of kinematics problems:

1 Draw a sketch. Set up a coordinate system. Choose a positive direction, usually to the right or upward. Remember that the velocities, accelerations and displacements in this direction will be positive.

2 Denote the known quantities in terms of v_0, v, v_{av}, t, a, x, x_0, y, or y_0.

3 What do you have to find? Express the quantity (quantities) in terms of the variables of Step 2 above.

4 Solve for the unknown in terms of the known quantities using the kinematics equations. It should be noted that if the problem involves a freely falling body, the acceleration of gravity is always $-g$ (since $+y$ is up).

5 Examine your results. Are the units correct? Does your answer make sense?

Distinction between average velocity and instantaneous velocity.
   Consider the motion of a particle as described by the distance–time graph. At time t_1 the distance from the origin is y_1 and at time t_2 the distance is y_2. The average velocity of the particle during the time interval

$$\Delta t = t_2 - t_1$$

is equal to

$$v_{av} = \frac{\Delta y}{\Delta t}$$
$$= \frac{y_2 - y_1}{t_2 - t_1} .$$

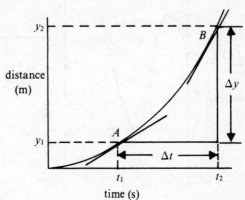

It should be noted that v_{av} is the slope of chord AB. However, the instantaneous velocity at time t_1 is the slope of the tangent at point A, and the instantaneous velocity at time t_2 is the slope of the tangent at point B.

   In a similar manner, consider the velocity–time graph of the motion of a particle moving with a variable acceleration. At t_1 the velocity of a particle is v_1 and at t_2 the velocity is v_2; the average acceleration of the particle during the time interval $\Delta t = t_2 - t_1$ is equal to

$$a_{av} = \frac{\Delta v}{\Delta t} = \frac{v_2 - v_1}{t_2 - t_1} .$$

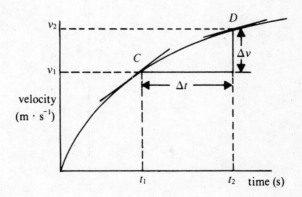

However, the instantaneous acceleration at time t_1 is the slope of the tangent at point C, and the instantaneous acceleration at time t_2 is the slope of the tangent at point D.

   It should be immediately apparent that when the average acceleration equals the instantaneous acceleration, the velocity–time graph is a straight line.

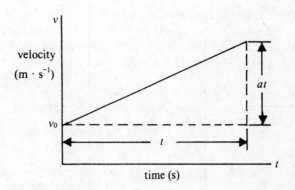

For motion with constant acceleration.   An examination of the displacement–time equation ($y - y_0 = v_0 t + \frac{1}{2}at^2$) reveals that if $a = 0$, the curve is a straight line, and if $a = \text{constant} = 0$, the graph is a parabola. In a similar manner an examination of the velocity–time equation ($v \neq v_0 + at$) indicates that the curve will be a straight line; for the particular case where $a = 0$, the line will be horizontal. In the graph shown above, the straight line has a positive slope indicating a positive acceleration. It is obvious that in an acceleration–time graph, constant acceleration will be represented by a horizontal line.

Graphical comparison of motion with variable acceleration and motion with constant acceleration.

(a)   variable acceleration
Distance–time graph
Equation of motion
$$y = t^3 - 6t^2 + 8t + 3$$

t	y
0	3
1	6
2	3
3	0
4	3

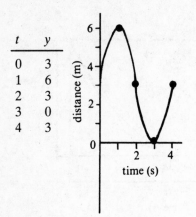

Velocity–time graph
Equation of motion
$$v = 3t^2 - 12t + 8$$

t	v
0	8
1	-1
2	-4
3	-1
4	8

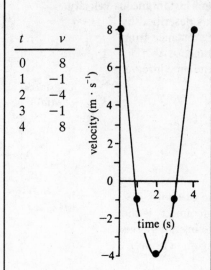

Acceleration–time graph
Equation of motion
$$a = 6t - 12$$

t	a
0	-12
1	-6
2	0
3	6
4	12

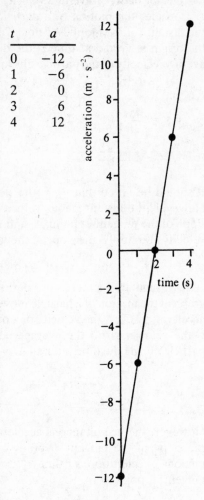

(b)   constant acceleration
Distance–time graph
Equation of motion
$$y = 4t - t^2$$

t	y
0	0
1	3
2	4
3	3
4	0

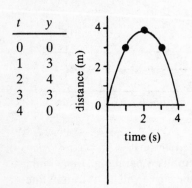

Velocity–time graph
Equation of motion
$$v = -2t + 4$$

t	v
0	4
1	2
2	0
3	-2
4	-4

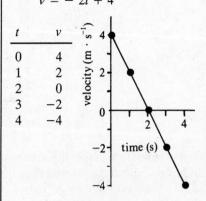

Acceleration–time graph
Equation of motion
$$a = -2$$

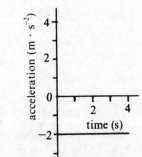

Relative velocities of bodies that move along a straight line.
Let

v_{AB} represent the velocity of A with respect to B.
v_{BC} represent the velocity of B with respect to C.
v_{AC} represent the velocity of A with respect to C;

$$v_{AC} = v_{AB} + v_{BC}$$
$$v_{AB} = v_{AC} - v_{BC}.$$

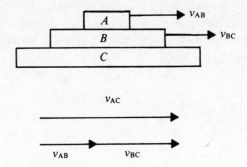

Velocities that do not lie along a straight line will be considered in chapter 3.

PROGRAMMED QUIZ

A bullet is fired vertically upward, reaches a height of 50 m, and falls back to the earth. Neglecting air resistance, the graph below gives the vertical height as a function of time. Answer frames 1–3.

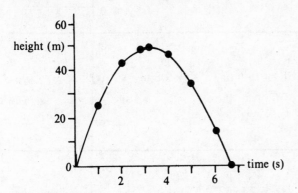

Table used to plot graph		calculated
t	y	v
0	0	31.3
1	26.4	21.5
2	43.0	11.7
3	49.8	1.9
3.19	50.0	0
4	46.5	−7.9
5	34.0	−15.0
6	11.4	−27.5
6.38	0	−31.3

1 Determine the instantaneous velocity at $t = 0$. Remember,

$$v = \frac{\Delta y}{\Delta t}.$$

Draw a tangent to the curve at $t = 0$ and select an arbitrary Δy and Δt.

1 At $t = 0$, $v = 31.3$ m · s^{-1} exactly (i.e., to three significant figures). The student should realize that the value obtained from the graph should be close to, but need not be exactly, this value.

2 Determine the instantaneous velocity at $t = 3$ s. Take a peek at the table used to plot the graph. Note that the bullet reached its maximum height at $t = 3.19$ s.

2 At $t = 3$ s, $v = 1.9$ m · s^{-1}. You should obtain a value close to this.

3 Determine the acceleration from

$$a = \frac{v - v_0}{\Delta t}.$$

3

$$a = \frac{1.9 \text{ m} \cdot \text{s}^{-1} - 31.3 \text{ m} \cdot \text{s}^{-1}}{3 \text{ s}}$$
$$= -9.8 \text{ m} \cdot \text{s}^{-2}$$

4 A ball is thrown vertically upward from a point 2 m above the ground with a speed of $19.6 \text{ m} \cdot \text{s}^{-1}$. Set up the coordinate system you will use to describe the motion of the ball. State what is given in terms of symbols.

4

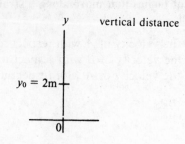

Given:

$$v_0 = 19.6 \text{ m} \cdot \text{s}^{-1}$$
$$v = 0$$
$$a = -g = -9.8 \text{ m} \cdot \text{s}^{-2}$$
$$y_0 = 2 \text{ m}$$

---

5 What is the velocity of the ball at its highest point? What is the acceleration of the ball at its highest point?

5

$$v = 0$$
$$a = -g = -9.8 \text{ m} \cdot \text{s}^{-2}$$

---

6 How long will it take the ball to reach its highest point?

6

$$v = v_0 + at = v_0 - gt$$
$$0 = 19.6 \text{ m} \cdot \text{s}^{-1} - 9.8 \text{ m} \cdot \text{s}^{-2} \, (t)$$
$$t = 2 \text{ s}$$

---

7 What is the average velocity of the ball?

7

$$v_{av} = \frac{v_0 + v}{2}$$
$$= \frac{19.6 \text{ m} \cdot \text{s}^{-1} + 0}{2} = 9.8 \text{ m} \cdot \text{s}^{-1}$$

---

8 Using the average velocity and the time for the ball to reach its highest point, what is the maximum height?

8

$$y - y_0 = v_{av} \, t$$
$$y - 2 \text{ m} = 9.8 \text{ m} \cdot \text{s}^{-1} \, (2 \text{ s})$$
$$y = 19.6 \text{ m} + 2 \text{ m} = 21.6 \text{ m}$$

---

9 Express the maximum height in terms of initial velocity, final velocity and acceleration. Substitute the numerical values for v, v_0, and g in the formula. Solve for y and compare with result of frame 8.

9

$$v^2 = v_0^2 + 2a(y - y_0) = v_0^2 - 2g(y - y_0)$$

$$y - y_0 = \frac{v^2 - v_0^2}{-2g}$$

$$y - 2 \text{ m} = \frac{0 - (19.6 \text{ m} \cdot \text{s}^{-1})^2}{-2(9.8 \text{ m} \cdot \text{s}^{-2})}$$
$$y = 21.6 \text{ m}$$

---

10 At what altitude will the velocity be 10 m · s⁻¹ downward?

10

$$v^2 = v_0{}^2 + 2a(y - y_0)$$
$$(-10 \text{ m} \cdot \text{s}^{-1})^2 = (19.6 \text{ m} \cdot \text{s}^{-1})^2 + $$
$$2(-9.8 \text{ m} \cdot \text{s}^{-2}) \times (y - 2 \text{ m})$$
$$y - 2 \text{ m} = 14.5 \text{ m}$$
$$y = 16.5 \text{ m}$$

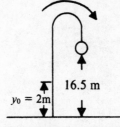

Note that the ball is moving downward.

16.5 m

$y_0 = 2$m

---

11 A bullet moving with a velocity of 300 m · s⁻¹ penetrates a distance of 0.15 m into a tree before stopping. Assuming a constant acceleration, compute the acceleration of the bullet. State what is given in terms of v_0, v, and x. Set up a coordinate system.

11

$O \longrightarrow x$

Given:

$$v_0 = 300 \text{ m} \cdot \text{s}^{-1} \qquad v = 0$$
$$x = 0.15 \text{ m} \qquad x_0 = 0$$

---

12 State the equation to be used, substitute, and solve for a.

12

$$v^2 = v_0{}^2 + 2a(x - x_0)$$
$$0 = (300 \text{ m} \cdot \text{s}^{-1})^2 + 2a(0.15 \text{ m} - 0)$$
$$a = -3 \times 10^5 \text{ m} \cdot \text{s}^{-2}$$

---

13 How long will the bullet penetrate the tree before it comes to a stop?

13

$$v = v_0 + at$$
$$0 = 300 \text{ m} \cdot \text{s}^{-1} - (3 \times 10^5 \text{ m} \cdot \text{s}^{-2})t$$
$$t = 10^{-3} \text{ s} = 0.001 \text{ s}$$

We also could have used

$$v_{av} = \frac{v_0 + v}{2} = \frac{300 \text{ m} \cdot \text{s}^{-1} + 0}{2} = 150 \text{ m} \cdot \text{s}^{-1}$$
$$x - x_0 = v_{av} t$$
$$t = \frac{x - x_0}{v_{av}} = \frac{0.15 \text{ m} - 0}{150 \text{ m} \cdot \text{s}^{-1}} = 0.001 \text{ s}$$

---

14 An automobile accelerates from 8 m · s⁻¹ to 30 m · s⁻¹ in 10 s. Compute the acceleration. State what is given in terms of v_0, v, and t. Set up a coordinate system.

14

$O \longrightarrow x$

Given:

$$v_0 = 8 \text{ m} \cdot \text{s}^{-1} \qquad v = 30 \text{ m} \cdot \text{s}^{-1}$$
$$t = 10 \text{ s} \qquad x_0 = 0$$

---

15 State the equation to be used. Substitute and solve for a.

15

$$a = \frac{v - v_0}{t} = \frac{30 \text{ m} \cdot \text{s}^{-1} - 8 \text{ m} \cdot \text{s}^{-1}}{10 \text{ s}}$$
$$= 2.2 \text{ m} \cdot \text{s}^{-2}$$

16 What is the distance the automobile travelled in 10 s?

16

$$x - x_0 = v_0 t + \tfrac{1}{2}at^2$$
$$x - 0 = (8 \text{ m} \cdot \text{s}^{-1})(10 \text{ s}) + \tfrac{1}{2}(2.2 \text{ m} \cdot \text{s}^{-2})(10 \text{ s})^2$$
$$x = 190 \text{ m}$$

We could also have used

$$x - x_0 = v_{av}\, t = \left(\frac{v_0 + v}{2} \right) t$$
$$x - 0 = \left(\frac{8 \text{ m} \cdot \text{s}^{-1} + 30 \text{ m} \cdot \text{s}^{-1}}{2} \right) (10 \text{ s})$$
$$x = 190 \text{ m}$$

---

17 An airplane starting from rest takes off from a landing field with a run of 900 m. If it moves with a constant acceleration of $2 \text{ m} \cdot \text{s}^{-2}$, compute the time it takes to make the run. Set up a coordinate system and state what is given in terms of v_0, a, and x.

17

Given:

$O \longmapsto\!\!\!\!\!\longrightarrow x$

$$v_0 = 0 \qquad\qquad a = 2 \text{ m} \cdot \text{s}^{-2}$$
$$x = 900 \text{ m} \qquad x_0 = 0$$

---

18 State the equation to be used, substitute, and solve for t.

18

$$x - x_0 = v_0\, t + \tfrac{1}{2}\, at^2$$
$$900 \text{ m} - 0 = 0 + \tfrac{1}{2}(2 \text{ m} \cdot \text{s}^{-2})\, t^2$$
$$t = 30 \text{ s}$$

---

19 With what velocity did it take off?

19

$$v = v_0 + at = 0 + 2 \text{ m} \cdot \text{s}^{-2}(30 \text{ s})$$
$$= 60 \text{ m} \cdot \text{s}^{-1}$$

The same result would be obtained by using
$$v^2 = v_0^2 + 2a(x - x_0)$$
$$= 0 + 2(2 \text{ m} \cdot \text{s}^{-2})(900 \text{ m} - 0)$$
$$v = 60 \text{ m} \cdot \text{s}^{-1}$$

STEP BY STEP SOLUTIONS OF PROBLEMS

Problem 1 A projectile is fired vertically upward from the ground with a velocity v_0. Answer frames 1–8.

1 Set up the coordinate system you will use to describe the motion of the projectile; let $y_0 = 0$.

1

2 What is the velocity of the ball at its highest point?

2 $v = 0$

3 How long will it take the projectile to rise to its highest point?

3

$$v = v_0 + at = v_0 - gt$$
$$0 = v_0 - gt$$
$$t = \frac{v_0}{g}$$

---

4 What is the maximum altitude of the projectile?

4

$$y - y_0 = v_0 t + \frac{at^2}{2}$$

$$y - 0 = v_0 \left(\frac{v_0}{g} \right) - \frac{g}{2} \left(\frac{v_0}{g} \right)^2$$

$$y = \frac{v_0^2}{2g}$$

We also could have used
$$v^2 = v_0^2 + 2a(y - y_0)$$
$$0 = v_0^2 - 2gy$$
$$y = \frac{v_0^2}{2g}$$

---

5 How long after the initial thrust upward will the projectile have a velocity of $\frac{v_0}{2}$ upward?

5

$$v = v_0 + at$$
Since $v = \frac{v_0}{2}$

$$\frac{v_0}{2} = v_0 - gt$$

$$t = \frac{v_0}{2g}$$

---

6 How long after the initial thrust upward will the projectile have a velocity of $\frac{v_0}{2}$ downward?

6

$$v = v_0 + at$$
Since $v = -\frac{v_0}{2}$

$$\frac{-v_0}{2} = v_0 - gt$$
(note that the final velocity is negative)

$$t = \frac{3}{2} \frac{v_0}{g}$$

$v = v_0/2$

---

7 When is the displacement of the projectile zero?

7

At $t = 0$ (the beginning) and at $t = \frac{2v_0}{g}$ (when the projectile returned to earth). It took $\frac{v_0}{g}$ seconds for the projectile to reach its maximum height and $\frac{v_0}{g}$ seconds for the projectile to return to the earth.

---

8 What are the magnitude and direction of the acceleration of the projectile when it is at its maximum height, moving upward, and moving downward?

8 At all times
$$a = -g = -9.8 \text{ m} \cdot \text{s}^{-2}$$

Problem 2 A body moving at $30 \text{ m} \cdot \text{s}^{-1}$ stops in 5 s. What was the body's deceleration if it is assumed to be constant? What distance did the body travel?

9 Set up a coordinate system you will use to describe the motion of the body. Let $x_0 = 0$.

9

$$O \vdash\!\!\longrightarrow$$
$$x$$

---

10 What is given in terms of v_0, v, v_{av}, x, a, and t?

10

$$v_0 = 30 \text{ m} \cdot \text{s}^{-1} \qquad v = 0 \qquad t = 5 \text{ s}$$

---

11 What unknown quantities must be found?

11 Find a, x.

---

12 Find a by using
$$a = \frac{v - v_0}{t}.$$

12

$$a = \frac{v - v_0}{t} = \frac{0 - 30 \text{ m} \cdot \text{s}^{-1}}{5 \text{ s}} = -6 \text{ m} \cdot \text{s}^{-2}$$

---

13 Find x by using the relationship for v_{av}.

13

$$v_{av} = \frac{v_0 + v}{2}$$
$$= \frac{30 \text{ m} \cdot \text{s}^{-1} + 0}{2} = 15 \text{ m} \cdot \text{s}^{-1}$$
$$x = v_{av} t = 15 \text{ m} \cdot \text{s}^{-1} (5 \text{ s}) = 75 \text{ m}$$

---

14 Find x by using v_0, a, and t.

14

$$x = v_0 t + \frac{at^2}{2}$$
$$= 30 \text{ m} \cdot \text{s}^{-1} (5 \text{ s}) + \tfrac{1}{2}(-6 \text{ m} \cdot \text{s}^{-2}) (5 \text{ s})^2$$
$$= 75 \text{ m}$$

Problem 3 A ball is thrown vertically up from the edge of a 98 m building and falls to the ground 6 s after leaving the thrower's hand. Assume that the thrower's hand is 2 m above the roof of the building. Find a) the initial velocity of the ball, b) the time to reach the maximum height, c) the maximum height, d) the velocity of the ball when it strikes the ground, and e) the position and velocity of the ball 1 s and 5 s after leaving the thrower's hand.

15 Draw a sketch and set up the coordinate system you will use to describe the motion of the ball. Let $y_0 = 0$.

15 Let the origin be the point at which the ball leaves the thrower's hand.

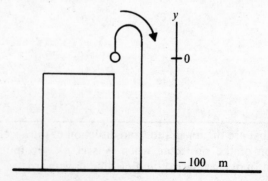

16 What is given in terms of v_0, v, v_{av}, y, a, and t in order to solve for a), b), c), and d)?

16 Given
$$y = -100 \text{ m}$$
$$t = 6 \text{ s}$$
$$a = -g = -9.8 \text{ m} \cdot \text{s}^{-2}$$

---

17 What unknown quantities must be found in a), b), c), and d)?

17 Find v_0
t (time to reach maximum height)
y (maximum height)
v (velocity of ball when it strikes the ground)

---

18 Find v_0.

18
$$y - y_0 = v_0 t + \tfrac{1}{2}at^2$$
$$-100 \text{ m} - 0 = v_0(6 \text{ s}) - \frac{9.8 \text{ m} \cdot \text{s}^{-2} (6 \text{ s})^2}{2}$$
$$-100 \text{ m} = (6 \text{ s})v_0 - 176.4 \text{ m}$$
$$v_0 = 12.73 \text{ m} \cdot \text{s}^{-1}$$

---

19 Find t (time to reach maximum height).

19
$$v = v_0 + at$$
$$0 = 12.73 \quad \cdot \text{s}^{-1} - 9.8 \text{ m} \cdot \text{s}^{-2} (t)$$
$$t = 1.30 \text{ s}$$

---

20 Find y (maximum height).

20
$$y - y_0 = v_0 t + \tfrac{1}{2}at^2$$
$$y - 0 = 12.73 \text{ m} \cdot \text{s}^{-1} (1.3 \text{ s}) + \tfrac{1}{2}(-9.8 \text{ m} \cdot \text{s}^{-2})$$
$$\times (1.3 \text{ s})^2$$
$$y = 8.27 \text{ m}$$
Another method
$$v_{av} = \frac{v_0 + v}{2} = \frac{12.73 \text{ m} \cdot \text{s}^{-1} + 0}{2} = 6.365 \text{ m} \cdot \text{s}^{-1}$$
$$y = v_{av} t = 6.365 \text{ m} \cdot \text{s}^{-1} (1.3 \text{ s}) = 8.27 \text{ m}$$

---

21 Find the velocity of the ball when it strikes the ground.

21
$$v = v_0 + at = 12.73 \text{ m} \cdot \text{s}^{-1} - 9.8 \text{ m} \cdot \text{s}^{-2} (6 \text{ s})$$
$$= -46.07 \text{ m} \cdot \text{s}^{-1}$$

---

22 Find the position of the ball 1 s after leaving the thrower's hand.

22
$$y - y_0 = v_0 t + \tfrac{1}{2}at^2$$
$$y - 0 = 12.73 \text{ m} \cdot \text{s}^{-1} (1 \text{ s}) + \tfrac{1}{2}(-9.8 \text{ m} \cdot \text{s}^{-2})$$
$$\times (1 \text{ s})^2$$
$$y = 7.83 \text{ m}$$

---

23 Find the velocity of the ball 1 s after leaving the thrower's hand.

23
$$v = v_0 + at = 12.73 \text{ m} \cdot \text{s}^{-1} - 9.8 \text{ m} \cdot \text{s}^{-2} (1 \text{ s})$$
$$= 2.93 \text{ m} \cdot \text{s}^{-1}$$

---

24 Find the position of the ball 5 s after leaving the thrower's hand.

24
$$y - y_0 = v_0 t + \tfrac{1}{2}at^2$$
$$y - 0 = 12.73 \ \text{m} \cdot \text{s}^{-1} \ (5 \ \text{s}) + \tfrac{1}{2}(- 9.8 \ \text{m} \cdot \text{s}^{-2})$$
$$\times (5 \ \text{s})^2$$
$$y = - 58.85 \ \text{m}$$

---

25 Find the velocity of the ball 5 s after leaving the thrower's hand.

25
$$v = v_0 + at = 12.73 \ \text{m} \cdot \text{s}^{-1} - 9.8 \ \text{m} \cdot \text{s}^{-2} \ (5 \ \text{s})$$
$$= - 36.27 \ \text{m} \cdot \text{s}^{-1}$$

---

26 In frames 21, 24 and 25, why are y and v negative?

26 The negative sign indicates that the ball is below the thrower's hand and that it is moving downward.

Problem 4 A ferry moving at constant velocity of $5 \ \text{m} \cdot \text{s}^{-1}$ passes a buoy in the river. A man is bicycling on the ferry at $2 \ \text{m} \cdot \text{s}^{-1}$ relative to the ferry in the same direction. a) How long will it take the man to reach the next buoy 50 m away? b) How long would it take him to reach the next buoy also 50 m away if he were cycling in the opposite direction?

27 Find v_{MR}, the relative velocity of the man to the river. Use v_{MF} for the velocity of the man relative to the ferry and v_{FR} for the velocity of the ferry relative to the river.

27
$$v_{MR} = v_{MF} + v_{FR} = 2 \ \text{m} \cdot \text{s}^{-1} + 5 \ \text{m} \cdot \text{s}^{-1}$$
$$= 7 \ \text{m} \cdot \text{s}^{-1}$$

---

28 Find the time.

28
$$x - x_0 = v_{av} \ t$$
$$50 \ \text{m} - 0 = (7 \ \text{m} \cdot \text{s}^{-1})t$$
$$t = 7.14 \ \text{s}$$

---

29 Find v_{MR} for part b.

29
$$v_{MR} = v_{MF} + v_{FR} = - 2 \ \text{m} \cdot \text{s}^{-1} + 5 \ \text{m} \cdot \text{s}^{-1}$$
$$= 3 \ \text{m} \cdot \text{s}^{-1}$$

---

30 Find the time.

30
$$x - x_0 = v_{av} \ t$$
$$50 \ \text{m} - 0 = (3 \ \text{m} \cdot \text{s}^{-1})t$$
$$t = 16.7 \ \text{s}$$

Problem 5 A stone is dropped from the top of a cliff 100 m high, and 2 s later a second stone is thrown vertically downward with a velocity of 30 m · s^{-1}. How far below the top of the cliff will the second stone overtake the first stone?

31 Set up a coordinate system you will use to describe the motion. Let $y_0 = 0$ (100 m above the ground).

31

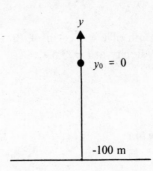

32 Let T = time for the second stone to overtake the first stone. What is the time of descent for the first stone when it is overtaken by the second stone?

32 $T + 2$ s = time of descent for the first stone.

33 What do we know about each stone?

33

first stone (dropped)	second stone (thrown downward)
$v_0 = 0$	$v_0 = -30$ m · s^{-1}
$a = -g = -9.8$ m · s^{-2}	$a = -g = -9.8$ m · s^{-2}
$t = T + 2$ s	$t = T$

34 What is the equation for the distance covered by the first stone?

34
$$y - y_0 = v_0 t + \tfrac{1}{2} at^2$$
$$y - 0 = 0 + \tfrac{1}{2} (-9.8 \text{ m} \cdot \text{s}^{-2}) (T + 2 \text{ s})^2$$

35 What is the equation for the distance covered by the second stone?

35
$$y - y_0 = v_0 t + \tfrac{1}{2} at^2$$
$$y - 0 = (-30 \text{ m} \cdot \text{s}^{-1}) T + \tfrac{1}{2} (-9.8 \text{ m} \cdot \text{s}^{-2}) T^2$$

36 Since the distances covered by the two stones are equal, equate the equations in frames 34 and 35 and solve for T.

36
$$-4.9 \text{ m} \cdot \text{s}^{-2} (T + 2 \text{ s})^2$$
$$= -30 \text{ m} \cdot \text{s}^{-1} T - 4.9 \text{ m} \cdot \text{s}^{-2} T^2$$
$$-4.9 \text{ m} \cdot \text{s}^{-2} (T^2 + 4 \text{ s } T + 4 \text{ s}^2)$$
$$= -30 \text{ m} \cdot \text{s}^{-1} T - 4.9 \text{ m} \cdot \text{s}^{-2} T^2$$
$$10.4 \text{ m} \cdot \text{s}^{-1} T = 19.6 \text{ m}$$
$$T = 1.88 \text{ s}$$

37 Either equation in frames 34 and 35 can be used to determine how far below the top of the cliff the second stone will overtake the first stone. Use the equation for the distance covered by the first stone.

37
$$y - y_0 = -4.9 \text{ m} \cdot \text{s}^{-2} (T + 2 \text{ s})^2$$
$$y - 0 = -4.9 \text{ m} \cdot \text{s}^{-2} (1.88 \text{ s} + 2 \text{ s})^2$$
$$y = -73.8 \text{ m}$$

PROGRAMMED TEST

1 *Problem 1* Referring to the distance–time graphs in Main Ideas, answer frames 2 and 3.

2 From the graph of $y = t^3 - 6t^2 + 8t + 3$, find the instantaneous velocity at $t = 3.5$ s.

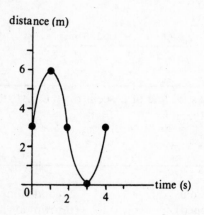

3 From the graph of $y = 4t - t^2$, find the instantaneous velocity at $t = 1.5$ s.

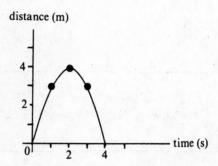

4 *Problem 2* At a July 4 celebration a solid propellant rocket fired vertically upward is accelerated until it reaches a speed of 60 m · s⁻¹ at a height of 100 m. At this point, the propellent is exhausted and the acceleration ceases. a) How much higher will the rocket go? b) Once the propellent is used up, how long will it take before the rocket falls back to earth? c) Find the time it took for the rocket to reach a speed of 60 m · s⁻¹.

2

$v = 2.75$ m · s⁻¹. Remember $v = \dfrac{\Delta y}{\Delta t}$, draw a tangent to the curve at $t = 3.5$ s and find the slope of the tangent.

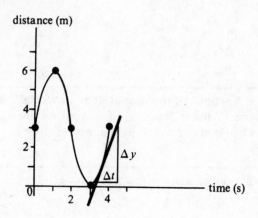

3 $v = 1$ m · s⁻¹. Draw a tangent to the curve at $t = 1.5$ s and find the slope of the tangent.

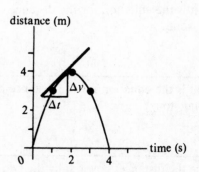

4 *Answer*
184 m, 13.7 s, 3.33 s

If you solved this problem correctly, go to frame 12. If you could not solve this problem, go through frames 5–11.

5 Set up a coordinate system you will use to describe the motion. Let $y_0 = 0$ (100 m above the ground).

5

6 What is given in part a)?

6

$v_0 = 60 \text{ m} \cdot \text{s}^{-1}$
$v = 0$
$a = -9.8 \text{ m} \cdot \text{s}^{-2}$

7 Solve for y.

7

$v^2 = v_0^2 + 2a(y - y_0)$
$0 = (60 \text{ m} \cdot \text{s}^{-1})^2 - 2(9.8 \text{ m} \cdot \text{s}^{-2})\,(y)$
$ = 3600 \text{ m}^2 \cdot \text{s}^{-2} - 19.6 \text{ m} \cdot \text{s}^{-2}\,(y)$
$y = 184 \text{ m}$

8 What is given in part b)?

8

$y = -100 \text{ m}$
$v_0 = 60 \text{ m} \cdot \text{s}^{-1}$
$a = -9.8 \text{ m} \cdot \text{s}^{-2}$

9 Solve for t in part b.

9

$y - y_0 = v_0 t + \tfrac{1}{2}at^2$
$-100 \text{ m} - 0 = (60 \text{ m} \cdot \text{s}^{-1})t - \tfrac{1}{2}(9.8 \text{ m} \cdot \text{s}^{-2})t^2$
$4.9 \text{ m} \cdot \text{s}^{-2}\, t^2 - 60 \text{ m} \cdot \text{s}^{-1}\, t - 100 \text{ m} = 0$
Use the quadratic formula to solve for t.

$t = \dfrac{-b \pm \sqrt{b^2 - 4ac}}{2a}$

$ = \dfrac{60 \pm \sqrt{(60)^2 - 4(4.9)\,(-100)}}{2(4.9)}$

$ = -1.49 \text{ s (extraneous)}$
$ = 13.7 \text{ s}$

10 What is given in part c?

10

$v_0 = 0$
$v = 60 \text{ m} \cdot \text{s}^{-1}$
$y = 100 \text{ m}$

11 Solve for t in part c. Note that the rocket was accelerating upward at 100 m.

11

$v_{av} = \dfrac{v_0 + v}{2} = \dfrac{0 + 60 \text{ m} \cdot \text{s}^{-1}}{2}$

$\phantom{v_{av}} = 30 \text{ m} \cdot \text{s}^{-1}$
$(y - y_0) = v_{av}\, t$
$(100 \text{ m}) = (30 \text{ m} \cdot \text{s}^{-1})t$
$t = 3.33 \text{ s}$

12 *Problem 3* A life raft is dropped from a helicopter that is 100 m above the water. a) If the helicopter was hovering over the water, how long would it take for the life raft to reach the water? b) If the helicopter was ascending at a constant speed of 15 m · s^{-1}, how long would it take for the life raft to reach the water? c) If the helicopter was descending at a constant speed of 15 m · s^{-1}, how long would it take for the life raft to reach the water?

12 *Answer*
4.52 s, 6.30 s, 3.23 s

If you solved this problem correctly, go to frame 20. If you could not solve this problem, go through frames 13–19.

---

13 Set up a coordinate system which you will use to describe the motion.

13

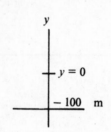

---

14 What is given for part a?

14

$v_0 = 0$
$a = -g = -9.8 \text{ m} \cdot \text{s}^{-2}$
$y = -100 \text{ m}$
$y_0 = 0$

---

15 Substitute in $y - y_0 = v_0 t + \frac{1}{2}at^2$ and solve for t.

15

$$y - y_0 = v_0 t + \frac{1}{2}at^2$$
$$-100 \text{ m} - 0 = \frac{1}{2}(-9.8 \text{ m} \cdot \text{s}^{-2})t^2$$
$$t^2 = \frac{100 \text{ m}}{4.9 \text{ m} \cdot \text{s}^{-2}} = 20.4 \text{ s}^2$$
$$t = 4.52 \text{ s}$$

---

16 What is given for part b?

16

$v_0 = +15 \text{ m} \cdot \text{s}^{-1}$
$a = -9.8 \text{ m} \cdot \text{s}^{-2}$
$y = -100 \text{ m}$
$y_0 = 0$
Note that the initial velocity is directed upward.

---

17 Substitute in $y - y_0 = v_0 t + \frac{1}{2}at^2$ and solve for t.

17

$$-100 \text{ m} = +15 \text{ m} \cdot \text{s}^{-1} t - \frac{1}{2}(9.8 \text{ m} \cdot \text{s}^{-2})t^2$$
$$(4.9 \text{ m} \cdot \text{s}^{-2})t^2 - 15 \text{ m} \cdot \text{s}^{-1}(t) - 100 \text{ m} = 0$$
Use the quadratic formula to solve for t.

$$t = \frac{-b \pm \sqrt{b^2 - 4ac}}{2a}$$
$$= \frac{15 \pm \sqrt{225 + 4(4.9)\,100}}{2(4.9)}$$
$$= 6.30 \text{ s}$$
$$= -3.23 \text{ s (extraneous)}$$

---

18 What is given for part c?

18

$v_0 = -15 \text{ m} \cdot \text{s}^{-1}$
$a = -9.8 \text{ m} \cdot \text{s}^{-2}$
$y = -100 \text{ m}$
$y_0 = 0$

Note that the initial velocity is directed downward.

---

19 Substitute in $y - y_0 = v_0 t + \tfrac{1}{2}at^2$ and solve for t.

19

$-100 \text{ m} = -15 \text{ m} \cdot \text{s}^{-1} - \tfrac{1}{2}(9.8 \text{ m} \cdot \text{s}^{-2})t^2$

$(4.9 \text{ m} \cdot \text{s}^{-2})t^2 + 15 \text{ m} \cdot \text{s}^{-1}(t) - 100 \text{ m} = 0$

Use the quadratic formula to solve for t.

$$t = \frac{-b \pm \sqrt{b^2 - 4ac}}{2a}$$

$$= \frac{-15 \pm \sqrt{225 + 4(4.9)\,100}}{2(4.9)}$$

$$= 3.23 \text{ s}$$
$$= -6.29 \text{ s (extraneous)}$$

---

20 **Problem 4** By this time you must have realized that $y - y_0 = v_0 t + \tfrac{1}{2}at^2$ (or $x - x_0 = v_0 t + \tfrac{1}{2}at^2$) is a very useful equation in kinematics when three out of four variables are given and we are required to solve for the fourth. If $y_0 = 0$, solve this equation for t in terms of v_0, a, and y and verify your result by checking for the value of t in Problem 3 in the Step by Step Solutions of Problems section, i.e., given

$v_0 = 12.73 \text{ m} \cdot \text{s}^{-1}$
$a = -9.8 \text{ m} \cdot \text{s}^{-2}$,
$y = -100 \text{ m}$,

find t.

20 **Answer**

$$t = -\frac{v_0}{a}\left(1 \pm \sqrt{1 + \frac{2ay}{v_0^2}}\right)$$

If you could not solve this problem go through frames 21–23.

---

21 Since we will have to use the quadratic formula to solve for t, rewrite the given equation in the form $ax^2 + bx + c = 0$.

21

$y = v_0 t + \tfrac{1}{2}at^2$
$\tfrac{1}{2}at^2 + v_0 t - y = 0$
$at^2 + 2v_0 t - 2y = 0$

---

22 Use the quadratic formula to solve for t.

22

$$t = \frac{-b \pm \sqrt{b^2 - 4ac}}{2a}$$

$$= \frac{-2v_0 \pm \sqrt{4v_0^2 + 8ay}}{2a}$$

$$= \frac{-v_0}{a} \pm \frac{v_0}{a}\sqrt{1 + \frac{2ay}{v_0^2}}$$

$$= \frac{-v_0}{a}\left(1 \pm \sqrt{1 + \frac{2ay}{v_0^2}}\right)$$

23 Substitute the numbers from Problem 3 in the formula.

23

$$t = \frac{-12.73}{-9.8} \left(1 \pm \sqrt{1 + \frac{2(-9.8)(-100)}{(12.73)^2}} \right)$$

$$= 1.3 \left(1 \pm \sqrt{1 + 12.1} \right)$$

$$= 1.3 \left(1 \pm \sqrt{13.1} \right)$$

$$= 1.3 \left(1 \pm 3.62 \right)$$

Since t cannot be negative, we will use $+3.62$.

$$t = 1.3 \,(4.62)$$

$$= 6 \text{ s}$$

3

Motion in a Plane

CHAPTER SUMMARY

In the previous chapters we discussed rectilinear motion, i.e., motion in a straight line. Here we consider motion in a plane — parabola, circle, ellipse, etc. In plane motion, the velocity vector can be resolved into x- and y-components. Since acceleration is also a vector, it too can be resolved into a_x and a_y. But often it is more useful to resolve the acceleration vector into components parallel and perpendicular to the path: the parallel component results in a change in the magnitude of the velocity, the perpendicular in a change in the direction. Based on this, the expression for centripetal acceleration is derived and period is defined. Motion in a uniform circle is emphasized and relative velocity is further discussed.

BASIC TERMS — *Give definitions or meanings for the following:*

plane motion (3-I)
position vector (3-1)
average velocity (3-1)
instantaneous velocity (3-1)
average acceleration (3-2)
instantaneous acceleration (3-2)
tangential component (3-3)

normal component (3-3)
projectile (3-4)
period (3-5)
circular motion (3-5)
uniform circular motion (3-5)
centripetal acceleration (3-5)
relative velocity (3-10)

PROGRAMMED QUIZ

1 If an object is moving in uniform circular motion is it accelerating?

1 Yes; although the speed is constant, the direction of the velocity vector is changing.

2 Can the acceleration vector be resolved into rectangular components? If yes, in what directions?

2 Yes, into x- and y-components or into components parallel and perpendicular to the path.

3 What effect does the component of *a* parallel to *v* have?

3 Changes the magnitude of *v* but not the direction.

4 If an object is moving in a straight line with an acceleration of 4 m · s^{-2}, what would be the component of a perpendicular to the path?

4 Zero, since the perpendicular component of a results in a change in the direction of the velocity. If there is no change in the direction, $a_\perp = 0$.

5 The acceleration of a projectile is always _____ .

5 $-g$.

6 As the radius of the circular path increases, the centripetal acceleration _____, provided that velocity remains the same.

6 Decreases;
$$a_\perp = \frac{v^2}{R} .$$

7 What is the distance covered by an object in uniform circular motion in one revolution?

7 Circumference = $2\pi R$

8 Is an object in uniform circular motion in equilibrium?

8 No, an object in equilibrium must either be at rest or in motion in a straight line at constant speed.

9 A plane flying west at 200 km · hr^{-1} experiences a wind of 50 km · hr^{-1} to the north. Depict the course of the plane graphically.

9

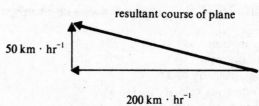

resultant course of plane

50 km · hr^{-1}

200 km · hr^{-1}

10 Where is the speed of a projectile the greatest? Where is it the least?

10 At both ends of the trajectory since v_y is maximum at these points; at the highest point since v_y is zero there (remember that throughout the trajectory v_x is constant and $v = \sqrt{v_x^2 + v_y^2}$).

11 If a ball is thrown upward making an angle θ_0 with the horizontal, at which point will the vertical component of the velocity be zero? the horizontal component?

11 At the highest point; never, the horizontal component of the velocity is always constant;
$$v_x = v_{0x} = v_0 \cos \theta_0 .$$

12 At each point on the trajectory draw in the vertical and horizontal components of the velocity vector. Indicate the magnitudes by appropriate lengths.

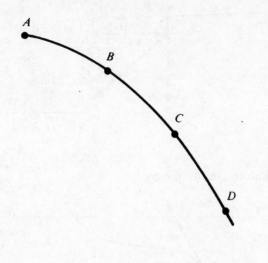

12

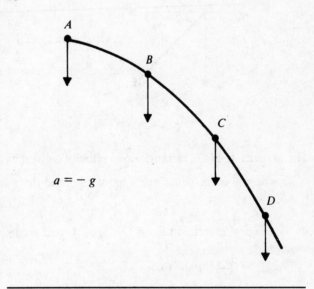

$v_x = v_{0x} = $ constant
v_y increases

---

13 Repeat frame 12 for the acceleration vector.

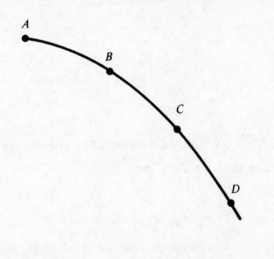

13

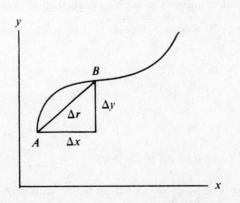

$a = -g$

MAIN IDEAS

1 The displacement of a particle from point A to point B over a time Δt is represented by Δr. The components of Δr are Δx and Δy.

2 Average velocity

$$v_{av} = \frac{\Delta r}{\Delta t}.$$

The components of v_{av} are

$$(v_x)_{av} = \frac{\Delta x}{\Delta t} \quad \text{and} \quad (v_y)_{av} = \frac{\Delta y}{\Delta t}.$$

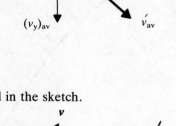

The magnitude of the average velocity is given by

$$|v_{av}| = \sqrt{(v_x)_{av}^2 + (v_y)_{av}^2}.$$

The direction of v_{av} is given by

$$\tan \theta = \frac{|(v_y)_{av}|}{|(v_x)_{av}|}$$

where θ is the acute angle between v_{av} and the x-axis as indicated in the sketch.

3 Instantaneous velocity

$$v = \lim_{\Delta t \to 0} \frac{\Delta r}{\Delta t}.$$

v is the tangent to the curve at A. The components of v are

$$v_x = \lim_{\Delta t \to 0} \frac{\Delta x}{\Delta t} \quad \text{and} \quad v_y = \lim_{\Delta t \to 0} \frac{\Delta y}{\Delta t}.$$

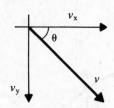

The magnitude of the instantaneous velocity is given by $|v| = \sqrt{v_x^2 + v_y^2}$ and the direction of v is given by $\tan \theta = \frac{|v_y|}{|v_x|}$ where θ is the acute angle between v and the x-axis as indicated in the sketch.

4 Average acceleration $a_{av} = \frac{\Delta v}{\Delta t}$. The x- and y-components of the average acceleration are

$$(a_x)_{av} = \frac{\Delta v_x}{\Delta t} \quad \text{and} \quad (a_y)_{av} = \frac{\Delta v_y}{\Delta t}.$$

The magnitude of the average acceleration is given by

$$|a_{av}| = \sqrt{(a_x)_{av}^2 + (a_y)_{av}^2}.$$

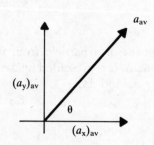

The direction of a_{av} is given by

$$\tan \theta = \frac{|(a_y)_{av}|}{|(a_x)_{av}|}, \text{ where } \theta \text{ is the acute angle between } a_{av} \text{ and the } x\text{-axis as indicated in the sketch.}$$

5 Instantaneous acceleration

$$\boldsymbol{a} = \lim_{\Delta t \to 0} \frac{\Delta \boldsymbol{v}}{\Delta t}.$$

The x- and y-components of instantaneous acceleration

$$a_x = \lim_{\Delta t \to 0} \frac{\Delta v_x}{\Delta t} \quad \text{and} \quad a_y = \lim_{\Delta t \to 0} \frac{\Delta v_y}{\Delta t}.$$

The magnitude of $\boldsymbol{a} = |a| = \sqrt{a_x^2 + a_y^2}$, and $\tan \theta = \dfrac{a_y}{a_x}$.

6 Normal (perpendicular) and tangential (parallel) components. If a particle travels along a curved path (our major concern will be circles), $\boldsymbol{a}$ can be resolved into a component normal to the curve $a_\perp$ and a component parallel to the curve $a_\parallel$. Note that the acceleration vector must always lie on the concave side of the curved path.

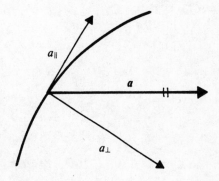

7 Two special cases of $\boldsymbol{a}$.

(i) When $\boldsymbol{a}$ is parallel to $\boldsymbol{v}$, its effect is to change the magnitude of $\boldsymbol{v}$. The direction will be unchanged.

(ii) When $\boldsymbol{a}$ is perpendicular to $\boldsymbol{v}$, its effect is to change the direction of $\boldsymbol{v}$. The magnitude will be unchanged.

8 Basic data pertaining to projectile motion.

v_0 = magnitude of initial velocity $\boldsymbol{v}_0$.

θ_0 = angle $\boldsymbol{v}_0$ makes with x-axis.

$v_{0x} = v_0 \cos \theta_0$ = horizontal component of v_0.

$v_{0y} = v_0 \sin \theta_0$ = vertical component of v_0.

$a_x = 0$ = the x-component of acceleration is zero (the horizontal component of velocity constant).

$a_y = -g$ (since the positive axis is upward).

$v_x = v_0 \cos \theta_0$ = horizontal component of v_x at any time t.

$v_y = v_0 \sin \theta_0 - gt$ = vertical component of v_y at any time t.

$$\left. \begin{array}{l} x = (v_0 \cos \theta_0)t \\ y = (v_0 \sin \theta_0)t - \tfrac{1}{2}gt^2 \end{array} \right\}$$ The position coordinates at a time t after the projectile leaves the origin. *Note*: At $t = 0$, $x = y = 0$

$R = \sqrt{x^2 + y^2}$ = distance of projectile from origin at any time.

$v = \sqrt{v_x^2 + v_y^2}$ = projectile's speed at any time.

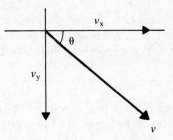

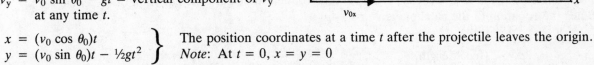

$\tan \theta = \dfrac{|v_y|}{|v_x|}$, where θ is the acute angle between the velocity vector and the x-axis as indicated in the sketch.

The path of a projectile is a parabola

$$y = (\tan \theta_0)x - \frac{g}{2v_0^2 \cos^2 \theta_0} x^2.$$

A parabola can be defined by the geometrical condition that every point on the curve is equidistant from a fixed point, called the focus, and a fixed line, called the directrix:

distance from directrix = distance from focus

$$p - y = \sqrt{(x - 0)^2 + (y + p)^2}.$$

Squaring both sides of this equation and simplifying, we get $x^2 = -4py$.

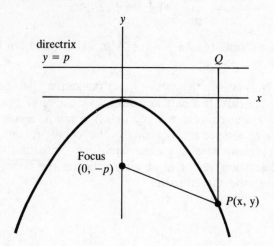

If we assume that the top section of a parabola can be approximated by the arc of a circle, the radius of curvature $R = 2f$. The equation of the circle is given by

$$x^2 + (y + R)^2 = R^2$$
$$x^2 + y^2 + 2Ry + R^2 = R^2$$
$$x^2 = -2Ry - y^2$$

When y is very small, $y = \Delta y$,

$$x^2 = -2R \, \Delta y - (\Delta y)^2.$$

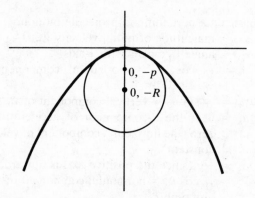

For infinitesimal valves of Δy, $(\Delta y)^2 \to 0$. Therefore, near the peak, the equation of the circle is $x^2 = -2Ry$. Since the equation of the parabola is $x^2 = -4py$,

$$2R = 4p$$
$$R = 2p = 2 \text{ (focal length)}.$$

9 Hints in solving projectile problems, i.e., translating projectile language to mathematics.

Draw a sketch. Set up a coordinate system. The positive y-axis should always be used for the upward direction. Make a list of known and unknown quantities.

	Equation
a. At the highest point (peak of the trajectory)	$v_y = 0$
b. To obtain the horizontal range (i.e., the horizontal distance from the starting point to the point at which the projectile returns to its original elevation). For a given v_0 and θ_0.	$y = 0$ $R = \dfrac{v_0^2 \sin 2\theta_0}{g}$
c. For what time after firing should fuse be set?	$t = T$
d. The projectile lands on a plateau or hill of elevation h or strikes a wall h meters above ground level	$y = h$
e. The projectile lands on the ground after being fired off a hill height h above ground level	$y = -h$
f. The projectile strikes a cliff or other vertical surface R meters from the gun	$x = R$

It should be understood that we make the following assumptions in our projectile problems:

i. motion is near surface of the earth;
ii. the surface of the earth is considered to be a plane surface; it follows that the path of a trajectory is a parabola,
iii. air resistance is neglected; and
iv. acceleration is constant ($a_x = 0$, $a_y = -g$).

10 Circular motion. For a particle moving in a circular path at uniform speed, $a_\perp = \dfrac{v^2}{R}$, where a is the centripetal acceleration, v is the magnitude of the velocity, and R is the radius of the circle. The time for one revolution is the period τ,

$$v = \frac{2\pi R}{\tau}.$$

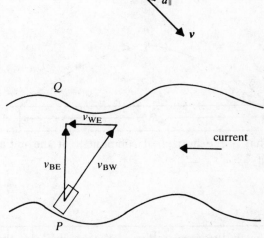

For a particle moving in a circular path at non-uniform speed, $a = \sqrt{a_\parallel{}^2 + a_\perp{}^2}$ where $a_\parallel$ is the component of the acceleration tangent to the circle (it is equal to the rate of change of the speed) and $a_\perp$ is the component of the acceleration normal to the circle.

$$\tan \theta = \frac{|a_\perp|}{|a_\parallel|}$$

where θ is the angle that the acceleration a makes with the velocity vector. In uniform circular motion, v is constant and $a_\parallel = 0$. Thus the only acceleration is $a_\perp$, which changes the direction but not the magnitude of v.

11 Relative velocity. Consider a barge crossing a river from P to Q. If there is a strong current, in what direction should the barge head upstream?

We now have a problem involving three different velocities with two different frames of reference (the water and the earth). Let

v_{BW} = velocity of the barge with respect to the water,
v_{BE} = velocity of the barge with respect to the earth, and
v_{WE} = velocity of the water with respect to the earth (river current).

Each velocity is labeled by two subscripts. The first subscript refers to the object, and the second refers to the reference frame in which the object has this velocity. Note that v_{WB}, for example, means the velocity of the water with respect to the barge. The velocity of the barge B relative to the water W has the same magnitude but opposite direction as the velocity of the water with respect to the barge. Thus $v_{BW} = -v_{WB}$.

What is the velocity of the barge crossing the river relative to the earth? Our subscript notation lends itself to the following procedure:

$$v_{BE} = v_{BW} + v_{WE}$$

Follow this rule:

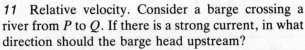

The common outer subscript of the first term and the inner subscript of the second term cancel each other. The resulting subscript is the inner subscript of the first term and the outer subscript of the second term. This rule can be generalized to any number of velocities. For example, if the captain on the barge walks across the barge with a velocity v_{CB} (the velocity of the captain with respect to the barge), his velocity relative to the earth is

$$v_{CE} = v_{CB} + v_{BW} + v_{WE}$$

$$
\begin{array}{cc}
v_{C\cancel{B}} & v_{C\cancel{W}} \\
+ \ v_{\cancel{B}W} & + \ v_{\cancel{W}E} \\
\hline
v_{CW} & v_{CE}
\end{array}
$$

It should be understood that this procedure can be used only when you have positive signs on the right side of the equation.

PROGRAMMED QUIZ

1 Frames 1–12 refer to this problem: A projectile is launched at an angle of 35° with respect to the horizontal. It has a muzzle velocity of $1000 \ \mathrm{m \cdot s^{-1}}$ and follows a parabolic path. What is the vertical component of the initial velocity?

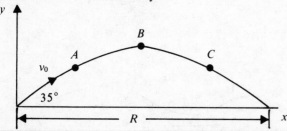

1

$$
\begin{aligned}
v_{0y} &= v_0 \sin \theta_0 \\
&= (1000 \ \mathrm{m \cdot s^{-1}}) \sin 35° \\
&= 574 \ \mathrm{m \cdot s^{-1}}
\end{aligned}
$$

2 What is the horizontal component of the initial velocity?

2

$$
\begin{aligned}
v_{0x} &= v_0 \cos \theta_0 \\
&= (1000 \ \mathrm{m \cdot s^{-1}}) \cos 35° \\
&= 819 \ \mathrm{m \cdot s^{-1}}
\end{aligned}
$$

3 What is the acceleration of the projectile at the point of firing? at B (maximum height)? at C?

3 $-9.8 \ \mathrm{m \cdot s^{-2}}$ at all points. The acceleration of the projectile is the same throughout the trajectory.

4 What is the vertical component of the velocity at the highest point?

4 $v_y = 0$

5 What is the horizontal component of the velocity at the highest point? at A? at C?

5 $v_x = v_{0x} = v_0 \cos \theta_0 = 819 \ \mathrm{m \cdot s^{-1}}$ at all points. The horizontal component of the velocity is constant throughout the trajectory.

6 What is the direction of v_y for the projectile going up, at the highest point, and coming down?

6 Up; at the highest point $v_y = 0$; down.

7 What is the maximum height that the projectile will reach?

7

$$v_y{}^2 = v_{0y}{}^2 + 2a(y - y_0) \qquad y_0 = 0$$

$$y = \frac{v_y{}^2 - v_{0y}{}^2}{2a} = \frac{0 - (574 \ \mathrm{m \cdot s^{-1}})^2}{2(-9.8 \ \mathrm{m \cdot s^{-2}})}$$

$$= 16{,}810 \ \mathrm{m}$$

8 How long does it take the projectile to reach the highest point?

8

$$v_y = v_{0y} + at$$
$$t = \frac{v_y - v_{0y}}{a}$$
$$= \frac{0 - 574 \text{ m} \cdot \text{s}^{-1}}{-9.8 \text{ m} \cdot \text{s}^{-2}} = 58.6 \text{ s}$$

---

9 What is the range R (horizontal distance from origin to point of impact)?

9 The time that the projectile is in the air is

$$2(58.6 \text{ s}) = 117 \text{ s}$$
$$R = v_x t = (819 \text{ m} \cdot \text{s}^{-1})(117 \text{ s})$$
$$= 95{,}800 \text{ m}$$

---

10 What is the magnitude of the velocity of the projectile just before impact?

10

$$v_x = 819 \text{ m} \cdot \text{s}^{-1}$$
$$v_y^2 = v_{0y} + 2a(y - y_0) \qquad y_0 = 0$$
since $y = 0$, $v_y = \pm \sqrt{v_{0y}^2} = -574 \text{ m} \cdot \text{s}^{-1}$
$$= \sqrt{(819 \text{ m} \cdot \text{s}^{-1})^2 + (574 \text{ m} \cdot \text{s}^{-1})^2}$$
$$= 1000 \text{ m} \cdot \text{s}^{-1}$$

---

11 If the initial velocity of the projectile is doubled, keeping the angle constant, what will be the new range R'?

11

$$R = \frac{v_0^2 \sin 2\theta_0}{g}$$
$$v_0' = 2v_0 = 2(1000 \text{ m} \cdot \text{s}^{-1}) = 2000 \text{ m} \cdot \text{s}^{-1}$$
$$R' = \frac{(2000 \text{ m} \cdot \text{s}^{-1})^2 \sin 2(35°)}{9.8 \text{ m} \cdot \text{s}^{-2}}$$
$$= 383{,}000 \text{ m} = 4R$$

It should be noted that for a given angle of elevation $R \propto v_0^2$. If v_0 is doubled, R will be quadrupled.

---

12 For maximum range, what must be the departure angle of the projectile? What will be the range at this angle?

12 45°;

$$R = \frac{v_0^2 \sin 2\,\theta_0}{g}$$
$$= \frac{(1000 \text{ m} \cdot \text{s}^{-1})^2 \sin 2(45°)}{9.8 \text{ m} \cdot \text{s}^{-2}}$$
$$= 102{,}000 \text{ m}$$

13 A body has x- and y-coordinates (3.0 m, 4.0 m) at time $t_1 = 5.0$ s and (5.0 m, 8.8 m) at time $t_2 = 5.4$ s. Find the components of the average velocity during this time interval.

13

$$(v_x)_{av} = \frac{\Delta x}{\Delta t} = \frac{x_2 - x_1}{t_2 - t_1}$$

$$= \frac{5.0\text{ m} - 3.0\text{ m}}{5.4\text{ s} - 5.0\text{ s}}$$

$$= \frac{2.0\text{ m}}{0.4\text{ m}} = 5.0\text{ m} \cdot \text{s}^{-1};$$

$$(v_y)_{av} = \frac{\Delta y}{\Delta t} = \frac{y_2 - y_1}{t_2 - t_1}$$

$$= \frac{8.8\text{ m} - 4.0\text{ m}}{5.4\text{ s} - 5.0\text{ s}}$$

$$= \frac{4.8\text{ m}}{0.4\text{ s}} = 12.0\text{ m} \cdot \text{s}^{-1}.$$

14 Find the magnitude of the average velocity.

14

$$|v_{av}| = \sqrt{(v_x)_{av}^2 + (v_y)_{av}^2}$$
$$= \sqrt{(5.0\text{ m} \cdot \text{s}^{-1})^2 + (12.0\text{ m} \cdot \text{s}^{-1})^2}$$
$$= 13.0\text{ m} \cdot \text{s}^{-1}$$

Note that this result can also be obtained by dividing the distance between the two points by the time interval.

$$|v_{av}| = \frac{\sqrt{(x_2 - x_1)^2 + (y_2 - y_1)^2}}{(t_2 - t_1)}$$

$$= \frac{\sqrt{(5.0\text{ m} - 3.0\text{ m})^2 + (8.8\text{ m} - 4.0\text{ m})^2}}{5.4\text{ s} - 5.0\text{ s}}$$

$$= 13\text{ m} \cdot \text{s}^{-1}.$$

15 Find the direction of the average velocity.

15

$$\tan \theta = \frac{|(v_y)_{av}|}{|(v_x)_{av}|}$$

$$= \frac{|12.0\text{ m} \cdot \text{s}^{-1}|}{|5.0\text{ m} \cdot \text{s}^{-1}|}$$

$$\theta = 67.4°$$

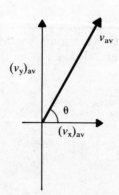

16 Consider the body in frame 13. At time $t_1 = 5.0$ s, the body has the following components of instantaneous velocity: $v_x = 2.0$ m $\cdot$ s^{-1} and $v_y = 4.0$ m $\cdot$ s^{-1}. At time $t_2 = 5.4$ s, the components of the instantaneous velocity are $v_x = 5.0$ m $\cdot$ s^{-1} and $v_y = 8.0$ m $\cdot$ s^{-1}. Find the components of the average acceleration during this time interval.

16

$$(a_x)_{av} = \frac{\Delta v_x}{\Delta t} = \frac{v_{2x} - v_{1x}}{t_2 - t_1}$$

$$= \frac{5.0 \text{ m} \cdot \text{s}^{-1} - 2.0 \text{ m} \cdot \text{s}^{-1}}{5.4 \text{ s} - 5.0 \text{ s}} = \frac{3.0 \text{ m} \cdot \text{s}^{-1}}{0.4 \text{ m} \cdot \text{s}^{-1}}$$

$$= 7.5 \text{ m} \cdot \text{s}^{-2}$$

$$(a_y)_{av} = \frac{\Delta v_y}{\Delta t} = \frac{v_{2y} - v_{1y}}{t_2 - t_1}$$

$$= \frac{8.0 \text{ m} \cdot \text{s}^{-1} - 4 \text{ m} \cdot \text{s}^{-1}}{5.4 \text{ s} - 5.0 \text{ s}} = \frac{4.0 \text{ m} \cdot \text{s}^{-1}}{0.4 \text{ s}}$$

$$= 10 \text{ m} \cdot \text{s}^{-2}$$

17 Find the magnitude of the average acceleration.

17

$$|a_{av}| = \sqrt{(a_x)_{av}{}^2 + (a_y)_{av}{}^2}$$

$$= \sqrt{(7.5 \text{ m} \cdot \text{s}^{-2})^2 + (10.0 \text{ m} \cdot \text{s}^{-2})^2}$$

$$= 12.5 \text{ m} \cdot \text{s}^{-2}$$

18 Find the direction of the average acceleration.

18

$$\tan \theta = \frac{|(a_y)_{av}|}{|(a_x)_{av}|}$$

$$= \frac{|10.0 \text{ m} \cdot \text{s}^{-2}|}{|7.5 \text{ m} \cdot \text{s}^{-2}|}$$

$$\theta = 53.1°$$

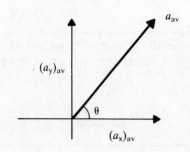

19 A projectile is launched at an angle θ_0 with respect to the horizontal with an initial velocity v_0. At any moment its direction of motion makes an angle θ with the horizontal. Derive a formula for θ as a function of time.

19

Since $\quad v_y = v_0 \sin \theta_0 - gt$

and $\quad v_x = v_0 \cos \theta_0$,

$$\tan \theta = \frac{v_y}{v_x} = \frac{v_0 \sin \theta_0 - gt}{v_0 \cos \theta_0}$$

$$= \frac{v_0 \sin \theta_0}{v_0 \cos \theta_0} - \frac{gt}{v_0 \cos \theta_0}$$

$$= \tan \theta_0 - \frac{gt}{v_0 \cos \theta_0}$$

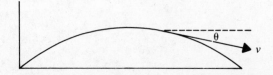

20 A mortar shell is launched from the edge of a cliff 120 m above ground level with an initial velocity of 150 m · s^{-1} at an angle of 40° with the horizontal. Determine the time required for the shell to hit the ground.

20

The shell will hit the ground 120 m below the origin.

$$y = (v_0 \sin \theta_0)t - \tfrac{1}{2} gt^2$$

since $y = -120$ m.

$$-120 \text{ m} = (150 \text{ m} \cdot \text{s}^{-1} \sin 40°)t - \tfrac{1}{2} 9.8 \text{ m} \cdot \text{s}^{-2} t^2$$
$$= 96.4 \text{ m} \cdot \text{s}^{-1} t - 4.9 \text{ m} \cdot \text{s}^{-2} t^2$$
$$4.9 \text{ m} \cdot \text{s}^{-2} t^2 - 96.4 \text{ m} \cdot \text{s}^{-1} t - 120 \text{ m} = 0$$

From the quadratic equation

$$t = \frac{-(-96.4) \pm \sqrt{(-96.4)^2 - 4(4.9\,(-120)}}{2(4.9)} \, ,$$

$$t = -1.173 \text{ s and} + 20.85 \text{ s}.$$

-1.173 s is extraneous; therefore $t = 20.85$ s.

---

21 Determine the distance, as measured from the base of the cliff, where the shell struck the ground.

21

$$x = (v_0 \cos \theta_0)t$$
$$= (150 \text{ m} \cdot \text{s}^{-1} \cos 40°)\,(20.85 \text{ s})$$
$$= 2396 \text{ m}$$

---

22 Determine the horizontal and vertical components of the shell's velocity at the instant it struck the ground.

22

$$v_x = v_0 \cos \theta_0$$
$$= 150 \text{ m} \cdot \text{s}^{-1} \cos 40°$$
$$= 114.9 \text{ m} \cdot \text{s}^{-1}$$
$$v_y = v_0 \sin \theta_0 - gt$$
$$= 150 \text{ m} \cdot \text{s}^{-1} \sin 40° - 9.8 \text{ m} \cdot \text{s}^{-2}\,(20.85 \text{ s})$$
$$= 96.42 \text{ m} \cdot \text{s}^{-1} - 204.3 \text{ m} \cdot \text{s}^{-1}$$
$$= -107.9 \text{ m} \cdot \text{s}^{-1}$$

---

23 Determine the magnitude of the velocity.

23

$$v = \sqrt{v_x{}^2 + v_y{}^2}$$
$$= \sqrt{(114.9 \text{ m} \cdot \text{s}^{-1})^2 + (-107.9 \text{ m} \cdot \text{s}^{-1})^2}$$
$$= 157.6 \text{ m} \cdot \text{s}^{-1}$$

---

24 Determine the angle made by the velocity vector with the horizontal.

24

$$\tan \theta = \frac{|v_y|}{|v_x|} = \frac{|-107.9 \text{ m} \cdot \text{s}^{-1}|}{|114.9 \text{ m} \cdot \text{s}^{-1}|}$$

$$\theta = 43.2°$$

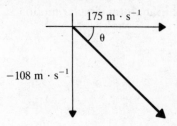

25 Find the angle by the formula derived in frame 19.

25

$$\tan \theta = \tan \theta_0 - \frac{gt}{v_0 \cos \theta_0}$$

$$= \tan 40° - \frac{(9.8 \text{ m} \cdot \text{s}^{-2})(20.85 \text{ s})}{(150 \text{ m} \cdot \text{s}^{-1}) \cos 40°}$$

$$= 0.8391 - 1.778 = -0.9389$$

$$= 43.2°$$

26 An unbanked circular speedway has a radius of 300 m. A car makes one complete circle at a speed of 35 m $\cdot$ s^{-1}. What is the centripetal acceleration of the car?

26

$$a_\perp = \frac{v^2}{R}$$

$$= \frac{(35 \text{ m} \cdot \text{s}^{-1})^2}{300 \text{ m}}$$

$$= 4.08 \text{ m} \cdot \text{s}^{-2}$$

27 How long does it take the car to make one complete circle?

27

$$v = \frac{2\pi R}{\tau}$$

$$\tau = \frac{2\pi R}{v} = \frac{2\pi (300 \text{ m})}{35 \text{ m} \cdot \text{s}^{-1}}$$

$$= 53.8 \text{ s}$$

28 The radius of the moon's orbit around the earth is 3.85×10^8 m. The moon travels around this orbit in 27.3 days. Find the magnitude of the moon's orbital velocity.

28

$$27.3 \text{ d} \times \frac{24 \text{ h}}{1 \text{ d}} \times \frac{3600 \text{ s}}{1 \text{ h}} = 2.36 \times 16^6 \text{ s}$$

$$v = \frac{2\pi R}{\tau} = \frac{2\pi (3.85 \times 10^8 \text{ m})}{2.36 \times 10^6 \text{ s}}$$

$$= 1.03 \times 10^3 \text{ m} \cdot \text{s}^{-1}$$

29 Find the radial acceleration of the moon toward the earth in $m \cdot s^{-2}$.

29

$$a_\perp = \frac{v^2}{R}$$

$$= \frac{(1.03 \times 10^3 \, m \cdot s^{-1})^2}{3.85 \times 10^8 \, m}$$

$$= 2.76 \times 10^{-3} \, m \cdot s^{-2}$$

---

30 Draw the velocity and radial acceleration vectors of a particle in uniform circular motion.

30

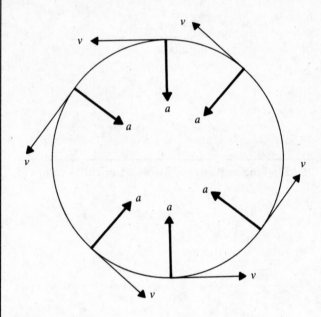

---

31 The speed of a barge in still water is $13.0 \, km \cdot h^{-1}$. At what upstream angle should the barge head if it is to travel directly across a river whose current has a speed of $5.0 \, km \cdot h^{-1}$?

31

$v_{BW} = 13 \, km \cdot h^{-1}$
$v_{WE} = 5 \, km \cdot h^{-1}$
$v_{BE} = ?$
$v_{BE} = v_{BW} + v_{WE}$

we have a right triangle.

$$\sin \theta = \frac{5 \, km \cdot h^{-1}}{13 \, km \cdot h^{-1}} = 0.3846$$

$$\theta = 22.6°$$

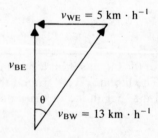

---

32 What is the speed of the barge with respect to the earth?

32 From the vector triangle, which is a 5–12–13 right triangle,

$$v_{BE} = 12 \, km \cdot h^{-1}$$

STEP BY STEP SOLUTIONS OF PROBLEMS

Problem 1 A mortar shell projected at an angle of 65° above the horizontal strikes a tower 25 m away at a point 15 m above the point of projection. a) Find the initial speed v_0 of the projectile. b) How long was it in the air? c) Find the magnitude and direction of the velocity of the projectile when it strikes the tower. d) Find the maximum height of the projectile. e) If the projectile had not struck the tower, what would have been the range R of the projectile? f) What would be the magnitude and direction of the velocity of the projectile upon impact?

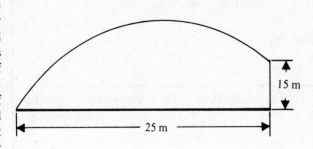

Since a_x and a_y are constant (i.e., $a_x = 0$ and $a_y = -g$), we can use the kinematic equations for constant acceleration ($x_0 = y_0 = 0$):

$$x = v_0 t + \tfrac{1}{2}a_x t^2$$
$$y = v_{0y} t + \tfrac{1}{2}a_y t^2$$

1 Since
$$v_x = v_{0x} = v_0 \cos \theta_0 \quad \text{and} \quad a_x = 0,$$
the first equation becomes:

1 $\quad x = (v_0 \cos \theta_0)t$

---

2 Since
$$v_{0y} = v_0 \sin \theta_0 \quad \text{and} \quad a_y = -g,$$
the second equation becomes:

2 $\quad y = (v_0 \sin \theta_0)t - \tfrac{1}{2}gt^2$

---

3 Substitute
$$x = 25 \text{ m}$$
$$y = 15 \text{ m}$$
and $\theta_0 = 65°$ in the equations in frames 1 and 2.

3
$$25 \text{ m} = (v_0 \cos 65°)t$$
$$15 \text{ m} = (v_0 \sin 65°)t - \tfrac{1}{2}(9.8 \text{ m} \cdot \text{s}^{-2})t^2$$

---

4 Solve the first equation in frame 3 for t, substitute in the second equation, and solve for v_0.

4
$$t = \frac{25 \text{ m}}{v_0 \cos 65°}$$
$$= \frac{59.1 \text{ m}}{v_0}$$
$$15 \text{ m} = v_0(0.906)\frac{59.1 \text{ m}}{v_0}$$
$$\quad - 4.9 \text{ m} \cdot \text{s}^{-2}\frac{(59.1 \text{ m})^2}{v_0^2}$$
$$v_0 = 21.1 \text{ m} \cdot \text{s}^{-1}$$

---

5 Substitute
$$v_0 = 21.1 \text{ m} \cdot \text{s}^{-1}$$
in the first equation to obtain t.

5
$$t = \frac{59.1 \text{ m}}{v_0}$$
$$= \frac{59.1 \text{ m}}{21.1 \text{ m} \cdot \text{s}^{-1}} = 2.80 \text{ s}$$

---

6 Find v_x and v_y;
$v_x = v_{0x} = v_0 \cos \theta_0$ and
$v_y = v_0 \sin \theta_0 - gt$.

6
$v_x = 21.1 \text{ m} \cdot \text{s}^{-1} \cos 65° = 8.92 \text{ m} \cdot \text{s}^{-1}$
$v_y = 21.1 \text{ m} \cdot \text{s}^{-1} \sin 65° - 9.8 \text{ m} \cdot \text{s}^{-2}$
$\qquad \times (2.80 \text{ s})$
$\quad = -8.34 \text{ m} \cdot \text{s}^{-1}$

---

7 Find the magnitude of the velocity vector by using $|v| = \sqrt{v_x^2 + v_y^2}$ and the direction of the velocity vector by using $\tan \theta = \dfrac{|v_y|}{|v_x|}$.

7
$$v = \sqrt{(8.92 \text{ m} \cdot \text{s}^{-1})^2 + (-8.3 \text{ m} \cdot \text{s}^{-1})^2}$$
$$\quad = 12.2 \text{ m} \cdot \text{s}^{-1}$$
$$\tan \theta = \frac{|-8.34 \text{ m} \cdot \text{s}^{-1}|}{|8.92 \text{ m} \cdot \text{s}^{-1}|}$$
$$\theta = 43.1° \text{ below the horizontal}$$

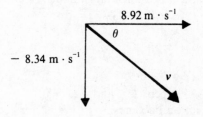

---

8 Find the maximum height by setting
$v_y = 0$ in
$v_y = v_0 \sin \theta_0 - gt$.
This equation will give you the time for the shell to reach its maximum height. Substitute this value of t in the equation in frame 2 to obtain the maximum height.

8
$21.1 \text{ m} \cdot \text{s}^{-1} (\sin 65°) - 9.8 \text{ m} \cdot \text{s}^{-2}(t) = 0$
$t = 1.95 \text{ s}$
$H = (v_0 \sin \theta_0)t - \frac{1}{2}gt^2$
$\quad = (21.1 \text{ m} \cdot \text{s}^{-1}) (\sin 65°) (1.95 \text{ s})$
$\qquad - \frac{1}{2}(9.8 \text{ m} \cdot \text{s}^{-2}) (1.95 \text{ s})^2$
$\quad = 18.7 \text{ m}$

---

9 Find the range by setting $y = 0$ in the equation in frame 2. Note that this quadratic equation has two roots at which
$y = 0$:
$\quad t = 0$ (the origin) and
$\quad t = \dfrac{2v_0 \sin \theta_0}{g}$
Substitute this value of t in
$\quad R = (v_0 \cos \theta_0)t$.

9
$y = 0 = (v_0 \sin \theta_0)t - \frac{1}{2}gt^2$
$0 = t(v_0 \sin \theta_0 - \frac{1}{2}gt)$
We have two values for t,
$\quad t = 0$ and
$\quad t = \dfrac{2v_0 \sin \theta_0}{g}$.
Substituting, we have
$\quad t = \dfrac{(2) (21.1 \text{ m} \cdot \text{s}^{-1}) \sin 65°}{9.8 \text{ m} \cdot \text{s}^{-2}} = 3.90 \text{ s}$
Note that this time is double the time for the shell to reach its maximum height:
$\quad R = 21.1 \text{ m} \cdot \text{s}^{-1} (\cos 65°) (3.90 \text{ s})$
$\qquad = 34.8 \text{ m}$

---

10 Find the velocity of the shell at the maximum range by using

$$|v| = \sqrt{v_x{}^2 + v_y{}^2}.$$

Remember v_x is always equal to $v_0 \cos \theta_0$. Also, we computed the time for maximum range in frame 9,

$$t = 3.90 \text{ s}.$$

Of course we knew the answer, but it's good to check.

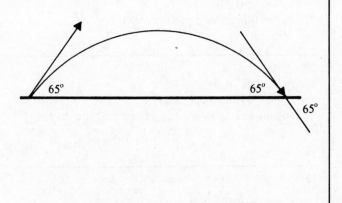

10

$$v_x = v_0 \cos \theta_0 = 8.92 \text{ m} \cdot \text{s}^{-1}$$
$$v_y = v_0 \sin \theta_0 - gt$$
$$= 21.1 \text{ m} \cdot \text{s}^{-1} (\sin 65°) - 9.8 \text{ m} \cdot \text{s}^{-2}$$
$$\times (3.90 \text{ s})$$
$$= -19.1 \text{ m} \cdot \text{s}^{-1}$$
$$|v| = \sqrt{v_x{}^2 + v_y{}^2}$$
$$= \sqrt{(8.92 \text{ m} \cdot \text{s}^{-1})^2 + (-19.1 \text{ m} \cdot \text{s}^{-1})^2}$$
$$= 21.1 \text{ m} \cdot \text{s}^{-1}$$
$$\tan \theta = \frac{|v_y|}{|v_x|}$$
$$= \frac{|-19.1 \text{ m} \cdot \text{s}^{-1}|}{|8.92 \text{ m} \cdot \text{s}^{-1}|}$$
$$\theta = 65° \text{ below the horizontal}$$

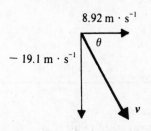

Problem 2 An anti-aircraft artillery gun fires a projectile with a muzzle velocity of 1000 m · s^{-1}. If the projectile is to explode at an altitude of 4000 m and a horizontal range of 3000 m from the gun site, find the angle of elevation of the gun and the fuse setting of the projectile. This is a standard anti-aircraft artillery problem. Given x, y, and v_0, find θ_0 and t.

---

11 Eliminate t from the basic kinematic equations
$$x = (v_0 \cos \theta_0)t$$
$$y = (v_0 \sin \theta_0)t - \tfrac{1}{2}gt^2$$

11 Solve the first equation for t and substitute in the second equation.

$$t = \frac{x}{v_0 \cos \theta_0}$$
$$y = v_0 \sin \theta_0 \frac{x}{v_0 \cos \theta_0} - \tfrac{1}{2} \frac{gx^2}{v_0{}^2 \cos^2 \theta_0}$$
$$= (\tan \theta_0) x - \frac{gx^2}{2v_0{}^2 \cos^2 \theta_0}$$

---

12 Substitute
$x = 3000$ m and
$y = 4000$ m.

12

$$4000 \text{ m} = \tan \theta_0 (3000 \text{ m})$$
$$- \frac{9.8 \text{ m} \cdot \text{s}^{-2} (3000 \text{ m})^2}{2(1000 \text{ m} \cdot \text{s}^{-1})^2 \cos^2 \theta_0}$$

---

13 Simplify; let
$$\tan \theta_0 = \frac{\sin \theta_0}{\cos \theta_0}.$$

13 $4000 \cos^2 \theta_0 + 44.1 = 3000 \sin \theta_0 \cos \theta_0$

---

14 Divide each term by 1000 and substitute
$$\sin \theta_0 = \sqrt{1 - \cos^2 \theta_0}.$$

14

$$4 \cos^2 \theta_0 + 0.0441 = 3 \cos \theta_0 \sqrt{1 - \cos^2 \theta_0}$$

---

15 Square both sides and collect similar terms.

15

$$16 \cos^4 \theta_0 + 0.353 \cos^2 \theta_0 + 0.00195$$
$$= 9 \cos^2 \theta_0 - 9 \cos^4 \theta_0$$
$$25 \cos^4 \theta_0 - 8.65 \cos^2 \theta_0 + 0.00195 = 0$$

16 Let $\cos^2 \theta_0 = q$ and solve the resulting quadratic for q.

16

$$25q^2 - 8.65q + 0.00195 = 0$$

$$q = \frac{8.65 \pm \sqrt{8.65^2 - 4(25)(0.00195)}}{2(25)}$$

$$= 0, 0.346$$

($q = 0$ is an extraneous root)

17 Solve $\cos^2 \theta_0 = 0.346$ for θ_0.

17

$$\cos^2 \theta_0 = 0.346$$
$$\cos \theta_0 = \pm 0.588$$

(again $\cos \theta_0 = -0.588$ is an extraneous root)

$$\theta_0 = 54.0°$$

18 Substitute
$\theta_0 = 54.0°$ in
$x = (v_0 \cos \theta_0)$ to obtain t.

18

$$t = \frac{x}{v_0 \cos \theta_0}$$

$$= \frac{3000 \text{ m}}{1000 \text{ m} \cdot \text{s}^{-1} (\cos 54°)}$$

$$= 5.10 \text{ s}$$

Problem 3 What is the radius of curvature of a projectile at the top of its trajectory in terms of θ_0 and v_0? What is its radial acceleration at this point?

19 Define a new system where the origin of the new set of axes is the peak (h, k) of the parabola.

19

$$x = x' + h$$
$$y = y' + k$$

where h, k are the x, y coordinates of the x', y' system

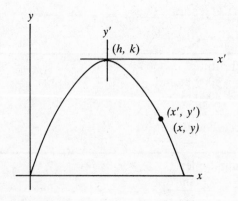

20 Find h. Remember that
$$\text{range} = \frac{v_0^2 \sin 2\theta_0}{g}$$

20

$$h = \frac{\text{range}}{2} = \frac{v_0^2 \sin 2\theta_0}{2g}$$

21 What is the equation of a parabolic trajectory?

21

$$y = (\tan \theta_0)\, x - \frac{g}{2v_0{}^2 \cos^2 \theta_0}\, x^2$$

---

22 For maximum height k,
$$x = \frac{R}{2} = \frac{v_0{}^2 \sin 2\theta_0}{2g}\,.$$
Substitute this in the equation for the parabolic trajectory. Remember $\sin 2\theta_0 = 2 \sin \theta_0 \cos \theta_0$

22

$$k = \tan \theta_0 \left(\frac{v_0{}^2 \sin 2\theta_0}{2g} \right) - \frac{g}{2v_0{}^2 \cos^2 \theta_0} \times$$
$$\left(\frac{v_0{}^2 \sin 2\theta_0}{2g} \right)^2$$

$$= \frac{\sin \theta_0}{\cos \theta_0} \left(\frac{v_0{}^2\, 2 \sin \theta_0 \cos \theta_0}{2g} \right) - \frac{g}{2v_0{}^2 \cos^2 \theta_0} \times$$
$$\left(\frac{v_0{}^2\, 2 \sin \theta_0 \cos \theta_0}{2g} \right)^2$$

$$= \frac{v_0{}^2 \sin^2 \theta_0}{g} - \frac{g}{2v_0{}^2 \cos^2 \theta_0} \times$$
$$\left(\frac{4\, v_0{}^4 \sin^2 \theta_0 \cos^2 \theta_0}{4g^2} \right)$$

$$= \frac{v_0{}^2 \sin^2 \theta_0}{g} - \frac{v_0{}^2 \sin^2 \theta_0}{2g}$$

$$= \frac{v_0{}^2 \sin^2 \theta_0}{2g}$$

---

23 What is the equation for a parabola in the x', y' system?

23 In the x, y system, the equation is $x^2 = -4py$. In the x', y' system, it is $x'^2 = -4py'$.

---

24 Translate this equation to the x, y system. Substitute $x' = x - h$ and $y' = y - k$.

24

$$x'^2 = -4py'$$
$$(x - h)^2 = -4p\,(y - k)$$
$$x^2 - 2hx + h^2 = -4py + 4pk$$

$$y = \left(\frac{h}{2p} \right) x - \frac{1}{4p}\, x^2 + \left(k - \frac{h^2}{4p} \right)$$

25 We now have two equations for a parabolic trajectory:

$$y = \left(\frac{h}{2p}\right) x - \frac{1}{4p} x^2 + \left(k - \frac{h^2}{4p}\right)$$

and

$$y = (\tan \theta_0)\, x - \frac{g}{2v_0^2 \cos^2 \theta_0} x^2.$$

Equate corresponding coefficients and solve for p.

25

$$\frac{h}{2p} = \tan \theta_0 \qquad \text{(coefficients of } x\text{)}$$

$$p = \frac{v_0^2 \cos^2 \theta_0}{2g}$$

$$\frac{1}{4p} = \frac{g}{2v_0^2 \cos^2 \theta_0} \qquad \text{(coefficients of } x^2\text{)}$$

$$p = \frac{v_0^2 \cos^2 \theta_0}{2g}$$

$$k - \frac{h^2}{4p} = 0 \qquad \text{(There is no constant term since the parabola passes through the origin.)}$$

$$p = \frac{v_0^2 \cos^2 \theta_0}{2g}$$

Note that we get the same value for p each time.

---

26 Find the radius of curvature from $R = 2p$.

26

$$R = 2p$$

$$= 2 \left(\frac{v_0^2 \cos^2 \theta_0}{2g}\right)$$

$$= \frac{v_0^2 \cos^2 \theta_0}{g}$$

---

27 Find the radial acceleration at the peak. Remember that $v = v_x = v_0 \cos \theta_0$.

27

$$a_\perp = \frac{v^2}{R}$$

$$= \frac{(v_0 \cos \theta_0)^2}{\dfrac{v_0^2 \cos^2 \theta_0}{g}}$$

$$= g$$

Problem 4 Prove that an object dropped vertically will hit the ground in the same time as an object projected horizontally.

28 Through what distance does an object fall in time t?

28

$$y = -\tfrac{1}{2} g t^2$$

---

29 Through what distance does an object fall if it is projected horizontally with a velocity v_0?

29

$$y = x \tan \theta_0 - \tfrac{1}{2} g \left(\frac{x}{v_0 \cos \theta_0}\right)^2$$

Since $\theta_0 = 0$,

$$y = -\tfrac{1}{2} g \left(\frac{x^2}{v_0^2}\right)$$

---

30 What is the range of an object projected horizontally?

30
$$x = (v_0 \cos \theta_0)t$$
since $\theta_0 = 0$,
$$x = v_0 t$$

---

31 Substitute this value of range in the equation for vertical distance.

31

$$y = -\tfrac{1}{2} g \left(\frac{x_2}{v_0^2} \right) = -\tfrac{1}{2} g \, \frac{(v_0 t)^2}{v_0^2}$$
$$= -\tfrac{1}{2} g t^2$$

Since the two vertical distances are the same, the two times are equal.

Problem 5 Two racing cars leave a corner at the same time at right angles to each other. Car 1 is traveling north at $9 \text{ m} \cdot \text{s}^{-1}$, and car 2 is traveling east at $12 \text{ m} \cdot \text{s}^{-1}$. What is the relative velocity of car 1 with respect to car 2?

32 Draw a sketch of the two cars with respect to a reference frame fixed to the earth.

32
v_{2E} is the velocity of car 2 with respect to the earth.
v_{1E} is the velocity of car 1 with respect to the earth.

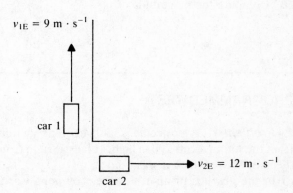

---

33 Since we are finding the relative velocity of car 1 with respect to car 2, we will assume that car 2 is at rest. What is the velocity of the earth with respect to car 2?

33 The earth is moving toward car 2 with velocity v_{E2}.

---

34 What is the velocity of car 1 with respect to car 2?

34 v_{12}

---

35 Write the vector equation of the velocity of car 1 as seen by car 2.

35
$$v_{12} = v_{1E} + v_{E2}$$
Velocity of car 1 with respect to car 2 is equal to the velocity of car 1 with respect to earth plus velocity of earth with respect to car 2.

$$\begin{aligned} & v_{1\cancel{E}} \\ + \; & v_{\cancel{E}2} \\ \hline & v_{12} \end{aligned}$$

---

36 But $v_{E2} = -v_{2E}$. Draw a vector diagram

36

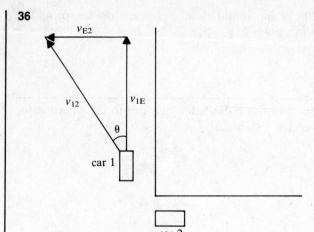

37 In what direction is car 1 seen moving by car 2?

37

$$\tan \theta = \frac{|v_{E2}|}{|v_{1E}|} = \frac{|12 \text{ m} \cdot \text{s}^{-1}|}{|9 \text{ m} \cdot \text{s}^{-1}|} = 1.333$$

$$\theta = 53.1°$$

38 Compute the magnitude of v_{12}.

38

$$v_{12} = \sqrt{(9 \text{ m} \cdot \text{s}^{-1})^2 + (12 \text{ m} \cdot \text{s}^{-1})^2}$$
$$= 15 \text{ m} \cdot \text{s}^{-1}$$

PROGRAMMED TEST

1 **Problem 1** A projectile is launched horizontally from the top of a cliff 200 m high. It falls 1850 m from the spot above which it was fired.
a) In the absence of air resistance, how long was it in the air?
b) What was the initial velocity?
c) Find the magnitude and direction of the velocity of the projectile just before impact.

1

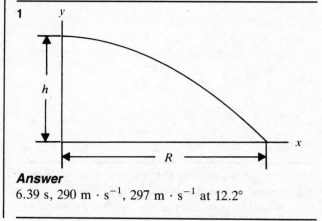

Answer
6.39 s, 290 m $\cdot$ s^{-1}, 297 m $\cdot$ s^{-1} at 12.2°

If you solved this problem correctly, go to frame 5. If you could not solve this problem, go through frames 2–4.

2 Find the time t.

2

$$y = v_{0y}t + \tfrac{1}{2}at^2$$
$$-200 \text{ m} = 0 - \tfrac{1}{2}(9.8 \text{ m} \cdot \text{s}^{-2})t^2$$
$$t = \pm 6.39 \text{ s}$$
$+6.39$ s is the desired answer

3 Find the initial speed. The initial speed is in the x-direction only (remember that it is constant throughout the trajectory).

3

$$v_{0x} = v_x = \frac{R}{t}$$
$$= \frac{1850 \text{ m}}{6.39 \text{ s}}$$
$$= 290 \text{ m} \cdot \text{s}^{-1}$$

4 We must find the *x*- and *y*-components of the velocity at this point in order to calculate the velocity just before impact.

4

$$v_y^2 = v_{0y}^2 + 2a(y - y_0)$$
$$= 0 - 2(9.8 \text{ m} \cdot \text{s}^{-2})(-200 \text{ m})$$
$$= -62.6 \text{ m} \cdot \text{s}^{-1}$$
$$v = \sqrt{v_x^2 + v_y^2}$$
$$= \sqrt{(290 \text{ m} \cdot \text{s}^{-1})^2 + (-62.6 \text{ m} \cdot \text{s}^{-1})^2}$$
$$= 297 \text{ m} \cdot \text{s}^{-1}$$
$$\tan \theta = \frac{|v_y|}{|v_x|}$$
$$= \frac{62.6 \text{ m} \cdot \text{s}^{-1}}{290 \text{ m} \cdot \text{s}^{-1}} = 0.216$$
$$\theta = 12.2°$$

below the *x*-axis

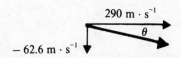

5 *Problem 2* An anti-aircraft gun has an angle of inclination of 75° and a muzzle velocity of 1100 m · s⁻¹ a) If the shell is to explode at an altitude of 1600 m, for what time after firing should the fuse be set? b) What will be the velocity at these times? c) If the shell does not explode, what would be the time for the shell to reach its maximum height? d) What would be the maximum height? e) What would be the range? f) Draw a sketch.

5

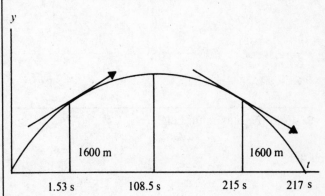

Answer
1.53 s or 215 s, 1090 m · s⁻¹ and
1090 m · s⁻¹, 108.5 s, 57600 m, 61800 m

If you solved this problem correctly, go to frame 11. If you could not solve this problem, go through frames 6–10.

6 Find the time for the shell to reach an altitude of 1600 m.

6

$$y = v_0 t + \tfrac{1}{2} a t^2$$
$$1600 \text{ m} = (1100 \text{ m} \cdot \text{s}^{-1})(\sin 75°)t$$
$$- \tfrac{1}{2}(9.8 \text{ m} \cdot \text{s}^{-2})t^2$$
$$4.9\, t^2 - 1063\, t + 1600 = 0$$
$$t = \frac{1063 \pm \sqrt{1063^2 - 4(4.9)(1600)}}{9.8}$$
$$= 1.53 \text{ s}, 215 \text{ s}$$

7 Find the velocities at these times.

$$v_x = v_0 \cos \theta_0 = (1100 \text{ m} \cdot \text{s}^{-1})(\cos 75°)$$
$$= 285 \text{ m} \cdot \text{s}^{-1} \text{ at all points}$$
$$v_y = v_0 \sin \theta_0 - gt$$
$$= (1100 \text{ m} \cdot \text{s}^{-1})(\sin 75°) - (9.8 \text{ m} \cdot \text{s}^{-2})$$
$$\times (1.53 \text{ s})$$
$$= 1050 \text{ m} \cdot \text{s}^{-1}$$
$$v = \sqrt{v_x{}^2 + v_y{}^2}$$
$$= \sqrt{(285 \text{ m} \cdot \text{s}^{-1})^2 + (1050 \text{ m} \cdot \text{s}^{-1})^2}$$
$$= 1090 \text{ m} \cdot \text{s}^{-1} \text{ (at } t = 1.53 \text{ s)}$$
$$v_y = (1100 \text{ m} \cdot \text{s}^{-1})(\sin 75°) - (9.8 \text{ m} \cdot \text{s}^{-2})$$
$$\times (215 \text{ s})$$
$$= -1050 \text{ m} \cdot \text{s}^{-1}$$
$$v = \sqrt{v_x{}^2 + v_y{}^2}$$
$$= \sqrt{(285 \text{ m} \cdot \text{s}^{-1})^2 + (-1050 \text{ m} \cdot \text{s}^{-1})^2}$$
$$= 1090 \text{ m} \cdot \text{s}^{-1} \text{ (at } t = 215 \text{ s)}$$

which agrees with our intuition.

8 To find the time for the shell to reach the maximum height, set $v_y = 0$.

$$v_y = v_0 \sin \theta_0 - gt = 0$$
$$t = \frac{v_0 \sin \theta_0}{g}$$
$$= \frac{1100 \text{ m} \cdot \text{s}^{-1}}{9.8 \text{ m} \cdot \text{s}^{-2}} \sin 75° = 108.5 \text{ s}$$

9 Find the maximum height.

$$H = (v_0 \sin \theta_0)t - \tfrac{1}{2}gt^2$$
$$= 1100 \text{ m} \cdot \text{s}^{-1} (\sin 75°)(108.5 \text{ s})$$
$$- \tfrac{1}{2}(9.8 \text{ m} \cdot \text{s}^{-2})(108.5 \text{ s})^2$$
$$= 57,600 \text{ m}$$

10 To find the range, we must first find t for the complete trajectory, and then find R.

$$y = v_0 \sin \theta_0\, t - \tfrac{1}{2}gt^2 = 0$$
$$0 = t(v_0 \sin \theta_0 - \tfrac{1}{2}gt)$$
$$t = 0,$$
$$t = \frac{2v_0 \sin \theta_0}{g}$$
$$= \frac{2(1100 \text{ m} \cdot \text{s}^{-1}) \sin 75°}{9.8 \text{ m} \cdot \text{s}^{-2}} = 217 \text{ s}$$

note that $t = 2(108.5 \text{ s})$
$$R = v_0 \cos \theta_0\,(t)$$
$$= (1100 \text{ m} \cdot \text{s}^{-1})(\cos 75°)(217 \text{ s})$$
$$= 61,800 \text{ m}$$

11 **Problem 3** A ball rolls off a horizontal table top 1 m above the floor with a horizontal speed of 4 $m \cdot s^{-1}$. Find a) the time it takes the ball to reach the floor, b) the horizontal distance covered, c) the magnitude and direction of the velocity of the ball just before it strikes the floor.

11

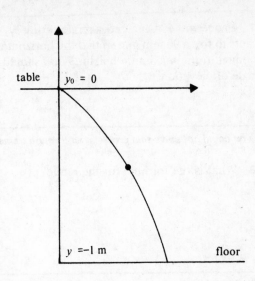

Answer

0.452 s, 1.81 m, 5.97 $m \cdot s^{-1}$

47.9° below the x-axis

If you solved this problem correctly, go to frame 17. If you could not solve this problem, go through frames 12–16.

12 State what is given.

12 Given

$v_{0x} = 4 \ m \cdot s^{-1}$ $v_{0y} = 0$

$a_x = 0$ $a_y = -g = -9.8 \ m \cdot s^{-1}$

$x_0 = 0$ $y - y_0 = -1 \ m$

13 Use $y - y_0 = v_{0y} t + \frac{1}{2}a_y t^2$ to find t.

13

$$-1 \ m - 0 = 0 - \frac{1}{2}(9.8 \ m \cdot s^{-2})t^2$$
$$t = 0.452 \ s$$

14 Use $x - x_0 = v_{0x} t + \frac{1}{2} a_x t^2$ to find x, the horizontal distance covered.

14

$x - 0 = (4 \ m \cdot s^{-1}) \ (0.452 \ s) + 0$

$x = 1.81 \ m$

15 Find the magnitude and direction of the velocity of the ball just before it strikes the ground. What is v_x?

Find v_y by using $v_y = v_{0y} + a_y t$.

Find v by using $v = \sqrt{v_x^2 + v_y^2}$

15

$v_x = v_{0x} = 4 \ m \cdot s^{-1}$

$v_y = 0 - (9.8 \ m \cdot s^{-2}) \ (0.452 \ s)$

    $= -4.43 \ m \cdot s^{-1}$

$v = \sqrt{(4 \ m \cdot s^{-1})^2 + (-4.43 \ m \cdot s^{-1})^2}$

   $= 5.97 \ m \cdot s^{-1}$

16 Find the angle.

16

$$\tan \theta = \frac{|-4.43 \ m \cdot s^{-1}|}{|4 \ m \cdot s^{-1}|}$$

$\theta = 47.9°$ below x-axis

17 Problem 4 An anti-aircraft artillery officer wants to fire a 90 mm gun so that the horizontal range is equal to the maximum height. What should be the angle of elevation θ_0?

If you could not solve this problem, go through frames 18–25.

18 What is the formula for the range?

19 What is the formula for the height?

20 What is the formula for the vertical component of the velocity vector?

21 What is v_y when the projectile reaches its maximum height?

22 Let $v_y = 0$ and solve for t.

23 Substitute this value of t in the equation for y in order to obtain an expression for the maximum height y_{max}.

24 Equate the expressions for maximum height and range and simplify.

17
Answer 76°

18
$$R = \frac{v_0^2 \sin 2\theta_0}{g}$$

19
$$y = (v_0 \sin \theta_0)t - \tfrac{1}{2}gt^2$$

20
$$v_y = v_0 \sin \theta_0 - gt$$

21
$$v_y = 0$$

22
$$0 = v_0 \sin \theta_0 - gt$$
$$t = \frac{v_0 \sin \theta_0}{g}$$

23
$$y_{max} = (v_0 \sin \theta_0)\left(\frac{v_0 \sin \theta_0}{g}\right) - \tfrac{1}{2} g \left(\frac{v_0 \sin \theta_0}{g}\right)^2$$
$$= \tfrac{1}{2} g(v_0^2 \sin^2 \theta_0)$$

24
$$\frac{v_0^2 \sin^2 \theta_0}{2g} = \frac{v_0^2 \sin 2\theta_0}{g}$$
$$\frac{\sin^2 \theta_0}{2} = \sin 2\theta_0$$

25 Substitute $\sin 2\theta_0 = 2 \sin \theta_0 \cos \theta_0$, simplify, and solve for θ_0.

25

$$\frac{\sin^2 \theta_0}{2} = 2 \sin \theta_0 \cos \theta_0$$

$$\frac{\sin \theta_0}{2} = 2 \cos \theta_0$$

$$\frac{\sin \theta_0}{\cos \theta_0} = \tan \theta_0 = 4$$

$$\theta_0 = 76°$$

4

Newton's Laws of Motion

CHAPTER SUMMARY

Newton's laws define all the principles of dynamics, the study of the causes of motion. Newton's first law deals with the situation where the vector sum of the forces acting on a body is zero. The second law relates force to acceleration when the vector sum of the forces is not zero, and the third law pertains to the mutual actions two bodies exert on one another. Force is discussed and illustrated, and the units of force are defined. Mass and weight are compared. The technique for finding the resultant of vectors is presented. This chapter includes the strategy for solving problems involving Newton's laws of motion, including a description of models and free-body diagrams.

BASIC TERMS — *Give definitions or meanings for the following:*

kinematics (4-I)
dynamics (4-I)
statics (4-I)
Newton's laws of motion (4-I)
empirical laws (4-I)
Philosophiae Naturalis Principia Mathematica (4-I)
force (4-1)
contact force (4-1)
vector (4-1)
resultant (4-1)
equilibrium (4-2)

mass (4-3)
newton (4-4)
dyne (4-4)
pound (4-4)
weight (4-5)
action and reaction (4-6)
tension (4-6)
free-body diagram (4-7)
frame of reference (4-8)
inertial frame of reference (4-8)

PROGRAMMED QUIZ

1 A horse is pulling a wagon. What force causes the horse to move forward?

1 The force that the ground exerts on the horse.

2 This is an example of Newton's _____ law of motion.

2 Third, since we are dealing with action and reaction forces.

75

3 In reference to Newton's third law of motion, the action and reaction forces act upon _____ bodies? (same or different)

3 Different. Either force may be considered the action and the other the reaction.

4 Describe the directions of the forces involved in Newton's third law of motion.

4 Opposite directions.

5 Give some applications of Newton's third law.

5 Rocket engine (the reaction force of expelled gases on the rocket will propel the rocket forward), water sprinkler, the firing of a rifle.

6 Describe an inertial reference frame. Give an example.

6 One in which Newton's first law is valid; a reference system which is attached to the earth, an aircraft moving at constant velocity and altitude over the earth.

7 What is the purpose of constructing models?

7 To enable us to simplify our understanding of phenomena.

8 What is a free-body (force) diagram?

8 Visualization of all the forces acting on a point particle depicted by lines with arrows to indicate the direction of the forces.

9 What are the four steps for solving equilibrium problems?

9

1 Draw a sketch.
2 draw a free-body diagram,
3 set up a rectangular coordinate system and resolve all forces acting on the particle into rectangular components,
4 set $\Sigma F_x = 0$ and $\Sigma F_y = 0$ and solve for unknown quantities.

10 The earth exerts a downward force on a body known as _____ .

10 Weight.

11 In reference to frame 10, what force (if any) does the body exert on the earth? This is an application of Newton's _____ law.

11 The body exerts an upward force of the same magnitude on the earth; third.

12 Write the first condition for equilibrium in mathematical symbols.

12

$R = 0$, $\Sigma F_x = 0$, $\Sigma F_y = 0$.

13 Which one of Newton's three laws deals with equilibrium?

13 The first law.

14 A bird is sitting at the center of a massless wire which is stretched between two poles. Explain why the wire sags regardless of how tightly the wire is stretched.

14

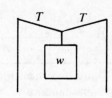

The sag provides the vertical components of the *T*s to balance *w*.

---

15 The acceleration due to gravity on the moon is about 1/6 of that on earth. If you weight 120 lb on earth, your weight on the moon would be _____.

15 20 lb;

$$w_m = mg_m$$
$$\text{but } g_m = \frac{g_E}{6}$$
$$\therefore w_m = \frac{mg_E}{6} = \frac{w_E}{6}$$
$$= \frac{120 \text{ lb}}{6} = 20 \text{ lb}.$$

---

16 Referring to frame 15, what would be your mass on the moon?

16 3.75 slugs; your mass on the moon would be the same as your mass on earth:

$$m = \frac{w_E}{g}$$
$$= \frac{120 \text{ lb}}{32 \text{ ft} \cdot \text{s}^{-2}}$$
$$= 3.75 \text{ slugs}.$$

---

17 A resultant force of 1 N is applied to a mass of 1 kg; the acceleration is _____. If the same force is applied to a mass of 10 kg, the acceleration would be _____.

17 $1 \text{ m} \cdot \text{s}^{-2}, 0.1 \text{ m} \cdot \text{s}^{-2}$;

$\Sigma F = ma$	$\Sigma F = ma$
$1 \text{ N} = 1 \text{ kg } (a)$	$1 \text{ N} = 10 \text{ kg}(a)$
$a = 1 \text{ m} \cdot \text{s}^{-2}$	$a = 0.1 \text{ m} \cdot \text{s}^{-2}$

---

18 An elevator weighs 5000 N. What is the tension in the cable when it is moving up at constant velocity? down at constant velocity?

18 5000 N in both cases; at constant velocity, the elevator is in equilibrium,
$$T = w.$$

---

19 Referring to frame 18, is the tension larger or smaller than 5000 N when it is accelerating upward? downward?

19 Larger than 5000 N; for the elevator to accelerate upward, $T - w$ must be positive. When the elevator is accelerating downward, the tension must be smaller than 5000 N since $w - T$ must be positive.

---

20 If a horizontal force of 3 N and a vertical force of 4 N act on a 1 kg body simultaneously, the acceleration will be _____.

20 $5 \text{ m} \cdot \text{s}^{-2}$;

$$\Sigma F_x = ma_x \qquad\qquad \Sigma F_y = ma_y$$
$$3 \text{ N} = 1 \text{ kg}(a_x) \qquad 4 \text{ N} = 1 \text{ kg}(a_y)$$
$$a_x = 3 \text{ m} \cdot \text{s}^{-2} \qquad\quad a_y = 4 \text{ m} \cdot \text{s}^{-2}$$
$$a = \sqrt{a_x^2 + a_y^2}$$
$$= \sqrt{(3 \text{ m} \cdot \text{s}^{-2})^2 + (4 \text{ m} \cdot \text{s}^{-2})^2}$$
$$= 5 \text{ m} \cdot \text{s}^{-2}$$

---

21 A weightless and frictionless pulley changes the _____ of the force only, not the _____ .

21 Direction, magnitude.

---

22 List the following units in order from smallest to largest: 1 gram, 1 kilogram, 1 slug. These are units of _____ .

22 I gram, 1 kilogram, 1 slug; mass.

---

23 List the following units in order from smallest to largest; 1 dyne, 1 pound, 1 newton. These are units of _____ .

23 1 dyne, 1 newton, 1 pound; force.

---

24 A body is accelerated by a resultant force acting on it. What will happen if the force is removed? This is an example of Newton's _____ law.

24 The body will continue its motion in a straight line at constant velocity; first.

---

25 In the equal-arm balance, mass is measured by balancing the _____ of the two objects.

25 Weights.

---

26 What is the relationship between gravitational mass and inertial mass?

26 Gravitational mass = inertial mass.

---

27 Is a force necessary to keep a body moving?

27 No, only to change its velocity.

---

28 If the sum of the forces in the y-direction is zero, is the object in equilibrium?

28 No, it is not accelerating in the y-direction but it may be accelerating in the x-direction if there is a resultant force in the x-direction.

---

29 In a problem involving Newton's second law, you were asked to find the acceleration. In setting up the problem you chose the wrong direction for *a*. Will you get the right answer?

29 Yes, your answer will be negative indicating that the acceleration is in the opposite direction. The magnitude will be correct.

---

30 What is included in a free-body diagram?

30 All the forces acting on the body, not the forces exerted by the body.

---

31 If a body is in equilibrium, could we use Newton's second law to determine the relationship between the forces?

31 Yes, set $\Sigma F = ma = 0$. Statics is that branch of dynamics which deals with bodies that have no acceleration.

---

32 If the resultant force acting on a body is doubled, will the velocity be doubled also?

32 No, according to Newton's second law the rate of change of velocity (acceleration) will be doubled.

MAIN IDEAS

In Chapters 2 and 3 we studied kinematics, the branch of mechanics dealing with the description of motion. The concepts of mass and force are introduced here in order to relate motion to its causes.

Dynamics is the study of systems in which $\Sigma F \neq 0$. It is based on Newton's second law of motion, $\Sigma F = ma$, where ΣF is the vector sum of all the forces acting on a body, *a* is the acceleration of the body, and *m* is the mass of the body. Although this chapter is primarily concerned with motion in one direction, it should be noted that if a body moves in a plane the above equation can be expressed in component form as $\Sigma F_x = ma_x$ and $\Sigma F_y = ma_y$. Since only straight-line motion is considered, motion along the *x*-axis implies that v_y and a_y are always equal to zero. Individual forces in some cases may have *y*-components, but $\Sigma F_y = 0$. Similarly, motion in the *y*-direction implies that v_x and a_x are equal to zero. Again, even if any individual forces have *x*-components, $\Sigma F_x = 0$.

Statics is a division of dynamics where acceleration is zero. Thus in statics we study the properties of bodies in equilibrium.

All of dynamics is based on three principles called Newton's laws of motion. The first law states that when the vector sum of the forces on a body is zero, the acceleration of the body is also zero (i.e., if $\Sigma F = 0$, then $a = 0$). The second law relates force to acceleration when the vector sum of the forces is not zero ($\Sigma F = ma$). The third law is a relation between the forces that two interacting bodies exert on each other.

Forces can be combined by vector addition. You should review the technique discussed in Chapter 1.

Consider the following problem: three forces F_1, F_2, F_3 lying in the $xy -$ plane act at point *0*. Find the magnitude and direction of the resultant force.

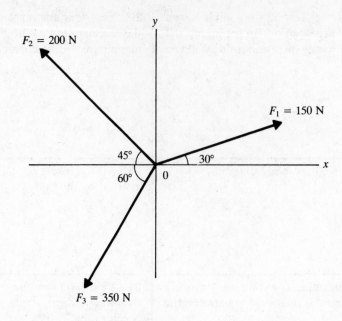

The computation for vector addition can be arranged systematically as follows:

Force	Angle	x-component	y-component
$F_1 = 150$ N	30°	+ 150 N cos 30° = + 130 N	+ 150 N sin 30° = + 75 N
$F_2 = 200$ N	45°	− 200 N cos 45° = − 141 N	+ 200 N sin 45° = + 141 N
$F_3 = 350$ N	60°	− 350 N cos 60° = − 175 N	− 350 N sin 60° = − 303 N
		$R_x = \Sigma F_x = -186$ N	$R_y = \Sigma F_y = -87$ N

$$R = \sqrt{R_x{}^2 + R_y{}^2}$$
$$= \sqrt{(-186 \text{ N})^2 + (-87 \text{ N})^2} = 205 \text{ N}$$

$$\tan \alpha = \frac{|R_y|}{|R_x|} = \frac{|-87 \text{ N}|}{|-186 \text{ N}|} = 0.468$$

$$\alpha = 25.1°$$

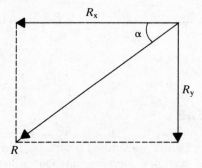

In solving problems involving the equilibrium of a particle, follow these four steps:

Step 1 Draw a sketch of the apparatus or structure indicating dimensions and angles.

Step 2 Choose a particle (such as a knot or ring) in equilibrium.
Draw a free-body diagram by indicating all the forces (denoted by arrows) acting on the particle. Do not show, in the free-body diagram, any of the forces exerted by the particle. (Remember, in accordance with Newton's third law, if a cable exerts a force on a particle, the particle exerts an equal and opposite force on the cable).

Step 3 Set up a rectangular coordinate system and resolve all forces acting on the particle into rectangular components.

Step 4 Set $\Sigma F_x = 0$ and $\Sigma F_y = 0$. Solve the simultaneous equations for the unknown quantities.

The various systems of units are summarized by the following table.

System of Units	Force	Mass	Acceleration
mks	newton (N)	kilogram (kg)	$m \cdot s^{-2}$
cgs	dyne (dyn)	gram (g)	$cm \cdot s^{-2}$
engineering	pound (lb)	slug	$ft \cdot s^{-2}$

Thus if one newton acts on a mass of 1 kg, it will produce an acceleration of $1\ m \cdot s^{-2}$. Note the equivalence of units: 1 N is equivalent to $1\ kg \cdot m \cdot s^{-2}$; 1 dyn is equivalent to $1\ g \cdot cm \cdot s^{-2}$; 1 lb is equivalent to $1\ slug \cdot ft \cdot s^{-2}$.

The weight of a body is the gravitational force exerted by the earth on a body. If a body (mass m described by an operational procedure) falls freely, its acceleration is g, and the force causing this acceleration is its weight w. Therefore , $\Sigma F = ma$ reduces to $w = mg$.

Inertial mass is determined by measuring the resultant force on a body and the resulting acceleration, and computing $m = \dfrac{\Sigma F}{a}$. On the other hand, gravitational mass is the property of a body that determines the magnitude of the gravitational force between any two bodies in accordance with Newton's law of gravitation. Experimental evidence indicates that inertial mass = gravitational mass.

Although Chapters 5 and 6 will be devoted to applications of Newton's second law, we will illustrate $\Sigma F = ma$ by considering the following problem:

Calculate the force required to accelerate a 40 kg object from rest to $2\ m \cdot s^{-1}$ in 3 seconds. What are the forces acting on the body?

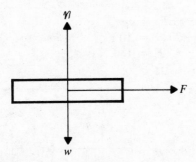

$F = $ applied horizontal force;
$w = $ downward force of gravity; ;
$\eta = $ upward force exerted by the floor.

Note that η and w are action–reaction forces. The object is exerting a force w on the floor, and the floor is exerting an equal and opposite force η on the object. If η and w were not equal to each other, the object would have motion in a vertical direction.

Before we can calculate the force, we must first calculate the acceleration using $v = v_0 + at$:

$$a = \frac{v - v_0}{t} = \frac{2\ m \cdot s^{-1} - 0}{2\ s} = 0.667\ m \cdot s^{-2}.$$

Substitute this value in Newton's second law:

$$\Sigma F_x = ma_x$$
$$= 40\ kg\ (0.677\ m \cdot s^{-2})$$
$$= 26.7\ N.$$

In solving problems involving the application of Newton's second law, follow six steps:

Step 1   Select a body which undergoes acceleration. Newton's second law will be applied to this body.

Step 2   Draw a free-body diagram by indicating all the forces, denoted by arrows, acting on the body. Do not show any of the forces exerted by the body. Assign symbols (or known values) to all quantities. The body's weight may be labeled as *mg*.

Step 3   Set up a rectangular coordinate system and resolve all forces acting on the body into rectangular components. In order to avoid duplication, remember that when a force is represented by its components, our convention is to draw two lines through the original force. When the direction of the acceleration is known in advance, take this direction as the +*x*- or *y*-axis.

Step 4 Repeat the above steps for each body separately. Note that the number of equations must equal the number of unknown quantities.

Step 5 Apply Newton's second law for each body ($\Sigma F_x = ma_x$, $\Sigma F_y = ma_y$) and solve the equations for the unknowns. In many instances, strings, cords, and ropes will be used to transmit forces. These will be considered to be massless and do not stretch. Bodies connected by a string will have accelerations of equal magnitude.

Step 6 Check special cases to verify that general analytical results agree with intuitive expectations.

PROGRAMMED QUIZ

1 How large a horizontal force is required to give a 10 kg mass an acceleration of 12 m · s^{-2} across a floor if there is no friction force opposing the motion?

1

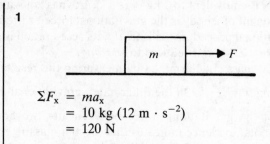

$$\Sigma F_x = ma_x$$
$$= 10 \text{ kg } (12 \text{ m} \cdot \text{s}^{-2})$$
$$= 120 \text{ N}$$

2 Same as frame 1 but a frictional force of 20 N opposes the motion.

2

$$\Sigma F_x = ma_x$$
$$F - 20 \text{ N} = 10 \text{ kg } (12 \text{ m} \cdot \text{s}^{-2})$$
$$F = 140 \text{ N}$$

3 A 2000 kg elevator has an upward acceleration of 4 m · s^{-2}. What is the tension in the support cable?

3

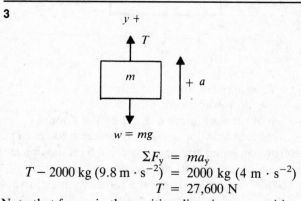

$$\Sigma F_y = ma_y$$
$$T - 2000 \text{ kg } (9.8 \text{ m} \cdot \text{s}^{-2}) = 2000 \text{ kg } (4 \text{ m} \cdot \text{s}^{-2})$$
$$T = 27{,}600 \text{ N}$$
Note that forces in the positive direction are positive.

4 The elevator in frame 3 is accelerating downward at 4 m · s^{-2}. What is the tension in the support cable?

4

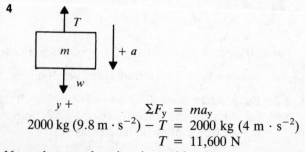

$$\Sigma F_y = ma_y$$
$$2000 \text{ kg } (9.8 \text{ m} \cdot \text{s}^{-2}) - T = 2000 \text{ kg } (4 \text{ m} \cdot \text{s}^{-2})$$
$$T = 11{,}600 \text{ N}$$
Note that acceleration is positive in the downward direction.

5 A 30 caliber bullet (0.0025 kg) traveling at 400 $m \cdot s^{-1}$ strikes a block of wood and penetrates it to a depth of 0.14 m. Assuming a constant retarding force, find the time for the bullet to stop.

5
Given:
$$v_0 = 400 \text{ m} \cdot \text{s}^{-1}$$
$$v = 0$$
$$x - x_0 = 0.14 \text{ m}$$
Find t:
$$v_{av} = \frac{v_0 + v}{2} = \frac{400 \text{ m} \cdot \text{s}^{-1} + 0}{2}$$
$$= 200 \text{ m} \cdot \text{s}^{-1}$$
$$x - x_0 = v_{av}\, t$$
$$t = \frac{x - x_0}{v_{av}} = \frac{0.14 \text{ m}}{200 \text{ m} \cdot \text{s}^{-1}} = 7 \times 10^{-4} \text{ s}$$

6 Find the acceleration.

6
$$a = \frac{v - v_0}{t}$$
$$= \frac{0 - 400 \text{ m} \cdot \text{s}^{-1}}{7 \times 10^{-4} \text{ s}}$$
$$= -5.71 \times 10^5 \text{ m} \cdot \text{s}^{-2}$$

7 Find the retarding force.

7

Apply Newton's second law:
$$\Sigma F_x = ma_x$$
$$-F = 0.0025 \text{ kg} \, (-5.71 \times 10^5 \text{ m} \cdot \text{s}^{-2})$$
$$F = 1.43 \times 10^3 \text{ N}$$

8 A single force of 20 N acts on a body of mass m The body starts from rest and travels in a straight line for a distance of 64 m in 8 s. Find the acceleration of the body.

8
$$x - x_0 = v_0\, t + \tfrac{1}{2}at^2$$
$$64 \text{ m} = 0 + \tfrac{1}{2}a\,(8 \text{ s})^2$$
$$a = 2 \text{ m} \cdot \text{s}^{-2}$$

9 Find the mass of the body.

9
$$\Sigma F_x = ma_x$$
$$m = \frac{\Sigma F_x}{a_x}$$
$$= \frac{20 \text{ N}}{2 \text{ m} \cdot \text{s}^{-2}}$$
$$= 10 \text{ kg}$$

10 A 2000 kg car is traveling at 120 km $\cdot$ h^{-1}. What is its speed in m $\cdot$ s^{-1}?

10
$$\frac{120 \text{ km}}{\text{h}} \times \frac{1000 \text{ m}}{1 \text{ km}} \times \frac{1 \text{ h}}{3600 \text{ s}} = 33.3 \text{ m} \cdot \text{s}^{-1}$$

11 What is the acceleration of the car if it is to come to a full stop in 80 m?

11

$$v^2 = v_0^2 + 2a\,(x - x_0)$$

$$a = \frac{v^2 - v_0^2}{2(x - x_0)}$$

$$= \frac{0 - (33.3 \text{ m} \cdot \text{s}^{-1})^2}{2(80 \text{ m})}$$

$$= -6.93 \text{ m} \cdot \text{s}^{-2}$$

---

12 Find the force acting on the car.

12

$$\Sigma F_x = ma_x$$

$$= 2000 \text{ kg}\,(-6.93 \text{ m} \cdot \text{s}^{-2})$$

$$= -1.39 \times 10^4 \text{ N}$$

---

13 What is the direction of the force?

13 The force is exerted in the direction opposite to the initial velocity.

STEP BY STEP SOLUTIONS OF PROBLEMS

Problem 1 Use the method of rectangular resolution to find the magnitude and direction of the resultant of the four forces acting on particle *P*.

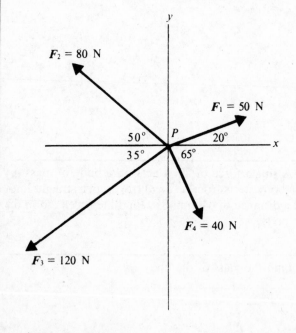

---

1 State what is given and what must be found.

1 Given

$$F_1 = 50 \text{ N at } 20°$$
$$F_2 = 80 \text{ N at } 50°$$
$$F_3 = 120 \text{ N at } 35°$$
$$F_4 = 40 \text{ N at } 65°$$

Find

R (Resultant)

(magnitude and direction)

---

2 Find the x- and y-components of $\boldsymbol{F}_1$.

2

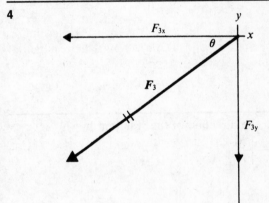

$$
\begin{aligned}
F_{1x} &= F_1 \cos \theta \\
&= +\ 50\ \text{N} \cos 20° \\
&= +\ 50\ \text{N}\ (0.940) \\
&= +\ 47.0\ \text{N}
\end{aligned}
\qquad
\begin{aligned}
F_{1y} &= F_1 \sin \theta \\
&= +\ 50\ \text{N} \sin 20° \\
&= +\ 50\ \text{N}\ (0.342) \\
&= +\ 17.1\ \text{N}
\end{aligned}
$$

---

3 Find the x- and y-components of $\boldsymbol{F}_2$.

3

$$
\begin{aligned}
F_{2x} &= F_2 \cos \theta \\
&= -\ 80.0\ \text{N} \cos 50° \\
&= -\ 80.0\ \text{N}\ (0.643) \\
&= -\ 51.4\ \text{N}
\end{aligned}
\qquad
\begin{aligned}
F_{2y} &= F_2 \sin \theta \\
&= +\ 80.0\ \text{N} \sin 50° \\
&= 80.0\ \text{N}\ (0.766) \\
&= +\ 61.3\ \text{N}
\end{aligned}
$$

---

4 Find the x- and y-components of $\boldsymbol{F}_3$.

4

$$
\begin{aligned}
F_{3x} &= F_3 \cos \theta \\
&= -\ 120\ \text{N} \cos 35° \\
&= -\ 120\ \text{N}\ (0.819) \\
&= -\ 98.3\ \text{N}
\end{aligned}
\qquad
\begin{aligned}
F_{3y} &= F_3 \sin \theta \\
&= -\ 120\ \text{N} \sin 35° \\
&= -\ 120\ \text{N}\ (0.574) \\
&= -\ 68.9\ \text{N}
\end{aligned}
$$

---

5 Find the x- and y-components of $\boldsymbol{F}_4$.

5

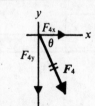

$$
\begin{aligned}
F_{4x} &= F_4 \cos \theta \\
&= +\ 40 \cos 65° \\
&= +\ 40\ \text{N}(0.423) \\
&= +\ 16.9\ \text{N}
\end{aligned}
\qquad
\begin{aligned}
F_{4y} &= F_4 \sin \theta \\
&= -\ 40\ \text{N} \sin 65° \\
&= -\ 40\ \text{N}(0.906) \\
&= -\ 36.2\ \text{N}
\end{aligned}
$$

6 Summarize in tabular form.

6

Force	Angle	x-components	y-components
$F_1 = 50$ N	20°	+ 47.0 N	+ 17.1 N
$F_2 = 80$ N	50°	− 51.4 N	+ 61.3 N
$F_3 = 120$ N	35°	− 98.3 N	− 68.9 N
$F_4 = 40$ N	65°	+ 16.9 N	− 36.2 N

---

7 Add the x-components and add the y-components.

7

$$R_x = \Sigma F_x = + 47.0 \text{ N} - 51.4 \text{ N} - 98.3 \text{ N} + 16.9 \text{ N}$$
$$= - 85.8 \text{ N}$$
$$R_y = \Sigma F_y = + 17.1 \text{ N} + 61.3 \text{ N} - 68.9 \text{ N} - 36.2 \text{ N}$$
$$= - 26.7 \text{ N}$$

---

8 Find the magnitude of the resultant by the Pythagorean theorem.

8

$$R = \sqrt{R_x{}^2 + R_y{}^2}$$
$$= \sqrt{(- 85.8 \text{ N})^2 + (-26.7 \text{ N})^2}$$
$$= 89.9 \text{ N}$$

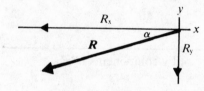

---

9 Find the direction of the resultant by
$$\tan \alpha = \frac{|R_y|}{|R_x|}.$$

9

$$\alpha = \arctan \frac{|R_y|}{|R_x|}$$
$$= \arctan \frac{26.7 \text{ N}}{85.8 \text{ N}} = \arctan 0.311$$
$$= 17.3°$$

Problem 2 Three blocks are connected by massless strings and are pulled to the right by a force T_1. If the rubbing surfaces are frictionless, find the acceleration of the blocks and the tensions in the connecting strings.

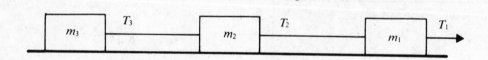

---

10 Select the bodies for analysis.

10

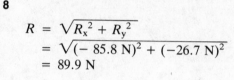

11 Draw the free-body diagrams for each body.

11

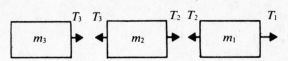

T_2 and T_3 are internal forces; m_1 pulls on m_2 with a force T_2, and in accordance with Newton's third law, m_2 exerts an equal and opposite force T_2 on m_1. Likewise m_2 pulls on m_3 with a force T_3, and m_3 exerts an equal and opposite force T_3 on m_2.

12 Set up a coordinate system. We are only concerned with the x-direction. $\mathcal{N}_1 = w_1 = m_1g$, $\mathcal{N}_2 = w_2 = m_2g$, and $\mathcal{N}_3 = w_3 = m_3g$.

12

13 Apply Newton's second law to each body.
$\Sigma F_x = ma_x$

13

For m_1; $T_1 - T_2 = m_1a_x$
For m_2; $T_2 - T_3 = m_2a_x$
For m_3; $T_3 = m_3a_x$

14 Solve for T_1, T_2, and T_3 in terms of m_1, m_2, m_3, and a_x. Add the three equations to solve for T_1. Solve for T_2.

14 Adding the three equations,
$$T_1 = (m_1 + m_2 + m_3)a_x$$
since $T_3 = m_3a_x$, substitute in the second equation to obtain
$$T_2 = (m_2 + m_3)a_x$$

15 Solve for a_x (remember that T_1, m_1, and m_3 are given quantities). Note that a_x could also have been obtained by considering the system to consist of three masses. Applying $\Sigma F_x = ma_x$ to the system, $T_1 = (m_1 + m_2 + m_3)a_x$.

15

$$T_1 = (m_1 + m_2 + m_3)a_x$$
$$a_x = \frac{T_1}{m_1 + m_2 + m_3}$$

Problem 3 An 80 kg physics professor is standing on a bathroom scale fastened to the floor of an elevator. What does the scale read (kg) when the elevator has an upward acceleration of 4.9 m · s^{-2}? What is the reading for a downward acceleration of 4.9 m · s^{-2}?

16 Draw a free-body diagram of the professor showing all the forces acting on him.

16

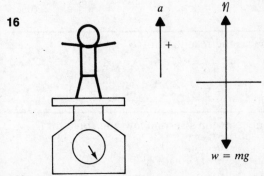

The forces on the professor are his weight w downward and the upward supporting force $\mathcal{N}$ exerted by the scale platform.

17 What is the direction of the resultant force?

17 Since the elevator is accelerating upward, the resultant force must be upward also.

---

18 What is the resultant force?

18

$$\Sigma F_y = \eta - w$$

---

19 Apply Newton's second law, $\Sigma F_y = ma_y$, and solve for η.

19

$$\eta - w = ma$$
$$\eta - mg = ma$$
$$\eta = m(g + a)$$
$$= 80 \text{ kg } (9.8 \text{ m} \cdot \text{s}^{-2} + 4.9 \text{ m} \cdot \text{s}^{-2})$$
$$= 1176 \text{ N}$$

---

20 What is the scale reading? Since the scale platform is exerting 1176 N on the professor, the professor is exerting 1176 N on the scale platform. Thus the apparent weight of the professor is 1176 N. To get the scale reading use $w = mg$.

20

$$m = \frac{w}{g} = \frac{1176 \text{ N}}{9.8 \text{ m} \cdot \text{s}^{-2}} = 120 \text{ kg}$$

---

21 What is the scale reading for a downward acceleration of $4.9 \text{ m} \cdot \text{s}^{-2}$. Use the same procedure to solve this problem. However, the acceleration a is positive downward. Draw a free-body diagram.

21

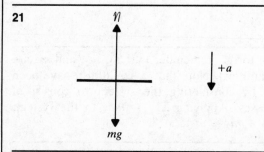

---

22 What is the direction of the resultant force?

22 Downward in the direction of the acceleration a.

---

23 What is the resultant force?

23

$$\Sigma F_y = w - \eta$$

---

24 Apply Newton's second law and solve for η.

24

$$w - \eta = ma$$
$$\eta = mg - ma$$
$$= m(g - a)$$
$$= 80 \text{ kg } (9.8 \text{ m} \cdot \text{s}^{-2} - 4.9 \text{ m} \cdot \text{s}^{-2})$$
$$= 392 \text{ N}$$

---

25 What is the scale reading?

25

$$w = mg$$
$$m = \frac{w}{g} = \frac{392 \text{ N}}{9.8 \text{ m} \cdot \text{s}^{-2}}$$
$$= 40 \text{ kg}$$

---

26 What would be happening if the scale read 0?

26 The scale and the professor would be falling freely.

PROGRAMMED TEST

1 *Problem 1* Use the method of *x*- and *y*-components to find the magnitude and direction of the resultant of the three forces in the diagram.

1

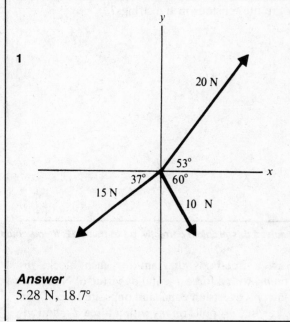

Answer
5.28 N, 18.7°

If you solved this problem correctly, go to frame 6. If you could not solve this problem, go through frames 2–5.

2 Tabulate the *x*- and *y*-components.

2

Force	Angle	*x*-components	*y*-components
20 N	53°	+ 20 N cos 53° = + 12 N	20 N sin 53° = + 16N
15 N	37°	− 15 N cos 37° = − 12 N	− 15 N sin 37° = − 9.03 N
10 N	60°	10 N cos 60° = + 5 N	− 10 N sin 60° = − 8.66 N

---

3 Find the sum of the *x*- and *y*-components.

3

$$R_x = \Sigma F_x = + 12 \text{ N} - 12 \text{ N} + 5 \text{ N} = + 5 \text{ N}$$
$$R_y = \Sigma F_y = + 16 \text{ N} - 9.03 \text{ N} - 8.66 \text{ N}$$
$$= 1.69 \text{ N}$$

---

4 Find the resultant by the Pythagorean theorem.

4

$$R = \sqrt{(5 \text{ N})^2 + (- 1.69 \text{ N})^2} = 5.28 \text{ N}$$

$R_y = - 1.66 \text{ N}$ $R_x = 5 \text{ N}$ R α

5 Find the angle using the tangent function.

5
$$\tan \alpha = \frac{|-1.69 \text{ N}|}{|5 \text{ N}|}$$
$$\alpha = 18.7°$$

---

6 **Problem 2** Three blocks connected by weightless strings (as shown) are initially at rest. The masses of the blocks, starting at the top, are 8, 6, and 4 kg. Through what distance will the system move in 2 seconds if an upward force of 250 N is acting on it? What are the tensions in the strings?

6

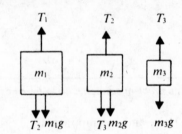

Answer
8.18 m, 139 N, 55.6 N

If you solved this problem correctly, go to frame 12. If you could not solve this problem, go through frames 7–11.

7 Draw a free-body diagram for each block; m_1 pulls on m_2 with a force T_2, and by virtue of Newton's third law, m_2 exerts an equal and opposite force T_2 on m_1. Likewise, m_2 pulls on m_3 with a force T_3, and m_3 exerts an equal and opposite force T_3 on m_2.

7

---

8 Applying Newton's second law to each block, $\Sigma F = ma$ becomes

8

for 8 kg block: $T_1 - T_2 - m_1 g = m_1 a$
$250 \text{ N} - T_2 - (8 \text{ kg})(9.8 \text{ m} \cdot \text{s}^{-2}) = 8 \text{ kg}\,(a)$
for 6 kg block: $T_2 - T_3 - m_2 g = m_2 a$
$T_2 - T_3 - (6 \text{ kg})(9.8 \text{ m} \cdot \text{s}^{-2}) = 6 \text{ kg}\,(a)$
for 4 kg block; $T_3 - m_3 g = m_3 a$
$T_3 - (4 \text{ kg})(9.8 \text{ m} \cdot \text{s}^{-2}) = 4 \text{ kg}\,(a)$

---

9 Note that we have three equations with three unknowns: T_2, T_3, and a. Solve for a by adding the three equations.

9

$$250 \text{ N} - T_2 - 78.4 \text{ N} = 8 \text{ kg}\,(a)$$
$$T_2 - T_3 - 58.8 \text{ N} = 6 \text{ kg}\,(a)$$
$$T_3 - 39.2 \text{ N} = 4 \text{ kg}\,(a)$$

$$250 \text{ N} - 176.4 \text{ N} = 18 \text{ kg}\,(a)$$
$$a = 4.09 \text{ m} \cdot \text{s}^{-2}$$

10 Solve for T_3 and T_2.

10
$$T_3 - 39.2 \text{ N} = 4 \text{ kg } (4.09 \text{ m} \cdot \text{s}^{-2})$$
$$T_3 = 55.6 \text{ N}$$
$$T_2 - 55.6 \text{ N} - 58.8 \text{ N} = 6 \text{ kg } (4.09 \text{ m} \cdot \text{s}^{-2})$$
$$T_2 = 139 \text{ N}$$

11 Knowing the acceleration, find the distance through which the system moves in 2 seconds.

11
$$y = y_0 + v_0 t + \tfrac{1}{2}at^2$$
$$= 0 + \tfrac{1}{2}(4.09 \text{ m} \cdot \text{s}^{-2}) (2 \text{ s})^2$$
$$= 8.18 \text{ m}$$

12 ***Problem 3*** An elevator and its load have a total mass of 1000 kg. Find the tension T in the supporting cable when the elevator, originally at rest, descends with constant acceleration through a distance of 40 m in 4 seconds.

12
Answer
4800 N

If you could not solve this problem, go through frames 13–17.

13 Draw a coordinate system and a free-body diagram.

13

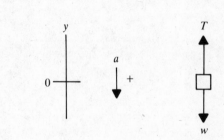

14 Find the acceleration by using
$$y = v_0 t + \tfrac{1}{2}at^2.$$

14
$$40 \text{ m} = 0 + \tfrac{1}{2}a (4 \text{ s})^2$$
$$a = 5 \text{ m} \cdot \text{s}^{-2}$$

15 What is the direction of the resultant force?

15 Downward in the direction of the acceleration.

16 What is the resultant force?

16
$$\Sigma F_y = w - T$$

17 Apply Newton's second law, $\Sigma F_y = ma$.

17
$$w - T = ma$$
$$mg - T = ma$$
$$T = m(g - a)$$
$$= 1000 \text{ kg } (9.8 \text{ m} \cdot \text{s}^{-2} - 5 \text{ m} \cdot \text{s}^{-2})$$
$$= 4800 \text{ N}$$

5

Applications of Newton's Laws — I

CHAPTER SUMMARY

This chapter deals with problem-solving strategies for problems in statics and dynamics. Contact forces are defined, with emphasis on the static and kinetic friction forces. An inertial reference system is presented on the basis of Newton's first law.

BASIC TERMS — *Give definitions or meanings for the following:*

gravitational interaction (5-1)
electromagnetic interaction (5-1)
strong interaction (5-1)
nuclear force (5-1)
weak interaction (5-1)
grand unified theory (5-1)
contact forces (5-2)

normal force (5-2)
friction force (5-2)
kinetic friction (5-2)
coefficient of kinetic friction (5-2)
static friction (5-2)
coefficient of static friction (5-2)

PROGRAMMED QUIZ

1 What are the four classes of forces found in nature? Give an example of each.

1 Gravitational interaction — weight; electromagnetic interaction — lightening; strong interaction — nuclear force; weak interaction — decay of some unstable particles.

2 Which interactions are dominant in the internal structure of stars? atoms?

2 Gravitational, electromagnetic.

3 Under what conditions will the weight of an object and the normal force have the same magnitude?

3 When the object is on a horizontal surface and the object is subjected to horizontal forces if any.

$$\Sigma F_x = 0; \quad T - \mathcal{F}_k = 0$$
$$\Sigma F_y = 0; \quad \mathcal{N} - w = 0$$
$$\mathcal{N} = w$$
$$\mathcal{F}_k = T$$

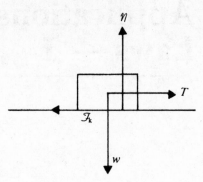

4 What is the smallest number of forces to act on a body in order for it to be in equilibrium? Illustrate. (Ignore zero forces.)

4 Two forces; a 10 N weight is supported by a cable; the two forces acting on it are the weight (10 N) and the tension (10 N).

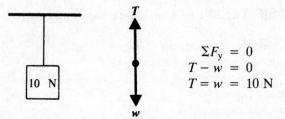

$$\Sigma F_y = 0$$
$$T - w = 0$$
$$T = w = 10 \text{ N}$$

If only one force acts on a body, the resultant cannot be zero; therefore the body cannot be in equilibrium.

5 What is friction?

5 A force, opposing motion, which exists when two objects are sliding past each other.

6 What is the direction of the friction force?

6 Parallel to the surface, opposite to the direction of the motion.

7 What is the difference between static and kinetic friction?

7 Static friction is the friction when motion is about to begin; kinetic friction when objects are in motion past each other.

8 What is the normal force? Illustrate.

8 If a block rests on a horizontal surface and is pulled to the right by a force T, the surface will react with a force P as indicated in the figure. The normal force is the vertical component of P. It is the normal ($\perp$) force exerted by the surface on the block. The horizontal component of P is called the force of friction; static friction if the motion is about to begin, kinetic if the block is in motion relative to the surfaces.

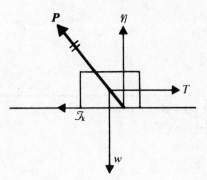

9 What are the four basic steps in solving problems dealing with the equilibrium of a particle?

9

Step 1 Draw a sketch.

Step 2 Choose a particle in equilibrium and draw a free-body diagram of this particle.

Step 3 Set up a rectangular coordinate system and resolve all forces acting on the particle into rectangular components.

Step 4 Set $\Sigma F_x = 0$ and $\Sigma F_y = 0$ and solve for the unknown quantities.

10 What are the six basic steps in solving problems dealing with Newton's second law?

10

Step 1 Select a body that undergoes acceleration.

Step 2 Draw a free-body diagram of this body.

Step 3 Set up a rectangular coordinate system and resolve all forces into rectangular components.

Step 4 Repeat the above steps for all other bodies.

Step 5 Apply Newton's second law to each body.

Step 6 Check special cases.

11 A child slides down a frictionless playground slide inclined at an angle θ with the horizontal. Draw a free-body diagram. What are the forces acting on the child?

11

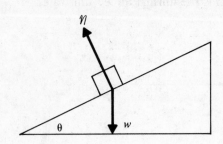

The forces acting on the child are the weight w and the normal force η exerted by the plane on the child.

12 Set up a coordinate system and resolve w into x- and y-components.

12

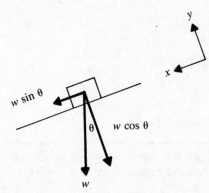

Take the x-axis parallel to the surface of the plane and the y-axis perpendicular to the surface. Note that the $+x$ direction coincides with the direction of the acceleration. Also, the angle between the vector w and the y-axis is θ.

13 What is ΣF_y?

13 $\Sigma F_y = \eta - w \cos \theta$

14 What is the acceleration in the y-direction?

14

$$a_y = 0$$

15 What does this mean with respect to Newton's second law?

15

$$\Sigma F_y = ma_y$$
$$\eta - w \cos \theta = 0$$
$$\eta = w \cos \theta$$

16 What is the child's acceleration down the incline?

16

$$\Sigma F_x = ma_x$$
$$w \sin \theta = ma_x$$
Remember that $w = mg$,
$$\therefore mg \sin \theta = ma_x$$
$$a_x = g \sin \theta$$

17 What does this mean?

17 Since the mass m does not appear in the final equation, it means that any body, regardless of its mass, will slide down a frictionless inclined plane with an acceleration $g \sin \theta$.

18 What happens when $\theta = 0°$?

18
$$a_x = g \sin 0° = 0$$
There is no acceleration.

19 What happens when $\theta = 90°$?

19
$$a_x = g \sin 90° = g$$
The object is falling freely.

MAIN IDEAS

In solving problems involving the equilibrium of a particle, follow these four steps:

Step 1 Draw a sketch of the apparatus or structure indicating dimensions and angles.

Step 2 Choose a particle (such as a knot or ring) in equilibrium.
Draw a free-body diagram by indicating all the forces (denoted by arrows) acting on the particle. Do not show, in the free-body diagram, any of the forces exerted by the particle. (Remember, in accordance with Newton's third law, if a cable exerts a force on a particle, the particle exerts an equal and opposite force on the cable.)

Step 3 Set up a rectangular coordinate system and resolve all forces acting on the particle into rectangular components.

Step 4 Set $\Sigma F_x = 0$ and $\Sigma F_y = 0$. Solve the simultaneous equations for the unknown quantities.

Before you can set up a free-body diagram, you must be familiar with the actions of various forces. Let us review some situations you will come in contact with.

The earth's force of gravity is represented by an arrow that passes through the center of gravity of the body.

Tensile forces act along flexible ropes, cords, or cables. If a rope (cord, or cable) is in equilibrium and if no forces act except at its ends, the tension is the same at both ends. Thus the tension at A is the same as the tension at B.

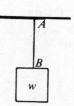

If a body (for example, a ladder leaning against a wall) is in contact with a frictionless surface, a force is depicted as acting perpendicular to the smooth surface.

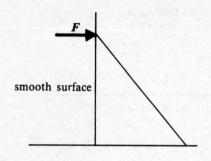

smooth surface

A hinge or pin may exert a force in any direction.

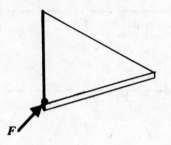

For rollers, the reaction is perpendicular to the surface with which the rollers are in contact.

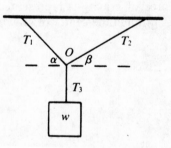

We will illustrate the four-step procedure by means of the following problem: A block of weight w hangs from a vertical cord that is knotted at point O to two other cords fastened to the ceiling as indicated in the sketch. If the weights of the cords are assumed to be negligible, find the tension in the three cords.

Step 1 Draw a sketch. (Given)

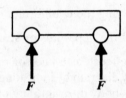

Step 2a (the block) Consider the forces acting on the hanging block.

Draw a free-body diagram.

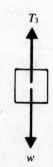

Step 3a (the block) Set up a rectangular coordinate system and resolve all forces acting on the block into rectangular components. Note: w and T_3 are vertical components.

Step 4a (the block) Set $\Sigma F_y = 0$:
$$T_3 - w = 0$$
$$T_3 = w$$

Step 2b (the knot O) Consider the forces acting on the knot O. Draw a free-body diagram.

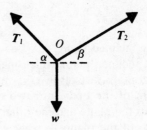

Step 3b (the knot O) Resolve all forces into horizontal and vertical components and replace each force by its components.

$T_{1x} = -T_1 \cos \alpha$
$T_{1y} = T_1 \sin \alpha$
$T_{2x} = T_2 \cos \beta$
$T_{2y} = T_2 \sin \beta$

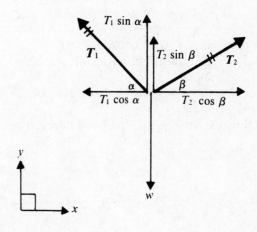

Step 4b (the knot O) This step requires that you set $\Sigma F_x = 0$ and $\Sigma F_y = 0$. Therefore

$$-T_1 \cos \alpha + T_2 \cos \beta = 0 \qquad (1)$$
$$T_1 \sin \alpha + T_2 \sin \beta - w = 0. \qquad (2)$$

The solution to the above pair of simultaneous equations may be obtained by eliminating one of the variables (T_1 or T_2) and reducing the problem to solving one linear equation with one unknown. To eliminate T_1 in the above set of equations, we multiply both sides of the two equations by appropriate quantities so that the coefficients of T_1 will be the same (or differ by a $-$ sign). It should be apparent that this can be accomplished by multiplying both sides of the first equation by sin α and both sides of the second equation by cos α. We thus obtain

$$- T_1 \sin \alpha \cos \alpha + T_2 \sin \alpha \cos \beta = 0$$
$$T_1 \sin \alpha \cos \alpha + T_2 \sin \beta \cos \alpha - w \cos \alpha = 0.$$

Adding the above, we obtain

$$T_2 (\sin \alpha \cos \beta + \cos \alpha \sin \beta) = w \cos \alpha$$

or

$$T_2 = \frac{w \cos \alpha}{\sin \alpha \cos \beta + \cos \alpha \sin \beta} = \frac{w \cos \alpha}{\sin (\alpha + \beta)}. \qquad (3)$$

Substituting the value of T_2 in Eq. (1), we obtain

$$T_1 = \frac{w \cos \beta}{\sin (\alpha + \beta)}. \qquad (4)$$

It should be noted that T_2 could have been eliminated by multiplying both sides of Eq. (1) by sin β (i.e., the coefficient of T_2 in Eq. (2)) and multiplying both sides of Eq. (2) by cos α (i.e., the coefficient of T_2 in Eq. (1)). Subsequent subtraction of both sides of Eq. (2) from Eq. (1) would result in a single equation with one variable (i.e., T_1).

A note on the inclined plane. A body (weight w) is resting on an inclined plane which makes an angle θ with the horizontal. If we resolve the vector representing the weight of the body into two components — one parallel to the plane and the other perpendicular to the surface of the plane — what is the angle between the weight vector and the normal to the surface?

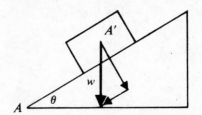

Consider triangles ABC and $A'BC'$:

  $\angle 1 = \angle 2$ (all right angles are equal to each other)

  $\angle 3 = \angle 4$ (vertical angles are equal to each other)

Therefore $\triangle ABC \sim \triangle A'BC'$ and thus $\angle A = \angle A' = \theta$.

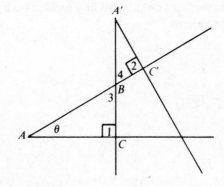

Friction. If the surface of one body slides over the surface of another body, each body, in accordance with Newton's third law, will exert a force on the other parallel to the surface. The force on each body is referred to as the frictional force and acts opposite to the direction of its motion relative to the body. The force of static friction is denoted $\mathcal{J}_s$ and the force of sliding or kinetic friction by $\mathcal{J}_k$.

$$\mu_s = \frac{\mathcal{J}_s}{\eta} = \text{coefficient of static friction,}$$

$$\mu_k = \frac{\mathcal{J}_k}{\eta} = \text{coefficient of sliding or kinetic friction.}$$

We will illustrate the basic concepts of equilibrium and friction forces by means of the following example.

  A block weighing w newtons rests on an inclined plane that makes an angle θ with the horizontal. The block is pulled up the plane at constant velocity by a force T newtons which makes an angle α with the plane. What is T? (The coefficient of kinetic friction $= \mu_k$.)

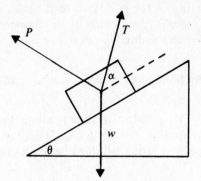

motion up the plane

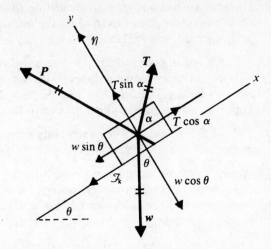

Free-body diagram. P denotes the contact force.

T, P and w resolved into components parallel and perpendicular to the plane.

Thus, there are six forces acting on the block: $T \cos \alpha$ and $T \sin \alpha$ (the components of T); $w \cos \theta$ and $w \sin \theta$ (the components of w); $\mathcal{F}_k$ (the force of friction, opposite in direction to the motion of the body); $\mathcal{N}$ (the normal force). Note that $\mathcal{F}_k$ and $\mathcal{N}$ are components of P. Setting up the equilibrium equations, we obtain

$$\Sigma F_x = 0, \qquad T \cos \alpha - w \sin \theta - \mathcal{F}_k = 0, \tag{5}$$
$$\Sigma F_y = 0, \qquad \mathcal{N} + T \sin \alpha - w \cos \theta = 0. \tag{6}$$
$$\text{But } \mathcal{F}_k = \mu_k \mathcal{N}. \tag{7}$$

Substituting the values $\mathcal{F}_k$ from (7) and $\mathcal{N}$ from (6) in Eq. (5), we obtain

$$T = \frac{w(\sin \theta + \mu_k \cos \theta)}{\cos \alpha + \mu_k \sin \alpha}. \tag{8}$$

Consider the various possibilities:

a) $$\theta = 0, \alpha = 0,$$

$$T = \frac{w(\sin 0 + \mu_k \cos 0)}{\cos 0 + \mu_k \sin 0} = \mu_k w.$$

In this case T is equal to the force of friction $\mathcal{F}_k$ and the normal force $\mathcal{N}$ is equal to the weight w.

b) $$\theta = 0, \qquad 0 < \alpha < 90°,$$

$$T = \frac{\mu_k w}{\cos \alpha + \mu_k \sin \alpha}.$$

c) $$0 < \theta < 90°, \alpha = 0,$$
$$T = w(\sin \theta + \mu_k \cos \theta).$$

d) $$0 < \theta < 90°, 0 < \alpha < 90°,$$

$$T = \frac{w(\sin \theta + \mu_k \cos \theta)}{\cos \alpha + \mu_k \sin \alpha}.$$

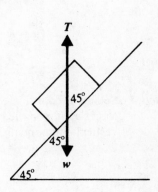

Note that when

$$\alpha = \theta = 45°, T = w.$$

It should be noted that the contact force has two components: $\mathcal{F}_k$ (the frictional component) and $\mathcal{N}$ (the normal component). In free-body diagrams it is often convenient to represent the contact force in terms of its components. If we know the direction of motion of a body, we know that the frictional force acting upon it is in the opposite direction. The normal force is a perpendicular force exerted by the surface on the body.

In solving problems involving the application of Newton's second law, follow six steps:

Step 1 Select a body that undergoes acceleration. Newton's second law will be applied to this body.

Step 2 Draw a free-body diagram by indicating all the forces, denoted by arrows, acting on the body. Do not show any of the forces exerted by the body. Assign symbols (or known values) to all quantities. The body's weight may be labeled as *mg*.

Step 3 Set up a rectangular coordinate system and resolve all forces acting on the body into rectangular components. In order to avoid duplication, remember that when a force is represented by its components, our convention is to draw two lines through the original force. When the direction of the acceleration is known in advance, take this direction as the positive direction.

Step 4 Repeat the above steps for each body separately. Note that the number of equations must equal the number of unknown quantities.

Step 5 Apply Newton's second law for each body ($\Sigma F_x = ma_x$, $\Sigma F_y = ma_y$) and solve the equations for the unknowns. In many instances, strings, cords, and ropes will be used to transmit forces. These will be considered to be massless and do not stretch. Bodies connected by a string will have accelerations of equal magnitude.

Step 6 Check special cases to verify that general analytical results agree with intuitive expectations.

We will illustrate the six steps by means of the following two problems.

Problem 1 A block whose mass is *m* is resting on a horizontal surface. The coefficient of kinetic friction between the block and surface is μ_k. An unknown force *T* is applied horizontally to the block giving it a velocity *v* in time *t*. If the block experiences a constant friction force, find *T*.

Step 1 Select the body for analysis. There is only one body.

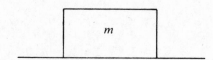

Step 2 Draw the free-body diagram. Note that *P*, the contact force between the horizontal surface and the block, will be resolved into its components, $\mathcal{F}_k$ and η in step 3.

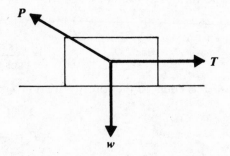

Step 3 Set up a coordinate system and resolve all forces acting on the body into horizontal and vertical components.

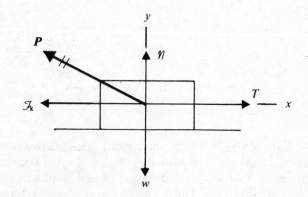

Step 4 There are no additional bodies.

Step 5 Apply Newton's second law.

The resultant of the forces in the x-direction is $\Sigma F_x = T - \mathcal{I}_k = ma_x$. (9)

The resultant of the forces in the y-direction is $\Sigma F_y = \mathcal{N} - w = ma_y = 0$. (10)

From (10) $\mathcal{N} = w = mg$.

Therefore $\mathcal{I}_k = \mu_k \mathcal{N} = \mu_k mg$.

Also $a_x = \dfrac{v - v_0}{t} = \dfrac{v}{t}$.

Substituting the values of $\mathcal{I}_k$ and a_x in (9) we obtain

$$T = \mathcal{I}_k + ma_x = \mu_k mg + \frac{mv}{t}.$$

Problem 2 Two known masses m_1 and m_2 are connected by a cord which passes over a frictionless pulley. This setup is known as Atwood's machine. If $m_2 > m_1$, find the acceleration of each mass and the tension in the cord.

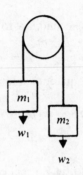

Step 1 Select the bodies for analysis. It should be noted that the pulley is massless and frictionless and only serves to change the direction of the force.

Step 2 Draw the free-body diagram for each body. The tension in the cord is the same throughout its length.

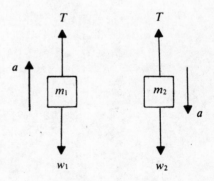

Step 3 and Step 4 Set up a coordinate system. Since $m_2 > m_1$, it is obvious that m_1 will accelerate upward and m_2 will accelerate downward. Thus the motion is clockwise. We usually choose the positive direction as the direction of the acceleration. However, it is not mandatory to do so. Negative results for acceleration and tension would signify that the direction is opposite to the one we chose.

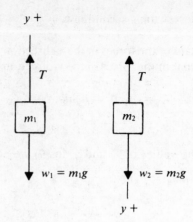

Step 5 Apply Newton's second law to each body. Remember that forces in the positive direction are positive,

for m_1: $\qquad\qquad\qquad T - m_1g = m_1a,$ $\qquad\qquad\qquad\qquad$ (11)

for m_2: $\qquad\qquad\qquad m_2g - T = m_2a.$ $\qquad\qquad\qquad\qquad$ (12)

Note that we have two equations and two unknowns, T and a; T can be eliminated by adding equations (11) and (12):

$$(m_2 - m_1)g = (m_1 + m_2)a,$$

$$a = \frac{(m_2 - m_1)g}{m_1 + m_2}.$$

Substituting the value of a in Eq. (11);

$$T - m_1g = \frac{m_1(m_2 - m_1)g}{m_1 + m_2},$$

$$T = \frac{2m_1m_2g}{m_1 + m_2}.$$

Step 6 Check special case. If $m_2 = m_1$, $T = m_1 g$, $a = 0$ and the Atwood's machine is in equilibrium. This agrees with our intuitive expectations.

PROGRAMMED QUIZ

1 If the coefficient of friction between automobile tires and the road is 0.4, what is the shortest distance in which an automobile can be stopped when traveling at $30 \text{ m} \cdot \text{s}^{-1}$?

1

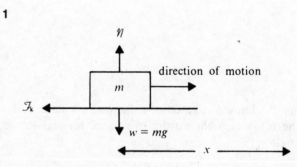

The retarding force $= \mathcal{F}_k = \mu_k \mathcal{N} = \mu_k w = \mu_k mg$ where m = mass of automobile.

Applying Newton's second law, $\Sigma F_x = ma_x$:

$$-\mathcal{F}_k = ma$$

$$-\mu_k mg = ma$$

$$a = -0.4(9.8 \text{ m} \cdot \text{s}^{-2}) = -3.92 \text{ m} \cdot \text{s}^{-2}$$

$$v^2 = v_0^2 + 2a(x - x_0) \qquad x_0 = 0$$

$$0 = (30 \text{ m} \cdot \text{s}^{-1})^2 + 2(-3.92 \text{ m} \cdot \text{s}^{-2})(x)$$

$$x = 115 \text{ m}$$

It is interesting to note that since $\mu_k mg = ma$, $\mu_k = \dfrac{a}{g}$.

2 Two blocks are being pulled along a horizontal surface by a force of 10 N. $\mathcal{F}_k$ for the 5 kg mass is 2 N, and $\mathcal{F}_k$ for the 2 kg mass is 1 N. Draw the free-body diagram for each mass.

2

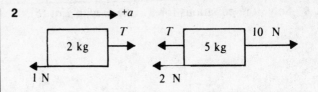

3 Apply Newton's second law to each body and solve for the tension in the connecting cord and the acceleration of the bodies.

3

$$\Sigma F_x = ma_x$$

For the 2 kg mass,

$$T - 1\,\text{N} = 2\,\text{kg}(a).$$

For the 5 kg mass,

$$10\,\text{N} - T - 2\text{N} = 5\,\text{kg}(a).$$

Add the two equations,

$$a = 1\,\text{m} \cdot \text{s}^{-2}.$$

Substitute the value of a in either equation:

$$T = 3\,\text{N}.$$

4 Solve the above problem for acceleration by considering both blocks and the connecting rope as a single system. Compare with results in frame 3.

4

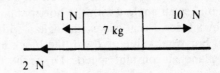

$$10\,\text{N} - 1\,\text{N} - 2\,\text{N} = 7\,\text{kg}(a)$$
$$a = 1\,\text{m} \cdot \text{s}^{-2}$$

(same answer as frame 3)

5 In frames 5–10 a block weighing w newtons is resting on a horizontal surface. It is pulled to the right at constant velocity by a force T acting at an angle α above the horizontal. The coefficient of sliding friction between the block and the surface is μ_k. Draw a sketch and free-body diagram.

5

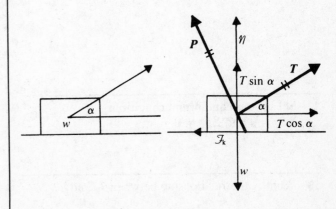

6 Compute ΣF_x, and ΣF_y.

6

$$\Sigma F_x = -\mathcal{F}_k + T \cos \alpha = 0$$
$$\Sigma F_y = \mathcal{N} - w + T \sin \alpha = 0$$

7 What is the relationship among $\mathcal{N}$, $\mathcal{F}_k$, and μ_k?

7

$$\mu_k = \frac{\mathcal{F}_k}{\mathcal{N}}$$

8 Solve the equations for T. Check with Eq. (8).

8
$$T = \frac{\mu_k w}{\mu_k \sin \alpha + \cos \alpha}$$

if $\theta = 0$, $T = \dfrac{w(\sin 0 + \mu_k \cos 0)}{\mu_k \sin \alpha + \cos \alpha}$

$$T = \frac{\mu_k w}{\mu_k \sin \alpha + \cos \alpha}$$

---

9 Solve the equation for w.

9
$$w = \frac{T(\cos \alpha + \mu_k \sin \alpha)}{\mu_k}$$

---

10 Solve the equation for μ_k.

10
$$\mu_k = \frac{T \cos \alpha}{w - T \sin \alpha}$$

---

11 A block weighing w newtons rests on an inclined plane that makes an angle θ with the horizontal. It is pulled up by a force T that makes an angle α with the horizontal. For what value of T will the block move down the plane at constant speed? Draw the free-body diagram.

11

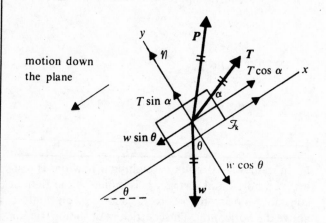

---

12 Set up the equilibrium conditions $\Sigma F_x = 0$ and $\Sigma F_y = 0$.

12
$$\Sigma F_x = 0; \ T \cos \alpha - w \sin \theta + \mathcal{F}_k = 0$$
$$\Sigma F_y = 0; \ \mathcal{N} + T \sin \alpha - w \cos \theta = 0$$

---

13 What is the relationship between $\mathcal{F}_k$ and $\mathcal{N}$?

13
$$\mathcal{F}_k = \mu_k \mathcal{N}$$

---

14 Solve the three equations in frames 12 and 13 for T.

14
$$T = \frac{w(\sin \theta - \mu_k \cos \theta)}{\cos \alpha - \mu_k \sin \alpha}$$

---

15 What is the value of T when $\alpha = 0$?

15
$$T = w(\sin \theta - \mu_k \cos \theta)$$

---

16 What is the value of μ_k when $T = 0$? What is happening?

16

$$w(\sin \theta - \mu_k \cos \theta) = 0$$
$$\mu_k = \frac{\sin \theta}{\cos \theta} = \tan \theta$$

The block is sliding down the plane at constant speed. If a block slides down an inclined plane at constant speed, the tangent of the slope angle of the inclined plane equals the coefficient of kinetic friction.

---

17 A block of mass m_1 moves on a level, frictionless surface. It is connected by a light, flexible cord over a small frictionless pulley to a second block of mass m_2. Draw the free-body diagrams and coordinate systems for these bodies. Why is the same T used to represent the tension in the cord in each case?

17

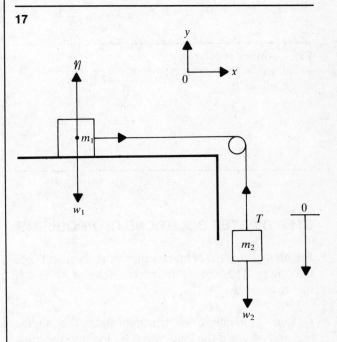

Since there is no friction in the pulley and the cord is considered to be massless, the tension is the same throughout the cord.

---

18 We have set up two coordinate systems. For block 1, the positive x-direction is to the right. For block 2, the positive y-direction is downward. Why?

18 In order for both bodies to accelerate in the positive x or y direction.

---

19 What is the relationship between a_x and a_y?

19

$a_x = a_y = a$.
Since the cord does not stretch, the speeds of the two bodies at any instant are equal and thus their accelerations have the same magnitude.

---

20 Apply Newton's second law to m_1.

20

$$\Sigma F_x = T = m_1 a$$
$$\Sigma F_y = \mathcal{N} - m_1 g = m_1 a_y = 0$$

Since body 1 has no acceleration in the y-direction (remember, we are using the coordinate system for body 1).

21 Apply Newton's second law to m_2.

21
$$\Sigma F_y = m_2g - T = m_2 a$$

---

22 Solve the two simultaneous equations for T and a.
$$T = m_1a$$
$$m_2g - T = m_2a$$

22
$$m_2g - T = m_2a$$
$$m_2g - m_1a = m_2a$$
$$a = \frac{m_2g}{m_1 + m_2}$$
$$T = \frac{m_1 m_2}{m_1 + m_2} g$$

---

23 Consider special cases:
if $m_1 = 0$,
if $m_2 = 0$.

23 If $m_1 = 0$, then
$$a = g, \qquad T = 0.$$
m_2 falls freely and there is no tension in the cord.
If $m_2 = 0$, then $a = 0$, $\qquad T = 0$.
There is no tension in the cord and no acceleration.
m_1 is at rest.

STEP BY STEP SOLUTIONS OF PROBLEMS

Problem 1   A 100 N block hangs from a vertical cord which is knotted to two other cords which are fastened to the ceiling. These two cords make angles of 30° and 50° respectively with the vertical. Determine the tensions in the three cords.

1 *Step 1* Draw a sketch indicating the angles (30° and 50°) and the load of 100 N. Identify the knot and the tensions.

1

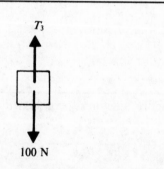

2 *Step 2a* (the block) Consider the forces acting on the hanging block. Draw a free-body diagram.

2

3 Since all the forces acting on the block are in the y-direction we can skip step 3 (resolve all forces into rectangular components).

Step 4a (the block)   Set $\Sigma F_y = 0$.

---

4 *Step 2b* (the knot O)   Consider the forces acting on the knot O. Draw a free-body diagram. (The two oblique cords make angles of 60° and 40°, respectively, with the horizontal axis.)

---

5 *Step 3b* (the knot O) Construct a set of rectangular axes. Resolve all forces into horizontal and vertical components and replace each force by its components.

---

6 *Step 4*   Set $\Sigma F_x = 0$ and $\Sigma F_y = 0$.

---

7 Using the method outlined, multiply both sides of the first equation by 0.866 and both sides of the second equation by 0.500.

---

8 Add the above equations and solve for T_2.

3

$$T_3 - 100 \text{ N} = 0$$
$$T_3 = 100 \text{ N}$$

The tension in the vertical cord is equal to the weight of the block.

4

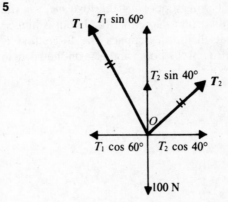

$$T_3 = 100 \text{ N}$$

5

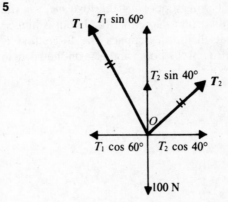

$$T_{1x} = -T_1 \cos 60° = -0.500 \, T_1$$
$$T_{1y} = T_1 \sin 60° = 0.866 \, T_1$$
$$T_{2x} = T_2 \cos 40° = 0.766 \, T_2$$
$$T_{2y} = T_2 \sin 40° = 0.643 \, T_2$$

6

$$\Sigma F_x = -0.500 \, T_1 + 0.766 \, T_2 = 0$$
$$\Sigma F_y = 0.866 \, T_1 + 0.643 \, T_2 - 100 \text{ N} = 0$$

7

$$-0.433 \, T_1 + 0.663 \, T_2 = 0$$
$$+0.433 \, T_1 + 0.322 \, T_2 - 50 \text{ N} = 0$$

8

$$0.985 \, T_2 = 50 \text{ N}$$
$$T_2 = 50.8 \text{ N}$$

---

9 Solve for T_1 by substituting this value of T_2 in the first equation in frame 6.

9

$$-0.500\,T_1 + 0.766\,(50.8\text{ N}) = 0$$
$$T_1 = 77.8\text{ N}$$

Problem 2 Find the tensions T and V in the cables and the force P exerted on the boom by the hinge for the arrangement shown in the sketch. From our discussion in Problem 1, the tension V in the vertical cord is equal to the weight of the block (1000 N).

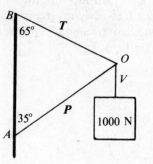

10 Since *Step 1* is given, we go on to *Step 2*. Draw the free-body diagram. Point O where the cable, the boom, and the wire supporting the load meet is the particle in equilibrium. Note that the boom is hinged at A and that the mast supplies the force that is transmitted through the boom and acts on the particle in equilibrium.

10

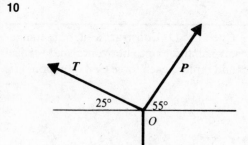

11 *Step 3* Construct a set of rectangular axes. Resolve all forces into horizontal and vertical components and replace each force by its components.

11

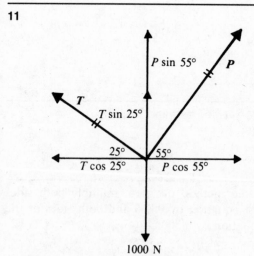

$$T_x = -T\cos 25° = -0.906\,T$$
$$T_y = T\sin 25° = +0.423\,T$$
$$P_x = P\cos 55° = +0.574\,P$$
$$P_y = P\sin 55° = +0.819\,P$$

---

12 *Step 4* Set $\Sigma F_x = 0$ and $\Sigma F_y = 0$. Solve for T and P.

12

$\Sigma F_x = -0.906\,T + 0.574\,P = 0$
$\Sigma F_y = +0.423\,T + 0.819\,P - 1000\ \text{N} = 0$
$\quad\ P = 920\ \text{N}$
$\quad\ T = 583\ \text{N}$

---

13 Check with values obtained from equations (*3*) and (*4*).

13

$$P = \frac{w\cos\alpha}{\sin(\alpha + \beta)}$$
$$= \frac{1000\ \text{N}\cos 25°}{\sin 80°}$$
$$= 920\ \text{N}$$
$$T = \frac{w\cos\beta}{\sin(\alpha + \beta)}$$
$$= \frac{1000\ \text{N}\cos 55°}{\sin 80°}$$
$$= 583\ \text{N}$$

Problem 3 A block weighing 20 N is placed on an inclined plane and connected to a 15 N block by a cord passing over a frictionless pulley. If the coefficient of sliding friction between the block and the plane is 0.1, for what two values of θ (the angle of inclination of the plane with the horizontal) will the block move with constant speed?

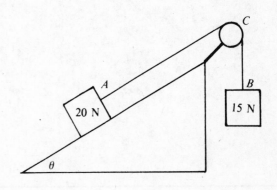

---

14 Since the sketch is given go on to *Step 2*. Draw the free-body diagram for A and B. What is the value of T? What is the tension in cord AC?

14 At B

$$\Sigma F_y = 0,$$
$$T - 15\ \text{N} = 0, \quad T = 15\ \text{N}.$$

Since a frictionless pulley changes the direction of the force, not the magnitude, the tension in cord AC is 15 N also.

15 The block can move with constant speed up or down the plane. Hence, we should have two values for θ. Draw the free-body diagram at A for constant speed up the plane. Note that $\mathcal{F}_k$ is opposite to the direction of motion.

15 At A

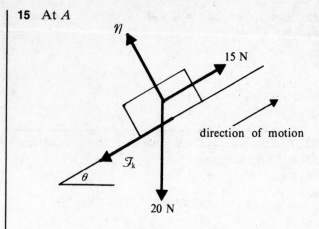

16 *Step 3* Set up a rectangular coordinate system (x-axis parallel to the plane, y-axis normal to the plane). Resolve all forces into rectangular components.

16

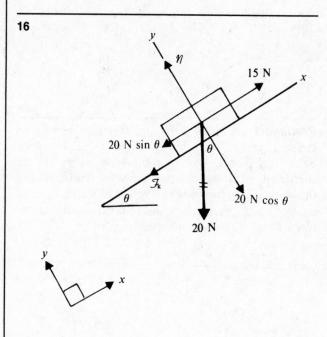

17 *Step 4* Set $\Sigma F_x = 0$ and $\Sigma F_y = 0$. Remember that $\mu_k = \dfrac{\mathcal{F}_k}{\mathcal{N}}$. Solve for θ.

17

$$\Sigma F_x = 0 \text{ yields}$$
$$15\text{ N} - 20\text{ N} \sin\theta - \mathcal{F}_k = 0.$$
$$\Sigma F_y = 0 \text{ yields}$$
$$\mathcal{N} - 20\text{ N} \cos\theta = 0.$$
$$\text{Since } \mathcal{F}_k = 0.1\,\mathcal{N},$$
$$15\text{ N} - 20\text{ N} \sin\theta - 0.1\,\mathcal{N} = 0.$$
Substituting $\mathcal{N} = 20$ N $\cos\theta$, we have
$$15\text{ N} - 20\text{ N} \sin\theta - 2\text{ N} \cos\theta = 0; \text{ where}$$
$$\cos\theta = \sqrt{1 - \sin^2\theta}.$$
After simplifying we obtain a quadratic equation in terms of $\sin\theta$:
$$\sin^2\theta - 1.49 \sin\theta + 0.548 = 0$$
$$\sin\theta = 0.831 \text{ or } \sin\theta = 0.659,$$
$$\theta = 56.2° \qquad \theta = 41.2°$$
Substituting in 15 N $- 20$ N $\sin\theta - 0.1\,\mathcal{N} = 0$, we see that $\theta = 56.2°$ does not check.

It is interesting to note that if we had set up the problem for the block to move down the plane we would have obtained the equation $15\text{ N} - 20\text{ N}\sin\theta + 2\text{ N}\cos\theta = 0$, which also would have yielded $\theta = 56.2°$ and $\theta = 41.2°$.

Thus the block moves up the plane at constant speed when $\theta = 41.2°$ and down the plane at constant speed when $\theta = 56.2°$.

The results of quadratic equations should always be checked with the original equation. Thus the student can verify that $\theta = 41.2°$ checks with $15\text{ N} - 20\text{ N}\sin\theta - 2\text{ N}\cos\theta = 0$ and $\theta = 56.2°$ checks with $15\text{ N} - 20\text{ N}\sin\theta + 2\text{ N}\cos\theta = 0$.

Problem 4 In the system shown in the figure a block having a mass $m_1 = 40$ kg is pulled to the right by a force $F = 300$ N at an angle $\theta = 35°$ with the horizontal. This block is attached by a massless cord passing over a small frictionless pulley to a second block having a mass $m_2 = 10$ kg. If the coefficient of kinetic friction between the first block and the horizontal surface is $\mu_k = 0.25$, what is the acceleration of the system and the tension is the cord connecting the two blocks?

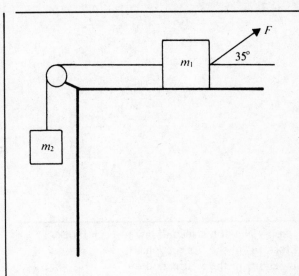

---

18 *Step 1* Consider block m_2.

18

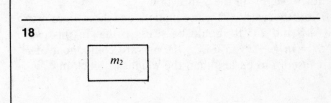

---

19 *Step 2* Draw the free-body diagram. Note that since m_2 is accelerating upward, T is not equal to w_2.

19

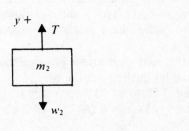

---

20 *Step 3* The only coordinate axis required is the y-axis, positive upward.

20

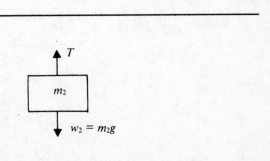

21 *Step 4* Repeat steps 1–3 for block m_1. Draw the free-body diagram for m_1. Specify a coordinate system: x-axis parallel to the horizontal surface (positive to the right) and a vertical y-axis (positive up). P, the contact force between the horizontal surface and block m_1 can be resolved into the normal force $\mathcal{N}$ and the force of kinetic friction $\mathcal{F}_k$. *Note:* F has an x-component $= F \cos \theta$ and a y-component $= F \sin \theta$.

21

22 Apply Newton's second law to each block.
for block m_2 in the y-direction
for block m_1 in the x-direction
substitute $\mathcal{F}_k = \mu_k \mathcal{N}$
for block m_1 in the y-direction
Note that we have three equations and three unknowns $(a, \mathcal{N}$ and $T)$. It should be stressed that in this case $\mathcal{N} = m_1 g - F \sin \theta$ i.e., the upward component of F caused $\mathcal{N}$ to be less than the weight of block m_1.

22

$$T - m_2 g = m_2 a$$
$$F \cos \theta - T - \mathcal{F}_k = m_1 a$$
$$F \cos \theta - T - \mu_k \mathcal{N} = m_1 a$$
$$F \sin \theta + \mathcal{N} - m_1 g = 0$$

$$T - m_2 g = m_2 a \qquad (13)$$
$$F \cos \theta - T - \mu_k \mathcal{N} = m_1 a \qquad (14)$$
$$F \sin \theta + \mathcal{N} - m_1 g = 0 \qquad (15)$$

23 Solve equation *(13)* for T and equation *(15)* for $\mathcal{N}$. Substitute the values for T and $\mathcal{N}$ in equation *(14)* and solve for a.
Substitute the numerical values given in the problem for the variables in the equation for a.

$m_1 = 40$ kg $\qquad \theta = 35°$
$m_2 = 10$ kg $\qquad \mu_k = 0.25$
$F = 300$ N

23

$$T = m_2(g + a)$$
$$\mathcal{N} = m_1 g - F \sin \theta$$
$$F \cos \theta - m_2(g + a) - \mu_k(m_1 g - F \sin \theta) = m_1 a$$
$$a = \frac{F(\cos \theta - \mu_k \sin \theta) - (\mu_k m_1 + m_2)g}{m_1 + m_2}$$

$$\frac{300 \text{ N} (\cos 35° + 0.25 \sin 35°) - [0.25 \,(40 \text{ kg}) + 10 \text{ kg}]\, 9.8 \text{ m} \cdot \text{s}^{-2}}{50 \text{ kg}}$$
$$= 1.85 \text{ m} \cdot \text{s}^{-2}$$
Substitute in $T = m_1(g + a)$
$$T = 10 \text{ kg} (9.8 \text{ m} \cdot \text{s}^{-2} + 1.85 \text{ m} \cdot \text{s}^{-2})$$
$$= 117 \text{ N}$$

Problem 5 Two blocks connected by a cord passing over a small frictionless pulley rest on a plane as shown in the figure. The coefficient of sliding friction between block m_1 and the plane is μ_{k1} and between block m_2 and its plane is μ_{k2}. What is the acceleration of the blocks and the tension in the cord?

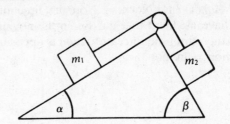

---

24 *Step 1* Consider block m_1.

24

---

25 Draw the free-body diagram. Assume that the system is moving to the right. Note that if, in a numerical problem, our assumption was incorrect, then our results would be negative in sign. $\mathcal{N}_1$ and $\mathcal{F}_{k1}$ are components of the contact force.

25

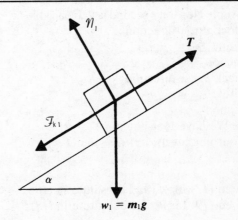

$\mathcal{F}_{k1}$ is opposite to the direction of motion.

---

26 Specify a coordinate system, x-axis parallel to the surface (positive to the right) and y-axis (positive up); w_1 is resolved into x- and y-components.

26

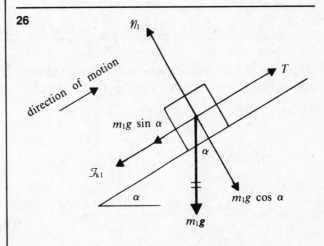

27 Repeat steps 1–3 for block m_2. Note the direction of $\mathscr{F}_{k2}$. We have assumed that the system is moving to the right; therefore, the force of friction is opposite to the direction of motion.

27

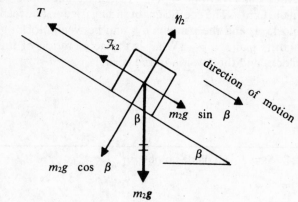

28 Apply Newton's second law to each block.
for block m_1, x-direction
substitute $\mathscr{F}_{k1} = \mu_{k1}\eta_1$
y-direction
for block m_2, x-direction
substitute $\mathscr{F}_{k2} = \mu_{k2}\eta_2$
y-direction
Note: We have four equations
and four unknowns: a, η_1, η_2 and T.

Solve eq (*17*) for η_1 and substitute in (*16*)
Solve eq (*19*) for η_2 and substitute in (*18*)

28

$$T - m_1g \sin \alpha - \mathscr{F}_{k1} = \eta_1 a$$
$$T - m_1g \sin \alpha - \mu_{k1}\eta_1 = m_1a$$
$$\eta_1 - m_1g \cos \alpha = 0$$
$$m_2g \sin \beta - T - J_{k2} = m_2a$$
$$m_2g \sin \beta - T - \mu_{k2}\eta_2 = m_2a$$
$$\eta_2 - m_2g \cos \beta = 0$$
$$T - m_1g \sin \alpha - \mu_{k1}\eta_1 = m_1a \qquad (16)$$
$$\eta_1 - m_1g \cos \alpha = 0 \qquad (17)$$
$$m_2g \sin \beta - T - \mu_{k2}\eta_2 = m_2a \qquad (18)$$
$$\eta_2 - m_2g \cos \beta = 0 \qquad (19)$$
$$T - m_1g \sin \alpha - \mu_{k1}m_1g \cos \alpha = m_1a \qquad (20)$$
$$m_2g \sin \beta - T - \mu_{k2}m_2g \cos \beta = m_2a \qquad (21)$$

Equations (*20*) and (*21*) represent a pair of simultaneous equations with two unknowns T and a. Add (*20*) and (*21*) and solve for a: $\qquad\qquad (22)$

$$a = \frac{m_2g(\sin \beta - \mu_{k2} \cos \beta) - m_1g(\sin \alpha + \mu_{k1} \cos \alpha)}{m_1 + m_2}.$$

Substitute Eq. (*22*) in Eq (*20*) to obtain T:

$$T = \frac{m_1m_2g(\sin \alpha + \sin \beta + \mu_{k1} \cos \alpha - \mu_{k2} \cos \beta)}{m_1 + m_2}.$$

Of course, Eq. (*22*) could also be substituted in Eq. (*21*) to obtain the same result.
Compute the acceleration a and the tension T in Problem 5 for the following numerical values:

$$m_1 = 100 \text{ kg}$$
$$\mu_{k1} = 0.3$$
$$\alpha = 40°$$
$$m_2 = 200 \text{ kg}$$
$$\mu_{k2} = 0.4$$
$$\beta = 60°$$
$$a = \frac{200 \text{ kg } (9.8 \text{ m} \cdot \text{s}^{-2}) (\sin 60° - 0.4 \cos 60°) - 100 \text{ kg } (9.8 \text{ m} \cdot \text{s}^{-2}) (\sin 40° + 0.3 \cos 40°)}{100 \text{ kg} + 200 \text{ kg}}$$
$$= 1.50 \text{ m} \cdot \text{s}^{-2}$$
$$T = \frac{100 \text{ kg } (200 \text{ kg}) (9.8 \text{ m} \cdot \text{s}^{-2}) (\sin 40° + \sin 60° + 0.3 \cos 40° - 0.4 \cos 60°)}{100 \text{ kg} + 200 \text{ kg}}$$
$$= 1005 \text{ N}$$

The student should verify the special cases for Problem 5

i $\beta = 90°$, $\mu_{k1} = \mu_k$

$$a = \frac{g(m_2 - m_1 \sin \alpha) - m_1 g \mu_k \cos \alpha}{m_1 + m_2}$$

$$T = \frac{m_1 m_2 g(\sin \alpha + 1 + \mu_k \cos \alpha)}{m_1 + m_2}$$

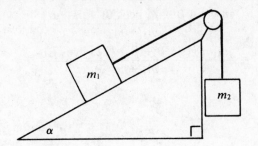

ii $\beta = 90°$, $\mu_k = 0$

$$a = \frac{g(m_2 - m_1 \sin \alpha)}{m_1 + m_2}$$

$$T = \frac{m_1 m_2 g(\sin \alpha + 1)}{m_1 + m_2}$$

iii $\alpha = \beta = 90°$ (Atwood's machine)

$$a = \frac{(m_2 - m_1)g}{m_1 + m_2}$$

$$T = \frac{2m_1 m_2 g}{m_1 + m_2}$$

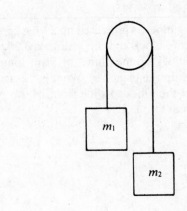

iv $\alpha = 0$, $\beta = 90°$, $\mu_{k1} = \mu_k$

$$a = \frac{(m_2 - m_1 \mu_k)g}{m_1 + m_2}$$

$$T = \frac{m_1 m_2 g(1 + \mu_k)}{m_1 + m_2}$$

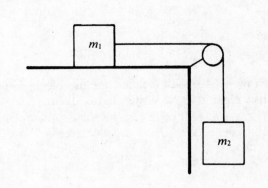

v $\alpha = 0$, $\beta = 90°$, $\mu_k = 0$

$$a = \frac{m_2 g}{m_1 + m_2}$$

$$T = \frac{m_1 m_2 g}{m_1 + m_2}$$

vi $\alpha = 0$

$$a = \frac{m_2 g (\sin \beta - \mu_{k2} \cos \beta) - m_1 g \mu_{k1}}{m_1 + m_2}$$

$$T = \frac{m_1 m_2 g (\sin \beta + \mu_{k1} - \mu_{k2} \cos \beta)}{m_1 + m_2}$$

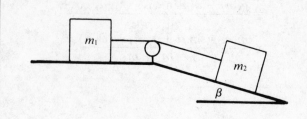

vii $\alpha = 0,\ \mu_{k1} = \mu_{k2} = 0$

$$a = \frac{m_2 g \sin \beta}{m_1 + m_2}$$

$$T = \frac{m_1 m_2 g \sin \beta}{m_1 + m_2}$$

Problem 6 A 10 kg block is projected up a long 25° incline with an initial velocity of 30 m · s⁻¹. The coefficient of friction between the block and the incline is 0.25. a) Find the friction force acting on the block. b) Find the acceleration of the block up the plane. c) How long does it take the block to move up the plane? d) How far does the block move up the plane? e) What is the acceleration of the block as it moves down the plane? f) How long does it take for the block to slide from its top position to its starting point? g) With what velocity does it reach its starting point?

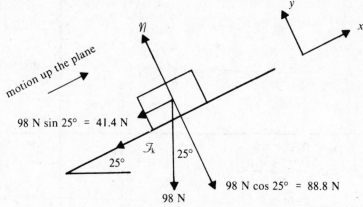

29 Draw a free-body diagram for the block. Note that its weight is 98 N. Write what is given.

29 Given:

$$v_0 = 30 \text{ m} \cdot \text{s}^{-1}$$
$$v = 0$$
$$m = 10 \text{ kg}$$
$$\theta = 25°$$
$$\mu_k = 0.25$$

30 Find the friction force.

30 No acceleration in the vertical direction.
$$\Sigma F_y = ma_y = 0$$
$$\mathcal{N} - 98 \text{ N} \cos 25° = 0$$
$$\mathcal{N} = 88.8 \text{ N}$$
$$\mathcal{F}_k = \mu_k \mathcal{N}$$
$$= 0.25\,(88.8 \text{ N}) = 22.2 \text{ N}$$

31 Find the acceleration of the block. The direction up the incline is taken as +.

31

$$\Sigma F_x = ma_x$$
$$-98 \text{ N} \sin 25° - \mathcal{F}_k = 10 \text{ kg } a$$
$$-41.4 \text{ N} - 22.2 \text{ N} = 10 \text{ kg } a$$
$$a = -6.36 \text{ m} \cdot \text{s}^{-2}$$

---

32 How long does it take the block to move up the plane?

32

$$v = v_0 + at$$
$$0 = 30 \text{ m} \cdot \text{s}^{-1} + (-6.36 \text{ m} \cdot \text{s}^{-2})t$$
$$t = 4.72 \text{ s}$$

---

33 How far does it move up the incline?

33

$$v_{av} = \frac{v_0 + v}{2}$$
$$= \frac{30 \text{ m} \cdot \text{s}^{-1} + 0}{2} = 15 \text{ m} \cdot \text{s}^{-1}$$
$$x = v_{av}t = 15 \text{ m} \cdot \text{s}^{-1} (4.72 \text{ s})$$
$$= 70.8 \text{ m}$$

---

34 Find the acceleration of the block down the plane. Note that now the positive direction is down the plane.

34

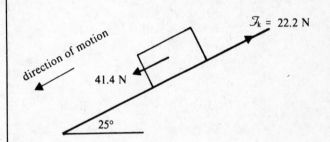

$$\Sigma F_x = ma_x$$
$$41.4 \text{ N} - 22.2 \text{ N} = 10 \text{ kg } a$$
$$a = 1.92 \text{ m} \cdot \text{s}^{-2}$$

---

35 How long does it take for the block to slide from its top position to its starting point?

35

$$x - x_0 = v_0 t + \tfrac{1}{2} at^2$$
$$70.8 \text{ m} - 0 = 0 + \tfrac{1}{2}(1.92 \text{ m} \cdot \text{s}^{-2})t^2$$
$$t = 8.59 \text{ s}$$

---

36 With what velocity does it arrive at its starting point?

36

$$v = v_0 + at$$
$$= 0 + (1.92 \text{ m} \cdot \text{s}^{-2}) (8.59 \text{ s})$$
$$= 16.5 \text{ m} \cdot \text{s}^{-1}$$

---

1 **_Problem 1_** Find the weight of the body and the tensions T and V. The tension in cable AC is 120 N.

1
Answer
236 N, 184 N

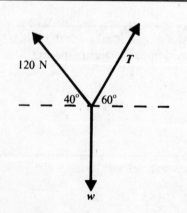

If you solved this problem correctly, go to frame 6. If you could not solve this problem, go through frames 2–5.

2 Since the sketch is given, we will proceed to _Step 2_. Consider the forces acting on the block. Draw a free-body diagram and solve for V.

2

$$\Sigma F_y = 0$$
$$V - w = 0$$
$$V = w$$

3 _Step 2_ (continued) Draw a free-body diagram for the knot C.

3

120 N

T

40° 60°

w

4 *Step 3* Set up the rectangular coordinate system and resolve all forces acting on C into rectangular components.

4

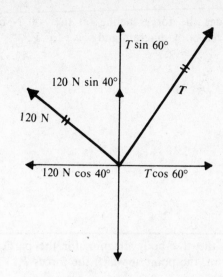

$$T_x = T \cos 60° = 0.500\ T$$
$$T_y = T \sin 60° = 0.866\ T$$
$$(120\ \text{N})_x = -120\ \text{N} \cos 40° = -91.9\ \text{N}$$
$$(120\ \text{N})_y = 120\ \text{N} \sin 40° = 77.1\ \text{N}$$

5 *Step 4* Set $\Sigma F_x = 0$, $\Sigma F_y = 0$ and solve for w and T.

5

$$\Sigma F_x = 0;\ 0.500\ T - 91.9\ \text{N} = 0$$
$$T = 184\ \text{N}$$
$$\Sigma F_y = 0;\ 0.866\ T + 77.1\ \text{N} - w = 0$$
$$w = 77.1\ \text{N} + 0.866\ (184\ \text{N}) = 236\ \text{N}$$

6 *Problem 2* A horizontal boom is hinged to a vertical mast at one end, and an 800 N body hangs from its other end. The boom is supported by a guy wire from its outer end to a point on the mast directly above the boom. If the tension in the wire is 1200 N, what is the angle that the wire makes with the boom? Also, find the force exerted on the boom by the hinge.

6
Answer
41.8°, 895 N

If you solved this problem correctly, go to frame 12. If you could not solve this problem, go through frames 7–11.

7 Draw a sketch.

7

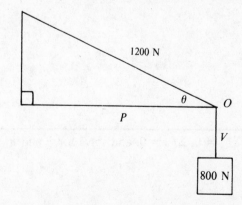

8 Consider the forces acting on the 800 N body. Draw a free-body diagram and solve for V.

8

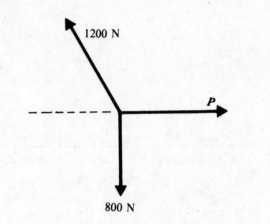

$$\Sigma F_y = 0$$
$$V - w = 0$$
$$V = w$$

---

9 Draw the free-body diagram for the particle in equilibrium, the point at which the forces P, V, and 1200 N meet.

9

1200 N

P

800 N

---

10 Resolve all forces into horizontal and vertical components and replace each force by its components.

10

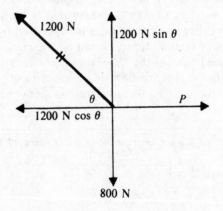

$$(1200\ \text{N})_x = -\ 1200\ \text{N} \cos \theta$$
$$(1200\ \text{N})_y = 1200\ \text{N} \sin \theta$$

---

11 Set $\Sigma F_x = 0$, $\Sigma F_y = 0$, and solve for P and θ

11

$$\Sigma F_y = 0;\ 1200\ \text{N} \sin \theta - 800\ \text{N} = 0$$
$$\sin \theta = 0.667,\ \theta = 41.8°$$
$$\Sigma F_x = 0;\ P - 1200\ \text{N} \cos \theta = 0$$
$$P = 1200\ \text{N} \cos 41.8° = 895\ \text{N}$$

---

12 **Problem 3** a) What downward force P_d parallel to the surface of an inclined plane with angle of inclination θ with the horizontal is required to push a block (weight w) down the plane at constant speed? The coefficient of friction is μ_k.

b) If $\theta = 20°$, $w = 150$ N, and $P_d = 2$ N, find μ_k.

c) What upward force P_u parallel to the plane is required to push the block up the plane at constant speed?

d) Find P_u if $\theta = 20°$ and $w = 150$ N.

e) Find an algebraic expression for P_u in terms of P_d, w, and θ.

12
Answer

$$P_d = w(\mu_k \cos\theta - \sin\theta),$$
$$0.378, \; P_u = w(\mu_k \cos\theta + \sin\theta),$$
$$105 \text{ N}, \; P_u = P_d + 2\,w \sin\theta$$

If you solved this problem correctly, go to frame 21. If you could not solve this problem, go through frames 13–20.

---

13 Draw a sketch.

13

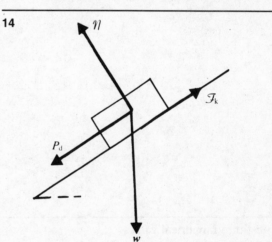

---

14 Draw the free-body diagram. Note that $\mathcal{F}_k$ is opposite to the direction of motion.

14

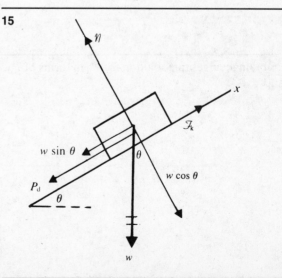

---

15 Resolve all forces into horizontal and vertical components and replace each force by its components.

15

16 Set $\Sigma F_x = 0$ and $\Sigma F_y = 0$ and solve for P_d.

16

$\Sigma F_x = 0; \mathcal{F}_k - w \sin \theta - P_d = 0$

$\Sigma F_y = 0; \mathcal{N} - w \cos \theta = 0$

$$\text{But } \mu_k = \frac{\mathcal{F}_k}{\mathcal{N}}$$

$\therefore \mu_k w \cos \theta - w \sin \theta - P_d = 0$

$$P_d = w(\mu_k \cos \theta - \sin \theta)$$

---

17 Substitute the values in the equation for P_d and solve for μ_k.

17

$$2 \text{ N} = 150 \text{ N}(0.94\mu_k - 0.342)$$
$$\mu_k = 0.378$$

---

18 Set up the free-body diagram for P_u. Set $\Sigma F_x = 0$ and $\Sigma F_y = 0$ and solve for P_u.

18

$\Sigma F_x = 0; P_u - w \sin \theta - \mathcal{F}_k = 0$

$\Sigma F_y = 0; \mathcal{N} - w \cos \theta = 0$

$$\mu_k = \frac{\mathcal{F}_k}{\mathcal{N}}$$

$P_u - w \sin \theta - \mu_k w \cos \theta = 0$

$P_u = w(\mu_k \cos \theta + \sin \theta)$

---

19 Substitute numerical values.

19

$$P_u = 150 \text{ N} [(0.378) (0.940) + 0.342]$$
$$= 105 \text{ N}$$

---

20 Obtain an algebraic solution for P_u in terms of P_d, w, and θ.

20 Solve $P_d = w(\mu_k \cos \theta - \sin \theta)$ for μ_k:

$$\mu_k = \frac{P_d + w \sin \theta}{w \cos \theta} .$$

Substitute this value in

$$P_u = w(\mu_k \cos \theta + \sin \theta)$$

$$= w\left(\frac{P_d + w \sin \theta}{w \cos \theta}\right) \cos \theta + w \sin \theta$$

$$= P_d + 2 w \sin \theta.$$

If $P_d = 2 \text{ N}$, $w = 150 \text{ N}$, $\theta = 20°$,

$$P_u = 2 \text{ N} + 2(150 \text{ N}) \sin 20° = 105 \text{ N}.$$

21 **_Problem 4_** A 5 kg block resting on a horizontal surface is connected by a cord passing over a frictionless pulley to a hanging 8 kg block. The coefficient of friction between the block and the horizontal surface is 0.6. Find the acceleration of each block and the tension in the cord.

21

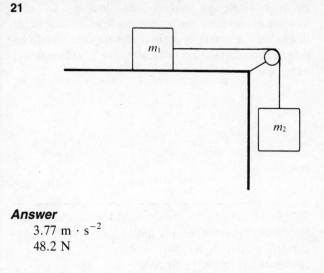

Answer
$3.77 \text{ m} \cdot \text{s}^{-2}$
48.2 N

If you solved this problem correctly, go to frame 30. If you could not solve this problem, go through frames 22–29.

22 *Step 1* Consider block $m_1 = 5$ kg.

22

m_1

23 *Step 2* Draw the free-body diagram for m_1.

23

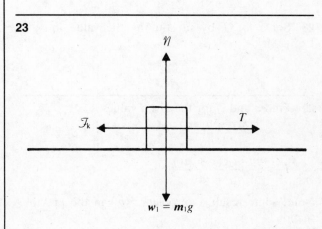

24 *Step 3* Specify a coordinate system, x-axis parallel to the surface (positive to the right) and y-axis (positive up). The contact force between the surface and block m_1, has been resolved into the normal force $\mathscr{N}$ and the kinetic friction $\mathscr{F}_k$. Note $\mathscr{F}_k$ is opposite to the direction of motion.

24

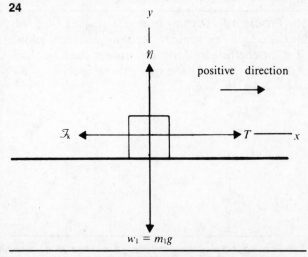

25 *Step 4* Repeat steps 1–3 for block m_2. In order to have m_1 and m_2 move in a positive direction, we designate the y-axis as positive downward. The direction of the acceleration is usually taken as the positive direction.

25

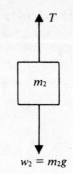

$$w_2 = m_2g$$

---

26 *Step 5* Apply Newton's second law to each body.
for block m_1 in the x-direction
substitute $\mathcal{F}_k = \mu_k \mathcal{N}$
for block m_1 in the y-direction
for block m_2 in the y-direction
Note that we have three equations and three unknowns (a, $\mathcal{N}$ and T).

26

$$T - \mathcal{F}_k = m_1a$$
$$T - \mu_k\mathcal{N} = m_1a$$
$$\mathcal{N} - m_1g = 0$$
$$m_2g - T = m_2a$$
$$T - \mu_k\mathcal{N} = m_1a \tag{23}$$
$$\mathcal{N} - m_1g = 0 \tag{24}$$
$$m_2g - T = m_2a \tag{25}$$

---

27 Solve for a by substituting $\mathcal{N} = m_1g$ in Eq. (23) and then adding Eq. (23) and (25).

27

$$a = \frac{g(m_2 - \mu_k m_1)}{m_1 + m_2}$$

---

28 Solve for T by substituting the value for a in Eq. (25).

28

$$T = \frac{m_1m_2g(1 + \mu_k)}{m_1 + m_2}$$

---

29 Find a and T for the given values,
$$a = \frac{g(m_2 - \mu_k m_1)}{m_1 + m_2},$$
$$T = \frac{m_1m_2g(1 + \mu_k)}{m_1 + m_2}.$$

Note: same result as problem 5(*iv*) in the previous section.

29

$$a = \frac{9.8 \text{ m} \cdot \text{s}^{-2}\,[8 \text{ kg} - 0.6(5 \text{ kg})]}{5 \text{ kg} + 8 \text{ kg}} = 3.77 \text{ m} \cdot \text{s}^{-2}$$

$$T = \frac{(5 \text{ kg})\,(8 \text{ kg})\,(9.8 \text{ m} \cdot \text{s}^{-2})\,(1 + 0.6)}{5 \text{ kg} + 8 \text{ kg}} = 48.2 \text{ N}$$

---

30 ***Problem 5*** Starting from rest, it takes 4 seconds for the 6 kg block to reach the floor 2 meters below. Find the coefficient of friction between the 8 kg block and the incline. The angle of the incline is 30° ($m_1 = 8$ kg, $m_2 = 6$ kg).

30

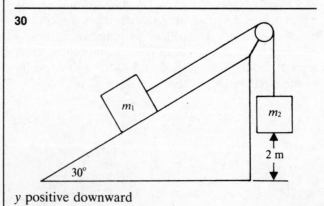

y positive downward

Answer 0.237

If you solved this problem correctly, go to frame 35. If you could not solve this problem, go through frames 31–34.

31 Find the acceleration.

31
$$y = y_0 + v_0t + \tfrac{1}{2}at^2$$
$$2\text{ m} = 0 + \tfrac{1}{2}(a)\,(4\text{ s})^2$$
$$a = 0.25\text{ m}\cdot\text{s}^{-2}$$

---

32 Draw the free-body diagrams and resolve all forces into rectangular components.

32

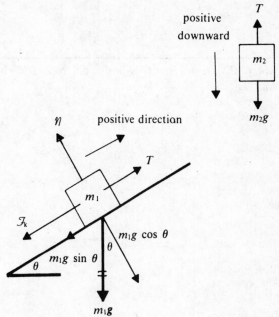

---

33 Apply Newton's second law to each body.

33
$$\Sigma F = ma$$
$$m_2g - T = m_2a$$
$$(6\text{ kg})\,(9.8\text{ m}\cdot\text{s}^{-2}) - T = (6\text{ kg})\,(0.25\text{ m}\cdot\text{s}^{-2})$$
$$T = 57.3\text{ N}$$
$$T - \mathcal{F}_k - m_1g\sin\theta = m_1a$$
$$57.3\text{ N} - \mathcal{F}_k - (8\text{ kg})\,(9.8\text{ m}\cdot\text{s}^{-2})\,(0.5) =$$
$$(8\text{ kg})\,(0.25\text{ m}\cdot\text{s}^{-2})$$
$$\mathcal{F}_k = 16.1\text{ N}$$

---

34 Find μ_k.

34
$$\mathcal{N} - mg\cos\theta = 0$$
$$\mathcal{F}_k = \mu_k\mathcal{N}$$
$$16.1\text{ N} = \mu_k\,(8\text{ kg})\,(9.8\text{ m}\cdot\text{s}^{-2})\,(0.866)$$
$$\mu_k = 0.237$$

---

35 **Problem 6** A block of mass m slides down an inclined plane that makes an angle θ with the horizontal. The motion of the block is opposed by a friction force $\mathcal{F}_k$, and it maintains a constant acceleration a. Express the acceleration in terms of $m, \mathcal{F}_k$, and θ.

35
Answer
$$a = \frac{mg\sin\theta - \mathcal{F}_k}{m}$$

If you could not solve this problem, go through frames 36–39.

36 *Step 1* Draw a sketch of the block.

36

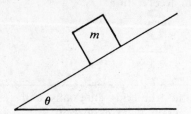

___

37 *Step 2* Draw the free-body diagram for the block.

37

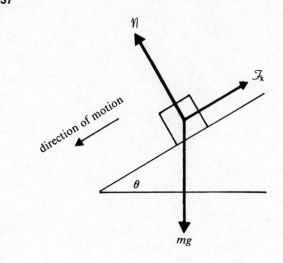

___

38 *Step 3* Specify a coordinate system (x-axis parallel to the plane and y-axis perpendicular to the plane). Resolve mg into components parallel and perpendicular to the plane.

38

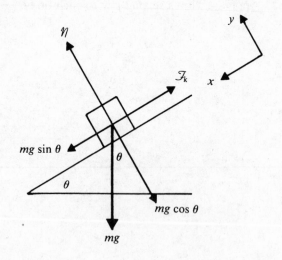

___

39 *Step 4* There are no additional bodies.

Step 5 Apply Newton's second law in the x-direction.

39

$$\Sigma F_x = ma_x$$
$$mg \sin \theta - \mathcal{F}_k = ma$$
$$a = \frac{mg \sin \theta - \mathcal{F}_k}{m}$$

___

6

Applications of Newton's Laws — II

MAIN IDEAS

In the previous chapter, Newton's laws of motion were applied to motion in a straight line. Here they are applied to circular motion such as satellite motion and the centrifuge. After an expression for radial force is derived, Newton's law of gravitation and the concept of weight are discussed, as well as gravitational field and apparent weight. It is a good idea to review the kinematics of circular motion studied in Chapter 3 before you do these problems.

BASIC TERMS — *Give definitions or meanings for the following:*

circular motion (6-I)
uniform circular motion (6-1)
radial force (6-1)
conical pendulum (6-1)
vertical circular motion (6-2)
weight (6-3)

Newton's law of gravitation (6-3)
gravitational field (6-4)
satellite motion (6-5)
newtonian synthesis (6-5)
centrifuge (6-6)

PROGRAMMED QUIZ

1 The force that the earth exerts on you is greater than, smaller than, or equal to the force that you exert on the earth?

1 Equal to; in Newton's law of gravitation the attractive forces exerted by each body on the other are equal in magnitude and opposite in direction.

2 In the motion of the moon around the earth, the force that provides the necessary centripetal acceleration is _____.

2 The gravitational attraction of the earth.

3 A small body attached to a cord is whirled in a vertical circle. Compare the tangential component of acceleration in this case with the tangential component of acceleration in uniform circular motion.

3 In uniform circular motion, the speed is constant; therefore there is no tangential component of acceleration. In motion in a vertical circle, the speed is greater when the object is coming down than when it is going up. Since the magnitude of the velocity is changing, there must be a tangential component of acceleration.

---

4 If you are whirling a ball on a string in a vertical circle and the string breaks, the ball will fly off in a _____ ; this is an example of _____ .

4 Straight line; inertia or Newton's first law. In order for the ball to travel in a vertical circular path the forces acting on the ball must furnish the required radial force. The forces in this case are the tension T in the string and the gravitational force w of the earth.

---

5 What is the actual force that you feel on your hand?

5 In order to keep the ball moving in a circular path, you must pull inward on the ball. In accordance with Newton's third law, the ball exerts on equal and opposite force on your hand.

---

6 If the speed of an object in uniform circular motion is doubled, the radial force is _____ .

6 Quadrupled;

$$F = \frac{mv^2}{R}$$
if $v' = 2v$
$$F' = \frac{m(2v)^2}{R}$$
$$= \frac{4mv^2}{R} = 4F.$$

---

7 An object is revolving uniformly in a circle in the clockwise direction. Show the tangential velocity at points 1 and 2 by arrows. Are the two velocity vectors equal?

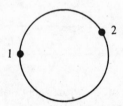

7

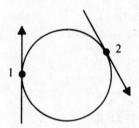

No, they are equal in magnitude but not in direction.

---

8 Referring to frame 7, use arrows to show the centripetal acceleration at both points. Are the two acceleration vectors equal?

8

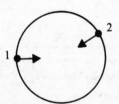

No, they are equal in magnitude but not in direction.

---

9 Referring to frame 7, use arrows to show the direction of the resultant force at both points. Are the two forces equal?

9 No, they are equal in magnitude but not in direction.

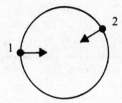

---

10 Is radial force a special kind of force?

10 No, it is the name for the resultant inward force that must provide the radial acceleration for circular motion.

---

11 Should the term mv^2/R be regarded as a force?

11 No. It is the sum of the physical forces exerted by strings, friction, gravitational interaction, electrical interaction, etc., which cause the body to accelerate toward the center of the circle.

---

12 You are in a fast moving automobile. Why is it that when you round a curve, you are pushed against the door?

12 You have the tendency to move in a straight line (Newton's first law).

---

13 What force causes you to move in a circular path?

13 The door of the car or the back of the seat exert the radial force on you.

---

14 In order for the car to move in a circular path it must have an inward (radial) force acting on it. What supplies this force?

14 The force of friction between the tires and the pavement (on a flat road).

---

15 Can the "apparent weightlessness" experienced by astronauts in a satellite orbiting the earth ever be experienced on earth?

15 Yes, in a free fall such as jumping off a cliff.

---

16 Under what conditions would an astronaut experience "real weightlessness?"

16 When the spaceship is far from the earth, the moon, the sun, and other celestial bodies.

---

17 Is an object's weight at the North Pole the same as its weight at the equator?

17 No. Because of the earth's rotation about its axis, the object at the equator will experience a radial acceleration toward the center of the earth. Its apparent weight would be $w = mg - \dfrac{mv^2}{R}$, where mg is its weight at the North Pole.

---

18 What is a gravitational field?

18 A mass alters the space surrounding it. This change is called a gravitational field.

---

19 How do we measure a gravitational field at any point?

19 We place a small test mass at the point. If the test mass experiences a gravitational force, then there is a gravitational field at that point.

---

20 Draw the gravitational field of the earth.

20

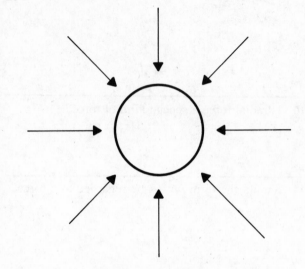

---

21 The sketch below shows three positions of the moon with respect to the earth. Even though the moon maintains a circular orbit about the earth, show how the moon "falls" toward the earth as it moves from position A to B and again as it moves from B to C.

21

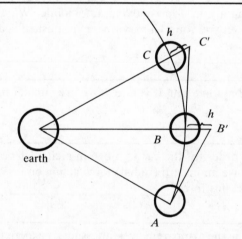

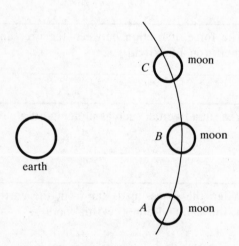

From Newton's first law, we know that the moon has a tendency to move in a straight line from A to B'. Because of the gravitational attraction of the earth, it falls a distance h to B. At position B, the moon is at the same distance from the earth as it was in position A. Again, at B, the moon heads for C' but falls back to C. Note that the time intervals from A to B and B to C are very small.

---

22 Why do we neglect the gravitational force of the sun in determining the weight of a body near the surface of the earth?

22 Because the distance between the sun and the earth is so great, the sun's gravitational attraction is negligible.

---

23 What is a centrifuge?

23 A rotating device for separating solids from liquids by whirling the container in a circle at high speeds.

MAIN IDEAS

1 Consider the case when the force on a particle is always normal to the curve. This means that $F_\parallel = 0$. Since $F_\parallel = ma_\parallel = 0$, $a_\parallel = 0$. It follows that the magnitude of the velocity will remain constant and the only effect of the force is to change the direction of motion.

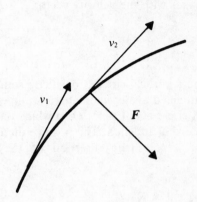

Similarly, when the force on a particle is parallel to the curve, $F_\perp = 0$. Since $F_\perp = ma_\perp$, $a_\perp = 0$; it follows that the magnitude of v will change but its direction will be constant; i.e., the particle moves in a straight line.

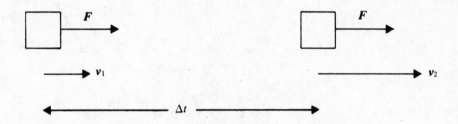

2 When a particle moves in a circular path at uniform speed,

$$a_\perp = \frac{v^2}{R},$$

Where $a_\perp$ is the centripetal (radial) acceleration, v is the magnitude of the velocity, and R is the radius of the circle. The period τ, the time for one revolution, is given by

$$\tau = \frac{2\pi R}{v}.$$

It is sometimes useful to express $a_\perp$ in terms of τ,

$$a_\perp = \frac{4\pi^2 R}{\tau^2}.$$

3 The particle's acceleration toward the center of the circle is caused by a net force also directed radially toward the center. In accordance with Newton's second law

$$\Sigma F = ma_\perp = \frac{mv^2}{R}.$$

There are various physical forces that may contribute to the net force ΣF which causes a body to travel in a circular path. These forces are: tension in a cord, force of friction between two surfaces, gravitational attraction, the magnetic force, and the electrical force.

4 Problem-solving strategy for circular motion.

1 Review the problem-solving hints for dynamics problems presented in Chapter 5.

2 Let the + direction be the direction of the radial acceleration which is toward the center of the circle.

3 Find the net force ΣF acting on the body in circular motion.

4 Set up Newton's second law,

$$\Sigma F = ma_\perp = \frac{mv^2}{R}.$$

5 For a particle moving in a circular path at non-uniform speed, $a = \sqrt{a_\parallel{}^2 + a_\perp{}^2}$ where $a_\parallel$ is the component of the acceleration tangent to the circle (it is equal to the rate of change of the speed) and $a_\perp$ is the component of the acceleration normal to the circle. Tan $\theta = \dfrac{a_\perp}{a_\parallel}$ where θ is the angle that the acceleration a makes with the velocity vector.

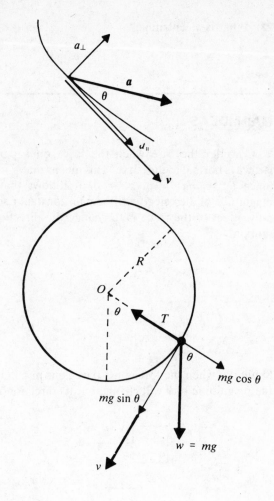

6 Motion in a vertical circle. Consider a small body of mass m attached to a cord of length R and whirling in a vertical circle about point O to which the other end of the cord is attached. The positive direction is towards the center (the direction of the radial acceleration).

$$F_\parallel = mg \sin \theta$$
$$F_\perp = T - mg \cos \theta$$
$$a_\parallel = \frac{F_\parallel}{m} = g \sin \theta$$
$$a_\perp = \frac{F_\perp}{m} = \frac{T - mg \cos \theta}{m} = \frac{v^2}{R}$$

At angle θ $\qquad\qquad\qquad\qquad T = m\left(\dfrac{v^2}{R} + g \cos \theta\right)$

At the lowest point ($\theta = 0$) $\qquad T = m\left(\dfrac{v^2}{R} + g\right)$

At the highest point ($\theta = 180°$) $\qquad T = m\left(\dfrac{v^2}{R} - g\right)$

When $T = 0$ $\qquad\qquad\qquad\qquad v \text{ critical} = \sqrt{Rg}$

7 Newton's law of gravitation is

$$F = \frac{Gm_1 m_2}{r^2},$$

where m_1 and m_2 are the masses of the bodies, r is the distance between their centers, F is the gravitational force of attraction that each body exerts on the other, G is the gravitational constant $= 6.670 \times 10^{-11}\ \text{N} \cdot \text{m}^2 \cdot \text{kg}^{-2}$. Experimental evidence indicates that inertial mass = gravitational mass.

8 The acceleration due to gravity g_p on any planet can be determined as follows: Consider a body having mass m and weight w_p on a particular plane (it should be noted that the mass will be the same on any planet), $w_p = mg_p = \dfrac{Gmm_p}{R_p{}^2}$; $g_p = \dfrac{Gm_p}{R_p{}^2}$, where m_p = mass of the planet; R_p = radius of the planet; G = gravitational constant.

9 The gravitational field $\bar{g}$ at a point in space. The mass of a body creates a change at each point in the space surrounding it. The gravitational field is measured by placing a test mass at that point. If the mass experiences a gravitational force, then there exists a gravitational field at that point:

$$\bar{g} = \frac{\bar{F}}{m}.$$

10 Important relationships for satellite motion.

$$v = \frac{\sqrt{Gm_E}}{r},$$

where

v = orbital speed,

m_E = mass of the earth,

r = radius of circular orbit measured from the center of the earth,

$$\tau = \frac{2\pi r^{3/2}}{\sqrt{Gm_E}}.$$

From Kepler's third law of motion, if two satellites are orbiting the same central mass, then

$$\frac{\tau_1^2}{r_1^3} = \frac{\tau_2^2}{r_2^3},$$

where τ_1 and r_1 are the period and orbit radius, respectively, of one satellite and τ_1 and r_2 are the period and orbit radius, respectively, of the second satellite.

11 Apparent weight or effective weight is the reading on a scale or the reaction of the floor platform or seat that an object is resting on.

12 Weightlessness. An object in free fall is said to have apparent weightlessness, even though the force of gravity is still acting on it, because a scale placed under it would read zero. The weightlessness experienced by astronauts in spaceships orbiting the earth is identical to free fall. Real weightlessness will be experienced if an astronaut is in outer space far from the gravitational influence of all celestial bodies.

PROGRAMMED QUIZ

1 If the mass of the moon is 7.15×10^{22} kg and the radius of the moon is 1.738×10^6 m, what is the acceleration due to gravity on the moon?

1

$$\begin{aligned} g_m &= \frac{Gm_m}{r_m^2} \\ &= \frac{6.67 \times 10^{-11}\,\text{N} \cdot \text{m}^2 \cdot \text{kg}^{-2}\,(7.15 \times 10^{22}\,\text{kg})}{(1.738 \times 10^6\,\text{m})^2} \\ &= 1.58\,\text{m} \cdot \text{s}^{-2} \end{aligned}$$

2 What is the mass of a body that weighs 10 N on the moon?

2

$$\begin{aligned} w_m &= mg_m \\ 10\,\text{N} &= m(1.58\,\text{m} \cdot \text{s}^{-2}) \\ m &= 6.33\,\text{kg} \end{aligned}$$

3 At what distance from the earth's center would a standard kilogram weigh 9.8 N?

3 Of course we know that on the surface of the earth a mass of 1 kg weighs 9.8 N. Hence the distance is equal to the radius of the earth. To verify this, use Newton's law of gravitation.

$$\begin{aligned} w &= mg \\ &= \frac{Gmm_E}{r^2} \end{aligned}$$

$$r = \sqrt{\frac{Gm_E}{g}}$$

$$= \sqrt{\frac{(6.67 \times 10^{-11}\,\text{N} \cdot \text{m}^2 \cdot \text{kg}^{-2})\,(5.98 \times 10^{24}\,\text{kg})}{9.8\,\text{m} \cdot \text{s}^{-2}}}$$

$= 6.38 \times 10^6$ m which is equal to the radius of the earth.

4 You discovered a new planet which has the same size as the earth but is 4 times as massive; compare your weight on the planet to your weight on earth.

4 Your weight on the planet would be 4 times your weight on earth:

$$g_E = \frac{Gm_E}{R_E{}^2} \; ; g_p = \frac{Gm_p}{R_p{}^2}$$

but $m_p = 4m_E$ and $R_p = R_E$ (given)

$$\therefore g_p = \frac{G(4m_E)}{R_E{}^2} = 4g_E$$

Since $w_p = mg_p = m(4g_E)$ and $w_E = mg_E$, where m is your mass, it follows that

$$w_p = 4w_E$$

---

5 An unbanked curve on a parkway has a radius of 300 m. A car rounds the curve at a speed of 35 m · s^{-1}. Draw a free-body diagram of the car (side and top views).

5

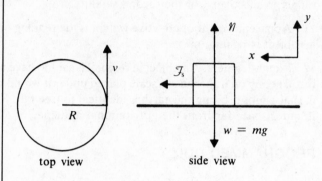

top view   side view

---

6 What is the radial acceleration of the car?

6

$$a_\perp = \frac{v^2}{R}$$

$$= \frac{(35 \text{ m} \cdot \text{s}^{-1})^2}{300 \text{ m}}$$

$$= 4.08 \text{ m} \cdot \text{s}^{-2}$$

---

7 Consider the vertical forces acting on the car. What is the value of η?

7 Since the car is not accelerating in the vertical direction, $a_y = 0$.

$$\Sigma F_y = ma_y = 0$$
$$\eta - mg = 0$$
$$\eta = mg$$

---

8 Friction causes the car to accelerate toward the center. We are using static friction because there is no relative motion between the tires and the roadway in the radial direction. What is the relationship for friction in terms of the mass of the car m, the coefficient of static friction μ_s, and g?

8

$$\mathcal{F}_s = \mu_s \, \eta$$
$$= \mu_s \, w = \mu_s \, mg$$

---

9 When a car rounds a curve on a level highway, the only force acting on it in a radial direction is the force of static friction. Why do we use static friction (and not kinetic friction) for a moving car?

9 There is no motion of the tires in the radial direction.

---

10 Explain why the force of static friction is directed toward the center of the curve when a car rounds a curve.

10 At any given moment, the walls of the tires in contact with the pavement are temporarily at rest and push outwardly against the road. The road reacts (Newton's third law) and exerts a radial force against the tires.

11 What must be the minimum coefficient of friction to keep the car from sliding?

11

$$\Sigma F_x = ma_x = ma_\perp$$
$$\mathcal{F}_s = \mu_s\, mg = ma_\perp$$
$$\mu_s = \frac{a_\perp}{g} = \frac{4.08 \text{ m} \cdot \text{s}^{-2}}{9.8 \text{ m} \cdot \text{s}^{-2}}$$
$$= 0.416$$

12 Since the gravitational force of the earth provides the radial force for a satellite orbiting the earth, find the period of the satellite using R = radius of orbit, v = constant speed, τ = period of satellite's orbit, M = mass of earth, G = universal gravitational constant.

12

$$\Sigma F = ma_\perp$$
$$\frac{GmM}{R^2} = \frac{mv^2}{R}$$
$$= \frac{m}{R}\left(\frac{2\pi R}{\tau}\right)^2$$

where $v = \dfrac{2\pi R}{\tau}$

$$\tau = 2\pi \sqrt{\frac{R^3}{GM}}$$

13 A massless cord 0.8 m long is whirling a 0.5 kg body in a vertical circle. What is the tension in the cord if the speed of the body is $6 \text{ m} \cdot \text{s}^{-1}$ at the top of the circle?

13

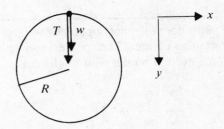

The direction of $a_\perp$ is positive. Consider the forces acting on the 0.5 kg body at the top of the circle.

$$F = \Sigma F_y = ma_y \text{ where } a_y = a_\perp = \frac{v^2}{R}$$

$$T + mg = \frac{mv^2}{R}$$

$$T = \frac{mv^2}{R} - mg$$

$$= \frac{(0.5 \text{ kg})\,(6 \text{ m} \cdot \text{s}^{-1})^2}{0.8 \text{ m}} - 0.5 \text{ kg}\,(9.8 \text{ m} \cdot \text{s}^{-2})$$

$$= 17.6 \text{ N}$$

14 What is the tension in the cord when the speed of the body is 6 m · s⁻¹ at the bottom of the circle?

14

The direction of $a_\perp$ is positive.
Consider the forces acting on the 0.5 kg body at the bottom of the circle.

$$F = \Sigma F_y = ma_y \text{ where } a_y = a_\perp = \frac{v^2}{R}$$

$$T - mg = \frac{mv^2}{R}$$

$$T = \frac{mv^2}{R} + mg$$

$$= 22.5 \text{ N} + 4.9 \text{ N} = 27.4 \text{ N}$$

15 An 80 kg pilot dives vertically at a velocity of 300 m · s⁻¹. He pulls out of the dive by changing his course to a circle in a vertical plane. If the radius of the circle is 1000 m, what is his acceleration at the lowest point?

15

$$a_\perp = \frac{v^2}{R}$$

$$= \frac{(300 \text{ m} \cdot \text{s}^{-1})^2}{1000 \text{ m}}$$

$$= 90 \text{ m} \cdot \text{s}^{-2}$$

16 How much does the pilot apparently weigh at the lowest point of his pullout? The apparent weight is the upward force exerted on the pilot by the seat.

16 The direction of $a_\perp$ is upward, therefore the upward direction is +.

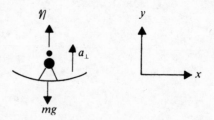

$$\Sigma F_y = ma_y$$

$$\eta - mg = \frac{mv^2}{R}$$

$$\eta = mg + \frac{mv^2}{R}$$

$$= 80 \text{ kg} \left[9.8 \text{ m} \cdot \text{s}^{-2} + \frac{(300 \text{ m} \cdot \text{s}^{-1})^2}{1000 \text{ m}} \right]$$

$$= 7980 \text{ N}$$

Note that η is the normal force exerted on the pilot by the seat.

17 The earth orbits the sun in a nearly circular orbit ($R = 1.49 \times 10^{11}$ m). If the period of the earth is 365.3 d, calculate the mass of the sun.

17

$$\tau^2 = \frac{4\pi^2}{Gm_{sun}} R^3$$

$$m_{sun} = \frac{4\pi^2 R^3}{G\tau^2}$$

$$= \frac{4\pi^2 (1.49 \times 10^{11} \text{ m})^3}{6.67 \times 10^{-11} \text{ N} \cdot \text{m}^2 \cdot \text{kg}^{-2} (31.56 \times 10^6 \text{ s})^2}$$

$$= 1.97 \times 30^{30} \text{ kg}$$

Note: 1 y = 365.3 d = 31.56×10^6 s

---

18 Two 10 kg spherical bodies are placed so that their centers are 40 cm apart. What is the magnitude of the gravitational force each body exerts on the other?

18

$$F = \frac{Gm_1m_2}{r^2}$$

$$= \frac{6.67 \times 10^{-11} \text{ N} \cdot \text{m}^2 \cdot \text{kg}^{-2} (10 \text{ kg}) (10 \text{ kg})}{(0.4 \text{ m})^2}$$

$$= 4.17 \times 10^{-8} \text{ N}$$

---

19 What is the force of gravity acting on a 9000 kg spaceship when it is in orbit three earth radii from the center of the earth?

19 Since the force of gravity is proportional to $1/r^2$, the weight of the spaceship is $\frac{1}{3^2} = \frac{1}{9}$ its weight at the surface of the earth.

$$w = \frac{1}{9} (9000 \text{ kg}) (9.8 \text{ m} \cdot \text{s}^{-2})$$

$$= 9800 \text{ N}$$

---

20 A satellite is in circular orbit about the earth. If the period of the satellite is 1 day, calculate its distance from the center of the earth. Since the moon and the satellite are both orbiting the same central mass (the earth), we can use Kepler's third law,

$$\frac{\tau_s^2}{r_s^3} = \frac{\tau_m^2}{r_m^3},$$

where

τ_s = period of satellite = 1 d,
τ_m = period of moon = 27.3 d,
r_s = distance of satellite from earth,
r_m = distance of moon from earth
$\quad = 3.8 \times 10^8$ m.

20

$$\frac{\tau_s^2}{r_s^3} = \frac{\tau_m^2}{r_m^3}$$

Invert both sides:

$$\frac{r_s^3}{\tau_s^2} = \frac{r_m^3}{\tau_m^2}$$

$$r_s^3 = r_m^3 \left(\frac{\tau_s}{\tau_m}\right)^2,$$

Take the cube root of each side:

$$r_s = r_m \left(\frac{\tau_s}{\tau_m}\right)^{2/3}$$

$$= 3.8 \times 10^8 \text{ m} \left(\frac{1 \text{ d}}{27.3 \text{ d}}\right)^{2/3}$$

$$= 3.8 \times 10^8 \text{ m} (0.110)$$

$$= 4.19 \times 10^7 \text{ m}$$

21 What is the acceleration due to gravity at this orbit? Use

$$g = \frac{Gm_{earth}}{r_s^2}$$

21

$$g = \frac{(6.67 \times 10^{-11}\,\text{N} \cdot \text{m}^2 \cdot \text{kg}^{-2})(5.98 \times 10^{24}\,\text{kg})}{(4.19 \times 10^7\,\text{m})^2}$$

$$= 0.227\,\text{m} \cdot \text{s}^{-2}$$

---

22 What is the orbital velocity of the satellite?

22

$$v = \frac{2\pi r_s}{\tau}$$

$$= \frac{2\pi(4.19 \times 10^7\,\text{m})}{86{,}400\,\text{s}}$$

$$= 3050\,\text{m} \cdot \text{s}^{-1}$$

Note: 1 d = 86,400 s

---

23 Any planet in our solar system can be considered as a satellite in circular orbit about the sun. What can you say about the ratio $\dfrac{\tau^2}{r^3}$, where

τ = planet's period about the sun,
r = radius of planet's orbit about the sun,
m = mass of sun.

23

$$\tau = 2\pi \sqrt{\frac{r^3}{GM}}$$

$$\tau^2 = \frac{4\pi^2 r^3}{GM}$$

$$\frac{\tau_2}{r^3} = \frac{4\pi^2}{GM}$$

Since the right side of the equation is a constant, the ratio of the square of the period of any planet revolving about the sun to the cube of the distance from the sun is a constant also. This is Kepler's third law, which can also be stated as

$$\frac{\tau_1^2}{r_1^3} = \frac{\tau_2^2}{r_2^3},$$

where τ and r are the periods and orbit radii, respectively, of the two planets.

STEP BY STEP SOLUTIONS OF PROBLEMS

Problem 1 Four point masses are fixed at positions as shown in the sketch. What is the magnitude and direction of the resultant force on the 1 kg mass at the origin?

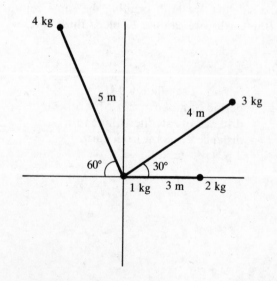

1 Find the force of attraction between the 1 kg and 2 kg masses using Newton's law of gravitation.

1

$$F_1 = \frac{Gm_1m_2}{r^2}$$

$$= \frac{(6.67 \times 10^{-11} \text{ N} \cdot \text{m}^2 \cdot \text{kg}^{-2})\,(1 \text{ kg})\,(2 \text{ kg})}{(3 \text{ m})^2}$$

$$= 1.48 \times 10^{-11} \text{ N}$$

2 Find the force of attraction between the 1 kg and 3 kg masses.

2

$$F_2 = \frac{(6.67 \times 10^{-11} \text{ N} \cdot \text{m}^2 \cdot \text{kg}^{-2})\,(1 \text{ kg})\,(3 \text{ kg})}{(4 \text{ m})^2}$$

$$= 1.25 \times 10^{-11} \text{ N}$$

3 Find the force of attraction between the 1 kg and 4 kg masses.

3

$$F_3 = \frac{(6.67 \times 10^{-11} \text{ N} \cdot \text{m}^2 \cdot \text{kg}^{-2})\,(1 \text{ kg})\,(4 \text{ kg})}{(5 \text{ m})^2}$$

$$= 1.07 \times 10^{-11} \text{ N}$$

4 Find the resultant of the three forces.

4

F	θ	x-component	y-component
1.48×10^{-11} N	0°	$+1.48 \times 10^{-11}$ N	0
1.25×10^{-11} N	30°	$+1.25 \times 10^{-11}$ N cos 30° $= +1.08 \times 10^{-11}$ N	$+1.25 \times 10^{-11}$ N sin 30° $= +0.625 \times 10^{-11}$ N
1.07×10^{-11} N	60°	-1.07×10^{-11} N cos 60° $= -0.535 \times 10^{-11}$ N	$+1.07 \times 10^{-11}$ N sin 60° $= +0.927 \times 10^{-11}$ N

$$\Sigma F_x = +2.03 \times 10^{-11} \text{ N} \qquad \Sigma F_y = +1.55 \times 10^{-11} \text{ N}$$

$$R = \sqrt{(\Sigma F_x)^2 + (\Sigma F_y)^2}$$

$$= \sqrt{(2.03 \times 10^{-11} \text{ N})^2 + (1.55 \times 10^{-11} \text{ N})^2}$$

$$= 2.55 \times 10^{-11} \text{ N}$$

$$\tan \alpha = \frac{|\Sigma F_y|}{|\Sigma F_x|} = \frac{|1.55 + 10^{-11} \text{ N}|}{|2.03 \times 10^{-11} \text{ N}|} = 0.764$$

$$\alpha = 37.4°$$

Problem 2 A small coin is placed on the outer edge of a record 26 cm in diameter. If the coefficient of static friction between the coin and the record is 0.2, what is the maximum period of rotation of the turntable before the coin slips off? What is its frequency in rev $\cdot$ min^{-1}?

5 Draw the free-body diagram of the coin.

5

6 Find ΣF in the y-direction.

6
$$\Sigma F_y = \eta - mg = 0$$
$$\eta = mg$$

---

7 The friction force supplies the radial force on the coin. Write the expression for ΣF in the x-direction. Solve for the velocity.

7
$$\Sigma F_x = \mathcal{F} = \frac{mv^2}{R}$$
but $\mathcal{F} = \mu_s \, \eta$
$$\mu_s \, \eta = \frac{mv^2}{R}$$
$$\mu_s \, mg = \frac{mv^2}{R}$$
$$v = \sqrt{\mu_s \, Rg}$$
$$= \sqrt{0.2 \, (9.8 \text{ m} \cdot \text{s}^{-2}) \, (0.13 \text{ m})}$$
$$= 0.505 \text{ m} \cdot \text{s}^{-1}$$

---

8 Find the period from
$$v = \frac{2\pi R}{\tau} .$$

8
$$\tau = \frac{2\pi R}{v}$$
$$= \frac{2\pi \, (0.13 \text{ m})}{0.505 \text{ m} \cdot \text{s}^{-1}}$$
$$= 1.62 \text{ s}$$

---

9 Find the frequency and convert to rev $\cdot$ min^{-1}.

9
$$f = \frac{1}{\tau} = \frac{1}{1.62 \text{ s}} = 0.62 \text{ rev} \cdot \text{s}^{-1}$$
$$\frac{0.62 \text{ rev}}{\text{s}} \times \frac{60 \text{ s}}{1 \text{ min}} = 37 \text{ rev} \cdot \text{min}^{-1}$$

Problem 3 A circular track of 120 m radius on a level road is banked for a velocity of 10 m $\cdot$ s^{-1}. What should be the minimum coefficient of friction between the tires and the road for an automobile rounding the curve at 25 m $\cdot$ s^{-1}?

10 Consider the general situation: velocity = v, radius = r, coefficient of static friction = μ_s, and banking angle = θ. Draw a free-body diagram of the automobile showing all the forces acting on it.

10

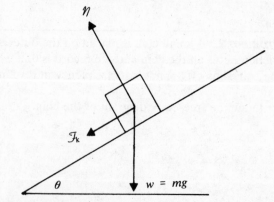

The forces acting on the automobile are its weight $w = mg$ and the reaction force of the road which is resolved into the normal force η and the force of static friction $\mathcal{F}_s$.

11 Choose a coordinate system such that the x-axis passes through the center of curvature of the track.

11

---

12 Resolve $\mathcal{N}$ and $\mathcal{J}_s$ into horizontal and vertical components along the x- and y-axis.

12

Horizontal comp of $\mathcal{N}$ = $\mathcal{N} \sin \theta$
Vertical comp of $\mathcal{N}$ = $\mathcal{N} \cos \theta$
Horizontal comp of $\mathcal{J}_s$ = $\mathcal{J}_s \cos \theta$
Vertical comp of $\mathcal{J}_s$ = $- \mathcal{J}_s \sin \theta$

---

13 Since there is no acceleration in the y-direction, we can state that $\Sigma F_y = ma_y = 0$.

13 $\Sigma F_y = \mathcal{N} \cos \theta - \mathcal{J}_s \sin \theta - mg = 0$

---

14 Substitute
$\mathcal{J}_s = \mu_s \mathcal{N}$ and solve for $\mathcal{N}$.

14

$$\mathcal{N} = \frac{mg}{\cos \theta - \mu_s \sin \theta}$$

---

15 The acceleration is caused by the horizontal components of $\mathcal{J}_s$ and $\mathcal{N}$ (which is equivalent to the horizontal component of the reaction force of the road). What is the value of ΣF_x?

15

$$F = \Sigma F_x = \mathcal{N} \sin \theta + \mathcal{J}_s \cos \theta$$
$$\text{Since } \mathcal{J}_s = \mu_s \mathcal{N}$$
$$\Sigma F_x = \mathcal{N} \sin \theta + \mu_s \mathcal{N} \cos \theta = \mathcal{N}(\sin \theta + \mu_s \cos \theta)$$

---

16 Substitute the value of $\mathcal{N}$ from the equation in frame 14 into this equation.

16

$$\Sigma F_x = \frac{mg(\sin \theta + \mu_s \cos \theta)}{\cos \theta - \mu_s \sin \theta}$$

---

17 Since
$$F_x = \frac{mv^2}{r}, \text{ solve for } v^2.$$

17

$$\frac{mv^2}{r} = \frac{mg(\sin \theta + \mu_s \cos \theta)}{\cos \theta - \mu_s \sin \theta}$$
$$v^2 = \frac{gr(\sin \theta + \mu_s \cos \theta)}{\cos \theta - \mu_s \sin \theta}$$

---

18 Solve for μ_s

18

$$\mu_s = \frac{v^2 \cos \theta - gr \sin \theta}{v^2 \sin \theta + gr \cos \theta}$$

---

19 What is the banking angle for $\mu_s = 0$?

19 If $\mu_s = 0$, $v^2 \cos \theta - gr \sin \theta = 0$ or
$\tan \theta = \dfrac{v^2}{gr}$.

---

20 Getting back to our problem, let us compute the banking angle for
$\quad r = 120$ m and
$\quad v = 10$ m · s^{-1}.

20

$$\tan \theta = \frac{(10 \text{ m} \cdot \text{s}^{-1})^2}{9.8 \text{ m} \cdot \text{s}^{-2} \, (120 \text{ m})}$$
$$\theta = 4.86°$$

---

21 Our problem requires that we find μ_s for
$\quad \theta = 4.86°$,
$\quad r = 120$ m and
$\quad v = 25$ m · s^{-1}.
Substitute these values in the equation in frame 18.

21

$$\mu_s = \frac{(25 \text{ m} \cdot \text{s}^{-1})^2 \cos 4.86° - 9.8 \text{ m} \cdot \text{s}^{-2} \, (120 \text{ m}) \sin 4.86°}{(25 \text{ m} \cdot \text{s}^{-1})^2 \sin 4.86° + 9.8 \text{ m} \cdot \text{s}^{-2} \, (120 \text{ m}) \cos 4.86°}$$
$$= 0.427$$

Problem 4 A cord is tied to a bucket of water and the bucket is swung in a vertical circle of radius 0.75 m. Determine the minimum velocity of the bucket if no water is to spill out of it.

22 Draw a free-body diagram. What are the forces acting on the body of water at the top of the circle? Determine the positive direction of the axis.

22

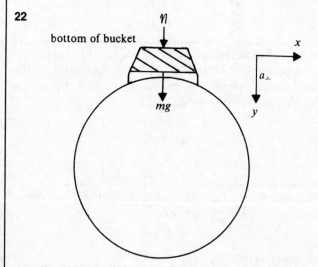

η (the reaction of the bottom of the bucket) and the weight of the water mg are the forces acting on the bucket of water. The direction of $a_\perp$ is downward at the top of the circle. Therefore the downward direction is +. The positive direction of a is always toward the center of the circular path.

23 What is the net force causing the body of water to move in a circular path? Apply Newton's second law.

23

$$\Sigma F_y = ma_y = ma_\perp$$
$$= \eta + mg$$
$$\eta + mg = \frac{mv^2}{R}$$

---

24 At minimum velocity, the water has no contact with the bottom of the bucket.
Therefore, $\eta = 0$. Solve for v_{min} and substitute the given values.

24 If

$$\eta = 0, \quad mg = \frac{mv_{min}^2}{R}$$
$$v_{min} = \sqrt{g\,R}$$
$$= \sqrt{(9.8 \text{ m} \cdot \text{s}^{-2})\,(0.75 \text{ m})}$$
$$= 2.71 \text{ m} \cdot \text{s}^{-1}$$

Problem 5 Compare the weight of an 80 kg explorer at the North Pole with her weight at the equator. Assume that the earth is spherical and therefore g has the same value everywhere on the earth's surface.

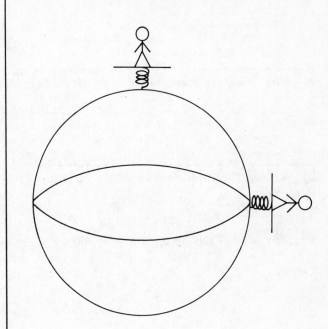

---

25 Draw a free-body diagram showing the forces acting on the explorer at the North Pole.

25

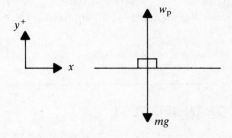

The forces acting on the explorer at the North Pole are the force of gravity mg and the force the scale platform exerts on her. This is her weight w_p.

26 Find the expression for her weight at the North Pole.

26
$$\Sigma F_y = 0$$
$$w_p - mg = 0$$
$$w_p = mg$$

---

27 At the equator the explorer is moving in a circular direction. Draw a free-body diagram.

27

The scale platform is exerting a force w_e on the explorer. This is her weight at the equator.

---

28 At the equator the explorer experiences an acceleration toward the center of the earth. Apply Newton's second law.

28
$$\Sigma F = ma_\perp$$
$$mg - w_e = \frac{mv^2}{R}$$
$$w_e = mg - \frac{mv^2}{R}$$

---

29 What is the explorer's weight at the North Pole?

29
$$w_p = mg$$
$$= (80 \text{ kg}) (9.8 \text{ m} \cdot \text{s}^{-2})$$
$$= 784 \text{ N}$$

---

30 What is the explorer's weight at the equator? Remember
$$v = \frac{2\pi R}{\tau},$$
and the period of the earth is 1 d = 86,400 s.

30
$$w_e = mg - \frac{mv^2}{R}$$
$$= mg - \frac{4\pi^2 \, mR}{\tau^2}$$
$$= 784 \text{ N} - \frac{4\pi^2 \, (80 \text{ kg}) \, (6.38 \times 10^6 \text{ m})}{(86,400 \text{ s})^2}$$
$$= 784 \text{ N} - 2.70 \text{ N}$$
$$= 781.3 \text{ N}$$

---

31 What is the percent difference between the explorer's weight at the North Pole and at the equator?

31
$$\% \text{ difference} = \frac{784 \text{ N} - 781.3 \text{ N}}{784 \text{ N}}$$
$$= 0.34\%$$

PROGRAMMED TEST

1 *Problem 1* A highway curve has a radius of 500 m. At what angle should it be banked so that a car traveling at 90 km $\cdot$ hr^{-1} will not skid?

1
Answer
7.29°

If you solved this problem correctly, go to frame 9. If you could not solve this problem, go through frames 2–8.

2 Draw a free-body diagram. Label the forces.

2

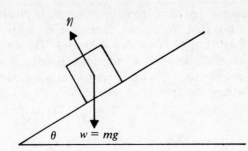

3 Choose a coordinate system such that the *x*-axis passes through the center of curvature. Note that the positive *x*-axis points toward the center. Resolve η into *x*- and *y*-components.

3

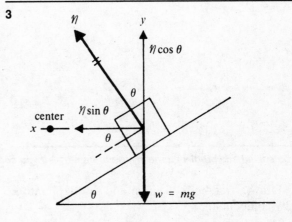

4 The horizontal component of the normal force causes the radial acceleration v^2/R. What is ΣF_x equal to?

4

$$\Sigma F_x = ma_x$$
$$\eta \sin \theta = \frac{mv^2}{R}$$

5 What is the vertical component of the normal force equal to? Remember $\Sigma F_y = ma_y$

5 Since there is no acceleration in the *y*-direction, $\Sigma F_y = 0$.

$$\eta \cos \theta - mg = 0$$
$$\eta \cos \theta = w = mg$$

6 Divide the equation in frame 4 by the equation in frame 5 to obtain the expression for the banking angle.

6

$$\tan \theta = \frac{v^2}{Rg}$$

7 Before we can substitute the numerical values in the above expression, we must convert $90 \text{ km} \cdot \text{hr}^{-1}$ to $\text{m} \cdot \text{s}^{-1}$.

7

$$\left(\frac{90 \text{ km}}{\text{hr}} \right) \left(\frac{1000 \text{ m}}{1 \text{ km}} \right) \left(\frac{1 \text{ hr}}{3600 \text{ s}} \right) = 25 \text{ m} \cdot \text{s}^{-1}$$

8 Solve for θ.

8

$$\tan \theta = \frac{v^2}{Rg}$$
$$= \frac{(25 \text{ m} \cdot \text{s}^{-1})^2}{(500 \text{ m}) (9.8 \text{ m} \cdot \text{s}^{-2})} = 0.128$$
$$\theta = 7.29°$$

9 Problem 2 A small block of mass m is placed inside an inverted frictionless cone that is rotating about a fixed vertical axis with a velocity v. The walls of the cone make an angle θ with the horizontal. For what values of v will the block remain at a constant height h above the apex of the cone?

9

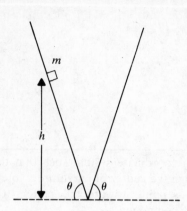

Answer
$$v = \sqrt{gh}$$

If you solved this problem correctly, go to frame 14. If you could not solve this problem, go through frames 10–13.

10 Draw a free-body diagram and resolve $\mathcal{N}$ into x- and y-components.

10

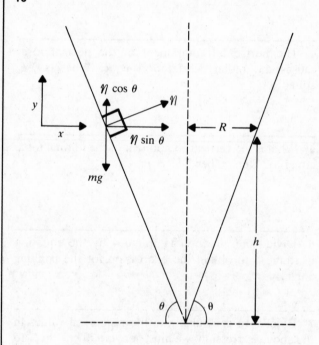

11 The horizontal component of the normal force causes the centripetal acceleration. What is ΣF_x equal to?

11

$$\Sigma F_x = ma_x$$
$$\mathcal{N} \sin \theta = \frac{mv^2}{R}$$

12 What is the vertical component of the normal force equal to?

12

$$\Sigma F_y = 0$$
$$\mathcal{N} \cos \theta = w = mg$$

13 Divide the equation from frame 11 by the equation in frame 12. Set $\tan \theta = \dfrac{h}{R}$ and solve for v.

13

$$\tan \theta = \frac{v^2}{Rg}$$
$$\frac{h}{R} = \frac{v^2}{Rg}$$
$$v = \sqrt{gh}$$

---

14 **Problem 3** The radius of a ferris wheel is 6 m, and it makes one revolution in 12 s. What is the difference in the apparent weight of a 50 kg passenger at the highest and lowest points?

14
Answer
164 N

If you solved this problem correctly, go to frame 20. If you could not solve this problem, go through frames 15–19.

---

15 Draw a free-body diagram for the passenger at the highest point.

15

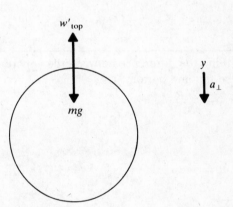

The apparent weight w' is the upward force exerted on the passenger by his supporting surface. The force of gravity is mg.

---

16 Apply Newton's second law at the top. Note that the + direction is toward the center. The direction of a is considered +.

16

$$\Sigma F_y = ma_y$$
$$mg - w'_{top} = \frac{mv^2}{R}$$
$$w'_{top} = m\left(g - \frac{v^2}{R}\right)$$

---

17 Draw a free-body diagram for the passenger at the lowest point.

17

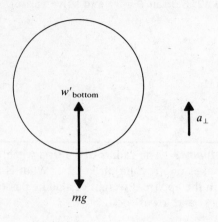

Note that the direction of $a_\perp$ is always toward the center of the circle. This direction is taken as +.

18 Apply Newton's second law to the lowest point.

18

$$\Sigma F_y = ma_y$$

$$w'_{bottom} - mg = \frac{mv^2}{R}$$

$$w'_{bottom} = m\left(g + \frac{v^2}{R}\right)$$

19 Find the difference between the apparent weight at the top and bottom. Use

$$v = \frac{2\pi R}{\tau}.$$

19

$$w'_{bottom} - w'_{top} = \text{difference in apparent weight.}$$

$$m\left(g + \frac{v^2}{R}\right) - m\left(g - \frac{v^2}{R}\right) = \frac{2mv^2}{R}$$

$$= \frac{2m}{R}\left(\frac{2\pi R}{\tau}\right)^2$$

$$= \frac{8\pi^2 mR}{\tau^2}$$

$$= \frac{8\pi^2\,(50\text{ kg})\,(6\text{ m})}{(12\text{ s})^2}$$

$$= 164\text{ N}$$

20 *Problem 4* What is the magnitude and direction of the resultant force on the moon during a solar eclipse? Find the force due to the radial acceleration of the moon.

mass of the sun = 1.99×10^{30} kg
mass of earth = 5.98×10^{24} kg
mass of moon = 7.36×10^{22} kg
distance from earth to moon = 3.8×10^8 m
distance from sun to moon = 1.49×10^{11} m

20
Answer
2.37×10^{18} N; 198×10^{18} N

If you solved this problem correctly, go to frame 27. If you could not solve this problem, go through frames 21–26.

21 What happens during a solar eclipse? Draw a diagram.

21 The moon blocks out the sun.

---

22 What is the force of attraction between the earth and the moon? Use Newton's law of gravitation.

22

$$F_1 = \frac{Gm_1m_2}{r^2}$$

$$= \frac{(6.67 \times 10^{-11} \text{ N} \cdot \text{m}^2 \cdot \text{kg}^{-2})\,(1.99 \times 10^{30} \text{ kg})\,(7.36 \times 10^{22} \text{ kg})}{(1.49 \times 10^{11} \text{ m})^2}$$

$$= 4.40 \times 10^{18} \text{ N}$$

---

23 What is the force of attraction between the moon and the sun?

23

$$F_2 = \frac{(6.67 \times 10^{-11} \text{ N} \cdot \text{m}^2 \cdot \text{kg}^{-2})\,(5.98 \times 10^{24} \text{ kg})\,(7.36 \times 10^{22} \text{ kg})}{(3.8 \times 10^8 \text{ m})^2}$$

$$= 2.03 \times 10^{18} \text{ N}$$

---

24 What is the resultant force?

24

$$4.40 \times 10^{18} \text{ N} - 2.03 \times 10^{18} \text{ N} = 2.37 \times 10^{18} \text{ N}$$

toward the sun.

---

25 Calculate the force due to the radial acceleration of the moon. Use

$$v = \frac{2\pi R}{\tau}.$$

The period of the moon is

$$27.3 \text{ d} \times \frac{86\ 400 \text{ s}}{1 \text{ d}} = 2.36 \times 10^6 \text{ s}$$

25

$$\Sigma F = \frac{mv^2}{R}$$

$$= \frac{m}{R}\left(\frac{2\pi R}{\tau}\right)^2$$

$$= \frac{4\pi^2 mR}{\tau^2}$$

$$= \frac{4\pi^2\,(7.36 \times 10^{22} \text{ kg})\,(3.8 \times 10^8 \text{ m})}{(2.36 \times 10^6 \text{ s})^2}$$

$$= 198 \times 10^{18} \text{ N}$$

---

26 What does this mean?

26 Since the radial force is approximately 100 times greater than the resultant force due to gravitational attraction, the moon does not move toward the sun.

27 **Problem 5** A spaceship is travelling from the earth toward the moon. At what distance from the center of the earth would the gravitational forces on the spaceship of the moon and the earth cancel? The distance from the earth to the moon is 3.8×10^8 m, $m_{\text{earth}} = 5.98 \times 10^{24}$ kg, $m_{\text{moon}} = 7.36 \times 10^{22}$ kg.

27

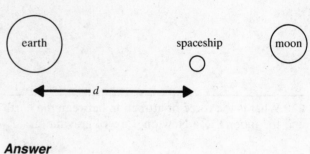

Answer

3.37×10^8 m

If you solved this problem correctly go to frame 31. If you would not solve this problem, go through frames 28–30.

28 Find an expression equating the force of attraction between the spaceship and moon to the force of attraction between the spaceship and earth. Use Newton's law of gravitation.

28

$$\frac{Gm_e m_s}{d^2} = \frac{Gm_m m_s}{(3.8 \times 10^8 \text{ m} - d)^2}$$

$$\frac{m_e}{d^2} = \frac{m_m}{(3.8 \times 10^8 \text{ m} - d)^2}$$

29 Substitute known values and simplify.

29

$$\frac{5.98 \times 10^{24} \text{ kg}}{d^2} = \frac{7.36 \times 10^{22} \text{ kg}}{(3.8 \times 10^8 \text{ m} - d)^2}$$

$$\frac{81.3}{d^2} = \frac{1}{(3.8 \times 10^8 \text{ m} - d)^2}$$

$$81.3 \, (3.8 \times 10^8 \text{ m} - d)^2 = d^2$$
$$81.3 \, (14.4 \times 10^{16} - 7.6 \times 10^8 d + d^2) = d^2$$
$$1.17 \times 10^{19} - 6.18 \times 10^{10} d + 81.3 \, d^2 = d^2$$
$$8.03 \, d^2 - 6.18 \times 10^{10} d + 1.17 \times 10^{19} = 0$$

30 Apply the quadratic formula.

30

$$d = \frac{6.18 \times 10^{10} \pm \sqrt{(6.18 \times 10^{10})^2 - 4(80.3)\,(1.17 \times 10^{19})}}{2(80.3)}$$

$$= 4.33 \times 10^8 \text{ m} \quad \text{or} \quad 3.37 \times 10^8 \text{ m}$$

4.33×10^8 is extraneous because d must be less than 3.8×10^8 m

31 *Problem 6* In order to produce "artificial gravity", space habitats will have to spin about their centers at constant angular rates. What should be the radius of a space habitat that must revolve at 1 rev · min^{-1} to produce an "artificial gravity" radial acceleration of 9.8 m · s^{-2}?

31

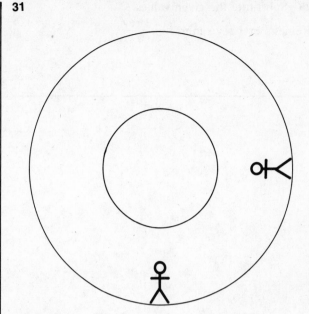

Answer
894 m

If you could not solve this problem correctly, go through frames 32–36.

32 Why is the astronaut "standing" on the outer rim of the habitat?

32 The spinning of the habitat produces a radial force toward the center. Since this force is acting on the astronaut, the astronaut is reacting by pushing on the outer rim.

33 What is the astronaut's apparent weight in the rotating space habitat?

33 The reaction of the floor of the habitat on the astronaut:
$w = mg$.

34 Apply Newton's second law

34

$$\Sigma F = ma_\perp = \frac{mv^2}{R}$$

$$mg = \frac{mv^2}{R}$$

$$g = \frac{v^2}{R}$$

35 Express g in terms of frequency. Remember $v = 2\pi Rf$. Solve for R.

35

$$g = \frac{v^2}{R} = \frac{(2\pi Rf)^2}{R} = 4\pi^2 Rf^2$$

$$R = \frac{g}{4\pi^2 f^2}$$

36 Substitute the given values.
Remember $1 \text{ rev} \cdot \text{min}^{-1} = \dfrac{1 \text{ rev}}{60 \text{ s}}$.

36

$$R = \frac{9.8 \text{ m} \cdot \text{s}^{-2}}{4\pi^2 \left(\frac{1}{60\text{s}}\right)^2}$$

$$= 894 \text{ m}$$

7

Work and Energy

CHAPTER SUMMARY

In this chapter, work and energy relationships are developed on the basis of Newton's laws of motion. Work is done when a force acts through a displacement. The force may be constant, such as in pulling an object, or it may vary, such as in compressing a spring. The work done on an object is related to the kinetic, gravitational potential, or elastic potential energies, or any combination of these. This is determined from the conditions for conservation of mechanical energy and by noting whether the forces are conservative or dissipative. Power relationships are also presented in this chapter.

BASIC TERMS — *Give definitions or meanings for the following:*

work (7-2)
joule (7-2)
erg (7-2)
foot pound (7-2)
elastic force (7-3)
restoring force (7-3)
Hooke's law (7-3)
kinetic energy (7-4)
work-energy theorem (7-4)

gravitational potential energy (7-5)
conservation of mechanical energy (7-5)
elastic potential energy (7-6)
conservative force (7-7)
dissipative force (7-7)
power (7-8)
watt (7-8)
horsepower (7-8)

PROGRAMMED QUIZ

1 Why is there no work done by the gravitational force when an object is moving along a horizontal surface?

1 Work is the product of the displacement and the component of the force parallel to the displacement. Since the gravitational force is perpendicular to the displacement, the work done by the gravitational force is zero.

2 What are the units of work in all three systems?

2 Joule (SI), erg (cgs), ft · lb (engineering).

3 What are the units of power in all three systems?

3 $J \cdot s^{-1}$ = watt (SI), erg $\cdot$ s^{-1} (cgs), ft $\cdot$ lb $\cdot$ s^{-1} (engineering).

---

4 Is horsepower a unit of power?

4 Yes; in the engineering system, 1 horsepower = 550 ft $\cdot$ lb $\cdot$ s^{-1}.

---

5 One method of finding the total work done on an object is to find the algebraic sum of the individual works. What is another method?

5 Finding the work done by the resultant force and multiplying this by the component of the displacement parallel to the force.

---

6 Show how the SI units of work and potential energy are equivalent.

6

Work	Potential energy
$(F \cos \theta)s$	mgy
$N \cdot m$	$kg \cdot m \cdot s^{-2} \cdot m = N \cdot m$

---

7 Show how the SI units of work and kinetic energy are equivalent.

7

Work	Kinetic energy
$(F \cos \theta)s$	$\frac{1}{2}mv^2$
$N \cdot m$	$kg(m \cdot s^{-1})^2 = kg \cdot m \cdot s^{-2} \cdot m = N \cdot m$

---

8 If the speed of an object is doubled, the kinetic energy is ____.

8

Quadrupled; $K = \frac{1}{2}mv^2$
  if $v' = 2v$,
    $K' = \frac{1}{2}m(4v^2) = 2mv^2 = 4K$.

---

9 If the weight of an object is doubled, the potential energy is ____.

9

Doubled, $U = mgy = wy$
  if $w' = 2w$,
    $U' = 2wy = 2mgy = 2U$.

---

10 What is total mechanical energy?

10 The sum of the kinetic and potential energies of the body.

---

11 The work of all forces acting on a body, with the exception of the elastic force and the gravitational force, equals _____ .

11 The change in the total mechanical energy of the body.

---

12 Is it possible for a body to acquire kinetic energy in a situation where the applied force is not moved?

12 Yes, when internal work is done on a system which consists of several moving parts which can do work on each other.

13 Which of the following are vectors? Which are scalars?
work, force, displacement, kinetic energy, potential energy, weight, mass, velocity, power, time.

13 Scalars: work, kinetic energy, potential energy, mass, power, time;
vectors: force, displacement, weight, velocity.

---

14 A kilowatt · hour is a unit of _____ .

14
Work; $P = \dfrac{W}{t}$; $W = P \cdot t$

---

15 When is a force which moves a body from one point to another conservative?

15 When the work is independent of the path taken.

---

16 What is an example of a conservative force? a nonconservative force?

16 Conservative: gravitational, the elastic force of a spring;
nonconservative: friction.

---

17 In calculating work, does the force have to be constant?

17 No; in the spring, for example, the elastic force increases as the spring is stretched.

---

18 When a stretched spring is released, what happens to the work that was done in stretching it?

18 In stretching, the work was transformed to elastic potential energy. When the spring is released, this potential energy may be transformed into kinetic energy or into work that will be done on another object.

---

19 Does potential energy depend on your choice of the origin in your coodinate system?

19 Yes. For example, the potential energy of a stone on top of a cliff height h: if $y = 0$ at top, $U = 0$; if $y = 0$ at base, $U = mgh$.

---

20 Does the change in potential energy depend on the choice of origin?

20 No; ΔU is the same, independent of where $y = 0$.

---

21 Give examples of conservation laws in physics.

21 Conservation of energy, conservation of momentum, conservation of angular momentum, conservation of electric charge.

---

22 What is the work-energy theorem?

22 The work done on a body is equal to the change in kinetic energy:
$W = K_2 - K_1 = \Delta K$

---

23 What is total mechanical energy?

23 The sum of kinetic and potential energies,
$E = K + U$

---

24 In a uniform gravitational field, the change of potential energy of a body depends on what?

24 The change in elevation.

---

25 Why can't we use the kinematics equations with constant acceleration in spring problems?

25 The elastic force is not constant.

MAIN IDEAS

1 If a body is acted upon by a constant force F and undergoes a displacement s along a straight line, then the work done by this force is
$W = (F \cos \theta) \cdot s$, where θ is the angle between F and s. Work is a scalar quantity.

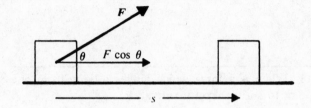

2 Units of work:

$$1 \text{ joule} = (1 \text{ newton})(1 \text{ meter}) \qquad 1 \text{ J} = 1 \text{ N} \cdot \text{m}$$
$$1 \text{ erg} = (1 \text{ dyne})(1 \text{ centimeter}) \qquad 1 \text{ erg} = 1 \text{ dyn} \cdot \text{cm}$$
$$1 \text{ ft} \cdot \text{lb} = (1 \text{ foot})(1 \text{ pound}) \qquad 1 \text{ J} = 0.7376 \text{ ft} \cdot \text{lb}$$

3 The work done by a varying force can be calculated as follows: Plot the component of F in the direction of the displacement as a function of s. Measure the area under the curve as the sum of the areas of the rectangles having dimensions $F_1 \cdot \Delta s_1$, $F_2 \cdot \Delta s_2$, $F_3 \cdot \Delta s_3$ etc. This area, which has dimensions of (force)(distance), represents work. This method can be illustrated by computing the work done when a spring is stretched. The force required to stretch an ideal spring is proportional to its elongation. The spring obeys Hooke's law $F = kx$, where F is the force exerted on the spring, k is the force constant which depends upon the nature and dimensions of the spring, and x is the displacement from the equilibrium position. The work done in changing the elongation of a spring from position x_1 to x_2 is $W = \frac{1}{2}kx_2^2 - \frac{1}{2}kx_1^2$.

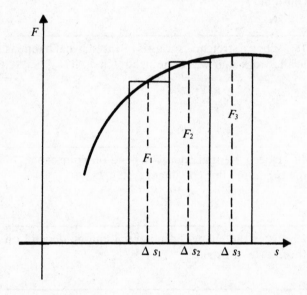

4 The kinetic energy K of a body is $K = \frac{1}{2}mv^2$, where m = mass of the body and v = speed of the body. The change in kinetic energy of a body is equal to the work of the resultant of the external forces acting on the body $W = K_2 - K_1 = \frac{1}{2}mv_2^2 - \frac{1}{2}mv_1^2 = \Delta K$. Kinetic energy is a scalar quantity. $W = \Delta K$ is known as the work-energy theorem.

Problem-solving strategy for problems involving the work-energy theorem:

Step 1 Identify all forces acting on the body.

Step 2 Set up a coordinate system and resolve all forces into components.

Step 3 Work is *positive* when the component of a force is in the same direction as the displacement. When the direction of a force is opposite to the direction of the displacement, the work is *negative*. (Since $W = Fs \cos \theta$, when the directions of the force and displacement are perpendicular to each other, the work is zero.)

Step 4 Find the total work done by the forces.

Step 5 Let subscript 1 denote the initial state and subscript 2 denote the final state:
$$W_{\text{tot}} = K_2 - K_1 = \Delta K.$$

5 Gravitational potential energy U is the energy a body possesses by virtue of its position with respect to some arbitrary elevation. $U = mgy$, where y is the height above the origin of coordinates.

6 Work done by a gravitational force: The potential energy will decrease when gravity does positive work [product of downward displacement (negative) and weight w (negative)]. The potential energy will increase when gravity does negative work [product of upward displacement (positive) and weight w (negative)]. $W_{grav} = - \Delta U = U_2 - U_1$, where ΔU means change in potential energy, i.e., final potential energy − initial potential energy.

7 When a body is not near the surface of the earth, the gravitational potential energy is given by $U = - Gmm_E/r$ where G is the universal gravitational constant, m is the mass of the body, m_E is the mass of the earth and r is the distance between m and the center of the earth. The total mechanical energy of a body not near the surface of the earth is $K + U = \frac{1}{2}mv^2 - Gmm_E/r$. If the gravitational force is the only force acting on the body, the total mechanical energy remains constant (or is conserved). Thus, for basic rocketry, $\frac{1}{2}mv_1^2 - Gmm_E/r_1 = \frac{1}{2}mv_2^2 - Gmm_E/r_2$. In order to obtain the escape velocity v_1, $r_1 =$ radius of the earth, $r_2 = \infty$ and $v_2 = 0$.

8 The total mechanical energy is defined as the sum of the kinetic and potential energies of the bodies ($K + U = E$). In reference to the figure, $\frac{1}{2}mv_1^2 + mgy_1 = K_1 + U_1 = E_1$ is the initial value of the total mechanical energy $K_2 + U_2 = E_2$, and $\frac{1}{2}mv_2^2 + mgy_2$ is the final value of the total mechanical energy. The work done by all forces (other than gravitational) W_{other} equals the change in the total mechanical energy of the body.

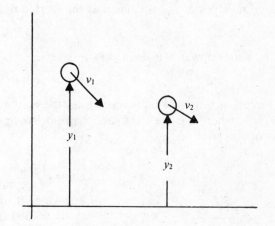

$W_{other} = (\frac{1}{2}mv_2^2 + mgy_2) - (\frac{1}{2}mv_1^2 + mgy_1)$. When $W_{other} = 0$, i.e., the total mechanical energy remains constant, $\frac{1}{2}mv_2^2 + mgy_2 = \frac{1}{2}mv_1^2 + mgy_1$ (a special case of the principle of conservation of mechanical energy). When

W_{other} is positive, $K_2 + U_2 > K_1 + U_1$,
W_{other} is negative, $K_2 + U_2 < K_1 + U_1$,
W_{other} is zero, $K_2 + U_2 = K_1 + U_1$.

Problem-solving strategy for conservation of mechanical energy:

Step 1 Let subscript 1 denote the initial state and subscript 2 the final state.

Step 2 Set up a coordinate system; up is +, down is −.

Step 3 Define K_1, K_2, U_1, and U_2.

Step 4 Identify all nongravitational forces that do work. Calculate W_{other}. Note that gravitational work is included in ΔU.

Step 5 Use $W_{other} = (\frac{1}{2}mv_2^2 + mgy_2) - (\frac{1}{2}mv_1^2 + mgy_1)$ to relate all quantities. $W_{other} = 0$ in problems involving conservation of energy.

9 The elastic potential energy of a spring is defined as $U = \frac{1}{2}kx^2$. As in the case for gravitational work, it follows that the work done by the elastic force (i.e., the restoring force of a spring) can be expressed in terms of a change in potential energy:

$W_{el} = U_1 - U_2 = \frac{1}{2}kx_1^2 - \frac{1}{2}kx_2^2$.

Let W_{other} equal work done on the mass by forces other than the elastic force. The work W_{other} of P equals the sum of the change in kinetic energy of the body and the change in its elastic potential energy,

$W_{other} = (\frac{1}{2}mv_2^2 - \frac{1}{2}mv_1^2) + (\frac{1}{2}kx_2^2 - \frac{1}{2}kx_1^2)$.

Restating this equation as

$W_{other} = (\frac{1}{2}mv_2^2 + \frac{1}{2}kx_2^2) - (\frac{1}{2}mv_1^2 + \frac{1}{2}kx_1^2)$

and noting that total mechanical energy is the sum of the kinetic and potential energies, we can say that the

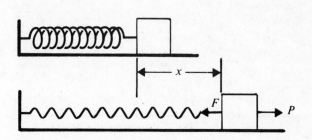

work of all forces acting on the body with the exception of the elastic force is equal to the change in the total mechanical energy of the body. If $W_{other} = 0$, the mechanical energy remains constant. In this case we have $\frac{1}{2}mv_1^2 + \frac{1}{2}kx_1^2 = \frac{1}{2}mv_2^2 + \frac{1}{2}kx_2^2$. The total energy $E + K + U$ is conserved.

10 Properties of the work done by a conservative force.

i It is independent of the path taken by the body between an initial and final position.
ii It is equal to the difference between the final and initial values of the potential energy of the body.
iii If a body can be made to return to its initial position, the work will be recovered.

Gravitational force and the elastic force of a spring are examples of conservative forces. A friction force is an example of a nonconservative or dissipative force.

11 Average power P_{av} is defined as the work ΔW done on an object divided by the time Δt taken to do it,

$$P_{av} = \frac{\Delta W}{\Delta t}.$$

Instantaneous power P is defined as

$$P = \lim_{\Delta t \to 0} \frac{\Delta W}{\Delta t}.$$

If a force F acting on a body accelerates the body to a velocity v, then the instantaneous power developed is $P = F \cdot v$, where v is the instantaneous velocity. In the case of average velocity, $P_{av} = F \cdot v_{av}$.
Units of power:

$$1 \text{ watt} = \frac{1 \text{ joule}}{1 \text{ second}} \; ; 1 \text{ W} = 1 \text{ J} \cdot \text{s}^{-1}$$
$$1 \text{ hp} = 550 \text{ ft} \cdot \text{lb} \cdot \text{s}^{-1}$$
$$= 33,000 \text{ ft} \cdot \text{lb} \cdot \text{min}^{-1} = 746 \text{ W}.$$

PROGRAMMED QUIZ

1 Frames 1 through 11 refer to the following problem: A 0.5 kg sled released from rest at the top of a 30° incline 2 m long reaches the bottom with a speed of 2 m · s^{-1}. What is its potential energy at the top?

1 Choose position 1 at the top and position 2 at the base; $y = 0$ at the base.
$$U_1 = mgy$$
$$= (0.5 \text{ kg}) (9.8 \text{ m} \cdot \text{s}^{-2}) (1 \text{ m})$$
$$= 4.9 \text{ J}$$

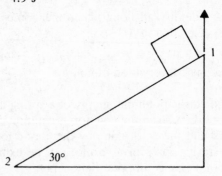

2 What is the potential energy at the base?

2 $U_2 = 0$

3 What is the change in potential energy as the sled slides down the incline?

3 Change in potential energy = final potential energy − initial potential energy.
$$\Delta U = U_2 - U_1 = 0 - 4.9 \text{ J} = -4.9 \text{ J}$$

4 What is the kinetic energy of the sled at the top of the incline?

4 $K_1 = 0$

---

5 What is the kinetic energy of the sled at the bottom?

5

$$\begin{aligned} K_2 &= \tfrac{1}{2}mv^2 \\ &= \tfrac{1}{2}(0.5 \text{ kg}) \,(2 \text{ m} \cdot \text{s}^{-1})^2 \\ &= 1.0 \text{ J} \end{aligned}$$

---

6 What is the change in kinetic energy of the sled as it slides down the incline?

6 $\Delta K = K_2 - K_1 = 1.0 \text{ J}$

---

7 How much work was done by forces other than the gravitational force?

7

$$\begin{aligned} W_{\text{other}} &= \Delta K + \Delta U \\ &= 1.0 \text{ J} - 4.9 \text{ J} = -3.9 \text{ J} \end{aligned}$$

---

8 If this work was done by the friction force, what must be the magnitude of the force?

8

$$\begin{aligned} W_{\text{other}} &= (\mathcal{F}_k \cos \theta)\, s \\ -3.9 \text{ J} &= \mathcal{F}_k \,(2 \text{ m}) \\ \mathcal{F}_k &= -1.95 \text{ N} \end{aligned}$$

Remember that $\mathcal{F}_k$ is always parallel to the surface,
$$\theta = 0, \cos 0° = 1$$

---

9 How long does it take for the sled to slide down? (Use power relationships.)

9

$$\begin{aligned} v_{\text{av}} &= \frac{v_0 + v}{2} \\ &= \frac{0 + 2\text{m} \cdot \text{s}^{-1}}{2} = 1 \text{ m} \cdot \text{s}^{-1} \\ P_{\text{av}} &= Fv_{\text{av}} \\ &= \frac{W_{\text{other}}}{t} \\ t &= \frac{-3.9 \text{ J}}{(-1.95 \text{ N})\,(1 \text{ m} \cdot \text{s}^{-1})} \\ &= 2 \text{ s} \end{aligned}$$

Note that W_{other} is the work done by the friction force.

---

10 What is the coefficient of kinetic friction between the sled and the surface of the incline?

10

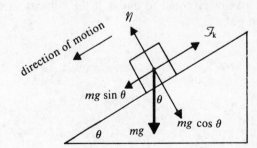

$$\begin{aligned} \mathcal{F}_k &= \mu_k \, \eta \\ &= \mu_k \,(mg \cos \theta) \\ 1.95 \text{ N} &= \mu_k \,(0.5 \text{ kg})\,(9.8 \text{ m} \cdot \text{s}^{-2})\,(\cos 30°) \\ \mu_k &= 0.460 \end{aligned}$$

---

11 Assuming that $\mu_k = 0$ and that the entire energy of the sled is in the form of kinetic energy just before it reaches the base, what would be its velocity?

11

$$K_2 = \tfrac{1}{2}mv_2^2$$
$$v_2^2 = \frac{2(4.9 \text{ J})}{0.5 \text{ kg}}$$
$$v_2 = 4.43 \text{ m} \cdot \text{s}^{-1}$$

---

12 Frames 12 through 15 refer to the following problem: A pendulum 2 m long is displaced to a height of 0.5 m (position 1) and released. Choosing $y = 0$ at the lowest point (position 2), what is the total mechanical energy at position 1?

12

$$K_1 + U_1 = 0 + mgy$$
$$= m(9.8 \text{ m} \cdot \text{s}^{-2})(0.5 \text{ m})$$
$$= (4.9 \text{ m}^2 \cdot \text{s}^{-2})m$$

---

13 What is the total mechanical energy at position 2?

13

$$K_2 + U_2 = \tfrac{1}{2}mv_2^2 + 0$$
$$= \tfrac{1}{2}mv_2^2$$

---

14 Since there are no forces acting on this system except for the gravitational force, the total mechanical energy at both points is the same. Find the velocity at the lowest point.

14

$$K_1 + U_1 = K_2 + U_2$$
$$(4.9 \text{ m}^2 \cdot \text{s}^{-2})m = \tfrac{1}{2}mv_2^2$$
$$v_2 = 3.13 \text{ m} \cdot \text{s}^{-1}$$

---

15 At what height (position 3) will the pendulum have a velocity equal to one half the velocity at the lowest point?

15

$$K_3 + U_3 = K_1 + U_1$$
where $K_1 = 0$

$$K_3 = \tfrac{1}{2}m\left(\frac{v_2}{2}\right)^2 = \tfrac{1}{4}(\tfrac{1}{2}mv_2^2) = \tfrac{1}{4}K_2$$

but $K_2 = U_1$
$\therefore 0.25\, K_2 = 0.25\, U_1$
Substituting $K_3 = 0.25\, U_1$ in the first equation,
$$0.25\, U_1 + U_3 = U_1$$
$$U_3 = 0.75\, U_1$$
$$mgh_3 = 0.75\, mg(0.5 \text{ m})$$
$$h_3 = 0.375 \text{ m}$$

16 A 10 N force acts on a 4 kg body moving initially in the direction of the force with a speed of $5 \text{ m} \cdot \text{s}^{-1}$. If the final velocity is $8 \text{ m} \cdot \text{s}^{-1}$, what is the change in kinetic energy of the body? (Use the work-energy theorem.)

16 Given:
$F = 10 \text{ N}$
$\theta = 0°$
$m = 10 \text{ kg}$
$v_1 = 5 \text{ m} \cdot \text{s}^{-1}$
$v_2 = 8 \text{ m} \cdot \text{s}^{-1}$
$s = ?$
$K_1 = \frac{1}{2}mv_1^2 = \frac{1}{2}(4 \text{ kg}) (5 \text{ m} \cdot \text{s}^{-1})^2 = 50 \text{ J}$
$K_2 = \frac{1}{2}mv_2^2 = \frac{1}{2}(4 \text{ kg}) (8 \text{ m} \cdot \text{s}^{-1})^2 = 128 \text{ J}$
$\Delta K = K_2 - K_1 = 128 \text{ J} - 50 \text{ J} = 78 \text{ J}$

---

17 Over what distance did the force act?

17
$W = (F \cos \theta) \, s = \Delta K$
$(10 \text{ N} \cos 0°) \, s = 78 \text{ J}$
$s = 7.8 \text{ m}$

---

18 Frames 18–21 refer to this problem: A 12 kg block is initially at rest on a horizontal frictionless plane. It is then pulled a distance of 8 m by a force of magnitude 20 N at an angle of 60° with the horizontal. What is the change in kinetic energy of the block?

18 Given:

$m = 12 \text{ kg} \qquad s = 8 \text{ m}$
$F = 20 \text{ N} \qquad v_1 = 0$
$\theta = 60° \qquad v_2 = ?$
$K_1 = 0$
$K_2 = \frac{1}{2}mv_2^2$

$\Delta K = K_2 - K_1 = \dfrac{mv_2^2}{2}$

---

19 Find the work done by the 20 N force.

19
$W = (F \cos \theta) \, s$
$= (20 \text{ N} \cos 60°) (8 \text{ m}) = 80 \text{ J}$

---

20 Use the work-energy theorem to find the final speed.

20
$W = \Delta K = \dfrac{mv_2^2}{2}$

$v_2 = \sqrt{\dfrac{2W}{m}}$

$= \sqrt{\dfrac{2(80 \text{ J})}{12 \text{ kg}}}$

$= 3.65 \text{ m} \cdot \text{s}^{-1}$

---

21 Check your answer by using Newton's second law and kinematics.

21

$F_x = F \cos \theta = 20 \text{ N} \cos 60° = 10 \text{ N}$
$\Sigma F_x = ma_x$
$10 \text{ N} = 12 \text{ kg} \, a_x$
$a_x = 0.833 \text{ m} \cdot \text{s}^{-2}$
$v_2^2 = v_1^2 + 2a(x - x_0)$
$= 0 + 2(0.833 \text{ m} \cdot \text{s}^{-2}) (8 \text{ m} - 0)$
$v_2 = 3.65 \text{ m} \cdot \text{s}^{-1}$ which agrees with the previous answer in frame 20.

22 The spring in a mechanical rifle has a force constant of $800 \text{ N} \cdot \text{m}^{-1}$. It is compressed 0.04 m from its initial position and a 0.10 kg pellet is put into the bore of the rifle against it and the spring is released. What can you say about the initial and final mechanical energy of the system?

22 The mechanical energy of the system consisting of the spring and the pellet remains constant.

$$K_1 + U_1 = K_2 + U_2$$
$$\tfrac{1}{2}mv_1^2 + \tfrac{1}{2}kx_1^2 = \tfrac{1}{2}mv_2^2 + \tfrac{1}{2}kx_2^2$$

---

23 Referring to the above, with what speed does the pellet leave the gun?

23 Since $v_1 = 0$ and $x_2 = 0$,

we have $\tfrac{1}{2}kx_1^2 = \tfrac{1}{2}mv_2^2$

$$v_2 = x_1 \sqrt{\frac{k}{m}}$$

$$= 0.04 \text{ m} \sqrt{\frac{800 \text{ N} \cdot \text{m}^{-1}}{0.10 \text{ kg}}}$$

$$= 3.58 \text{ m} \cdot \text{s}^{-1}$$

---

24 In terms of the work-energy theorem, what is the meaning of $\tfrac{1}{2}kx_1^2 = \tfrac{1}{2}mv_2^2$?

24 The work done by the spring on the block is equal to the change in kinetic energy of the block (i.e., $W = \Delta K$).

---

25 A force of 2600 N stretches a spring 0.13 m. What is the spring constant?

25

$$F = kx$$
$$k = \frac{F}{x} = \frac{2600 \text{ N}}{0.13 \text{ m}} = 2 \times 10^4 \text{ N} \cdot \text{m}^{-1}$$

---

26 What is the potential energy of this spring when it is stretched 0.13 m?

26

$$U = \tfrac{1}{2}kx^2$$
$$= \tfrac{1}{2}(2 \times 10^4 \text{ N} \cdot \text{m}^{-1}) (0.13 \text{ m})^2$$
$$= 169 \text{ J}$$

---

27 By what amount would an 80 kg mass stretch this spring? Draw a free-body diagram.

27

From Newton's second law,
$$\Sigma F_y = ma_y.$$
Since $a_y = 0$,
$$\Sigma F_y = 0$$
$$F_{spring} - mg = 0$$
$$kx - mg = 0$$
$$x = \frac{mg}{k} = \frac{(80 \text{ kg}) (9.8 \text{ m} \cdot \text{s}^{-2})}{2 \times 10^4 \text{ N} \cdot \text{m}^{-1}} = 0.0392 \text{ m}$$

STEP BY STEP SOLUTIONS OF PROBLEMS

Problem 1   A 15 kg block is pushed 30 m up an inclined plane that makes an angle of 25° with the horizontal by a constant force of 140 N acting parallel to the plane. The coefficient of kinetic friction between the block and the plane is 0.32. a) How much work is done by the force? b) Compute the increase in kinetic energy of the block. c) Compute the increase in potential energy of the block. d) Compute the work done against friction. e) Show that the sum of all the works equals the change in kinetic energy of the block. f) If the block was pushed up in 5.06 s find the average power expended.

1   Draw a free-body diagram of the block and resolve the forces into components parallel and perpendicular to the incline.

1

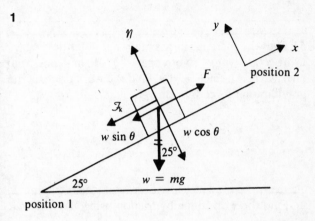

2   Find the magnitude of the components of w.

2

$$
\begin{aligned}
w_\parallel &= w \sin \theta \\
&= 15 \text{ kg}(9.8 \text{ m} \cdot \text{s}^{-2})\,(\sin 25°) \\
&= 62.1 \text{ N} \\
w_\perp &= w \cos \theta \\
&= 15 \text{ kg}(9.8 \text{ m} \cdot \text{s}^{-2})\cos 25° \\
&= 133 \text{ N}
\end{aligned}
$$

(Note $w_\perp = \eta$ since $\Sigma F_y = 0$.

3   Find the force of friction from $\mathcal{J}_k = \mu_k \eta$.

3

$$
\begin{aligned}
\mathcal{J}_k &= (0.32)\,(133 \text{ N}) \\
&= 42.6 \text{ N}
\end{aligned}
$$

4   Find the work done by the force of 140 N using $W = Fs$.

4

$$
\begin{aligned}
W &= (140 \text{ N})\,(30 \text{ m}) \\
&= 4200 \text{ J}
\end{aligned}
$$

5   Using Newton's second law, find the acceleration of the block. (In order to find the increase in kinetic energy of the block, we must know its velocity. In order to find the velocity of the block we must know the acceleration.)

5

$$
\begin{aligned}
\Sigma F &= ma \\
140 \text{ N} - \mathcal{J}_k - w \sin \theta &= ma \\
140 \text{ N} - 42.6 \text{ N} - 62.1 \text{ N} &= 15 \text{ kg } (a) \\
a &= 2.35 \text{ m} \cdot \text{s}^{-2}
\end{aligned}
$$

6 Find the final velocity of the block using $v_2{}^2 = v_1{}^2 + 2a(x - x_0)$.

6
$$v_2{}^2 = 0 + 2(2.35 \text{ m} \cdot \text{s}^{-2}) (30 \text{ m})$$
$$v_2 = 11.9 \text{ m} \cdot \text{s}^{-1}$$

---

7 Find the increase in kinetic energy using $K = \frac{1}{2}mv^2$. Note that the original kinetic energy $K_1 = 0$ since $v_1 = 0$.

7
$$K = \frac{1}{2}(15 \text{ kg}) (11.9 \text{ m} \cdot \text{s}^{-1})^2$$
$$= 1060 \text{ J}$$
$$\Delta K = K_2 - K_1 = 1060 \text{ J}$$

---

8 Find the increase in gravitational potential energy using $U_2 = mgy_2$. Note that the original potential energy $U_1 = 0$ since $y_1 = 0$. Find the work done by the gravitational force by using $W_{\text{gravity}} = -\Delta U$.

8
$$U_2 = (15 \text{ kg}) (9.8 \text{ m} \cdot \text{s}^{-2}) (30 \text{ m sin } 25°)$$
$$= 1860 \text{ J}$$
$$\Delta U = U_2 - U_1 = 1860 \text{ J}$$
$$W_{\text{gravity}} = -1860 \text{ J}$$

---

9 Find the work done by friction using $W_{\mathcal{J}} = -\mathcal{J}_k s$.

9
$$W_{\mathcal{J}} = -(42.6 \text{ N}) (30 \text{ m})$$
$$= -1280 \text{ J}$$
$\mathcal{J}_k$ is directed down the plane, the displacement is up the plane, hence $W_{\mathcal{J}}$ is negative.

---

10 Add the answers from frames 4, 8, and 9. These should equal the answer of frame 7, thus verifying that $W = \Delta K$ (i.e., the total work W is equal to the change in kinetic energy ΔK).

10 $4200 \text{ J} - 1860 \text{ J} - 1280 \text{ J} = 1060 \text{ J}$

---

11 Find the average power expended in pushing the block up the incline. Use $P = \dfrac{W}{t}$.

11
$$P = \frac{4200 \text{ J}}{5.06 \text{ s}}$$
$$= 830 \text{ watts}$$

Problem 2 The system shown in the figure is released from rest when the 20 kg mass is 4 m above the floor. Using the principle of conservation of energy, determine the velocity v with which the 20 kg mass strikes the floor.

$m_A = 5 \text{ kg}$
$m_B = 20 \text{ kg}$

---

12 What is the gravitational potential energy of the system before the larger mass is released? Use $U_1 = m_A g y_A + m_B g y_B$, where y is measured from the floor.

12
$$U_1 = 0 + 20 \text{ kg} (9.8 \text{ m} \cdot \text{s}^{-2}) (4 \text{ m})$$
$$= 784 \text{ J}$$

---

13 What is the kinetic energy of the system before the larger mass is released?

13 $K_1 = 0$

---

14 What is the gravitational potential energy of the system when the 20 kg mass strikes the floor? Use $U_2 = m_A g y_A + m_B g y_B$.

14

$$U_2 = (5 \text{ kg}) (9.8 \text{ m} \cdot \text{s}^{-2}) (4 \text{ m}) + 0$$
$$= 196 \text{ J}$$

---

15 What is the final kinetic energy of the system? Remember that both masses have the same acceleration. Use $K_2 = \frac{1}{2}m_A v_A^2 + \frac{1}{2}m_B v_B^2$.

15

$$K_2 = \frac{1}{2}(5 \text{ kg} + 20 \text{ kg})v^2$$
$$= 12.5 \text{ kg}(v^2)$$

---

16 Since the total mechanical energy of the system is conserved, the sum of the original kinetic and potential energies equals the sum of the final kinetic and potential energies. Use $U_1 + K_1 = U_2 + K_2 + 0$. Find v.

16

$$784 \text{ J} = 196 \text{ J} + 12.5 \text{ kg}(v^2)$$
$$v = 6.86 \text{ m} \cdot \text{s}^{-1}$$

Problem 3 A 4 kg block is dropped from a height of 0.5 m onto a spring whose force constant is 2450 $N \cdot m^{-1}$. Find the maximum distance that the spring will be compressed.

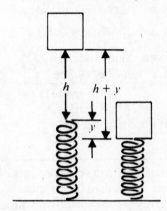

---

17 What is the total kinetic energy before the mass is released onto the spring?

17 0

---

18 What is the total kinetic energy when maximum compression occurs?

18 0

---

19 Find the loss in gravitational potential energy. Use $U(\text{gravitational}) = mg(h + y)$.

19

$$U = 4 \text{ kg} (9.8 \text{ m} \cdot \text{s}^{-2}) (0.5 \text{ m} + y)$$
$$= 19.6 \text{ N} \cdot \text{m} + 39.2 \text{ N} (y)$$

---

20 Find the gain in the elastic potential energy of the spring. Use $U(\text{elastic}) = \frac{1}{2}ky^2$.

20

$$U = \frac{1}{2}ky^2$$
$$= \frac{1}{2}(2450 \text{ N} \cdot \text{m}^{-1})y^2$$
$$= 1225 \text{ N} \cdot \text{m}^{-1}(y^2)$$

---

21 Since the total mechanical energy is conserved, the loss in gravitational potential energy is equal to the gain in elastic energy.

21

$$19.6 \text{ N} \cdot \text{m} + 39.2 \text{ N} (y) = 1225 \text{ N} \cdot \text{m}^{-1} (y^2)$$
$$1225 y^2 - 39.2y - 19.6 = 0$$

---

22 Solve for y using the quadratic equation.

$$y = \frac{-b \pm \sqrt{b^2 - 4ac}}{2a}$$

where $a = 1225$, $b = -39.2$, $c = -19.6$.

22

$$y = \frac{39.2 \pm \sqrt{(-39.2)^2 - 4(1225)(-19.6)}}{2(1225)}$$

$= 0.143$ m

$= -0.111$ m (extraneous)

---

23 What does the -0.111 m represent?

After being fastened to the spring, the block and the spring rebound upward through a vertical distance equal to $y_1 + y_2 = 0.143$ m $+ 0.111$ m $= 0.254$ m. The work done by the elastic force of the spring (in moving the block upward) is equal to the change in the elastic potential energy of the spring. This in turn is equal to the gain in the gravitational potential energy of the block. Thus,

$$mg(y_1 + y_2) = \tfrac{1}{2}(ky_1^2 - ky_2^2)$$

$$k = \frac{2\,mg}{y_1 - y_2} :$$

Substitute the given values and verify k:

$$k = \frac{2(4 \text{ kg})(9.8 \text{ m} \cdot \text{s}^{-2})}{0.143 \text{ m} - 0.111 \text{ m}}$$

$= 2450$ N $\cdot$ m^{-1},

which checks with our original value.

23 The height to which the mass and spring would rebound if they were fastened together after contact.

$y_1 = 0.143$ m

$y_2 = 0.111$ m

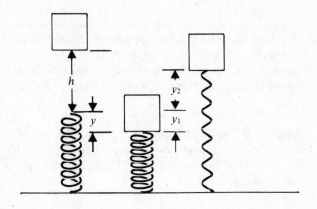

Problem 4 A ball is thrown vertically upward. If air resistance is taken into account, prove that the time during which the ball rises is less than the time during which it falls to the ground. Assume uniform acceleration up and down (not necessarily the same) and that the air offers the same resistance in each direction. (*Hint:* Use potential and kinetic energies.)

24 Draw a diagram depicting the motion and kinetic and potential energies of the ball for the initial and final positions of the upward and downward flights.

24

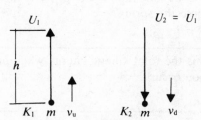

---

25 If air resistance is taken into account what statement can you make concerning the initial kinetic energy K_1 and the potential energy U_1 when the ball reaches its maximum height?

25 $K_1 > U_1$

---

26 What statement can you make about the initial kinetic energy U_2 of the ball at its maximum height and the kinetic energy when the ball strikes the ground?

26 $U_2 = U_1 > K_2$

---

27 Find v_u and v_d in terms of height h and time t_u and t_d.

$$(v_\text{u})_\text{av} = \frac{h}{t_\text{u}}$$

$$(v_\text{d})_\text{av} = \frac{h}{t_\text{d}}$$

27

$$(v_\text{u})_\text{av} = \frac{v_\text{u} + 0}{2}, \ v_\text{u} = 2(v_\text{u})_\text{av} = \frac{2h}{t_\text{u}}$$

$$(v_\text{d})_\text{av} = \frac{0 + v_\text{d}}{2}, \ v_\text{d} = 2(v_\text{d})_\text{av} = \frac{2h}{t_\text{d}}$$

---

28 Compare K_1 and K_2. Express K_1 and K_2 in terms of the above. Substitute in the inequality $K_1 > K_2$ and compare t_u and t_d.

28

$$K_1 > K_2$$
$$\tfrac{1}{2}mv_\text{u}^2 > \tfrac{1}{2}mv_\text{d}^2$$
$$v_\text{u}^2 > v_\text{d}^2$$
$$v_\text{u} > v_\text{d}$$
$$\frac{2h}{t_\text{u}} > \frac{2h}{t_\text{d}}$$
$$\frac{1}{t_\text{u}} > \frac{1}{t_\text{d}} \ \text{or}$$
$$t_\text{u} < t_\text{d}$$

Problem 5 A ball of mass m is tied to a string of length l, and the other end of the string is tied to a rigid support. The ball is held out with the string taut as in the diagram and then released. What is the speed of the ball at the lowest point? What is the tension in the string at this point?

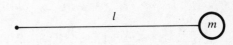

29 Draw a sketch showing the ball at the highest, lowest, and in-between positions. Denote the highest position as 1 and the lowest as 2. What are U and K at these points?

29

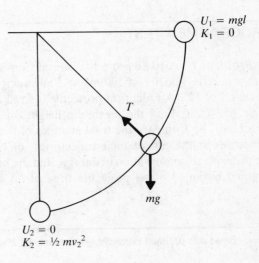

$U_1 = mgl$
$K_1 = 0$

$U_2 = 0$
$K_2 = \tfrac{1}{2} mv_2^2$

---

30 What is the work done by the tension?

30 Zero, since the tension of the string is perpendicular to the path of the ball at each point.
$$W_\text{other} = 0.$$

---

31 Apply the principle of conservation of energy and solve for v_2.

31

$$K_1 + U_1 = K_2 + U_2$$
$$0 + mg\,l = \tfrac{1}{2}mv_2^2 + 0$$
$$v = \sqrt{2gl}$$

---

32 Using the formula for radial acceleration, $a_\perp = \dfrac{v^2}{R}$ toward the center, find the tension in the string at the lowest point.

32

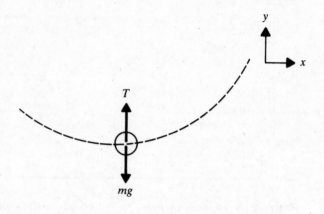

$$\Sigma F_y = ma_y$$
$$T - mg = m\left(\frac{v^2}{l}\right)$$
$$T = m\left(\frac{v^2}{l} + g\right)$$

PROGRAMMED TEST

1 *Problem 1* A 10 kg projectile is fired from a gun with a muzzle velocity of 500 m · s^{-1} at an angle of elevation of 60°. An identical projectile is fired at an angle of 90°. a) Find the maximum height for both projectiles. b) Compare the total energies of the two projectiles at the top of their trajectories. c) Using the principle of conservation of energy, find the height attained by an identical projectile fired at an angle of 35°.

1 *Answer*
9570 m, 1280 m, both have the same energy $= 1.25 \times 10^6$ J, 4190 m.

If you solved this problem correctly, go to frame 12. If you could not solve this problem, go through frames 2–11.

---

2 Using the equations developed in chapter 3, find the height for the projectile fired at 60°.

2

$$h = \frac{v_0^2 \sin^2 \theta_0}{2g}$$
$$= \frac{(500 \text{ m} \cdot \text{s}^{-1})^2 \sin^2 (60°)}{2(9.8 \text{ m} \cdot \text{s}^{-2})}$$
$$= 9570 \text{ m}$$

---

3 Find the height reached by the second projectile using the same equation.

3
$$h = \frac{(500 \text{ m} \cdot \text{s}^{-1})^2 \sin^2 (90°)}{2(9.8 \text{ m} \cdot \text{s}^{-2})}$$
$$= 12,800 \text{ m}$$

---

4 At the top of the trajectories, the projectiles have velocities in the *x*-direction only. Find the velocity for the first projectile.

4
$$v = v_0 \cos \theta_0$$
$$= 500 \text{ m} \cdot \text{s}^{-1} (\cos 60°)$$
$$= 250 \text{ m} \cdot \text{s}^{-1}$$

---

5 Find the kinetic energy of the first projectile at the top of its trajectory.

5
$$K = \tfrac{1}{2}mv^2$$
$$= \tfrac{1}{2}(10 \text{ kg}) (250 \text{ m} \cdot \text{s}^{-1})^2$$
$$= 313,000 \text{ J}$$

---

6 Find the gravitational potential energy of the first projectile at maximum height.

6
$$U = mgy$$
$$= 10 \text{ kg} (9.8 \text{ m} \cdot \text{s}^{-2}) (9570 \text{ m})$$
$$= 938,000 \text{ J}$$

---

7 Find the total energy at the top for the first projectile.

7 $313,000 \text{ J} + 938,000 \text{ J} = 1,250,000 \text{ J}$

---

8 Find the kinetic energy of the second projectile at the top.

8 0 since $v = 0$

---

9 Calculate the gravitational potential energy at the top for the second projectile. This is equal to its total energy.

9
$$U = mgy$$
$$= 10 \text{ kg} (9.8 \text{ m} \cdot \text{s}^{-2}) (12,800 \text{ m})$$
$$= 1,250,000 \text{ J}$$

---

10 The third projectile will also have the same total energy at maximum height. Find the height using the principle of conservation of energy.

10
$$1,250,000 \text{ J} = \tfrac{1}{2}mv^2 + mgy$$
$$= \tfrac{1}{2}(10 \text{ kg}) (500 \text{ m} \cdot \text{s}^{-1} \cos 35°)^2$$
$$+ (10 \text{ kg}) (9.8 \text{ m} \cdot \text{s}^{-2})y$$
$$y = 4200 \text{ m}$$

---

11 Check your result by using
$$h = \frac{v_0^2 \sin^2 \theta_0}{2g}$$

11
$$h = \frac{(500 \text{ m} \cdot \text{s}^{-1})^2 \sin^2 35°}{2(9.8 \text{ m} \cdot \text{s}^{-2})} = 4200 \text{ m}$$

---

12 ***Problem 2*** Starting from rest, a 10 kg block slides down an incline 13 m long, height 5 m. a) If the surface is frictionless, what is its speed at the bottom? b) Find the speed if the coefficient of friction is 0.3.

12
Answer
$9.90 \text{ m} \cdot \text{s}^{-1}, 5.25 \text{ m} \cdot \text{s}^{-1}$

If you solved this problem correctly, go to frame 20. If you could not solve this problem, go through frames 13–19.

13 Draw a free-body diagram and resolve the forces into components parallel and perpendicular to the incline. Label the top position 1 and the bottom position 2. Designate the angle of the incline as θ.

13

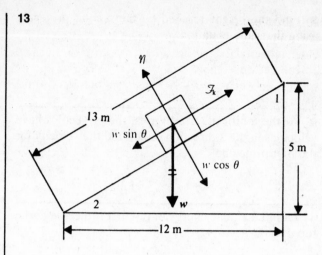

14 What is the total mechanical energy at the top?

14

Total mechanical energy
$$= \frac{1}{2}mv_1^2 + mgy_1$$
$$= 0 + 10 \text{ kg} (9.8 \text{ m} \cdot \text{s}^{-2}) (5 \text{ m})$$
$$= 490 \text{ J}$$

15 What is the total mechanical energy at the bottom?

15

$$\text{Total mechanical energy} = \frac{1}{2}mv_2^2 + mgy_2$$
$$= \frac{1}{2}(10 \text{ kg}) v_2^2 + 0$$
$$= 5 \text{ kg } v_2^2$$

16 Since the only force acting on the body is the gravitational, total mechanical energy is conserved. Write the relationship and solve for the velocity.

16

$$5 \text{ kg } v_2^2 = 490 \text{ J}$$
$$v_2 = 9.90 \text{ m} \cdot \text{s}^{-1}$$

17 Find the friction force.
$$\sin \theta = \tfrac{5}{13} = 0.385$$
$$\cos \theta = \tfrac{12}{13} = 0.923$$

17

$$J_k = \mu_k \eta = \mu_k mg \cos \theta$$
$$= (0.3) (10 \text{ kg}) (9.8 \text{ m} \cdot \text{s}^{-2}) (0.923)$$
$$= 27.1 \text{ N}$$

18 What is the work done by the friction force? Since the friction force acts in a direction opposite to the displacement, the work is negative.

18

$$W_{\mathcal{F}} = -\mathcal{F}_k s$$
$$= -27.1 \text{ N} (13 \text{ m})$$
$$= -352 \text{ J}$$

19 The work done by the friction force is equal to the change in the total mechanical energy of the block. Write the relationship and solve for the velocity.

19

$$W_{\text{other}} = \Delta E = E_2 - E_1$$
$$= (\tfrac{1}{2}mv_2^2 + mgy_2) - (\tfrac{1}{2}mv_1^2 + mgy_1)$$
$$-352 \text{ J} = 5 \text{ kg } v_2^2 - 490 \text{ J}$$
$$v_2 = 5.25 \text{ m} \cdot \text{s}^{-1}$$

20 **Problem 3** A block of mass 2 kg compresses a horizontal spring by 0.3 m. When it is released the block moves across a horizontal tabletop a distance of 2.3 m before coming to rest. If the coefficient of friction between the block and the table is 0.2, find the force constant.

20

Answer
$200 \text{ N} \cdot \text{m}^{-1}$

If you solved this problem correctly, go to frame 25. If you could not solve this problem, go through frames 21–24.

21 The nonconservative force acting on the block is friction. Find the work done by the friction force. The negative sign indicates that the direction of the friction force is opposite to the displacement.

21
$$\begin{aligned} W_{\text{other}} &= -\mathcal{F}_k x_2 = -\mu_k m g x_2 \\ &= -0.2(2 \text{ kg})(9.8 \text{ m} \cdot \text{s}^{-2})(2.3 \text{ m}) \\ &= -9.02 \text{ J} \end{aligned}$$

---

22 What is the total mechanical energy when the block is at x_1? ($K_1 = 0$ since the velocity is 0.)

22
$$\begin{aligned} E_1 &= \tfrac{1}{2} k x_1{}^2 \\ &= \tfrac{1}{2} k (0.3 \text{ m})^2 = 0.045 \text{ m}^2 \, (k) \end{aligned}$$

---

23 What is the total mechanical energy when the block is at x_2? ($K_2 = 0$ since the velocity is 0.)

23
$$E_2 = 0$$

---

24 The work done by the friction force W_{other} is equal to the change in the total mechanical energy. Find k from this relationship.

24
$$\begin{aligned} W_{\text{other}} &= E_2 - E_1 \\ -9.02 \text{ J} &= 0 - 0.045 \text{ m}^2 \, (k) \\ k &= 200 \text{ N} \cdot \text{m}^{-1} \end{aligned}$$

---

25 **Problem 4** The minus sign in front of $U = -Gmm_E/r$ denotes that the potential energy is negative at any finite distance from the center of the earth. The potential energy is zero at infinity and decreases as the body approaches the earth. Does this agree with $W_{\text{grav}} = -\Delta U$ (i.e., the work done by the gravitational force is equal to the negative of the change in potential energy)? Illustrate by means of the following example: A body of mass m is released from rest at point 1 in outer space, a distance $4 \times$ earth's radius from the center of the earth, and moves under the influence of the earth's gravitational field at point 2, a distance $2 \times$ earth's radius from the center of the earth. Prove that $W_{\text{grav}} = -\Delta U$.

If you could not solve this problem, go through frames 26–29.

26 What is the potential energy of the body at point 1?

26
$$\begin{aligned} U_1 &= \frac{-Gmm_E}{4R} \\ &= \frac{-C}{4} \end{aligned}$$
where $C = \dfrac{Gmm_E}{R}$

27 What is the potential energy of the body at point 2?

27

$$U_2 = \frac{-Gmm_\mathrm{E}}{2R}$$

$$= \frac{-C}{2}$$

---

28 What is the change in potential energy?

28

$$\Delta U = U_2 - U_1$$

$$= \frac{-C}{2} - \left(-\frac{C}{4}\right) = -\frac{C}{2} + \frac{C}{4}$$

$$= \frac{-C}{4}$$

---

29 What is the work done by the gravitational force?

29

$$W_\mathrm{grav} = -\Delta U = -\left(-\frac{C}{4}\right) = +\frac{C}{4}$$

which states that the work done by the gravitational field is positive. This is as it should be since the force and displacement are in the same direction.

8

Impulse and Momentum

CHAPTER SUMMARY

In this chapter we again refer to Newton's laws of motion. Here we develop the concepts of impulse and momentum and conservation of momentum. Momentum is conserved in all collisions; since momentum is a vector, the equation for conservation of momentum can be written in terms of x- and y-components for collisions where the objects do not follow a straight line. In perfectly elastic collisions kinetic energy is conserved as well as momentum (in completely inelastic collisions the particles stick together and some kinetic energy is lost). Special situations that lend themselves to momentum considerations are recoil, center of mass, rocket propulsion, and collisions involving massless particles (e.g., the photon).

BASIC TERMS — *Give definitions or meanings for the following:*

impulse (8-1)
momentum (linear) (8-1)
conservation of (linear) momentum (8-2)
internal force (8-2)
external force (8-2)
isolated system (8-2)

inelastic collision (8-3)
elastic collision (8-3)
ballistic pendulum (8-3)
center of mass (8-5)

PROGRAMMED QUIZ

1 If the impulse of a body is doubled, the change in momentum is _____.

1 Doubled; $J = mv_2 - mv_1$.

---

2 No kinetic energy is lost in a completely elastic collision. Does this mean that each body has the same kinetic energy before and after the collision?

2 No, the kinetic energy may be transferred from one body to another based on the ratio of the masses.

---

3 In the firing of a rifle, why is the total momentum of the system zero before firing?

3 Because both the bullet and the gun are at rest.

4 In frame 3, how is the total momentum conserved?

4 The forward momentum of the bullet and gases must equal the backward momentum of the rifle.

---

5 Show how the units of impulse and momentum are equivalent.

5

$$J = \Delta p$$
$$1 \, \text{N} \cdot \text{s} = 1 \, \text{kg} \cdot \text{m} \cdot \text{s}^{-1}$$
$$1(\text{kg} \cdot \text{m} \cdot \text{s}^{-2})\text{s} = 1 \, \text{kg} \cdot \text{m} \cdot \text{s}^{-1}$$

---

6 Can you give an example of a situation where conservation of momentum does not apply?

6 No, no exception has ever been found.

---

7 In all collisions momentum is conserved. Can there be a collision where kinetic energy is also conserved?

7 Yes, in a completely elastic collision, i.e., one where the forces of interaction between the bodies are conservative.

---

8 As the velocity of a body decreases, does the momentum increase, decrease, or stay the same?

8 Decrease.

---

9 Give an example of a collision in which some kinetic energy is transformed into heat.

9 A rubber ball collides with a wall. Due to the distortion, heat is generated as the molecules rub against each other.

---

10 Is momentum a vector or a scalar? What about impulse?

10 Both momentum and impulse are vectors since they have magnitude and direction.

---

11 Write Newton's second law in terms of impulse and momentum.

11

$$F = ma$$
$$F = m\frac{v - v_0}{t}$$
$$Ft = mv - mv_0$$
$$J = \Delta p$$

---

12 Give an example of a completely elastic collision.

12 Collision between atoms.

---

13 If $p_1 = 5 \, \text{kg} \cdot \text{m} \cdot \text{s}^{-1}$ at $0°$ and $p_2 = 12 \, \text{kg} \cdot \text{m} \cdot \text{s}^{-1}$ at $90°$, find Δp.

13

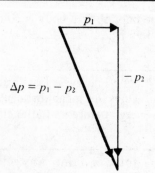

$13 \, \text{kg} \cdot \text{m} \cdot \text{s}^{-1}$

---

14 Give an example of a completely inelastic collision.

14 A car collides with a truck and the two vehicles stick together.

15 If the momentum of a particle is constant, can it be moving in uniform circular motion?

15 No, constant momentum means that the velocity must be constant in magnitude and direction. Also, in uniform circular motion the object is accelerating; therefore, there must be a resultant force acting on it.

16 Define a collision.

16 An event in which two or more objects come together (or separate) in a brief period of time.

17 In conservation of momentum is it important to know what is going on during the collision?

17 No, only the conditions before and after the collision.

18 If we have two cars and the total momentum of the system is zero, does this mean that the cars are at rest?

18 Not necessarily; momentum is a vector. If the cars are moving in opposite directions with momenta that are equal in magnitude, the total momentum (vector sum) will be zero.

19 If the two cars in frame 18 collide and stick together what will be their velocity?

19 Since the momentum before collision was zero, the momentum after the collision must be zero. Since the cars are stuck together they cannot move in opposite directions. Therefore, they must be at rest.

20 Why is the principle of conservation of momentum more general than the principle of conservation of mechanical energy?

20 Mechanical energy is conserved only when the internal forces of a system are conservative; conservation of momentum holds for any type of internal force, conservative or not.

21 Can impulse and momentum be expressed in terms of their components?

21 Yes, they are both vector quantities.

MAIN IDEAS

A constant force F is acting on a particle of mass m during a time interval $t_2 - t_1$. If v_1 and v_2 are the velocities of the particle at t_1 and t_2 respectively, then it follows from Newton's second law that

$$F = ma = m\,\frac{v_2 - v_1}{t_2 - t_1}.$$
$$F(t_2 - t_1) = mv_2 - mv_1.$$

This equation states that the impulse of the force is equal to the change in momentum, where impulse $= J = F(t_2 - t_1)$; momentum at $t_2 = mv_2$, momentum at $t_1 = mv_1$. In general, momentum $= p = mv$. Impulse and momentum are vector quantities. The units of impulse and momentum are:

impulse	momentum
$N \cdot s$	$kg \cdot m \cdot s^{-1}$
$dyn \cdot s$	$g \cdot cm \cdot s^{-1}$
$lb \cdot s$	$slug \cdot ft \cdot s^{-1}$

Units of momentum and impulse are equivalent: $1 \text{ kg} \cdot \text{m} \cdot \text{s}^{-1} = (1 \text{ kg} \cdot \text{m} \cdot \text{s}^{-2})\text{s} = 1 \text{ N} \cdot \text{s}$.

The principle of conservation of linear momentum. If the resultant of all external forces acting on a collection of particles is zero (i.e., $\Sigma F_{ext} = 0$), the vector sum of the momenta of the particles will remain constant.

Total momentum of a system.

$$P = p_1 + p_2 + \ldots = m_1 v_1 + m_2 v_2 + \ldots$$

Consider the collision of two bodies. If the kinetic energy is conserved, the collision is defined as completely elastic. If the bodies adhere to one another and move as a single body after colliding with each other, the collision is defined as completely inelastic.

Problem-solving strategy for conservation of momentum:

Step 1 Set up a coordinate system.

Step 2 Label all vectors and resolve velocity into *x*- and *y*-components.

Step 3 Express conservation of momentum in component from.

$P_1 = P_2$ total momentum before collision = total momentum after collision

$P_{1x} = P_{2x}$ sum of *x*-components before collision = sum of *x*-components after collision.

$P_{1y} = P_{2y}$ sum of *y*-components before collision = sum of *y*-components after collision.

Step 4 Solve for unknown quantities using the strategy you learned in solving equilibrium problems.

Step 5 If the collision is elastic, use the principle of conservation of energy.

$K_1 = K_2$ total kinetic energy before collision = total kinetic energy after collision.

Step 6 Since conservation of energy and conservation of momentum in the *x*- and *y*-directions will give us three equations, we can have only three unknowns. Additional information must be obtained from geometrical considerations or from one or both final velocity magnitudes.

Consider the elastic collision of two particles
A and *B*:

m_A = mass of *A*,
m_B = mass of *B*,
v_{A1} = velocity of *A* before collision,
v_{A2} = velocity of *A* after collision,
v_{B1} = velocity of *B* before collision,
v_{B2} = velocity of *B* after collision,
P_1 = total momentum before collision,
P_2 = total momentum after collision,
K_1 = total kinetic energy before collision,
K_2 = total kinetic energy after collision.

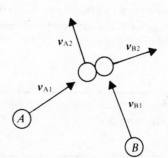

Applying the principles of conservation of kinetic energy and momentum, we have conservation of kinetic energy, $K_1 = K_2$,

$$\tfrac{1}{2}m_A v_{A1}^2 + \tfrac{1}{2}m_B v_{B1}^2 = \tfrac{1}{2}m_A v_{A2}^2 + \tfrac{1}{2}m_B v_{B2}^2. \tag{1}$$

Conservation of momentum, $P_1 = P_2$,

$$m_A v_{A1} + m_B v_{B1} = m_A v_{A2} + m_B v_{B2}. \tag{2}$$

Since momentum is a vector quantity, we can resolve the velocity vectors of the momentum equation into horizontal and vertical components and thus reduce the equation to the following:

$$m_A v_{A1x} + m_B v_{B1x} = m_A v_{A2x} + m_B v_{B2x} \tag{3}$$
$$m_A v_{A1y} + m_B v_{B1y} = m_A v_{A2y} + m_B v_{B2y}, \tag{4}$$

where $v_{A1x}, v_{B1x}, v_{A2x}, v_{B2x}$ = horizontal components of $v_{A1}, v_{B1}, v_{A2}, v_{B2}$ respectively; $v_{A1y}, v_{B1y}, v_{A2y}, v_{B2y}$ = vertical components of $v_{A1}, v_{B1}, v_{A2}, v_{B2}$ respectively. Eq. (*1*), (*3*), and (*4*) can be applied to elastic collisions where the velocities do not all lie on a single line. Since we have only three equations, additional information required to reduce the number of unknowns to three can be obtained from geometrical considerations.

A special case. Two particles moving along the same line have a completely inelastic collision, (i.e., they stick together after colliding with each other and have a common final velocity). From Eq. (*2*) we have

$m_A v_{A1} + m_B v_{B1} = (m_A + m_B)v_2$, where $v_2 = v_{A2} = v_{B2}$.

Consider the situation where we have a spring compressed by two blocks which are at rest on a level frictionless surface. The system is released.

If the spring is not attached to the blocks it expands to its natural unstressed length and drops to the surface. The original momentum of the system is zero. Since there are no external forces acting on the system, the momentum will remain constant and thus equal zero at all times. From the principle of conservation of momentum, we have $m_A v_A + m_B v_B = 0$. Although the original kinetic energy is zero, the final kinetic energy due to the original elastic potential energy is $K = \frac{1}{2} m_A v_A^2 + \frac{1}{2} m_B v_B^2$. Similarly, in the firing of a rifle, the total momentum of the system is zero at all times. Thus, it follows from the principle of conservation of momentum that the forward momentum of the bullet and gases must equal the backward momentum of the rifle.

Center of mass. Consider a collection of particles having masses $m_1, m_2, \ldots, m_n$. Let the coordinates of m_1 be (x_1, y_1), those of m_2 (x_2, y_2), \ldots, and m_n (x_n, y_n). The center of mass of the collection of particles is defined as the point with coordinates (X, Y) where

$$X = \frac{m_1 x_1 + m_2 x_2 + \ldots + m_n x_n}{m_1 + m_2 + \ldots + m_n} , \quad Y = \frac{m_1 y_1 + m_2 y_2 + \ldots + m_n y_n}{m_1 + m_2 + \ldots + m_n} .$$

The velocity of the center of mass is given by $V = \dfrac{m_1 v_1 + m_2 v_2 + \ldots + m_n v_n}{m_1 + m_2 + \ldots + m_n}$.

If the total mass $M = m_1 + m_2 + \ldots + m_n$, then $MV = m_1 v_1 + m_2 v_2 + \ldots + m_n v_n$.
The acceleration of the center of mass is given by

$$A = \frac{m_1 a_1 + m_2 a_2 + \ldots + m_n a_n}{m_1 + m_2 + \ldots + m_n} , \quad MA = m_1 a_1 + m_2 a_2 + \ldots + m_n a_n.$$

The center of mass moves as though all the mass of the collection of particles were concentrated at that point. Thus $\Sigma F_{ext} = MA$.

Rocket propulsion is an application of Newton's third law. The forward force on the rocket is the reaction to the backward force on the ejected propellant. The acceleration of the rocket is given by

$$a = \frac{\Delta v}{\Delta t} = \frac{v_r}{m} \frac{\Delta m}{\Delta t} ,$$

where

v_r = relative velocity of ejected fuel,

$\dfrac{\Delta m}{\Delta t}$ = mass of fuel ejected per unit time,

m = mass of rocket at take-off.

The resultant force on the rocket is

$$F = v_r \cdot \frac{\Delta m}{\Delta t}$$

(Newton's second law).

PROGRAMMED QUIZ

1 Car A is moving to the right with a constant velocity v_A. What is the momentum of the car?

1 $p_A = m_A v_{A1}$

2 Car B is moving to the left with constant velocity v_B. Assuming the same coordinate system as in frame 1, what is the momentum of car B?

2 $p_B = -m_B v_{B1}$

3 The two cars collide. Write the expression for conservation of momentum.

3

$P_1 = P_2$

$m_A v_{A1} - m_B v_{B1} = m_A v_{A2} + m_B v_{B2}$, where v_{A2} and v_{B2} are the final velocities of car A and B respectively.

4 If the collision is completely elastic, is kinetic energy conserved? If yes, write down the expression.

4 Yes; $K_1 = K_2$,
$$\tfrac{1}{2}(m_A v_{A1}^2 + m_B v_{B1}^2) = \tfrac{1}{2}(m_A v_{A2}^2 + m_B v_{B2}^2).$$

---

5 Rewrite the expression for conservation of momentum if the collision was completely inelastic.

5 $m_A v_{A1} - m_B v_{B1} = (m_A + m_B)v_2$, where v_2 is the final velocity of both cars.

---

6 If instead of car B, car A collided with a wall and the collision lasted for a time t, what would be the force that the wall exerted on the car?

6
$$Ft = m_A v_{A2} - m_A v_{A1}$$
$$F = \frac{m_A v_{A2} - m_A v_{A1}}{t}$$

---

7 What would be the acceleration of car A after the collision?

7
$$F = ma$$
$$a = \frac{F}{m} = \frac{m_A v_{A2} - m_A v_{A1}}{t(m_A)}$$
$$= \frac{v_{A2} - v_{A1}}{t}$$

---

8 Frames 8–20 are related to the following problem: Two blocks A and B of mass 4 and 1 kg respectively have a compressed spring between them. Initially the system is at rest. As the spring is released, it expands exerting equal and opposite forces on the blocks and then drops to the surface. If the velocity of block A is $-2\ \mathrm{m \cdot s^{-1}}$, what is the velocity of block B?

8
$$P_1 = P_2$$
$$m_A v_{A1} + m_B v_{B1} = m_A v_{A2} + m_B v_{B2}$$
$$0 = 4\ \mathrm{kg}(-2\ \mathrm{m \cdot s^{-1}}) + (1\ \mathrm{kg})(v_{B2})$$
$$v_{B2} = 8\ \mathrm{m \cdot s^{-1}}$$

---

9 What is the ratio of the velocities?

9
$$0 = m_A v_{A2} + m_B v_{B2}$$
$$\frac{v_{A2}}{v_{B2}} = \frac{-m_B}{m_A}$$
$$\frac{2}{8} = \frac{1}{4}$$

---

10 What was the original kinetic energy of the system?

10 0 (system was at rest).

---

11 Find the final kinetic energy of block A.

11
$$K_A = \tfrac{1}{2}mv_{A2}^2 = \tfrac{1}{2}(4\ \mathrm{kg})(-2\ \mathrm{m \cdot s^{-1}})^2$$
$$= 8\ \mathrm{J}$$

---

12 Find the final kinetic energy of block B.

12
$$K_B = \tfrac{1}{2}mv_{B2}^2 = \tfrac{1}{2}(1\ \mathrm{kg})(8\ \mathrm{m \cdot s^{-1}})^2$$
$$= 32\ \mathrm{J}$$

13 What is the ratio of the kinetic energies? Note that

$$\frac{v_{A2}}{v_{B2}} = \frac{m_B}{m_A}.$$

13

$$\frac{\tfrac{1}{2}m_A v_{A2}{}^2}{\tfrac{1}{2}m_B v_B{}^2} = \frac{m_A}{m_B}\left(\frac{v_{A2}}{v_{B2}}\right)^2 = \frac{m_B}{m_A}$$

$$\frac{8}{32} = \frac{1}{4}$$

---

14 What was the source of this kinetic energy?

14 The elastic potential energy of the spring.

---

15 Find the impulse of the force on block B.

15

$$\begin{aligned} J_B &= m_B v_{B2} - m_B v_{B1} \\ &= 1 \text{ kg } (8 \text{ m} \cdot \text{s}^{-1}) - 0 \\ &= 8 \text{ N} \cdot \text{s} \end{aligned}$$

---

16 If the force acts for 0.5 s, calculate the force.

16

$$J_B = F_B t$$
$$F_B = \frac{8 \text{ N} \cdot \text{s}}{0.5 \text{ s}} = 16 \text{ N}$$

---

17 Since the forces are equal and opposite and act for the same period of time, what is the impulse on block A?

17

$$\begin{aligned} J_A &= F_A t \\ &= (-16 \text{ N})(0.5 \text{ s}) \\ &= -8 \text{ N} \cdot \text{s} \end{aligned}$$

---

18 Find the work done on block A.

18

$$\begin{aligned} W_A &= \tfrac{1}{2}m_A v_{A2}{}^2 - \tfrac{1}{2}m_A v_{A1}{}^2 \\ &= \tfrac{1}{2}(4 \text{ kg})(-2 \text{ m} \cdot \text{s}^{-1})^2 - 0 \\ &= 8 \text{ J} \end{aligned}$$

---

19 Through what distance does block A move?

19

$$W_A = F_A s_A$$
$$s_A = \frac{8 \text{ J}}{-16 \text{ N}} = -0.5 \text{ m}$$

---

20 Through what distance does block B move?

20

$$W_B = F_B s_B = \tfrac{1}{2}m_B v_{B2}{}^2 - \tfrac{1}{2}m_B v_{B1}{}^2$$
$$s_B = \frac{\tfrac{1}{2}(1 \text{ kg})(8 \text{ m} \cdot \text{s}^{-1})^2 - 0}{16 \text{ N}}$$
$$= 2 \text{ m}$$

In frame 13 we have shown that although the final momenta of the two bodies are equal in magnitude, the final kinetic energies are inversely proportional to their corresponding masses. The change in momentum of a body equals the impulse of the force acting on it. The forces on the two bodies are equal in magnitude and act for equal times; hence they produce equal and opposite changes in momentum. Remember, the momentum of this system remains constant and is equal to zero. On the other hand, the change in kinetic energy is equal to the work of the force. The points of application of the two forces move through different distances (except when $m_A = m_B$). Thus the acceleration, velocity and displacement of the smaller body are greater than those of the larger body. It follows that more work is done on the smaller body.

21 What is the center of mass of the earth–moon system ($m_e = 5.98 + 10^{24}$ kg, $m_m = 7.36 \times 10^{22}$ kg)? The distance between the earth and the moon is 3.8×10^8 m. Set up a coordinate system with the origin at the center of the earth. Use

$$x = \frac{m_1 x_1 + m_2 x_2}{m_1 + m_2}.$$

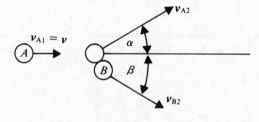

$$x = \frac{m_e x_e + m_m x_m}{m_e + m_m}$$

$$= \frac{(5.98 \times 10^{24} \text{ kg}) (0) + (7.36 \times 10^{22} \text{ kg}) (3.8 \times 10^8 \text{ m})}{5.98 \times 10^{24} \text{ kg} + 7.36 \times 10^{22} \text{ kg}}$$

$$= 4.62 \times 10^6 \text{ m}$$

from the center of the earth.

---

22 A small rocket burns 0.08 kg of fuel per second, ejecting it as a gas with a velocity relative to the rocket of 6000 m · s⁻¹. What is the propelling force on the rocket? Use

$$F = v_r \frac{\Delta m}{\Delta t}.$$

22

$$F = (6000 \text{ m} \cdot \text{s}^{-1}) (0.08 \text{ kg} \cdot \text{s}^{-1})$$

$$= 480 \text{ N}$$

STEP BY STEP SOLUTIONS OF PROBLEMS

Problem 1 A particle B is resting on a frictionless surface and is struck by a second particle which was originally traveling at a speed v. After the collision, particle A is deflected through an angle α from its original direction and particle B acquires a velocity at an angle β as noted in the figure. Assume that the particles have the same mass m and that this is not a perfectly elastic collision. Compute the speed of each particle after the collision.

1 What is the momentum of each particle before impact?

1 Particle A has momentum mv. Particle B has zero momentum.

---

2 What is the momentum of each particle after impact?

2 Particle A: mv_{A2}. Particle B: mv_{B2}.

---

3 Set up Eq. (3) and (4), conservation of momentum for the horizontal and vertical directions for this problem.

3

$$\begin{aligned} P_{1x} &= P_{2x} & mv &= mv_{A2x} + mv_{B2x} \\ P_{1y} &= P_{2y} & 0 &= mv_{A2y} - mv_{B2y} \end{aligned}$$

4 Divide through by m and substitute: $v_{A2x} = v_{A2} \cos \alpha$, $v_{B2x} = v_{B2} \cos \beta$, $v_{A2y} = v_{A2} \sin \alpha$, $- v_{B2y} = - v_{B2} \sin \beta$.

4
$$v = v_{A2} \cos \alpha + v_{B2} \cos \beta$$
$$0 = v_{A2} \sin \alpha - v_{B2} \sin \beta$$

---

5 Eliminate v_{B2} by multiplying the first equation by $\sin \beta$ and the second by $\cos \beta$.

5
$$v \sin \beta = v_{A2} \sin \beta \cos \alpha + v_{B2} \sin \beta \cos \beta$$
$$0 = v_{A2} \cos \beta \sin \alpha - v_{B2} \sin \beta \cos \beta$$

---

6 Add the equations.

6 $v \sin \beta = v_{A2} (\sin \beta \cos \alpha + \cos \beta \sin \alpha)$

---

7 Substitute $\sin (\beta + \alpha) = \sin \beta \cos \alpha + \cos \beta \sin \alpha$ and solve for v_{A2}.

7
$$v_{A2} = \frac{v \sin \beta}{\sin (\alpha + \beta)}$$

---

8 Substitute the value for v_{A2} in the second equation in frame 4 and solve for v_{B2}.

8
$$v_{B2} = \frac{v \sin \alpha}{\sin (\alpha + \beta)}$$

---

9 Solve for v_{A2} and v_{B2} if $v = 25 \text{ m} \cdot \text{s}^{-1}$, $\alpha = 20°$, and $\beta = 40°$.

9
$$v_{A2} = \frac{(25 \text{ m} \cdot \text{s}^{-1}) \sin 40°}{\sin 60°} = 18.6 \text{ m} \cdot \text{s}^{-1}$$
$$v_{B2} = \frac{(25 \text{ m} \cdot \text{s}^{-1}) \sin 20°}{\sin 60°} = 9.87 \text{ m} \cdot \text{s}^{-1}$$

---

10 If particle A has a mass m_1 and particle B has a mass m_2, find v_{A2} and v_{B2}. Follow frames 1–8.

10
$$P_{1x} = P_{2x} \qquad m_1 v = m_1 v_{A2x} + m_2 v_{B2x}$$
$$P_{1y} = P_{2y} \qquad 0 = m_1 v_{A2y} - m_2 v_{B2y}$$

$$m_1 v = m_1 v_{A2} \cos \alpha + m_2 v_{B2} \cos \beta$$
$$0 = m_1 v_{A2} \sin \alpha - m_2 v_{B2} \sin \beta$$

$$m_1 v \sin \beta = m_1 v_{A2} \sin \beta \cos \alpha + m_2 v_{B2} \sin \beta \cos \beta$$
$$0 = m_1 v_{A2} \cos \beta \sin \alpha - m_2 v_{B2} \sin \beta \cos \beta$$

$$m_1 v \sin \beta = m_1 v_{A2} (\sin \beta \cos \alpha + \cos \beta \sin \alpha)$$
$$v_{A2} = \frac{v \sin \beta}{\sin (\alpha + \beta)} \quad \text{no change in } v_{A2}$$

$$v_{B2} = \frac{m_1 v \sin \alpha}{m_2 \sin (\alpha + \beta)}$$

Problem 2 Suppose the collision in the previous problem is perfectly elastic. After impact, the first particle moves with speed v_1 in the first quadrant at an angle α with the x-axis and the second with speed v_2 in the fourth quadrant at an angle β with the x-axis. Find the speed of each particle after collision in terms of v, α, and β. Prove that $\alpha + \beta = \pi/2$.

11 Write the conservation of momentum equations for the system as expressed by the equations in frame 4.

11
$$v = v_{A2} \cos \alpha + v_{B2} \cos \beta \qquad (5)$$
$$0 = v_{A2} \sin \alpha - v_{B2} \sin \beta \qquad (6)$$

12 Square both sides and add. Note that $\sin^2 \alpha + \cos^2 \alpha = 1$.

12
$$\begin{aligned} v^2 &= v_{A2}^2 \cos^2 \alpha + 2v_{A2}v_{B2} \cos \alpha \cos \beta \\ &\quad + v_{B2}^2 \cos^2 \beta \\ 0 &= v_{A2}^2 \sin^2 \alpha - 2v_{A2}v_{B2} \sin \alpha \sin \beta \\ &\quad + v_{B2}^2 \sin^2 \beta \\ v^2 &= v_{A2}^2 + v_{B2}^2 + 2v_{A2}v_{B2} (\cos \alpha \cos \beta \\ &\quad - \sin \alpha \sin \beta) \qquad (7) \end{aligned}$$

13 Since this is a perfectly elastic collision, write the expression for conservation of energy.

13 $\tfrac{1}{2}mv^2 = \tfrac{1}{2}mv_{A2}^2 + \tfrac{1}{2}mv_{B2}^2$

14 Divide through by $\tfrac{1}{2}m$.

14 $v^2 = v_{A2}^2 + v_{B2}^2$

15 From the above and Eq. (7), we have
$$2v_{A2}v_{B2} (\cos \alpha \cos \beta - \sin \alpha \sin \beta) = 0.$$
What does this equal?

15
$$2v_{A2}v_{B2} \cos (\alpha + \beta) = 0$$
Since $v_{A2}v_{B2} \neq 0$, $\cos (\alpha + \beta) = 0$ or
$$\alpha + \beta = \pi/2$$
It should be noted that α and β are complementary angles.

16 Solve for v_{A2} by eliminating v_{B2} between Eq. (5) and Eq. (6). Solve Eq. (6) for v_{B2}.

16
$$v_{B2} = v_{A2} \frac{\sin \alpha}{\sin \beta}$$

17 Substitute this expression in Eq. (5) and solve for v_{A2}. Note that $\sin (\alpha + \beta) = \sin \alpha \cos \beta + \cos \alpha \sin \beta$.

17
$$\begin{aligned} v &= v_{A2} \cos \alpha + v_{A2} \frac{\sin \alpha}{\sin \beta} \cos \beta \\ &= \frac{v_{A2}(\sin \alpha \cos \beta + \cos \alpha \sin \beta)}{\sin \beta} \\ v_{A2} &= \frac{v \sin \beta}{\sin (\alpha + \beta)} = v \sin \beta, \\ &\quad \text{since } \alpha + \beta = \pi/2 \end{aligned}$$

18 Solve for v_{B2} by substituting the above in Eq. (6).

18
$$v \sin \alpha \sin \beta - v_{B2} \sin \beta = 0$$
Note that the direction of particle B is $\pi/2 - \alpha$.

Problem 3 If a particle A of very large mass makes a perfectly elastic collision with a particle B of very small mass that is at rest, prove that the final velocity of particle B will be twice the velocity of A.

19 What is the total momentum before collision?

19 $P_1 = m_A v_{A1}$

20 What is the total momentum after collision?

20 $P_2 = m_A v_{A2} + m_B v_{B2}$

21 Write the equation for conservation of momentum.

21

$$P_1 = P_2$$
$$m_A v_{A1} = m_A v_{A2} + m_B v_{B2}$$

---

22 Write the equation for conservation of energy. Note that the ½ term has been cancelled.

22

$$K_1 = K_2$$
$$m_A v_{A1}{}^2 = m_A v_{A2}{}^2 + m_B v_{B2}{}^2$$

---

23 Divide the equations in frames 21 and 22 by m_A.

23

$$v_{A1} = v_{A2} + \frac{m_B}{m_A} v_{B2}$$

$$v_{A1}{}^2 = v_{A2}{}^2 + \frac{m_B}{m_A} v_{B2}{}^2$$

---

24 Square the first equation and substitute in the second.

24

$$v_{A2}{}^2 + 2\frac{m_B}{m_A} v_{A2} v_{B2} + \frac{m_B{}^2}{m_A{}^2} v_{B2}{}^2$$
$$= v_{A2}{}^2 + \frac{m_B}{m_A} v_{B2}{}^2$$

---

25 Divide through by $\dfrac{m_B v_{B2}}{m_A}$ and simplify.

25

$$v_{B2} \left(1 - \frac{m_B}{m_A} \right) = 2v_{A2}$$

---

26 Since $m_A \gg m_B$, what happens to $\dfrac{m_B}{m_A}$?

26 Approaches zero.

---

27 What is v_{B2}?

27 $v_{B2} = 2v_{A2}$

Problem 4   A 0.003 kg bullet traveling in a horizontal direction with a velocity of 800 m · s^{-1} is fired into a 0.5 kg block initially at rest on a level surface. The bullet passes through the block and emerges with its velocity reduced to 200 m · s^{-1}. The block slides a distance of 3 m along the surface from its initial position. Find a) the velocity v_{B2} of the block at the moment of collision, b) the work done by the friction force, c) the coefficient of friction, d) the decrease in kinetic energy of the bullet as it emerges from the block, e) the kinetic energy the block had at the moment of collision.

Before collision

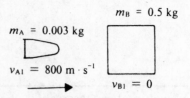

After collision

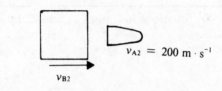

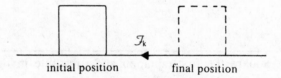

28   Find v_{B2} by applying the law of conservation of momentum.

28

$$P_1 = P_2$$
$$m_A v_{A1} + m_B v_{B1} = m_A v_{A2} + m_B v_{B2}$$
$$m_A v_{A1} + 0 = m_A v_{A2} + m_B v_{B2}$$
$$v_{B2} = \frac{m_A\, v_{A1} - v_{A2}}{m_B}$$
$$= \frac{0.003 \text{ kg } (800 \text{ m} \cdot \text{s}^{-1} - 200 \text{ m} \cdot \text{s}^{-1})}{0.5 \text{ kg}}$$
$$= 3.6 \text{ m} \cdot \text{s}^{-1}$$

29   Find the work done by the friction force $\mathcal{F}_k$ applying the work-energy theorem.

29

$$W = K_2 - K_1$$
$$= 0 - \tfrac{1}{2}(0.5 \text{ kg}) (3.6 \text{ m} \cdot \text{s}^{-1})^2 = -3.24 \text{ J}$$

The moment the block was struck by the bullet it had an initial velocity of 3.6 m · s^{-1}. The final velocity of the block (after sliding 3 m) is 0. The work done by friction is negative because it opposes the motion.

30   Find the coefficient of friction by using the definitions of work and the coefficient of friction.

30   Work done by friction

$$W = -\mathcal{F}_k s = -\mu_k \, \mathcal{N}s = -\mu_k m_B g s$$
$$\mu_k = \frac{-(-3.24 \text{ J})}{0.5 \text{ kg } (9.8 \text{ m} \cdot \text{s}^{-2}) (3 \text{ m})} = 0.220$$

31 Find the decrease in kinetic energy of the bullet.

31
$$K_1 = \tfrac{1}{2}m_A v_{A1}^2$$
$$= \tfrac{1}{2}(0.003 \text{ kg}) (800 \text{ m} \cdot \text{s}^{-1})^2 = 960 \text{ J}$$
$$K_2 = \tfrac{1}{2}m_A v_{A2}^2$$
$$= \tfrac{1}{2}(0.003 \text{ kg}) (200 \text{ m} \cdot \text{s}^{-1})^2 = 60 \text{ J}$$
$$\Delta K = K_2 - K_1 = 60 \text{ J} - 960 \text{ J} = -900 \text{ J}$$

32 Find the kinetic energy the block had at the moment of collision.

32
$$K = \tfrac{1}{2}m_B v_{B2}^2$$
$$= \tfrac{1}{2}(0.5 \text{ kg}) (3.6 \text{ m} \cdot \text{s}^{-1})^2 = 3.24 \text{ J}$$

33 During the collision the bullet lost 960 J − 60 J = 900 J of energy, but the block gained only 3.24 J of energy. What happened to the 900 J − 3.24 J = 896.76 J?

33 Since this is a highly inelastic collision, the energy that is lost is transformed into heat energy, chemical energy, sound energy, energy of deformation, etc.

Problem 5 Block A and Block B are on a frictionless horizontal surface. Block A, having mass $m_A = 4$ kg, moves with an initial velocity $v_A = 3$ m $\cdot$ s^{-1} parallel to the x-axis. It collides with block B, which has mass $m_B = 2$ kg and is initially at rest. After the collision, the velocity of A is $v_{A2} = 1.5$ m $\cdot$ s^{-1} in the first quadrant at an angle α with the x-axis. Assuming that the collision is perfectly elastic, find the final speed v_{B2} of the 2 kg block and the angles α and β.

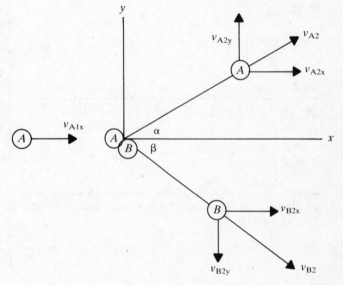

34 Since the collision is elastic, apply the principle of conservation of energy:
$$K_1 = K_2$$
$$\tfrac{1}{2}m_A v_{A1}^2 = \tfrac{1}{2}m_A v_{A2}^2 + \tfrac{1}{2}m_B v_{B2}^2.$$

34
$$\tfrac{1}{2}(4 \text{ kg}) (3 \text{ m} \cdot \text{s}^{-1})^2 = \tfrac{1}{2}(4 \text{ kg}) (1.5 \text{ m} \cdot \text{s}^{-1})^2 +$$
$$\tfrac{1}{2}(2 \text{ kg}) (v_{B2})^2$$
$$v_{B2} = 3.67 \text{ m} \cdot \text{s}^{-1}$$

35 Apply the principle of conservation of momentum in the x-direction:
$$P_{1x} = P_{2x}$$
$$m_A v_{A1x} = m_A v_{A2x} + m_B v_{B2x}.$$

35
$$(4 \text{ kg}) (3 \text{ m} \cdot \text{s}^{-1}) = (4 \text{ kg}) (1.5 \text{ m} \cdot \text{s}^{-1}) \cos \alpha +$$
$$(2 \text{ kg}) (3.67 \text{ m} \cdot \text{s}^{-1}) \cos \beta$$
$$12 = 6 \cos \alpha + 7.34 \cos \beta$$

36 Apply the principle of conservation of momentum in the y-direction:

$$P_{1y} = P_{2y}$$
$$0 = m_A v_{A2y} + m_B v_{B2y}.$$

36

$$0 = (4 \text{ kg}) (1.5 \text{ m} \cdot \text{s}^{-1}) \sin \alpha -$$
$$(2 \text{ kg}) (3.67 \text{ m} \cdot \text{s}^{-1}) \sin \beta$$
$$0 = 6 \sin \alpha - 7.34 \sin \beta$$

---

37 We now have two equations with α and β. Eliminate α by solving the equation in frame 35 for $\cos \alpha$ and the equation in frame 36 for $\sin \alpha$.

37

$$12 = 6 \cos \alpha + 7.34 \cos \beta$$
$$6 \cos \alpha = 12 - 7.34 \cos \beta$$
$$\cos \alpha = 2 - 1.22 \cos \beta$$

$$0 = 6 \sin \alpha - 7.34 \sin \beta$$
$$\sin \alpha = 1.22 \sin \beta$$

---

38 Square both sides of the above equations and add them.

38

$$\cos^2 \alpha = 4 - 4.88 \cos \beta + 1.49 \cos^2 \beta$$
$$\sin^2 \alpha = 1.49 \sin^2 \beta$$

$$\sin^2 \alpha \cos^2 \alpha = 1.49 \sin^2 \beta + 4 - 4.88 \cos \beta$$
$$\sin^2 \alpha + \cos^2 \alpha = 1.49 (\sin^2 \beta + \cos^2 \beta) + 4 - 4.88 \cos \beta$$

---

39 $\sin^2 \alpha + \cos^2 \alpha = 1$. Solve for β.

39

$$1 = 1.49 + 4 - 4.88 \cos \beta$$
$$\cos \beta = 0.920$$
$$\beta = 23.1°$$

---

40 Substitute the value of β in the equation in frame 37 and solve for α.

40

$$\sin \alpha = 1.22 \sin \beta$$
$$\sin \alpha = 1.22 \sin 23.1°$$
$$\alpha = 28.6°$$

PROGRAMMED TEST

1 **Problem 1** A hockey puck B resting on a smooth ice surface is struck by a second puck A which was originally travelling at $50 \text{ m} \cdot \text{s}^{-1}$. After colliding, the speed of puck A is reduced to $35 \text{ m} \cdot \text{s}^{-1}$ and is deflected through an angle α from its original direction. Puck B acquires a velocity of $25 \text{ m} \cdot \text{s}^{-1}$ at an angle β with the original velocity of A. Assume that the two pucks have the same mass and that the collision is not perfectly elastic. a) Find α and β. b) What fraction of the original kinetic energy of A is lost?

1

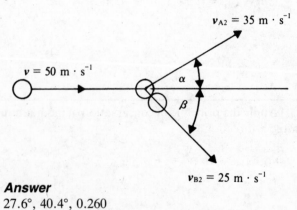

Answer
27.6°, 40.4°, 0.260

If you solved this problem correctly, go to frame 10. If you could not solve this problem, go through frames 2–9.

2 Write the expression for conservation of momentum in the x- and y-directions:
$$P_{1x} = P_{2x} \quad \text{and} \quad P_{1y} = P_{2y}$$

2
$$mv = mv_{A2x} + mv_{B2x}$$
$$0 = mv_{A2y} + mv_{B2y}$$

---

3 Divide by m and resolve the velocities into horizontal and vertical components.

3
$$50 \text{ m} \cdot \text{s}^{-1} = 35 \text{ m} \cdot \text{s}^{-1} \cos \alpha + 25 \text{ m} \cdot \text{s}^{-1} \cos \beta$$
$$0 = 35 \text{ m} \cdot \text{s}^{-1} \sin \alpha - 25 \text{ m} \cdot \text{s}^{-1} \sin \beta$$

---

4 Divide both equations by 5, transpose $7 \cos \alpha$ and $7 \sin \alpha$ to the left side of the equations respectively, square both sides and add.

4 $100 \text{ m}^2 \cdot \text{s}^{-2} - 140 \text{ m}^2 \cdot \text{s}^{-2} \cos \alpha + 49 \text{ m}^2 \cdot \text{s}^{-2}$
$\times (\sin^2 \alpha + \cos^2 \alpha) = 25 \text{ m}^2 \cdot \text{s}^{-2} (\sin^2 \beta + \cos^2 \beta)$

---

5 Solve for α; remember that $(\sin^2 \alpha + \cos^2 \alpha) = 1$ and $(\sin^2 \beta + \cos^2 \beta) = 1$.

5
$$140 \text{ m}^2 \cdot \text{s}^{-2} \cos \alpha = 124 \text{ m}^2 \cdot \text{s}^{-2}$$
$$\alpha = 27.6°$$

---

6 Substitute this value in the equation in frame 3 and solve for β.

6
$$25 \text{ m} \cdot \text{s}^{-1} \sin \beta = 35 \text{ m} \cdot \text{s}^{-1} (\sin 27.6°)$$
$$\beta = 40.4°$$

---

7 To find the fraction of the original kinetic energy that was lost, find the original kinetic energy.

7
$$K = \tfrac{1}{2}mv^2 = \frac{m}{2} (50 \text{ m} \cdot \text{s}^{-1})^2$$
$$= 1250 \text{ m}^2 \cdot \text{s}^{-2} \, (m)$$

---

8 What is the final kinetic energy?

8
$$K = \tfrac{1}{2}m (25 \text{ m} \cdot \text{s}^{-1})^2 + \tfrac{1}{2}m (35 \text{ m} \cdot \text{s}^{-1})^2$$
$$= \frac{m}{2} (625 \text{ m}^2 \cdot \text{s}^{-2} + 1225 \text{ m}^2 \cdot \text{s}^{-2})$$
$$= 926 \text{ m}^2 \cdot \text{s}^{-2} \, (m)$$

---

9 The fraction of original kinetic energy lost equals
$$\frac{K_{\text{original}} - K_{\text{final}}}{K_{\text{original}}}.$$

9
$$\frac{K_{\text{original}} - K_{\text{final}}}{K_{\text{original}}} =$$
$$\frac{1250 \text{ m}^2 \cdot \text{s}^{-2} \, (m) - 925 \text{ m}^2 \cdot \text{s}^{-2} \, (m)}{1250 \text{ m}^2 \cdot \text{s}^{-2} \, (m)} = 0.260$$

---

10 *Problem 2* Derive the general solution for α and β in problem 1.

10
Answer
$$\cos \alpha = \frac{v^2 + v_{A2}{}^2 - v_{B2}{}^2}{2vv_{A2}}$$
$$\cos \beta = \frac{v^2 + v_{B2}{}^2 - v_{A2}{}^2}{2vv_{B2}}$$

If you solved this problem correctly, go to frame 16. If you could not solve this problem, go through frames 11–15.

11 Write the expressions for conservation of momentum in the x- and y-direction.

11

$$mv = mv_{A2x} + mv_{B2x}$$
$$0 = mv_{A2y} + mv_{B2y}$$

---

12 Divide both equations by m and resolve the velocities into horizontal and vertical components.

12

$$v = v_{A2} \cos \alpha + v_{B2} \cos \beta$$
$$0 = v_{A2} \sin \alpha - v_{B2} \sin \beta$$

---

13 Transpose $v_{A2} \cos \alpha$ and $v_{A2} \sin \alpha$ to the left sides of the equations respectively, square both sides and add.

13

$$v^2 = 2vv_{A2} \cos \alpha - v_{A2}{}^2 + v_{B2}{}^2$$

---

14 Solve for $\cos \alpha$.

14

$$\cos \alpha = \frac{v^2 + v_{A2}{}^2 - v_{B2}{}^2}{2vv_{A2}}$$

---

15 Solve for $\cos \beta$.

15

$$\cos \beta = \frac{v^2 - v_{A2}{}^2 + v_{B2}{}^2}{2vv_{B2}}$$

---

16 *Problem 3* In problem 1, we assumed that both pucks had the same mass. If puck A has mass m_1 and puck B has mass m_2, find $\cos \alpha$ and $\cos \beta$.

16
Answer

$$\cos \alpha = \frac{v^2 + v_{A2}{}^2 - \left(\frac{m_2}{m_1}\right)^2 v_{B2}{}^2}{2vv_A{}^2}$$

$$\cos \beta = \frac{\left(\frac{m_1}{m_2}\right)(v^2 - v_{A2}{}^2) + \left(\frac{m_2}{m_1}\right)(v_{B2})^2}{2vv_{B2}}$$

If you solved this problem correctly, go to frame 22. If you could not solve this problem, go through frames 17–21.

---

17 Write the expression for conservation of momentum in the x- and y-directions.

17

$$P_{1x} = P_{2x}$$
$$P_{1y} = P_{2y}$$

---

18 Resolve the velocities into horizontal and vertical components.

18

$$m_1 v = m_1 v_{A2} \cos \alpha + m_2 v_{B2} \cos \beta$$
$$0 = m_1 v_{A2} \sin \alpha + m_2 v_{B2} \sin \beta$$

---

19 Divide both sides by m_2 and transpose the cos α and sin α terms to the left side of the equations. Square both sides and add.

19

$$\frac{m_1}{m_2} v - \frac{m_1}{m_2} v_{A2} \cos \alpha = v_{B2} \cos \beta$$

$$\frac{m_1}{m_2} v_{A2} \sin \alpha = v_{B2} \sin \beta$$

$$\left(\frac{m_1}{m_2}\right)^2 (v^2 - 2vv_{A2} \cos \alpha + v_{A2}{}^2 \cos^2 \alpha) = v_{B2}{}^2 \cos^2 \beta$$

$$\left(\frac{m_1}{m_2}\right)^2 v_{A2}{}^2 \sin^2 \alpha = v_{B2}{}^2 \sin^2 \beta$$

$$\left(\frac{m_1}{m_2}\right)^2 (v^2 - 2vv_{A2} \cos \alpha + v_{A2}{}^2) = v_{B2}{}^2$$

---

20 Solve for cos α.

20

$$\cos \alpha = \frac{v^2 + v_{A2}{}^2 - \left(\dfrac{m_2}{m_1}\right)^2 v_{B2}{}^2}{2vv_{A2}}$$

---

21 Substitute this expression in the equation of frame 18. Solve for cos β.

21

$$m_2 v_{B2} \cos \beta = m_1 v - m_1 v_{A2} \cos \alpha$$

$$= m_1 v - m_1 v_{A2} \left[\frac{m_1{}^2 v^2 + m_1{}^2 v_{A2}{}^2 - m_2{}^2 v_{B2}{}^2}{2m_1{}^2 v v_{A2}} \right]$$

$$\cos \beta = \frac{\left(\dfrac{m_1}{m_2}\right)(v^2 - v_{A2}{}^2) + \left(\dfrac{m_2}{m_1}\right)(v_{B2})^2}{2vv_{B2}}$$

---

22 **Problem 4** A 0.3 kg body moving at 8 m · s^{-1} on a frictionless surface collides head on with a 0.5 kg body moving at 2 m · s^{-1} in the opposite direction. Find the speed v of the bodies if they stick together after the collision.

22
Answer
1.75 m · s^{-1}

If you solved this problem correctly, go to frame 26. If you could not solve this problem, go through frames 23–25.

---

23 What kind of collision is this?

23 This is a completely inelastic collision.

---

24 Draw a sketch showing the relationship of the masses before and after the collision. Indicate the velocities.

24

---

25 Apply the principle of conservation of momentum. Solve for v.

25
$$m_A v_{A1} + m_B v_{B1} = (m_A + m_B)v$$
where $v = v_{A2} = v_{B2}$,
$$(0.3 \text{ kg})(8 \text{ m} \cdot \text{s}^{-1}) + (0.5 \text{ kg})(-2 \text{ m} \cdot \text{s}^{-1}) = (0.8 \text{ kg})v$$
$$v = 1.75 \text{ m} \cdot \text{s}^{-1}$$
in the direction of the motion of the 0.3 kg body.

---

26 Problem 5 Find the speeds of the bodies if the collision is completely elastic.

26
Answer
$$v_{A2} = -4.5 \text{ m} \cdot \text{s}^{-1}$$
$$v_{B2} = 5.5 \text{ m} \cdot \text{s}^{-1}$$

If you solved this problem correctly, go to frame 35. If you could not solve this problem, go through frames 27–34.

---

27 Write the equation for the conservation of momentum.

27
$$(0.3 \text{ kg})(8 \text{ m} \cdot \text{s}^{-1}) + (0.5 \text{ kg})(-2 \text{ m} \cdot \text{s}^{-1})$$
$$= (0.3 \text{ kg})v_{A2} + (0.5 \text{ kg})v_{B2}$$

---

28 Since this is a perfectly elastic collision, write the equation for conservation of energy.

28
$$\tfrac{1}{2}(0.3 \text{ kg})(8 \text{ m} \cdot \text{s}^{-1})^2 + \tfrac{1}{2}(0.5 \text{ kg})(-2 \text{ m} \cdot \text{s}^{-1})^2$$
$$= \tfrac{1}{2}(0.3 \text{ kg})v_{A2}^2 + \tfrac{1}{2}(0.5 \text{ kg})v_{B2}^2$$

---

29 Simplify both equations.

29
$$3v_{A2} + 5v_{B2} = 14 \text{ m} \cdot \text{s}^{-1}$$
$$3v_{A2}^2 + 5v_{B2}^2 = 212 \text{ m}^2 \cdot \text{s}^{-2}$$

---

30 Solve the first equation for v_{B2}.

30
$$v_{B2} = \frac{14 \text{ m} \cdot \text{s}^{-1} - 3v_{A2}}{5}$$

---

31 Square both sides, substitute the value of v_{B2}^2 in the second equation in frame 23 and simplify.

31
$$v_{B2}^2 = \frac{196 \text{ m}^2 \cdot \text{s}^{-2} - 84 \text{ m} \cdot \text{s}^{-1} v_{A2} + 9v_{A2}^2}{25}$$
$$3 v_{A2}^2 + 5 (7.84 \text{ m}^2 \cdot \text{s}^{-2} - 3.36 \text{ m} \cdot \text{s}^{-1} v_{A2}$$
$$+ 0.36 v_{A2}^2) = 212 \text{ m}^2 \cdot \text{s}^{-2}$$
$$2va_2^2 - 7 v_{A2} - 72 = 0$$

---

32 Solve the quadratic equation for v_{A2}.

32
$$v_{A2} = 8 \text{ and } -4.5$$

---

33 Substitute the values of v_{A2} in the first equation in frame 29 to obtain v_{B2}.

33
$$v_{B2} = -2 \text{ and } 5.5$$

---

34 Which are the correct answers for v_{A2} and v_{B2}?

34 The correct solution is
$$v_{A2} = -4.5 \text{ m} \cdot \text{s}^{-1} \text{ and}$$
$$v_{B2} = 5.5 \text{ m} \cdot \text{s}^{-1}$$
The solution
$$v_{A2} = 8 \text{ m} \cdot \text{s}^{-1} \text{ and}$$
$$v_{B2} = -2 \text{ m} \cdot \text{s}^{-1}$$
means that the bodies passed through each other and is therefore considered unacceptable.

---

35 **Problem 6** A 3 kg mass and a 5 kg mass are resting on a frictionless table and compressing a spring. When the masses are released, the 5 kg mass acquires a speed of $2 \text{ m} \cdot \text{s}^{-1}$. Find the speed of the 3 kg mass and the energy stored in the spring.

35

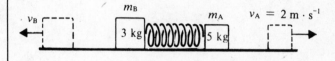

Answer
$-3.33 \text{ m} \cdot \text{s}^{-1}$; 26.6 J

If you could not solve this problem, go through frames 36–40.

36 What do we call the energy stored in the spring when the spring is compressed?

36 Elastic potential energy.

---

37 What is the initial momentum of the system?

37 Zero.

---

38 What is the final momentum of the system?

38 Zero.

---

39 Calculate the velocity v of the 3 kg mass from the principle of conservation of momentum.

39

$$m_A v_A + m_B v_B = 0$$
$$(5 \text{ kg})(2 \text{ m} \cdot \text{s}^{-1}) + (3 \text{ kg})(v) = 0$$
$$v = -3.33 \text{ m} \cdot \text{s}^{-1}$$

---

40 Calculate the energy stored in the spring. The source of this energy is the original elastic potential energy of the system.

40 This energy is equal to the total kinetic energy
$$= \tfrac{1}{2}(3 \text{ kg})(-3.33 \text{ m} \cdot \text{s}^{-1})^2 + \tfrac{1}{2}(5 \text{ kg})(2 \text{ m} \cdot \text{s}^{-1})^2$$
$$= 26.6 \text{ J}$$

9

Rotational Motion

CHAPTER SUMMARY

Up to this point we have considered bodies as point masses. In this chapter we deal with the rotation of rigid bodies. The definition and kinematic equations for describing the rotational motion of rigid bodies are analogous to those for motion in a straight line. On the basis of the relationships between angular and linear velocities and accelerations, quantities such as torque, work, and power in rotational motion are presented. Angular impulse is equal to a change in angular momentum, and, as in translation, angular momentum is conserved for an isolated system. Moment of inertia is introduced on the basis of the kinetic energy of rotation. The discussion is extended to certain situations where the axis of rotation is not stationary.

BASIC TERMS — *Give definitions or meanings for the following:*

rigid body (9-I)
angular velocity (9-1)
radian (9-1)
angular acceleration (9-1)
average angular velocity (9-1)
average angular acceleration (9-1)
instantaneous angular velocity (9-1)
instantaneous angular acceleration (9-1)
tangential component of acceleration (9-3)

radial component of acceleration (9-3)
moment of inertia (9-4)
torque (9-5)
moment (9-5)
moment arm (9-5)
angular momentum (9-9)
angular impulse (9-9)
conservation of angular momentum (9-10)
precession (9-11)

PROGRAMMED QUIZ

1 What is the rotation analog of the following: mass, force, acceleration, momentum, displacement (quantity and symbol)?

1 Mass — moment of inertia I,
force — torque Γ,
acceleration — angular acceleration α,
momentum — angular momentum L,
displacement — angular displacement θ.
Note: Rotational quantities associated with an axis can be represented by vectors, but this is not necessary for the problem that we are considering.

2 What is the relationship between radians and degrees?

2 2π rad $= 360°$, 1 rad $= 57.3°$.

---

3 What are the units of radians?

3 No units; a radian is a ratio of two lengths, the arclength divided by the radius.

---

4 In using the rotational analogs of the kinematic formulas, can the angular velocity be expressed in revolutions per minute?

4 No, angular velocity must be expressed in radian measure.

---

5 If we consider a rotating rigid body as being composed of numerous particles, what quantity is common to all of them?

5 Angular velocity.

---

6 If a body has a greater moment of inertia than another, does this indicate that its mass is greater also?

6 Not necessarily. Moment of inertia depends on the way mass is distributed in relation to the axis of rotation. Therefore a body with a larger moment of inertia may have a smaller mass than another.

---

7 Show how the SI units of rotational kinetic energy equal joules. (*Note*: The radian is a dimensionless quantity).

7 $K = \frac{1}{2}I\omega^2 = \frac{1}{2}\text{kg} \cdot \text{m}^2 (\text{rad} \cdot \text{s}^{-1})^2 = \text{N} \cdot \text{m} = \text{J}$.

---

8 What is Newton's second law for rotating bodies?

8 $\Sigma\Gamma = I\alpha$.

---

9 If the resultant of the external forces acting on a body is 0, is the body in equilibrium?

9 It is in translational equilibrium, but it need not be in rotational equilibrium.

---

10 Compare the moment of inertia of a hollow cylinder with that of a solid cylinder. Both have the same mass and radius, and moments are taken about the axis of rotational symmetry.

10 The moment of inertia of the hollow cylinder is greater than that of the solid cylinder. The further the mass is from the axis of rotation, the greater the moment of inertia.

---

11 For a given displacement and force, when will the magnitude of the torque be maximum?

11 When the force is perpendicular to the displacement.

---

12 Can the moment of inertia of a rigid body be negative?

12 No, the moment of inertia is the sum of mr^2, which are positive quantities.

---

13 What is a rigid body?

13 A body of definite size and shape which can undergo both translational and rotational motion.

---

14 If the instantaneous velocity of a motor is doubled, what will be the instantaneous power, assuming constant torque?

14

$P = \Gamma\omega$ if $\omega' = 2\omega$
$P' = \Gamma(2\omega) = 2\Gamma\omega = 2P$.

---

15 How would you solve a problem where rotational and translational motion occur simultaneously?

15 Use $\Sigma F = ma$ and $\Sigma \Gamma = I\alpha$ provided that the axis of rotation passes through the center of mass of the body and does not change direction.

---

16 A sphere is rolling without slipping. What is the relationship between linear and angular acceleration?

16 $a = r\alpha$.

---

17 A skater is spinning holding her arms extended horizontally. What happens when she drops her hands to her sides?

17 Angular momentum is conserved. When the skater drops her hands to her sides, her moment of inertia decreases, therefore her angular velocity increases.

---

18 What are the units of torque in all three systems?

18 N · m (SI); dyne · cm (cgs); lb · ft (engineering).

MAIN IDEAS

1 One radian (1 rad) is the angle subtended at the center of a circle by an arc equal in length to the radius of the circle. In general, θ (rad) $= \dfrac{s}{R}$, where s is equal to the length of the arc and R is the radius of the circle.

2 The orientation of a rigid body is given by the angle θ made by an initial reference line and a final reference line (both passing through the axis of rotation). Angular displacement is given by $\Delta\theta = \theta_2 - \theta_1$ where θ_1 is the position at time t_1 and θ_2 is the position at time t_2.

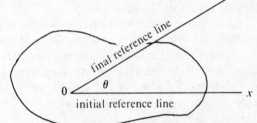

3 The basic concepts for rotational motion may be defined in a manner similar to the one used in translational motion. Thus

$$\text{average angular velocity} = \omega_{av} = \frac{\Delta\theta}{\Delta t},$$

$$\text{instantaneous angular velocity} = \omega = \lim_{\Delta t \to 0} \frac{\Delta\theta}{\Delta t},$$

$$\text{average angular acceleration} = \alpha_{av} = \frac{\omega_2 - \omega_1}{t_2 - t_1} = \frac{\Delta\omega}{\Delta t},$$

$$\text{instantaneous angular acceleration} = \alpha = \lim_{\Delta t \to 0} \frac{\Delta\omega}{\Delta t}.$$

4 Equations for rotational motion are analogous to equations for translational motion if we substitute θ for x, y or s; ω for v; and α for a.

Translation	Rotation
$a = $ constant	$\alpha = $ constant
$v = v_0 + at$	$\omega = \omega_0 + \alpha t$
$x = x_0 + v_0 t + \frac{1}{2}at^2$	$\theta = \theta_0 + \omega_0 t + \frac{1}{2}\alpha t^2$
$x = x_0 + \dfrac{v_0 + v}{2} t$	$\theta = \theta_0 + \dfrac{\omega_0 + \omega}{2} t$
$v^2 = v_0^2 + 2a(x - x_0)$	$\omega^2 = \omega_0^2 + 2\alpha(\theta - \theta_0)$

5 Relations between linear and rotational quantities: $s = r\theta$, $v = r\omega$. $a_\parallel = r\alpha$, $a_\perp = \dfrac{v^2}{r} = \omega^2 r$, where s is the arclength, r is the radius of the circle, v is the tangential speed of a particle on the circle, $a_\parallel$ is the tangential acceleration, and $a_\perp$ is the centripetal acceleration.

6 The moment of inertia I of a body about an axis of rotation is obtained as follows: Subdivide the body into many small parts which we shall call particles, multiply the mass of each particle by the square of tis distance from the axis, obtain the sum of these products:

$$I = \sum_{i=1}^{\infty} m_i r_i^2 = (m_1 r_1^2 + m_2 r_2^2 + m_3 r_3^2 + \ldots)$$

7 Parallel-axis theorem, $I_p = I_{cm} + Md_2$, where I_p = moment of inertia about an axis parallel to the axis passing through the center of mass cm and d is the perpendicular distance between the two axes.

8 The rotational kinetic energy K of a rigid body is $K = \frac{1}{2}I\omega^2$.

9 Total kinetic energy of a rigid body that has both translational and rotational motion is
$$K = \frac{1}{2}MV^2 + \frac{1}{2}I_c\omega^2,$$
where
M = mass of moving body,
V = center-of-mass velocity,
ω = angular velocity through center of mass,
I_c = moment of inertia about axis through center of mass.

10 The moment of a force or torque Γ is the tendency of a force to produce rotation about a specified axis (called the axis of rotation). The torque of a force is the product of the magnitude of the force F and the perpendicular distance from the axis of rotation to the line of action of the force. Thus $\Gamma_1 = F_1 l_1$, $\Gamma_2 = F_2 l_2$. The effect of a force will be to produce clockwise or counterclockwise rotation about the axis. We shall use the convention that counterclockwise torques are positive and clockwise torques are negative. Thus $\Gamma_1 = + F_1 l_1$ and $\Gamma_2 = - F_2 l_2$. Use the symbol $\bigodot +$ to indicate the positive direction of rotation.

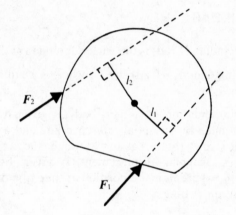

11 The rotational analog of Newton's second law is $\Sigma\Gamma = I\alpha$.

12 Work done by a constant torque equals the product of the torque and the angular displacement: $W = \Gamma \cdot \Delta\theta$.

13 Power = rate of doing work = $P = \Gamma\omega$.

14 Angular momentum = $L = mvr = pr = I\omega$.

15 Angular impulse = $J_\theta = \Gamma \Delta t$.

16 Conservation of angular momentum: the total angular momentum of an isolated system is conserved.

17 To find the direction of vectors ω and L, wrap the fingers of your right hand about the axis of rotation with your fingers pointing in the direction of rotation. Your thumb will point in the direction of ω and L.

18 The gyroscope. The forces acting on a gyroscope are its weight w acting downward at the center of mass and the upper force P at the pivot point. Precession is the motion of the axis of the gyroscope:
Ω = precession angular velocity
= rate at which the axis moves
$$= \frac{\Delta\phi}{\Delta t} = \frac{\Gamma}{L} = \frac{wR}{I\omega}$$
where
ω = angular velocity of gyroscope flywheel or rotor,
I = moment of inertia of flywheel or rotor,
R = horizontal distance of the center of mass from the pivot support.

19 Additional equations for rotational motion which are analogous to equations for translational motion if we substitute I for m and Γ for F are as follows:

Translation	Rotation
$\Sigma F = ma$	$\Sigma \Gamma = I\alpha$
$K = \dfrac{mv^2}{2}$	$K = \dfrac{I\omega^2}{2}$
$\Delta W = F\Delta s$	$\Delta W = \Gamma\Delta\theta$
instantaneous power $= P = Fv$	$P = \Gamma\omega$
impulse $= J = F\Delta t$	angular impulse $= J_\theta = \Gamma\Delta t$
momentum $= p = mv$	angular momentum $= L = I\omega$

20 Problem solving strategy for rotational dynamics:

a) Select a body for analysis.
b) Draw a free-body diagram. Label weight $w = mg$ immediately.
c) Set up coordinate axes for each body. Indicate the positive sense of rotation for each rotating body by the symbol ⟳(+) .

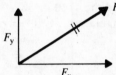

d) Resolve forces into components. Cross out the original force so that there will be no repetition.
e) Apply Newton's second law for each body:
$$\Sigma F = ma,$$
$$\Sigma \Gamma = I\alpha.$$
Solve for unknown quantities. Remember, if the line of action of a force goes through the point we are using to calculate torques, the torque of that force is zero. Write separate equations for each body. Also bear in mind the kinematic relation between two motions:
$$v = \omega r,$$
$$a = \alpha r.$$
f) Check special cases.

PROGRAMMED QUIZ

1 A pie is cut into 8 equal pieces. What is the angle (in radians) of each piece?

1

$$\frac{2\pi \text{ rad}}{8} = \frac{\pi}{4} \text{ rad}$$

---

2 The angular velocity of a flywheel increases from 300 to 1800 rev · min^{-1} in 5 s at a constant rate. Answer frames 2–15. What is the initial angular velocity in rad · s^{-1}?

2

$$\omega_0 = \left(\frac{300 \text{ rev}}{\text{min}}\right)\left(\frac{1 \text{ min}}{60 \text{ s}}\right)\left(\frac{2\pi \text{ rad}}{1 \text{ rev}}\right)$$

$$= 10\,\pi \text{ rad} \cdot \text{s}^{-1}$$

---

3 What is the final angular velocity in rad · s^{-1}?

3

$$\omega = \left(\frac{1800 \text{ rev}}{\text{min}}\right)\left(\frac{1 \text{ min}}{60 \text{ s}}\right)\left(\frac{2\pi \text{ rad}}{1 \text{ rev}}\right)$$

$$= 60\pi \text{ rad} \cdot \text{s}^{-1}$$

4 What is the angular acceleration?

4

$$\alpha = \frac{\omega - \omega_0}{t}$$
$$= \frac{60\pi \text{ rad} \cdot \text{s}^{-1} - 10\pi \text{ rad} \cdot \text{s}^{-1}}{5 \text{ s}}$$
$$= 10\pi \text{ rad} \cdot \text{s}^{-2}$$

---

5 During this period, how many revolutions were made by the flywheel?

5

$$\theta = \theta_0 + \omega_0 t + \tfrac{1}{2}\alpha t^2$$
$$= 0 + 10\pi \text{ rad} \cdot \text{s}^{-1} (5 \text{ s})$$
$$\quad + \tfrac{1}{2}(10\pi \text{ rad} \cdot \text{s}^{-2}) (5 \text{ s})^2$$
$$= 175\pi \text{ rad}$$

$$(175\pi \text{ rad}) \left(\frac{1 \text{ rev}}{2\pi \text{ rad}} \right) = 87.5 \text{ rev}$$

---

6 If the flywheel is 0.4 m in diameter, what is the linear speed of a point on its rim when the angular speed is 1800 rev $\cdot$ min^{-1}?

6

$$v = r\omega$$
$$= (0.2 \text{ m}) (60\pi \text{ rad} \cdot \text{s}^{-1})$$
$$= 12\pi \text{ m} \cdot \text{s}^{-1}$$

---

7 What is the radial acceleration of this point at the same speed?

7

$$a_\perp = \omega^2 r$$
$$= (60\pi \text{ rad} \cdot \text{s}^{-1})^2 (0.2 \text{ m})$$
$$= 720\pi^2 \text{ m} \cdot \text{s}^{-2}$$

---

8 What is the tangential acceleration of this point in the 0.5 s time period?

8

$$a_\parallel = r\alpha$$
$$= (0.2 \text{ m}) (10\pi \text{ rad} \cdot \text{s}^{-2})$$
$$= 2\pi \text{ m} \cdot \text{s}^{-2}$$

---

9 If it started from rest and assuming the same acceleration, how long had the flywheel been in motion before it reached an angular velocity of 10 π rad $\cdot$ s^{-1}?

9

$$\omega = \omega_0 + \alpha t$$
$$10\pi \text{ rad} \cdot \text{s}^{-1} = 0 + 10\pi \text{ rad} \cdot \text{s}^{-2}(t)$$
$$t = 1 \text{ s}$$

---

10 The flywheel has a moment of inertia of 40 kg $\cdot$ m^2. What constant torque is required for it to accelerate at this rate?

10

$$\Sigma\Gamma = I\alpha$$
$$= (40 \text{ kg} \cdot \text{m}^2) (10\pi \text{ rad} \cdot \text{s}^{-2})$$
$$= 400\pi \text{ N} \cdot \text{m}$$

---

11 What is its final kinetic energy?

11

$$K = \tfrac{1}{2}I\omega^2$$
$$= \tfrac{1}{2}(40 \text{ kg} \cdot \text{m}^2) (60\pi \text{ rad} \cdot \text{s}^{-1})^2$$
$$= 72{,}000\pi^2 \text{ J}$$

---

12 What is the instantaneous power developed by the agent exerting the torque at the end of the 5 s time interval?

12
$$P = \Gamma\omega$$
$$= 400\pi \text{ N} \cdot \text{m} \ (60\pi \text{ rad} \cdot \text{s}^{-1})$$
$$= 24,000\pi \text{ watts}$$

---

13 What is the angular momentum at this point?

13
$$L = I\omega$$
$$= 40 \text{ kg} \cdot \text{m}^2 \ (60\pi \text{ rad} \cdot \text{s}^{-1})$$
$$= 2400 \ \pi^2 \text{ kg} \cdot \text{m}^2 \cdot \text{s}^{-1}$$

---

14 Using this value, calculate the mass of the flywheel.

14
$$L = mvr$$
$$m = \frac{2400\pi \text{ kg} \cdot \text{m}^2 \cdot \text{s}^{-1}}{12\pi \text{ m} \cdot \text{s}^{-1} \ (0.2 \text{ m})}$$
$$= 1000 \text{ kg}$$

---

15 What must be the angular impulse during the 5 s time interval?

15
$$L_0 = I\omega_0$$
$$= 40 \text{ kg} \cdot \text{m}^2 \ (10\pi \text{ rad} \cdot \text{s}^{-1})$$
$$= 400\pi \text{ kg} \cdot \text{m}^2 \cdot \text{s}^{-1}$$
$$J_\theta = L - L_0$$
$$= (2400\pi - 400\pi) \text{ kg} \cdot \text{m}^2 \cdot \text{s}^{-1}$$
$$= 2000\pi \text{ kg} \cdot \text{m}^2 \cdot \text{s}^{-1}$$

In frames 16–18, find the torque about O due to F (and w if stated).

16

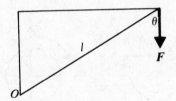

16 $\Gamma_0 = -Fl \sin\theta$ (clockwise)

17

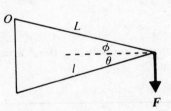

17
$$\Gamma_0 = -FL \cos\phi \text{ or}$$
$$-Fl \cos\theta \text{ (clockwise)}$$

18

18 $\Gamma_0 = Fl \cos\theta$ (counterclockwise)

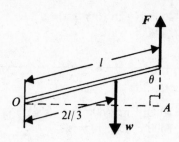

19 $\Gamma_0 = Fl \sin \theta - 2/3 \, wl \sin \theta$

The perpendicular distance from the axis of rotation to the line of action of F is equal to $OA = l \sin \theta$. Therefore, F produces a counterclockwise torque $= Fl \sin \theta$. The perpendicular distance from the axis of rotation to the line of action of w is equal to $2/3 \, l \sin \theta$. Therefore w produces a clockwise torque $= 2/3 \, wl \sin \theta$.

---

20 The mass of the rotor and frame of a gyroscope is 0.20 kg. The moment of inertia of the rotor about its axis is 1.8×10^{-4} kg $\cdot$ m^2, and its angular velocity is 500 rad $\cdot$ s^{-1}. The gyroscope is supported on a single pivot. Its center of gravity is 0.04 m from the pivot along the horizontal. Find the precession angular velocity.

20

$w = (0.20 \text{ kg}) (9.8 \text{ m} \cdot \text{s}^{-2}) = 1.96 \text{ N}$
$R = 0.04 \text{ m}$
$I = 1.8 \times 10^{-4} \text{ kg} \cdot \text{m}^2$
$\omega = 500 \text{ rad} \cdot \text{s}^{-1}$

$$\Omega = \frac{wR}{I\omega}$$

$$= \frac{(1.96 \text{ N}) (0.04 \text{ m})}{(1.8 \times 10^{-4} \text{ kg} \cdot \text{m}^2) (500 \text{ rad} \cdot \text{s}^{-1})}$$

$$= 0.871 \text{ rad} \cdot \text{s}^{-1}$$

STEP BY STEP SOLUTIONS OF PROBLEMS

Problem 1 A cord is wrapped around the rim of a flywheel which is mounted on frictionless bearings on a horizontal shaft through its center. A mass m is suspended from one end of the cord. The moment of inertia of the wheel is I, and the radius is R. Find the angular acceleration of the wheel, the linear acceleration of m, and the tension in the cord.

1 Draw a free-body diagram for the mass and the flywheel. (P is the force exerted on the flywheel at the axle. M is the mass of the flywheel.)

1

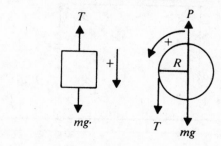

The positive direction is the direction of the acceleration.

---

2 Using Newton's second law, write the equation for the motion of the mass.

2

$$\Sigma F = ma$$
$$mg - T = ma$$

---

3 The torque on the flywheel is due to the tension in the cord. Write Newton's second law for the flywheel.

3

$$\Sigma \Gamma = I\alpha$$
$$TR = I\alpha \qquad\qquad (1)$$

The torques due to Mg and P (about the axle) are 0.

4 Solve for α by solving and eliminating T in the above equations. Note that $a = \alpha R$.

4

$$mg = ma + \frac{I\alpha}{R}$$

$$= mR\alpha + \frac{I\alpha}{R}$$

$$\alpha = \frac{mg}{MR + \dfrac{I}{R}} \qquad (2)$$

5 Solve for a, using $a = \alpha R$.

5

$$a = \frac{mg}{m + \dfrac{I}{R^2}}$$

6 Substitute the value of α in Eq. (1) and solve for T.

6

$$T = \frac{mg}{1 + \dfrac{mR^2}{I}} \qquad (3)$$

If $m = 10$ kg, $M = 2$ kg, $R = 0.5$ m, $s = 10$ m, show that the work done in unwinding 10 m of cord equals the gain in kinetic energy of the wheel.

7 In order to calculate the work done, first find the torque from $\Gamma = TR$; substitute Eq. (3) for T.

7

$$I = MR^2$$
$$= (2 \text{ kg}) (0.5 \text{ m})^2$$
$$= 0.5 \text{ kg} \cdot \text{m}^2$$

$$\Gamma = \frac{mg}{1 + \dfrac{mR^2}{I}} (R)$$

$$= \frac{10 \text{ kg} (9.8 \text{ m} \cdot \text{s}^{-2})}{1 + \dfrac{(10 \text{ kg}) (0.5 \text{ m})^2}{0.5 \text{ kg} \cdot \text{m}^2}} (0.5 \text{ m})$$

$$= 8.17 \text{ N} \cdot \text{m}$$

8 Calculate the angular displacement using $\theta = s/R$.

8

$$\theta = \frac{10 \text{ m}}{0.5 \text{ m}}$$
$$= 20 \text{ rad}$$

9 Work done is equal to $\Gamma\theta$.

9

$$W = \Gamma\theta$$
$$= (8.17 \text{ N} \cdot \text{m}) (20 \text{ rad})$$
$$= 163 \text{ J}$$

10 To find the kinetic energy of the wheel first find the numerical value for α from Eq. (2).

10

$$\alpha = \frac{mg}{mR + \dfrac{I}{R}}$$

$$= \frac{10 \text{ kg } (9.8 \text{ m} \cdot \text{s}^{-2})}{10 \text{ kg } (0.5 \text{ m}) + \dfrac{0.5 \text{ kg} \cdot \text{m}^2}{0.5 \text{ m}}}$$

$$= 16.3 \text{ rad} \cdot \text{s}^{-2}$$

---

11 Find the angular velocity from $\omega^2 = \omega_0^2 + 2\alpha\theta$.

11

$$\omega^2 = 0 + 2(16.3 \text{ s}^{-2})(20 \text{ rad})$$
$$\omega = 25.5 \text{ rad} \cdot \text{s}^{-1}$$

---

12 Find the kinetic energy from $K = \frac{1}{2}I\omega^2$ and compare with the answer in frame 9.

12

$$K = \frac{1}{2}(0.5 \text{ kg} \cdot \text{m}^2)(25.5 \text{ s}^{-1})^2$$
$$= 163 \text{ J}$$

Problem 2 Two blocks connected by a cord pass over a pulley in the form of a thin cylindrical shell of mass M and radius R. The blocks are sliding over frictionless surfaces as indicated in the figure. Find the angular acceleration of the pulley and the tension in each part of the string.

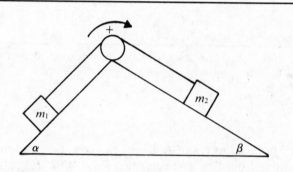

---

13 Draw a free-body digram for m_1, m_2, and the pulley. Remember that for the pulley to have an angular acceleration $T_1 \neq T_2$. Assume that m_1 is moving up the plane and m_2 is moving down.

13

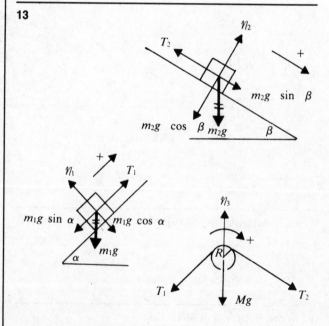

$\mathcal{N}_3$ is the force exerted on the pulley at the axle.

14 Write Newton's second law for the pulley. The moment of inertia of the pulley is MR^2.

14
$$T_2R - T_1R = I\alpha = MR^2\alpha$$
The torques due to η_3 and Mg (about the axle) are 0.

15 Since the string does not slip or stretch $a = R\alpha$. Substitute in the above equation.

15 $\quad T_2 - T_1 = Ma \quad\quad\quad\quad\quad (4)$

16 Write Newton's second law for m_1 and m_2. Note that $a_1 = a_2 = a$.

16
$$\Sigma F = ma$$
$$T_1 - m_1g \sin \alpha = m_1a \quad\quad (5)$$
$$m_2g \sin \beta - T_2 = m_2a \quad\quad (6)$$

17 Add Eqs. (4), (5), and (6) are solve for a.

17
$$a = \frac{(m_2 \sin \beta - m_1 \sin \alpha)}{m_1 + m_2 + M} g$$

18 Substitute the value of a in Eq. (5) and Eq. (6) in order to solve for T_1 and T_2, respectively.

18
$$T_1 = \frac{m_1g[m_2(\sin \alpha + \sin \beta) + M \sin \alpha]}{m_1 + m_2 + M}$$
$$T_2 = \frac{m_2g[m_1(\sin \alpha + \sin \beta) + M \sin \beta]}{m_1 + m_2 + M}$$

The student should verify the special cases for Problem 2.

i) $\quad \beta = 90°$
$$a = \frac{(m_2 - m_1 \sin \alpha)g}{m_1 + m_2 + M}$$
$$T_1 = \frac{m_1g[m_2(\sin \alpha + 1) M \sin \alpha]}{m_1 + m_2 + M}$$
$$T_2 = \frac{m_2g[m_1(\sin \alpha + 1) + M]}{m_1 + m_2 + M}$$

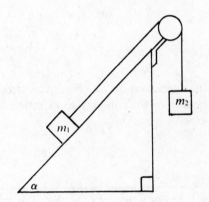

ii) $\quad \alpha = \beta = 90°$ (Atwood's machine)
$$a = \frac{(m_2 - m_1)g}{m_1 + m_2 + M}$$
$$T_1 = \frac{m_1g(2m_2 + M)}{m_1 + m_2 + M}$$
$$T_2 = \frac{m_2g(2m_1 + M)}{m_1 + m_2 + M}$$

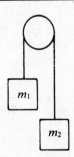

iii) $\alpha = 0°$, $\beta = 90°$

$$a = \frac{m_2 g}{m_1 + m_2 + M}$$

$$T_1 = \frac{m_1 m_2 g}{m_1 + m_2 + M}$$

$$T_2 = \frac{m_2 g(m_1 + M)}{m_1 + m_2 + M}$$

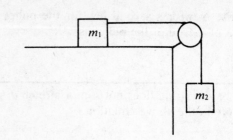

---

iv) $\alpha = 0$

$$a = \frac{m_2 g \sin \beta}{m_1 + m_2 + M}$$

$$T_1 = \frac{m_1 m_2 g \sin \beta}{m_1 + m_2 + M}$$

$$T_2 = \frac{m_2 g \sin \beta \, (m_1 + M)}{m_1 + m_2 + M}$$

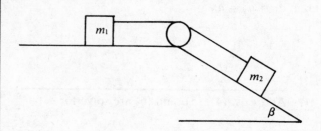

Problem 3 A solid cylinder, radius 0.2 m, is pivoted about a horizontal axis through its center. A 10 kg mass is hanging from a rope which is wrapped around the cylinder. If the mass falls 4 m in the first 8 s after it is released, find the moment of inertia of the wheel. What is the force exerted on the cylinder by its bearings?

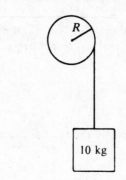

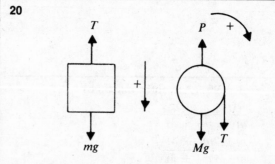

---

19 Find the acceleration of the mass from the kinematic equations for constant acceleration.

19

$$y - y_0 = v_0 t + \tfrac{1}{2}at^2$$
$$4 \text{ m} = 0 + \tfrac{1}{2}a \, (8 \text{ s})^2$$
$$a = 0.125 \text{ m} \cdot \text{s}^{-2}$$

---

20 Draw a free-body diagram for the mass and the cylinder.

20

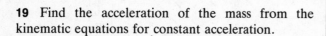

---

21 Write Newton's second law for the 10 kg mass and solve for T.

21

$$\Sigma F = ma$$
$$mg - T = ma$$
$$(10 \text{ kg})(9.8 \text{ m} \cdot \text{s}^{-2}) - T = (10 \text{ kg})(0.125 \text{ m} \cdot \text{s}^{-2})$$
$$T = 96.75 \text{ N}$$

22 What is the angular acceleration of the wheel? ($a = \alpha R$).

22

$$\alpha = \frac{a}{R}$$
$$= \frac{0.125 \text{ m} \cdot \text{s}^{-2}}{0.2 \text{ m}}$$
$$= 0.625 \text{ rad} \cdot \text{s}^{-2}$$

23 Write Newton's second law for the wheel and solve for I.

23

$$\Sigma\Gamma = I\alpha$$
$$TR = I\alpha$$
$$I = \frac{96.75 \text{ N}(0.2 \text{ m})}{0.625 \text{ s}^{-2}}$$
$$= 31.0 \text{ kg} \cdot \text{m}^2$$

24 Find the mass of the cylinder using

$$I = \frac{MR^2}{2}.$$

24

$$M = \frac{2I}{R^2}$$
$$= \frac{2(31 \text{ kg} \cdot \text{m}^2)}{(0.2 \text{ m})^2}$$
$$= 1550 \text{ kg}$$

25 Find the force exerted by the bearings.

25

$$P = Mg + T$$
$$= (1550 \text{ kg}) (9.8 \text{ m} \cdot \text{s}^{-2}) + 96.75 \text{ N}$$
$$= 15,300 \text{ N}$$

PROGRAMMED TEST

1 *Problem 1* A solid cylinder rolls without slipping down an incline of 40°. Find the acceleration and the minimum coefficient of friction needed to prevent slipping.

Answer

1 4.20 m · s⁻², 0.280

If you solved this problem correctly, go to frame 8. If you could not solve this problem, go through frames 2–7.

2 Draw a free-body diagram.

2

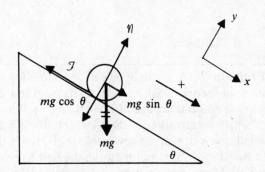

3 Write Newton's second law for the linear and angular motion. The moment of inertia of a solid cylinder is $MR^2/2$.

3
$$\Sigma F_x = ma$$
$$mg \sin \theta - \mathcal{F} = ma \qquad (7)$$
$$\Sigma \Gamma = I\alpha$$
$$\mathcal{F}R = \frac{MR^2\alpha}{2}$$

---

4 Since the cylinder rolls without slipping $a = R\alpha$. Substitute this relationship in the previous equation and solve for a.

4
$$\mathcal{F}R = \frac{mR^2}{2}\left(\frac{a}{R}\right)$$
$$a = \frac{2\mathcal{F}}{m} \qquad (8)$$

---

5 Substitute in Eq. (7) and solve for $\mathcal{F}$.

5
$$mg \sin \theta - \mathcal{F} = 2\mathcal{F}$$
$$\mathcal{F} = \frac{mg \sin \theta}{3}$$

---

6 Substitute in Eq. (8) and find the numerical value for the acceleration.

6
$$a = \frac{2(mg \sin \theta)}{3\,m}$$
$$= \frac{2}{3}(9.8 \text{ m} \cdot \text{s}^{-2}) \sin 40°$$
$$= 4.20 \text{ m} \cdot \text{s}^{-2}$$

---

7 Find the minimum coefficient of friction to prevent slipping. (Note that this is the smallest value the coefficient of static friction may have).

7
$$\mu_s = \frac{\mathcal{F}}{\mathcal{N}}$$
$$= \frac{1/3\ mg \sin \theta}{mg \cos \theta} = \frac{\tan \theta}{3} = \tan \frac{40°}{3}$$
$$= 0.280$$

---

8 ***Problem 2*** A grinding wheel, mass 200 kg and moment of inertia of 550 kg · m², starts from rest and develops a constant torque of 1200 N · m. a) What is the angular acceleration of the flywheel? b) What is its angular velocity after 5 revolutions? c) How much work was done by the motor during the first 5 revolutions? d) How much power was expended by the motor at the end of the first 5 revolutions?

8
Answer
2.18 rad · s⁻², 11.7 rad · s⁻¹, 37700 J, 14000 watts

If you solved this problem correctly, go to frame 13. If you could not solve this problem, go through frames 9–12.

9 Find the angular acceleration.

9
$$\Gamma = I\alpha$$
$$\alpha = \frac{1200 \text{ N} \cdot \text{m}}{550 \text{ kg} \cdot \text{m}^2}$$
$$= 2.18 \text{ rad} \cdot \text{s}^{-2}$$

---

10 To find the angular velocity after 5 revolutions, use the kinematic equations.

10
$$\omega^2 = \omega_0^2 + 2\alpha(\theta - \theta_0)$$
$$= 0 + 2(2.18 \text{ s}^{-2})(10\,\pi)$$
$$\omega = 11.7 \text{ rad} \cdot \text{s}^{-1}$$

---

11 Find the work done in the first five revolutions (1 rev = 2π rad).

11
$$W = \Gamma\theta$$
$$= (1200 \text{ N} \cdot \text{m})(10\,\pi)$$
$$= 37,700 \text{ J}$$

---

12 Find the power expended at the end of this time period.

12
$$P = \Gamma\omega$$
$$= (1200 \text{ N} \cdot \text{m})(11.7 \text{ s}^{-1})$$
$$= 14,000 \text{ watts}$$

---

13 **Problem 3** A 10 kg block is at rest on a horizontal frictionless surface. A cord which is attached to the block passes over a pulley of 0.2 m radius. The other end of the cord is attached to a hanging block of same mass. When the system is released the blocks move 5 m in 2 s. a) What is the tension in each part of the cord? b) What is the moment of inertia of the pulley?

13

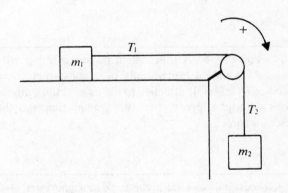

Answer
25 N, 73 N, 0.768 kg · m²

If you solved this problem correctly go to frame 18. If you could not solve this problem, go through frames 14–17.

14 Find the acceleration of the system from the kinematic equations (remember that *a* is the same throughout).

14
$$y - y_0 = v_0 t + \tfrac{1}{2}at^2$$
$$5 \text{ m} = 0 + \tfrac{1}{2}a(2 \text{ s})^2$$
$$a = 2.5 \text{ m} \cdot \text{s}^{-2}$$

15 Draw a free-body diagram for each mass and the pulley. Each block has the same acceleration.

15

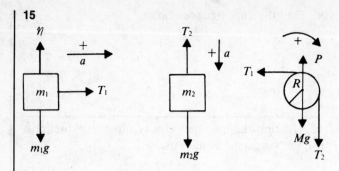

---

16 Use Newton's second law for both blocks to find T_1 and T_2.

16

$$\Sigma F = ma$$
$$T_1 = m_1 a$$
$$= (10 \text{ kg})(2.5 \text{ m} \cdot \text{s}^{-2}) = 25 \text{ N}$$
$$m_2 g - T_2 = m_2 a$$
$$(10 \text{ kg})(9.8 \text{ m} \cdot \text{s}^{-2}) - T_2 = (10 \text{ kg})(2.5 \text{ m} \cdot \text{s}^{-2})$$
$$T_2 = 73 \text{ N}$$

---

17 Use Newton's second law for the pulley, substituting $a = \alpha r$, to find the moment of inertia of the pulley.

17

$$\Sigma \Gamma = I\alpha$$
$$T_2 R - T_1 R = I\alpha$$
$$T_2 R - T_1 R = \frac{Ia}{R}$$
$$T_2 R^2 - T_1 R^2 = Ia$$
$$73 \text{ N}(0.2 \text{ m})^2 - 25 \text{ N}(0.2 \text{ m})^2 = I(2.5 \text{ m} \cdot \text{s}^{-2})$$
$$I = 0.768 \text{ kg} \cdot \text{m}^2$$

---

18 *Problem 4* A thin walled hollow cylinder with mass M is pulled horizontally by a constant force F applied by a handle attached to the axle. If the cylinder rolls without slipping, find the acceleration and the friction force.

18
Answer

$$a = \frac{F}{2M}$$
$$\mathcal{F}_k = \frac{F}{2}$$

If you could not solve this problem, go through frames 19–25.

19 Draw a free-body diagram. Set up a coordinate system.

19

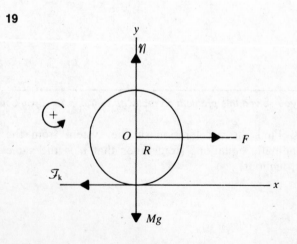

20 Apply Newton's second law in the x-direction.

20
$$\Sigma F_x = ma$$
$$F - \mathcal{I}_k = Ma$$

21 Take torques of all forces about the axle O of the cylinder.

21 The only force which has a nonzero torque is $\mathcal{I}_k$:
$$\Gamma = \mathcal{I}_k R$$
Note that the lines of action of η, F, and Mg pass through O and therefore have zero moment arms.

22 Express $\Sigma\Gamma$ in terms of I and α. Newton's second law for rotation is $\Sigma\Gamma = I\alpha$.

22 $\Sigma\Gamma = \mathcal{I}_k R = I\alpha$

23 Substitute for I and solve for $\mathcal{I}_k$:
$$I = MR^2$$

23
$$\mathcal{I}_k R = MR^2\alpha$$
$$\mathcal{I}_k = MR\alpha$$

24 But $R\alpha = a$. Substitute $\mathcal{I}_k = Ma$ in Newton's second law and solve for a.

24
$$F - \mathcal{I}_k = Ma$$
$$F - Ma = Ma$$
$$F = 2Ma$$
$$a = \frac{F}{2M}$$

25 Substitute this value in the expression for $\mathcal{I}_k$.

25
$$\mathcal{I}_k = M\left(\frac{F}{2M}\right)$$
$$= \frac{F}{2}$$

10

Equilibrium of a Rigid Body

CHAPTER SUMMARY

Chapter 2 was devoted to translational equilibrium, $\Sigma F = 0$. As was mentioned in that chapter, for a body to be in equilibrium, a second condition must be satisfied: The condition for rotational equilibrium states that the sum of the moments about any axis must be zero, $\Sigma \Gamma = 0$. A force that always acts on objects is the weight, which can be considered to be concentrated at the center of gravity. This must be included in the calculations unless it is stated that the object is of negligible weight. A couple is a pair of forces that produces rotation.

BASIC TERMS — *Give definitions or meanings for the following:*

first condition for equilibrium (10-1)
second condition for equilibrium (10-1)
center of gravity (10-2)

center of mass (10-2)
couple (10-4)

PROGRAMMED QUIZ

1 Why does a couple have no effect in producing translation of the body on which it acts?

1 Because the resultant force is zero.

2 Two forces equal in magnitude, opposite in direction, with parallel lines of action are acting on an object. Is the object in equilibrium?

2 It is in translational equilibrium since $\Sigma F = 0$, but it is not in rotational equilibrium since a couple, as such forces are called, produces rotation.

3 Write the two conditions of equilibrium in symbols.

3
$\Sigma F = 0$ and
$\Sigma \Gamma = 0$.

4 Where is the center of gravity of a homogeneous sphere, cube, or circular disk?

4 At the geometric center.

5 If $\Sigma\Gamma = 0$ about a particular axis, what can we say about $\Sigma\Gamma$ about any other axis?

5 Equals zero also.

---

6 In problems involving the second condition of equilibrium, must the torques be calculated about the center of gravity?

6 No, they may be calculated about any arbitrary axis.

---

7 A single force acting on a body will produce rotation. What is the exception?

7 If the line of action of the force is through the center of gravity, the force will produce translation only.

---

8 What must be done to bring equilibrium to an object acted on by a couple?

8 Another couple having an equal and opposite torque must be applied to the object.

---

9 Can there be a single force acting on an object if the torque is zero?

9 Yes, the moment arm may be zero.

---

10 Must the center of gravity be within the body?

10 No, in an "L" shaped body, for example, the center of gravity is outside.

---

11 If a body is suspended from one point and does not rotate, does this mean that it is suspended at its center of gravity?

11 No, but a vertical line from the point of suspension will pass through the center of gravity.

---

12 If a ladder rests against a frictionless wall, in what direction is the force that the ladder exerts on the wall?

12 Perpendicular to the wall.

---

13 Referring to frame 12, what are the forces that the ladder exerts on the ground?

13 A horizontal force equal to the reaction force of the wall on the ladder and a vertical force equal to the weight of the ladder.

---

14 Why is the concept of center of gravity so important in solving problems in equilibrium?

14 In equilibrium problems we can regard the entire weight of the object as concentrated at its center of gravity.

MAIN IDEAS

1 Conditions for equilibrium

First: The resultant of all the external forces acting on a body in equilibrium must equal zero. Thus, $\Sigma F = 0$ or $\Sigma F_x = 0$, $\Sigma F_y = 0$.

Second: The sum of all external torques acting on a body must equal zero. It should be noted that the axis of rotation could be at any point. Also, once the axis is chosen, it must be used for torques. Thus, $\Sigma \Gamma = 0$ (about any arbitrary axis).

2 A rigid body moving in uniform translational motion (without rotation) is in equilibrium. However, a rigid body rotating about a fixed axis at constant angular velocity is not in equilibrium because the individual particles in the body have accelerations.

3 The center of gravity of a body is a point where all the weight may be considered to be concentrated.

$$X = \frac{w_1 x_1 + w_2 x_2 + \dots}{W} = \frac{\Sigma w x}{W}, \qquad (1)$$

$$Y = \frac{w_1 y_1 + w_2 y_2 + \dots}{W} = \frac{\Sigma w y}{W}, \qquad (2)$$

where w_1, w_2, ... represent the weights of small particles having coordinates (x_1, y_1), (x_2, y_2), ..., which make up the body and $W = w_1 + w_2 + \dots$. The following hints will be useful in solving center of gravity problems.

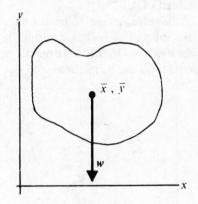

i) If x_1, y_1 is the center of gravity, of body 1, x_2, y_2 the center of gravity of body 2, x_3, y_3 the center of gravity of body 3, and if w_1, w_2 and w_3 are the weights of each body, respectively, then the center of gravity of the composite body can be calculated from Eqs. (*1*) and (*2*).

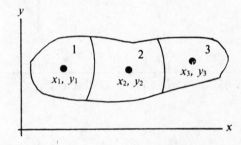

ii) In the case of uniform sheets of metal, machine parts, etc., the coordinates of the center of area are given by:

$$X = \frac{A_1 x_1 + A_2 x_2 + \dots}{A} = \frac{\Sigma A x}{A},$$

$$Y = \frac{A_1 y_1 + A_2 y_2 + \dots}{A} = \frac{\Sigma A y}{A}.$$

4 A couple is a pair of nonconcurrent forces equal in magnitude and oppositely directed. The resultant torque of a couple about any point is *lF*.

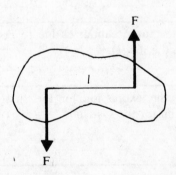

5 In solving problems involving the equilibrium of a body, follow these five steps.

Step 1 Draw a sketch (if not given) of all the apparatus or structures indicating dimensions and angles.

Step 2 Choose a body (e.g., a beam or a tie rod). Draw a force diagram by indicating all the forces (denoted by arrows) acting on the body. Do not show in the free-body diagram any of the forces exerted by the body.

Step 3 Set up a rectangular coordinate system and resolve all forces acting on the body into rectangular components.

Step 4 Set $\Sigma F_x = 0$ and $\Sigma F_y = 0$.

Step 5 Since torques may be computed about any axis, select a point through which the lines of action of two or more forces, especially one or more unknowns, pass. Set $\Sigma \Gamma = 0$ and solve the resulting equations for the unknown quantities. Include the symbol $\underset{+}{\bigcirc}$ to indicate the choice of positive direction.

PROGRAMMED QUIZ

1 Frames 1–10 refer to the following diagram: A boom length l, hinged at O, is supported by a cable fixed at height h above O. The cable makes an angle θ with the boom. Find the torque about O due to F.

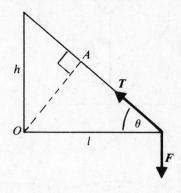

1 $\Gamma_0 = -Fl$

2 Find the torque about O due to T.

2
$$\Gamma_0 = Tl \sin \theta$$
The perpendicular distance from the axis of rotation to the line of action of T is equal to $OA = l \sin \theta$.

3 Are there any other forces acting on this system?

3 Yes, the weight of the boom at $l/2$, and the forces on the hinge F_H to the right and F_V upward.

4 Find the torque about O due to the weight of the boom.

4 $\Gamma_0 = -\frac{1}{2}wl$

5 Find the torque about O due to F_V and F_H (the forces on the hinge).

5 0, since the moment arm is zero.

6 Write the expression for the first condition of equilibrium for the system.

6
$$\Sigma F_y = T \sin \theta - F - w + F_V = 0$$
$$\Sigma F_x = -T \cos \theta + F_H = 0$$

7 Write an expression for the second condition for equilibrium. Choose an axis through O.

7 $-Fl - \frac{1}{2}wl + Tl \sin \theta = 0$

8 Given $F = 100$ N, $w = 50$ N, and $\theta = 30°$; find T.

8
$$T = \frac{F + w/2}{\sin \theta} = \frac{100 \text{ N} + 25 \text{ N}}{\sin 30°} = 250 \text{ N}$$

---

9 To find the force on the hinge, first find F_H and F_V.

9
$$F_H = T \cos \theta = 250 \text{ N}(\cos 30°) = 217 \text{ N}$$
$$F_V = F + w - T \sin \theta$$
$$= 100 \text{ N} + 50 \text{ N} - 250 \text{ N}(\sin 30°)$$
$$= 25 \text{ N}$$

---

10 Find the force on the hinge.

10
$$F = \sqrt{F_H^2 + F_V^2} = \sqrt{(217 \text{ N})^2 + (25 \text{ N})^2}$$
$$= 218 \text{ N}$$

---

11 What can be the maximum weight of a uniform 6 m board that is to be lifted by two people? One can lift up to 500 N and the other can lift 700 N.

11
$$\Sigma F_y = 0$$
$$0 = -500 \text{ N} + 700 \text{ N} - w$$
$$w = 1200 \text{ N}$$

---

12 Where is the weight concentrated?

12 At 3 m, the midpoint.

---

13 Referring to frame 11, the person who is lifting 500 N is at the left end; where must the other person lift? Compute torques about the left end.

13
$$\Sigma \Gamma_L = 0$$
$$0 = -1200 \text{ N}(3 \text{ m}) + 700 \text{ N}(l)$$
$$l = 5.14 \text{ m}$$

---

14 Compute torques about the other end.

14
$$\Sigma \Gamma_R = 0$$
$$0 = -500 \text{ N}(6 \text{ m}) + 1200 \text{ N}(3 \text{ m})$$
$$- 700 \text{ M}(l)$$
$$l = 0.86 \text{ m}$$

---

15 What is the relationship between the answers of frames 13 and 14?

15 They are both at the same point; 5.14 m from the left end is equal to 0.86 m from the right.

---

16 Find the center of gravity of two homogeneous cubes that are attached to each other as in the figure. One cube has a mass of 2 kg and is 0.50 m on a side, the other has a mass of 1 kg and is 0.25 m on a side. Measure distances from the unattached end of the 2 kg cube.

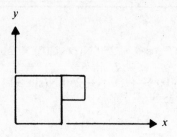

16

$$X = \frac{w_1 x_1 + w_2 x_2}{W}$$

$$= \frac{m_1 g x_1 + m_2 g x_2}{Mg}$$

$$= \frac{2 \text{ kg}(0.25 \text{ m}) + 1 \text{ kg}(0.625) \text{ m}}{3 \text{ kg}}$$

$$= 0.375 \text{ m}$$

$$Y = \frac{w_1 y_1 + w_2 y_2}{W}$$

$$= \frac{m_1 g y_1 + m_2 g y_2}{Mg}$$

$$= \frac{2 \text{ kg}(0.25 \text{ m}) + 1 \text{ kg}(0.375 \text{ m})}{3 \text{ kg}}$$

$$= 0.292 \text{ m}$$

STEP BY STEP SOLUTIONS OF PROBLEMS

Problem 1 Find the tension in the cable CD and the force F exerted on the strut AC at pin A.

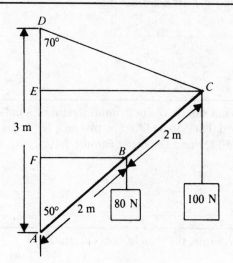

1 *Step 1* Draw a sketch (given). Calculate AE, CE, and BF, the perpendicular distances from the axis of rotation to the lines of action of the respective forces.

1

$AE = (4 \text{ m}) \cos 50° = 2.57 \text{ m}$
$CE = (4 \text{ m}) \sin 50° = 3.06 \text{ m}$
$BF = (2 \text{ m}) \sin 50° = 1.53 \text{ m}$

---

2 *Step 2* Choose AC as the body under consideration. Draw a free-body diagram.

2

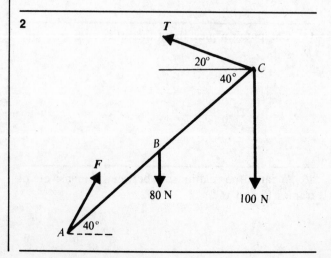

3 *Step 3* Construct a set of rectangular axes and resolve into horizontal and vertical components all forces acting on the body. Note that we have arbitrarily decided that F_V should be acting upward. If our choice was incorrect, F_V will turn out to have a negative value indicating that F_V is actually downward.

3

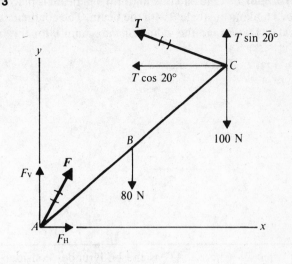

4 *Step 4* Set $\Sigma F_x = 0$, $\Sigma F_y = 0$.

4

$\Sigma F_x = F_H - T \cos 20° = 0$
$\Sigma F_y = F_V + T \sin 20° - 80 \text{ N} - 100 \text{ N} = 0$

5 *Step 5* Take torques about A. This is a good choice because the torques of F_H and F_V will be zero. Set $\Sigma\Gamma_A = 0$. Note that the perpendicular distance from A to the line of action of the 80 N force is 1.53 m and that the perpendicular distance from A to the line of action of the 100 N force is 3.06 m.

5

$\Sigma\Gamma_A = 0$
$T \sin 20°(3.06 \text{ m}) + T \cos 20°(2.57 \text{ m})$
$- (100 \text{ N})(3.06 \text{ m}) - (80 \text{ N})(1.53 \text{ m}) = 0$
$T = 123 \text{ N}$

Note $\circlearrowright$ +

6 Calculate $F_H = T \cos 20°$.
Calculate $F_V = 180 \text{ N} - T \sin 20°$.

6

$F_H = T \cos 20° = (123 \text{ N}) \cos 20° = 116 \text{ N}$
$F_V = 180 \text{ N} - T \sin 20° = 180 \text{ N} - (123 \text{ N}) \sin 20°$
$= 138 \text{ N}$

7 Find F by using
$$F = \sqrt{F_H^2 + F_V^2}.$$

7

$F = \sqrt{(116 \text{ N})^2 + (138 \text{ N})^2}$
$= 180 \text{ N}$
$\theta = \arctan \dfrac{|138 \text{ N}|}{|116 \text{ N}|} = 50.0°$

Problem 2 One end of a uniform 4 m beam is placed against a vertical wall. The other end is held by a massless cord making an angle θ with the beam. The coefficient of static friction between the end of the beam and the wall is 0.4. Determine the value for maximum θ for the beam to remain in equilibrium.

8 *Step 1* Draw a sketch.

8

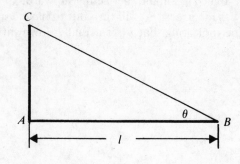

9 *Step 2* Choose AB as the body under consideration. Draw a free-body diagram.

9

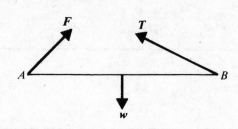

10 *Step 3* Construct a set of rectangular axes and resolve into horizontal and vertical components all forces acting on the body. Again, as in the previous problem, we have arbitrarily decided that F_V should be acting upward. If our choice was incorrect, F_V will turn out to have a negative value indicating that F_V is actually acting downward.

10

11 *Step 4* Set $\Sigma F_x = 0$; $\Sigma F_y = 0$.

11

$$\Sigma F_x = F_H - T \cos \theta = 0 \qquad (3)$$
$$\Sigma F_y = F_V + T \sin \theta - mg = 0 \qquad (4)$$

12 *Step 5* Take torques about A, since the moments of F_H, F_V, and $T \cos \theta$ will be zero. Set $\Sigma \Gamma_A = 0$. Solve Eq. (5) for T and substitute in Eq. (3) in order to obtain the value for F_H. Also substitute $T = mg/\sin \theta$ in Eq. (4) in order to obtain the value for F_V.

12

$$\Sigma \Gamma_A = 0$$
$$lT \sin \theta - l/2 \, mg = 0 \qquad (5)$$
$$T = \frac{mg}{2 \sin \theta}$$

$$F_H = T \cos \theta = \frac{mg}{2 \sin \theta} \cos \theta \qquad (6)$$

$$F_V = mg - T \sin \theta = \frac{mg}{2} . \qquad (7)$$

13 What is happening at point A? F_V is the force of static friction $\mathcal{I}_s$ and F_H is the normal force $\mathcal{N}$. It follows that

$$\mu_s = \frac{\mathcal{I}_s}{\mathcal{N}} = \frac{F_V}{F_H}.$$

Substitute the values of F_H and F_V from Eq. (6) and (7), respectively, in this equation.

13

$$\mu_s = \frac{F_V}{F_H} = \frac{mg/2}{\dfrac{mg \cos \theta}{2 \sin \theta}} = \frac{\sin \theta}{\cos \theta} = \tan \theta$$

---

14 What is the value of θ for $\mu_s = 0.4$?

14

$$\tan \theta = 0.4$$
$$\theta = 21.8°$$

---

15 Find the tension T in the cable for a beam weighing 200 N.

15

$$T = \frac{mg}{2 \sin \theta} = \frac{200 \text{ N}}{2 \sin 21.8°}$$
$$= 269 \text{ N}$$

Problem 3 Find the centroid of the composite figure consisting of a square (2 m × 2 m), an isosceles triangle, base 2 m, height 3 m and a semicircle of radius 1 m. We are given the following information on the centers of gravity.

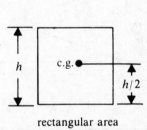

rectangular area

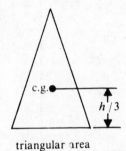

triangular area

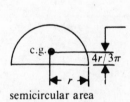

semicircular area

---

16 Set up a coordinate system and designate the area of the square as A_1, the area of the triangle as A_2, and the area of the semicircle as A_3.

16

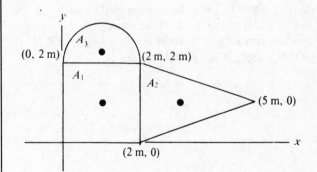

---

17 What are the coordinates of the centroids of each area?

17

$A_1(1, 1)$
$A_2(3, 1)$
$A_3(1, 2.424)$

The ordinate of A_3 is

$$2 + \frac{4r}{3\pi} = 2.424$$

---

18 Find the area of each figure. Find $A = A_1 + A_2 + A_3$.

18

$$A_1 = (2 \text{ m}) (2 \text{ m}) = 4 \text{ m}^2$$

$$A_2 = \frac{(2 \text{ m}) (3 \text{ m})}{2} = 3 \text{m}^2$$

$$A_3 = \frac{\pi (1 \text{ m})^2}{2} = 1.57 \text{ m}^2$$

$$A = 8.57 \text{ m}^2$$

19 Find

$$X = \frac{A_1 x_1 + A_2 x_2 + A_3 x_3}{A}.$$

19

$$X = \frac{4 \text{ m}^2 (1 \text{ m}) + 3 \text{ m}^2 (3 \text{ m}) + 1.57 \text{ m}^2 (1 \text{ m})}{8.57 \text{ m}^2}$$

$$= 1.70 \text{ m}$$

20 Find

$$Y = \frac{A_1 y_1 + A_2 y_2 + A_3 y_3}{A}.$$

20

$$Y = \frac{4 \text{ m}^2 (1 \text{ m}) + 3 \text{ m}^2 (1 \text{ m}) + 1.57 \text{ m}^2 (2.424 \text{ m})}{8.57 \text{ m}^2}$$

$$= 1.26 \text{ m}$$

21 Using a scale of 1 cm is equal to 1 m, sketch the composite figure and indicate the coordinates of the centroid.

21

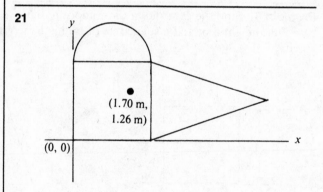

PROGRAMMED TEST

1 *Problem 1* Find the tension in the cable and the components of the force on the strut at A. The strut is nonuniform (c.g. 2 m from A) and weighs 100 N. A 400 N weight is hanging 4 m from A.

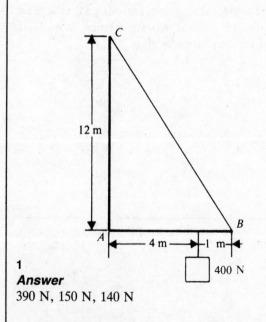

1
Answer
390 N, 150 N, 140 N

If you solved this problem correctly, go to frame 7. If you could not solve this problem, go through frames 2–6.

2 Since the sketch was given, we will proceed with *Step 2.* Choose *AB* as the body under consideration. Draw a free-body diagram.

2

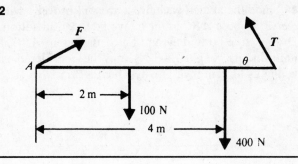

3 *Step 3* Construct a set of rectangular axes and resolve into horizontal and vertical components all forces acting on the body. Note that $\triangle ABC$ is a 5, 12, 13 right triangle, $\therefore \sin \theta = 12/13$, $\cos \theta = 5/13$.

3

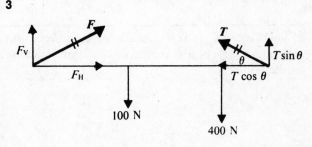

4 Set $\Sigma F_x = 0$; $\Sigma F_y = 0$.

4

$$\Sigma F_x = F_H - T \cos \theta = 0$$
$$F_H - 0.385\ T = 0$$
$$\Sigma F_y = F_V + T \sin \theta - 100\ \text{N} - 400\ \text{N} = 0$$
$$F_V + 0.923\ T - 500\ \text{N} = 0$$

5 Take torques about *A*. Why is this a good choice? (The torques of F_H, F_V and $T \cos \theta$ will be zero.) Set $\Sigma \Gamma_A = 0$.

5

$$\Sigma \Gamma_A = 0$$
$$T \sin \theta (5\ \text{m}) - 100\ \text{N}(2\ \text{m}) - (400\ \text{N})(4\ \text{m}) = 0$$
$$T(4.62\ \text{m}) - 1800\ \text{N} \cdot \text{m} = 0$$
$$T = 390\ \text{N}$$

6 Find F_H and F_V.

6

$$F_H = 0.385T = 0.385(390\ \text{N})$$
$$= 150\ \text{N}$$
$$F_V = 500\ \text{N} - 0.923T = 500\ \text{N} - 0.923(390\ \text{N})$$
$$= 140\ \text{N}$$

7 **Problem 2** The uniform 6 m boom in the figure weighs 300 N. Find the tension in the cable and the force exerted on the boom by the vertical mast.

7

Answer
650 N, 789 N, 41.7°

If you solved this problem correctly, go to frame 14. If you could not solve this problem, go through frames 8–13.

8 Since the sketch was given, we will proceed with *Step 2.* Choose *ABC* as the body under consideration. Draw a free-body diagram. Since the boom *ABC* is uniform, its weight (300 N) may be considered as acting as its center of gravity which is 3 m from *A*.

8

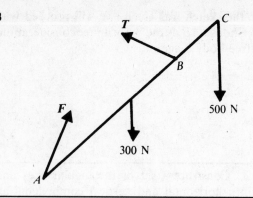

9 Construct a set of rectangular axes and resolve into horizontal and vertical components all forces acting on the body.

9

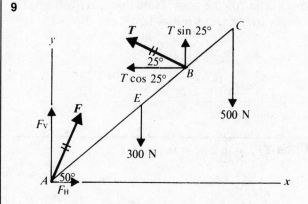

10 Set $\Sigma F_x = 0$; $\Sigma F_y = 0$.

10

$\Sigma F_x = F_H - T \cos 25° = 0$
$\Sigma F_y = F_V + T \sin 25° - 800\ N = 0$

11 Take torques about *A*. To repeat, this is a good choice. Since the perpendicular distances from the axis of rotation *A* to the lines of action of F_V and F_H are zero, the torques will be zero.
Note: The $\perp$ distance from *A* to the 300 N force is 3 m cos 50° = 1.93 m; $\perp$ distance from *A* to the 500 N force is 6 m cos 50° = 3.86 m. The $\perp$ distance from *A* to $T \sin 25° = 4$ m cos 50° = 2.57 m, and the $\perp$ distance from *A* to $T \cos 25° = 4$ m cos 40° = 3.06 m.

11

$\Sigma \Gamma_A = 0$
$T \sin 25°(2.57\ m) + T \cos 25°(3.06\ m)$
$\quad - 300\ N(1.93\ m) - 500\ N(3.86\ m) = 0$
$\quad T = 650\ N$

Note ⟳ +

12 Calculate F_H, F_V,
$F_H = T \cos 25°$, $F_V = 800\ N - T \sin 25°$.

12

$F_H = T \cos 25° = 650\ N(\cos 25°) = 589\ N$
$F_V = 800\ N - T(\sin 25°)$
$\quad = 800\ N - 650\ N(\sin 25°) = 525\ N$

13 Find *F* by using $F = \sqrt{F_H{}^2 + F_V{}^2}$. Draw a sketch.
$\text{Tan}\ \theta = \dfrac{|F_V|}{|F_H|}$.

13

$F = \sqrt{(589\ N)^2 + (525\ N)^2}$
$\quad = 789\ N$
$\tan \theta = \dfrac{|F_V|}{|F_H|} = \dfrac{525\ N}{589\ N}$
$\quad \theta = 41.7°$

14 **Problem 3** A uniform ladder 5 m long weighing 300 N rests against a vertical frictionless wall with its lower end 3 m from the wall. A man weighing 700 N climbs slowly up the ladder and it starts to slip when he has climbed 2 m along the ladder. Find the coefficient of static friction between the ladder and the floor.

14

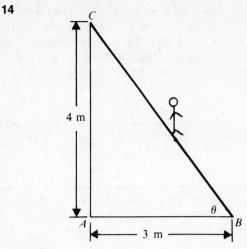

Answer

0.323

If you could not solve this problem go through frames 15–20.

15 Since the sketch was given, we will proceed with *Step 2*; choose *CB* (the ladder) as the body under consideration. Draw a free-body diagram. Since the wall is frictionless, it exerts a horizontal force on the ladder.

15

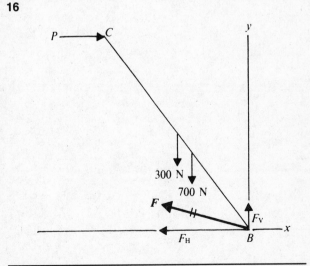

---

16 *Step 3* Construct a set of rectangular axes and resolve into horizontal and vertical components all forces acting on the body. Note that $\triangle ABC$ is a 3, 4, 5 right triangle, $\sin \theta = 4/5$, $\cos \theta = 3/5$.

16

---

17 *Step 4* Set $\Sigma F_x = 0$; $\Sigma F_y = 0$.

17

$$\Sigma F_x = P - F_H = 0$$
$$\Sigma F_y = F_V - 1000 \text{ N} = 0$$

---

18 *Step 5* Take torques about *B*. *Note*: The $\perp$ distance from *B* to the line of action of the 700 N force is 2 m cos θ = 1.2 m; the $\perp$ distance from *B* to the line of action of the 300 N force is 2.5 m cos θ = 1.5 m; the $\perp$ distance from *B* to the line of action of *P* is 4 m.

18

$\Sigma\Gamma_B = 0$

$700\text{ N}(1.2\text{ m}) + 300\text{ N}(1.5\text{ m}) - P(4\text{ m}) = 0$

$\qquad P = 323\text{ N}$

---

19 Calculate F_H. Note that, from frame 17, $F_V = 1000$ N.

19 $\quad F_H = P = 323$ N

---

20 Calculate $\mu_s = \mathcal{I}_s / \mathcal{N}$, where $\mathcal{I}_s = F_H$ and $\mathcal{N} = F_V$.

20

$$\mu_s = \frac{F_H}{F_V}$$

$$= \frac{323\text{ N}}{1000\text{ N}} = 0.323$$

Note the difference between this problem and Problem 2 in the Step by Step Solution of Problems section. In this case F_H is the force of static friction $\mathcal{I}_s$ and F_V is the normal force $\mathcal{N}$. In the problem cited, the reverse is true; i.e., F_H is the normal force $\mathcal{N}$ and F_V is the force of static friction $\mathcal{I}_s$.

11

Periodic Motion

CHAPTER SUMMARY

Previously we dealt with bodies in motion in a circle with constant speed or in a straight line with constant acceleration; here we are concerned with a special case of motion where the acceleration is not constant but varies due to a variable restoring force. Simple harmonic motion is best exemplified in the spring and the simple pendulum. Equations for displacement, velocity and acceleration in simple harmonic motion are developed on the basis of the circle of reference. In addition, equations for angular harmonic motion, of which the physical pendulum is an example, are derived and damped and forced oscillations are studied.

BASIC TERMS — *Give definitions or meanings for the following:*

periodic motion (11-I)
oscillation (11-I)
cycle (11-1)
hertz (11-1)
frequency (11-1)
period (11-1)
amplitude (11-1)
simple harmonic motion (11-1)
circle of reference (11-3)
phasor (11-3)

angular frequency (11-3)
phase angle (11-3)
angular simple harmonic motion (11-4)
isochronous (11-4)
simple pendulum (11-5)
physical pendulum (11-6)
damped oscillation (11-7)
damping (11-7)
forced oscillation (11-7)
resonance (11-7)

PROGRAMMED QUIZ

1 Frames 1–6 refer to a particle in simple harmonic motion. What is the relationship between the frequency and the amplitude?

1 No relation, the frequency is independent of the amplitude.

2 At which point is the speed of the object maximum?

2 At the equilibrium position, since
$v = \omega \sqrt{A^2 - x^2}$, $v_{max} = \omega A$ at this point.

3 What is the relationship between maximum potential and maximum kinetic energies?

3 The maximum potential energy is equal to the maximum kinetic energy:

$$U = \frac{1}{2}kx^2,$$
$$U_{max} = \frac{1}{2}kA^2;$$
$$K = \frac{k}{2}(A^2 - x^2),$$
$$K_{max} = \frac{k}{2}A^2.$$

4 At the equilibrium position, what is the acceleration of the particle? Why doesn't it stop here?

4 The acceleration is zero but the velocity is not zero. Therefore the particle overshoots this point.

5 Write an expression for the force on the particle in terms of Newton's second law and Hooke's law.

5 $F = ma = -kx$.

6 What kind of force is this?

6 F is a restoring force. When the displacement is to the right, F acts to the left.

7 What is a hertz a unit of? What does 1 hertz equal?

7 Frequency; 1 Hz = 1 cycle $\cdot$ s^{-1}

8 In simple harmonic motion total mechanical energy is conserved. What does this mean?

8 The sum of the kinetic and potential energies is a constant; $E = \frac{1}{2}mv^2 + \frac{1}{2}kx^2 = $ constant.

9 Why isn't mass included in the equation for the frequency of a simple pendulum?

9 The mass appears on both sides of the equation since the restoring force is proportional to the mass. Therefore, the mass cancels out.

10 Why does a clock keep constant time even though it may run down and the amplitude become smaller?

10 The period is independent of the amplitude. Therefore, the period is constant even though the amplitude decreases.

11 How can oil deposits be found using a simple pendulum?

11 An area with an oil deposit has a different density than the surroundings, therefore the acceleration due to gravity is different. This can be determined by measuring the period with the simple pendulum.

12 How are these two equations for simple harmonic motion related:
$$x = A \sin(\omega t + \theta_0) \text{ and } x = B \sin \omega t + C \cos \omega t?$$

12

$$x = A \sin(\omega t + \theta_0)$$
$$= A(\sin \omega t \cos \theta_0 + \cos \omega t \sin \theta_0).$$
If $\theta_0 = $ constant, then $A \cos \theta_0 = B$ and $A \sin \theta_0 = C$
$$\therefore x = B \sin \omega t + C \cos \omega t$$

13 Which would you take with you to keep time on the moon: a pendulum or a mass on a spring?

13 A mass on a spring since its period is not dependent on the acceleration due to gravity.

---

14 What is the relationship between uniform circular and simple harmonic motion?

14 Simple harmonic motion is the projection of a point moving around a circle at constant speed.

---

15 What is the product of the frequency and the period equal to?

15 One; since
$$f = \frac{1}{\tau} \; ; f\tau = 1$$

MAIN IDEAS

1 Characteristics of simple harmonic motion. It is motion in a straight line, periodic or oscillating, and the acceleration of the body at any time is proportional to the negative of the displacement (i.e., the acceleration vector is oppositely directed to the displacement vector).

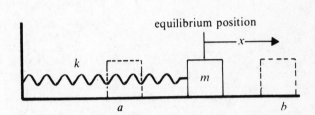

2 Hooke's law. If the spring in the figure obeys Hooke's law, then $F = -kx$, where F is the restoring force, k is the force constant, and x is the displacement from the equilibrium position. From Newton's second law it follows that $a = -\dfrac{k}{m} x$. If the body moves from a to b and back again, we say that it has made one complete vibration or cycle. The period τ of this motion is the time required to make one cycle. The frequency f is the number of cycles or vibrations completed per second, $f = \dfrac{1}{\tau}$, 1 cycle/s = 1 Hz (hertz). The amplitude A of the motion is the maximum value of the displacement. When a mass m is executing simple harmonic motion, the total mechanical energy $E = K + U$ = constant. At maximum displacement, $v = 0$ and $x = A$. Thus we have $\frac{1}{2}mv^2 + \frac{1}{2}kx^2 = \frac{1}{2}kA^2$. Solving for v we obtain

$$v = \pm \sqrt{\frac{k}{m}} \sqrt{A^2 - x^2} \text{ and } v_{\max} = A \sqrt{\frac{k}{m}}$$

(since v = maximum at $x = 0$).

A plot of $U = \frac{1}{2}kx^2$ is very informative. Draw a horizontal line at ordinate $U = \frac{1}{2}kA^2$ intersecting the parabola at two points. Construct a vertical line at any x (for example B) between $-A$ and A. $BC = U$ represents the potential energy and $CD = K$ the kinetic energy.

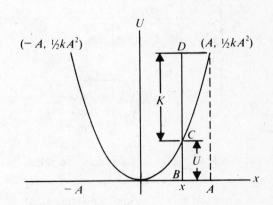

3 Circle of reference. A particle Q is rotating in a circle of radius A with uniform speed v and angular speed ω. Q will experience a centripetal acceleration $a_\perp = \dfrac{v_\parallel^2}{A} = \omega^2 A$ which is directed toward O.

Remember that $\omega = 2\pi f$, where f is the number of revolutions per second.

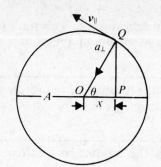

Consider the motion (SHM) of P, the projection of Q on the x-axis:

displacement of $P = x = A \cos \theta$,
acceleration of $P = -a_\perp \cos \theta$,
velocity of $P = -v_\parallel \sin \theta$.

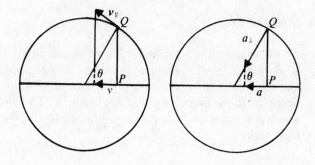

4 Summary of the instantaneous values of the displacement, restoring force, acceleration and velocity at $\dfrac{\pi}{2}$ intervals in the motion of a particle executing SHM at the end of a spring.

Displacement x	Restoring Force F	Acceleration a	Velocity v
A	$-kx$	$-A\omega^2$	0
0	0	0	$-A\omega$
$-A$	$-kx$	$A\omega^2$	0
0	0	0	$A\omega$
A	$-kx$	$-A\omega^2$	0

5 Summary of useful relationships for SHM.

force $\qquad\qquad\qquad\qquad\qquad\qquad\qquad F = -kx$
acceleration as a function of displacement $\qquad a = -\omega^2 x$
displacement as a function of time $\qquad\qquad x = A \cos \omega t$

velocity as a function of displacement $\qquad v = \pm\omega\sqrt{A^2 - x^2}$
velocity as a function of time $\qquad\qquad v = -\omega A \sin \omega t$
acceleration as a function of time $\qquad\qquad a = -\omega^2 A \cos \omega t$

potential energy	$U = \frac{1}{2}kx^2$
kinetic energy	$K = \frac{1}{2}mv^2 = \frac{1}{2}k(A^2 - x^2)$
total mechanical energy	$E = \frac{1}{2}mv^2 + \frac{1}{2}kx^2 = \frac{1}{2}kA^2$
period	$\tau = 2\pi\sqrt{\dfrac{-x}{a}} = 2\pi\sqrt{\dfrac{m}{k}}$
period of simple pendulum	$\tau = 2\pi\sqrt{\dfrac{L}{g}}$
angular velocity	$\omega^2 = \dfrac{k}{m}$

6 Angular harmonic motion. If a body, pivoted about an axis, experiences a restoring torque such that $\Gamma = -k'\theta$, where k' = torque constant and θ is the angular displacement, then the body is undergoing angular harmonic motion.

7 Physical pendulum. An irregularly shaped body is pivoted at O, distance h from the center of gravity. The period of oscillation of the physical pendulum is

$\tau = 2\pi\sqrt{\dfrac{I}{mgh}}$ where m is the mass of the body,

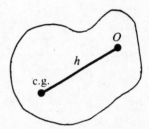

I the moment of inertia about O, and h the distance from O to the center of gravity.

8 Center of percussion. Consider a point C, distance L from O. Assume that the entire mass of the body is concentrated at C and that this point mass is suspended from a string of length L. Then the resulting simple pendulum would have the same period as the original physical pendulum. Point C is defined as the center of percussion or oscillation.

9 Damped and forced oscillations (resonance). Dissipative forces like friction will cause a decrease in amplitude of an oscillating system. This type of motion is called damped oscillation. By applying a driving force to the system, we can maintain oscillations of constant amplitude. The amplitude of a forced oscillation will be greatest when the driving frequency is close to the natural frequency of the system. When there is a small amount of damping, the driving frequency passes through the natural oscillation frequency of the system and resonance occurs.

10 Problem solving strategy:

Step 1 Identify the basic physical quantities of the system such as m, k, τ, ω. Identify the quantities that describe the motion such as A, v_{max}, ϕ_0, x, v, t.

Step 2 If the problem does not involve time t, use $a = -\dfrac{k}{m}x$ or $v = \pm\sqrt{\dfrac{k}{m}}\sqrt{A^2 - x^2}$.

Step 3 When information is given involving x, v, and a at various times t, use

$$x = A\cos(\omega t + \phi_0),$$
$$v = -\omega A\sin(\omega t + \phi_0),$$
$$a = -\omega^2 A\cos(\omega t + \phi_0) = -\omega^2 x.$$

Step 4 If $x_0 \neq 0$ and $v_0 \neq 0$, use

$$A^2 = v_0^2 + \frac{v_0^2}{\omega^2} \quad \text{and} \quad \tan\phi_0 = -\frac{v_0}{\omega_0 x_0}.$$

Step 5 When energy quantities are required; use
$$E = \frac{1}{2}mv^2 + \frac{1}{2}kx^2 = \text{constant} \quad \text{and} \quad E = \frac{1}{2}kA^2.$$

1 Frames 1–11 refer to the following problem: A 0.5 kg body suspended from a spring is undergoing simple harmonic motion due to an elastic restoring force of force constant $k = 50$ N $\cdot$ m^{-1}. Construct a graph of U (elastic potential energy) as a function of x (displacement) over a range of x from -0.3 m to $+0.3$ m.

1

x (cm)	$\frac{1}{2}kx^2 = U$(J)
-0.3	2.25
-0.2	1.00
-0.1	0.25
0	0
$+0.1$	0.25
$+0.2$	1.00
$+0.3$	2.25

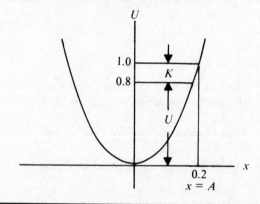

2 If the initial potential energy is 0.8 J and the initial kinetic energy is 0.2 J, what is the amplitude of oscillation? Check answer with graph.

2

$$\frac{1}{2}kA^2 = E = K + U$$

$$\frac{1}{2}(50 \text{ N} \cdot \text{m}^{-1})A^2 = 0.2 \text{ J} + 0.8 \text{ J} = 1.0 \text{ J}$$

$$A = 0.2 \text{ m}$$

(*Note*: At the endpoint the energy is all potential.) Graphically, find the displacement for $U = 1$ J.

3 What is the speed of the body at the midpoint of its path?

3 At the midpoint the energy is all kinetic and thus the speed has a maximum value,

$$\frac{1}{2}mv_{\max}^2 = \frac{1}{2}kA^2 = E$$

$$\frac{1}{2}(0.5 \text{ kg})v_{\max}^2 = 1.0 \text{ J}$$

$$v_{\max} = 2 \text{ m} \cdot \text{s}^{-1}$$

4 What is the potential energy when the displacement is $\frac{1}{2}$ the amplitude? Check with graph.

4

$$U = \frac{1}{2} kx^2$$

$$= \frac{1}{2} (50 \text{ N} \cdot \text{m}^{-1}) (0.1 \text{ m})^2$$

$$= 0.25 \text{ J}$$

Graphically, find U for $x = 0.1$ m.

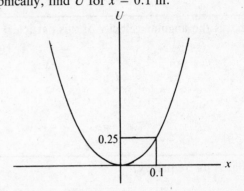

5 At what displacement are the kinetic and potential energies equal? Check with graph.

5

$$K + U = E$$
$$\text{if } K = U, \text{ then } 2U = E$$
$$2(\frac{1}{2} kx^2) = E$$
$$x^2 = \frac{1 \text{ J}}{50 \text{ N} \cdot \text{m}^{-1}}$$
$$x = 0.141 \text{ m}$$

Graphically, find x for $U = 0.5$ J.

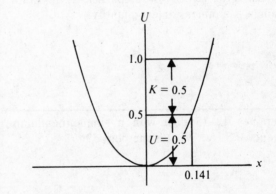

6 Draw a circle of reference for the motion of the body. Remember that the amplitude of the motion is equal to the radius of the circle of reference.

6

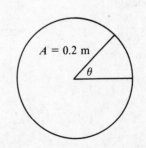

7 Based on the circle of reference, what is the angular displacement of the particle at this point?

7

$$x = A \cos \theta$$

$$\cos \theta = \frac{0.1414 \text{ m}}{0.2 \text{ m}}$$

$$\theta = 45°$$

---

8 What is the angular velocity of this particle?

8

$$\omega^2 = \frac{k}{m}$$

$$= \frac{50 \text{ N} \cdot \text{m}^{-1}}{0.5 \text{ kg}}$$

$$\omega = 10 \text{ rad} \cdot \text{s}^{-1}$$

---

9 What is its frequency?

9

$$\omega = 2\pi f$$

$$f = \frac{10 \text{ s}^{-1}}{2\pi} = 1.59 \text{ s}^{-1}$$

---

10 Find the time required for the particle to move through the angle $\theta = 45°$. ($180° = \pi$ rad; $45° = \frac{\pi}{4}$ rad.)

10

$$\theta = \omega t$$

$$= 45° = 0.785 \text{ rad} = 10 \text{ rad} \cdot \text{s}^{-1}(t)$$

$$t = 0.0785 \text{ s}$$

---

11 What is the velocity of the particle at this point? (A radian is a dimensionless quantity.)

11

$$v = -\omega A \sin \omega t$$
$$= -(10 \text{ rad} \cdot \text{s}^{-1})(0.2 \text{ m}) \sin [(10 \text{ rad} \cdot \text{s}^{-1})(0.0785 \text{ s})]$$
$$= -2 \text{ m} \cdot \text{s}^{-1} \sin (0.785 \text{ rad})$$
$$= -1.41 \text{ m} \cdot \text{s}^{-1}$$

---

12 Frames 12–15 deal with a simple pendulum, frequency 0.8 Hz. What is the period?

12

$$\tau = \frac{1}{f}$$

$$= \frac{1}{0.8 \text{ s}^{-1}} = 1.25 \text{ s}$$

---

13 What is its length?

13

$$\tau = 2\pi \sqrt{\frac{L}{g}}$$

$$L = \frac{\tau^2 g}{4\pi^2}$$

$$= \frac{(1.25 \text{ s})^2 (9.8 \text{ m} \cdot \text{s}^{-2})}{4\pi^2}$$

$$= 0.388 \text{ m}$$

---

14 What is its frequency on the moon where $g_{moon} = \frac{1}{6} g_{earth}$?

14

$$\tau_{moon} = 2\pi \sqrt{\frac{L}{g_{moon}}} = 2\pi \sqrt{\frac{L}{g_{earth}/6}}$$

$$= \sqrt{6}\left(2\pi \sqrt{\frac{L}{g_{earth}}}\right) = \sqrt{6}\,\tau_{earth}$$

But $f_{moon} = \dfrac{1}{\tau_{moon}}$

$$= \frac{1}{\sqrt{6}(1.25\ s)}$$

$$= 0.327\ Hz$$

---

15 At what distance from the center of gravity must a physical pendulum be suspended if it is to have the same period? The moment of inertia of the physical pendulum is $0.2\ kg \cdot m^2$; the mass is $0.4\ kg$.

15

$$\tau = 2\pi \sqrt{\frac{I}{mgh}}$$

$$h = \frac{4\pi^2 I}{mg\tau^2}$$

$$= \frac{4\pi^2\ (0.2\ kg \cdot m^2)}{0.4\ kg\ (9.8\ m \cdot s^{-2})\ (1.25\ s)^2}$$

$$= 1.29\ m$$

---

16 A $0.20\ kg$ mass attached to a spring is in SHM in a horizontal plane. If the spring has a force constant of $2 \times 10^4\ N \cdot m^{-1}$ and a total vibrational energy of 4 J, find the amplitude of vibration.

16

Total energy $E = K + U$

$$= \tfrac{1}{2}mv^2 + \tfrac{1}{2}kx^2$$

At the maximum displacement from equilibrium, $v = 0$.

$$E = \tfrac{1}{2}m\ (0)^2 + \tfrac{1}{2}kA^2$$

$$A = \sqrt{\frac{2E}{k}} = \sqrt{\frac{2(4\ J)}{2 \times 10^4\ N \cdot m^{-1}}}$$

$$= 2 \times 10^{-2}\ m$$

---

17 Find the maximum velocity.

17 The maximum velocity occurs at the equilibrium position, $x = 0$.

$$E = \tfrac{1}{2}m(v_{max})^2 + \tfrac{1}{2}k(0)^2$$

$$v_{max} = \pm \sqrt{\frac{2E}{m}} = \sqrt{\frac{2(4\ J)}{0.20\ kg}}$$

$$= \pm 6.32\ m \cdot s^{-1}$$

---

18 Find the period, the time required to complete one vibration.

18

$$\tau = 2\sqrt{\frac{m}{k}}$$

$$= 2\sqrt{\frac{0.20\ kg}{2 \times 10^4\ N \cdot m^{-1}}}$$

$$= 0.0199\ s$$

19 An object of mass 0.20 kg hangs from a long spiral spring. It is pulled down 0.15 m below its equilibrium position and released. If it is oscillating with a period of 1.8 s, find the spring constant k.

19

$$\tau = 2\pi \sqrt{\frac{m}{k}}$$

$$k = \frac{4\pi^2 m}{\tau^2}$$

$$= \frac{4\pi^2 (0.20 \text{ kg})}{(1.8 \text{ s})^2}$$

$$= 2.44 \text{ N} \cdot \text{m}^{-1}$$

---

20 Through what distance was the spring stretched by the mass?

20

$$F = k\Delta y$$
$$mg = k\Delta y$$
$$(0.20 \text{ kg})(9.8 \text{ m} \cdot \text{s}^{-2}) = (2.44 \text{ N} \cdot \text{m}^{-1}) \Delta y$$
$$\Delta y = 0.803 \text{ m}$$

---

21 What is the velocity of the mass as it passes through the equilibrium position? At the equilibrium position $y = 0$.

21

$$\tfrac{1}{2}mv^2 + \tfrac{1}{2}ky^2 = \tfrac{1}{2}kA^2$$
$$\tfrac{1}{2}mv^2 = \tfrac{1}{2}kA^2$$

$$v = \sqrt{\frac{k}{m}}\, A$$

$$= \sqrt{\frac{2.44 \text{ N} \cdot \text{m}^{-1}}{0.20 \text{ kg}}}\, (0.15 \text{ m})$$

$$= 0.524 \text{ m} \cdot \text{s}^{-1} \text{ upward}$$

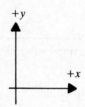

---

22 What is the acceleration of the mass when it is 0.04 m above the equilibrium position?

22

$$a = -\frac{k}{m}\, y$$

$$= \frac{-2.44 \text{ N} \cdot \text{m}^{-1}}{0.20 \text{ kg}}\, (0.04 \text{ m})$$

$$= -0.488 \text{ m} \cdot \text{s}^{-2}$$

The acceleration vector is directed downward.

23 How much time is required for the mass to move from 0.04 m below its equilibrium position to a point 0.04 m above it? Use $y = -A \cos \omega t$.

	$y = +0.15$ m
$t = t_2$	$y = +0.04$ m
	$y = 0$
$t = t_1$	$y = -0.04$ m
$t = t_0$	$y = -0.15$ m

Find the time t_1 for the mass to go from $y = -0.15$ m to $y = -0.04$ m and the time t_2 for the mass to go from $y = -0.15$ m to $y = +0.04$ m

23

$$\omega = \frac{2\pi}{\tau} = \frac{2\pi}{1.8 \text{ s}} = 3.49 \text{ s}^{-1}$$

$$y = -A \cos 3.49t$$

At $t = 0$,

$$y = -A \cos \omega \cdot 0 = -A.$$

At t_1, $y = -0.04$ m,

$$-0.04 = -0.15 \cos 3.49t_1$$

$$\cos 3.49t_1 = 0.267$$

$$3.49t_1 = 74.5°$$

$$= 74.5° \left(\frac{\pi \text{ rad}}{180°} \right)$$

$$= 1.30 \text{ rad}$$

$$t_1 = 0.373 \text{ s}.$$

At t_2, $y = +0.04$ m,

$$+0.04 = -0.15 \cos 3.49t_2$$

$$\cos 3.49t_2 = 0.267$$

$$3.49t_2 = 105.5° \left(\frac{\pi \text{ rad}}{180°} \right)$$

$$= 1.84 \text{ rad}$$

$$t_2 = 0.528 \text{ s}.$$

$$t_2 - t_1 = 0.528 \text{ s} - 0.373 \text{ s}$$

$$= 0.155 \text{ s}$$

STEP BY STEP SOLUTIONS OF PROBLEMS

Problem 1 A 4 kg body hangs from a spring and oscillates with a period of 1.5 s upon being pulled down 0.12 m below its equilibrium position and released. Find a) the force constant of the spring, b) the maximum velocity, c) the maximum acceleration, d) the total energy of the system, e) the time required for the body to move 0.06 m upward from its initial position.

1 Find the force constant by using

$$\tau = 2\pi \sqrt{\frac{m}{k}} .$$

1

$$k = \frac{4\pi^2 m}{\tau^2}$$

$$= \frac{4\pi^2 (4 \text{ kg})}{(1.5 \text{ s})^2}$$

$$= 70.1 \text{ N} \cdot \text{m}^{-1}$$

2 Using $v = \pm \omega \sqrt{A^2 - x^2}$, find the maximum velocity. Remember that $\omega = 2\pi f = \frac{2\pi}{\tau}$, , since $\tau = 1/f$.

2 The maximum velocity occurs at the equilibrium position, $x = 0$. Thus, $v_{max} = \pm \omega A$.

$$v_{max} = \pm \frac{2\pi A}{\tau}$$

$$= \pm \frac{2\pi (0.12 \text{ m})}{1.5 \text{ s}}$$

$$= \pm 0.502 \text{ m} \cdot \text{s}^{-1}$$

3 Using $a = -\omega^2 x$, find the maximum acceleration. Note that we could also have used $a = -\dfrac{k}{m} x$.

3 The maximum acceleration occurs at the top and bottom of the oscillation, $x = \pm A$. Therefore,

$$a_{max} = \mp \omega^2 A = \mp \frac{4\pi^2 A}{\tau^2}$$

$$= \mp \frac{4\pi^2 (0.12 \text{ m})}{(1.5 \text{ s})^2}$$

$$= \mp 2.10 \text{ m} \cdot \text{s}^{-1}$$

---

4 To find the total energy of the system, we use $E = K + U$ where E = total energy, K = kinetic energy of the body = $\frac{1}{2}mv^2$, and U = elastic potential energy = $\frac{1}{2}kx^2$. At maximum displacement ($x = A$), $v = 0$. Hence $E = \frac{1}{2}kA^2$.

4

$$E = \frac{1}{2} kA^2$$

$$= \frac{1}{2} (70.1 \text{ N} \cdot \text{m}^{-1}) (0.12 \text{ m})^2$$

$$= 0.505 \text{ J}$$

---

5 Verify that the total energy of the system is 0.505 J when the body is 0.04 m above its equilibrium position.

5

$$\omega = \frac{2\pi}{\tau} = \frac{2\pi}{1.5 \text{ s}} = 4.19 \text{ s}^{-1}$$

$$v = \omega \sqrt{A^2 - x^2}$$

$$= 4.19 \text{ s}^{-1} \sqrt{(0.12 \text{ m})^2 - (0.04 \text{ m})^2}$$

$$= 0.474 \text{ m} \cdot \text{s}^{-1}$$

$$E = K + U = \frac{1}{2} mv^2 + \frac{1}{2} kx^2$$

$$= \frac{1}{2} (4 \text{ kg}) (0.474 \text{ m} \cdot \text{s}^{-1})^2 + \frac{1}{2} (70.1 \text{ N} \cdot \text{m}^{-1})$$

$$(0.04 \text{ m})^2$$

$$= 0.505 \text{ J}$$

---

6 In order to find the time required for the body to move 0.06 m upward from its initial position, we make use of the reference circle and the equation $\omega = \theta/t$.

6 When the body moves 0.06 m up from its initial position, the corresponding reference point moves from Q_1 to Q_2 through an angle of 60°. Since the reference point has a constant angular velocity $\omega = 4.19 \text{ s}^{-1}$ and $60° = \dfrac{\pi}{3}$ rad, $t = \dfrac{\theta}{\omega}$,

$$t = \frac{\pi/3}{4.19 \text{ s}^{-1}}$$

$$= 0.250 \text{ s}.$$

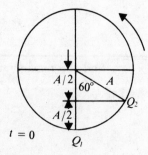
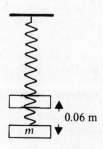

Problem 2 A mass of 6 kg is suspended from a spring. a) What additional force should be applied to the mass so that the spring will oscillate at 1.5 Hz when it is stretched 0.08 m? b) What force is exerted by the spring on the mass when it is at the lowest point? equilibrium? the highest point? c) Compute the total energy of the system when the body is 0.03 m below the equilibrium position.

7 Calculate the period from $\tau = 1/f$.

7

$$\tau = \frac{1}{1.5 \text{ s}^{-1}} = 0.667 \text{ s}$$

---

8 Calculate the spring constant from

$$\tau = 2\pi \sqrt{\frac{m}{k}} \, .$$

8

$$k = \frac{4\pi^2 \, m}{\tau^2}$$

$$= \frac{4\pi^2 \, (6 \text{ kg})}{(0.667 \text{ s})^2} = 532 \text{ N} \cdot \text{m}^{-1}$$

---

9 The additional force can be obtained from Hooke's law.

9

$$F = kx$$
$$= (532 \text{ N} \cdot \text{m}^{-1}) \, (0.08 \text{ m}) = 42.6 \text{ N}$$

---

10 The upward force that the spring exerts on the body is equal to the weight of the body and the elastic restoring force; $F = mg - kx$.

10 At the lowest point,
$$F = 6 \text{ kg} (9.8 \text{ m} \cdot \text{s}^{-2}) - (532 \text{ N} \cdot \text{m}^{-1}) \, (-0.08 \text{ m})$$
$$= 101 \text{ N}.$$
At equilibrium,
$$F = 6 \text{ kg} (9.8 \text{ m} \cdot \text{s}^{-2}) - 532 \, (0) = 58.8 \text{ N}.$$
At the highest point,
$$F = 6 \text{ kg} (9.8 \text{ m} \cdot \text{s}^{-2}) - (532 \text{ N} \cdot \text{m}^{-1}) \, (0.08 \text{ m})$$
$$= 16.2 \text{ N}.$$

---

11 In order to calculate the total energy, we must determine the kinetic energy and the elastic potential energy. Since $K = \frac{1}{2}mv^2$, we must first find ω and v.

11

$$\omega = 2\pi f = 2\pi \, (1.5 \text{ s}^{-1}) = 9.42 \text{ s}^{-1}$$
$$v = \omega \sqrt{A^2 - x^2}$$
$$= 9.42 \text{ s}^{-1} \sqrt{(0.08 \text{ m})^2 - (0.03 \text{ m})^2}$$
$$= 0.699 \text{ m} \cdot \text{s}^{-1}$$
$$K = \frac{1}{2} mv^2 = \frac{1}{2} \, (6 \text{ kg}) \, (0.699 \text{ m} \cdot \text{s}^{-1})^2$$
$$= 1.47 \text{ J}$$
$$U = \frac{1}{2} kx^2 = \frac{1}{2} \, (532 \text{ N} \cdot \text{m}^{-1}) \, (0.03 \text{ m})^2$$
$$= 0.239 \text{ J}$$
$$E = K + U = 1.47 \text{ J} + 0.239 \text{ J} = 1.71 \text{ J}$$
This result checks with

$$E = \frac{1}{2} kA^2$$

$$= \frac{1}{2} \, (532 \text{ N} \cdot \text{m}^{-1}) \, (0.08 \text{ m})^2$$

$$= 1.70 \text{ J}$$

Problem 3   Two springs are attached to a block and to fixed supports as shown. Find the effective force constant, i.e., the value k_{eff} for a single spring which will give the same resultant force on the block.

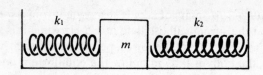

12   Displace the block a distance x to the right and draw a free-body diagram depicting F_1 due to spring 1 and F_2 due to spring 2. Spring 1 is stretched and spring 2 is compressed; thus spring 1 is pulling on the block to the left and spring 2 is pusing on the block to the left.

12

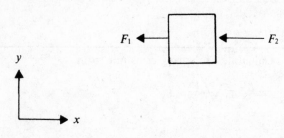

13   Using $F_1 = -k_1x_1$, $F_2 = -k_2x_2$ and $x_1 = x_2 = x$, find the resultant force on m.

13

$$\Sigma F_x = F_1 + F_2$$
$$= -k_1x_1 - k_2x_2$$
$$= -k_1x - k_2x$$
$$= -(k_1 + k_2)x$$

14   What is k_{eff}? Why?

14 $k_{eff} = k_1 + k_2$ because a single spring with a force constant $(k_1 + k_2)$ will give the same resultant force on the block equivalent to the combination of these two springs.

Problem 4   What is the effective force constant of two springs which are connected in parallel as shown in the diagram? The block m is on a horizontal frictionless surface. If the block is displaced from equilibrium, what will be its period?

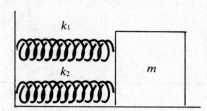

15   Displace the block a distance x to the right. Draw a free-body diagram and determine the resultant force on the block.

15

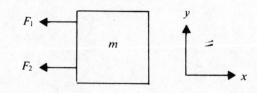

$$\Sigma F_x = F_1 + F_2$$

16   What is F_1 equal to in terms of the stretch (displacement) of the springs? What about F_2?

16

$$F_1 = -k_1x_1$$
$$F_2 = -k_2x_2$$

17 What is the relationship between x_1, x_2 and x?	**17** $x_1 = x_2 = x$
18 Substitute the above in the equation in frame 15.	**18** $$\Sigma F_x = -k_1 x - k_2 x$$ $$= -(k_1 + k_2)x$$
19 What is k_{eff}? Why?	**19** $$k_{eff} = k_1 + k_2.$$ In accordance with our definition, a single spring with a force constant $(k_1 + k_2)$ will have the same result-ant force as two springs connected in parallel.
20 What will be the period of this block?	**20** $$\tau = 2\pi \sqrt{\frac{m}{k_{eff}}} = 2\pi \sqrt{\frac{m}{k_1 + k_2}}$$

The effective force constant of n springs connected in parallel is $k_{eff} = k_1 + k_2 + \ldots k_n$.

PROGRAMMED TEST

1 ***Problem 1*** A small body is undergoing simple harmonic motion on a frictionless horizontal surface with an amplitude of 0.13 m. At a point 0.05 m from equilibrium the velocity is $0.24 \text{ m} \cdot \text{s}^{-1}$. a) What is the period? b) What is the displacement and the acceler-ation when the velocity is $\pm 0.10 \text{ m} \cdot \text{s}^{-1}$?	**1** ***Answer*** $3.14 \text{ s}, 0.12 \text{ m}, -0.48 \text{ m} \cdot \text{s}^{-2}$

If you solved this problem correctly, go to frame 5. If you could not solve this problem, go through frames 2–4.

2 Compute the period by calculating ω.	**2** $$v = \pm \omega \sqrt{A^2 - x^2}$$ $$0.24 \text{ m} \cdot \text{s}^{-1} = \omega \sqrt{(0.13 \text{ m})^2 - (0.05 \text{ m})^2}$$ $$\omega = 2 \text{ s}^{-1}$$ $$\tau = \frac{2\pi}{\omega} = \frac{2\pi}{2 \text{ s}^{-1}} = 3.14 \text{ s}$$
3 Solve for the displacement.	**3** $$v = \pm \omega \sqrt{A^2 - x^2}$$ $$0.10 \text{ m} \cdot \text{s}^{-1} = \pm 2 \text{ s}^{-1} \sqrt{(0.13 \text{ m})^2 - x^2}$$ $$0.01 \text{ m}^2 \cdot \text{s}^{-2} = \pm 4 \text{ s}^{-2} (0.0169 \text{ m}^2 - x^2)$$ $$x = 0.12 \text{ m}$$
4 Find the acceleration at $x = 0.12$ m.	**4** $$a = -\omega^2 x = -(2 \text{ s}^{-1})^2 (0.12 \text{ m}) = -0.48 \text{ m} \cdot \text{s}^{-2}$$ If the body is moving to the right, the acceleration will be directed toward the left.

5 *Problem 2* When a 1 kg mass is hung from a spring, it stretches by 0.04 m. The spring is now stretched 0.05 m from its equilibrium position and released. Find a) the force constant of the spring, b) the period of the motion, c) the maximum velocity, and d) the maximum acceleration.

5

Answer

$196 \text{ N} \cdot \text{m}^{-1}$, 0.448 s, $0.7 \text{ m} \cdot \text{s}^{-1}$, $-9.8 \text{ m} \cdot \text{s}^{-2}$

If you solved this problem correctly, go to frame 10. If you could not solve this problem, go through frames 6–9.

6 Find the force constant using Hooke's law.

6

$$F = ky$$
$$k = \frac{F}{y} = \frac{mg}{y}$$
$$= \frac{1 \text{ kg } (9.8 \text{ m} \cdot \text{s}^{-2})}{0.05 \text{ m}}$$
$$= 196 \text{ N} \cdot \text{m}^{-1}$$

7 Find the period.

7

$$\tau = 2\pi \sqrt{\frac{m}{k}}$$
$$= 2\pi \sqrt{\frac{1 \text{ kg}}{196 \text{ N} \cdot \text{m}^{-1}}}$$
$$= 0.448 \text{ s}$$

8 Before you can find the maximum velocity, calculate f and ω.

8

$$f = \frac{1}{\tau}$$
$$= \frac{1}{0.448 \text{ s}} = 2.23 \text{ Hz}$$
$$\omega = 2\pi f = 2\pi(2.23 \text{ s}^{-1}) = 14.0 \text{ s}^{-1}$$
$$v_{max} = \omega A = (14.0 \text{ s}^{-1})(0.05 \text{ m}) = 0.7 \text{ m} \cdot \text{s}^{-1}$$

9 Compute the acceleration. Remember that the acceleration is maximum at $x = A$.

9

$$a = -\omega^2 x$$
$$a_{max} = -\omega^2 A = -(14.0 \text{ s}^{-1})^2 (0.05 \text{ m})$$
$$= -9.8 \text{ m} \cdot \text{s}^{-2}$$

10 *Problem 3* What is the effective force constant of two springs which are connected in series? What is the general relationship for n springs connected in series?

10

Answer

$$k = \frac{k_1 k_2}{k_1 + k_2} \; ; \frac{1}{k} = \frac{1}{k_1} + \frac{1}{k_2} + \frac{1}{k_3} + \cdots + \frac{1}{k_n}$$

If you could not solve this problem, go through frames 11–19.

11 Displace the block a distance x to the right. Consider the point A where the two springs are joined together as a point particle. Draw the free-body diagram of this point particle noting the forces exerted by each spring on the other.

11

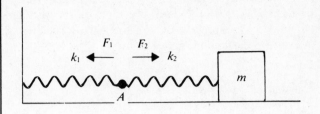

12 Express F_1 and F_2 in terms of their displacements and spring constants.

12

$$F_1 = -k_1x_1$$
$$F_2 = -k_2x_2$$

13 What is the relationship between F_1 and F_2?

13 In accordance with Newton's third law, F_1 is equal in magnitude to F_2.

$$\therefore k_1x_1 = k_2x_2$$

14 Express the displacement x_2 in terms of x by using $x = x_1 + x_2$.

14

$$x_2 = \frac{k_1}{k_2}x_1 \quad x_1 = \frac{k_1}{k_2}(x - x_2)$$

$$x_2 = \frac{k_1}{k_2}x \quad - \frac{k_1x_2}{k_2}$$

$$x_2 + \frac{k_1x_2}{k_2} = \frac{k_1}{k_2}x$$

$$x_2\left(\frac{k_2 + k_1}{k_2}\right) = \frac{k_1}{k_2}x$$

$$x_2 = \left(\frac{k_1}{k_1 + k_2}\right)x$$

15 Consider the forces acting on the block. Draw a free-body diagram.

15

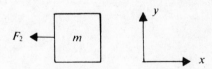

$$\Sigma F_x = F_2 = -k_2x_2$$

16 Substitute the expression from frame 14 for x_2.

16

$$\Sigma F_x = -k_2\frac{k_1}{k_1 + k_2}x$$

$$= -\frac{k_1k_2}{k_1 + k_2}x$$

17 What is k_{eff}?

17

$$k_{eff} = \frac{k_1 k_2}{k_1 + k_2}$$

In accordance with our definition, a single spring with a force constant

$$\frac{k_1 k_2}{k_1 + k_2}$$

will give the same resultant force on two springs connected in series.

18 Rewrite k_{eff} another way.

18

$$\frac{1}{k_{eff}} = \frac{1}{k_1} + \frac{1}{k_2}$$

19 Generalize for n springs in series.

19

$$\frac{1}{k_{eff}} = \frac{1}{k_1} + \frac{1}{k_2} + \cdots + \frac{1}{k_n}$$

12

Elasticity

CHAPTER SUMMARY

Up to this point we have dealt with rigid bodies that did not change their shape under the action of applied forces. In this chapter we are concerned with bodies that are deformed by tensile, shearing or compressive stresses. Each stress has a corresponding strain which describes the relative change in the dimensions of the body. The relationships between stress and strain are developed and the various elastic moduli (Young's, shear and bulk) and the force constant are defined.

BASIC TERMS — *Give definitions or meanings for the following:*

tension (12-1)
compression (12-1)
stress (12-1)
tensile stress (12-1)
pascal (12-1)
Poisson's ratio (12-1)
compressive stress (12-1)
tensile strain (12-1)
compressive strain (12-1)
Hooke's law (12-1)
elastic modulus (12-1)
Young's modulus (12-1)
force constant (12-1)
volume strain (12-2)
bulk modulus (12-2)

bulk stress (12-2)
pressure (12-2)
atmosphere (12-2)
compressibility (12-2)
shear stress (12-3)
shear modulus (12-3)
shear strain (12-3)
elasticity (12-4)
plasticity (12-4)
brittle (12-4)
ductile (12-4)
proportion limit (12-4)
yield point (12-4)
elastic limit (12-4)
breaking stress (12-4)

PROGRAMMED QUIZ

1 Compare what happens to a body under tensile, compressive or shearing stress.

1 Tension stretches objects, compression shrinks them and shear twists them.

2 Draw a sketch for frame 1.

2

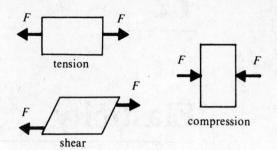

3 What does elastic limit refer to?

3 Maximum stress that can be applied to a body without deforming it permanently.

4 What are the common units of the elastic constants in the SI and engineering systems?

4 Pascal, lb · in.$^{-2}$

5 What is 1 Pa equal to?

5 $1 \text{ N} \cdot \text{m}^{-2}$

6 Does the volume of an object under shearing stress change?

6 No, only the shape.

7 Can liquids be under tensile or shearing stress?

7 No, they do tend to resist compression.

8 Which is the only elastic modulus that applies to liquids?

8 Bulk modulus.

9 What is the direction of the force exerted by a fluid on its container?

9 Always normal to the surface of the container.

10 What is the proportional limit?

10 Maximum strain up to which materials obey Hooke's law.

11 Why is the bulk modulus relationship negative?

11

$$B = -\frac{V\Delta p}{\Delta V};$$

an increase in pressure produces a decrease in volume. If Δp is positive, ΔV is negative and B is a positive quantity.

12 Frames 12–15 refer to the following stress-strain diagram for a material under tension. What is the behaviour of the material between *0* and *1*?

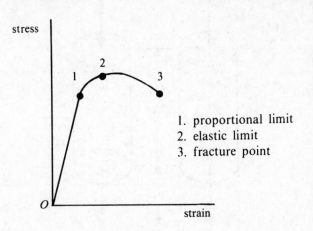

1. proportional limit
2. elastic limit
3. fracture point

12 Stress and strain are proportional; material obeys Hooke's law.

---

13 What is the behaviour of the material between *0* and *2*?

13 Elastic.

---

14 What is the behaviour of the material between *2* and *3*?

14 Plastic.

---

15 Is the material ductile or brittle?

15 Brittle because fracture occurs soon after the elastic limit is passed.

---

16 What does the breaking stress or ultimate strength refer to?

16 The stress required to cause actual fracture of a material.

---

17 What does the term fluid apply to?

17 Liquids and gases.

---

18 In reference to a spring, what is the unit of the force constant or spring constant k? What is $1/k$ called?

18 $N \cdot m^{-1}$; the compliance of the spring.

---

19 What is meant by the statement that the pressure in a fluid is the same in all directions?

19 The force on a surface is normal to the surface.

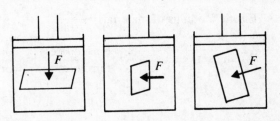

MAIN IDEAS

1 Consider rod a of length l_0 and cross-sectional area A subject to the action of equal and opposite "stretching" forces F applied normal to the cross-sectional surfaces. The rod is said to be under tension and has a tensile stress $= \dfrac{F}{A}$.

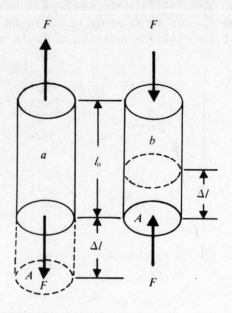

2 The forces on rod b tend to compress the rod and thus the rod is said to be under a compressive stress, which is also defined as $\dfrac{F}{A}$.

3 In reference to rod a, tensile strain $= \dfrac{\Delta l}{l_0}$ and in reference to rod b, compressive strain $= -\dfrac{\Delta l}{l_0}$. Volume strain $= \dfrac{\Delta V}{V}$, where V is the original volume and ΔV is the change in volume.

4 Consider an arbitrary cross-section of the rod. Let A' be the area of this cross-section. Resolve F into $F_\perp$, the component of F which is perpendicular to A', and $F_\parallel$, the component of F which is parallel to the surface A'. Normal stress on $A' = \dfrac{F_\perp}{A'}$, shearing stress on $A' = \dfrac{F_\parallel}{A'}$.

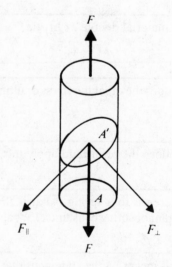

5 Hydrostatic pressure $p = \dfrac{F}{A}$.

6 Units. Stress and pressure: one pascal $= 1$ Pa $= 1$ N $\cdot$ m^{-2}, one atmosphere $= 1$ atm $= 1.013 \times 10^5$ Pa $= 14.7$ lb $\cdot$ in^{-2}; strain: no units.

7 Elastic modulus of material $= \dfrac{\text{stress}}{\text{strain}}$.

Young's modulus $= Y = \dfrac{\text{tensile stress}}{\text{tensile strain}} = \dfrac{\text{compressive stress}}{\text{compressive strain}}$

$= \dfrac{F/A}{\Delta l/l_0} = \dfrac{Fl_0}{A\Delta l}$.

8 If a material (such as a rod or bar) is under a tensile or compressive stress, there is a change in length and a simultaneous change in the transverse dimension (width or diameter). If w is the original width or diameter and Δw the change in width or diameter, then $\dfrac{\Delta w}{w} = -\dfrac{\sigma \Delta l}{l}$, where σ is known as Poisson's ratio.

9 The bulk modulus of a material $B = -V\dfrac{\Delta p}{\Delta V}$, where V = original volume, ΔV = change in volume, and Δp = change in pressure. Note, an increase in pressure is accompanied by a decrease in volume. Thus ΔV is negative when Δp is positive. When Δp is negative, ΔV will be positive. Therefore B will always have a positive value.

10 Young's modulus may be restated as

$$F_\perp = \frac{YA}{l_0}\,\Delta l.$$

Substituting k for $\dfrac{YA}{l_0}$ and x for Δl, we have $F_\perp = kx$, which is Hooke's law. If a material returns to its original length when a deforming force is removed, the material is said to exhibit elastic behaviour.

11 Structural members composed of two materials in series. Consider the beams composed of two materials in series as in the figure. Since the tensile or compressive forces are transmitted from one end of the beam to the other, $F = F_a = F_b$. The total elongation or reduction will be $\Delta l = \Delta l_a + \Delta l_b$. Using the modulus relationship, we have

$$\Delta l = \frac{Fl_a}{A_a Y_a} + \frac{Fl_b}{A_b Y_b} = F\left(\frac{l_a}{A_a Y_a} + \frac{l_b}{A_b Y_b}\right).$$

If both materials have the same cross sectional areas. i.e., $A_a = A_b = A$, then

$$\Delta l = \frac{F}{A}\left(\frac{l_a}{Y_a} + \frac{l_b}{Y_b}\right).$$

It should be noted that $\text{stress}_a = \dfrac{F}{A_a}$ and $\text{stress}_b = \dfrac{F}{A_b}$.

12 Structural members composed of two materials in parallel. Consider the beams composed of two materials in parallel as in the figure. Since the two materials act as a unit (e.g., reinforced concrete), their elongation or reduction will be the same; $\Delta l_a = \Delta l_b = \Delta l$. Therefore both materials have the same strain, $\dfrac{\Delta l_a}{l_0} = \dfrac{\Delta l_b}{l_0} = \dfrac{\Delta l}{l_0}$. Since

$$Y = \frac{\text{stress}}{\text{strain}}, \frac{\text{stress}_a}{Y_a} = \frac{\text{stress}_b}{Y_b}.$$

Hence the total load F carried by both members is $F = \text{stress}_a A_b + \text{stress}_b A_b$.

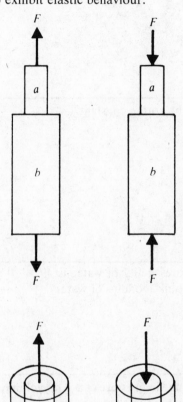

PROGRAMMED QUIZ

1 A metal rod 5 m long, cross-sectional area 5×10^{-5} m^2, is under a tension of 10,000 N. Answer frames 1–4. What is the stress?

1

$$\begin{aligned}
\text{stress} &= \frac{F}{A}\\
&= \frac{10{,}000\ \text{N}}{5 \times 10^{-5}\ \text{m}^2}\\
&= 2.00 \times 10^8\ \text{Pa}
\end{aligned}$$

2 If it stretches 0.6 cm, what is the strain?

2

$$\text{strain} = \frac{\Delta l}{l_0}$$
$$= \frac{0.006 \text{ m}}{5 \text{ m}}$$
$$= 1.2 \times 10^{-3}$$

Strain has no units.

---

3 What is Young's modulus for this material?

3

$$Y = \frac{l_0 F}{A \Delta l} = \frac{\text{stress}}{\text{strain}}$$
$$= \frac{(5 \text{ m})(10{,}000 \text{ N})}{(5 \times 10^{-5} \text{ m}^2)(0.006 \text{ m})} = \frac{2.00 \times 10^8 \text{ Pa}}{1.2 \times 10^{-3}}$$
$$= 1.67 \times 10^{11} \text{ Pa}$$

---

4 What is the spring constant?

4

$$F = \frac{YA}{l_0} \cdot \Delta l = kx \qquad \text{where } x = \Delta l$$
$$\therefore k = \frac{YA}{l_0}$$
$$= \frac{(1.67 \times 10^{11} \text{ N} \cdot \text{m}^{-2})(5 \times 10^{-5} \text{ m}^2)}{5 \text{ m}}$$
$$= 1.67 \times 10^6 \text{ N} \cdot \text{m}^{-1}$$

---

5 The compressibility of water is 49×10^{-11} Pa^{-1}. What is the bulk modulus of water?

5

$$k = \frac{1}{B}$$
$$B = \frac{1}{49 \times 10^{-11} \text{ Pa}^{-1}} = 2.04 \times 10^9 \text{ Pa}$$

---

6 If the change in pressure on a 2 m^3 volume of water is 10^6 Pa, what is the change in volume?

6

$$k = -\frac{1}{V} \frac{\Delta V}{\Delta p}$$
$$\Delta V = -(49 \times 10^{-11} \text{ Pa})(2 \text{ m}^3)(10^6 \text{ Pa})$$
$$= -9.8 \times 10^{-4} \text{ m}^3$$

---

7 What does the negative sign in frame 6 indicate?

7 That the volume decreases as the pressure increases.

---

8 What was the volume strain of the water?

8

$$\text{volume strain} = \frac{\Delta V}{V}$$
$$= \frac{9.8 \times 10^{-4} \text{ m}^3}{2 \text{ m}^3} = 4.9 \times 10^{-4}$$

---

9 What was the force exerted on the water if the area was 2m²?

9

$$F = pA$$
$$= (10^6 \text{ N} \cdot \text{m}^{-2}) (2 \text{ m}^2)$$
$$= 2 \times 10^6 \text{ N}$$

10 A force is acting on the corner of a square block 0.8 m on a side, displacing the corner 0.02 m. What is the shear strain?

10

$$\text{shear strain} = \frac{x}{h}$$
$$= \frac{0.02 \text{ m}}{0.8 \text{ m}}$$
$$= 0.025$$

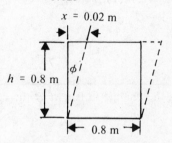

11 What is the strain in terms of an angle?

11

$$\text{shear strain} = \tan \phi = \phi$$
$$\phi = \arctan 0.025 = 0.025 \text{ rad}$$
$$= 1.43°$$

12 If the shear modulus of the material is 0.6×10^{11} Pa, what is the shear stress?

12

$$S = \frac{\text{shear stress}}{\text{shear strain}}$$
$$\text{shear stress} = 0.6 \times 10^{11} \text{ Pa } (0.025)$$
$$= 15 \times 10^8 \text{ Pa}$$

13 What force must be applied parallel to the area to produce this shear stress?

13

$$\text{shear stress} = \frac{F_{\parallel}}{A}$$
$$F_{\parallel} = (15 \times 10^8 \text{ N} \cdot \text{m}^{-2}) (0.8 \text{ m})^2$$
$$= 9.6 \times 10^8 \text{ N}$$

14 If Poisson's ratio for this material is 0.25, what is Young's modulus?

14

$$S = \frac{Y}{2(1 + \sigma)}$$
$$Y = 2(0.6 \times 10^{11} \text{ Pa}) (1 + 0.25)$$
$$= 1.5 \times 10^{11} \text{ Pa}$$

15 What is the bulk modulus for this material?

15

$$B = \frac{Y}{3(1 - 2\sigma)}$$
$$= \frac{1.5 \times 10^{11} \text{ Pa}}{3[1 - 2(0.025)]}$$
$$= 1 \times 10^{11} \text{ Pa}$$

16 A circular steel column 0.25 m in diameter and 4 m long is placed vertically and is required to support a load of 10^5 N. What is the stress in the column?

16

$$\text{stress} = \frac{F}{A}$$
$$= \frac{F}{\pi r^2}$$
$$= \frac{10^5 \text{ N}}{\pi(0.125 \text{ m})^2}$$
$$= 2.04 \times 10^6 \text{ Pa}$$

17 What is the strain in the column? (Young's modulus $= 2 \times 10^{11}$ Pa.)

17

$$Y = \frac{\text{stress}}{\text{strain}}$$
$$\text{strain} = \frac{2.04 \times 10^6 \text{ Pa}}{2 \times 10^{11} \text{ Pa}} = 1.02 \times 10^{-5}$$

18 What is the change in length of the column?

18

$$\text{strain} = \frac{\Delta l}{l_0}$$
$$\Delta l = (4 \text{ m}) (1.02 \times 10^{-5})$$
$$= 4.08 \times 10^{-5} \text{ m}$$

STEP BY STEP SOLUTIONS OF PROBLEMS

Problem 1   A circular steel rod 2 m long and 4 cm in diameter is placed under a tension of 15,000 N. Find the elongation, stress, and strain if Young's modulus for this material is 2×10^{11} Pa.

1 Find the cross sectional area using
$$A = \frac{\pi d^2}{4}.$$

1

$$A = \frac{\pi(0.04 \text{ m})^2}{4}$$
$$= 1.26 \times 10^{-3} \text{ m}^2$$

2 Solve the equation for Young's modulus for Δl and substitute the numerical values. Remember that $1 \text{ Pa} = 1 \text{ N} \cdot \text{m}^{-2}$.

2

$$Y = \frac{F/A}{\Delta l/l_0}$$
$$\Delta l = \frac{F l_0}{YA}$$
$$= \frac{15000 \text{ N } (2 \text{ m})}{(2 \times 10^{11} \text{ N} \cdot \text{m}^{-2}) (1.26 \times 10^{-3} \text{ m}^2)}$$
$$= 1.19 \times 10^{-4} \text{ m}$$

3 Find the stress using
$$\text{stress} = \frac{F}{A}.$$

3

$$\text{stress} = \frac{15000 \text{ N}}{1.26 \times 10^{-3} \text{ m}^2}$$
$$= 1.19 \times 10^7 \text{ Pa}$$

4 Find the strain using

$$\text{strain} = \frac{\Delta l}{l_0}.$$

4

$$\text{strain} = \frac{\Delta l}{l_0}$$

$$= \frac{1.19 \times 10^{-4} \text{ m}}{2 \text{ m}}$$

$$= 5.95 \times 10^{-5}$$

Problem 2 A 0.5 kg body on a steel wire 1 m long and 0.2 cm in diameter (Young's modulus = 2×10^{11} Pa) is whirled in a vertical circle. The angular velocity at the bottom of the circle is 6 rev · s^{-1}. Calculate the elongation of the wire when the body is at the lowest point. Assume that the wire is massless.

5 In order to find the required tension in the cable, consider the forces acting on the 0.5 kg body when it is at the bottom of the circle. Express the net force acting on the body in terms of angular velocity and solve for the tension. As you will recall $v = \omega R$ and 1 rev = 2π rad.

5

$$\Sigma F_y = ma_y$$

$$= T - mg = \frac{mv^2}{R}$$

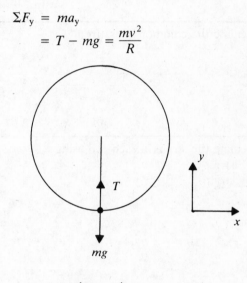

$$T = m\left(\frac{v^2}{R} + g\right) = m(\omega^2 R + g)$$

$$= 0.5 \text{ kg } [144 \, \pi^2 \text{ s}^{-2} \, (1 \text{ m}) + 9.8 \text{ m} \cdot \text{s}^{-2}]$$

$$= 715 \text{ N}$$

---

6 Solve for Δl in the equation for Young's modulus. Find A as in frame 1.

6

$$\Delta l = \frac{Fl_0}{YA}$$

$$= \frac{715 \text{ N } (1 \text{ m})}{(2 \times 10^{11} \text{ N} \cdot \text{m}^{-2}) \, (3.14 \times 10^{-6} \text{ m}^2)}$$

$$= 1.14 \times 10^{-3} \text{ m} = 1.14 \text{ mm}$$

If the breaking stress of the wire is 7.2×10^8 Pa, will this wire break at this point?

7 Calculate the stress from

$$\text{stress} = \frac{F}{A}$$

7

$$\text{stress} = \frac{F}{A}$$

$$= \frac{715 \text{ N}}{3.14 \times 10^{-6} \text{ m}^2}$$

$$= 2.28 \times 10^8 \text{ Pa}$$

---

8 Will the wire break?

8 No, since the stress of 2.28×10^8 Pa is less than the breaking stress.

Problem 3 A copper and a steel rod are joined end to end. Each rod is 0.8 m long and 0.03 m in diameter. The combination is subjected to a tensile force of 5,000 N. Calculate the strain, elongation and change in diameter for each rod. Young's modulus for copper is 1.1×10^{11} Pa, for steel it is 2×10^{11} Pa; Poisson's ratio is 0.32 for copper and 0.19 for steel.

9 Calculate the cross sectional area of the rods from
$$A = \frac{\pi d^2}{4}.$$

9
$$A = \frac{\pi(0.03 \text{ m})^2}{4}$$
$$= 7.07 \times 10^{-4} \text{ m}^2$$

10 Calculate the common stress from
$$\text{stress} = \frac{P}{A}.$$

10
$$\text{stress} = \frac{5000 \text{ N}}{7.07 \times 10^{-4} \text{ m}^2}$$
$$= 7.07 \times 10^6 \text{ Pa}$$

11 Calculate the strain in each rod using
$$Y = \frac{\text{stress}}{\text{strain}}.$$

11
$$\text{copper: strain} = \frac{\text{stress}}{Y}$$
$$= \frac{7.07 \times 10^6 \text{ Pa}}{1.1 \times 10^{11} \text{ Pa}}$$
$$= 6.43 \times 10^{-5}$$
$$\text{steel: strain} = \frac{7.07 \times 10^6 \text{ Pa}}{2 \times 10^{11} \text{ Pa}}$$
$$= 3.54 \times 10^{-5}$$

12 Calculate the elongation in each rod from
$$\text{strain} = \frac{\Delta l}{l_0}$$

12
$$\text{copper: } \Delta l = \text{strain } (l_0)$$
$$= (6.43 \times 10^{-5}) \, (0.8 \text{ m})$$
$$= 5.14 \times 10^{-5} \text{ m}$$
$$\text{steel: } \Delta l = (3.54 \times 10^{-5}) \, (0.8 \text{ m})$$
$$= 2.83 \times 10^{-5} \text{ m}$$

13 Calculate the change in diameter for each rod using
$$\frac{\Delta d}{d} = -\frac{\sigma \Delta l}{l_0} = -\sigma \, (\text{strain}).$$

13 copper:
$$\Delta d = -\frac{\sigma \Delta l}{l_0} d$$
$$= -0.32 \frac{(5.14 \times 10^{-5})}{0.8 \text{ m}} (0.03 \text{ m})$$
$$= -6.17 \times 10^{-7} \text{ m}$$
steel:
$$\Delta d = -0.19 \frac{(2.83 \times 10^{-5} \text{ m})}{0.8 \text{ m}} (0.03 \text{ m})$$
$$= -2.02 \times 10^{-7} \text{ m}$$
Δd could also be obtained by using $\Delta d = -d\sigma$ (strain).

PROGRAMMED TEST

1 Problem 1 A 0.5 kg body on a steel wire is whirled in a horizontal circle of 1 m radius. The diameter of the wire is 0.2 cm. What is the maximum angular velocity the body can have without breaking the wire if the breaking strength of steel is 7.2×10^8 Pa?

1

Answer

$10.7 \text{ rev} \cdot \text{s}^{-1}$

If you solved this problem correctly go to frame 6. If you could not solve this problem go through frames 2–5.

---

2 Calculate the cross sectional area of the wire.

2

$$A = \frac{\pi d^2}{4}$$
$$= \frac{\pi (0.002 \text{ m})^2}{4}$$
$$= 3.14 \times 10^{-6} \text{ m}^2$$

---

3 Calculate the maximum force ($F_{\max}$) that can be sustained by the wire without breaking.

3

$$\text{breaking stress} = \frac{F_{\max}}{A}$$
$$F_{\max} = (7.2 \times 10^8 \text{ N} \cdot \text{m}^{-2})$$
$$\times (3.14 \times 10^{-6} \text{ m}^2)$$
$$= 2.26 \times 10^3 \text{ N}$$

---

4 The tension in the wire is the only force acting on the 0.5 kg body. Express the tension T in terms of the velocity v.

4

$$\Sigma F_x = m a_x$$
$$T = \frac{m v^2}{R}$$

---

5 Express the above equation in terms of angular velocity ω. Substitute the given values and solve for ω. Convert your answer to $\text{rev} \cdot \text{s}^{-1}$.

5

$$F_{\max} = T = m \, \omega^2 R$$
$$\omega^2 = \frac{2.26 \times 10^3 \text{ N}}{(0.5 \text{ kg}) (1 \text{ m})}$$
$$\omega = 67.2 \text{ rad} \cdot \text{s}^{-1}$$
$$= 67.2 \, \frac{\text{rad}}{\text{s}} \times \frac{1 \text{ rev}}{2\pi \text{ rad}} = 10.7 \text{ rev} \cdot \text{s}^{-1}$$

---

6 Problem 2 An elevator cable can support a maximum stress of 7×10^7 Pa. If the total weight of the loaded elevator is 20,000 N and the maximum upward acceleration is $1.5 \text{ m} \cdot \text{s}^{-2}$, what should be the diameter of the cable?

6

Answer

0.020 m

If you solved this problem correctly, go to frame 10. If you could not solve this problem go through frames 7–9.

7 Use Newton's second law to find the tension in the cable.

7

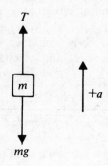

$$\Sigma F_y = ma_y$$
$$T - mg = ma_y$$
$$T - 20{,}000 \text{ N} = \frac{20{,}000 \text{ N}}{9.8 \text{ m} \cdot \text{s}^{-2}} (1.5 \text{ m} \cdot \text{s}^{-2})$$
$$T = 23{,}100 \text{ N}$$

---

8 Find the area of the cable from the stress relationship.

8

$$\text{stress} = \frac{F}{A}$$
$$A = \frac{23{,}100 \text{ N}}{7 \times 10^7 \text{ N} \cdot \text{m}^{-2}}$$
$$= 3.30 \times 10^{-4} \text{ m}^2$$

---

9 Find the diameter.

9

$$A = \frac{\pi d^2}{4}$$
$$d = \sqrt{\frac{4(3.3 \times 10^{-4} \text{ m}^2)}{\pi}}$$
$$= 0.0205 \text{ m}$$

---

10 ***Problem 3*** A brass bar 0.3 cm square and 6 m long is stretched with a force of 500 N at each end. Find the stress, strain, total elongation and fractional change in the thickness of the bar.
    ($Y = 0.91 \times 10^{11}$ Pa, $\sigma = 0.26$)

10
Answer
5.56×10^7 Pa, 6.11×10^{-4}, 3.67 mm, 1.63×10^{-4}

If you could not solve this problem, go through frames 11–14.

11 Find the stress.

11

$$\text{stress} = \frac{F}{A}$$
$$= \frac{500 \text{ N}}{(0.003 \text{ m})^2}$$
$$= 5.56 \times 10^7 \text{ Pa}$$

---

12 Find the strain using Young's modulus.

12

$$Y = \frac{\text{stress}}{\text{strain}}$$

$$\text{strain} = \frac{5.56 \times 10^7 \text{ Pa}}{0.91 \times 10^{11} \text{ Pa}}$$

$$= 6.11 \times 10^{-4}$$

---

13 What is the total elongation?

13

$$\text{strain} = \frac{\Delta l}{l_0}$$

$$\Delta l = (6.11 \times 10^{-4})\,(6\text{ m})$$

$$= 3.67 \times 10^{-3} \text{ m} = 3.67 \text{ mm}$$

---

14 Find the fractional change in the thickness of the bar using Poisson's ratio.

14

$$\frac{\Delta w}{w} = -\frac{\sigma \Delta l}{l_0},$$

$$= -0.26\,\frac{(3.67 \times 10^{-3} \text{ m})}{6 \text{ m}}$$

$$= -1.59 \times 10^{-4}$$

13

Fluid Mechanics

CHAPTER SUMMARY

In the beginning of the text we covered statics — the study of objects at rest. We will now study fluids at rest. The properties of fluids such as density (specific gravity) and hydrostatic pressure are described, as well as phenomena such as surface tension, surface film and capillarity. Archimedes' principle and pressure gauges are discussed in detail. The second part of the chapter deals with fluid dynamics. After defining an ideal fluid and various aspects of fluid flow, the discussion turns to the mathematical relationships of a moving fluid: the continuity equation, Bernoulli's equation, Poiseuille's law and Stokes' law. Laminar and turbulent flows are considered as well as viscosity. Many applications are presented in each section, including applications in medicine.

BASIC TERMS — *Give definitions or meanings for the following:*

fluid dynamics (13-I)
fluid statics (13-I)
fluid (13-I)
density (13-1)
specific gravity (13-1)
pressure (13-2)
Pascal's law (13-2)
Torr (13-2)
gauge pressure (13-2)
absolute pressure (13-2)
mercury barometer (13-2)
atmosphere (13-2)
bar (13-2)
Archimedes' principle (13-3)
buoyancy (13-3)
buoyant force (13-3)
surface tension (13-4)
capillarity (13-4)
meniscus (13-4)

contact angle (13-4)
turbulent flow (13-5)
ideal fluid (13-5)
line of flow (13-5)
steady (stationary) flow (13-5)
streamline (13-5)
flow tube (13-5)
laminar (streamline) flow (13-5)
continuity equation (13-5)
Bernoulli's equation (13-6)
Torricelli's theorem (13-7)
viscosity (13-8)
Poiseuille's law (13-8)
Stokes' law (13-8)
poise (13-8)
newtonian fluid (13-8)
pressure gradient (13-8)
turbulence (13-9)

PROGRAMMED QUIZ

1 What is the difference between hydrostatics, hydrodynamics and aerodynamics?

1 Hydrostatics is the study of fluids at rest, hydrodynamics of fluids in motion, and aerodynamics is a branch of hydrodynamics dealing with the flow of gases, particularly air.

2 What are the units of specific gravity?

2 No units since it is a ratio of the density of a substance to the density of water.

3 Give an application of Pascal's law.

3 Hydraulic lift; small force over a small area produces a pressure which is equal to that of a large force over a large area.

4 What is gauge pressure?

4 Pressure in excess of atmospheric pressure; absolute pressure minus atmospheric pressure.

5 What are some devices used to measure pressure?

5 Manometer, barometer.

6 What are some devices used to produce a vacuum?

6 Rotary oil pump, mercury or oil diffusion pump.

7 The fact that we "weigh" less in water is an application of _____.

7 Archimedes' principle.

8 What does a hydrometer measure?

8 Density of liquids.

9 Surface tension causes what phenomena?

9 Soap films, bubbles, meniscus.

10 What happens when a pressure of 10×10^5 Pa is applied to the piston in a cylinder of fluid?

10 The pressure is increased by 10×10^5 Pa everywhere in the cylinder.

11 Two identical dams are built on two lakes which have the same depth. One lake has twice the volume of the other. What is the ratio of the total force on each dam?

11 $F = pA$, since the pressure and the area of both dams are the same, the forces are equal.

12 Archimedes' principle is most closely related to which physical quantity?

12 Specific gravity.

13 The floating of an iceberg can be explained by _____.

13 Archimedes' principle.

14 In a hydraulic press, the force of the output piston is much greater than that of the input piston. What quantity cannot be exceeded by the output piston?

14 Work.

---

15 What is the usual unit of surface tension? How is it related to the SI unit?

15
$$\text{Dyn} \cdot \text{cm}^{-1};$$
$$1 \text{ N} \cdot \text{m}^{-1} = 1000 \text{ dyn} \cdot \text{cm}^{-1}$$

---

16 Why is a drop of liquid in free fall in a vacuum spherical in shape?

16 A surface under tension will contract until it has the minimum area for the particular boundaries and pressures. A spherical area is the smallest area for a given volume.

---

17 An object suspended by a string is submerged in water. Will the tension in the string be the same as the tension when it was suspended in air?

17 The tension when the object is submerged in the water will be less since the tension in the string is the actual weight less the upward buoyant force.

---

18 What is a fluid?

18 A fluid is any substance that can flow. It includes both liquids and gases.

---

19 State Archimedes' principle.

19 When a body is immersed in a fluid, the fluid exerts an upward force on the body equal to the weight of the fluid that is displaced by the body.

---

20 State Pascal's law.

20 Pressure applied to an enclosed fluid is transmitted undiminished to every portion of the fluid and the walls of the containing vessel.

---

21 Bernoulli's equation is based on what physical principle?

21 Conservation of energy.

---

22 Torricelli's theorem is a special case of what mathematical relationship?

22 Bernoulli's equation.

---

23 What is a newtonian fluid?

23 One for which the relationship for viscosity, $F = \eta A \frac{v}{l}$, holds.

---

24 In streamline flow of an incompressible fluid through a tube, what is conserved? This is mathematically represented by what relationship?

24 Mass; equation of continuity.

---

25 What is the effect of viscosity in a fluid?

25 Viscosity is an internal friction; it impedes (limits) the flow of a fluid.

---

26 What is an incompressible fluid?

26 One where the density is constant.

---

27 Can an element of fluid flow through the sides of a flow tube?

27 No, a flow tube is a bundle of streamlines and streamlines may never cross. Therefore an element must follow the streamline until it reaches the end of the flow tube.

---

28 The Venturi tube relationship is a special case of what equation? What situation?

28 Bernoulli's equation; for two points at the same elevation.

---

29 What are some situations where the fluid flow is similar to that of a Venturi tube?

29 Lift on an aircraft wing and the curved flight of a spinning ball (due to a pressure difference between the upper and lower surfaces).

---

30 Write Bernoulli's equation for hydrostatics.

30 Bernoulli's equation is
$$p_1 - p_2 = \tfrac{1}{2}\rho(v_2{}^2 - v_1{}^2) + \rho g(y_2 - y_1)$$
in hydrostatics, $v_1 = v_2 = 0$
$$\therefore p_1 - p_2 = \rho g(y_2 - y_1).$$

---

31 What is the usual unit of viscosity? What is it equal to?

31 Poise; 1 poise $= 1 \, \mathrm{dyn} \cdot \mathrm{s} \cdot \mathrm{cm}^{-2} = 10^{-1} \, \mathrm{N} \cdot \mathrm{s} \cdot \mathrm{m}^{-2}$

---

32 Is pressure a scalar or a vector quantity?

32 Pressure is a scalar quantity. Regardless of the orientation of an area, the force due to a fluid at rest acting on the area is always perpendicular to the area.

---

33 What is the viscosity of an ideal fluid?

33 Zero.

---

34 Which law would you use to calculate the velocity of a sphere falling in a viscous fluid?

34 Stokes' law.

---

35 In all of the equations in this chapter is the pressure gauge atmospheric or absolute?

35 Absolute pressure.

---

36 Explain why a pitched ball, which has been given a spin, follows the curve as shown.

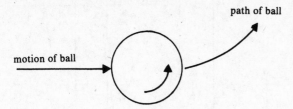

The diagram shows a spinning ball traveling to the right and at the same time it is rotating around a horizontal axis. Instead of the ball moving, imagine the rotating ball is stationary in a wind tunnel and that the air is moving to the left.

36

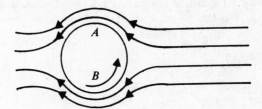

Since the surface of the ball at A is moving in the same direction as the air, the velocity of the air will be increased at this point; at B, the motion of the ball's surface retards the motion of the air thus decreasing its velocity. Since the velocity of the air is greater at A than at B, it follows from Bernouilli's principle that the pressure of the air at B will be greater than at A. Due to a difference in pressure between the upper and lower surfaces of the ball, the ball will experience a net force upwards and follow the circular path.

high air velocity
low pressure

high pressure
low air velocity

37 Why is there an upward lift on an airplane wing? Imagine that the wing is stationary in a wind tunnel and that the air is moving to the right as shown.

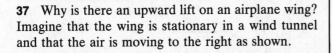

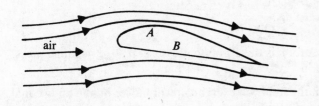

37 Air passing over the top surface will travel over a longer path and thus achieve a higher velocity than the air that flows along the undersurface. In accordance with Bernouilli's principle, it follows that the pressure of the air at B will be greater than the pressure at A. Due to this difference in pressure Δp, the airplane wing will experience an upward lift $F_L = \Delta p A$, where A is the wing area. The mgy term in Bernouilli's equation is neglected because of the small variation in y, i.e. the wing thickness is small.

MAIN IDEAS

Fluid statics, the study of fluids (liquids or gases) at rest

1 The density of a homogeneous material is defined as $\rho = \dfrac{m}{V}$, where ρ is the density, m is the mass, and V is the volume.

2 Units of density: In SI, $kg \cdot m^{-3}$; in the cgs system, $g \cdot cm^{-3}$.

3 The specific gravity of a substance is the ratio of its density to that of water. Specific gravity has no units.

4 The pressure at any point in a fluid is defined as $p = \dfrac{\Delta F}{\Delta A}$, where p is the pressure, ΔF the normal force and ΔA the area acted upon by the normal force. The unit of pressure is the pascal; $1 \, Pa = 1 \, N \cdot m^{-2}$. Pressure is a scalar, no direction can be assigned to it.

5 The relationship between the pressure p at any point in a fluid with respect to its elevation y (positive upwards) is $\Delta p = -\rho g \Delta y$. Thus an increase in elevation (positive Δy) will result in a decrease in pressure.

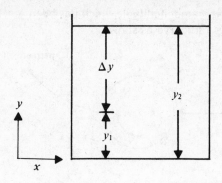

6 Let us take our y-coordinate as positive downward in a fluid of uniform density ρ. Let p_a be the atmospheric pressure. The pressure at depth h is given by $p = p_a + \rho g h$.

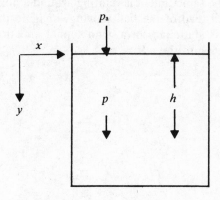

7 Pascal's law: Pressure applied to a confined fluid is transmitted undiminished throughout the fluid and to the walls of the confining vessel. The hydraulic press is an application of Pascal's law,

$$p = \frac{f}{a} = \frac{F}{A}.$$

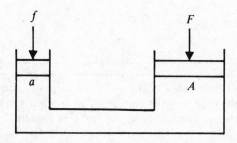

8 Difference between absolute pressure and gauge pressure: p is the absolute pressure, $p - p_a$ = gauge pressure. 1 atmosphere (1 atm) = 1.013×10^5 Pa = 14.7 lb · in^{-2}; 10^5 N · m^{-2} = 1 bar.

9 Archimedes' principle: If a body is immersed in a fluid, the fluid will exert an upward force on the body equal to the weight of the fluid displaced by the body. This upward force is referred to as the buoyant force. Archimedes' principle enables us to find the specific gravity of a solid object (specific gravity > 1) by using

$$\text{specific gravity} = \frac{\text{weight in air}}{\text{weight in air} - \text{apparent weight in water}} = \frac{\text{weight in air}}{\text{apparent loss of weight in water}}$$

10 Forces against a dam (water height = h, width = L). The average pressure is $p_{av} = \dfrac{\rho g h}{2}$ and the total force on the wall of the dam is $F_{tot} = p_{av} A = \frac{1}{2}\rho g h^2 L$.

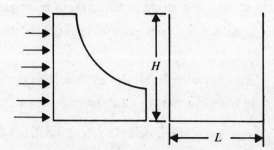

11 Surface tension $= \gamma = \dfrac{F}{2l}$, where F is the inward force exerted by a liquid over a length l.

12 Pressure difference across a surface film. The pressure difference between the inside and outside of a soap bubble is given by $p - p_a = \dfrac{4\gamma}{R}$, (soap bubble) where p is the inside pressure, p_a the outside pressure, R the radius and γ is the surface tension of the soap solution. Since a liquid drop has only one surface film,

$$p - p_a = \frac{2\gamma}{R} \qquad \text{(liquid drop).}$$

13 Capillarity: A meniscus is defined as the concave or convex surface of a liquid standing in a tube. The distance y from the midpoint of the meniscus to the liquid surface is given by

$$y = \frac{2\gamma_{LV}\cos\theta}{\rho g r}$$

where γ_{LV} is the surface tension (of the liquid-vapor film) ρ the density of the liquid, r the radius of the tube and θ is the angle between the edge of the tube and the surface of the liquid. The liquid rises if $\theta < 90°$ and is depressed if $\theta > 90°$.

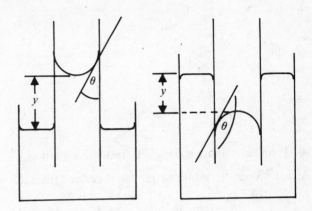

Fluid dynamics, the study of fluids in motion

1 Continuity equation. Consider a tube of flow as indicated in the figure. The quantity of fluid crossing A_1 is equal to the quantity of fluid crossing A_2 in any given time interval: $\rho A_1 v_1 \Delta t = \rho A_2 v_2 \Delta t$ or $A_1 v_1 = A_2 v_2$, where ρ is the density of the fluid, v_1 and v_2 the velocities at two different points with corresponding cross-sectional areas A_1 and A_2 and Δt the time interval.

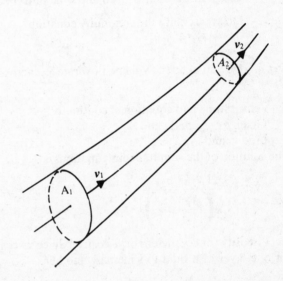

2 Bernoulli's equation. Consider two points of a tube of flow as indicated in the figure:

$$p_1 + \rho g y_1 + \tfrac{1}{2}\rho v_1^2 = p_2 + \rho g y_2 + \tfrac{1}{2}\rho v_2^2,$$

where the fluid flow is due to a difference in pressure $(p_1 - p_2)$ and a gravitational field (elevation difference) $(y_1 - y_2)$. The work done by the gravitational force and by the force due to the pressure is equal to the change in kinetic energy.

Bernouilli's equation may also be written as $p + \rho g y + \tfrac{1}{2}\rho v^2 = $ constant. It should be noted that p is the absolute pressure and that a consistent set of units must be used. In SI units, pressure is expressed in Pa, density in $kg \cdot m^{-3}$ and velocity in $m \cdot s^{-1}$.

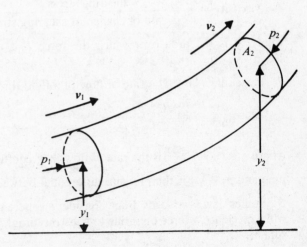

3 Special cases of Bernoulli's equation.

$v_1 = v_2 = 0$ (hydrostatic equation)

$y_1 = y_2$ (venturi tube)

$$p_1 - p_2 = \rho g(y_2 - y_1)$$
$$p_1 - p_2 = \tfrac{1}{2}\rho(v_2^2 - v_1^2)$$

$p_1 = p_2, v_1 = 0$ (a tank of fluid open to the atmosphere; fluid from small opening)

$$v_2 = \sqrt{2gh}$$

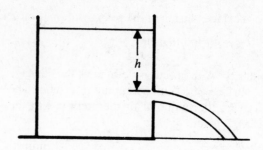

4 Problem solving strategy: Bernoulli's equation.

Step 1 Since Bernoulli's equation is derived from the work-energy theorem, identify points 1 and 2 in reference to

$$p_1 + \rho g y_1 + \tfrac{1}{2}\rho v_1^2 = p_2 + \rho g y_2 + \tfrac{1}{2}\rho v_2^2$$

and indicate what is given and what must be determined.

Step 2 Do you require the continuity equation?

$$A_1 v_1 = A_2 v_2$$

Step 3 Do you need the volume flow rate $\dfrac{\Delta V}{\Delta t}$ across an area A or its corresponding mass flow rate $\dfrac{\Delta m}{\Delta t} = \rho A v$?

5 Venturi tube and equation of continuity.

Given p_1, p_2, ρ, A_1 and A_2

Find v_1 and v_2.

$$p_1 - p_2 = \tfrac{1}{2}\rho(v_2^2 - v_1^2)$$
$$A_1 v_1 = A_2 v_2$$

The solution of the simultaneous equations is

$$v_1^2 = \frac{2(p_1 - p_2)}{\rho\left(\dfrac{A_1^2}{A_2^2} - 1\right)} \qquad v_2^2 = \frac{2(p_1 - p_2)}{\rho\left(1 - \dfrac{A_2^2}{A_1^2}\right)}$$

6 Viscosity (or coefficient of viscosity). Since viscosity is an internal friction of a fluid, a force F must be exerted for one layer of a fluid to slide past another.

$$\text{viscosity} = \eta = \frac{\text{shearing stress}}{\text{rate of change of shearing strain}} = \frac{F/A}{\Delta l/l\Delta t} = \frac{F/A}{v/l},$$

where A is the area over which the force F is applied and v/l is the velocity gradient. Units: 1 poise $= 1 \text{ dyn} \cdot \text{s} \cdot \text{cm}^{-2} = 10^{-1} \text{ N} \cdot \text{s} \cdot \text{m}^{-2}$

7 Poiseuille's law. The rate of flow of a fluid through a pipe is given by:

$$Q = \frac{\Delta v}{\Delta t} = \frac{\pi}{8} \cdot \frac{R^4}{\eta} \cdot \frac{p_1 - p_2}{L},$$

where $Q = \dfrac{\Delta v}{\Delta t}$ is the rate of flow, η = coefficient of viscosity, L = length of pipe, R = interior radius of pipe and $p_1 - p_2$ is the pressure differential between the ends of the pipe.

8 Stokes' law — viscous drag. Consider a sphere moving in a viscous fluid at a relative velocity v. The sphere will experience a force on it due to a viscous drag: $F = 6\pi\eta r v$, where η is the viscosity and r is the radius of the sphere.

9 Terminal velocity of a sphere of density ρ falling in a fluid of density ρ', $v_T = \dfrac{2\, r^2 g}{9\,\eta}(\rho - \rho')$, where v_T = terminal velocity, r = the radius of the sphere and η the viscosity.

10 Reynolds number — turbulent flow in a pipe or tube. Non-laminar flow is called turbulent flow. $N_R = \dfrac{\rho v D}{\eta}$, where ρ is the density of the fluid, η the viscosity, v the average velocity and D the diameter of the pipe.

$\qquad$ If $N_R < 2000$, the flow is laminar,
$\qquad\quad N_R > 3000$, the flow is turbulent,
$\quad 2000 < N_R < 3000$, the flow is unstable.

PROGRAMMED QUIZ

1 Find the mass of a 12 cm^3 block of aluminum if the density of aluminum is $2.7\,\text{g} \cdot \text{cm}^{-3}$.

1
$$\rho = \frac{m}{V}$$
$$m = (2.7\,\text{g} \cdot \text{cm}^{-3})\,(12\,\text{cm}^3) = 32.4\,\text{g}$$

---

2 What is the density of seawater in SI units if the specific gravity is 1.03?

2
$$\text{specific gravity} = \frac{\rho_{\text{seawater}}}{\rho_{\text{water}}}$$
$$\rho_{\text{seawater}} = (1.03)\,(1000\,\text{kg} \cdot \text{m}^{-3})$$
$$= 1030\,\text{kg} \cdot \text{m}^{-3}$$

---

3 A tank 0.5 m deep is filled to the top with seawater. What is the pressure at the bottom of the tank due to the water?

3
$$
\begin{aligned}
p &= \rho g h \\
&= (1030\,\text{kg} \cdot \text{m}^{-3})\,(9.8\,\text{m} \cdot \text{s}^{-2})\,(0.5\,\text{m}) \\
&= 5050\,\text{Pa}
\end{aligned}
$$

---

4 What is the absolute pressure at the bottom of the tank (atmospheric pressure is 1.013×10^5 Pa)?

4
$$
\begin{aligned}
p &= p_a + \rho g h \\
&= 1.013 \times 10^5\,\text{Pa} + 0.0505 \times 10^5\,\text{Pa} \\
&= 1.06 \times 10^5\,\text{Pa}
\end{aligned}
$$

---

5 In operating a lift, how much force must you exert if you wish to lift a 2000 kg car? The two pistons are 0.03 m and 0.24 m in radius.

5
$$
p = \frac{f}{a} = \frac{F}{A}
$$
$$
= \frac{f}{\pi r^2} = \frac{F}{\pi R^2}
$$
$$
f = \frac{(2000\,\text{kg})\,(9.8\,\text{m} \cdot \text{s}^{-2})\,(0.03\,\text{m})^2}{(0.24\,\text{m})^2}
$$
$$
= 306\,\text{N}
$$

---

6 What forces act on an iceberg? What is the relationship between them?

6 Its weight and the buoyant force. The weight is equal to the buoyant force.

---

7 What is the buoyant force equal to? Relate this to the quantities in frame 6.

7 The weight of the displaced water.
$$\text{weight} = \text{buoyant force}$$
$$m_i g = m_w g$$
$$\rho_i g V_i = \rho_w g V_w$$

8 If the density of ice and seawater is 0.92 and $1.03 \text{ g} \cdot \text{cm}^{-3}$ respectively, what volume of the iceberg lies below the water?

8 The volume of iceberg underneath the water is equal to the volume of the displaced water. Therefore, from frame 7,

$$\frac{V_w}{V_i} = \frac{\rho_i}{\rho_w} = \frac{0.92 \text{ g} \cdot \text{cm}^{-3}}{1.03 \text{ g} \cdot \text{cm}^{-3}} = 0.893$$

---

9 What force is required to lift a circular wire 1 cm in diameter out of a soap solution (surface tension $25 \text{ dyn} \cdot \text{cm}^{-3}$)?

9

$$\gamma = \frac{F}{2l} = \frac{F}{2\pi d}$$
$$= 2\pi (25 \text{ dyn} \cdot \text{cm}^{-1}) (1 \text{ cm})$$
$$= 157 \text{ dyn}$$

---

10 A soap bubble, $\gamma = 25 \text{ dyn} \cdot \text{cm}^{-1}$, has a radius of 8 mm. Calculate the difference between the pressure of the liquid and the outside air.

10

$$p - p_a = \frac{4\gamma}{R}$$
$$= \frac{4(25 \text{ dyn} \cdot \text{cm}^{-1})}{0.8 \text{ cm}}$$
$$= 125 \text{ dyn} \cdot \text{cm}^{-2}$$

---

11 A block of metal weighs 60 N in air and 53 N when fully immersed in water. What is the specific gravity of the metal?

11

specific gravity

$$= \frac{\text{weight in air}}{\text{weight in air} - \text{apparent weight in water}}$$
$$= \frac{60 \text{ N}}{60 \text{ N} - 53 \text{ N}} = 8.57$$

---

12 What is the density of the metal?

12

$$(\text{specific gravity})_m = \frac{\rho_m}{\rho_w}$$
$$\text{where } \rho_m = \text{density of metal}$$
$$\rho_w = \text{density of water}$$
$$\rho_m = (8.57 (10^3 \text{ kg} \cdot \text{m}^{-3})$$
$$= 8.57 \times 10^3 \text{ kg} \cdot \text{m}^{-3}$$

---

13 What is the volume of the block?

13

$$\rho_m = \frac{m_m}{V_m}$$
$$V_m = \frac{m_m}{\rho_m} = \frac{w_m}{\rho_m g} \text{ since } w = mg$$
$$= \frac{60 \text{ N}}{(8.57 \times 10^3 \text{ kg} \cdot \text{m}^{-3}) (9.8 \text{ m} \cdot \text{s}^{-2})}$$
$$= 7.14 \times 10^{-4} \text{ m}^3$$

---

14 If the block weighs 54.4 N when completely submerged in a liquid, find the buoyant force.

14 buoyant force $= 60 \text{ N} - 54.4 \text{ N} = 5.6 \text{ N}$

---

15 Find the density of this liquid if the buoyant force is equal to the weight of the displaced liquid.

15

$$w_1 = \rho_1 V_1 g$$

$$\rho_1 = \frac{5.6 \text{ N}}{(7.14 \times 10^{-4} \text{ m}^3)\,(9.8 \text{ m} \cdot \text{s}^{-2})}$$

$$= 800 \text{ kg} \cdot \text{m}^{-3}$$

Note that the volume of the displaced liquid = volume of the block.

---

16 What is the specific gravity of this liquid?

16

$$(\text{specific gravity})_1 = \frac{\rho_1}{\rho_w}$$

$$= \frac{8 \times 10^2 \text{ kg} \cdot \text{m}^{-3}}{1 \times 10^3 \text{ kg} \cdot \text{m}^{-3}}$$

$$= 0.8$$

---

17 A block of wood floats on water with 0.8 of its volume submerged. What is the buoyant force acting on it in terms of ρ, V and g? (The volume of the displaced water = 0.8 volume of the block.)

17 The block will be buoyed up by a force equal to the weight of the displaced water.

$$w_b = w_w$$

$$\rho_b V_b g = \rho_w\,(0.8\,V)g$$

since $\rho = \dfrac{m}{V}$, $w = mg = \rho V g$

---

18 What is the density of the block in terms of the density of water?

18 $\rho_b = 0.8\,\rho_w$

---

19 What is the block's specific gravity?

19 specific gravity $= \dfrac{\rho_b}{\rho_w} = 0.8$

---

20 Water flows from one pipe, 4 cm in diameter to another, 2 cm in diameter. If the velocity is 6 m · s^{-1} in the first pipe find the velocity in the second.

20

$$A_1 v_1 = A_2 v_2$$

$$v_2 = \frac{\pi(2 \text{ cm})^2\,(6 \text{ m} \cdot \text{s}^{-1})}{\pi(1 \text{ cm})^2}$$

$$= 24 \text{ m} \cdot \text{s}^{-1}$$

---

21 If the pressure is 5×10^5 Pa in the first pipe, what will be the pressure in the second if it is 4 m above the first?

21

$$p_1 - p_2 = \tfrac{1}{2}\rho(v_2^2 - v_1^2) + \rho g(y_2 - y_1)$$

$$p_2 = 5 \times 10^5 \text{ N} \cdot \text{m}^{-2} - \tfrac{1}{2}(1 \times 10^3 \text{ kg} \cdot \text{m}^{-3})$$

$$\times [(24 \text{ m} \cdot \text{s}^{-1})^2 - (6 \text{ m} \cdot \text{s}^{-1})^2]$$

$$- (1 \times 10^3 \text{ kg} \cdot \text{m}^{-3})\,(9.8 \text{ m} \cdot \text{s}^{-2})\,(4 \text{ m})$$

$$= 1.91 \times 10^5 \text{ Pa}$$

---

22 What will be the pressure if the water is turned off?

22

$$p_1 - p_2 = \rho g(y_2 - y_1)$$

$$p_2 = 5 \times 10^5 \text{ N} \cdot \text{m}^{-2}$$

$$- (1 \times 10^3 \text{ kg} \cdot \text{m}^{-3})\,(9.8 \text{ m} \cdot \text{s}^{-2})\,(4 \text{ m})$$

$$= 4.61 \times 10^5 \text{ Pa}$$

23 Water flows out of the second pipe into the atmosphere. Calculate the horizontal reaction force on the system.

23

$$F = \rho A v^2$$
$$= (1 \times 10^3 \text{ kg} \cdot \text{m}^{-3}) \, \pi(0.01 \text{ m})^2$$
$$\times (24 \text{ m} \cdot \text{s}^{-1})^2$$
$$= 181 \text{ N}$$

---

24 Water has a viscosity of 0.656 centipoise at 40°C. Find the viscosity in $\text{N} \cdot \text{s} \cdot \text{m}^{-2}$.

24

$$1 \text{ cp} = 10^{-2} \text{ poise}$$
$$0.656 \text{ cp} = 6.56 \times 10^{-3} \text{ poise}$$
$$1 \text{ poise} = 10^{-1} \text{ N} \cdot \text{s} \cdot \text{m}^{-2}$$
$$6.56 \times 10^{-3} \text{ poise} = 6.56 \times 10^{-4} \text{ N} \cdot \text{s} \cdot \text{m}^{-2}$$

---

25 An aluminum sphere falls through water (viscosity 1 cp). If the terminal velocity is $350 \text{ m} \cdot \text{s}^{-1}$, find the radius of the sphere. (The density of aluminum is $2700 \text{ kg} \cdot \text{m}^{-3}$ and the density of water is $1000 \text{ kg} \cdot \text{m}^{-3}$.)

25 Assuming laminar flow and including buoyancy, we can use

$$v_T = \frac{2r^2 g}{9 \eta} (\rho - \rho')$$

$$r^2 = \frac{9(1 \times 10^{-3} \text{ N} \cdot \text{s} \cdot \text{m}^{-2}) (350 \text{ m} \cdot \text{s}^{-1})}{2(9.8 \text{ m} \cdot \text{s}^{-2}) (2700 \text{ kg} \cdot \text{m}^{-3} - 1000 \text{ kg} \cdot \text{m}^{-3})}$$

$$= 0.00972 \text{ m}$$

---

26 A hole is made 5 m below the water surface in a large open tank whose side walls are vertical. What is the velocity of the efflux of the water?

26

$$v = \sqrt{2gh}$$
$$= \sqrt{2(9.8 \text{ m} \cdot \text{s}^{-2}) (5 \text{ m})}$$
$$= 9.90 \text{ m} \cdot \text{s}^{-1}$$

STEP BY STEP SOLUTIONS OF PROBLEMS

Problem 1 A homogeneous body floats with 0.25 of its volume in water and 0.60 of its volume in oil as shown in the figure. If the specific gravity of the body is 0.735, find the density of the oil.

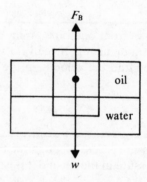

1 According to Archimedes' principle, what is the relationship between w and F_B?

1 Since the body is in equilibrium its weight w is equal to the buoyant force F_B.

---

2 Calculate the weight of the displaced water and oil. Use $\rho = \frac{m}{V}$ and $w = mg$. Let V = total volume of the body and ρ_0 = density of oil.

2

$$\text{weight of displaced oil} = 0.60 \, V \rho_0 g$$
$$\text{weight of displaced water} = 0.25 \, V (1.00 \text{ g} \cdot \text{cm}^{-3}) g$$

3 What is the weight of the body?

3 weight of the body $= V (0.735 \text{ g} \cdot \text{cm}^{-3})g$

---

4 Apply Archimedes' principle, the weight of the body = weight of the displaced water + weight of the displaced oil.

4

$$V(0.735 \text{ g} \cdot \text{cm}^{-3})g = 0.25V(1.00 \text{ g} \cdot \text{cm}^{-3})g + 0.60V\rho_o g$$

---

5 Divide through by Vg and solve for ρ_o.

5

$$\rho_o = 0.808 \text{ g} \cdot \text{cm}^{-3}$$

Problem 2 A dam has a rectangular vertical cross section and is 15 m long. If the water stands 10 m high, find a) the water pressure 8 m below the water level and b) the total force on the dam.

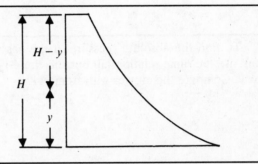

---

6 To find the pressure at any elevation use $p = \rho g(H-y)$, where y is the distance from the bottom.

6

$$p = (1000 \text{ kg} \cdot \text{m}^{-3}) (9.8 \text{ m} \cdot \text{s}^{-2})$$
$$\times (10 \text{ m} - 2 \text{ m})$$
$$= 78,400 \text{ Pa}$$

---

7 Find the average pressure from

$$p_{\text{av}} = \frac{\rho g h}{2}.$$

7

$$p_{\text{av}} = \frac{(1000 \text{ kg} \cdot \text{m}^{-3}) (9.8 \text{ m} \cdot \text{s}^{-2}) (10 \text{ m})}{2}$$
$$= 49,000 \text{ Pa}$$

---

8 Find the area of the dam.

8

$$A = LH = (15 \text{ m}) (10 \text{ m}) = 150 \text{ m}^2$$

---

9 The total force is the product of the average pressure and area.

9

$$F_{\text{tot}} = p_{\text{av}} A$$
$$= (49,000 \text{ N} \cdot \text{m}^{-2}) (150 \text{ m}^2)$$
$$= 7.35 \times 10^6 \text{ N}$$

Problem 3 In the mercury manometer depicted in the figure, $y_1 = 4$ cm, $y_2 = 9$ cm. Atmospheric pressure is 990 millibars. Find a) the absolute pressure at the bottom of the U-tube, b) the absolute pressure in the open tube at a depth of 5 cm below the free surface, c) the absolute pressure of the gas in the tank and d) the gauge pressure of the gas in terms of the height of mercury.

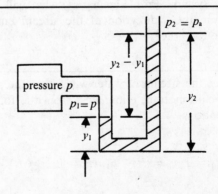

10 The absolute pressure can be calculated from $p = p_a + \rho g y_2$. Note that 990 millibars $= 0.990 \times 10^5$ Pa and the density of mercury is 13.6×10^3 kg $\cdot$ m^{-3}.

10
$$p = 0.990 \times 10^5 \text{ N} \cdot \text{m}^{-2}$$
$$+ (13.6 \times 10^3 \text{ kg} \cdot \text{m}^{-3}) (9.8 \text{ m} \cdot \text{s}^{-2})$$
$$\times (0.09 \text{ m})$$
$$= 1.11 \text{ Pa}$$

11 Use the same relationship to find the absolute pressure in the open tube at 5 cm below the surface.

11
$$p = p_a + \rho g y$$
$$= 0.990 \times 10^5 \text{ N} \cdot \text{m}^{-2}$$
$$+ (13.6 \times 10^3 \text{ kg} \cdot \text{m}^{-3}) (9.8 \text{ m} \cdot \text{s}^{-2})$$
$$\times (0.05 \text{ m})$$
$$= 1.06 \text{ Pa}$$

12 To find the absolute pressure of the gas in the tank use the same relationship but substitute $y_2 - y_1$ for y. Compare the answer with frame 11.

12
$$p = p_a + \rho g (y_2 - y_1)$$
$$= 0.990 \times 10^5 \text{ N} \cdot \text{m}^{-2}$$
$$+ (13.6 \times 10^3 \text{ kg} \cdot \text{m}^{-3}) (9.8 \text{ m} \cdot \text{s}^{-2})$$
$$\times (0.09 \text{ m} - 0.04 \text{ m})$$
$$= 1.06 \text{ Pa}$$

13 Calculate the gauge pressure which equals $p - p_a$, and is proportional to the difference in height of the mercury columns.

13
$$y_2 - y_1 = 0.05 \text{ m of mercury}$$

Problem 4 Consider a large open tank filled with water to a height H. At a depth h_1 below the surface, a small hole is made in the wall. a) At what distance R from the base of the tank does the emerging stream strike the ground? b) At what height h_2 above the bottom of the tank should a second hole be made in order for the emerging water to have the same range R?

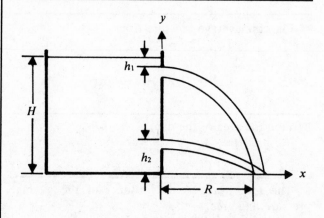

14 Let the foot of the tank be the origin of our co-ordinate system. Fron kinematics, what will be the velocity in the x-direction of the stream emerging from the top hole?

14
$$v_{0x} = \sqrt{2gh_1}$$

15 Since the stream of water will follow the pattern of projectile motion, eliminate t from the following two equations:
$$x = x_0 + v_{0x}t$$
$$y = y_0 + v_{0y}t - \tfrac{1}{2}gt^2$$
(note: $x_0 = 0$, $y_0 = H - h_1$, $v_{0y} = 0$, $x = R$)

15
$$R = v_{0x}t = \sqrt{2gh_1}\, t \quad \text{and}$$
$$y = 0 = (H - h_1) - \tfrac{1}{2}gt^2$$
$$\therefore \tfrac{1}{2}gt^2 = \tfrac{1}{2}g \left(\frac{R^2}{2gh_1} \right) = H - h_1$$
$$R = 2\sqrt{h_1(H - h_1)}$$

16 To find h_2, follow the same procedure. First find v_{0x} and substitute in the two kinematic equations given in frame 15.

16

$$v_{0x} = \sqrt{2g(H - h_2)}$$
$$R = \sqrt{2g(H - h_2)}\, t$$
$$y = 0 = h_2 - \tfrac{1}{2}gt^2$$

---

17 Eliminate t and solve for R.

17

$$t = \frac{R}{\sqrt{2g(H - h_2)}}$$
$$\tfrac{1}{2}gt^2 = \tfrac{1}{2}g\,\frac{R^2}{2g(H - h_2)} = h_2$$
$$R = 2\sqrt{h_2(H - h_2)}$$

---

18 But R in frame 15 must equal R in frame 17. Equate and solve for h_2.

18

$$h_2(H - h_2) = h_1(H - h_1)$$
$$h_2 = h_1$$

Problem 5 Water is pumped from a pipeline 2 m above the ground to a water tower 15 m above the ground. If the pipeline velocity and gauge pressure are $8 \text{ m} \cdot \text{s}^{-1}$ and 2×10^5 Pa, respectively, and water enters the tower at one atmosphere, with what velocity does the water enter the tank?

19 Tabulate what is given and what must be found. Note that we will use Bernoulli's equation, therefore we must use absolute pressures. Absolute pressure = p_a + gauge pressure.

19 Given:
$$p_1 = 1.01 \times 10^5 \text{ Pa} + 2 \times 10^5 \text{ Pa}$$
$$p_2 = 1.01 \times 10^5 \text{ Pa}$$
$$y_1 = 2 \text{ m} \qquad y_2 = 15 \text{ m}$$
$$v_1 = 8 \text{ m} \cdot \text{s}^{-1}$$
$$\rho = 10^3 \text{ kg} \cdot \text{m}^{-3}$$
Find v_2

---

20 Solve Bernoulli's equation
$$p_1 + \rho g y_1 + \tfrac{1}{2}\rho v_1^2 = p_2 + \rho g y_2 + \tfrac{1}{2}\rho v_2^2 \text{ for } v_2.$$

20

$$v_2^2 = \frac{2(p_1 - p_2)}{\rho} + 2g(y_1 - y_2) + v_1^2$$
$$= \frac{2(3.01 \times 10^5 \text{ Pa} - 1.01 \times 10^5 \text{ Pa})}{10^3 \text{ kg} \cdot \text{m}^{-3}}$$
$$+ 2(9.8 \text{ m} \cdot \text{s}^{-2})$$
$$\times (2 \text{ m} - 15 \text{ m}) + (8 \text{ m} \cdot \text{s}^{-1})^2$$
$$v_2 = 14.5 \text{ m} \cdot \text{s}^{-1}$$

Problem 6 Water is flowing in a horizontal pipe of variable cross section. If the discharge ratio from the pipe is $4 \times 10^{-3} \text{ m}^3 \cdot \text{s}^{-1}$, find the velocities at two points where the cross-sectional areas are 0.005 m^2 and 0.001 m^2 respectively. Also, find the pressure difference between these two points.

21 Find the velocities from the discharge rate equation, $Q = Av$.

21
$$A_1 v_1 = Q$$
$$(0.005 \text{ m}^2)v_1 = 4 \times 10^{-3} \text{ m}^3 \cdot \text{s}^{-1}$$
$$v_1 = 0.8 \text{ m} \cdot \text{s}^{-1}$$
$$A_2 v_2 = Q$$
$$(0.001 \text{ m}^2)v_2 = 4 \times 10^{-3} \text{ m}^3 \cdot \text{s}^{-1}$$
$$v_2 = 4 \text{ m} \cdot \text{s}^{-1}$$

22 Find the pressure difference by using Bernoulli's equation,

$$p_1 + \rho g y_1 + \tfrac{1}{2}\rho v_1{}^2 = p_2 + \rho g y_2 + \tfrac{1}{2}\rho v_2{}^2.$$

22 Since the pipe is horizontal, $y_1 = y_2$, and the equation reduces to:

$$
\begin{aligned}
p_1 - p_2 &= \tfrac{1}{2}\rho(v_2{}^2 - v_1{}^2) \\
&= \tfrac{1}{2}(10^3 \text{ kg} \cdot \text{m}^{-3}) \\
&\quad [(4 \text{ m} \cdot \text{s}^{-1})^2 - (0.8 \text{ m} \cdot \text{s}^{-1})^2] \\
&= 7680 \text{ Pa}
\end{aligned}
$$

PROGRAMMED TEST

1 *Problem 1* A block of wood whose density is $0.85 \text{ g} \cdot \text{cm}^{-3}$ floats in a liquid of density $1.1 \text{ g} \cdot \text{cm}^{-3}$. The total volume of the wood is 27 cm^3. Find a) the mass of the wood, b) the mass of the displaced liquid, c) the volume of the displaced liquid, d) the volume of wood which appears above the surface and e) the specific gravity of the wood.

1 *Answer*
23.0 g, 23.0 g, 20.9 cm³, 6.1 cm³, 0.85

If you solved this problem correctly, go to frame 8. If you could not solve this problem, go through frames 2–7.

2 Find the mass of the wood from the density relation.

2

$$\rho = \frac{m}{V}$$
$$m = (0.85 \text{ g} \cdot \text{cm}^{-3})(27 \text{ cm}^3) = 23.0 \text{ g}$$

3 What is the buoyant force on the wood?

3

$$F_B = w = 23.0 \text{ g} \, (g)$$

4 What is the mass of the displaced liquid?

4 Weight of displaced liquid = buoyant force
$$m_1 g = 23.0 \text{ g} \, (g)$$
$$m_1 = 23.0 \text{ g}$$

5 Find the volume of the displaced liquid from density relations.

5

$$\rho = \frac{m}{V}$$

$$V = \frac{23.0 \text{ g}}{1.1 \text{ g} \cdot \text{cm}^{-3}} = 20.9 \text{ cm}^3$$

6 The volume of wood which appears above the surface can be found by subtracting the volume of the displaced liquid from the total volume of the wood.

6

$$27 \text{ cm}^3 - 20.9 \text{ cm}^3 = 6.1 \text{ cm}^3$$

7 The specific gravity of the wood can be found by dividing the density of wood by the density of water.

7

$$\frac{0.85 \text{ g} \cdot \text{cm}^{-3}}{1.00 \text{ g} \cdot \text{cm}^{-3}} = 0.85$$

8 Problem 2 A hollow sphere has an outer radius of 12 cm and a density of 2.7 g · cm^{-3}. What should be the inner radius in order for it to float half submerged in water.

8 Answer

11.2 cm

If you solved this problem correctly, go to frame 13. If you could not solve this problem, go through frames 9–12.

9 What is the volume of the sphere? Let V_o = volume of outer sphere and V_i = volume of inner sphere.

9

$$V = V_o - V_i$$

---

10 What is the weight of the sphere?

10

$$\rho = \frac{m}{V}$$
$$w_s = mg = \rho_s Vg$$

---

11 What is the weight of the displaced water? Note that the volume of the displaced water is $\frac{1}{2}V_o$.

11

$$w_w = \frac{\rho_w V_o g}{2}$$

---

12 This is equal to the buoyant force on the sphere which equals the weight of the sphere. Write the relationship and solve for r.

12

$$F_B = w_w = w_s$$
$$\frac{\rho_w V_o g}{2} = \rho_s Vg \quad \text{where } V = V_o - V_i$$
$$V_o - V_i = \frac{\rho_w V_o}{2\rho_s}$$
$$V_i = V_o \left(1 - \frac{\rho_w}{2\rho_s}\right)$$
$$\frac{4}{3}\pi r_i^3 = \frac{4}{3}\pi (12 \text{ cm})^3 \left(1 - \frac{1.00 \text{ g} \cdot \text{cm}^{-3}}{2(2.7 \text{ g} \cdot \text{cm}^{-3})}\right)$$
$$r_i = 11.2 \text{ cm}$$

---

13 Problem 3 A cubical copper block floats on mercury. If the densities of copper and mercury are 8.9 and 13.6 g · cm^{-3} respectively, find the fraction of the block which is above the mercury surface. If water is poured over the mercury, what must be the minimal depth of the water layer so that the block is submerged?

13 Answer

0.346, 0.373 of block's height

If you solved this problem correctly, go to frame 20. If you could not solve this problem, go through frames 14–19.

14 The weight of the block is equal to the weight of the displaced mercury. Write the relationship in terms of the densities. Use $w = mg$ and $\rho = \frac{m}{V}$.

14

$$w_b = w_m$$
$$\rho_b V_b g = \rho_m V_m g$$

---

15 What is the ratio of the volume of the displaced mercury to the volume of the block?

15

$$\frac{V_m}{V_b} = \frac{\rho_b}{\rho_m} = \frac{8.9 \text{ g} \cdot \text{cm}^{-3}}{13.6 \text{ g} \cdot \text{cm}^{-3}} = 0.654$$

---

16 This is the fraction of the block under the mercury. What fraction is above?

16 $1 - 0.654 = 0.346$

---

17 When water is poured over the mercury, the weight of the block is equal to the weight of the displaced mercury and displaced water. What is this in terms of densities?

17

$$w_b = w_m + w_w \qquad (1)$$
$$\rho_b V_b g = \rho_m V_m g + \rho_w V_w g$$

---

18 What is the volume of the mercury in terms of the other volumes?

18

$$V_m = V_b - V_w$$

---

19 Use this relationship to eliminate V_m in Eq. (1) and find V_w / V_b.

19

$$\rho_b V_b = \rho_m (V_b - V_w) + \rho_w V_w$$
$$(\rho_m - \rho_w) V_w = (\rho_m - \rho_b) V_b$$
$$\frac{V_w}{V_b} = \frac{\rho_m - \rho_b}{\rho_m - \rho_w}$$
$$= \frac{13.6 \text{ g} \cdot \text{cm}^{-3} - 8.9 \text{ g} \cdot \text{cm}^{-3}}{13.6 \text{ g} \cdot \text{cm}^{-3} - 1 \text{ g} \cdot \text{cm}^{-3}}$$
$$= 0.373 \text{ of block's height}$$

---

20 *Problem 4* Prove that if a solid object (specific gravity > 1) is fully submerged in water its specific gravity $= \dfrac{\text{weight in air}}{\text{apparent loss of weight in water}}$

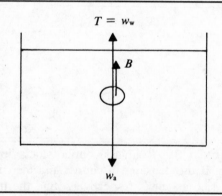

If you solved this problem correctly go to frame 26. If you could not solve this problem, go through frames 21–25.

---

21 When the body is immersed in water, then $T = w_w$ = tension in the cord = weight in water w_a = weight of object in air. Find ΣF_y.

21 $\Sigma F_y = w_w + B - w_a = 0$

---

22 What is the buoyant force equal to? Use $w = mg$ and $\rho = m/V$ and substitute in the first equation.

22 In accordance with Archimedes' principle, the body is buoyed up by a force equal to the weight of the displaced water.
$$B = \rho V_w g$$
$$\Sigma F_y = w_w + \rho_w V_w g - w_a = 0$$

---

23 Express the volume of the object in terms of its density and weight. Remember that the weight of the object is w_s.

23

$$\rho_{obj} = \frac{m_{obj}}{V_{obj}}$$

$$V_{obj} = \frac{m_{obj}}{\rho_{obj}} = \frac{w_a}{\rho_{obj}g}$$

---

24 Since $V_{obj} = V_w$ substitute in the equation for ΣF_y and solve for ρ_{obj}.

24

$$\Sigma F_y = w_w + \rho_w \frac{w_a g}{\rho_{obj}g} - w_a = 0$$

$$\rho_{obi} = \left(\frac{w_a}{w_a - w_w}\right)\rho_w$$

---

25 Find the specific gravity by dividing both sides of the equation by ρ_w.

25

$$\text{specific gravity} = \frac{\rho_{obj}}{\rho_w} = \frac{w_a}{w_a - w_w}$$

---

26 *Problem 5* A pipeline has a variable cross-sectional area. If the velocity of the water is $3 \text{ m} \cdot \text{s}^{-1}$ at a point where the diameter is 0.1 m, find the velocity at a point where the diameter is 0.3 m. What is the discharge rate?

26 *Answer*
$0.333 \text{ m} \cdot \text{s}^{-1}$, $2.36 \times 10^{-2} \text{ m}^3 \cdot \text{s}^{-1}$

If you solved this problem correctly, go to frame 29. If you could not solve this problem, go through frames 27–28.

27 Find v_2 from the continuity equation.

27

$$A_1 v_1 = A_2 V_2$$
$$v_2 = \frac{A_1 v_1}{A_2}$$
$$= \frac{\pi(\frac{1}{2}d_1)^2 v_1}{\pi(\frac{1}{2}d_2)^2}$$
$$= \frac{(0.1 \text{ m})^2 (3 \text{ m} \cdot \text{s}^{-1})}{(0.3 \text{ m})^2}$$
$$\doteq 0.333 \text{ m} \cdot \text{s}^{-1}$$

---

28 Find the discharge rate.

28

$$Q = A_1 v_1$$
$$= \pi[(\frac{1}{2})(0.1 \text{ m})]^2 (3 \text{ m} \cdot \text{s}^{-1})$$
$$= 2.36 \times 10^{-2} \text{ m}^3 \cdot \text{s}^{-1}$$

---

29 *Problem 6* Water stands at a height of 10 m in a closed tank. A pressure of $3 \times 10^4 \text{ Pa}$ (gauge) is applied to the water by compressed air at the top of the tank. Calculate the speed with which a stream of water will emerge from a small hole in the side of the tank 6 m below the water level.

29 *Answer*
$13.3 \text{ m} \cdot \text{s}^{-1}$

If you solved this problem correctly, go to frame 32. If you could not solve this problem, go through frames 30–31.

30 Use Bernoulli's equation and solve for v_2. Let $p_1 = p =$ absolute pressure at the surface of the water and take the bottom of the tank as the reference level. Then $y_1 = h$, $y_2 = 0$, $p_2 = p_a$, $v_1 = 0$.

30

$$p_1 + \rho g y_1 + \tfrac{1}{2}\rho v_1^2 = p_2 + \rho g y_2 + \tfrac{1}{2}\rho v_2^2$$
$$p + \rho g h + \tfrac{1}{2}\rho v_1^2 = p_a + \tfrac{1}{2}\rho v_2^2$$
$$v_2^2 = \frac{2(p - p_a)}{\rho} + 2gh$$

---

31 Substitute the values and solve. Note that $p - p_a$ is the gauge pressure.

31

$$v_2^2 = \frac{2(3 \times 10^4 \text{ Pa})}{10^3 \text{ kg} \cdot \text{m}^{-3}} + 2(9.8 \text{ m} \cdot \text{s}^{-2})(6 \text{ m})$$
$$v_2 = 13.3 \text{ m} \cdot \text{s}^{-1}$$

---

32 *Problem 7* A liquid flowing through a 2 m long pipe of radius 0.01 m undergoes a pressure drop of 8 Pa. If the flow velocity at the center is $0.1 \text{ m} \cdot \text{s}^{-1}$, find the viscosity of the liquid.

32 *Answer*
1.0 cp

If you could not solve the problem go through frames 33–35.

---

33 Determine what is given in terms of the equation
$$v = \frac{p_1 - p_2}{4\eta L}(R^2 - r^2),$$
where v = velocity,
$p_1 - p_2$ = pressure difference,
$\quad L$ = length of pipe,
$\quad R$ = inner radius of pipe,
$\quad r$ = distance from center,
$\quad \eta$ = coefficient of viscosity.

33 Given:
$$v = 0.1 \text{ m} \cdot \text{s}^{-1}$$
$$p_1 - p_2 = 8 \text{ Pa}$$
$$L = 2 \text{ m}$$
$$R = 0.01 \text{ m}$$
$$r = 0$$
Find η

---

34 Solve for η and substitute the given values.

34

$$\eta = \frac{(p_1 - p_2)R^2}{4vL}$$
$$= \frac{(8 \text{ N} \cdot \text{m}^{-2})(0.01 \text{ m})^2}{4(0.1 \text{ m} \cdot \text{s}^{-1})(2 \text{ m})}$$
$$= 0.001 \text{ N} \cdot \text{s} \cdot \text{m}^{-2}$$

---

35 Convert to centipoise:
1 poise $= 10^{-1} \text{ N} \cdot \text{s} \cdot \text{m}^{-2}$
$\quad$ 1 cp $= 10^{-2}$ poise

35

$$(0.001 \text{ N} \cdot \text{s} \cdot \text{m}^{-2})\left(\frac{1 \text{ poise}}{10^{-1} \text{ N} \cdot \text{s} \cdot \text{m}^{-2}}\right) = 0.01 \text{ poise}$$

$$(0.01 \text{ poise})\left(\frac{1 \text{ cp}}{0.01 \text{ poise}}\right) = 1.0 \text{ cp}$$

Note: the viscosity of water at 20° C is 1.005 poise.

14

Temperature and Expansion

CHAPTER SUMMARY

In this chapter, we begin our discussion of thermodynamics, the study of energy transformations and their relationship to the properties of matter. Temperature is described as a fourth fundamental physical quantity and the Kelvin, Celsius, Fahrenheit and Rankine temperature scales are defined. The concepts of thermal equilibrium and the zeroth law of thermodynamics are developed and the remainder of the chapter is devoted to thermal expansion and stresses.

BASIC TERMS — *Give definitions or meanings for the following:*

temperature (14-1)
thermal equilibrium (14-1)
zeroth law of thermodynamics (14-1)
insulator (14-1)
conductor (14-1)
thermometric property (14-2)
thermometer (14-2)
Celsius scale (14-3)
Fahrenheit scale (14-3)

absolute temperature scale (14-4)
absolute zero (14-4)
Rankine scale (14-4)
triple point (14-4)
Kelvin scale (14-4)
thermal expansion (14-5)
coefficient of linear expansion (14-5)
coefficient of volume expansion (14-5)
thermal stress (14-6)

PROGRAMMED QUIZ

1 Which scales have the same degree magnitudes?	**1** Fahrenheit and Rankine; Celsius and Kelvin.
2 What are the zero points in all four scales?	**2** 0 K, − 273°C, 0°R, − 460°F.
3 What are the ice points in all four scales?	**3** 273 K, 0°C, 492°R, 32°F.
4 What are the steam points in all four scales?	**4** 373 K, 100°C, 672°R, 212°F.

5 A sensitive thermometer is placed in contact with two substances. In each case the reading is the same. What can we say about the two substances?

5 They are in thermal equilibrium.

---

6 What is the difference between "20°F" and "20 F°"?

6 20°F is an actual temperature, 20 F° is a temperature interval.

---

7 Can the coefficient of volume expansion be negative?

7 Yes (ex: water between 0°C and 4°C and rubber) but usually it is positive.

---

8 Which type of thermometer is the most precise?

8 Resistance thermometer.

---

9 Are the melting, boiling and triple points of a particular substance constant?

9 Only the triple point is constant; the melting and boiling points change with pressure.

---

10 If α for brass is 2.0×10^{-5} (C°)$^{-1}$, what is β?

10 $\beta = 3\alpha = 3(2.0 \times 10^{-5}(\text{C}°)^{-1}) = 6.0 \times 10^{-5}(\text{C}°)^{-1}$

---

11 In what state is a substance at the triple point?

11 Solid, liquid and/or gas.

---

12 A temperature change of 5° on the Celsius scale corresponds to how many degrees on the Fahrenheit scale?

12 9°.

---

13 Why does a bimetallic strip bend upon heating?

13 If the two metals have different coefficients of linear expansion, one metal will expand more than the other causing the strip to bend.

---

14 If a ring is heated the outer circumference will expand. What about the inner circumference?

14 It will expand also.

---

15 Give common examples of thermal expansion.

15 Telephone wires sag in summer, you heat the cover to remove it from a jar, spaces are left in rail-road tracks, mercury rises in a thermometer.

MAIN IDEAS

1 Temperature may be considered as our fourth indefinable term. The others are length, mass, and time. Temperature may be described in terms of properties of matter (e.g., length of a mercury column L, the pressure of a gas p and electrical resistance R). These properties are referred to as state coordinates or thermometric properties.

2 Thermal equilibrium. If two or more bodies are in contact with each other and there is no change in their state co-ordinates (for example the height of a mercury column remains unchanged), then the bodies are said to be in thermal equilibrium.

3 Zeroth law of thermodynamics. If system A is in thermal equilibrium with C and B is in thermal equilibrium with C then A and B are in thermal equilibrium with each other.

4 Thermometer. A device which is capable of indicating quantitative measures of temperature. Important characteristics of a thermometer include sensitivity, accuracy, reproducibility and speed in achieving thermal equilibrium with other systems.

5 Thermocouple. When two dissimilar metals, such as copper and iron, are joined together as shown, then a temperature difference between the two junctions will produce an electromotive force.

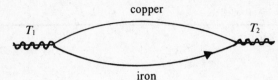

6 Triple point. Solid, liquid and gaseous states of a substance are in thermal equilibrium at one definite temperature and pressure known as the triple point. The triple point pressure and temperature of water are 610 Pa and 0.01°C respectively.

7 Temperature scales. The standard fixed point in thermometry is the triple point of water, 273.16 K (read 273.16 Kelvin — the Kelvin has the same magnitude as one degree on the Celsius scale).

8 Celsius temperature is defined by $T_C = T_K - 273.15°$, where T_C denotes Celsius temperature and T_K denotes the temperature on the Kelvin scale.

9 Fahrenheit temperature is defined by $T_F = T_R - 459.67°$, where T_R represents the Rankine temperature.

The following points should be noted: $T_R = \frac{9}{5} T$, one degree on the Fahrenheit scale has the same magnitude as one degree on the Rankine scale and $-459.67°R$ corresponds to -273.15 K.

10 Conversion from Fahrenheit → Celsius and vice versa. $T_F = \frac{9}{5} T_C + 32°$ and $T_C = \frac{5}{9} (T_F - 32°)$ where the ratio $\frac{5}{9} = \frac{5\,C°}{9\,F°}$.

11 Difference between °C and C°: 20°C refers to an actual temperature. 20 C° refers to a temperature interval or change.

12 Coefficient of linear expansion α. Consider a body of length L_0 which undergoes a change in length ΔL during a temperature change ΔT. Thus, $\alpha = \frac{1}{L_0} \cdot \frac{\Delta L}{\Delta T}$.

13 Coefficient of volume expansion β. In a similar manner, if a body of volume V_0 undergoes a change in volume ΔV during a temperature change ΔT,

$$\beta = \frac{1}{V_0} \frac{\Delta V}{\Delta T}.$$

14 Relationship between α and β.
$\beta = 3\alpha$.

15 Thermal stresses. Consider a rod of length L_0 fastened at each end. If the temperature is reduced ($\Delta T = -$), then

$$\frac{\Delta L}{L_0} = \alpha \Delta T \quad (\Delta L \text{ and } \Delta T \text{ are negative})$$
$$F = -AY\alpha\,\Delta T \quad (\text{since } \Delta T = -, F \text{ is } +).$$

If ΔT is positive, then F and F/A are negative. F is the compressive force and F/A the compressive stress.

PROGRAMMED QUIZ

In frames 1–3, change 65°F to the appropriate scale:
1 Rankine.

1

$$T_F = T_R - 460°$$
$$T_R = 65° + 460° = 525°R$$

2 Kelvin.

2

$$T_R = \frac{9}{5} T$$

$$T = \frac{5}{9} (525°) = 292 \text{ K}$$

---

3 Celsius.

3

$$T_F = \frac{9}{5} T_C + 32°$$

$$T_C = \frac{5}{9} (65° - 32°) = 18.3°C$$

---

4 Fill in the missing numbers on the two scales.

	F	C
steam point		
body temperature	98.6°	
hot day	95°	
cool room	50°	
ice point		
cold day		−5°

4

	F	C
steam point	212°	100°
body temperature	98.6°	37°
hot room	95°	35°
cool room	50°	10°
ice point	32°	0°
cold day	23°	−5°

$$T_C = \frac{5}{9} (T_F - 32°)$$

$$= \frac{5}{9} (98.6° - 32°) = 37°C$$

$$= \frac{5}{9} (95° - 32°) = 35°C$$

$$= \frac{5}{9} (50° - 32°) = 10°C$$

$$T_F = \frac{9}{5} T_C + 32°$$

$$= \frac{9}{5} (- 5° + 32°) = 23°F$$

---

5 A gas thermometer registers a pressure of 6 cm of mercury when in contact with water at the normal boiling point. What pressure will it read when in contact with water at the triple point?

5

$$\frac{T(X)}{T(X_3)} = \frac{X}{X_3}$$

$$X_3 = \frac{273 \text{ K}}{373 \text{ K}} (6 \text{ cm}) = 4.39 \text{ cm of Hg}$$

---

6 An aluminum pendulum shaft is measured to be 0.80 m at a temperature of 20°C. What is the change in length at 30°C?

6

$$\Delta L = \alpha L_0 \Delta T$$
$$= (2.4 \times 10^{-5} \, (C°)^{-1})$$
$$\times (0.80 \text{ m}) (30°C - 20°C)$$
$$= 1.92 \times 10^{-4} \text{ m}$$

---

7 What is the new length?

7 $0.80 \text{ m} + 2 \times 10^{-4} = 0.8002 \text{ m}$

---

8 Which of the dimensions will increase, which will decrease when this piece of copper is heated?

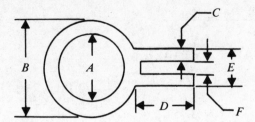

8 All the dimensions will increase, including the inner ones.

---

9 A steel liner in the form of a thin cylinder (outside diameter 90.2 mm at 20°C) is to be inserted in the bore of a 90 mm brass cannon. To what temperature should the cannon be heated so that the liner can be inserted? (α for brass $= 2.0 \times 10^{-5}$ [C°]$^{-1}$.)

9

$$\Delta L = \alpha L_0 \Delta T$$
$$\Delta T = \frac{2 \times 10^{-4} \text{ m}}{2 \times 10^{-5} \text{ (C°)}^{-1} (0.09 \text{ m})}$$
$$= 111 \text{ C°}$$
$$T_f - 20 \text{ °C} = 111 \text{ C°}$$
$$T_f = 131\text{°C}$$

---

10 A steel railroad rail 20 m in length is laid on a winter day when the temperature is 0°C. What is the expansion of the rail when the temperature rises to 30°C? (α for steel $= 1.2 \times 10^{-5}$[C°]$^{-1}$.)

10

$$\Delta L = \alpha L \Delta T$$
$$= 1.2 \times 10^{-5}\text{(C°)}^{-1} (20 \text{ m}) (30 \text{ C°})$$
$$= 7.2 \times 10^{-3} \text{ m}$$

---

11 If the cross sectional area of this rail is 4×10^{-3} m^2, what is the compression of the rail if it is firmly lodged between two other rails? The force of compression is the force that would be required to compress the rail back to its original length (the modulus of elasticity of steel $= 2 \times 10^{11}$ Pa).

11

$$Y = \frac{\text{compressive stress}}{\text{compressive strain}} = \frac{F_\perp/A}{\Delta l/l_0}$$
$$F_\perp = \frac{YA\Delta l}{l_0}$$
$$= \frac{2 \times 10^{11} \text{ Pa } (4 \times 10^{-3} \text{ m}^2) (7.2 \times 10^{-3} \text{ m})}{20 \text{ m}}$$
$$= 2.88 \times 10^5 \text{ N}$$

---

12 A 10 cm bimetallic strip consists of a thin strip of copper on top welded to a similar piece of steel on the bottom. The left end of the strip is clamped rigidly as shown. If the bimetallic strip is heated 10 C°, compute the increase in length for each strip and show how the strip will bend. ($\alpha_{copper} = 1.7 \times 10^{-5}$[C°]$^{-1}$, $\alpha_{steel} = 1.2 \times 10^{-5}$ [C°]$^{-1}$.)

12 for copper,
$$\Delta L = 1.7 \times 10^{-5} \text{ (C°)}^{-1} (0.10 \text{ m}) (10 \text{ C°})$$
$$= 1.7 \times 10^{-5} \text{ m}$$
for steel,
$$\Delta L = 1.2 \times 10^{-5} \text{ (C°)}^{-1} (0.10 \text{ m}) (10 \text{ C°})$$
$$= 1.2 \times 10^{-5} \text{ m}$$
Since copper expands more than steel, the bimetallic strip will bend downward.

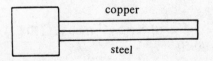

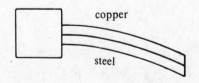

13 A steel tank contains 200 1 of alcohol at 10°C. When the tank and alcohol are heated to 35°C, the volume of the tank increases by 0.18 1. How many liters of alcohol overflow? ($\beta_{\text{steel}} = 3.6 \times 10^{-5} \text{ [C°]}^{-1}$, $\beta_{\text{ethyl alcohol}} = 75 \times 10^{-5} \text{ [C°]}^{-1}$)

13

$$(\Delta V)_{\text{al}} = \beta_{\text{al}} V_0 \Delta T$$
$$(\Delta V)_{\text{s}} = \beta_{\text{s}} V_0 \Delta T$$
$$\frac{(\Delta V)_{\text{al}}}{(\Delta V)_{\text{s}}} = \frac{\beta_{\text{al}}}{\beta_{\text{s}}}$$
$$(\Delta V)_{\text{al}} = \frac{\beta_{\text{al}}}{\beta_{\text{s}}} (\Delta V)_{\text{s}}$$
$$= \frac{75 \times 10^{-5} \text{ (C°)}^{-1}}{3.6 \times 10^{-5} \text{ (C°)}^{-1}} (0.181)$$
$$= 3.75 \text{ 1}$$

STEP BY STEP SOLUTIONS OF PROBLEMS

Problem 1 A steel measuring tape was calibrated at a temperature of 20°C. When the temperature was 10°C, the distance between the two points was measured as 35.0 m. What is the true distance between the two points?

1 Draw a sketch to represent the lengths of the tape at 10°C and 20°C.

1

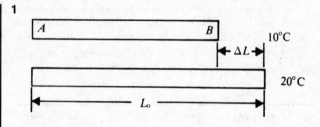

2 The tape would give a true reading of 35.0 m if the temperature was 20°C. Since the temperature is 10°C, the tape contracted by ΔL. Hence the true reading is $L_0 - \Delta L$. Find ΔL.

2

$$\Delta L = L_0 \alpha \Delta T$$
$$= 35.0 \text{ m } [1.2 \times 10^{-5} \text{ (C°)}^{-1}] (10 \text{ C°})$$
$$= 4.2 \times 10^{-3} \text{ m} = 4.2 \text{ mm}$$

3 Find $L_0 - \Delta L$.

3

$$L_0 - \Delta L = 35.0 \text{ m} - 0.0042 \text{ m}$$
$$= 34.9958 \text{ m}$$

Problem 2 A steel bridge has a continuous span of 600 m which is fixed at one end and is free to move at the other. a) What would be the change in length of the bridge between a winter temperture of $-30°C$ and a hot summer's day of 40°C? b) If both ends of the bridge were rigidly fixed at 40°C, compute the additional stress on the bridge at the winter temperature of $-30°C$.

4 Given:
$$\alpha = 1.2 \times 10^{-5} \text{ (C°)}^{-1}$$
$$L = 600 \text{ m}$$
$$\Delta T = 40°C - (-30°C) = 70 \text{ C°}$$
Find ΔL by using
$$\Delta L = \alpha L_0 \Delta T$$

4

$$\Delta L = 1.2 \times 10^{-5} \text{ (C°)}^{-1} (600 \text{ m}) (70 \text{ C°})$$
$$= 0.504 \text{ m}$$

5 What would be the fractional change in length if the bridge was free to contract?

5

$$\frac{\Delta L}{L_0} = \alpha \Delta T$$

6 Since the bridge is rigidly fixed at both ends, the tensile stress must increase by an amount that will produce a strain which is equal and opposite to the fractional change in length. What is this strain?

6

From $Y = \dfrac{F/A}{\Delta L/L_0}$,

we have $\dfrac{\Delta L}{L_0} = \dfrac{F}{AY}$

7 In order to calculate the stress on the span, we note that the strain $(\Delta L/L_0)$ due to the thermal expansion plus the elastic strain must equal 0. Express this condition.

7

$$\alpha \Delta T + \frac{F}{AY} = 0$$

$$\frac{F}{A} = -Y\alpha\Delta T$$

8 Find the numerical value of the stress by substituting $Y = 2 \times 10^{11}$ Pa, $\alpha = 1.2 \times 10^{-5}$ $(C°)^{-1}$, $\Delta T = 70$ C°.

8

$$\frac{F}{A} = -2 \times 10^{11} \text{ Pa } [1.2 \times 10^{-5} \text{ (C°)}^{-1}] \text{ (70 C°)}$$

$$= -1.68 \times 10^8 \text{ Pa}$$

Problem 3 A grandfather's clock has a brass pendulum which has a period of 2 s (calibrated at 20°C). a) What is the fractional change in length $\Delta L/L_0$ of the pendulum when the temperature rises to 30°C? b) How many seconds per day will the clock gain or lose? ($\alpha = 2.0 \times 10^{-5}$ $(C°)^{-1}$.)

9 Since $\Delta L = \alpha L_0 \Delta T$, solve for $\Delta L/L_0$ and substitute $\alpha = 2.0 \times 10^{-5}$ $(C°)^{-1}$ and $\Delta T = 10$ C°.

9

$$\frac{\Delta L}{L_0} = \alpha \Delta T = 2.0 \times 10^{-5} \text{ (C°)}^{-1} \text{ (10 C°)}$$

$$= 2 \times 10^{-4}$$

10 We recall from Chapter 11 that the period of a physical pendulum is $\tau = 2\pi\sqrt{I/mgh}$, where I is the moment of inertia of the pendulum about the axis through its pivot, h is the distance from the pivot to the center of gravity and m is the mass of the pendulum. Also, $I = mL_0^2/3$ and $h = L_0/2$. Express the period in terms of L and g.

10

$$\tau_0 = 2\pi \sqrt{\frac{I}{mgh}}$$

$$= 2\pi \sqrt{\frac{mL_0^2}{3mgL_0/2}}$$

$$= 2\pi \sqrt{\frac{2L_0}{3g}}$$

τ_0 is the period when the length of the pendulum $= L_0$

11 When the temperature rises, the length will increase by ΔL. What is the new period?

11

$$\tau = 2\pi \sqrt{\frac{2(L_0 + \Delta L)}{3g}}$$

12 Substitute $\Delta L = \alpha L_0 \Delta T$ and simplify. Express τ (the new period) in terms of τ_0.

12

$$\tau = 2\pi \sqrt{\frac{2(L_0 + \alpha L_0 \Delta T)}{3g}}$$

$$= 2\pi \sqrt{\frac{2L_0(1 + \alpha \Delta T)}{3g}}$$

$$= 2\pi \sqrt{\frac{2L_0}{3g}}(1 + \alpha \Delta T)^{1/2}$$

$$= \tau_0(1 + \alpha \Delta T)^{1/2} \qquad (1)$$

---

13 Use the binomial theorem to expand $(1 + \alpha \Delta T)^{1/2}$ and retain the first two terms. Why?

13

$$(1 + \alpha \Delta T)^{1/2} = 1 + \tfrac{1}{2}\alpha \Delta T + \dots$$
$$= 1 + \tfrac{1}{2}\alpha \Delta T$$

The first two terms are the only significant ones. The squares, cubes, etc. of α are infinitesimal in value.

---

14 Substitute the value of $(1 + \alpha \Delta T)^{1/2}$ in Eq. (1) and solve for τ in terms of τ_0 (note: $\alpha = 2 \times 10^{-5}$ $(C°)^{-1}$).

14

$$\tau = \tau_0[1 + \tfrac{1}{2}(2 \times 10^{-5}\ (C°)^{-1} \cdot 10\ C°)]$$
$$= \tau_0(1 + 1 \times 10^{-4})$$

---

15 What will be the change in the period?

15

$$\tau - \tau_0 = \tau_0 \times 10^{-4}$$
$$= 2 \times 10^{-4}\ \frac{s}{period}$$

Note that the pendulum at 30°C requires more time (2×10^{-4}s) to make one vibration. Thus there will be a loss of time per day.

---

16 Since there are 86,400 s in a day, the pendulum beats 86,400/2 = 43,200 periods per day at 20°C. How many seconds per day will the clock lose?

16 The total loss in time per day

$$= 2 \times 10^{-4}\ \frac{s}{period} \cdot 43,200\ \frac{periods}{day}$$
$$= 8.64\ s/day$$

PROGRAMMED TEST

1 *Problem 1* At what temperature do the Celsius and Fahrenheit scales coincide?

1 *Answer*
$-40°C = -40°F$

If you solved this problem correctly go to frame 3. If you could not solve this problem go through frame 2.

2 Use the relationship $T_F = \frac{9}{5} T_C + 32°$ where T_F = Fahrenheit temperature, T_C = Celsius temperature and the ratio $\frac{9}{5} = \frac{9\ F°}{5\ C°}$.

2

Let $T_F = T_C = X$

$$T_F = \frac{9}{5} T_C + 32°$$

$$X = \frac{9}{5} X + 32°$$

$$5X = 9X + 160°$$

$$-4X = 160°$$

$$X = -40°F = -40°C$$

---

3 **Problem 2** A pycnometer measures 100 cm^3 at 20°C. If it is filled to the brim with mercury at this temperature and heated to 100°C, how much mercury will overflow?

$$\beta_{glass} = 1.5 \times 10^{-5}\ (C°)^{-1},$$
$$\beta_{Hg} = 18.2 \times 10^{-5}\ (C°)^{-1}.$$

3 **Answer**
1.34 cm^3

If you solved this problem correctly, go to frame 6. If you could not solve this problem, go through frames 4–5.

4 Since the volume of the mercury and the glass will increase, the overflow will be the increase in volume of the mercury ΔV_{Hg} minus the increase in volume of the glass ΔV_g. Write the mathematical expression for the overflow.

4

$$\text{overflow} = \Delta V = \Delta V_{Hg} - \Delta V_g$$

---

5 Compute ΔV by using $\Delta V = V_0 \beta \Delta T$ for both mercury and glass.

5

$$\begin{aligned}\Delta V &= V_0 \beta_{Hg} \Delta T - V_0 \beta_g \Delta T\\ &= V_0 \Delta T (\beta_{Hg} - \beta_g)\\ &= 100\ \text{cm}^3\ (80\ C°)\ [18.2 \times 10^{-5}\ (C°)^{-1}\\ &\quad - 1.5 \times 10^{-5}\ (C°)^{-1}]\\ &= 1.34\ \text{cm}^3\end{aligned}$$

---

6 **Problem 3** Consider a body under hydrostatic pressure. a) Find the increase in pressure if the body is not permitted to expand when the temperature of the body is raised. b) What hydrostatic pressure is required to prevent a brass block from expanding when its temperature is raised 40 C°?

6 **Answer**
$\Delta p = B\beta\Delta T$, 1.46×10^8 Pa

If you could not solve this problem, go through frames 7–10.

7 Determine the fractional change in volume, if the body is free to expand, from the relationship $\Delta V = \beta V_0 \Delta T$.

7

$$\frac{\Delta V}{V_0} \beta \Delta T \tag{2}$$

8 Use the definition of the bulk modulus to determine the fractional change.

8

$$B = -\frac{\Delta p}{\Delta V/V_0}$$

$$\frac{\Delta V}{V_0} = -\frac{\Delta p}{B} \qquad (3)$$

---

9 The problem requires that the total fractional change in volume must be zero. Equate equations (2) and (3) and solve for Δp.

9

$$-\frac{\Delta p}{B} + \beta\Delta T = 0$$

$$\Delta p = B\beta\Delta T$$

---

10 For part b:
Given $B = 0.61 \times 10^{11}\,\text{Pa}$
$\beta = 6.0 \times 10^{-5}(\text{C}°)^{-1}$
$\Delta T = 40\,\text{C}°$
Find Δp.

10

$$\Delta p = 0.61 \times 10^{11}\,\text{Pa}\,[6.0 \times 10^{-5}\,(\text{C}°)^{-1}]\,(40\,\text{C}°)$$
$$= 1.46 \times 10^8\,\text{Pa}$$

Note: $\dfrac{\Delta V}{V_0} = \beta\Delta T$ represents the expansion of the body and $\dfrac{-\Delta V}{V_0} = \dfrac{\Delta p}{B}$ represents the corresponding compression of the body back to its original volume.

15

Quantity of Heat

CHAPTER SUMMARY

This chapter begins with a discussion of heat transfer or heat flow. Ideally, the word heat refers to a method of energy transfer. Although any energy unit can be used to measure heat transfer, units based on thermal energy are developed. On the basis of these definitions, specific heat capacity, molar heat capacity, change of phase, heat of fusion and heat of vaporization are introduced.

BASIC TERMS — *Give definitions or meanings for the following:*

heat transfer (15-1)
calorie (15-2)
British thermal unit (Btu) (15-2)
specific heat capacity (15-3)
molar heat capacity (15-3)
calorimetry (15-3)
rule of Dulong and Petit (15-4)
phase (15-5)
heat of fusion (15-5)

phase change (15-5)
phase equilibrium (15-5)
heat of vaporization (15-5)
latent heat (15-5)
supercooled (15-5)
heat of sublimation (15-5)
heat of combustion (15-5)
sublimation (15-5)

PROGRAMMED QUIZ

1 To what physical quantity is heat most closely related?

1 Energy.

2 Which common substance requires a large amount of heat for a given increase in temperature, i.e. has a large specific heat capacity?

2 Water.

3 What happens to the temperature as ice melts to water?

3 Stays the same.

4 You can cool a cup of hot tea by putting a metal spoon in it. Should the specific heat capacity of the metal be as high or as low as possible?

4 As high as possible so that a large amount of heat will be transmitted from the tea to the spoon, thus lowering the temperature of the tea.

---

5 What is the relationship between the heat of vaporization of a substance and the heat of condensation?

5 Equal; the same amount of heat is necessary to change a substance from liquid to vapor as the amount of heat that must be removed to change it from vapor to liquid.

---

6 What are some units of quantity of heat?

6 Calorie, kilocalorie, British thermal unit, joule, ft · lb.

---

7 What happens when a body at a higher temperature is placed in contact with a body of lower temperature?

7 Heat flows from the body at a higher temperature to the body at a lower temperature until they achieve thermal equilibrium.

---

8 Can an energy transfer occur without heat flow? If yes, give an example.

8 Yes; in stirring a liquid vigorously, energy is transferred by means of work.

---

9 When can you add heat to a substance without a resulting change in temperature?

9 During a phase change.

---

10 What are the units of the heat of vaporization?

10 Cal · g^{-1}, J · g^{-1}, J · kg^{-1}, Btu · $lb.^{-1}$
The units are the same for the heat of fusion.

---

11 What happens to the heat that flows into 1 kg of water at 20°C?

11 It raises the temperature of the body.

---

12 Is the specific heat capacity of a substance constant?

12 No, it changes with temperature.

---

13 What are some thermal properties of matter?

13 Heat conductivity, heat of combustion, heat of fusion, heat of vaporization.

---

14 What is the difference between a calorie, an international table calorie and a thermochemical calorie?

14 A calorie is the quantity of heat necessary to raise the temperature of 1 gram of water from 14.5°C to 15.5°C. Therefore it is referred to as a 15° calorie. The IT cal is equal to this and the thermochemical calorie is a 17° calorie.

---

15 The quantity of heat required to raise the temperature of a sample of metal depends only on how many molecules the sample contains (not on the mass of an individual molecule). This is known as what law?

15 Dulong and Petit law,

$$C = Mc = \frac{\Delta Q}{n\Delta T}$$. The only variable is n.

MAIN IDEAS

1 Heat transfer or heat flow refers to energy transfer from a body of higher temperature to one at lower temperature. Consider body A at temperature T_2 in contact with body B at temperature T_1 where $T_2 > T_1$. The temperature of A will decrease and the temperature of B will increase until they have both achieved thermal equilibrium, i.e., $T_2 = T_1$. The energy transferred from A to B is referred to as heat transfer or heat flow.

2 Quantity of heat — used only with respect to an interaction in which there is an energy transfer from one system to another due to a temperature difference. Although the joule should be used to measure the quantity of heat, a unit which is often used is the calorie. One calorie (cal) is the amount of heat required to raise the temperature of 1 gram of water from 14.5°C to 15.5°C (1 cal = 4.186 J). In a similar manner, 1 British thermal unit (Btu) is the amount of heat needed to raise the temperature of 1 lb of water from 63°F to 64°F.

3 Specific heat capacity (or specific heat) of a substance = $c = \dfrac{\Delta Q}{m \Delta T}$, where m = mass, ΔQ = change in heat (joules or calories) and ΔT = change in temperature. If the specific heat is constant during the temperature change, then $\Delta Q = mc\Delta T$. Specific heat is expressed in cal $\cdot$ g^{-1} (C°)$^{-1}$ or J $\cdot$ kg^{-1} (C°)$^{-1}$. Note that specific heat is temperature dependent; therefore the expression "specific heat capacity" refers to the mean specific heat capacity over the temperature interval.

4 Molar heat capacity (or molar specific heat) = $C = Mc = \dfrac{\Delta Q}{n \Delta T}$, where M = molecular mass of the substance in grams and $n = \dfrac{m}{M}$ is the number of moles (mol) of the substance. If $m = M$, we have 1 mol which is the mass in grams numerically equal to the molecular mass. (For example, since 32 is the molecular mass of oxygen, 1 mole of oxygen is 32 grams of oxygen). If C is constant, $Q = nC\Delta T$.

5 Specific heat at constant pressure or volume. Since pressure and volume are the commonly used state parameters, the specific heat is measured by holding one of the variables constant: Thus c_p = specific heat at constant pressure, C_p = molar specific heat at constant pressure, c_v = specific heat at constant volume, C_v = molar specific heat at constant volume.

6 Law of Dulong and Petit. The average molar specific heat (at constant pressure) for all metals except the lightest ≈ 25 J $\cdot$ mol^{-1} $\cdot$ (C°)$^{-1}$ ≈ 6 cal $\cdot$ mol^{-1} (C°)$^{-1}$.

7 Change of phase — matter may exist as a solid, liquid, or gas. Under appropriate conditions of temperature and pressure and by applying the proper amount of heat, a solid may change into a liquid and a liquid into a gas. The heat of fusion of a substance is the amount of heat per unit mass that must be supplied to a material at its melting point to convert it to a liquid at the same temperature. The heat of vaporization is the quantity of heat per unit mass that must be supplied to a material at its boiling point to convert it to a gas at the same temperature. $Q = m L_v$ is used for the phase transition from liquid to vapor and $Q = m L_f$ is used for the transition from solid to liquid.

8 Hints for solving problems.

    a. When heat flows into a material, the temperature of the material increases and thus ΔT is + and ΔQ is +. When heat flows out of a material, the temperature decreases and thus $\Delta T = -$ and ΔQ is −. Use $Q = mc\Delta T$ provided that the substance does not change its phase and pressure is kept constant.

    b. If there is a change of phase, use $Q = mL_f$ at the melting point and $Q = mL_v$ at the boiling point. When ice melts, the heat of fusion is positive (heat is entering). When water freezes, the heat of fusion is negative.

    c. In order to achieve thermal equilibrium, heat exchanges involve the principle of conservation of energy.

    d. The concepts of potential energy mgh and kinetic energy $\frac{1}{2}mv^2$ play an important role (in conjunction with the principle of conservation of energy) in many energy exchange problems.

    e. As usual, be careful of units.

Remember that during a phase change there is no change in temperature.

PROGRAMMED QUIZ

1 In order to raise the temperature of 1 kg of a substance from 0°C to 100°C, 47000 J of heat are needed. What is the specific heat of this substance?

1
$$c = \frac{\Delta Q}{m\Delta T}$$
$$= \frac{47000 \text{ J}}{1 \text{ kg } (100 \text{ C}°)}$$
$$= 470 \text{ J} \cdot \text{kg}^{-1} (\text{C}°)^{-1}$$

---

2 What is this substance? Refer to a table of specific heat capacities.

2 Iron.

---

3 How much heat is required to raise the temperature of 5 g of ice at −20°C to its melting point? The specific heat capacity of ice is 2.30 J $\cdot$ g^{-1}. (C°)$^{-1}$.

3
$$\Delta Q = mc\Delta T$$
$$= (5 \text{ g}) [2.30 \text{ J} \cdot \text{g}^{-1}. (\text{C}°)^{-1}] (20 \text{ C}°)$$
$$= 230 \text{ J}$$

---

4 Find the heat needed to melt 15 g of ice at its melting point. The heat of fusion of water is 335 J $\cdot$ g^{-1}.

4
$$Q = mL_f$$
$$= 15 \text{ g } (335 \text{ J} \cdot \text{g}^{-1}) = 5025 \text{ J}$$

---

5 How much heat must be removed from 5g of steam at 100°C to condense it to water at 100°C? The heat of vaporization of water is 2256 J $\cdot$ g^{-1}.

5
$$Q = mL_v$$
$$= 5 \text{ g } (2256 \text{ J} \cdot \text{g}^{-1}) = 11280 \text{ J}$$

---

6 Originally, 1 kg of iron is at a temperature of 20°C. If 8000 J of heat are added to the iron, what will be its final temperature? Refer to frame 1 for the specific heat.

6

$$\Delta Q = mc (T_2 - T_1)$$
$$T_2 - T_1 = \frac{8000 \text{ J}}{1 \text{ kg } (470 \text{ J} \cdot \text{kg}^{-1}. (\text{C}°)^{-1})}$$
$$T_2 - 20°C = 17C°$$
$$T_2 = 37°C$$

---

7 What is the specific heat capacity of a substance whose molecular mass is 27 g $\cdot$ mol^{-1} and molar heat capacity is 24.6 J $\cdot$ mol^{-1} $\cdot$ (C°)$^{-1}$?

7
$$C = Mc$$
$$c = \frac{24.6 \text{ J} \cdot \text{mol}^{-1} \cdot (\text{C}°)^{-1}}{27 \text{ g} \cdot \text{mol}^{-1}}$$
$$= 0.911 \text{ J} \cdot \text{g}^{-1} \cdot (\text{C}°)^{-1}$$

---

8 What is the molecular mass M of water? The atomic mass of hydrogen is 1 and that of oxygen is 16.

8 Since a molecule of water (H_2O) consists of 2 hydrogen atoms and 1 oxygen atom, $M = 2 \text{ g} \cdot \text{mol}^{-1} + 16 \text{ g} \cdot \text{mol}^{-1} = 18 \text{ g} \cdot \text{mol}^{-1}$.

9 Heat capacity is defined as $\dfrac{Q}{\Delta T}$. Compare the heat capacities of equal masses of water, aluminum, iron and lead.

9 Since $\dfrac{Q}{\Delta T} = mc$,

mc_w: mc_a: mc_i: mc_1, where the subscripts w, a, i, and l refer to water, aluminum, iron and lead respectively. Dividing through by m and substituting the values of the specific heat capacities, we have
    4.186: 0.91: 0.47: 0.130.
Dividing through by 4.186: we have:
    1: 0.217: 0.112: 0.031.

---

10 Compare the heat capacities of equal volumes of the same substances.

10 mc_w: mc_a: mc_i: mc_1,

since $\rho = \dfrac{m}{V}$,

$\rho_w V c_w$: $\rho_a V c_a$: $\rho_i V c_i$: $\rho_1 V c_1$.
Divide through by V, use specific gravities in lieu of densities and substitute the values of the specific heat capacities.
    (1) (4.186): (2.7) (0.91): (7.8) (0.47): (11.3) (0.130)
    1: 0.587: 0.875: 0.350.

---

11 How much heat must be added to 100 kg of water to raise its temperature by 10C°?

11
$$\Delta Q = mc\Delta T$$
$$= (100 \text{ kg}) (4190 \text{ J} \cdot \text{g}^{-1} \, [\text{C}°]^{-1}) (10\text{C}°)$$
$$= 4.19 \times 10^6 \text{ J}$$

---

12 Express the above answer in calories.

12
$$\Delta Q = mc\Delta T$$
$$= (10^5 \text{ g}) (1 \text{ cal} \cdot \text{g}^{-1} \, [\text{C}°]^{-1}) (10\text{C}°)$$
$$= 10^6 \text{ cal}$$

---

13 Calculate the quantity of heat in calories that must be added to 400 g of ice at 0°C in order to melt it.

13
$$Q = mL_f$$
$$= 400 \text{ g} (79.7 \text{ cal} \cdot \text{g}^{-1})$$
$$= 3.18 \times 10^4 \text{ cal}$$

---

14 Calculate the heat required to raise the temperature of the melted ice from 0°C to 100°C.

14
$$\Delta Q = mc\Delta T$$
$$= 400 \text{ g} (1 \text{ cal} \cdot \text{g}^{-1} \, [\text{C}°]^{-1}) (100\text{C}°)$$
$$= 4 \times 10^4 \text{ cal}$$

---

15 Calculate the heat required to convert the 400 g of water at 100°C to steam at 100°C.

15
$$Q = mL_v$$
$$= 400 \text{ g} (539 \text{ cal} \cdot \text{g}^{-1})$$
$$= 2.16 \times 10^5 \text{ cal}$$

---

16 In reference to frames 13, 14, 15, how much heat was required to convert 400 g of ice at 0°C to steam at 100°C?

16
$$Q = 3.18 \times 10^4 \text{ cal} + 4 \times 10^4 \text{ cal} + 2.16 \times 10^5 \text{ cal}$$
$$= 2.88 \times 10^5 \text{ cal}$$

17 If all the potential energy of a waterfall 100 m high is converted into thermal energy, what is the temperature difference between the top and bottom of the falls?

18 If 10 g of water at 20°C is poured into 100 g of water at 80°C, what is the final temperature of the water?

17
$$U = \Delta Q$$
$$mgy = mc\Delta T$$

$$\Delta T = \frac{(9.8 \text{ m} \cdot \text{s}^{-2})(100 \text{ m})}{4190 \text{ J} \cdot \text{kg}^{-1} \cdot (\text{C}°)^{-1}}$$
$$= 0.234\text{C}°$$

18 The 10 g of water will gain heat.
$$\Delta Q = mc\Delta T$$
$$= (10 \text{ g})(1 \text{ cal} \cdot \text{g}^{-1} \cdot [\text{C}°]^{-1})(T_f - 20)$$
$$= 10(T_f - 20)$$
The 100 g of water will lose heat.
$$\Delta Q = mc\Delta T$$
$$= 100 \text{ g}(1 \text{ cal} \cdot \text{g}^{-1} \cdot [\text{C}°]^{-1})(T_f - 80)$$
$$= 100(T_f - 80)$$
In accordance with the law of conservation of energy, the sum of the heat gained and heat lost equals zero.
$$10(T_f - 20) + 100(T_f - 80) = 0$$
$$10 T_f - 200 + 100 T_f - 8000 = 0$$
$$110 T_f = 8200$$
$$T_f = 74.5°\text{C}$$

STEP BY STEP SOLUTIONS OF PROBLEMS

Problem 1 100 g of unknown metal shot at a temperature of 95°C is poured into a 140 g aluminum calorimeter containing 200 g of water. If the initial temperature of the water and calorimeter was 16°C and the final temperature was 20°C, find the specific heat of the metal.

1 This is the standard laboratory calorimetry experiment. It should be emphasized that when heat "flows" into a substance, the temperature of the substance increases and thus ΔT is +. When heat "flows" out of a substance, the temperature decreases, and thus ΔT is −. Let us tabulate the given data using subscripts c, w, and x for calorimeter, water, and unknown metal respectively.

1 Given:

$m_c = 140$ g	$T_c = 16°$C
$m_w = 200$ g	$T_w = 16°$C
$m_x = 100$ g	$T_x = 95°$C
$c_c = 0.22 \text{ cal} \cdot \text{g}^{-1} \cdot (\text{C}°)^{-1}$	
$c_w = 1 \text{ cal} \cdot \text{g}^{-1} \cdot (\text{C}°)^{-1}$	
$T_f = 20°$C	

Find: c_x

2 Calculate the heat lost by the metal.

2
$$(\Delta Q)_x = m_x c_x (\Delta T)_x$$
$$= 100 \text{ g} \cdot c_x \cdot (20°\text{C} - 95°\text{C})$$
$$= (-7500 \text{ g} \cdot \text{C}°) c_x$$

3 Calculate the heat gained by the aluminum in the calorimeter.

3
$$(\Delta Q)_c = m_c c_c (\Delta T)_c$$
$$= 140 \text{ g}(0.22 \text{ cal} \cdot \text{g}^{-1}[\text{C}°]^{-1})(4 \text{ C}°)$$
$$= +123 \text{ cal}$$

4 Calculate the heat gained by the water.

4
$$(\Delta Q)_w = m_w c_w (\Delta T)_w$$
$$= 200 \text{ g}(1 \text{ cal} \cdot \text{g}^{-1}[\text{C}°]^{-1})(4 \text{ C}°)$$
$$= +800 \text{ cal}$$

5 In accordance with the law of conservation of energy, the sum of the heat losses and gains equals zero. Solve for c_x.

5

$$(\Delta Q)_x + (\Delta Q)_c + (\Delta Q)_w = 0$$
$$(-7500 \text{ g} \cdot \text{C}°)c_x + 123 \text{ cal} + 800 \text{ cal} = 0$$
$$c_x = \frac{923 \text{ cal}}{7500 \text{ g} \cdot \text{C}°}$$
$$= 0.123 \text{ cal} \cdot \text{g}^{-1} \cdot (\text{C}°)^{-1}$$

Note that if heat lost is treated as negative and heat gained as positive, then the sum equals zero.

Problem 2 How much heat (J) is required to convert 0.1 kg of ice at $-20°$C to steam at 100°C?

6 This problem has four parts. We must find the amount of heat a) to raise the temperature of ice from $-20°$C to 0° C, b) to convert the ice at 0° C to water at 0°C, c) to raise the temperature of water from 0°C to 100°C, and d) to convert the water at 100°C to steam at 100°C. Solve part a) by using $\Delta Q = mc\Delta T$, where $c = 2300 \text{ J} \cdot \text{kg}^{-1} (\text{C}°)^{-1}$.

6

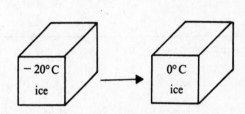

$$\Delta Q = 0.1 \text{ kg } [2300 \text{ J} \cdot \text{kg}^{-1} (\text{C}°)^{-1}] (20 \text{ C}°)$$
$$= 4600 \text{ J}$$

---

7 Solve part b) by using $Q = mL_f$ where $L_f = 335{,}000 \text{ J} \cdot \text{kg}^{-1}$.

7

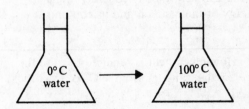

$$Q = 0.1 \text{ kg } (335{,}000 \text{ J} \cdot \text{kg}^{-1})$$
$$= 33{,}500 \text{ J}$$

---

8 Solve part c) by using $\Delta Q = mc\Delta T$.

8

$$\Delta Q = 0.1 \text{ kg } [4190 \text{ J} \cdot \text{kg}^{-1} (\text{C}°)^{-1}] (100 \text{ C}°)$$
$$= 41{,}900 \text{ J}$$

9 Solve d) by using $Q = mL_v$, where
$L_v = 2.26 \times 10^6 \text{ J} \cdot \text{kg}^{-1}$.

9

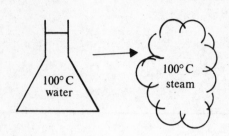

$$Q = 0.1 \text{ kg} (2.26 \times 10^6 \text{ J} \cdot \text{kg}^{-1})$$
$$= 226{,}000 \text{ J}$$

---

10 Add a + b + c + d.

10

$$\begin{array}{r} 4600 \text{ J} \\ 33500 \text{ J} \\ 41900 \text{ J} \\ 226000 \text{ J} \\ \hline 306000 \text{ J} \end{array}$$

Problem 3 A 0.5 kg metal canteen containing 0.75 kg of water and 0.1 kg of ice is dropped from an aircraft to the ground. After landing, the temperature of the canteen and its contents is found to be 25°C. If the velocity of the canteen just before impact is 445 m · s^{-1}, what is the specific heat of the canteen? (Assume that no energy is imparted to the ground upon impact.)

11 Tabulate the given information using subscripts c, i and w for canteen, ice, and water respectively.

11 Given:

$$
\begin{array}{ll}
m_c = 0.5 \text{ kg} & T_c = 0°C \\
m_w = 0.75 \text{ kg} & T_w = 0°C \\
m_i = 0.1 \text{ kg} & T_i = 0°C \\
c_w = 4190 \text{ J} \cdot \text{kg}^{-1} \text{ (C°)}^{-1} \\
L_f = 335{,}000 \text{ J} \cdot \text{kg}^{-1} \\
T_f = 25°C \\
v_f = 445 \text{ m} \cdot \text{s}^{-1}
\end{array}
$$

Find c_c.

---

12 The kinetic energy of the canteen just before impact will manifest itself as a temperature increase in the canteen and its contents. What is the kinetic energy of the canteen and its contents?

12 The total mass is equal to 0.5 kg + 0.75 kg + 0.1 kg = 1.35 kg
$$K = \tfrac{1}{2}mv^2 = \tfrac{1}{2} (1.35 \text{ kg}) (445 \text{ m} \cdot \text{s}^{-1})^2$$
$$= 134{,}000 \text{ J}$$

---

13 How much heat is required to raise the temperature of the canteen from 0°C to 25°C? Use $\Delta Q = mc\Delta T$.

13

$$\Delta Q_c = 0.5 \text{ kg} (c_c) (25 \text{ C°})$$
$$= 12.5 \text{ kg} \cdot \text{C°}(c_c)$$

---

14 How much heat is required to convert 0.1 kg of ice at 0°C to 0.1 kg of water at 0°C? Use $Q = mL_f$.

14

$$Q_i = 0.1 \text{ kg} (335{,}000 \text{ J} \cdot \text{kg}^{-1})$$
$$= 33{,}500 \text{ J}$$

15 The total amount of water at 0°C is now 0.85 kg. How much heat is required to raise the temperature of the water to 25°C? Use $\Delta Q = mc\Delta T$.

15

$$\Delta Q_w = 0.85 \text{ kg } (4190 \text{ J} \cdot \text{kg}^{-1}) (C°)^{-1} (25C°)$$
$$= 89{,}000 \text{ J}$$

---

16 Equate the kinetic energy to the sum of Q_c, Q_i and Q_w and solve for c_c.

16

$$K = Q_c + Q_i + Q_w$$
$$134{,}000 \text{ J} = 12.5 \text{ kg} \cdot C° (c_c) + 33{,}500 \text{ J} + 89{,}000 \text{ J}$$
$$c_c = 920 \text{ J} \cdot \text{kg}^{-1} (C°)^{-1}$$

PROGRAMMED TEST

1 **Problem 1** What must be the initial velocity of a silver bullet at a temperature of 20°C so that the heat developed when it is brought to a complete stop shall be sufficient to melt it? (specific heat = 234 J · kg^{-1} (C°)$^{-1}$, heat of fusion = 88300 J · kg^{-1}, melting point = 961°C. Assume that all the energy stays in the bullet.

1 **Answer**
785 m · s^{-1}

If you solved this problem correctly, go to frame 3. If you could not solve this problem, go through frame 2.

2 Assuming that all the heat is supplied to the bullet, from the principle of conservation of energy, we know that the initial kinetic energy is equal to the heat required to raise the temperature of the bullet to its melting point + the heat required to melt the bullet. Note that the rise in temperature = 961°C − 20°C = 941 C°.

2

$$K = \tfrac{1}{2}mv^2 = mc\,\Delta T + mL_f$$
divide through by m
$$\frac{v^2}{2} = c\,\Delta T + L_f$$
$$= 234 \text{ J} \cdot \text{kg}^{-1} \cdot (C°)^{-1} (941 \text{ C}°) + 88300 \text{ J} \cdot \text{kg}^{-1}$$
$$= 220{,}000 \text{ J} \cdot \text{kg}^{-1} + 88300 \text{ J} \cdot \text{kg}^{-1}$$
$$v = 785 \text{ m} \cdot \text{s}^{-1}$$

---

3 **Problem 2** How much steam at 100°C is required to melt 1 kg of ice at 0°C? (Assume that the condensed steam will end up as water at 0°C.)

3 **Answer**
0.125 kg

If you solved this problem correctly, go to frame 7. If you could not solve this problem, go through frames 4–6.

4 Tabulate the given information.

4

$$L_v = 2.26 \times 10^6 \text{ J} \cdot \text{kg}^{-1}$$
$$L_f = 3.35 \times 10^5 \text{ J} \cdot \text{kg}^{-1}$$
$$m_i = 1 \text{ kg}$$
$$c_w = 4190 \text{ J} \cdot \text{kg}^{-1} \cdot (C°)^{-1}$$
$$T_{i(steam)} = 100°C$$
$$T_{f(water)} = 0°C$$

---

5 In accordance with the principle of conservation of energy, the heat lost by the steam = heat gained by the ice. Noting that the condensed steam at 100°C should be treated as water, write the equation for heat lost = heat gained. Solve for m_s.

5

$$L_v m_s + m_s c_w (\Delta T)_s = m_i L_f$$
$$m_s = \frac{m_i L_f}{L_v + c_w (\Delta T)_s}$$

6 Substitute the given values and solve for m_s.

6

$$m_s = \frac{1 \text{ kg } (335{,}000 \text{ J} \cdot \text{kg}^{-1})}{2.26 \times 10^6 \text{ J} \cdot \text{kg}^{-1} + 4190 \text{ J} \cdot \text{kg}^{-1} (\text{C}°)^{-1} (100 \text{ C}°)}$$
$$= 0.125 \text{ kg}$$

---

7 *Problem 3* In order to determine the heat of fusion of ice, 10 g of ice at a temperature of 0°C are dropped into an aluminum calorimeter of mass 50 g containing 480 g of water at a temperature of 20°C. When the ice melts the final temperature is 18°C. Find the heat of fusion of ice.

7 *Answer*
80.2 cal $\cdot$ g^{-1}

If you could not solve this problem, go through frames 8–12.

8 Calculate the heat lost by the warm water.

8

$$\begin{aligned}(\Delta Q)_w &= m_w c_w (T_f - T_0) \\ &= 480 \text{ g } (1 \text{ cal} \cdot \text{g}^{-1} [\text{C}°]^{-1}) (18°\text{C} - 20°\text{C}) \\ &= -960 \text{ cal}\end{aligned}$$

---

9 Calculate the heat lost by the calorimeter.

9

$$\begin{aligned}(\Delta Q)_c &= m_c c_c (T_f - T_o) \\ &= 50 \text{ g } (0.22 \text{ cal} \cdot \text{g}^{-1} [\text{C}°]^{-1}) (18°\text{C} - 20°\text{C}) \\ &= -22 \text{ cal}\end{aligned}$$

---

10 Calculate the heat required to melt the ice (the ice gains heat).

10

$$\begin{aligned}(Q)_{ice} &= m_{ice} L_f \\ &= +10 \text{ g } L_f\end{aligned}$$

---

11 Calculate the heat required to raise the temperature of the 10 g of ice water to the thermal equilibrium temperature of 18°C.

11

$$\begin{aligned}(\Delta Q)_{ice\ w} &= m_{ice\ w}\, c_w (T_f - T_o) \\ &= 10 \text{ g } (1 \text{ cal} \cdot \text{g}^{-1} \cdot [\text{C}°]^{-1}) (18 \text{ C}°) \\ &= +180 \text{ cal}\end{aligned}$$

---

12 Express the sum of the heat losses and gains to zero and solve for L_f.

12

$$-960 \text{ cal} - 22 \text{ cal} + 10 \text{ g } L_f + 180 \text{ cal} = 0$$
$$10 \text{ g } L_f = 802 \text{ cal}$$
$$L_f = 80.2 \text{ cal} \cdot \text{g}^{-1}$$

16

Heat Transfer

CHAPTER SUMMARY

The three modes of heat transfer, conduction, convection and radiation, are discussed in detail and quantities such as thermal conductivity and the convection coefficient are defined. The Stefan-Boltzmann law for the rate of radiation of energy is presented and the ideal radiator is considered.

BASIC TERMS — *Give definitions or meanings for the following:*

conduction (16-1)
thermal conductivity (16-1)
heat current (16-1)
temperature gradient (16-1)
thermal resistance (16-1)

convection (16-2)
radiation (16-3)
Stefan-Boltzmann law (16-3)
Stefan-Boltzmann constant (16-3)
blackbody (16-5)

PROGRAMMED QUIZ

1 What medium is required for heat transfer by radiation?

1 No medium since electromagnetic waves do not require any material for propagation.

2 On what does the natural direction of the heat flow between two bodies depend?

2 On their temperatures; heat flows from the body at the higher temperature to the one at the lower temperature.

3 Why does the heated material move in natural or free convection?

3 Because its density becomes less than that of the surrounding material.

4 Why are metals good conductors of heat?

4 Metals contain free electrons which can travel a great distance before colliding and transferring their energy. Therefore, the rate of energy transferred to the colder end of the body is increased.

5 This property of metals has what other physical implications?

5 They are also good conductors of electricity.

6 If the entire body is at the same temperature, can heat be transferred by conduction?

6 No, for heat transfer by conduction the ends of the body must be at different temperatures so that some molecules can give up their energy to others.

7 What bodies emit electromagnetic radiation?

7 All bodies; the rate of emission increases with temperature and decreases with reflectivity.

8 What is the relationship between the temperature of the radiator and the wavelength of the most intense radiation?

8 The higher the temperature, the shorter the wavelength.

9 Why do thermopane windows have a vacuum space between the two glass panes?

9 A vacuum prevents heat transfer by conduction or convection.

10 A blackbody is in thermal equilibrium with its surroundings. How much radiant energy does it absorb?

10 All radiant energy incident on it.

11 A substance with a high thermal conductivity is a good conductor or insulator?

11 Conductor.

12 Can convection take place in a solid?

12 No, since there can be no flow of the heated material.

13 By what type of heat transfer do we receive energy from the sun?

13 Radiation.

14 Why does a metal object feel colder to the touch than a wooden object at the same temperature?

14 Since metal is a good conductor it conducts the heat from your skin, thus cooling it, more readily than the wood.

15 What is the relationship between the absorption and emission properties of an object?

15 A good absorber is a good emitter.

16 What is the value of k for a perfect insulator?

16 $k = 0$. A good heat conductor has a large value of k. A good insulator has a small value of k.

MAIN IDEAS

1 Conduction is the transfer or flow of heat in a body due to temperature differences between different parts of the body. It must be emphasized that no part of the heated material flows. Thermal energy is passed along from one molecule to the next while each individual molecule retains its original position. The quantity of heat flowing through a body per unit time (heat current) is given by $H = \dfrac{kA(T_2 - T_1)}{L}$, where the thermal conductivity k is an intrinsic property of the material, A is the cross-sectional area, $T_2 - T_1$ is the temperature difference and L is the distance between the two points whose temperature difference we are considering. When T_2 and T_1 do not change with time and the heat flows at a constant rate, the condition is referred to as a steady state heat flow. H is measured in watts.

2 Temperature gradient. If the body has a non-uniform cross-sectional area, then the above equation would be written as $H = - kA\,\dfrac{\Delta T}{L}$, where $\dfrac{\Delta T}{L}$ is called the temperature gradient. The direction of heat flow is the direction of increasing x. Since heat flows in the direction of decreasing T, a minus sign is introduced in order to maintain H as a positive quantity.

3 Unit for k: $1\ \mathrm{J} \cdot (\mathrm{s} \cdot \mathrm{m} \cdot \mathrm{C}°)^{-1} = 1\ \mathrm{cal} \cdot (\mathrm{s} \cdot \mathrm{cm} \cdot \mathrm{C}°)^{-1}$.

4 Thermal resistance R of a slab of building material of thickness L is defined by
$$H = \frac{A(T_2 - T_1)}{R},$$
where $R = \dfrac{L}{k}$. Usually H is expressed in $\mathrm{BTU} \cdot \mathrm{hr}^{-1}$.

5 Problem solving hints for heat conductivity.

Step 1 Use
$$H = \frac{kA(T_2 - T_1)}{L}$$
for a single body where the direction of heat flow is parallel to L and perpendicular to A.

Step 2 If you have a heat flow through two different materials 1 and 2, then denote the temperature at the interface as T_3.

1	2
T_1 $\qquad$ T_3	T_2

The temperature differences are now $T_3 - T_1$ for material 1 and $T_2 - T_3$ for material 2. This treatment is analogous to two resistors in an electric circuit connected in series.

Step 3 Be careful of algebraic signs. If $T_2 - T_1$ is positive, this means that region 1 has gained heat.

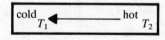

If $T_2 - T_1$ is negative, region 1 has lost heat.

Remember, heat flows in the direction of decreasing T (from hot to cold).

Step 4 For two parallel heat flow paths.
$$H = H_1 + H_2.$$
Each body may have different values of L, A, and k.

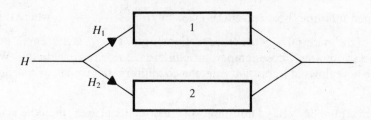

6 Convection is a mode of heat transfer that involves the actual motion of the fluid. The heated material is moved from one point to another. The convection current is given by $H = hA\,(\Delta T)^{5/4}$ where h is the convection coefficient, A is the surface area and ΔT is the temperature difference between the surface and the main body of fluid. The SI unit for h is $W \cdot m^{-2}\,(C°)^{-5/4}$.

7 Radiation. Energy is continually emitted from all bodies in the form of electromagnetic waves. This energy, referred to as radiant energy, travels at the speed of light and is transmitted most readily through a vacuum. Electromagnetic waves from 0.4×10^{-6} m (violet) to 0.7×10^{-6} m (red) in length make up the visible spectrum. Wavelengths larger than 0.7×10^{-6} m are called infrared and can be detected by the body in the form of heat. Radiation is the mechanism by which the sun's energy reaches the earth.

8 Stefan-Boltzmann law. The radiation of energy per unit time for a surface is given by $H = Ae\sigma T^4$, where A is the surface area, e is a dimensionless quantity called the emissivity, T is the absolute temperature and σ is a universal physical constant called the Stefan-Boltzmann constant $= 5.6699 \times 10^{-8}$ W $\cdot$ m^{-2} $\cdot$ K^{-4}.

9 Radiative equilibrium. A body is said to have reached radiative equilibrium when its rate of radiation equals the rate at which it receives energy from other radiating bodies. A good absorber of radiant energy is a good emitter and vice versa.

10 Blackbody. A body which absorbs all the radiant energy which is incident on it is called a blackbody or an ideal radiator. This body is also an ideal emitter of radiant energy. The emissivity e of a blackbody is 1. The emissivity of a smooth copper surface is ≈ 0.3.

PROGRAMMED QUIZ

1 If the absolute temperature of a body is doubled, the radiant energy emitted is _____.

1 Increased 16 times, $H \propto T^4$ and $H' \propto T'^4$ if $T' = 2T$, then $H' \propto (2T)^4 \propto 16T^4$
$\therefore H' = 16H$

---

2 What is the heat current if 10 J of heat flow through an object in 1 minute?

2
$$H = \frac{Q}{t}$$
$$= \frac{10\text{ J}}{60\text{ s}} = 0.167 \text{ J} \cdot \text{s}^{-1}$$

---

3 The heat flow through an aluminum rod, 1 m long and 1×10^{-4} m^2 in cross-sectional area, is 2 J $\cdot$ s^{-1}. Find the temperature difference between both ends of the rod ($k = 205$ J $\cdot$ s^{-1} $\cdot$ m^{-1} $\cdot$ (C°)$^{-1}$).

3
$$H = \frac{kA(T_2 - T_1)}{L}$$
$$T_2 - T_1 = \frac{(2\text{ J} \cdot \text{s}^{-1})\,(1\text{ m})}{205\text{ J} \cdot \text{s}^{-1} \cdot \text{m}^{-1} \cdot (C°)^{-1}\,(1 \times 10^{-4}\text{ m}^2)}$$
$$= 97.6 \text{ C}°$$

4 What is the rate of heat flow from a container made completely of glass, filled with a liquid at 80°C, if the temperature of the surroundings is 20°C? The container has an area of 0.1 m² and a thickness of 0.2 cm; $k = 0.8$ J · s⁻¹ · m⁻¹ · (C°)⁻¹).

4

$$H = \frac{kA(T_2 - T_1)}{L}$$
$$= \frac{(0.8 \text{ J} \cdot \text{s}^{-1} \cdot \text{m}^{-1} \cdot (\text{C°})^{-1}) (0.1 \text{ m}^2) (60 \text{ C°})}{0.002 \text{ m}}$$
$$= 2400 \text{ J} \cdot \text{s}^{-1}$$

5 A vertical wall is maintained at a constant temperature of 90°C. On both sides of the wall the air temperature is 30°C. How much heat is lost per 1 m² of wall by natural convection on both sides? $h = 2.0$ W · m⁻². (C°)⁻⁵ᐟ⁴.

5

$$H = A\,h(\Delta T)^{5/4}$$
$$= (1 \text{ m}^2) [2.0 \text{ W} \cdot \text{m}^{-2} (\text{C°})^{-5/4}] (60 \text{ C°})^{5/4}$$
$$= 334 \text{ W} \quad \text{on each side.}$$

Heat lost by both sides
$$= 2(334 \text{ W}) = 668 \text{ W}$$

6 What is the rate of energy radiation from a 0.2 m² area of a blackbody at a temperature of 200 K? Note $e = 1$.

6

$$H = Ae\sigma(T^4)$$
$$= (0.2 \text{ m}^2) (1)$$
$$\times (5.6699 \times 10^{-8} \text{ W} \cdot \text{m}^{-2} \cdot \text{K}^{-4}) (200 \text{ K})^4$$
$$= 18.1 \text{ W}$$

STEP BY STEP SOLUTIONS OF PROBLEMS

Problem 1 One end of a 1 m copper rod with a uniform cross section of 2×10^{-4} m² is kept in steam, and the other end is in contact with a block of ice at 0°C. How much ice melts in 10 hours?

1 Tabulate the given data. The quantity of heat H flowing through the rod is given by
$$H = \frac{kA(T_2 - T_1)}{L}.$$

1

$$A = 2 \times 10^{-4} \text{ m}^2$$
$$L = 1 \text{ m}$$
$$k = 385 \text{ J} \cdot \text{s}^{-1} \cdot \text{m}^{-1} \cdot (\text{C°})^{-1}$$
$$t = 10 \text{ hours} = 36000 \text{ s}$$
$$L_f = 335{,}000 \text{ J} \cdot \text{kg}^{-1}$$
$$(T_2 - T_1) = 100 \text{ C°}$$

2 Since H is the rate of flow, Ht is the amount of heat which flows in the time t. Let m_i be the mass of the ice that will melt in this time. Therefore, $Ht = m_i L_f$. Solve for m_i.

2

$$m_i L_f = Ht = \frac{kA(T_2 - T_1)}{L} t$$
$$m_i = \frac{kA(T_2 - T_1)}{L_f L} t$$

3 Substitute the values and solve for m_i.

3 $m_i =$

$$\frac{385 \text{ J} \cdot \text{s}^{-1} \cdot \text{m}^{-1} \cdot (\text{C°})^{-1} (2 \times 10^{-4} \text{ m}^2) (100 \text{ C°}) (36000 \text{ s})}{(335{,}000 \text{ J} \cdot \text{kg}^{-1}) (1 \text{ m})}$$
$$= 0.827 \text{ kg}$$

Problem 2 A composite rod is made up of equal lengths and cross-sections of aluminum, brass and copper. The free aluminum end is maintained at 100°C and the free copper end is immersed in ice at 0°C. If the surface of the rod is insulated to prevent heat flow radially, find the temperature at each junction.

4 Make a sketch of the composite rod and denote the temperature at the aluminum-brass junction as T_B and the temperature at the brass-copper junction as T_C.

4

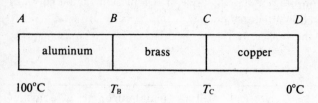

aluminum	brass	copper

$100°C$ T_B T_C $0°C$

---

5 The heat current $H = kA(T_2 - T_1)/L$ is the same in each rod. If the heat current was greater in one section of the rod than the other, the heat energy would "accumulate" at the junction raising its temperature until the heat current was the same throughout the rod. Solve the heat current equation for HL/A for each section of the rod. Note that H, L and A are constants.

5

$$\frac{HL}{A} = k(T_2 - T_1)$$

Heat flow$_{AB}$ = 205 J $\cdot$ (s $\cdot$ m $\cdot$ C°)$^{-1}$ $(100°C - T_B)$

Heat flow$_{BC}$ = 109 J $\cdot$ (s $\cdot$ m $\cdot$ C°)$^{-1}$ $(T_B - T_C)$

Heat flow$_{CD}$ = 385 J $\cdot$ (s $\cdot$ m $\cdot$ C°)$^{-1}$ (T_C)

---

6 Set heat flow$_{AB}$ = heat flow$_{BC}$ and heat flow$_{BC}$ = heat flow$_{CD}$. We now have 2 equations with two unknowns.

6

205 J $\cdot$ (s $\cdot$ m $\cdot$ C°)$^{-1}$ $(100°C - T_B)$
= 109 J $\cdot$ (s $\cdot$ m $\cdot$ C°)$^{-1}$ $(T_B - T_C)$
109 J $\cdot$ (s $\cdot$ m $\cdot$ C°)$^{-1}$ $(T_B - T_C)$ = 385 J $\cdot$ (s $\cdot$ m $\cdot$ C°)$^{-1}$ (T_C)
$$109\,T_B = 494\,T_C$$

---

7 Solve for T_B and T_C.

7 $T_B = 70.7°C$, $T_C = 15.6°C$

Problem 3 Find the rate at which the sun loses energy if we assume that it is radiating as a blackbody. The radius of the sun is 7.00×10^8 m and the temperature is 5.8×10^3 K.

8 We will use $H = Ae\sigma T^4$. Tabulate the given data.

8

$e = 1$ (blackbody)
$\sigma = 5.67 \times 10^{-8}$ W $\cdot$ m^{-2} $\cdot$ K^{-4}
$R = 7.00 \times 10^8$ m
$T = 5.8 \times 10^3$ K

---

9 Find the surface area of the sun.

9

$$A = 4\pi R^2$$
$$= 4\pi(7.00 \times 10^8 \text{ m})^2 = 6.16 \times 10^{18} \text{ m}^2$$

---

10 Solve for H.

10

$$H = Ae\sigma T^4$$
$$= (6.16 \times 10^{18} \text{ m}^2)\,(1)$$
$$\times (5.67 \times 10^{-8} \text{ W} \cdot \text{m}^{-2} \cdot \text{K}^{-4})$$
$$\times (5.80 \times 10^3 \text{ K})^4$$
$$= 3.95 \times 10^{26} \text{ W}$$

PROGRAMMED TEST

1 **_Problem 1_** Two rods of lengths L_1 and L_2 of uniform cross-sectional areas and different thermal conductivities are joined together as in the figure. If the temperatures of the free ends are maintained at T_A and T_B respectively ($T_A > T_B$), find the junction temperature T.

1

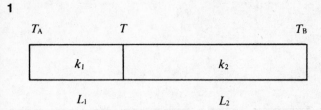

Answer

$$T = \frac{\dfrac{k_1}{L_1} T_A + \dfrac{k_2}{L_2} T_B}{\dfrac{k_1}{L_1} + \dfrac{k_2}{L_2}}$$

If you solved this problem correctly, go to frame 4. If you could not solve this problem, go through frames 2–3.

2 Solve the heat current equation for H/A for each rod.

2

$$\frac{H}{A} = \frac{k_1}{L_1} (T_A - T)$$
$$\frac{H}{A} = \frac{k_2}{L_2} (T - T_B)$$

3 Equate and solve for T.

3

$$\frac{k_1}{L_1} (T_A - T) = \frac{k_2}{L_2} (T - T_B)$$

$$T = \frac{\dfrac{k_1}{L_1} T_A + \dfrac{k_2}{L_2} T_B}{\dfrac{k_1}{L_1} + \dfrac{k_2}{L_2}}$$

4 **_Problem 2_** The temperature of the filament in a 50 watt incandescent lamp is 2500 K. Find the surface area if the emissivity is 0.35.

4 **Answer**
6.45×10^{-5} m^2

If you solved this problem correctly, go to frame 7. If you could not solve this problem, go through frames 5–6.

5 Tabulate the given information in terms of the variables in the Stefan-Boltzmann law.

5

$T = 2500$ K
$e = 0.35$
$\sigma = 5.67 \times 10^{-8}$ W $\cdot$ m^{-2} $\cdot$ K^{-4}
$H = 50$ watts

6 Solve the Stefan-Boltzmann law for A and substitute the numerical values.

6

$$H = Ae\sigma T^4$$
$$A = \frac{H}{e\sigma T^4}$$

$$= \frac{50 \text{ W}}{(0.35)\,(5.67 \times 10^{-8} \text{ W} \cdot \text{m}^{-2} \cdot \text{K}^{-4})\,(2500 \text{ K})^4}$$
$$= 6.45 \times 10^{-5} \text{ m}^2 = 0.645 \text{ cm}^2$$

---

7 **Problem 3** A 1 meter long compound bar has a solid brass inner core 0.01 m in diameter surrounded by a copper casing whose outside diameter is 0.02 m. The bar is thermally insulated; one end is maintained at 100°C and the other at 0°C. Find the total heat current.

7 **Answer**
$9.95 \text{ J} \cdot \text{s}^{-1}$

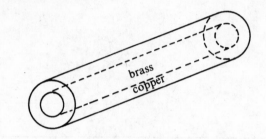

If you could not solve the problem, go through frames 8–10.

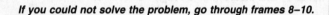

8 Find the cross-sectional areas of both metals.

8

$$A_{\text{brass}} = \pi r^2$$
$$= \pi (0.005 \text{ m})^2 = 7.85 \times 10^{-5} \text{ m}^2$$
$$A_{\text{copper}} = \pi (R^2 - r^2)$$
$$= \pi \left[(0.01 \text{ m})^2 - (0.005 \text{ m})^2 \right]$$
$$= 2.36 \times 10^{-4} \text{ m}^2$$

---

9 Find the heat current through each rod.

9

$$H = \frac{kA(T_2 - T_1)}{L}$$

$$H_{\text{brass}} =$$
$$\frac{109 \text{ J } (\text{s} \cdot \text{m} \cdot \text{C}°)^{-1}\,(7.85 \times 10^{-5} \text{ m}^2)\,(100 \text{ C}°)}{1 \text{ m}}$$
$$= 0.85 \text{ J} \cdot \text{s}^{-1}$$

$$H_{\text{copper}} =$$
$$\frac{385 \text{ J } (\text{s} \cdot \text{m} \cdot \text{C}°)^{-1}\,(2.36 \times 10^{-4} \text{ m}^2)\,(100 \text{ C}°)}{1 \text{ m}}$$
$$= 9.09 \text{ J} \cdot \text{s}^{-1}$$

---

10 Find the sum of the heat currents.

10 $0.856 \text{ J} \cdot \text{s}^{-1} + 9.09 \text{ J} \cdot \text{s}^{-1} = 9.95 \text{ J} \cdot \text{s}^{-1}$

17

Thermal Properties of Matter

CHAPTER SUMMARY

We have studied the relationships between volume and temperature and pressure separately, here we combine all three in the equation of state. In addition, pVT-surfaces for an ideal gas and pV diagrams for a real substance are described. Phase diagrams are presented with special emphasis on the triple point and the critical point. Other phenomena which are discussed: vapor pressure, freezing and boiling points, and humidity.

BASIC TERMS — *Give definitions or meanings for the following:*

state coordinate (17-1)
equilibrium state (17-1)
equation of state (17-1)
ideal gas (17-2)
partial pressure (17-2)
Boyle's law (17-2)
Charles' law (17-2)
ideal gas constant (17-2)
standard temperature and pressure (17-2)
pV-diagram (17-3)
phase equilibrium (17-4)

pVT-surface (17-4)
isotherm (17-4)
critical point (17-4)
phase diagram (17-4)
sublimation (17-4)
triple point (17-4)
vapor pressure (17-5)
absolute humidity (17-5)
relative humidity (17-5)
dew point (17-5)
humidity (17-5)

PROGRAMMED QUIZ

1 When we say that the volume of gas is proportional to its temperature does this mean in any scale?

1 The temperature must be absolute temperature.

2 Why does the pressure of a gas increase as the temperature is raised if the volume is kept constant?

2 Because the molecules have higher speeds and therefore collide more often and with greater impulse with the wall.

3 Why does the pressure of a gas increase if the volume is reduced while the temperature is kept constant?

3 Because the molecules collide with the walls more often.

4 Why does the air feel dry in a heated room?

4 When the air is heated, its volume expands but the actual moisture content remains the same. Thus the amount of water vapor per unit volume of air is decreased. But at a higher temperature the air can hold more moisture. Since relative humidity is a comparison between the amount of water vapor actually present and that which the air could hold if saturated at the same temperature, a higher temperature gives you a sensation of dryness.

5 What do we mean by an equilibrium state of a given mass?

5 The temperature and pressure are the same at all points.

6 When do real gases approximate ideal gases?

6 At low pressures.

7 Can solid, liquid and vapor phases of a substance ever exist in equilibrium?

7 Yes, along the triple line.

8 What happens to a substance at a temperature higher than the critical point?

8 The distinction between liquid and vapor disappears; it changes gradually and continuously from low density, large compressibility to high density, small compressibility.

9 What happens to the freezing point of a liquid when another substance has been dissolved in it? the boiling point?

9 The freezing point is lowered but the boiling point may be either raised or lowered depending on the dissolved substance.

10 What is the difference between absolute and relative humidity?

10 Absolute humidity is the mass of water vapor per unit volume; relative humidity is the ratio of partial pressure to the vapor pressure at the same temperature or the density of water vapor in the air at a given temperature as compared to the density at saturation.

11 Draw a graph of pressure as a function of volume for a fixed mass of gas at constant temperature.

11

12 Draw a graph of pressure as a function of temperature for a fixed mass of gas at constant volume.

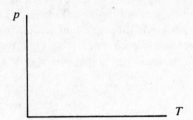

12

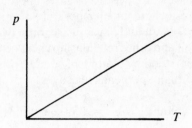

13 Draw a graph of volume as a function of temperature for a fixed mass of gas at constant pressure.

13

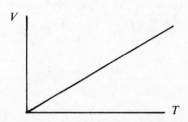

14 What is meant by the dew point?

14 The dew point is the temperature at which the water vapor in the atmosphere begins to condense.

15 What is meant by critical temperature? critical pressure?

15 Critical temperature is the temperature above which pressure alone cannot condense a gas to a liquid. Critical pressure is the pressure required to liquify a gas at its critical temperature.

16 If alcohol is rubbed on your body, the alcohol evaporates leaving you with a sensation of cold. Explain.

16 In order to evaporate, the alcohol must draw heat from your body. Therefore, the temperature of your body drops.

MAIN IDEAS

1 Equations of state. The "state" of a material may be described by its mass m, volume V, pressure p and temperature T. In mathematical form this would be represented as $f(m, V, p, T) = 0$, i.e., the state is a function of four variables. We define an equilibrium state as one where, for a given volume and mass, the pressure and temperature are the same throughout the material.

2 The ideal gas. An ideal gas is one where the "point molecules" do not exert attractive forces on one another. The equation of state is $pV = nRT$, where $n = m/M$ is the number of moles of gas, m is the total mass, M the molecular mass (mass per mole) and R is the universal gas constant. $R = 8.314 \text{ J} \cdot \text{mol}^{-1} \cdot \text{K}^{-1} = 1.99 \text{ cal} \cdot \text{mol}^{-1} \cdot \text{K}^{-1}$.

3 The general gas law. For a specified mass or fixed number of moles of an ideal gas, nR is constant. Hence $\dfrac{p_1 V_1}{T_1} = \dfrac{p_2 V_2}{T_2} = $ constant, where the subscripts 1 and 2 refer to two states of the same mass of gas at different pressures, volumes and temperatures.

4 Boyle's law. If $T = $ constant, $p_1 V_1 = p_2 V_2 = $ constant.

5 Charles' law. If $p = $ constant, $\dfrac{V_1}{T_1} = \dfrac{V_2}{T_2} = $ constant.

6 Gay-Lussac's law. If V = constant, $\frac{p_1}{T_1} = \frac{p_2}{T_2}$ = constant.

7 Phases of a substance. Real gases approach ideal gases at low pressure. However, the similarity ceases at high pressures, where, at a temperature drop, the gas will change to a liquid or solid phase. Substances can exist in either the solid, liquid or gas phase, or in two phases simultaneously, or along the triple line in all three phases. The triple line and other relationships between the phases of a substance such as the critical point and triple point are best understood by plotting p, V and T for a given mass on a three dimensional graph where p, V and T are the three mutually perpendicular axes.

8 Specific volume $v = \frac{V}{m} = \frac{1}{\rho}$ is sometimes plotted along the volume axis.

9 Triple point. For any substance there is only one pressure and temperature at which all three phases can coexist. For water $p = 0.00610$ Pa, $T = 273.16$ K.

10 Critical point. A point on a p vs T diagram (see the figure for water) above which there is no distinction between liquid and gas.

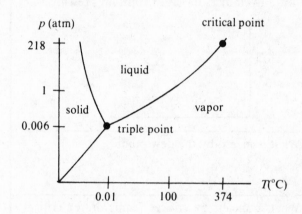

11 Partial pressure. In a mixture of gases, the partial pressure of each gas is the pressure that gas would exert by itself if it occupies the entire volume. The total pressure is the sum of the partial pressures.

12 Absolute humidity = mass of water vapor per unit volume.

13 Relative humidity (%) = $\dfrac{\text{partial pressure of water vapor}}{\text{vapor pressure at same temperature}}$ (100%). If the vapor is saturated, the relative humidity = 100%. If no water vapor is present, the relative humidity = 0%.

14 The dew point is the temperature at which the water vapor in the air becomes saturated.

15 Vapor pressure is the pressure at which vapor and liquid are in equilibrium.

16 Problem solving hints for ideal gases.

Step 1 Since ideal gases are associated with many variables — p, v, T, n, m, M — and perhaps two states, make a list of what is given and what must be found.

Step 2 Be consistent with your units. If you are using SI units, remember 1 Pa = 1 N · m^{-2} and T is always in Kelvins. Also, the molecular mass M is usually given in grams per mole. It may be necessary to convert to kg · mole^{-1}. For example, the molecular mass of oxygen is 32 g · mole^{-1} = 32 × 10^{-3} kg · mole^{-1}.

PROGRAMMED QUIZ

1 A tank, volume 0.10 m^3, is filled with 20 moles of oxygen at a temperature of 50°C. What is the absolute pressure of the gas? (Remember that the temperature must be converted to kelvins.)

1

$$pV = nRT$$

$$p = \frac{(20 \text{ mol}) (8.314 \text{ J} \cdot \text{mol}^{-1} \cdot \text{K}^{-1}) (323 \text{ K})}{0.10 \text{ m}^3}$$

$$= 5.37 \times 10^5 \text{ Pa}$$

2 What is the gauge pressure?

2

$$p = p_g + p_a$$
$$p_g = 5.37 \times 10^5 \text{ Pa} - 1.01 \times 10^5 \text{ Pa}$$
$$= 4.36 \times 10^5 \text{ Pa}$$

---

3 What is the mass of the oxygen?

3

$$m = nM$$
$$= (20 \text{ mol}) (32 \text{ g} \cdot \text{mol}^{-1}) = 640 \text{ g}$$

---

4 If the relative humidity is 70%, what is the partial pressure of water vapor in the atmosphere at 15°C? (The pressure for this temperature is 0.0169×10^5 Pa.)

Vapor pressure of water

$T(°C)$	Vapor pressure ($\times 10^5$ Pa)
0	0.00610
5	0.00868
10	0.0119
15	0.0169
20	0.0233

4 Relative humidity =

$$(100\%) \ \frac{\text{partial pressure of water vapor}}{\text{vapor pressure at same temperature}}$$

partial pressure of water vapor =
$$\frac{(70\%) \, (0.0169 \times 10^5 \text{ Pa})}{100\%}$$
$$= 0.0118 \times 10^5 \text{ Pa}$$

---

5 Keeping the same partial pressure, what would be the temperature for the formation of dew? (Extrapolate from table in frame 4.)

5 10°C

---

6 What do we mean by a gas at normal temperature and pressure?

6 Temperature of 0°C = 273 K
and a pressure of 1 atm = 1.01×10^5 Pa

---

7 A gas at normal temperature and pressure has a volume of 1.2 m³. If the volume is reduced to 1 m³, what is the new pressure, assuming temperature is kept constant?

7

$$p_1 V_1 = p_2 V_2$$
$$p_2 = \frac{(1.01 \times 10^5 \text{ Pa}) \, (1.2 \text{ m}^3)}{1 \text{ m}^3}$$
$$= 1.21 \times 10^5 \text{ Pa}$$

---

8 If the temperature had been brought up to 30°C while the volume was reduced, what would have been the new pressure?

8

$$\frac{p_1 V_1}{T_1} = \frac{p_2 V_2}{T_2}$$
$$p_2 = \frac{(1.01 \times 10^5 \text{ Pa}) \, (1.2 \text{ m}^3) \, (303 \text{ K})}{(273 \text{ K}) \, (1 \text{ m}^3)}$$
$$= 1.345 \times 10^5 \text{ Pa}$$

---

9 What is the specific volume of aluminum if its density is 2700 kg · m⁻³?

9

$$\rho = \frac{1}{v}$$
$$v = \frac{1}{2700 \text{ kg} \cdot \text{m}^{-3}} = 3.70 \times 10^{-4} \text{ m}^3 \cdot \text{kg}^{-1}$$

10 Air is made up mostly of nitrogen, oxygen and argon. At STP, the nitrogen, oxygen and argon have pressures of 8.15×10^4 Pa, 1.92×10^4 Pa and 0.066×10^4 Pa respectively. Find the pressure of air at STP, using Dalton's law.

10

$$p = p_N + p_O + p_A$$
$$= 8.15 \times 10^4 \text{ Pa} + 1.92 \times 10^4 \text{ Pa} + 0.066 \times 10^4 \text{ Pa}$$
$$= 1.01 \times 10^5 \text{ Pa}$$

---

11 How many cylinders of helium are required to fill a 680 m³ balloon at normal atmospheric pressure if the helium is stored in cylinders of volume 2.8 m³ at an absolute pressure of 16×10^5 Pa? Assume that there is no change in the temperature of the helium.

11

$$\frac{P_1 V_1}{T_1} = \frac{P_2 V_2}{T_2}$$

Since $T_1 = T_2$

$$V_2 = \left(\frac{P_1}{P_2}\right) V_1$$

$$= \left(\frac{16 \times 10^5 \text{ Pa}}{1.01 \times 10^5 \text{ Pa}}\right) (2.8 \text{ m}^3)$$

$$= 44.4 \text{ m}^3 \cdot \text{cylinder}^{-1}$$

Each cylinder will release 44.4 m³ of helium at atmospheric pressure into the balloon. Therefore, we will require

$$\frac{680 \text{ m}^3}{44.4 \text{ m}^3 \cdot \text{cylinder}^{-1}} = 15.3 \text{ cylinders.}$$

STEP BY STEP SOLUTIONS OF PROBLEMS

Problem 1 A diving bell in the form of a circular cylinder 3 m high, open at the bottom and closed at the top is lowered to a depth of 100 m in a lake. To what height will the water rise within the diving bell when it reaches the bottom? The surface temperature of the water is 25°C and the temperature at the bottom is 10°C.

1 Make a sketch of the problem and tabulate the given data. Use subscript 1 for surface data and subscript 2 for data at the bottom of the lake.

1

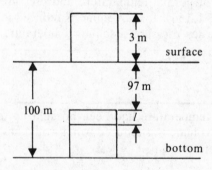

$$T_1 = 25°C = 298 \text{ K}$$
$$p_1 = 1.01 \times 10^5 \text{ Pa}$$
$$V_1 = 3 \text{ m } (A)$$
(the volume of a cylinder = area × height)
$$T_2 = 10°C = 283 \text{ K}$$
$$V_2 = Al$$
$$h = 100 \text{ m}$$

2 Use the ideal gas law and solve for unknowns.

2

$$\frac{p_1 V_1}{T_1} = \frac{p_2 V_2}{T_2}$$

$$\frac{(1.01 \times 10^5 \text{ Pa}) \, (3 \text{ m}) \, (A)}{298 \text{ K}} = \frac{p_2 \, (Al)}{283 \text{ K}}$$

$$p_2 l = 2.877 \times 10^5 \text{ Pa} \cdot \text{m}$$

---

3 Solve for $p_2 = p_1 + \rho g h$.

3

$$p_2 = 1.01 \times 10^5 \text{ Pa} + (1 \times 10^3 \text{ kg} \cdot \text{m}^{-3})$$
$$\times \, (9.8 \text{ m} \cdot \text{s}^{-2}) \, (97 + l)$$
$$= 1.052 \times 10^6 \text{ Pa} + 9800 \, l \, (\text{Pa} \cdot \text{m}^{-1})$$

---

4 Substitute this value of p_2 in the equation in frame 2. Dividing through by 9800, you get a quadratic equation.

4

$$(1.052 \times 10^6 \text{ Pa} + 9800 \, l \, \text{Pa} \cdot \text{m}^{-1})l$$
$$= 2.877 \times 10^5 \text{ Pa} \cdot \text{m}$$
$$l^2 + 107.3l - 29.36 = 0$$

---

5 Solve for l.

5 $l = 0.25$ m

---

6 To what height will the water rise in the diving bell?

6 $3 \text{ m} - 0.25 \text{ m} = 2.75 \text{ m}$

Problem 2 A demonstration barometer 1 m long with a cross section of 1 cm^2 indicated a true reading of 76 cm of mercury before a small amount of air was introduced into the tube causing the column to drop to a height of 68 cm. The room temperature was 20°C. Assuming that the air is nitrogen with a molecular mass $M = 28 \text{ g} \cdot \text{mol}^{-1}$, what mass of air entered the tube?

7 Draw a sketch and tabulate the data.

7

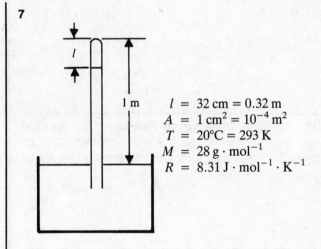

$l = 32 \text{ cm} = 0.32 \text{ m}$
$A = 1 \text{ cm}^2 = 10^{-4} \text{ m}^2$
$T = 20°\text{C} = 293 \text{ K}$
$M = 28 \text{ g} \cdot \text{mol}^{-1}$
$R = 8.31 \text{ J} \cdot \text{mol}^{-1} \cdot \text{K}^{-1}$

---

8 Solve the equation of state for an ideal gas for m. Substitute $V = Al$.

8

$$pV = \frac{m}{M} RT$$

$$m = \frac{pVM}{RT} = \frac{plAM}{RT}$$

---

9 Since the height of the mercury column has dropped by 8 cm, what is the pressure of the air above the mercury in Torr?

9 80 Torr (1 Torr = 1 mm of Hg)

---

10 Express this pressure in Pa.

10

$$\frac{80}{760} \, (1.01 \times 10^5 \, \text{Pa}) = 1.06 \times 10^4 \, \text{Pa}$$

---

11 Substitute the numerical values and solve for m.

11

$$m = \frac{(1.06 \times 10^4 \, \text{Pa}) \, (0.32 \, \text{m}) \, (10^{-4} \, \text{m}^2) \, (28 \, \text{g} \cdot \text{mol}^{-1})}{8.31 \, \text{J} \cdot \text{mol}^{-1} \cdot \text{K}^{-1} \, (293 \, \text{K})}$$
$$= 3.90 \times 10^{-3} \, \text{g} = 3.90 \, \text{mg}$$

Problem 3 If a balloon has a diameter of 6 m at the earth's surface where the pressure is 1 atm and the temperature is 17°C, what will be the diameter of the balloon if it rises to an altitude where the pressure is 0.2 atm and the temperature is −23°C?

12 Tabulate the given information. Use subscript 1 for conditions at the earth's surface and 2 for conditions above the earth.

12

$$p_1 = 1 \, \text{atm} \qquad\qquad p_2 = 0.2 \, \text{atm}$$
$$d_1 = 6 \, \text{m} \qquad\qquad r_1 = 3 \, \text{m}$$
$$T_1 = 17°C = 290 \, \text{K}$$
$$T_2 = -23°C = 250 \, \text{K}$$
find d_2

---

13 Assuming an ideal gas in the balloon, use the ideal gas law to solve for V_2. It must be stressed that the temperature is absolute, the pressure is the actual pressure, not gauge.

13

$$\frac{p_1 V_1}{T_1} = \frac{p_2 V_2}{T_2}$$
$$V_2 = \frac{p_1 T_2}{p_2 T_1} \, (V_1)$$

---

14 Substitute $\frac{4}{3} \pi r^3$ for V and solve for r_2 and d_2. It should be noted that mixed units may be used for pressure and volume provided that the equation is balanced.

14

$$\frac{4}{3} \pi r_2^{\,3} = \frac{1 \, \text{atm} \, (250 \, \text{K})}{0.2 \, \text{atm} \, (290 \, \text{K})} \left(\frac{4}{3} \pi\right) (3 \, \text{m})^3$$
$$r_2^{\,3} = 116 \, \text{m}^3$$
$$r_2 = 4.88 \, \text{m}$$
$$d_2 = 9.76 \, \text{m}$$

PROGRAMMED TEST

1 Problem 1 A 4 l bottle with a stopcock contains oxygen at 290 K and atmospheric pressure. The bottle is heated to a temperature of 420 K with the stopcock open. The stopcock is then closed and the bottle and its contents are cooled to the original temperature. a) What is the final pressure of the oxygen in the bottle? b) How many grams of oxygen remain?

1 Answer

6.97×10^4 Pa, 3.71 g

If you solved this problem correctly, go to frame 6. If you could not solve this problem, go through frames 2–5.

2 Tabulate the given quantities. Use subscript 1 for the heated system and subscript 2 for the cooled system.

2

$p_1 = 1.01 \times 10^5$ Pa
$T_1 = 420$ K
$V_1 = V_2 = 4$ l
$T_2 = 290$ K
find p_2

3 Use the ideal gas law to solve for p_2. Note that $V_1 = V_2$.

3

$$\frac{p_1}{T_1} = \frac{p_2}{T_2}$$

$$p_2 = \frac{(1.01 \times 10^5 \text{ Pa}) (290 \text{ K})}{420 \text{ K}}$$

$$= 6.97 \times 10^4 \text{ Pa}$$

4 Use $pV = nRT$ and solve for n.

4

$$n = \frac{pV}{RT}$$

$$= \frac{(6.97 \times 10^4 \text{ Pa}) (4 \times 10^{-3} \text{ m}^3)}{8.314 \text{ J} \cdot \text{mol}^{-1} \cdot \text{K}^{-1} (290 \text{ K})}$$

$$= 0.116 \text{ mol}$$

5 Find the mass of oxygen remaining. The molecular mass of oxygen is 32 g · mol^{-1}.

5

$$m = nM$$

$$= 0.116 \text{ mol} (32 \text{ g} \cdot \text{mol}^{-1})$$

$$= 3.71 \text{ g}$$

6 Problem 2 One mole of an ideal gas at NTP, i.e., normal temperature and pressure, occupies a volume of 22.4 liters. a) Determine the universal gas constant R and b) find the ratio of the density of oxygen to that of water at NTP.

6 Answer

8.31 J · mol^{-1} · K^{-1}, 1.43×10^{-3}

If you solved this problem correctly, go to frame 13. If you could not solve this problem, go through frames 7–12.

7 Solve for R in the equation of state.

7

$$pV = nRT$$

$$R = \frac{pV}{nT}$$

8 Substitute the given values. Note that since $1 \text{ cm}^3 = 10^{-6} \text{ m}^3$, $22.4 \text{ l} = 0.0224 \text{ m}^3$; NTP is 273 K and 1.013×10^5 Pa.

8

$$R = \frac{(1.013 \times 10^5 \text{ Pa})(0.0224 \text{ m}^3)}{(1 \text{ mol})(273 \text{ K})}$$
$$= 8.31 \text{ J} \cdot \text{mol}^{-1} \cdot \text{K}^{-1}$$

---

9 Substitute $\frac{m}{M} = n$ in the equation of state.

9

$$pV = \frac{mRT}{M}$$

---

10 Since $\rho = \frac{m}{V}$, substitute $m = \rho V$ in the equation above and solve for ρ.

10

$$\rho = \frac{pM}{RT}$$

---

11 To solve for the density of oxygen substitute $M = 32 \text{ g} = 0.032 \text{ kg}$ and the other numerical values.

11

$$\rho_{\text{oxygen}} = \frac{(1.013 \times 10^5 \text{ Pa})(0.032 \text{ kg})}{(8.31 \text{ J} \cdot \text{mol}^{-1} \cdot \text{K}^{-1})(273 \text{ K})}$$
$$= 1.43 \text{ kg} \cdot \text{m}^{-3}$$

---

12 The density of water is $1000 \text{ kg} \cdot \text{m}^{-3}$. Compute the ratio of the density of oxygen to the density of water.

12

$$\frac{\rho_{\text{oxygen}}}{\rho_{\text{water}}} = \frac{1.43 \text{ kg} \cdot \text{m}^{-3}}{1000 \text{ kg} \cdot \text{m}^{-3}} = 1.43 \times 10^{-3}$$

---

13 *Problem 3* A flask containing 4 g of oxygen at an absolute pressure of 12 atm and a temperature of 37°C develops a leak during a certain time period and the pressure drops to one-half of its original value as the temperature decreases to 17°C. a) What is the volume of the flask? b) How many grams of oxygen leaked out in this period?

13 *Answer*
2.65×10^{-4} m³, 1.86 g

If you could not solve this problem, go through frames 14–19.

14 Tabulate the given information. Use subscript 1 for the original state.

14

$m_1 = 4$ g	$R = 8.314 \text{ J} \cdot \text{mol}^{-1} \cdot \text{K}^{-1}$
$p_1 = 12$ atm	$p_2 = 6$ atm
$T_1 = 310$ K	$T_2 = 290$ K

---

15 How many moles are there in 4 g of oxygen?

15

$$n = \frac{m}{M}$$
$$= \frac{4 \text{ g}}{32 \text{ g} \cdot \text{mol}^{-1}} = 0.125 \text{ mol}$$

---

16 Use the equation of state and solve for V.

16

$$pV = nRT$$
$$V = \frac{(0.125 \text{ mol}) (8.314 \text{ J} \cdot \text{mol}^{-1} \cdot \text{K}^{-1}) (310 \text{ K})}{(12) (1.013 \times 10^5 \text{ Pa})}$$
$$= 2.65 \times 10^{-4} \text{ m}^3 = 265 \text{ cm}^3$$

---

17 Use the equation of state to find how many moles of oxygen remain in the flask.

17

$$p_2 V_2 = nRT_2$$
$$n = \frac{(6) (1.013 \times 10^5 \text{ Pa}) (2.65 \times 10^{-4} \text{ m}^3)}{(8.314 \text{ J} \cdot \text{mol}^{-1} \cdot \text{K}^{-1}) (290 \text{ K})}$$
$$= 6.68 \times 10^{-2} \text{ mol}$$

---

18 How many grams of oxygen remain in the flask?

18

$$m = Mn = (32 \text{ g} \cdot \text{mol}^{-1}) (0.0668 \text{ mol})$$
$$= 2.14 \text{ g}$$

---

19 How many grams of oxygen leaked out?

19

$$4 \text{ g} - 2.14 \text{ g} = 1.86 \text{ g}$$

18

The First Law of Thermodynamics

CHAPTER SUMMARY

Work is calculated for a thermodynamic system undergoing a volume change, the heat (energy) transfer is analyzed and both are discussed in terms of the change in the internal energy. When heat is added to a system, some of the energy remains within the system, thus increasing its internal energy; the remainder leaves the system as it does work against its surroundings. This is known as the first law of thermodynamics. The internal energy, heat capacities and adiabatic processes of an ideal gas are also presented. The following processes are described: isochoric, isothermal and isobaric.

BASIC TERMS — *Give definitions or meanings for the following:*

thermodyamic system (18-1)
path (18-2)
free expansion (18-3)
first law of thermodynamics (18-4)
internal energy (18-4)

isothermal process (18-5)
isobaric process (18-5)
adiabatic process (18-5)
isochoric process (18-5)
molar heat capacity (18-7)

PROGRAMMED QUIZ

1 What is an adiabatic process? Express this mathematically.

1 One in which no heat enters or leaves the system; $Q = 0$.

2 Write the first law of thermodynamics for an adiabatic process.

2 $U_2 - U_1 = \Delta U = -W$.

3 What is an isochoric process? Express this mathematically.

3 One in which the volume remains constant, i.e. the system does no work; $W = 0$.

4 Write the first law of thermodynamics for an isochoric process.

4 $U_2 - U_1 = \Delta U = Q$.

---

5 What is an isothermal process?

5 One in which the temperature is constant although heat is added or removed slowly enough for the system to be in thermal equilibrium, i.e. the change in internal energy is 0, $\Delta U = 0$. This is true only for the special case of an ideal gas where the internal energy of the system depends only on the temperature.

---

6 Express this mathematically. Write the first law of thermodynamics for an isothermal process.

6
$$0 = \Delta U = Q - W$$
$$Q = W.$$

---

7 What is an isobaric process? Express this mathematically.

7 $W = p(V_2 - V_1)$.
The process takes place at constant pressure.

---

8 What does the internal energy of an ideal gas depend on? a real gas?

8 The internal energy of an ideal gas depends on temperature only. The same is true of a gas at low pressure. Otherwise, the internal energy of a real gas depends on temperature, pressure and volume.

---

9 On a pV-diagram, do the work, heat taken in and expended and the internal energy depend on the path taken?

9 The work and the heat taken in and expended depend on the path; the internal energy is independent of the path.

---

10 What type of process is a phase change at a given pressure?

10 Isothermal, since there is no temperature change.

---

11 The first law of thermodynamics can be considered a generalization of what law that we have studied previously?

11 The law of conservation of mechanical energy.

---

12 In order to be able to use the ideal gas equation of state, must the state of the gas change slowly or quickly?

12 The state of the gas must change slowly enough to insure that the pressure and temperature are uniform throughout the gas, yet it must be fast enough to prevent appreciable heat exchange with the surroundings.

---

13 How can thermal energy be added to a system?

13 By the transfer of thermal energy or the performance of work.

---

14 How can you perform an adiabatic process without insulating the material?

14 Perform it quickly.

---

15 What is the relationship between the molar heat capacity of an ideal gas at constant pressure and at constant volume?

15 The difference between the molar heat capacity of an ideal gas at constant pressure and at constant volume equals the universal gas constant,
$$C_p - C_v = R.$$

---

16 What happens when a system under pressure expands? Illustrate.

16 It does work against its surroundings.

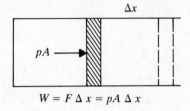

$$W = F \Delta x = pA \Delta x$$

---

17 Apply the first law of thermodynamics to boiling water. What happens to the heat of vaporization?

17 Most of the heat of vaporization remains in the system as an increase in internal energy. The remainder leaves the system as it does work against its surroundings while expanding from liquid to vapor.

---

18 Diesel engines do not require spark plugs. How is the fuel ignited?

18 When diesel fuel is injected into a cylinder at the end of a compression stroke, the high temperature attained during the process causes the fuel to ignite spontaneously.

---

19 An ideal gas expands slowly to three times its original volume in an isothermal process. If 1200 J of work is done in this process, find the heat added to the gas and its change in internal energy.

19 For an ideal gas
$$\Delta U = nC_v \Delta T$$
Since $\Delta T = 0$ (isothermal process)
$$\Delta U = 0$$
$$Q = \Delta U + W = 0 + 1200 \text{ J}$$
$$= 1200 \text{ J}$$

---

20 Do this problem for an adiabatic process.

20
$$Q = 0 \quad \text{(adiabatic process)}$$
$$\Delta U = Q - W$$
$$= 0 - 1200 \text{ J}$$
$$= -1200 \text{ J}$$

MAIN IDEAS

1 A thermodynamic system is one which interacts with its surroundings. The interactions which we will be concerned with are heat transfer to and work done by the system.

2 Work done by a thermodynamic system during a volume change (variable pressure). Consider a gas at pressure p and volume V. If the piston is displaced by Δx, the work done is $\Delta W = pA\Delta x$. Since $A\Delta x = \Delta V$, $\Delta W = p\Delta V$ where ΔV is the change in volume. For a variable pressure, $W = p_1\Delta V_1 + p_2\Delta V_2 + \cdots$, which is equal to the area under the curve in the pV-diagram.

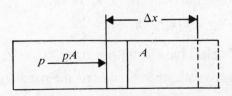

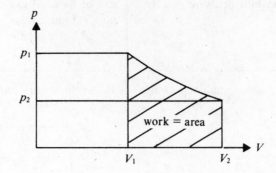

3 Work done by a thermodynamic system during a volume change (constant pressure). In this case $W = p(V_2 - V_1)$.

4 Positive and negative work, positive and negative heat. The work done by the substance is positive if the volume increases. The work done is negative if the volume decreases. Heat is considered to be positive when it enters a system. Heat is negative when it leaves the system. Work and heat transfer depend upon the path taken to go from one state to another.

5 The first law of thermodynamics. $\Delta U = U_2 - U_1 = Q - W$, where ΔU is the change in the internal energy of the system, Q is the heat entering the system and W is the work done by the system against its surroundings. This law may be rewritten as $Q = W + \Delta U$ which states that, when a quantity of heat Q enters a system, some of it (W) leaves the system in the form of work done by the system on its surroundings and the remainder (ΔU) is stored in the system as increased internal energy. Although the internal energy of a system may be defined as the sum of all the kinetic and potential energies of its constituent particles, it is desirable to define the internal energy change ΔU as $\Delta U = Q - W$. Even though Q and W are path dependent, in any thermodynamic process ΔU depends only on the initial and final states and not on the path leading from one to the other.

6 The principle of conservation of energy. Consider an isolated system, i.e. one into which there is no flow of heat and which does no external work. Therefore, we can say that $W = Q = 0$ and $\Delta U = 0$. That is, the internal energy of the system remains constant. This is the mathematical statement of the principle of conservation of energy. It must be emphasized that the energy of a system can only be changed by the performance of work or by a flow of heat across its boundaries.

7 An isochoric process is one in which the volume of a system does not change. This implies that the system does no work ($W = 0$). Therefore, $\Delta U = U_2 - U_1 = Q$.

8 An isothermal process is one which occurs at constant temperature. For the special case where the internal energy depends only on the temperature, $\Delta U = 0$ and thus $Q = W$.

9 An isobaric process occurs at constant pressure. We have shown that in this case $W = p(V_2 - V_1)$.

10 An adiabatic process is one in which no heat is gained or lost by the system. Since $Q = 0$, it follows from the first law of thermodynamics that $\Delta U = - W$.

11 Molar heat capacity at constant volume C_v and molar heat capacity at constant pressure C_p. The flow of heat at constant volume is given by $Q = nC_v \Delta T$, where n is the number of moles. Since the volume is constant, no work is done. Hence $W = 0$ and from the first law $\Delta U = Q$. Thus $\Delta U = nC_v\Delta T$. The flow of heat at constant pressure is given by $Q = nC_p\Delta T$. The work $W = p\Delta V = nRT$. For all ideal gases, $C_p - C_v = R$.

12 Adiabatic relations: (p, V, γ and T, V, γ). When a gas undergoes an adiabatic process, $T_1V_1^{\gamma-1} = T_2V_2^{\gamma-1}$ and $p_1V_1^\gamma = p_2V_2^\gamma$, where $\gamma = \dfrac{C_p}{C_v}$.

13 Problem solving strategy: ($Q = \Delta U + W$) problems.

a) Q is positive when heat enters the system. Q is negative when heat leaves the system.

b) W is positive if the system does work against its surroundings. W is negative when work is done on the system by its surroundings.

c) The internal energy change ΔU depends only on the initial and final states of a system. It is independent of the path. In this pV-diagram, the internal energy is the same for each path:

$$\Delta U_{132} = \Delta U_{142} = \Delta U_{12}$$

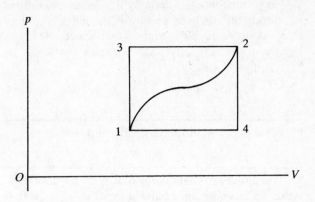

d) All quantities must be expressed in consistent units. Make sure that your equations are balanced.

e) Be careful with symbols.

m = mass of a gas,

M = mass of one mole (usually expressed in grams per mole),

$n = \dfrac{m}{M}$ = number of moles,

c_p = specific heat at constant pressure,

c_v = specific heat at constant volume,

C_p = heat capacity of one mole at constant pressure,

C_v = heat capacity of one mole at constant volume.

PROGRAMMED QUIZ

1 Six moles of an ideal gas are heated at constant pressure from 310 K to 390 K. Calculate the work done by the gas.

1
$$W = p(V_2 - V_1)$$
$$= pV_2 - pV_1$$
since $pV = nRT$,
$$W = nRT_2 - nRT_1$$
$$= nR(T_2 - T_1)$$
$$= (6 \text{ mol}) (8.314 \text{ J} \cdot \text{mol}^{-1} \cdot \text{K}^{-1})$$
$$(390 \text{ K} - 310 \text{ K})$$
$$= 3991 \text{ J}$$

2 A system takes in 1000 J of heat and does 600 J of work. What is the change in the internal energy?

2
$$\Delta U = Q - W$$
$$= 1000 \text{ J} - 600 \text{ J} = 400 \text{ J}$$

3 A liquid is changed to a vapor at a constant pressure of 1 atmosphere (1.013×10^5 Pa). The volume of the liquid was 2×10^{-6} m^3. The volume of the vapor is 2400×10^{-6} m^3. What type of process is this?

3 A process at constant pressure is isobaric.

4 How much work was done in this process?

4
$$W = p(V_2 - V_1)$$
$$= (1.013 \times 10^5 \text{ N} \cdot \text{m}^{-2}) (2400 - 2)$$
$$\times 10^{-6} \text{ m}^3$$
$$= 242.9 \text{ J}$$

5 How much work is done by 0.5 moles of an ideal gas during an adiabatic process if the initial and final temperatures are 20°C and 50°C respectively? The molar heat capacity at constant volume is $21.1 \text{ J} \cdot \text{mol}^{-1} \cdot \text{K}^{-1}$.

5
$$W = nC_v(T_1 - T_2)$$
$$= 0.5 \text{ mol } (21.1 \text{ J} \cdot \text{mol}^{-1} \cdot \text{K}^{-1})$$
$$\times (293 \text{ K} - 323 \text{ K})$$
$$= -317 \text{ J}$$

---

6 What is the significance of the negative sign?

6 Work is negative, the process is a compression.

---

7 The initial internal energy of a system was 4000 J. After undergoing an adiabatic process, it is 3000 J. How much heat entered the system?

7 0, no heat enters or leaves the system in an adiabatic process.

---

8 How much work was done on the system?

8
$$\Delta U = -W$$
$$U_2 - U_1 = -W$$
$$3000 \text{ J} - 4000 \text{ J} = -W$$
$$1000 \text{ J} = +W$$

---

9 What does the positive sign indicate?

9 Work is positive, as when a system expands.

---

10 What is the new pressure of a gas $\gamma = 1.40$ if originally the volume was 0.4 m^3 and the pressure was 1.0×10^5 Pa, and it is compressed quickly to a volume of 0.03 m^3?

10 If a compression of a gas is carried out very rapidly, the process is approximately adiabatic.
$$p_1 V_1{}^\gamma = p_2 V_2{}^\gamma$$
$$p_2 = (1.0 \times 10^5 \text{ Pa}) \left(\frac{0.4 \text{ m}^3}{0.03 \text{ m}^3}\right)^{1.40}$$
$$= 3.76 \times 10^6 \text{ Pa}$$

---

11 In reference to the above, if the original temperature is 293 K, what is the final temperature?

11
$$T_1 V_1{}^{\gamma-1} = T_2 V_2{}^{\gamma-1}$$
$$T_2 = T_1 \left(\frac{V_1}{V_2}\right)^{\gamma-1}$$
$$= (293 \text{ K}) \left(\frac{0.4 \text{ m}^3}{0.03 \text{ m}^3}\right)^{1.4-1}$$
$$= 826 \text{ K}$$

---

12 An internal energy change of 1000 J in an isochoric process means what?

12
$$U_2 - U_1 = Q = 1000 \text{ J}$$
1000 J of heat were added to a substance in a rigid container of fixed volume to produce this energy change.

---

13 Frames 13–16 refer to the thermodynamic process shown in the *p-V* plane. When the system is taken from state 1 to state 2 along path 1-3-2, 100 J of heat flow into the system and 40 J of work are done. Along path 1-4-2, the system does 20 J of work ($W_{142} = 20$ J). How much heat flows into the system, i.e. what is Q_{142}?

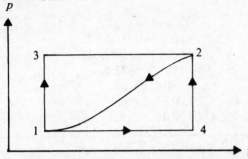

14 When the system is returned from state 2 to state 1 along the curved path, the work done by the system is 25 J. How much heat does the system absorb or liberate, i.e. $Q_{21} = ?$

15 If $U_1 = 0$ and $U_4 = 35$ J, find the heat absorbed or liberated in the process $1 \rightarrow 4$.

16 Find the heat absorbed in the process $4 \rightarrow 2$.

13 Since ΔU is independent of path,
$$\Delta U_{12} = Q_{132} - W_{132}$$
$$= 100 \text{ J} - 40 \text{ J} = 60 \text{ J}$$
$$\Delta U_{12} = Q_{142} - W_{142} \text{ or}$$
$$Q_{142} = \Delta U_{12} + W_{142}$$
$$= 60 \text{ J} + 20 \text{ J} = 80 \text{ J}$$

14 Since $\Delta V < 0$ for the process from state 2 to state 1, W_{21} is negative, $W_{21} = -25$ J.
Also, $\Delta U_{21} = -\Delta U_{12} = -60$ J (from above)
$$Q_{21} = \Delta U_{21} + W_{21}$$
$$= -60 \text{ J} - 25 \text{ J} = -85 \text{ J}$$
Since Q_{21} is negative, the system is liberating heat for this process.

15 $\Delta U_{14} = U_4 - U_1 = 35 \text{ J} - 0 = 35 \text{ J}$
$W_{142} = 20$ J (from frame 12)
$W_{42} = 0$ because $\Delta V = 0$ in the process from $4 \rightarrow 2$
$W_{142} = W_{14} + W_{42}$
$20 \text{ J} = W_{14} + 0$
$W_{14} = 20 \text{ J}$
$\Delta U_{14} = Q_{14} - W_{14}$
$Q_{14} = \Delta U_{14} + W_{14}$
$\quad = 35 \text{ J} + 20 \text{ J} = 55 \text{ J}$

The positive value means that heat is absorbed in the process.

16 $W_{42} = 0$ since $\Delta V = 0$ for the process from state 4 to state 2.
$$\Delta U_{42} = U_2 - U_4$$
$$= (U_2 - U_1) - (U_4 - U_1)$$
$$= \Delta U_{12} - \Delta U_{14}$$
$$= 60 \text{ J} - 35 \text{ J} = 25 \text{ J}$$
$$\Delta U_{42} = Q_{42} - W_{42}$$
$$Q_{42} = \Delta U_{42} + W_{42}$$
$$= 25 \text{ J} + 0 = 25 \text{ J}$$

The positive value means that heat is absorbed in the process.

STEP BY STEP SOLUTIONS OF PROBLEMS

Problem 1 A cylinder contains 2 moles of carbon dioxide at a temperature of 20°C. The cylinder is provided with a frictionless piston which maintains a constant pressure of 3 atm on the gas. The gas is heated until its temperature increases to 150°C. a) Draw a diagram representing the process in the pV-plane. b) How much work is done by the gas in this process? c) On what is this work done? d) What is the internal energy change of the gas? e) How much heat was supplied to the gas? f) Compare e) with the amount of heat flowing into the gas.

1 Tabulate the given data.

1

$$n = 2 \text{ mol}$$
$$T_1 = 20°C = 293 \text{ K}$$
$$p_1 = p_2 = 3 \text{ atm} = 3.039 \times 10^5 \text{ Pa}$$
$$T_2 = 150°C = 423 \text{ K}$$
$$R = 8.314 \text{ J} \cdot \text{mol}^{-1} \cdot \text{K}^{-1}$$
$$C_v = 20.85 \text{ J} \cdot \text{mol}^{-1} \cdot \text{K}^{-1}$$
$$C_p = 29.16 \text{ J} \cdot \text{mol}^{-1} \cdot \text{K}^{-1}$$

2 Draw a diagram for this process in the pV-plane. Note that the pressure is constant.

2

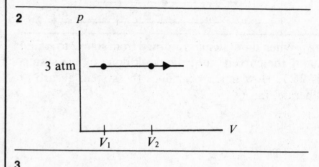

3 How much work is done by the gas in this process?

3

$W = p\Delta V$ but from the equation of state since p is constant,
$$pV = nRT$$
$$p\Delta V = nR\Delta T$$
$$\therefore W = nR\Delta T$$
$$= 2 \text{ mol } (8.314 \text{ J} \cdot \text{mol}^{-1} \cdot \text{K}^{-1}) (130 \text{ K})$$
$$= 2160 \text{ J}$$

4 On what is this work done?

4 On the piston.

5 Find the change in internal energy.

5

$$\Delta U = nC_v\Delta T$$
$$= 2 \text{ mol } (20.85 \text{ J} \cdot \text{mol}^{-1} \cdot \text{K}^{-1}) (130 \text{ K})$$
$$= 5420 \text{ J}$$

6 What is the heat supplied to the gas?

6

$$Q = \Delta U + W$$
$$= 5420 \text{ J} + 2160 \text{ J}$$
$$= 7580 \text{ J}$$

7 What is the heat flowing into the gas?

7

$$Q = nC_p\Delta T$$
$$= 2 \text{ mol } (29.16 \text{ J} \cdot \text{mol}^{-1} \cdot \text{K}^{-1}) (130 \text{ K})$$
$$= 7580 \text{ J}$$

The heat flowing into the gas is equal to the heat supplied to the gas.

Problem 2 A mass of 10 kg of water at 100°C is boiled at a pressure of 1 atm until it is completely converted into steam. a) Compute the work done by the water (steam) and b) compute the increase in internal energy. The density of water at 100°C = 958 kg · m^{-3}, the density of steam at 100°C = 0.598 kg · m^{-3}, the heat of vaporization of water = 2256 J · g^{-1}.

8 Tabulate the given data.

8
$$m = 10 \text{ kg}$$
$$L_v = 2256 \text{ J} \cdot \text{g}^{-1}$$
$$p = 1 \text{ atm} = 1.013 \times 10^5 \text{ Pa}$$
$$\rho_w = 958 \text{ kg} \cdot \text{m}^{-3}$$
$$\rho_s = 0.598 \text{ kg} \cdot \text{m}^{-3}$$

9 What is the work (at constant pressure) done by the water-steam in the vaporizing process?

9
$$W = p\Delta V$$
$$= p(V_s - V_w)$$

10 Express this relationship in terms of densities. Use $\rho = m/V$.

10
$$W = p\left(\frac{m}{\rho_s} - \frac{m}{\rho_w}\right)$$
$$= mp\left(\frac{1}{\rho_s} - \frac{1}{\rho_w}\right)$$

11 Substitute the numerical values and find W.

11
$$W = (10 \text{ kg})(1.013 \times 10^5 \text{ N} \cdot \text{m}^{-2})$$
$$\times \left(\frac{1}{0.598 \text{ kg} \cdot \text{m}^{-3}} - \frac{1}{958 \text{ kg} \cdot \text{m}^{-3}}\right)$$
$$= 1.69 \times 10^6 \text{ J}$$

12 Compute the heat added to the water; use $Q = mL_v$.

12
$$Q = (10^4 \text{ g})(2256 \text{ J} \cdot \text{g}^{-1})$$
$$= 22.56 \times 10^6 \text{ J}$$

Since heat is entering this system, Q is positive.

13 Compute the increase in internal energy using the first law of thermodynamics.

13
$$\Delta U = Q - W$$
$$= 22.56 \times 10^6 \text{ J} - 1.69 \times 10^6 \text{ J}$$
$$= 20.9 \times 10^6 \text{ J}$$

Problem 3 One mole of oxygen is taken from point 1 to point 3 along the path indicated by arrows. Compute a) the heat flowing into the system, b) the work done by the system and c) the change in the internal energy along the path segments 1→2 and 2→3.

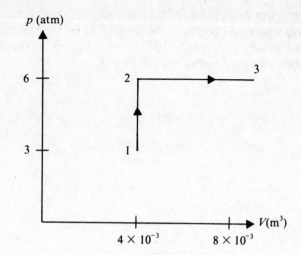

---

14 Tabulate the given data.

14
$$n = 1 \text{ mol}$$
$$p_1 = 3 \text{ atm} = 3.039 \times 10^5 \text{ Pa}$$
$$p_2 = 6 \text{ atm} = 6.078 \times 10^5 \text{ Pa}$$
$$p_3 = 6 \text{ atm} = 6.078 \times 10^5 \text{ Pa}$$
$$R = 8.314 \text{ J} \cdot \text{mol}^{-1} \cdot \text{K}^{-1}$$
$$C_v = 21.1 \text{ J} \cdot \text{mol}^{-1} \cdot \text{K}^{-1}$$
$$C_p = 29.41 \text{ J} \cdot \text{mol}^{-1} \cdot \text{K}^{-1}$$
$$M = 32 \text{ g}$$
$$V_1 = 4 \times 10^{-3} \text{ m}^3$$
$$V_2 = 4 \times 10^{-3} \text{ m}^3$$
$$V_3 = 8 \times 10^{-3} \text{ m}^3$$

---

15 In order to use the relation $Q_{12} = nC_v(\Delta T)_{12}$, we must compute $(\Delta T)_{12}$ from the ideal gas law, $(\Delta T)_{12} = T_2 - T_1$ (note that $V_1 = V_2$).

15
$$(\Delta T)_{12} = \frac{p_2 V_2}{nR} - \frac{p_1 V_1}{nR}$$
$$= \frac{(p_2 - p_1)V_1}{nR}$$

---

16 Substitute the numerical values and solve for $(\Delta T)_{12}$.

16
$$(\Delta T)_{12} =$$
$$\frac{(6.078 \times 10^5 \text{ Pa} - 3.039 \times 10^5 \text{ Pa})(4 \times 10^{-3} \text{ m}^3)}{1 \text{ mol} (8.314 \text{ J} \cdot \text{mol}^{-1} \cdot \text{K}^{-1})}$$
$$= 146 \text{ K}$$

---

17 Solve for Q_{12}.

17
$$Q_{12} = nC_v(\Delta T)_{12}$$
$$= 1 \text{ mol} (21.1 \text{ J} \cdot \text{mol}^{-1} \cdot \text{K}^{-1})(146 \text{ K})$$
$$= 3080 \text{ J}$$

---

18 Find the work done by the system between points 1 and 2 using $W = p\Delta V$.

18 Since $(\Delta V)_{12} = 0$
$$W_{12} = 0$$

---

19 Find $(\Delta U)_{12}$.

19
$$(\Delta U)_{12} = Q_{12} - W_{12}$$
$$= 3080 \text{ J} - 0$$
$$= 3080 \text{ J}$$

---

20 Find $(\Delta T)_{23}$. Note that $p_2 = p_3$.

20
$$(\Delta T)_{23} = \frac{p_3 V_3}{nR} - \frac{p_2 V_2}{nR} = \frac{p_2(V_3 - V_2)}{nR}$$
$$= \frac{(6.078 \times 10^5 \text{ Pa})(8 \times 10^{-3} \text{ m}^3 - 4 \times 10^{-3} \text{ m}^3)}{1 \text{ mol } (8.314 \text{ J} \cdot \text{mol}^{-1} \cdot \text{K}^{-1})}$$
$$= 292 \text{ K}$$

21 Solve for Q_{23}.

21
$$Q_{23} = nC_p (\Delta T)_{23}$$
$$= 1 \text{ mol } (29.41 \text{ J} \cdot \text{mol}^{-1} \cdot \text{K}^{-1})(292 \text{ K})$$
$$= 8590 \text{ J}$$

22 Find the work done by the system between points 2 and 3.

22
$$W_{23} = p(\Delta V)_{23}$$
$$= (6.078 \times 10^5 \text{ Pa})(4 \times 10^{-3} \text{ m}^3)$$
$$= 2430 \text{ J}$$

23 Find $(\Delta U)_{23}$.

23
$$(\Delta U)_{23} = Q_{23} - W_{23}$$
$$= 8590 \text{ J} - 2430 \text{ J}$$
$$= 6160 \text{ J}$$

PROGRAMMED TEST

1 *Problem 1* Nitrogen gas occupies a volume of 8 liters at STP. If it is compressed to a volume of 4 l, find the final pressure and temperature if the process is adiabatic ($\gamma = 1.4$).

1 *Answer*

2.64 atm, 360 K

If you solved this problem correctly, go to frame 5. If you could not solve this problem, go through frames 2–4.

2 Find the final pressure.

Given $V_1 = 8 \text{ l}$ $T_1 = 273 \text{ K}$

$V_2 = 4 \text{ l}$ $p_1 = 1 \text{ atm}$

Find p_2, T_2

2
$$p_1 V_1^\gamma = p_2 V_2^\gamma$$
$$p_2 = 1 \text{ atm } \left(\frac{8 \text{ l}}{4 \text{ l}}\right)^{1.4}$$
$$= 2.64 \text{ atm}$$

3 Find the final temperature.

3
$$T_1 V_1^{\gamma-1} = T_2 V_2^{\gamma-1}$$
$$T_2 = 273 \text{ K } \left(\frac{8 \text{ l}}{4 \text{ l}}\right)^{0.4}$$
$$= 360 \text{ K}$$

4 Find the final temperature using another method.

4
$$\frac{p_1 V_1}{T_1} = \frac{p_2 V_2}{T_2}$$
$$T_2 = \frac{(2.64 \text{ atm})(4 \text{ l})(273 \text{ K})}{(1 \text{ atm})(8 \text{ l})}$$
$$= 360 \text{ K}$$

5 **_Problem 2_** Two moles of helium are taken from point 1 to point 3. Show that the change in internal energy is independent of the path, i.e. $(\Delta U)_{123} = (\Delta U)_{143}$

5

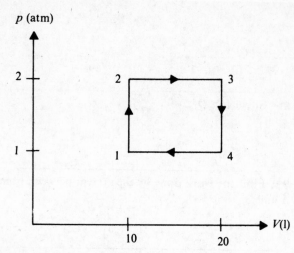

Answer
$$\Delta U_{123} = \Delta U_{143} = 4560 \text{ J}$$

If you solved this problem correctly, go to frame 26. If you could not solve this problem, go through frames 6–25.

6 Tabulate the given data.

6
$$n = 2 \text{ mol}$$
$$p_1 = 1 \text{ atm} = 1.013 \times 10^5 \text{ Pa}$$
$$p_2 = 2 \text{ atm} = 2.026 \times 10^5 \text{ Pa}$$
$$p_3 = 2 \text{ atm} = 2.026 \times 10^5 \text{ Pa}$$
$$p_4 = 1 \text{ atm} = 1.013 \times 10^5 \text{ Pa}$$
$$R = 8.31 \text{ J} \cdot \text{mol}^{-1} \cdot \text{K}^{-1}$$
$$C_v = 12.47 \text{ J} \cdot \text{mol}^{-1} \cdot \text{K}^{-1}$$
$$C_p = 20.78 \text{ J} \cdot \text{mol}^{-1} \cdot \text{K}^{-1}$$
$$M = 4 \text{ g}$$
$$V_1 = 10 \text{ l} = 1 \times 10^{-2} \text{ m}^3$$
$$V_2 = 10 \text{ l} = 1 \times 10^{-2} \text{ m}^3$$
$$V_3 = 20 \text{ l} = 2 \times 10^{-2} \text{ m}^3$$
$$V_4 = 20 \text{ l} = 2 \times 10^{-2} \text{ m}^3$$

7 Find $(\Delta T)_{12}$ using the ideal gas law.

7
$$(\Delta T)_{12} = \frac{(p_2 - p_1)V_1}{nR}$$
$$= \frac{(2.026 \times 10^5 \text{ Pa} - 1.013 \times 10^5 \text{ Pa})(1 \times 10^{-2} \text{ m}^3)}{(2 \text{ mol})(8.31 \text{ J} \cdot \text{mol}^{-1} \cdot \text{K}^{-1})}$$
$$= 61 \text{ K}$$

8 Solve for Q_{12}.

8
$$Q_{12} = nC_v(\Delta T)_{12}$$
$$= (2 \text{ mol})(12.47 \text{ J} \cdot \text{mol}^{-1} \cdot \text{K}^{-1})(61 \text{ K})$$
$$= 1520 \text{ J}$$

9 Find W_{12}.

9
$$W_{12} = p(\Delta V)_{12} = 0$$

10 Find $(\Delta U)_{12}$.

10 $(\Delta U)_{12} = Q_{12} - W_{12}$
$= 1520 \text{ J} - 0$
$= 1520 \text{ J}$

11 Find $(\Delta T)_{23}$.

11
$\Delta T_{23} = \dfrac{p_2(V_3 - V_2)}{nR}$

$= \dfrac{(2.026 \times 10^5 \text{ Pa})(2 \times 10^{-2} \text{ m}^3 - 1 \times 10^{-2} \text{ m}^3)}{(2 \text{ mol})(8.31 \text{ J} \cdot \text{mol}^{-1} \cdot \text{K}^{-1})}$

$= 122 \text{ K}$

12 Solve for Q_{23}.

12 $Q_{23} = nC_p(\Delta T)_{23}$
$= 2 \text{ mol } (20.78 \text{ J} \cdot \text{mol}^{-1} \cdot \text{K}^{-1})(122 \text{ K})$
$= 5070 \text{ J}$

13 Solve for W_{23}.

13 $W_{23} = p_2(\Delta V)_{23}$
$= (2.026 \times 10^5 \text{ Pa})(1 \times 10^{-2} \text{m}^3)$
$= 2030 \text{ J}$

14 Find $(\Delta U)_{23}$.

14 $(\Delta U)_{23} = Q_{23} - W_{23}$
$= 5070 \text{ J} - 2030 \text{ J}$
$= 3040 \text{ J}$

15 Find $(\Delta U)_{13} = (\Delta U)_{12} + (\Delta U)_{23}$.

15 $(\Delta U)_{13} = 1520 \text{ J} + 3040 \text{ J} = 4560 \text{ J}$

16 Find $(\Delta T)_{14}$.

16
$(\Delta T)_{14} = \dfrac{p_1(V_4 - V_1)}{nR}$

$= \dfrac{(1.013 \times 10^5 \text{ Pa})(2 \times 10^{-2} \text{ m}^3 - 1 \times 10^{-2} \text{ m}^3)}{(2 \text{ mol})(8.31 \text{ J} \cdot \text{mol}^{-1} \cdot \text{K}^{-1})}$

$= 61 \text{ K}$

17 Find Q_{14}.

17 $Q_{14} = nC_p(\Delta T)_{14}$
$= 2 \text{ mol } (20.78 \text{ J} \cdot \text{mol}^{-1} \cdot \text{K}^{-1})(61 \text{ K})$
$= 2535 \text{ J}$

18 Find W_{14}.

18
$W_{14} = p_1(\Delta V)_{14}$
$= (1.013 \times 10^5 \text{ Pa}) (1 \times 10^{-2} \text{ m}^3)$
$= 1013 \text{ J}$

19 Find $(\Delta U)_{14}$.

19
$(\Delta U)_{14} = Q_{14} - W_{14}$
$= 2535 \text{ J} - 1013 \text{ J}$
$= 1520 \text{ J}$

20 Solve for $(\Delta T)_{43}$.

20

$$(\Delta T)_{43} = \frac{(p_3 - p_4)V_3}{nR}$$

$$= \frac{(2.026 \times 10^5 \text{ Pa} - 1.013 \times 10^5 \text{ Pa})(2 \times 10^{-2}\text{m}^3)}{2 \text{ mol } (8.31 \text{ J} \cdot \text{mol}^{-1} \cdot \text{K}^{-1})}$$

$$= 122 \text{ K}$$

---

21 Find Q_{43}.

21

$$\begin{aligned}Q_{43} &= nC_v(\Delta T)_{43} \\ &= (2 \text{ mol}) (12.47 \text{ J} \cdot \text{mol}^{-1} \cdot \text{K}^{-1}) (122 \text{ K}) \\ &= 3040 \text{ J}\end{aligned}$$

---

22 Find W_{43}.

22

$$W_{43} = p_4(\Delta V)_{43} = 0$$

---

23 Find $(\Delta U)_{43}$.

23

$$\begin{aligned}(\Delta U)_{43} &= Q_{43} - W_{43} \\ &= 3040 \text{ J} - 0 \\ &= 3040 \text{ J}\end{aligned}$$

---

24 Find $(\Delta U)_{13} = (\Delta U_{14}) + (\Delta U)_{43}$

24

1520 J + 3040 J = 4560 J

---

25 Compare with frame 15.

25 ΔU_{13} for both paths = 4560 J thus the change in internal energy is independent of the path.

---

26 *Problem 3* One mole of helium is initially at a temperature of 30°C and a volume of 30 1. The helium is first expanded at constant pressure until the volume is doubled and then adiabatically until the temperature returns to its initial value. Find a) the total heat supplied in the process, b) the total change in internal energy of the helium, c) the total work done by the helium, d) the final volume of the helium, e) the pressure for the first expansion and f) the final pressure. g) Draw a pV-diagram for the entire process.

26 *Answer*
   6300 J, 0, 6300 J, 169 1, 8.39 $\times$ 10⁵ Pa, 1.49 $\times$ 10⁵ Pa; the pV-diagram is given in frame 36.

If you could not solve this problem, go through frames 27–36.

27 Find the temperature at the end of the expansion at constant pressure. Note that during this expansion the volume is doubled.

27

$$\frac{V_1}{T_1} = \frac{V_2}{T_2}$$

$$T_2 = \frac{303 \text{ K}(60 \text{ 1})}{30 \text{ 1}}$$

$$= 606 \text{ K}$$

28 Find the heat supplied for the expansion at constant pressure.

28
$$Q = nC_p \Delta T$$
$$= (1 \text{ mol})(20.78 \text{ J} \cdot \text{mol}^{-1} \cdot \text{K}^{-1})(606 \text{ K} - 303 \text{ K})$$
$$= 6300 \text{ J}$$

---

29 How much heat is supplied for the adiabatic process?

29 0, no heat flows in or out during an adiabatic process.

---

30 What is the total heat supplied?

30 6300 J + 0 = 6300 J

---

31 What is the total change in the internal energy of the helium?

31 0, the internal energy of an ideal gas depends on temperature only. Since the initial temperature = final temperature, the change in internal energy = 0.

---

32 Find the total work done by the helium.

32
$$\Delta U = Q - W$$
$$W = 6300 \text{ J} - 0$$
$$= 6300 \text{ J}$$

---

33 Find the final volume V_3 of the helium.

33 $T_2 V_2^{\gamma-1} = T_3 V_3^{\gamma-1}$ where $\gamma = 1.67$ for helium gas.

$$V_3^{(0.67)} = \frac{606 \text{ K}}{303 \text{ K}}(0.06 \text{ m}^3)^{(0.67)}$$

$$V_3 = 0.169 \text{ m}^3 = 169 \text{ l}$$

---

34 Since the first expansion occurs at constant pressure, we can find the pressure from the equation of state.

34
$$p\Delta V = nR\Delta T$$

$$p = \frac{1 \text{ mol} (8.31 \text{ J} \cdot \text{mol}^{-1} \cdot \text{K}^{-1})(606 \text{ K} - 303 \text{ K})}{(6 \times 10^{-3} \text{ m}^3 - 3 \times 10^{-3} \text{ m}^3)}$$

$$= 8.39 \times 10^5 \text{ Pa}$$

---

35 Find the final pressure p_3.

35

$$\frac{p_2 V_2}{T_2} = \frac{p_3 V_3}{T_3}$$

$$p_3 = \frac{(8.39 \times 10^5 \text{ Pa})(60 \text{ l})(303 \text{ K})}{(606 \text{ K})(169 \text{ l})}$$

$$= 1.49 \times 10^5 \text{ Pa}$$

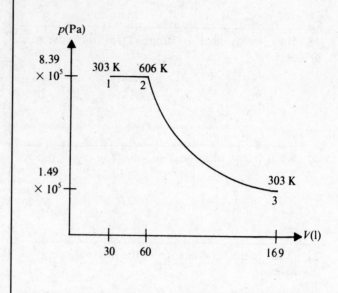

19

The Second Law of Thermodynamics

CHAPTER SUMMARY

The first law of thermodynamics states that when heat is added to a system some of the energy remains within the system thus increasing its internal energy; the remainder leaves the system as it does work against its surroundings. The essence of the first law is that energy is conserved. The second law stipulates that it is impossible for thermal energy, on its own, to flow from a region of low temperature to one at a higher temperature and that only a fraction of the thermal energy may be converted into work. This means that heat engines, such as the internal combusion engine, steam engine and the refrigerator, may not be 100% efficient; the Carnot cycle represents the processes of a maximum efficiency idealized engine. In addition, the Carnot cycle can be used to define the Kelvin temperature scale and absolute zero. The second law of thermodynamics is also presented in terms of entropy.

BASIC TERMS — *Give definitions or meanings for the following:*

reversible process (19-1)
equilibrium process (19-1)
irreversible process (19-1)
cyclic process (19-2)
heat engine (19-2)
thermal efficiency (19-2)
working substance (19-2)
internal combustion engine (19-3)
compression ratio (19-3)
Otto cycle (19-3)
diesel cycle (19-3)

refrigeration (19-4)
performance coefficient (19-4)
energy efficiency rating (19-4)
heat pump (19-4)
second law of thermodynamics (19-5)
thermal pollution (19-6)
Carnot cycle (19-6)
entropy (19-7)
Kelvin temperature scale (19-8)
absolute zero (19-8)

PROGRAMMED QUIZ

1 Why is the entropy of the universe increasing? What is the significance of the increase of entropy that accompanies every natural process?

1 Because most processes are irreversible. The increase in entropy represents the extent to which the universe becomes more disordered or random in that process. Energy becomes more unavailable and the universe is referred to as becoming "rundown."

2 When is the change in entropy equal to zero?

2 Only in a reversible process.

3 On what does the natural direction of heat flow between two reservoirs depend?

3 Their temperatures; heat flows from the hotter reservoir to the colder.

4 This is the basis of what physical principle?

4 The second law of thermodynamics.

5 What processes are involved in a Carnot cycle?

5 Two reversible adiabatic processes and two reversible isothermal processes.

6 What do we mean when we say that heat engines usually operate in a cycle?

6 They return to the same point in terms of thermodynamic properties.

7 What happens to the heat that a heat engine takes in?

7 Some of it is converted into work, the rest is exhausted at a lower temperature.

8 In a heat engine, what does the difference between the heat intake and heat exhaust equal?

8 The work output.

9 Does the efficiency of a Carnot engine depend on the working substance? If not, what does it depend on?

9 No, it depends only on the operating temperatures,

$$e = 1 - \frac{T_C}{T_H} .$$

10 The efficiency of the internal combustion engine is a function of what quantities?

10 The compression ratio and the value of γ of the working substance.

11 When can a heat engine be 100% efficient?

11 If it is frictionless and its exhaust temperature is 0 K.

12 One way of expressing the second law of thermodynamics: it is impossible to have a process whose only function is to transfer heat from _____ to _____ .

12 A cold region; a warm region.

13 Can we reach absolute zero?

13 No, we can only approach it.

14 What is a reservoir?

14 A large source of heat, the temperature of which does not change appreciably when heat is added or removed.

---

15 Can a real thermodynamic process be reversible?

15 No, for a process to be reversible, it must be done very slowly so that it could be considered a series of equilibrium states. Real processes are done more quickly, and turbulence and friction would be present.

---

16 Give some examples of irreversible processes, i.e. processes that take place in one direction.

16 Heat flows from a body of high temperature to a body of lower temperature; gases and liquids by their own accord tend to mix, not to unmix; iron rusts; rocks crumble; people grow old, Humpty Dumpty.

---

17 What is the difference between the operation of a refrigerator and a heat engine?

17 A heat engine takes in heat from a hot reservoir, converts a part of the heat energy into mechanical work output, and rejects the difference as heat to a cold reservoir. On the other hand, a refrigerator takes in heat from a cold reservoir, the compressor supplies a mechanical work input and heat is rejected to a hot reservoir.

---

18 What are the algebraic signs for W, Q_H and Q_C for the heat engine and refrigerator?

18

	Q_C	W	Q_H
heat engine	−	+	+
refrigerator	+	−	−

---

19 Draw a schematic flow diagram of a heat engine.

19

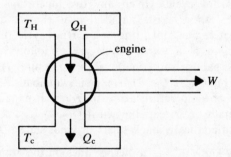

---

20 Draw a schematic flow diagram of a refrigerator.

20

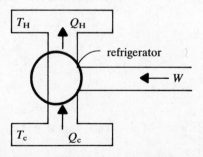

MAIN IDEAS

1 Heat engines. A heat engine is a system or device for converting "heat" into "work". The following processes are common to all heat engines: a) heat is taken in from a source at high temperature, mechanical work is done and the heat is expelled to a lower temperature and b) heat engines usually operate in a cycle, i.e. they return to a point at which all thermodynamic variables are the same as they were at the initial stage. If Q and W are the net work and heat, respectively, which occur during a cycle, then $\Delta U = 0$ and $Q = W$. A heat engine absorbs heat Q_H from a high temperature reservoir and expels heat Q_C to a low temperature reservoir. In accordance with the first law of thermodynamics, the work done by the engine $W = Q_H + Q_C$. The thermal efficiency of the heat engine is defined by $e = \dfrac{W}{Q_H} = \dfrac{Q_H + Q_C}{Q_H}$. A positive value of Q_H means that heat is entering the working substance and a negative value of Q_C means that energy is transferred out of the working substance. The thermal efficiency of an internal combustion engine is defined by $e = 1 - \dfrac{1}{r^{\gamma-1}}$, where r = compression ratio ≈ 8 and $\gamma = 1.4$.

2 Refrigerators. A refrigerator is a heat engine operating in reverse. Heat Q_C is taken in from a low temperature reservoir (a storage chamber) and the heat Q_H is expelled into a high temperature reservoir (the environment). The performance coefficient $K = \dfrac{-Q_C}{W} = \dfrac{-Q_C}{Q_H + Q_C}$.

3 The second law of thermodynamics can be expressed in two equivalent forms. Lord Kelvin stated that, "It is not possible to have a process whereby the only result is the extraction of heat from a reservoir and the conversion of all this heat into work." Rudolf Claudius stated that, "It is not possible to have a process whereby heat is removed from a reservoir at one temperature and absorbed in equal quantity by a reservoir at a higher temperature." In other words, heat does not on its own accord flow from a body of low temperature to a body at a higher temperature. If no other changes are taking place in a system or its environment, it is impossible to remove heat from a reservoir and convert it completely to work.

4 Carnot cycle. Given any two operating temperatures, there exists an ideal heat engine, called a Carnot engine, operating in a Carnot cycle. The four processes of a Carnot cycle are as follows: 1) The gas expands isothermally at temperature T_H (AB), absorbing heat Q_H. 2) It expands adiabatically (BC) until its temperature drops to T_C. 3) It expands isothermally (CD) expelling heat Q_C. 4) It is compressed adiabatically back to its original state (DA).

AB and DC are isotherms, lines on the graph connecting points of equal temperature. BC and AD are adiabats, lines on the graph representing an adiabatic process, i.e. no heat enters or leaves the system ($Q = 0$).

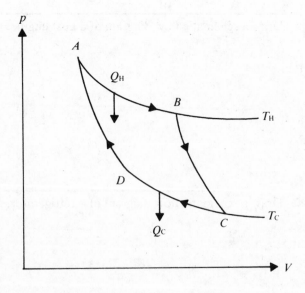

The efficiency of a Carnot engine $e = 1 - \dfrac{T_C}{T_H}$. The performance coefficient for a Carnot refrigerator $K = \dfrac{T_C}{T_H - T_C}$. We can now restate the second law of thermodynamics. Regardless of the working substance, all

Carnot engines operating between the same two temperatures have the same efficiency.

5 Kelvin temperatures may be defined as $\dfrac{T_H}{T_C} = \dfrac{|Q_H|}{|Q_C|}$, where T_H is the Kelvin temperature of the hotter re-

servoir and T_C the temperature of the colder reservoir. Absolute zero ($T = 0$ K) is a temperature we may approach but never reach. This is sometimes referred to as the third law of thermodynamics.

6 Entropy. So far we have described the state of a system in terms of such quantities as pressure, volume and temperature. A system may also be described in terms of the probabilities of having particular states. The measure of such a probability is referred to as entropy. We will define a change in entropy as follows. Consider two states of a system and a number of reversible paths connecting them. $S_2 - S_1 = \Delta S = \Delta Q/T$, where ΔQ is the heat added to the system and T is the absolute temperature. This definition holds only for reversible equilibrium processes. Since ΔS is independent of the path leading from the initial to the final states, compute entropy changes in non-equilibrium processes as follows: Find a path connecting the given initial and final states which consists entirely of reversible equilibrium processes and compute the entropy change.

7 Problem solving strategy: Heat engines and refrigerators.

a) Remember the sign conventions for W, Q_C and Q_H. Each Q is positive if it represents heat entering the working substance of an engine or other system, negative if it leaves the system.

b) A problem may involve the rate of heat transfer (heat current). Then $H = \dfrac{Q}{t}$.

c) The total internal energy change in any cyclic process is zero.

PROGRAMMED QUIZ

1 A diesel engine takes in 6000 J of heat and delivers 2000 J of work per cycle. The heat is obtained by burning diesel fuel with a heat of combustion of 5.00×10^4 J $\cdot$ g^{-1}. What is the thermal efficiency of the engine?

1

$$
\begin{aligned}
\text{Efficiency} &= \frac{\text{work output}}{\text{heat energy input}} \\
&= \frac{W}{Q_H} \\
&= \frac{2000 \text{ J}}{6000 \text{ J}} = 0.333 = 33.3\%
\end{aligned}
$$

2 How much heat Q_C is discarded in each cycle? Remember the total internal energy change in any cyclic process is zero.

2 From the first law of thermodynamics for a cyclic process,

$$
\begin{aligned}
\Delta U &= 0 = Q - W \\
Q &= W = Q_H + Q_C \\
Q_C &= W - Q_H \\
&= 2000 \text{ J} - 6000 \text{ J} \\
&= -4000 \text{ J}
\end{aligned}
$$

This means that 4000 J of heat leave the engine during each cycle.

3 What mass of fuel is burned in each cycle?

3

$$
Q_H = mL_C
$$
where L_C = heat of combustion,
$$
\begin{aligned}
m &= \frac{Q_H}{L_C} \\
&= \frac{6000 \text{ J}}{5.00 \times 10^4 \text{ J} \cdot \text{g}^{-1}} \\
&= 0.12 \text{ g}
\end{aligned}
$$

4 If the engine goes through 60 cycles per second, what is its power output in watts and in horsepower?

$$\text{Power} = \frac{\text{work}}{\text{cycle}} \cdot \frac{\text{cycles}}{\text{second}}$$
$$= (2000 \text{ J}) (60 \text{ s}^{-1})$$
$$= 1.2 \times 10^5 \text{ W}$$

$$(1.2 \times 10^5 \text{ W}) \left(\frac{1 \text{ hp}}{746 \text{ W}} \right) = 161 \text{ hp}$$

---

5 An ice-making machine operates in a Carnot cycle. It takes heat from water at 0°C and rejects heat to a room at 20°C. If 40 kg of water at 0°C are converted into ice at 0°C, how much heat Q_H is rejected to the room? Comment on the algebraic sign.

5

$$T_H = 20°C = 293 \text{ K}$$
$$T_C = 0°C = 273 \text{ K}$$
$$Q_C = mL_f$$
$$= (40 \text{ kg}) (3.34 \times 10^5 \text{ J} \cdot \text{kg}^{-1})$$
$$= 1.34 \times 10^7 \text{ J}$$

This heat is absorbed by the ice-making machine.

Since $\dfrac{T_H}{T_C} = \dfrac{-Q_H}{Q_C}$

$$Q_H = -Q_C \left(\frac{T_H}{T_C} \right)$$

$$= - (1.34 \times 10^7 \text{ J}) \left(\frac{293 \text{ K}}{273 \text{ K}} \right)$$

$$= - 1.44 \times 10^7 \text{ J}.$$

Q_4 is negative because this heat is rejected by the ice-making machine.

---

6 How much energy must be supplied to the ice-making machine? Comment on the algebraic sign.

From the first law of thermodynamics for a cyclic process,
$$\Delta U = 0 = Q - W$$
$$Q = W = Q_C + Q_H$$
$$= 1.34 \times 10^7 \text{ J} - 1.44 \times 10^7 \text{ J}$$
$$= - 1.00 \times 10^6 \text{ J}.$$

W is negative because the energy is being supplied to the ice-making machine.

---

7 What is the efficiency of a diesel engine whose compression ratio is 20? (Use $\gamma = 1.40$.)

$$e = 1 - \frac{1}{r^{\gamma - 1}}$$

$$= 1 - \frac{1}{20^{0.40}} = 69.8\%$$

---

8 The combustion temperature in a diesel engine is 2000 K and the exhaust temperature is 1200 K. What is the maximum efficiency of the engine?

The Carnot efficiency is the maximum possible efficiency.

$$e = 1 - \frac{T_C}{T_H}$$

$$= 1 - \frac{1200 \text{ K}}{2000 \text{ K}} = 40\%$$

---

9 What is the performance coefficient of a Carnot refrigerator that operates between two heat reservoirs at temperatures of 500 K and 400 K?

9

$$K = \frac{T_C}{T_H - T_C}$$
$$= \frac{400 \text{ K}}{500 \text{ K} - 400 \text{ K}} = 4$$

---

10 Frames 10–20 refer to this pV-diagram of the Carnot cycle. What do T_H and T_C represent? What do AD and BC represent?

10 Isotherms, adiabats.

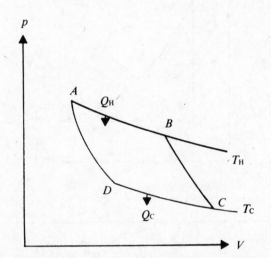

---

11 In the process AB, the gas _____.

11 Expands isothermally at temperature T_H.

---

12 During the process AB does the engine absorb or reject heat?

12 Absorbs heat Q_H.

---

13 In the process BC, the gas _____.

13 Expands adiabatically until its temperature drops to T_C.

---

14 During the process BC does the engine absorb or reject heat?

14 Neither, there is no heat flow.

---

15 In the process CD, the gas _____.

15 Is compressed isothermally at temperature T_C.

---

16 During the process CD, does the engine absorb or reject heat?

16 It rejects heat Q_C.

---

17 In the process DA, the gas _____.

17 Is compressed adiabatically back to its central state.

---

18 During the process DA, does the engine absorb or reject heat?

18 Neither, there is no heat flow.

---

19 What quantity is represented by the area enclosed by the four curves representing the four processes?

19 The net work done by the working substance of the Carnot engine.

20 What is the change in the internal energy of this Carnot engine in one cycle?

20 Zero, the Carnot cycle returns to its original state.

STEP BY STEP SOLUTIONS OF PROBLEMS

Problem 1 A heat engine carries 0.2 mol of an ideal gas through the cyclic process shown in the figure. Process 1–2 is at constant volume, process 2–3 is adiabatic and process 3–1 is at a constant pressure of 2 atm. Use $\gamma = 1.67$ and $C_v = 12.47 \text{ J} \cdot \text{mol}^{-1} \cdot \text{K}^{-1}$. Find a) the pressure and volume at each vertex point and b) the net work done by the gas in the entire process. ($T_1 = 290$ K, $T_2 = 650$ K, $T_3 = 440$ K).

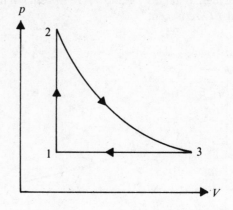

1 Tabulate the given data.

1

$n = 0.2$ mol
$p_1 = p_3 = 2$ atm $= 2.026 \times 10^5$ Pa
$T_1 = 290$ K
$T_2 = 650$ K
$T_3 = 440$ K
$C_v = 12.47 \text{ J} \cdot \text{mol}^{-1} \cdot \text{K}^{-1}$
$\gamma = 1.67$
$R = 8.314 \text{ J} \cdot \text{mol}^{-1} \cdot \text{K}^{-1}$

2 Find V_1 from the equation of state.

2

$$\frac{p_1 V_1}{T_1} = nR$$

$$V_1 = \frac{(0.2 \text{ mol})(8.314 \text{ J} \cdot \text{mol}^{-1} \cdot \text{K}^{-1})(290 \text{ K})}{2.026 \times 10^5 \text{ Pa}}$$

$$= 0.00238 \text{ m}^3$$

3 Find p_2 from the equation of state. Note that $V_2 = V_1$.

3

$$p_2 = \frac{nRT_2}{V_2}$$

$$= \frac{(0.2 \text{ mol})(8.314 \text{ J} \cdot \text{mol}^{-1} \cdot \text{K}^{-1})(650 \text{ K})}{0.00238 \text{ m}^3}$$

$$= 4.54 \times 10^5 \text{ Pa}$$

4 Find V_3 from the equation of state. Note that $p_3 = p_1$.

4

$$V_3 = \frac{nRT_3}{p_3}$$

$$= \frac{(0.2 \text{ mol})(8.314 \text{ J} \cdot \text{mol}^{-1} \cdot \text{K}^{-1})(440 \text{ K})}{2.026 \times 10^5 \text{ Pa}}$$

$$= 0.00361 \text{ m}^3$$

5 In order to find the net work done by the gas, we must find the work done for each process. What is W_{12}?

5 Process 1-2 is isochoric, i.e. there is no change in volume,
$$W = 0.$$

6 Process 2-3 is adiabatic. Find W_{23}.

6
$$W_{23} = nC_v(T_2 - T_3)$$
$$= (0.2 \text{ mol})(12.47 \text{ J} \cdot \text{mol}^{-1} \cdot \text{K}^{-1})(650 \text{ K} - 440 \text{ K})$$
$$= 524 \text{ J}$$

7 Find W_{31}. Note that process 3-1 is isobaric.

7
$$W_{31} = p(V_1 - V_3)$$
$$= 2.026 \times 10^5 \text{ Pa}(2.38 \times 10^{-3} \text{ m}^3 - 3.61 \times 10^{3} \text{ m}^3)$$
$$= - 249 \text{ J}$$

8 What is the significance of the negative sign?

8 Process 3-1 is a compression, therefore the work done is negative.

9 Find the net work $= W_{12} + W_{23} + W_{31}$.

9 $0 + 524 \text{ J} + (- 249 \text{ J}) = 275 \text{ J}$

Problem 2 Find the thermal efficiency of an engine which operates on the following cycle: a) Starts with n mol of an ideal gas at p_0, V_0. b) Quadruples the pressure at constant volume. c) Triples the volume at constant pressure. d) Changes to ¼ the pressure at constant volume. e) Changes to 1/3 the volume at constant pressure, thus completing the cycle. (Use $C_v = 1.5$ R.)

10 Draw a pV-diagram for the entire process. Indicate the pressure and the volume at each vertex. Indicate by an arrow in which cycle heat enters the system.

10
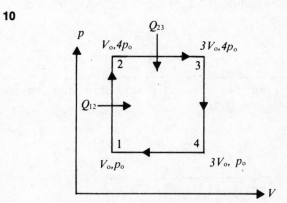

11 The efficiency of the engine is the ratio of the net work done during the cycle to the heat flowing into the engine. Since no work is done during cycles 1-2 and 3-4 (no change in volume), calculate W_{23} and W_{41}.

11
$$W_{23} = p_2(V_3 - V_2) = 4p_0(2V_0) = 8p_0V_0$$
$$W_{41} = p_4(V_1 - V_4) = p_0(- 2V_0) = - 2p_0V_0$$

12 Find the net work.

12
$$W = W_{12} + W_{23} + W_{34} + W_{41}$$
$$= 6p_0V_0$$

13 Check: the net work is represented by the area enclosed by the four processes.

13
$$W = (3V_0 - V_0)(4p_0 - p_0) = 6p_0V_0$$

14 Find the temperature at each vertex from the equation of state.

14

$$\frac{pV}{T} = nR$$

$$T_1 = \frac{p_0 V_0}{nR}$$

$$T_2 = \frac{4p_0 V_0}{nR}$$

$$T_3 = \frac{12p_0 V_0}{nR}$$

$$T_4 = \frac{3p_0 V_0}{nR}$$

---

15 Find Q_{12}. Note that V is constant.

15

$$Q_{12} = nC_v(\Delta T)_{12} = nC_v(T_2 - T_1)$$

$$= nC_v \left(\frac{4p_0 V_0}{nR} - \frac{p_0 V_0}{nR} \right)$$

$$= \frac{3C_v}{R} p_0 V_0$$

---

16 Find Q_{23}. Note that p is constant.

16

$$Q_{23} = nC_p(\Delta T)_{23} = nC_p(T_3 - T_2)$$

$$= nC_p \frac{(12p_0 V_0)}{nR} - \frac{4p_0 V_0}{nR}$$

$$= \frac{8C_p}{R} p_0 V_0$$

---

17 Substitute for C_p using $C_p - C_v = R$.

17

$$Q_{23} = \frac{8(R + C_v)}{R} p_0 V_0$$

$$= 8p_0 V_0 + \frac{8C_v}{R} p_0 V_0$$

---

18 Find the heat flowing into the engine, $Q_H = Q_{12} + Q_{23}$.

18

$$Q_H = \frac{3C_v}{R} p_0 V_0 + \frac{8C_v}{R} p_0 V_0 + 8p_0 V_0$$

$$= \frac{11C_v}{R} p_0 V_0 + 8p_0 V_0$$

---

19 Substitute $C_v = 1.5R$.

19

$$Q_H = 24.5 \, p_0 V_0$$

---

20 Find the efficiency of the engine.

20

$$\text{Efficiency} = \frac{W}{Q_H} = \frac{6 p_0 V_0}{24.5 p_0 V_0} = 24.5\%$$

Problem 3 Heat is added to 10 kg of ice at $0°C$ until it is all melted. a) What is the change in the entropy of the water? b) Consider the source of heat as a reservoir at $40°C$ (i.e. its temperature will not change). What is the reservoir's change in entropy? c) What is the total change in entropy?

21 How much heat is required to convert 10 kg of ice at $0°C$ to water at $0°C$?

21

$$Q = mL_f$$

$$= 10 \text{ kg}(335 \times 10^3 \text{ J} \cdot \text{kg}^{-1})$$

$$= 3.35 \times 10^6 \text{ J}$$

22 Find the change in entropy of the water.

22

$$S_2 - S_1 = \frac{Q}{T}$$
$$= \frac{3.35 \times 10^6 \text{ J}}{273 \text{ K}}$$
$$= 1.227 \times 10^4 \text{ J} \cdot \text{K}^{-1}$$

23 Find the change in entropy of the reservoir. Note that heat is leaving the reservoir. The reservoir loses as much heat as the ice gains.

23

$$S_2 - S_1 = \frac{-Q}{T}$$
$$= \frac{-3.35 \times 10^6 \text{ J}}{313 \text{ K}}$$
$$= -1.07 \times 10^4 \text{ J} \cdot \text{K}^{-1}$$

24 What is the total change in entropy of the ice and the reservoir?

24

$$S_2 - S_1 = 1.227 \times 10^4 \text{ J} \cdot \text{K}^{-1} + (-1.07 \times 10^4 \text{ J} \cdot \text{K}^{-1})$$
$$= 1570 \text{ J} \cdot \text{K}^{-1}$$

PROGRAMMED TEST

1 *Problem 1* A heat engine contains 2 l of hydrogen at a pressure of 3 atm and a temperature of 300 K. The hydrogen goes through the following cycle: *1*) heated at constant pressure to 600 K, *2*) cooled at constant volume to 250 K, *3*) cooled at constant pressure to 125 K, *4*) heated at constant volume to 300 K. Calculate a) the net work done by the hydrogen, b) the net heat flowing into the hydrogen and c) the efficiency of the engine.
($c_v = 20.42 \text{ J} \cdot \text{mol}^{-1} \cdot \text{K}^{-1}$, $c_p = 28.74 \text{ J} \cdot \text{mol}^{-1} \cdot \text{K}^{-1}$)

1 *Answer*
356 J, 2976 J, 12%

If you solved this problem correctly, go to frame 16. If you could not solve this problem, go through frames 2–15.

2 Sketch the four processes in a pV-diagram.

2

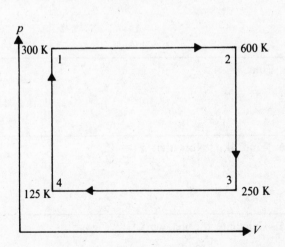

3 Find n using the equation of state.	**3** $$\frac{p_1 V_1}{T_1} = nR$$ $$n = \frac{(3.039 \times 10^5 \text{ Pa})(2 \times 10^{-3} \text{ m}^3)}{(300 \text{ K})(8.32 \text{ J} \cdot \text{mol}^{-1} \cdot \text{K}^{-1})}$$ $$= 0.244 \text{ mol}$$
4 Find V_2 from the equation of state. Note that $p_1 = p_2$.	**4** $$\frac{p_2 V_2}{T_2} = nR$$ $$V_2 = \frac{(0.244 \text{ mol})(8.32 \text{ J} \cdot \text{mol}^{-1} \cdot \text{K}^{-1})(600 \text{ K})}{3.039 \times 10^5 \text{ Pa}}$$ $$= 0.00401 \text{ m}^3$$
5 Find p_3 from the equation of state. Note that $V_3 = V_2$.	**5** $$\frac{p_3 V_3}{T_3} = nR$$ $$p_3 = \frac{(0.244 \text{ mol})(8.32 \text{ J} \cdot \text{mol}^{-1} \cdot \text{K}^{-1})(250 \text{ K})}{0.00401 \text{ m}^3}$$ $$= 1.27 \times 10^5 \text{ Pa}$$
6 Although we know that $T_4 = 125$ K, check.	**6** $$T_4 = \frac{p_4 V_4}{nR}$$ $$= \frac{(1.27 \times 10^5 \text{ Pa})(2 \times 10^{-3} \text{ m}^3)}{(0.244 \text{ mol})(8.32 \text{ J} \cdot \text{mol}^{-1} \cdot \text{K}^{-1})}$$ $$= 125 \text{ K}$$
7 Find W_{12}.	**7** $$W_{12} = p_1(V_2 - V_1)$$ $$= 3.039 \times 10^5 \text{ Pa}(0.00401 \text{ m}^3 - 0.002 \text{ m}^3)$$ $$= 611 \text{ J}$$
8 Find W_{23}. Note that $V_2 = V_3$.	**8** $$W_{23} = 0 \text{ since } V_2 = V_3.$$
9 Find W_{34}.	**9** $$W_{34} = p_3(V_4 - V_3)$$ $$= 1.27 \times 10^5 \text{ Pa}(0.002 \text{ m}^3 - 0.00401 \text{ m}^3)$$ $$= -255 \text{ J}$$
10 Find W_{41}. Note that $V_4 = V_1$.	**10** $$W_{41} = 0.$$
11 Calculate the net work.	**11** $$W = W_{12} + W_{23} + W_{34} + W_{41} = 611 \text{ J} + (-255 \text{ J})$$ $$= 356 \text{ J}$$

12 To compute the efficiency, we must first find the heat flowing into the engines. The heat flows in during the processes 4-1 and 1-2. Compute Q_{41}. (Note that volume is constant.)

12

$Q_{41} = nC_v(\Delta T)_{41}$
$= (0.244 \text{ mol})(20.42 \text{ J} \cdot \text{mol}^{-1} \cdot \text{K}^{-1})(175 \text{ K})$
$= 872 \text{ J}$

---

13 Compute Q_{12}. (Note that pressure is constant.)

13

$Q_{12} = nC_p(\Delta T)_{12}$
$= (0.244 \text{ mol}(28.74 \text{ J} \cdot \text{mol}^{-1} \cdot \text{K}^{-1})(300 \text{ K})$
$= 2104 \text{ J}$

---

14 Compute total heat added.

14

$$Q_H = Q_{41} + Q_{12}$$
$$= 872 \text{ J} + 2104 \text{ J} = 2976 \text{ J}$$

---

15 Compute the efficiency.

15

$$\text{Efficiency} = \frac{W}{Q_4}$$
$$= \frac{356 \text{ J}}{2976 \text{ J}}$$
$$= 12.0\%$$

---

16 *Problem 2* What is the relationship between the performance coefficient K of a Carnot refrigerator and the efficiency e of a Carnot engine?

16 *Answer*

$$K = \frac{1 - e}{e}$$

If you solved this problem correctly, go to frame 22. If you could not solve this problem, go through frames 17–21.

17 What is e equal to?

17

$$e = \frac{T_H - T_C}{T_H}$$

---

18 Solve for T_C.

18

$$T_C = T_H(1 - e)$$

---

19 What is K equal to?

19

$$K = \frac{T_C}{T_H - T_C}$$

---

20 Substitute the value of T_C from frame 18 in this equation.

20

$$K = \frac{T_H(1 - e)}{T_H - T_H(1 - e)}$$

---

21 Simplify.

21

$$K = \frac{1 - e}{e}$$

22 Problem 3   A Carnot refrigerator takes heat from water at 0°C and rejects heat to a room at 20°C. If 20 kg of water at 0°C are converted to ice at 0°C find a) how much heat is rejected to the room and b) how much energy must be supplied to the refrigerator.

22 Answer

$- 7.19 \times 10^6$ J, 4.9×10^5 J

If you could not solve this problem, go through frames 23–26.

---

23 How much heat does the refrigerator take in from the cold reservoir (i.e. the 20 kg of water)?

23 $Q_C = mL_f$

$= (20 \times 10^3 \text{g}) (335 \text{ J} \cdot \text{g}^{-1})$

$= 6.70 \times 10^6$ J

---

24 How much heat does the refrigerator reject to the hot reservoir (i.e. the room)?

24

$$\frac{Q_C}{Q_H} = \frac{- T_C}{T_H}$$

$$Q_H = -\left(\frac{293 \text{ K}}{273 \text{ K}}\right) 6.70 \times 10^6 \text{ J}$$

$$= - 7.19 \times 10^6 \text{ J}$$

Note that the $-$ sign indicates that heat is flowing out of the refrigerator.

---

25 From the first law of thermodynamics for a cyclic process, the work done by the compressor $W = Q_C + Q_H$. Find W.

25 $W = 6.70 \times 10^6 \text{ J} - 7.19 \times 10^6 \text{ J}$

$$= - 4.9 \times 10^5 \text{ J}$$

The minus sign means that work must be done on the compressor motor.

---

26 How much energy must be supplied to the refrigerator?

26 4.9×10^5 J

20

Molecular Properties of Matter

CHAPTER SUMMARY

This chapter is concerned with the molecular model of matter. In a previous chapter, we discussed an ideal gas from a macroscopic viewpoint, here we again are concerned with an ideal gas, this time in terms of its microscopic properties. This provides the framework for a mathematical analysis called the kinetic theory of gases. Molar heat capacity is one of the outcomes of the kinetic theory and this theory is also used to discuss the distribution of molecular speeds. The chapter ends with a discussion of crystals and their heat capacities.

BASIC TERMS — *Give definitions or meanings for the following:*

molecule (20-1)

short-range order (20-1)

long-range order (20-1)

potential well (20-1)

mole (20-2)

Avogadro's number (20-2)

Boltzmann constant (20-3)

degree of freedom (20-4)

rule of Dulong and Petit (20-6)

crystal (20-6)

osmosis (20-7)

diffusion (20-7)

PROGRAMMED QUIZ

1 What do we mean when we say that the molecules of a gas are in equilibrium?

1 Each molecule has the same average energy over a period of time.

2 What determines whether a substance will be in the solid, liquid or gaseous state?

2 The molecular motion and the forces between the molecules.

3 What does the average kinetic energy per molecule depend on?

3

Only on the temperature; $\frac{1}{2} m (v^2)_{av} = \frac{3}{2} kT$.

4 What is the basic objective of kinetic theory?

4 To relate the thermodynamic laws in terms of the averages of the microscopic variables.

---

5 Why are average quantities used in the kinetic theory?

5 Because of the great numbers of particles involved.

---

6 What laws do the molecules in an ideal gas obey?

6 Newton's laws of motion (for example, conservation of energy, conservation of momentum).

---

7 How can we describe the motion of the molecules in a gas?

7 Random, i.e. in all directions at various speeds.

---

8 $C_v = \dfrac{3}{2} R$ for a monatomic ideal gas; what is C_p in terms of R? What is C_p/C_v?

8

$$C_p - C_v = R$$
$$C_p = R + \frac{3}{2} R = \frac{5}{2} R$$
$$\frac{C_p}{C_v} = \frac{5/2\,R}{3/2\,R} = \frac{5}{3} = 1.67$$

---

9 A monatomic gas has how many degrees of freedom?

9 Three, one for each velocity component needed to describe its motion.

---

10 What force holds molecules together? Is it attractive or repulsive?

10 Electrical force; it is attractive at larger distances, at close distances the outer charges overlap resulting in a repulsive force between the molecules.

---

11 Does molar heat capacity depend on the number of atoms in a molecule of a gas?

11 Yes, polyatomic gases have larger molar heat capacities than monatomic gases.

---

12 What is the reason for this?

12 Some of the energy goes into increasing the rotational and vibrational kinetic energy of the molecules. Only translational kinetic energy affects the temperature.

---

13 What is the principle of equipartition of energy?

13 The energy of a large number of weakly interacting molecules in equilibrium is, on the average, divided equally among the independent ways that the molecules can possess energy (e.g. translation, rotation, vibration).

---

14 The pressure exerted on the walls of a container by a confined gas is due to what?

14 The collisions of the gas molecules with the walls.

---

15 In our discussion of molecules, why do we neglect the force of gravitation?

15 Because it is negligible as compared with the electrical force.

---

16 What is the Boltzmann constant?

16 It is a gas constant on a "per molecule" basis;
$$c = \frac{R}{N_A}$$
where R = gas constant and
N_A = Avogadro's number.

---

17 What determines the heat capacity of a crystal?

17 The kinetic and potential energies associated with molecular vibrations.

MAIN IDEAS

1 Molecules. Matter consists of minute particles called molecules. The molecules of a particular substance have the same structure, mass and the same electrical, mechanical and chemical properties. The forces that hold together the molecules of a liquid or solid are mainly electrical.

2 Mole. A mole of any substance contains as many entities as there are atoms in 12 grams of carbon 12. The word entity denotes atoms, electrons, molecules, eggs, basketballs, etc. Thus, we can speak of a mole of atoms, a mole of molecules or a mole of any type of particles.

3 Avogadro's number (N_A). One mole of any pure chemical compound contains 6.022×10^{23} molecules. Thus $N_A = 6.022 \times 10^{23}$ molecules $\cdot$ mol^{-1}.

4 Molecular (or atomic) mass M. The molecular mass of a substance is the mass in grams of one mole of the substance. This means that 1 mole of carbon 12 atoms has a mass of 12 g. Similarly, the molecular mass of CO_2 is 44 g; since the atomic mass of carbon is 12 g and the atomic mass of oxygen is 16 g, 12 g + 2(16 g) = 44 g. The unit of M is g $\cdot$ mol^{-1} or kg $\cdot$ mol^{-1}.

5 The mass m of a single molecule is given by $m = M/N_A$. The unit of m is g $\cdot$ molecule^{-1} or kg $\cdot$ molecule^{-1}.

6 The kinetic theory of an ideal gas is concerned with the macroscopic properties of matter by applying the laws of mechanics to the average behavior of molecules. Consider a cubic box ($V = l^3$) containing N identical molecules, each of mass m. Assume, at first, that the speed of the molecules in the x-direction is v_x. When a molecule strikes the surface AB, it rebounds in a perfectly elastic collision and travels toward the surface OC and thus shuttles up and back between the opposite surfaces.

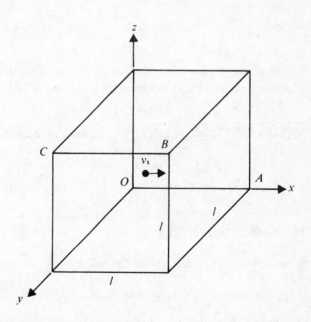

The pressure on the surface AB or OC will be $p = \dfrac{Nmv_x^2}{V}$ and the force of the molecular bombardment will be

$F = \dfrac{Nmv_x^2}{l}$. It should be noted that since v_x is not the same for all molecules we resort to the concept of the average value of the square of the speed. Since $(v^2)_{av} = (v_x^2)_{av} + (v_y^2)_{av} + (v_z^2)_{av}$ and $(v_x^2)_{av} = (v_y^2)_{av} = (v_z^2)_{av}$, then $(v_x^2)_{av} = \frac{1}{3}(v^2)_{av}$. The product pV may now be written as $pV = \frac{1}{3}Nm(v^2)_{av} = \frac{2}{3}U$, where $U =$ internal energy of the gas, assumed to be entirely kinetic. It also follows that the average translational kinetic energy of a single molecule $= (E_k)_{av} = \frac{1}{2}m(v^2)_{av} = \frac{3}{2}kT$, where $(v^2)_{av}$ is the average of the square of the speeds of the molecules and $k = \dfrac{R}{N_A} = 1.38 \times 10^{-23}$ J $\cdot$ (molecule)$^{-1} \cdot$ K^{-1} is called the Boltzmann constant. $v_{rms} = \sqrt{(v^2)_{av}} = \sqrt{\dfrac{3kT}{m}} = \sqrt{\dfrac{3RT}{M}}$ is called the "root-mean-square" speed. It is the square root of the mean of the squared molecular speeds. The ideal-gas equation $pV = nRT$ may be written as $pV = NkT$ (since $N = N_A n$ and $R = N_A k$). Thus k may be regarded as a gas constant on a "per molecule" basis instead of the "per mole" basis used for R.

7 Molar heat capacity of a gas. $C_v = \frac{3}{2}R$, $C_p - C_v = R$, $\gamma = \dfrac{C_p}{C_v}$ for a monatomic gas.

8 Crystals. The molecules of a solid assume a fixed relationship with respect to one another and oscillate about this position. If the molecular arrangement assumes a definite geometric pattern, we call the solid a crystal. The internal energy of a crystal is $U = 3NkT = 3nRT$, where N is the number of molecules. It should be noted that the energy of a crystal is double the energy of the same number of molecules of an ideal gas at the same temperature. The law of Dulong and Petit, $C = 3R$, can be derived from the kinetic theory.

9 Diffusion. Diffusion is the random movement of one kind of molecules through a substance consisting of another kind. The rate of diffusion (mol $\cdot$ s^{-1}) across an area A is given by $Q = \dfrac{DA(C_2 - C_1)}{L}$, where D is the diffusion constant (m$^2 \cdot$ s^{-1}) and C_1 and C_2 are concentration constants (mol $\cdot$ m^{-3}) of the two regions separated by distance L.

10 Osmosis. Osmosis is a special case of the diffusion process in which fluid molecules pass through a semi-permeable membrane. Osmotic pressure Π occurs when the concentrations on the two sides of the membrane are different.

$\Pi = CRT = \dfrac{nRT}{V}$, where $C =$ number of moles n of solute per unit volume V of solute.

11 Problem solving strategy.

a) Be careful of symbols. In the formula $n = \dfrac{m}{M}$, $n =$ number of moles, $M =$ mass per mole, and $m =$ total mass. In the formula $M = N_A m$, $m =$ mass of a single molecule and M is the mass of a mole. In $n = \dfrac{N}{N_A}$, $n =$ number of moles an $N =$ number of molecules. The Boltzmann constant $k = \dfrac{R}{N_A}$ is the gas constant per molecule, and R is the gas constant per mole.

b) Check units on both sides of an equation. Although N is a dimensionless quantity, express it as the unit "molecules" for balancing equations only. Thus k would be written as 1.38×10^{-23} J $\cdot$ K$^{-1} \cdot$ molecule^{-1}.

PROGRAMMED QUIZ

1 Compare the root-mean-square speed of a helium atom to that of an oxygen molecule at the same temperature and pressure.

1

$$\frac{v_{rms_H}}{v_{rms_O}} = \frac{\sqrt{\dfrac{3kT}{m_H}}}{\sqrt{\dfrac{3kT}{m_O}}}$$

$$= \sqrt{\frac{m_O}{m_H}} = \sqrt{\frac{32\ g}{4\ g}} = \sqrt{8}$$

---

2 What is the kinetic energy of 1 molecule at 310 K?

2

$$U = \frac{3}{2}\,kT$$
$$= \frac{3}{2}\,(1.38 \times 10^{-23}\ \text{J} \cdot \text{mol}^{-1} \cdot \text{K}^{-1})\,(310\ \text{K})$$
$$= 6.42 \times 10^{-21}\ \text{J}$$

---

3 Does the kinetic energy depend on the substance?

3 No, only on the temperature.

---

4 Referring to frame 2, what is the kinetic energy if the absolute temperature is doubled?

4

$$U = \frac{3}{2}\,kT$$
if $T' = 2T$, then
$$U' = \frac{3}{2}\,kT' = 3kT = 2U$$
$$U' = 2(6.42 \times 10^{-21}\ \text{J}) = 1.28 \times 10^{-20}\ \text{J}$$

---

5 How many molecules are there in one mole of a gas?

5 Avogrado's number,
$$N_A = 6.022 \times 10^{23}$$

---

6 One mole of nitrogen gas has a mass of 28 g. What is the mass of one nitrogen molecule?

6

$$M = N_A m$$
$$m = \frac{28\ \text{g} \cdot \text{mol}^{-1}}{6.022 \times 10^{23}\ \text{molecules} \cdot \text{mol}^{-1}}$$
$$= 4.65 \times 10^{-23}\ \text{g} \cdot \text{molecule}^{-1}$$

---

7 What is the volume of 0.5 mole of a gas at 300 K and 1 atm pressure?

7

$$pV = nRT$$
$$V = \frac{(0.5\ \text{mol})\,(8.31\ \text{J} \cdot \text{mol}^{-1} \cdot \text{K}^{-1})\,(300\ \text{K})}{1.013 \times 10^5\ \text{Pa}}$$
$$= 1.23 \times 10^{-2}\ \text{m}^3$$

8 How many molecules are there in 0.5 mol?

8

$$n = \frac{N}{N_A}$$

$$N = (0.5 \text{ mol}) (6.022 \times 10^{23} \text{ molecules} \cdot \text{mol}^{-1})$$

$$= 3.01 \times 10^{23} \text{ molecules}$$

---

9 Calculate the volume in frame 7 using $pV = NkT$.

9

$$V = \frac{NkT}{p}$$

$$= \frac{(3.01 \times 10^{23}) (1.38 \times 10^{-23} \text{ J} \cdot \text{K}^{-1}) (300 \text{ K})}{1.013 \times 10^5 \text{ Pa}}$$

$$= 1.23 \times 10^{-2} \text{ m}^3$$

---

10 Find $(v)_{av}$ and v_{rms} for the following:
$v_1 = 2 \text{ m} \cdot \text{s}^{-1}$ and $v_2 = 5 \text{ m} \cdot \text{s}^{-1}$.

10

$$(v)_{av} = \frac{v_1 + v_2}{2}$$

$$= \frac{2 \text{ m} \cdot \text{s}^{-1} + 5 \text{ m} \cdot \text{s}^{-1}}{2}$$

$$= 3.5 \text{ m} \cdot \text{s}^{-1}$$

$$v_{rms} = \sqrt{\frac{v_1^2 + v_2^2}{2}}$$

$$= \sqrt{\frac{(2 \text{ m} \cdot \text{s}^{-1})^2 + (5 \text{ m} \cdot \text{s}^{-1})^2}{2}}$$

$$= 3.81 \text{ m} \cdot \text{s}^{-1}$$

The root-mean-square speed v_{rms} is about 10% greater than the arithmetic average $(v)_{av}$.

---

11 What is the concentration in $\text{mol} \cdot \text{m}^{-3}$ of sodium and chlorine ions when 30.0 g of NaCl is dissolved in 2.00 liters of water? Sodium chloride has a molecular mass $M = 58.4 \text{ g} \cdot \text{mol}^{-1}$. The molecules are dissociated into Na^+ and Cl^- ions. Therefore the total ion concentration is twice the number of moles of NaCl per cubic meter.

11

$$\rho = \frac{m}{V} = \frac{30 \text{ g}}{2 \text{ l}} \cdot \frac{1 \text{ l}}{10^{-3} \text{ m}^3}$$

$$= 15 \times 10^3 \text{ g} \cdot \text{m}^{-3}$$

$$C = \frac{n}{V} = \frac{m}{MV} \qquad \left(\text{since } n = \frac{m}{M} \right)$$

but $\rho = \dfrac{m}{V}$

$$\therefore C = \frac{\rho}{M} = \frac{15 \times 10^3 \text{ g} \cdot \text{m}^{-3}}{58.4 \text{ g} \cdot \text{mol}^{-1}}$$

$$= 257 \text{ mol} \cdot \text{m}^{-3}$$

which represents the concentration of NaCl molecules. The concentration of ions is 514 $\text{mol} \cdot \text{m}^{-3}$.

12 What is the osmotic pressure of this solution across a semipermeable membrane with a salt water solution on one side and fresh water on the other at a temperature of 30°C?

12

$$K = C + 273 = 30 + 273 = 303 \text{ K}$$
$$\Pi = CRT$$
$$= (514 \text{ mol} \cdot \text{m}^{-3})(8.314 \text{ J} \cdot \text{mol}^{-1} \cdot \text{K}^{-1})(303 \text{ K})$$
$$= 1.29 \times 10^6 \text{ Pa}$$

---

13 What minimum concentration of sucrose in maple syrup would be needed for the osmotic pressure in the roots to push the sap to a height of 8.0 m at a temperature of 20°C?

13 The osmotic pressure Π is equal to the hydrostatic pressure $\rho g h$.

$$\Pi = CRT = \rho g h$$
$$C = \frac{\rho g h}{RT}$$

Assume that the density of sucrose is equal to the density of pure water.

$$C = \frac{(1 \times 10^3 \text{ kg} \cdot \text{m}^{-3})(9.8 \text{ m} \cdot \text{s}^{-2})(8.0 \text{ m})}{(8.314 \text{ J} \cdot \text{mol}^{-1} \cdot \text{K}^{-1})(293 \text{ K})}$$
$$= 32.2 \text{ mol} \cdot \text{m}^{-3}$$

STEP BY STEP SOLUTIONS OF PROBLEMS

Problem 1 The v_{rms} of a particle is $1 \text{ m} \cdot \text{s}^{-1}$ at a temperature of 300 K. a) Find the mass. b) If the particle is an ice crystal, how many molecules does it contain? c) Assuming that the particle is spherical, find the radius.

1 Find the mass of the particle from $\frac{1}{2}m(v^2)_{\text{av}} = \frac{3}{2}kT$.

Note $v_{\text{rms}} = \sqrt{(v^2)_{\text{av}}}$,
$$v_{\text{rms}}^2 = (v^2)_{\text{av}}$$

1

$$m = \frac{3kT}{v_{\text{rms}}^2}$$
$$= \frac{3(1.38 \times 10^{-23} \text{ J} \cdot \text{K}^{-1})(300 \text{ K})}{(1 \text{ m} \cdot \text{s}^{-1})^2}$$
$$= 1.24 \times 10^{-20} \text{ kg}$$

---

2 What is the molecular mass of ice (water)?

2 $18 \text{ g} = 0.018 \text{ kg}$; H_2O is composed to two atoms of hydrogen (2 g) and one of oxygen (16 g).

---

3 What is the number of moles?

3

$$n = \frac{m}{M}$$
$$= \frac{1.24 \times 10^{-20} \text{ kg}}{0.018 \text{ kg} \cdot \text{mol}^{-1}} = 6.89 \times 10^{-19} \text{ mol}$$

---

4 One mole contains Avogadro's number of molecules. Find the number of molecules in this particle.

4

$$n = \frac{N}{N_A}$$
$$N = (6.89 \times 10^{-19} \text{ mol})\left(\frac{6.02 \times 10^{23} \text{ molecules}}{\text{mol}}\right)$$
$$= 4.15 \times 10^5 \text{ molecules}$$

5 Find the volume of one particle from the density relationship (the density of water $= 1000 \text{ kg} \cdot \text{m}^{-3}$).

5

$$\rho = \frac{m}{V}$$

$$V = \frac{1.24 \times 10^{-20} \text{ kg}}{10^3 \text{ kg} \cdot \text{m}^{-3}}$$

$$= 1.24 \times 10^{-23} \text{ m}^3$$

---

6 Find the radius using

$$V = \frac{4}{3}\pi r^3$$

for the volume of a sphere.

6

$$r^3 = \frac{3V}{4\pi}$$

$$= \frac{3(1.24 \times 10^{-23} \text{ m}^3)}{4\pi}$$

$$= 2.96 \times 10^{-24} \text{ m}^3$$

$$r = 1.44 \times 10^{-8} \text{ m} = 1.44 \times 10^{-6} \text{ cm}$$

Problem 2 Consider a nitrogen molecule at a temperature of 300 K. a) What is the average translational kinetic energy? b) What is the average value of the square of its speed $(v^2)_{av}$? c) What is the root-mean-square speed v_{rms}? d) What is the momentum of the molecule traveling at this speed? e) What is the average force that the molecule exerts on the walls of the container? Assume that the molecule is bouncing back and forth perpendicular to two opposite walls and the container is a 1 liter cube. f) What is the pressure on the walls of the container? g) How many molecules would be required to produce an average pressure of 1 atm?

7 Find the average translational kinetic energy.

7

$$\frac{1}{2}m(v^2)_{av} = \frac{3}{2}kT$$

$$= \frac{3}{2}(1.38 \times 10^{-23} \text{ J} \cdot \text{K}^{-1})(300 \text{ K})$$

$$= 6.21 \times 10^{-21} \text{ J}$$

---

8 Find the mass of one molecule of nitrogen. The atomic mass of nitrogen is $14 \text{ g} \cdot \text{mol}^{-1}$ and one molecule of N_2 contains 2 atoms of nitrogen. Therefore the molecular mass $M = 28 \text{ g} \cdot \text{mol}^{-1}$.

8

$$m = \frac{M}{N_A}$$

$$= \frac{28 \text{ g} \cdot \text{mol}^{-1}}{6.02 \times 10^{23} \text{ molecules} \cdot \text{mol}^{-1}}$$

$$= 4.65 \times 10^{-23} \text{ g} = 4.65 \times 10^{-26} \text{ kg}$$

---

9 Find the average value of the square of the speed.

9

$$(v^2)_{av} = \frac{3kT}{m}$$

$$= \frac{3(1.38 \times 10^{-23} \text{ J} \cdot \text{K}^{-1})(300 \text{ K})}{4.65 \times 10^{-26} \text{ kg}}$$

$$= 2.67 \times 10^5 \text{ m}^2 \cdot \text{s}^{-2}$$

---

10 What is the root-mean-square speed?

$$v_{rms} = \sqrt{(v^2)_{av}}$$

10

$$v_{rms} = \sqrt{2.67 \times 10^5 \text{ m}^2 \cdot \text{s}^{-2}}$$

$$= 517 \text{ m} \cdot \text{s}^{-1}$$

11 What is the momentum?

11

$$\begin{aligned} \text{momentum} &= mv_{\text{rms}} \\ &= (4.65 \times 10^{-26}\ \text{kg})\ (517\ \text{m} \cdot \text{s}^{-1}) \\ &= 2.40 \times 10^{-23}\ \text{kg} \cdot \text{m} \cdot \text{s}^{-1} \end{aligned}$$

---

12 What is the distance between opposite walls of a 1 liter cubic container?

12

0.10 m since $11 = 0.001\ \text{m}^3$

---

13 Find the average force from pressure relationships. Note that N, the number of molecules $= 1$.

13

$$p = \frac{F}{A} = \frac{Nm(v^2)_{\text{av}}}{V}$$

$$= \frac{Nm(v^2)_{\text{av}}}{A \cdot l}$$

$$F = \frac{Nm(v^2)_{\text{av}}}{l}$$

$$= \frac{(1)\ (4.65 \times 10^{-26}\ \text{kg})\ (2.67 \times 10^5\ \text{m}^2 \cdot \text{s}^{-2})}{0.10\ \text{m}}$$

$$= 1.24 \times 10^{-19}\ \text{N}$$

---

14 What is the pressure on the walls of the container?

14

$$p = \frac{F}{A}$$

$$= \frac{1.24 \times 10^{-19}\ \text{N}}{(0.10\ \text{m})^2} = 1.24 \times 10^{-17}\ \text{Pa}$$

---

15 How many molecules would be required to produce a pressure of 1 atm?

15

$$\frac{1.013 \times 10^5\ \text{Pa}}{1.24 \times 10^{-17}\ \text{Pa}} = 8.17 \times 10^{21}\ \text{molecules}$$

Problem 3 a) Assuming that the atmosphere is primarily composed of nitrogen, compare the speed of propagation ($350\ \text{m} \cdot \text{s}^{-1}$) of sound waves in air at 27°C with the v_{rms} and $\sqrt{(v_x^2)_{\text{av}}}$ of the nitrogen molecule. b) Find the velocity of sound in air at 27°C using $c = \sqrt{\gamma RT/M}$. Assume that air is 75% nitrogen and 25% oxygen.

16 Give the v_{rms} for nitrogen which you found in frame 10.

16

$$v_{\text{rms}} = 517\ \text{m} \cdot \text{s}^{-1}$$

17

Find $(v_x^2)_{\text{av}}$ using $(v_x^2)_{\text{av}} = \frac{1}{3}(v^2)_{\text{av}}$

since $(v^2)_{\text{av}} = (v_x^2)_{\text{av}} + (v_y^2)_{\text{av}} + (v_z^2)_{\text{av}}$ and
$(v_x^2)_{\text{av}} = (v_y^2)_{\text{av}} = (v_z^2)_{\text{av}}$.

17

$$(v_x^2)_{\text{av}} = \frac{1}{3}(v^2)_{\text{av}} = \frac{1}{3}(517\ \text{m} \cdot \text{s}^{-1})^2$$

$$= 8.91 \times 10^4\ \text{m}^2 \cdot \text{s}^{-2}$$

---

18 Find $\sqrt{(v_x^2)_{\text{av}}}$.

18 $\sqrt{(v_x^2)_{\text{av}}} = \sqrt{8.91 \times 10^4\ \text{m}^2 \cdot \text{s}^{-2}} = 298\ \text{m} \cdot \text{s}^{-1}$

Hence $\sqrt{(v_x^2)}$ is approximately equal to the speed of the propagation of sound waves in air.

19 Find the molecular mass of air. Assume that a mole of air is composed of 75% nitrogen and 25% oxygen.

19 Since nitrogen has a molecular mass of 28 g, a mole of air contains 75% (28 g) = 21 g of nitrogen. Similarly, the molecular mass of oxygen is 32 g. Hence a mole of air contains 25% (32 g) = 8 g of oxygen. Therefore a mole of air has a molecular mass of 21 g + 8 g = 29 g = 0.029 kg.

20 Find the speed of propagation of sound at 27°C using $c = \sqrt{\gamma RT/M}$.

20
$$c = \sqrt{\frac{1.4 \ (8.34 \text{ J} \cdot \text{mol}^{-1} \cdot \text{K}^{-1}) \ (300 \text{ K})}{0.029 \text{ kg} \cdot \text{mol}^{-1}}}$$
$$= 348 \text{ m} \cdot \text{s}^{-1}$$
which corresponds to the speed of propagation of sound waves in air at 27°C.

PROGRAMMED TEST

1 **Problem 1** How many molecules are present in 1 cm^3 of air at a pressure of 10^{-15} atm and a temperature of 310 K?

1 **Answer**
2.37×10^4

If you solved this problem correctly, go to frame 4. If you could not solve this problem, go through frames 2–3.

2 Tabulate the given data.

2
$$p = 10^{-15} \text{ atm} = 10^{-15} \ (1.013 \times 10^5 \text{ Pa})$$
$$V = 1 \text{ cm}^3 = 10^{-6} \text{ m}^3$$
$$T = 310 \text{ K}$$
$$k = 1.38 \times 10^{-23} \text{ J} \cdot \text{K}^{-1}$$

3 Find the number of molecules using $pV = NkT$.

3
$$N = \frac{pV}{kT}$$
$$= \frac{(1.013 \times 10^{-10} \text{ Pa}) \ (10^{-6} \text{ m}^3)}{(1.38 \times 10^{-23} \text{ J} \cdot \text{K}^{-1}) \ (310 \text{ K})}$$
$$= 2.37 \times 10^4 \text{ molecules}$$

4 **Problem 2** A copper cube is 1 cm on a side. Find a) the mass of the cube, b) the number of moles of copper in the cube, c) the number of atoms of copper, d) the mass of a copper atom and e) the dimensions of a copper atom by assuming it is a cube.

4 **Answer**
8.9 g, 0.140, 8.43×10^{22}, 1.06×10^{-22} g, 2.28×10^{-8} cm

If you solved this problem correctly, go to frame 12. If you could not solve this problem, go through frames 5–11.

5 Find the mass of the cube from density considerations. Use $\rho = 8.9 \text{ g} \cdot \text{cm}^{-3}$.

5
$$\rho = \frac{m}{V}$$
$$m = 8.9 \text{ g} \cdot \text{cm}^{-3} \ (1 \text{ cm})^3 = 8.9 \text{ g}$$

6 What is the molecular mass of copper?

6
$$M = 63.5 \text{ g} \cdot \text{mol}^{-1}$$

---

7 How many moles of copper in the cube?

7
$$n = \frac{m}{M}$$
$$= \frac{8.9 \text{ g}}{63.5 \text{ g} \cdot \text{mol}^{-1}} = 0.140 \text{ mol}$$

---

8 How many atoms is this?

8 $0.140(6.02 \times 10^{23}) = 8.43 \times 10^{22}$

---

9 Find the mass of a copper atom.

9 Since the cube contains 8.43×10^{22} atoms and has a mass of 8.9 g, it follows that the mass of an atom
$$= \frac{8.9 \text{ g}}{8.43 \times 10^{22}} = 1.06 \times 10^{-22} \text{ g}$$

---

10 Find the volume of a copper atom from the density relationship.

10
$$\rho = \frac{m}{V}$$
$$V = \frac{1.06 \times 10^{-22} \text{ g}}{8.9 \text{ g} \cdot \text{cm}^{-3}} = 1.19 \times 10^{-23} \text{ cm}^3$$

---

11 Find the size by assuming that the atom has a cubical shape.

11
$$V = l^3$$
$$l^3 = 11.9 \times 10^{-24} \text{ cm}^3$$
$$l = 2.28 \times 10^{-8} \text{ cm}$$
It should be noted that the diameter of a copper atom is 2.56×10^{-8} cm.

---

12 **Problem 3** In order for a projectile, mass m, to "escape" the earth's gravitational field, it must be launched vertically with a kinetic energy greater than mgR. At what temperature will an average nitrogen molecule attain this energy?

If you could not solve this problem, go through frames 13–15.

12 **Answer**
$$1.41 \times 10^5 \text{ K}$$

---

13 Write the mass of a nitrogen molecule which was found in frame 8 of the previous section.

13 4.65×10^{-26} kg

---

14 Find the kinetic energy $= mgR$. (The earth's radius $= 6.38 \times 10^6$ m.)

14
$$K = mgR$$
$$= (4.65 \times 10^{-26} \text{ kg})(9.8 \text{m} \cdot \text{s}^{-2})$$
$$\times (6.38 \times 10^6 \text{ m})$$
$$= 2.91 \times 10^{-18} \text{ J}$$

15 Find the temperature for this kinetic energy for a single molecule to "escape" the earth's gravitational field.

15

$$U = \frac{3}{2}kT$$

$$T = \frac{2(2.91 \times 10^{-18} \text{ J})}{3(1.38 \times 10^{-23} \text{ J} \cdot \text{K}^{-1})}$$

$$= 1.41 \times 10^5 \text{ K}$$

21

Mechanical Waves

CHAPTER SUMMARY

All matter exhibits wave properties. In this chapter we are concerned only with mechanical waves, many of which are periodic, with special emphasis on water waves. The mathematical expressions for the speed of transverse and longitudinal waves are derived, and longitudinal waves are considered (in relation to the previous chapter) as an adiabatic process consisting of compressions and rarefactions of an ideal gas. The mathematical representation of a traveling wave is presented as an extra topic.

BASIC TERMS — *Give definitions or meanings for the following:*

wave (21-I)
mechanical wave (21-I)
medium (21-I)
sinusoidal wave (21-I)
wave speed (21-1)
transverse wave (21-1)
longitudinal wave (21-1)
periodic wave (21-2)
wavelength (21-2)

condensation (21-2)
rarefaction (21-2)
polarization (21-3)
sound (21-4)
adiabatic bulk modulus (21-5)
wave number (21-6)
phase (21-6)
propagation constant (21-6)
wave function (21-7)

PROGRAMMED QUIZ

1 A transverse wave is moving to the right. What is the motion of the particles of the medium?

1 At right angles to the direction of travel of the wave.

2 A water wave eventually slows down to zero speed. What happens to its energy?

2 It is dissipated — very often as heat.

3 Can mechanical waves propagate anywhere?

3 No, they require an elastic medium for propagation.

4 The motion of the mechanical waves presented in this chapter reminds you of what type of motion that you have already studied?

4 Simple harmonic motion.

5 What are some terms used in wave motion which are the same as the terms used in simple harmonic motion? Give definitions.

5 Period — time for one cycle; frequency — number of cycles per second; angular frequency — the product of 2π and frequency.

6 Identify each term in this expression:
$y = A \sin(\omega t - kx)$.

6

y = displacement
A = amplitude
sin = waveform
ω = angular frequency
t = time
k = wave number
x = position

7 Identify each element.

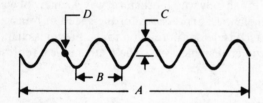

7

A = train of 5 waves
B = wavelength
C = amplitude
D = equilibrium position

8 Can longitudinal waves propagate in a solid? in a gas?

8 Yes, yes.

9 Can transverse waves propagate in a solid? in a gas?

9 Yes, no.

10 Two strings of equal length and different weights are under the same tension. Will the speed of a transverse wave be the same in both?

10 No, the speed will be less in the heavier string, $c = \sqrt{T/\mu}$.

11 As the temperature of an ideal gas decreases, what happens to the speed of a longitudinal wave propagating through the gas?

11 Decreases, $c = \sqrt{\gamma RT/M}$.

12 Is the motion of the waveform the same as the motion of a particle in the medium?

12 No, the waveform moves along the medium at constant speed. A particle has no net movement; it oscillates about its equilibrium position.

13 In a gas, the sensation of sound is associated with what type of wave?

13 Longitudinal.

14 Are water waves transverse or longitudinal?	**14** Both transverse and longitudinal.
15 Why does a water wave slow down as it is approaching the shore?	**15** Since the depth decreases, the speed decreases, $c \approx \sqrt{gh}$, where h = depth of the water.

MAIN IDEAS

1 Mechanical waves. Two essential elements for the production of mechanical waves are a vibrating source and an elastic medium. A transverse wave is produced when the particles of a medium vibrate perpendicularly to the direction of propagation of the wave disturbance. A longitudinal wave is produced when the particles of the medium vibrate parallel to the direction of the wave disturbance. If one end of a medium is vibrating periodically, the displacement of the particles of the medium will vary with time in accordance with the simple harmonic relation $y = A \sin \omega t$ or $y = A \cos \omega t$, where A is the amplitude of vibration, t is the time and $\omega = 2\pi f$ is the angular frequency (f is the frequency of vibration). The speed of propagation c of the wave is equal to the product of the frequency and wavelength, $c = f\lambda$, where λ is the distance between two successive points on the wave having the same phase.

2 Mathematical representation of a traveling wave. $y = A \sin \omega \left(t - \dfrac{x}{c} \right) = A \sin 2\pi f \left(t - \dfrac{x}{c} \right) = A \sin 2\pi$

$\left(\dfrac{t}{\tau} - \dfrac{x}{\lambda} \right)$, where $\tau = 1/f$ is the period of vibration. This equation can also be expressed as $y = A \sin (\omega t - kx)$, where $k = 2\pi/\lambda$ and is called the propagation constant or the wave number and $\omega = 2\pi f$.

3 Speed of a transverse wave in a vibrating string. $c = \sqrt{T/\mu}$, where T is the tension in the string and μ = mass per unit length.

4 Speed of a longitudinal wave in a vibrating fluid. $c = \sqrt{B_{ad}/\rho}$, where B_{ad} = adiabatic bulk modulus and ρ = density of fluid.

5 Speed of a longitudinal wave in a solid bar. $c = \sqrt{Y/\rho}$, where Y is Young's modulus and ρ = density of the solid.

6 Speed of a longitudinal wave in an ideal gas. $c = \sqrt{\gamma RT/M}$, where R is the universal gas constant = 8.314 $J \cdot mol^{-1} \cdot K^{-1}$, M the molecular mass, T the Kelvin temperature, $\gamma = C_p/C_v$.

7 Be careful: the symbol T is used for both tension and temperature.

PROGRAMMED QUIZ

1 What is the frequency of a wave whose wavelength is 1.5 m and speed is 360 m · s⁻¹?	**1** $c = f\lambda$ $f = \dfrac{360 \text{ m} \cdot \text{s}^{-1}}{1.5 \text{ m}} = 240 \text{ s}^{-1}$
2 What is the period of this wave?	**2** $\tau = \dfrac{1}{f} = \dfrac{1}{240 \text{ s}^{-1}} = 4.17 \times 10^{-3} \text{ s}$
3 What is the wave number of the wave?	**3** $k = \dfrac{2\pi}{\lambda} = \dfrac{2\pi}{1.5 \text{ m}} = 4.19 \text{ m}^{-1}$
4 What is the angular frequency of this wave?	**4** $\omega = 2\pi f = 2\pi(240 \text{ s}^{-1}) = 1510 \text{ s}^{-1}$

5 A string, 1.40 m long, has a mass of 0.05 kg. What is μ?

5

$$\mu = \frac{m}{L} = \frac{0.05 \text{ kg}}{1.4 \text{ m}} = 3.57 \times 10^{-2} \text{ kg} \cdot \text{m}^{-1}$$

---

6 What is the tension in the above string if the speed of a transverse pulse in the string is 18 m · s⁻¹?

6

$$c = \sqrt{\frac{T}{\mu}}$$
$$T = (18 \text{ m} \cdot \text{s}^{-1})^2 (0.0357 \text{ kg} \cdot \text{m}^{-1})$$
$$= 11.6 \text{ N}$$

---

7 What is the speed of a longitudinal wave in oxygen at 300 K? The molecular mass of oxygen is 32 g.

7

$$c = \sqrt{\frac{\gamma R T}{M}}$$
$$= \sqrt{\frac{1.40(8.314 \text{ J} \cdot \text{mol}^{-1} \cdot \text{K}^{-1})\,(300 \text{ K})}{0.032 \text{ kg} \cdot \text{mol}^{-1}}}$$
$$= 330 \text{ m} \cdot \text{s}^{-1}$$

---

8 What is the speed of a water wave at a depth of 5 m?

8

$$c = \sqrt{gh} = \sqrt{(9.8 \text{ m} \cdot \text{s}^{-2})\,(5 \text{ m})}$$
$$= 7 \text{ m} \cdot \text{s}^{-1}$$

STEP BY STEP SOLUTIONS OF PROBLEMS

Problem 1 A steel wire is connected between two poles. At 30°C, the tension in the wire is 0. If the wire is plucked at a temperature of 0°C, what will be the speed of propagation of the transverse pulse in the wire?

1 Tabulate the given data.

1

$$Y = 2 \times 10^{11} \text{ Pa}$$
$$\rho = 7.8 \times 10^3 \text{ kg} \cdot \text{m}^{-3}$$
$$\alpha = 1.2 \times 10^{-5} \text{ (C°)}^{-1}$$
$$\Delta T = 30 \text{ C°}$$

---

2 Write the equation for the speed of propagation of a transverse pulse in a string.

2 $c = \sqrt{T/\mu}$ where T is the tension and μ is the mass per unit length.

---

3 A decrease in temperature causes the wire to contract; the contraction produces a tensile stress. Express this tension in terms of the modulus of elasticity and the coefficient of linear expansion.

3

$$\frac{\text{stress}}{\text{strain}} = \frac{F/A}{\Delta L/L_0} = Y$$
$$F = \frac{YA\Delta L}{L_0}$$
$$\text{but } \frac{\Delta L}{L_0} = \alpha \Delta T$$
$$\therefore F = YA\alpha\Delta T = \text{tension}$$

4 Express μ in terms of the density ($\rho = m/V$).

4

$$\mu = \frac{m}{L_0} = \frac{\rho V}{L_0} = \frac{\rho A L_0}{L_0} = \rho A$$

5 Substitute the above in the equation for the speed of propagation of a transverse wave.

5

$$c^2 = \frac{T}{\mu} = \frac{AY\alpha\Delta T}{\rho A} = \frac{Y\alpha\Delta T}{\rho}$$

6 Substitute the numerical values and solve for c.

6

$$c^2 = \frac{(2 \times 10^{11}\,\text{Pa})\,[1.2 \times 10^{-5}\,(\text{C}°)^{-1}]\,(30\,\text{C}°)}{7.8 \times 10^3\,\text{kg}\cdot\text{m}^{-3}}$$

$$c = 96.1\,\text{m}\cdot\text{s}^{-1}$$

Problem 2   What is the speed of sound in nitrogen at 27°C? What is the ratio of the speed of sound in a diatomic gas to the root-mean-square speed of a gas molecule at the same temperature?

7 Tabulate the data.

7

$$M = 28\,\text{g}\cdot\text{mol}^{-1} = 28 \times 10^{-3}\,\text{kg}\cdot\text{mol}^{-1}$$
$$T = 27°\text{C} = 300\,\text{K}$$
$$\gamma = 1.40$$
$$R = 8.31\,\text{J}\cdot\text{mol}^{-1}\cdot\text{K}^{-1}$$

8 Use the equation for the speed of a longitudinal wave in an ideal gas to find c.

8

$$c = \sqrt{\frac{\gamma RT}{M}}$$

$$= \sqrt{\frac{(1.40)\,(8.31\,\text{J}\cdot\text{mol}^{-1}\cdot\text{K}^{-1})\,(300\,\text{K})}{0.028\,\text{kg}\cdot\text{mol}^{-1}}}$$

$$= 353\,\text{m}\cdot\text{s}^{-1}$$

9 Write the expression for the v_{rms} of a gas.

9

$$v_{\text{rms}} = \sqrt{\frac{3RT}{M}}$$

10 Find the ratio of c to v_{rms}.

10

$$\frac{c}{v_{\text{rms}}} = \frac{\sqrt{\dfrac{\gamma RT}{M}}}{\sqrt{\dfrac{3RT}{M}}} = \sqrt{\frac{\gamma}{3}}$$

11 Substitute the value of γ.

11

$$\frac{c}{v_{\text{rms}}} = \sqrt{\frac{1.40}{3}} = 0.683$$

Problem 3 A copper pipe 200 m long is struck at one end. This results in the propagation of two longitudinal waves, one in the pipe and the other in the air. What is the time interval between the two sounds that a person at the other end will hear?

12 Tabulate the data.	**12** $$l = 200 \text{ m}$$ $$Y_c = 1.1 \times 10^{11} \text{ Pa}$$ $$\rho_c = 8.9 \text{ g} \cdot \text{cm}^{-3} = 8.9 \times 10^3 \text{ kg} \cdot \text{m}^{-3}$$ $$c_a = 345 \text{ m} \cdot \text{s}^{-1}$$
13 Using the subscript c for copper and a for air, find the speed of propagation of a longitudinal wave in copper.	**13** $$c_c = \sqrt{\frac{Y_c}{\rho_c}}$$ $$= \sqrt{\frac{1.1 \times 10^{11} \text{ Pa}}{8.9 \times 10^3 \text{ kg} \cdot \text{m}^{-3}}}$$ $$= 3.52 \times 10^3 \text{ m} \cdot \text{s}^{-1}$$
14 How much time is required for the wave to travel through the copper wire?	**14** $$t_c = \frac{l}{c_c}$$ $$= \frac{200 \text{ m}}{3.52 \times 10^3 \text{ m} \cdot \text{s}^{-1}} = 0.0568 \text{ s}$$
15 Find the time required for the wave to travel through the same distance in air.	**15** $$t_a = \frac{l}{c_c}$$ $$= \frac{200 \text{ m}}{345 \text{ m} \cdot \text{s}^{-1}} = 0.580 \text{ s}$$
16 Find the time interval.	**16** $$\text{time interval} = t_a - t_c$$ $$= 0.580 \text{ s} - 0.0568 \text{ s}$$ $$= 0.523 \text{ s}$$

PROGRAMMED TEST

1 *Problem 1* In a sonometer, one end of a steel wire is attached to a fixed support and a 1 kg mass is hung from the other end which passes over a frictionless pulley 0.8 m from the fixed support. If the mass of the wire is 0.01 kg, with what speed will a transverse wave be propagated in the wire? What about a longitudinal wave?	**1** *Answer* $$28 \text{ m} \cdot \text{s}^{-1}, 5060 \text{ m} \cdot \text{s}^{-1}$$

If you solved this problem correctly, go to frame 7. If you could not solve this problem, go through frames 2–6.

2 Tabulate the given data.

2
$$m = 0.01 \text{ kg}$$
$$M = 1 \text{ kg}$$
$$l = 0.8 \text{ m}$$
$$\rho = 7.8 \times 10^3 \text{ kg} \cdot \text{m}^{-3}$$
$$Y = 2 \times 10^{11} \text{ Pa}$$

---

3 Find the tension in the wire.

3
$$T = Mg = 1 \text{ kg} (9.8 \text{ m} \cdot \text{s}^{-2}) = 9.8 \text{ N}$$

---

4 Find μ.

4
$$\mu = \frac{m}{l} = \frac{0.01 \text{ kg}}{0.8 \text{ m}} = 0.0125 \text{ kg} \cdot \text{m}^{-1}$$

---

5 Find the speed of the transverse wave.

5
$$c = \sqrt{\frac{T}{\mu}} = \sqrt{\frac{9.8 \text{ N}}{0.0125 \text{ kg} \cdot \text{m}^{-1}}}$$
$$= 28 \text{ m} \cdot \text{s}^{-1}$$

---

6 Find the speed of the longitudinal wave.

6
$$c = \sqrt{\frac{Y}{\rho}} = \sqrt{\frac{2 \times 10^{11} \text{ Pa}}{7.8 \times 10^3 \text{ kg} \cdot \text{m}^{-3}}}$$
$$= 5060 \text{ m} \cdot \text{s}^{-1}$$

---

7 **Problem 2** A transverse sinusoidal wave is generated at one end of a horizontal string by an electrically driven tuning fork which has a frequency of 512 Hz. The other end of the string passes over a frictionless pulley and supports a mass of 10 kg. If $\mu = 0.03 \text{ kg} \cdot \text{m}^{-1}$, find a) the speed of the transverse wave in the string, b) the wavelength and c) the period.

7 **Answer**
$57.2 \text{ m} \cdot \text{s}^{-1}, 0.112 \text{ m}, 1.95 \times 10^{-3} \text{ s}$

If you solved this problem correctly, go to frame 12. If you could not solve this problem, go through frames 8–11.

---

8 Find the tension T.

8
$$T = Mg = 10 \text{ kg} (9.8 \text{ m} \cdot \text{s}^{-2}) = 98 \text{ N}$$

---

9 Find the speed of the transverse wave.

9
$$c = \sqrt{\frac{T}{\mu}} = \sqrt{\frac{98 \text{ N}}{0.03 \text{ kg} \cdot \text{m}^{-1}}}$$
$$= 57.2 \text{ m} \cdot \text{s}^{-1}$$

---

10 Find the wavelength.

10
$$c = f\lambda$$
$$\lambda = \frac{57.2 \text{ m} \cdot \text{s}^{-1}}{512 \text{ s}^{-1}} = 0.112 \text{ m}$$

---

11 What is the period?

11
$$\tau = \frac{1}{f} = \frac{1}{512\ \text{s}^{-1}} = 1.95 \times 10^{-3}\ \text{s}$$

---

12 **Problem 3** The equation of a transverse wave is $y = 6 \sin (4\pi t - 0.2\ \pi x)$, where x and y are in cm and t is in seconds. Find a) the amplitude, b) wavelength, c) frequency, d) period and e) speed of propagation of the wave.

12 **Answer**
6 cm, 10 cm, 2 s^{-1}, 0.5 s, 20 cm · s^{-1}

If you could not solve this problem, go through frames 13–20.

13 What is the general equation of the wave function?

13
$$y = A \sin (\omega t - kx)$$

---

14 What are ω and k equal to?

14 $\omega = 4\pi\ \text{s}^{-1}$ and $k = 0.2\pi\ \text{cm}^{-1}$

---

15 What is the amplitude?

15 $A = 6$ cm

---

16 Find the wavelength.

16
$$k = \frac{2\pi}{\lambda}$$
$$\lambda = \frac{2\pi}{0.2\pi\ \text{cm}^{-1}} = 10\ \text{cm}$$

---

17 Find the frequency.

17
$$\omega = 2\pi f$$
$$f = \frac{4\pi\ \text{s}^{-1}}{2\pi} = 2\ \text{s}^{-1}$$

---

18 What is the period?

18
$$\tau = \frac{1}{f} = \frac{1}{2\ \text{s}^{-1}} = 0.5\ \text{s}$$

---

19 Find the speed of propagation.

19 $c = f\lambda = (2\ \text{s}^{-1})(10\ \text{cm}) = 20\ \text{cm} \cdot \text{s}^{-1}$

---

20 Check: $\omega = ck$.

20
$$\omega = ck$$
$$4\pi\ \text{s}^{-1} = (20\ \text{cm} \cdot \text{s}^{-1})(0.2\pi\ \text{cm}^{-1})$$
$$4\pi\ \text{s}^{-1} = 4\pi\ \text{s}^{-1}\ \text{(checks)}$$

22

Reflections and Normal Modes

CHAPTER SUMMARY

In this chapter we again are concerned with mechanical waves, but here the waves are propagated in media with certain boundary conditions at one or both ends. In a string that is fixed at one end, for example, a pulse which originates at the other end will travel toward the fixed end and be reflected. The interference of incident and reflected trains of waves results in a standing wave which can be algebraically calculated by the principle of superposition. The reinforcement and interference of longitudinal waves and longitudinal standing waves are discussed as well as the phenomenon of resonance whereby vibrating bodies receive energy most readily at certain frequencies. The properties of vibrating bodies must be included in the design of many musical instruments such as organ pipes and various equipment such as loudspeakers and microphones.

BASIC TERMS — *Give definitions or meanings for the following:*

boundary condition (21-1)
standing waves (22-2)
principle of superposition (22-2)
node (22-2)
antinode (22-2)
fundamental frequency (22-3)
harmonics (22-3)
harmonic series (22-3)

overtone (22-3)
normal mode (22-3)
pressure node (22-4)
pressure antinode (22-4)
interference (22-6)
forced oscillation (22-7)
resonance (22-7)

PROGRAMMED QUIZ

1 An opera singer can break a window by singing the appropriate note. This is an example of what phenomenon?

1 Resonance.

2 Relate the principle of conservation of energy to constructive and destructive interference.

2 The energy is divided unevenly between the location of destructive (minimum energy) and constructive (maximum energy) interference. The total energy is constant.

3 A standing wave on a string must have a _____ at its fixed end.

3 Node.

---

4 What is the separation between a node and an antinode equal to?

4 1/4 wavelength.

---

5 What is the minimum length of a vibrating string in terms of wavelength?

5 1/2 wavelength; the end points must be nodes.

---

6 What is the motion of a vibrating string at a node? At an antinode?

6 Permanently at rest; the string executes simple harmonic motion about its equilibrium position.

---

7 What is the lowest frequency of the stretched string called?

7 Fundamental frequency.

---

8 The other frequencies are called _____ .

8 Overtones.

---

9 Overtones whose frequencies are integral multiples of the fundamental are called _____ .

9 Harmonics.

---

10 In longitudinal waves, what is analogous to constructive and destructive interference?

10 Reinforcement and interference.

---

11 A guitar string has a fundamental frequency of 256 Hz. How many nodes are there between the ends for the first overtone?

11 One node.

---

12 Under what conditions can a standing wave be produced in a stretched string?

12 If the frequency of the two waves traveling in opposite directions is one of the natural frequencies of the string.

---

13 In a longitudinal wave in a pipe, there will be a _____ at the open end of the pipe and a _____ at the closed end.

13 Displacement antinode, displacement node.

---

14 What is Kundt's tube used for ?

14 To measure the speed of sound in metal rods and gases.

---

15 What do the fundamental frequencies and overtones of an organ pipe depend on?

15 Length of pipe and temperature.

MAIN IDEAS

1 A standing wave is produced by two trains of waves traveling in opposite directions. By the principle of superposition, the amplitude of the standing wave is the algebraic sum of the instantaneous amplitudes of the individual waves. The shape of a vibrating string is a sine curve whose amplitude varies with time. Consider the wave functions of two waves with equal amplitudes, periods and wavelengths traveling in opposite directions:

$y_1 = A \sin(\omega t - kx)$ traveling to the right,

$y_2 = -A \sin(\omega t + kx)$ traveling to the left.

The two wave functions have opposite amplitudes A and $-A$ because the reflected wave is inverted. The wave function for $y_1 + y_2$ is given by

$y_1 + y_2 = (-2A \cos \omega t)\sin kx.$

2 Vibration of a string fixed at both ends. Consider a string under tension. If it is bowed, a transverse disturbance will travel to both ends where reflections will occur. Displacement nodes will be formed at both ends and at every half-wavelength. We can satisfy this condition by adjusting the string length to fit an integral number of half-wavelengths or by setting up a particular wave whose half-wavelengths will fit into the fixed length of the string:

Fundamental or first harmonic

$$f_1 = \left(\frac{c}{2L}\right) = \frac{1}{2L}\sqrt{\frac{T}{\mu}}$$

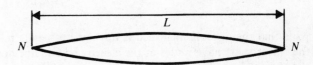

Second harmonic

$$f_2 = 2\left(\frac{c}{2L}\right) = 2\left(\frac{1}{2L}\sqrt{\frac{T}{\mu}}\right)$$

Third harmonic

$$f_3 = 3\left(\frac{c}{2L}\right) = 3\left(\frac{1}{2L}\sqrt{\frac{T}{\mu}}\right)$$

In general the nth harmonic is given by

$$f_n = \frac{n}{2L}\sqrt{\frac{T}{\mu}}.$$

The wave speed c is the same for all frequencies and depends only on the tension and the mass per unit length:

$$c = \sqrt{\frac{T}{\mu}}.$$

Be careful: the symbol T is used for both tension and temperature.

3 The vibrating air column.

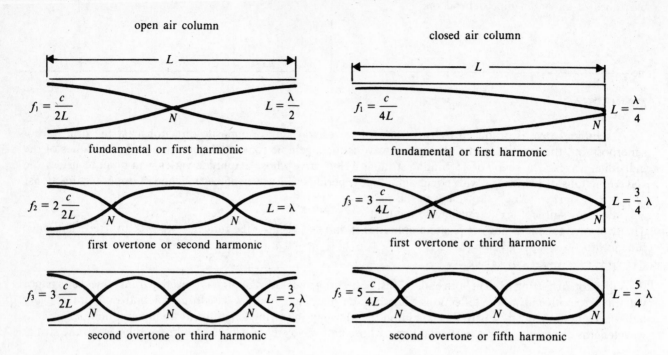

open air column

$$f_1 = \frac{c}{2L} \qquad L = \frac{\lambda}{2}$$

fundamental or first harmonic

$$f_2 = 2\frac{c}{2L} \qquad L = \lambda$$

first overtone or second harmonic

$$f_3 = 3\frac{c}{2L} \qquad L = \frac{3}{2}\lambda$$

second overtone or third harmonic

closed air column

$$f_1 = \frac{c}{4L} \qquad L = \frac{\lambda}{4}$$

fundamental or first harmonic

$$f_3 = 3\frac{c}{4L} \qquad L = \frac{3}{4}\lambda$$

first overtone or third harmonic

$$f_5 = 5\frac{c}{4L} \qquad L = \frac{5}{4}\lambda$$

second overtone or fifth harmonic

Note that the air column which is open at both ends must have antinodes at both ends. In the closed air column the waves must have nodes at the closed end and antinodes at the open end; thus we may only have the odd-numbered harmonics.

4 Clamped rods. The mode of vibration of a clamped rod depends upon where the rod is clamped. Longitudinal vibrations are produced along the rod when it is stroked lengthwise with a rosined cloth. Rods clamped at one end produce a series of standing waves that correspond to those of the closed pipe.

The fundamental note has a node at the clamped end.

$$f_1 = \frac{c}{4L} \qquad\qquad L = \frac{\lambda}{4}$$

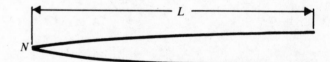

The third harmonic or first overtone has a node at $L/3$ from the free end.

$$f_3 = 3\left(\frac{c}{4L}\right) \qquad L = \frac{3\lambda}{4}$$

The fifth harmonic or second overtone has nodes at $L/5$ and $3L/5$ from the free end.

$$f_5 = 5\left(\frac{c}{4L}\right) \qquad L = \frac{5\lambda}{4}$$

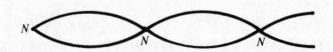

Rods clamped at the midpoint produce a series of standing waves that correspond to those of the open pipe.

Fundamental or first harmonic

$$f_1 = \frac{c}{2L} \qquad\qquad L = \frac{\lambda}{2}$$

The third harmonic or second overtone

$$f_3 = 3\left(\frac{c}{2L}\right) \qquad L = \frac{3\lambda}{2}$$

The fifth harmonic or third overtone

$$f_5 = 5\left(\frac{c}{2L}\right) \qquad L = \frac{5\lambda}{2}$$

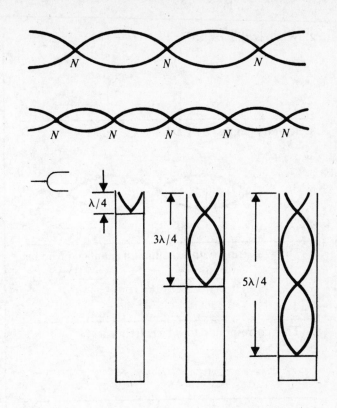

5 Resonance. A vibrating tuning fork will cause an air column which is closed at one end to vibrate if the air column has the same natural frequency as the tuning fork. This phenomenon is referred to as resonance and can be noted by an increase in the intensity of the sound produced. The length of the air column is related to an odd number of quarter wavelengths of the sound in air. Thus for the appropriate tuning fork and tube, the resonance points are $\lambda/4$, $3\lambda/4$, $5\lambda/4$,......

6 The Kundt's tube apparatus shown in the figure may be used to determine the speed of sound in a metal rod. When the metal rod is rubbed with a rosined cloth, standing waves will be set up in the air column as a result of the interference of the incident and reflected waves. The nodes of the standing waves will be identified by little piles of cork dust. The distance between two successive nodes is half a wavelength of the sound in the tube. Since the metal rod is clamped at its center, the fixed point is the node of the longitudinal wave in the rod and the loops of the wave will be at the ends of the rod. Hence the length of the rod is $= \frac{1}{2}\lambda_m$. Since the frequency of the sound produced by the metal $=$ frequency of the sound of the air in the tube,

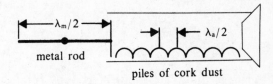

$$f = \frac{c_m}{\lambda_m} = \frac{c_a}{\lambda_a} .$$

Kundt's tube can also be used to measure the speed of sound in gases.

PROGRAMMED QUIZ

1 Draw the resultant of the two waves.

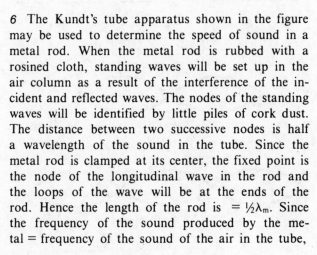

1

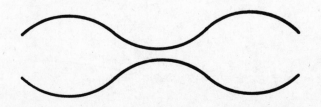

2 What is this called?

2 Maximum destructive interference.

---

3 Identify points *ABCDE*.

3 *A*, *C*, *E* are nodes; *B* and *D* are antinodes.

---

4 Draw a string with a minimum number of nodes.

4

---

5 This corresponds to which frequency?

5 Fundamental.

---

6 Draw the first and second overtones for the above string.

6

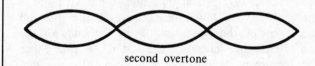

first overtone

second overtone

---

7 What is the wavelength in each case in terms of the length of the string?

7

$\lambda_1 = 2L$ (fundamental)
$\lambda_2 = L$ (first overtone)
$\lambda_3 = \dfrac{2L}{3}$ (second overtone)

---

8 What are the three frequencies equal to?

8

$f_1 = \dfrac{c}{2L}$

$f_2 = \dfrac{c}{L}$

$f_3 = \dfrac{3c}{2L}$

---

9 The fundamental frequency of an open organ pipe is 220 Hz. If the speed of sound in air is 348 m · s⁻¹, what is the length of the pipe?

9

$$f_1 = \frac{c}{2L}$$

$$L = \frac{348 \text{ m} \cdot \text{s}^{-1}}{2(220 \text{ s}^{-1})}$$

$$= 0.791 \text{ m}$$

---

10 What is the frequency of the first overtone (second harmonic)?

10

$$f_2 = 2f_1$$

$$= 2(220 \text{ Hz}) = 440 \text{ Hz}$$

---

11 Find the tension of a steel string, $L = 0.8$ m and $\mu = 0.004$ kg · m⁻¹, whose fundamental frequency is middle C (262 vib · s⁻¹).

11

$$f_1 = \frac{1}{2L} \sqrt{\frac{T}{\mu}}$$

$$T = f_1^2 (4L^2)\mu$$

$$= (262 \text{ s}^{-1})^2 (4) (0.8 \text{ m})^2 (0.004 \text{ kg} \cdot \text{m}^{-1})$$

$$= 703 \text{ N}$$

---

12 A pipe which is closed at one end is vibrating in the first overtone. The frequency of the tone is 440 Hz. Calculate the velocity of the sound in air at 20°C if the velocity at 0°C is 331 m · s⁻¹.

12

$$\frac{v_1}{v_2} = \sqrt{\frac{T_1}{T_2}}$$

$$\frac{331 \text{ m} \cdot \text{s}^{-1}}{v_2} = \sqrt{\frac{273 \text{ K}}{293 \text{ K}}}$$

$$v_2 = 343 \text{ m} \cdot \text{s}^{-1}$$

---

13 Calculate the wavelength of the above sound.

13

$$c = f\lambda$$

$$\lambda = \frac{343 \text{ m} \cdot \text{s}^{-1}}{440 \text{ s}^{-1}} = 0.780 \text{ m}$$

---

14 Calculate the length of the pipe.

14

$$L = \frac{\lambda}{4}$$

$$= \frac{0.780 \text{ m}}{4}$$

$$= 0.195 \text{ m}$$

STEP BY STEP SOLUTIONS OF PROBLEMS

Problem 1 A steel wire 1 m long having a mass of 0.006 kg is under a tension of 800 N. What is the fundamental frequency of vibration? How many overtones can be heard by a person capable of hearing frequencies up to 7320 Hz?

1 Find the mass per unit length of the wire.

1

$$\mu = \frac{m}{L} = \frac{0.006 \text{ kg}}{1 \text{ m}} = 0.006 \text{ kg} \cdot \text{m}^{-1}$$

2 What is the fundamental frequency?

2

$$f_1 = \frac{1}{2L} \sqrt{\frac{T}{\mu}}$$

$$= \frac{1}{2(1 \text{ m})} \sqrt{\frac{800 \text{ N}}{0.006 \text{ kg} \cdot \text{m}^{-1}}}$$

$$= 183 \text{ Hz}$$

---

3 Find the number of harmonics that the person is capable of hearing.

3

$$nf_1 = f_n$$

$$n = \frac{7320 \text{ Hz}}{183 \text{ Hz}} = 40$$

---

4 How many overtones in this?

4 $40 - 1 = 39$

Problem 2 A 550 Hz standing wave in a column of methane produces waves that are 40 cm between nodes at 20°C. Find $\gamma = C_p/C_v$.

5 Tabulate the data.

5

$$T = 20°C = 293 \text{ K}$$
$$f = 550 \text{ Hz}$$
$$R = 8.314 \text{ J} \cdot \text{mol}^{-1} \cdot \text{K}^{-1}$$
$$\text{distance between nodes} = 40 \text{ cm}$$

---

6 Find the wavelength.

6 Since the distance between nodes

$$= \frac{\lambda}{2}, \lambda = 80 \text{ cm} = 0.80 \text{ m}$$

---

7 Find the speed of propagation.

7

$$c = f\lambda$$
$$= (550 \text{ s}^{-1}) (0.80 \text{ m}) = 440 \text{ m} \cdot \text{s}^{-1}$$

---

8 What is the molecular mass of methane?

8 methane is CH_4
$$(12 + 4) \text{ g} = 16 \text{ g} = 0.016 \text{ kg}$$

---

9 Find γ by using $c = \sqrt{\gamma RT/M}$.

9

$$\gamma = \frac{c^2 M}{RT}$$

$$= \frac{(440 \text{ m} \cdot \text{s}^{-1})^2 (0.016 \text{ kg})}{(8.314 \text{ J} \cdot \text{mol}^{-1} \cdot \text{K}^{-1}) (293 \text{ K})}$$

$$= 1.27$$

Problem 3 The speed of a longitudinal wave in a helium-argon mixture at 300 K is 1200 m · s^{-1}. What is the composition of the mixture by mole fractions?

10 Tabulate the data. Use subscripts a for argon and h for helium.

10

$$
\begin{aligned}
M_a &= 40 \text{ g} = 0.040 \text{ kg} \\
M_h &= 4 \text{ g} = 0.004 \text{ kg} \\
\gamma &= 1.67 \\
R &= 8.314 \text{ J} \cdot \text{mol}^{-1} \cdot \text{K}^{-1} \\
c &= 1200 \text{ m} \cdot \text{s}^{-1} \\
T &= 300 \text{ K}
\end{aligned}
$$

11 Denote k to be the fractional molecular mass of argon. What is the fractional molecular mass of helium?

11 $(1 - k)$

12 Write the mathematical expression for the weighted average molecular mass M_{av}.

12

$$
\begin{aligned}
M_{av} &= kM_a + (1 - k)M_h \\
\text{or } M_{av} &= k(M_a - M_h) + M_h
\end{aligned}
$$

13 What is the mathematical relationship for the speed of propagation of a wave in an ideal gas? Solve for M_{av}.

13

$$
c = \sqrt{\frac{\gamma R T}{M_{av}}}
$$

$$
M_{av} = \frac{\gamma R T}{c^2}
$$

14 Equate the two expressions for M_{av} and solve for k.

14

$$
k(M_a - M_h) + M_h = \frac{\gamma R T}{c^2}
$$

$$
k = \frac{\dfrac{\gamma R T}{c^2} - M_h}{M_a - M_h}
$$

15 Substitute the numerical values.

15

$$
k = \frac{\dfrac{(1.67)(8.314 \text{ J} \cdot \text{mol}^{-1} \cdot \text{K}^{-1})(300 \text{ K})}{(1200 \text{ m} \cdot \text{s}^{-1})^2} - 0.004 \text{ kg}}{0.040 \text{ kg} - 0.004 \text{ kg}}
$$

$$
= 0.0308
$$

16 What is the fractional molecular mass of helium?

16 $1 - k = 1 - 0.0308 = 0.969.$

PROGRAMMED TEST

1 Problem 1 The following results were obtained in a resonance experiment. A long tube containing air at a pressure of 1 atm and a temperature of 388 K is open at one end and closed at the other by a movable piston. A tuning fork vibrating at 1000 Hz produces resonance at 10, 30 and 50 cm from the open end. a) Find the speed of sound in air at this temperature. b) Find γ for air.

1 Answer

$400 \text{ m} \cdot \text{s}^{-1}$, 1.43

If you solved this problem correctly, go to frame 6. If you could not solve this proble, go through frames 2–5.

2 Find the wavelength. Remember that resonance occurs at $\lambda/4$, $3\lambda/4$ and $5\lambda/4$.

2

Since $\dfrac{\lambda}{4} = 10$ cm

$$\lambda = 40 \text{ cm} = 0.40 \text{ m}$$

Check with the other resonance points:

$$\frac{3}{4}\lambda = 30 \text{ cm}; \quad \lambda = 0.40 \text{ m}$$

$$\frac{5}{4}\lambda = 50 \text{ cm}; \quad \lambda = 0.40 \text{ m}$$

---

3 Find the speed of sound in air.

3
$$\begin{aligned} c &= f\lambda \\ &= (1000 \text{ s}^{-1})(0.40 \text{ m}) \\ &= 400 \text{ m} \cdot \text{s}^{-1} \end{aligned}$$

---

4 What is the molecular mass of air?

4

$28.8 \text{ g} \cdot \text{mol}^{-1} = 0.0288 \text{ kg} \cdot \text{mol}^{-1}$

---

5 Find γ from the expression for the speed of a wave in an ideal gas.

5

$$c = \sqrt{\frac{\gamma RT}{M}}$$

$$\gamma = \frac{(0.0288 \text{ kg} \cdot \text{mol}^{-1})(400 \text{ m} \cdot \text{s}^{-1})^2}{(8.31 \text{ J} \cdot \text{mol}^{-1} \cdot \text{K}^{-1})(388 \text{ K})}$$

$$= 1.43$$

---

6 Problem 2 a) What is the ratio of the speed of sound in air to the speed of sound in helium? b) What frequency does an organ pipe produce in air if it produces a frequency of 1290 Hz in helium at the same temperature?

6 Answer

0.341, 440 Hz

If you solved this problem correctly, go to frame 14. If you could not solve this problem, go through frames 7–13.

7 What is the relationship for the speed, γ, R, temperature and molecular mass of air and of helium?

7

$$c_a = \sqrt{\frac{\gamma_a R T}{M_a}}$$

$$c_h = \sqrt{\frac{\gamma_h R T}{M_h}}$$

---

8 Noting that R and T are constants, find the relationship between c_a and c_h.

8

$$\frac{c_a}{c_h} = \frac{\sqrt{\dfrac{\gamma_a}{M_a}}}{\sqrt{\dfrac{\gamma_h}{M_h}}} = \sqrt{\frac{\gamma_a M_h}{\gamma_h M_a}}$$

---

9 Substitute the numerical values and solve.

9

$$\frac{c_a}{c_h} = \sqrt{\frac{(1.4)(4\ \text{g})}{(1.67)(28.8\ \text{g})}} = 0.341$$

---

10 What is the relationship for the speed, frequency and wavelength of sound in helium and in air?

10

$$c_h = f_h \lambda_h$$
$$c_a = f_a \lambda_a$$

---

11 What do we know about λ_a and λ_h?

11 Since the wavelength is a function of the length of the pipe,

$$\lambda_a = \lambda_h = \text{constant.}$$

---

12 What is the relationship between c_h and c_a?

12

$$\frac{c_a}{c_h} = \frac{f_a}{f_h}$$

---

13 Find the frequency in air.

13

$$f_a = \frac{c_a}{c_h}\ (f_h)$$

$$= (0.341)(1290\ \text{Hz})$$
$$= 440\ \text{Hz}$$

---

14 **Problem 3** A 1 m long copper rod is clamped at its center and set into longitudinal vibration. The resulting sound produces standing waves in a Kundt's tube containing air at 300 K. Heaps of cork dust within the tube are found to be 9.9 cm apart. Find the speed of the longitudinal waves in the copper rod. (Use speed in air = 348 m · s^{-1} at 300 K.)

14 **Answer**

3515 m · s^{-1}

If you could not solve this problem, go through frames 15–20.

15 Find the wavelength of the sound in copper.

15 Since the rod is clamped at its center, the length of the rod

$$1\ \text{m} = \frac{\lambda_c}{2}\ .$$

$$\lambda_c = 2\ \text{m}$$

---

16 Find the wavelength of the sound in the air tube.

16 The distance between two heaps of cork dust =

$$9.9 \text{ cm} = \frac{\lambda_a}{2} \ .$$

$$\lambda_a = 19.8 \text{ cm} = 0.198 \text{ m}$$

---

17 What is the relationship between the speed, frequency and wavelength in copper and in air?

17 $c_c = f_c \lambda_c$
$c_a = f_a \lambda_a$

---

18 What do you know about f_c and f_a?

18 $f_c = f_a = \text{constant}$

---

19 Find the ratio of the speed of sound in copper to the speed of sound in air.

19 $\dfrac{c_c}{c_a} = \dfrac{\lambda_c}{\lambda_a}$

---

20 Substitute the numerical values and solve for c_c.

20

$$c_c = \frac{(348 \text{ m} \cdot \text{s}^{-1})(2 \text{ m})}{0.198 \text{ m}}$$

$$= 3515 \text{ m} \cdot \text{s}^{-1}$$

23

Sound

CHAPTER SUMMARY

The mathematical representation of sound waves is presented in terms of pressure and amplitude. Loudness, intensity, intensity level and pitch are also defined, and the mathematical relationships are developed. A significant portion of the chapter deals with the ear and hearing and our perception of musical notes and beats. In addition, the Doppler effect, sources of sound and many applications of acoustic phenomena in medicine and our everyday lives are discussed.

BASIC TERMS — *Give definitions or meanings for the following:*

sound (23-I)
pressure amplitude (23-1)
intensity (23-1)
intensity level (23-1)
decibel (23-1)
threshold of hearing (23-2)
threshold of pain (23-2)
loudness (23-2)
loudness level (23-2)

sone (23-2)
phon (23-2)
pitch (23-2)
timbre (23-2)
beat frequency (23-3)
beats (23-3)
Doppler effect (23-4)
sonar (23-6)
transducer (23-6)

PROGRAMMED QUIZ

1 What is the unit of intensity of sound?

1 $W \cdot m^{-2}$, however it should be noted that acousticians use $W \cdot cm^{-2}$ which is a hybrid unit.

2 Why do we use a logarithmic scale for the intensity level of sound?

2 Because our ear is sensitive over an extremely large range of intensities.

3 How is loudness represented in a mathematical description of sound?

3 Since loudness is a purely subjective term it is not possible to measure it with instruments. Therefore, in physics we deal with a similar quantity — intensity which is objective and measurable.

4 Can sound waves travel through a vacuum?

4 No, they require a medium for propagation.

5 What is the pitch of a sound wave related to?

5 Frequency.

6 Beats are the result of what phenomenon?

6 Constructive and destructive interference.

7 Can standing waves on a string produce sound?

7 Yes, ex: violin.

8 What happens to the density of a medium as sound waves pass through it?

8 The sound wave alternately compresses and rarefies the medium resulting in a fluctuation of the density.

9 What would be a source of sound?

9 Some kind of vibrating object; the frequency of vibration is equal to the frequency of the resulting sound wave.

10 What happens when an observer moves toward a stationary source of sound?

10 He intercepts more wave fronts per unit time; therefore the frequency increases.

11 What are three subjective sensations of sound? What objective quantities are associated with them?

11 Pitch − frequency; loudness − intensity; quality − overtone structure.

12 Why can we hear the sound from a source which is obstructed? What is this phenomenon called?

12 Because sound waves "bend" around corners; diffraction.

13 When will two musical notes sound pleasing to the ear?

13 If their frequencies are in the ratio of small whole numbers.

14 The normal human ear responds to what intensities?

14 0–120 dB.

15 The normal human ear is most sensitive to what frequencies?

15 Between 2000 and 3000 Hz.

MAIN IDEAS

1 Audible sound waves lie in the 20–20,000 Hz range.

2 Pressure amplitude. Sound waves may be considered as fluctuations in pressure about normal atmospheric pressure. The maximum difference in the pressure variation is defined as the pressure amplitude $p_{max} = BkA$, where B is the bulk modulus of air, k the propagation constant and A the amplitude of the wave.

3 The velocity amplitude V of a wave is the maximum velocity of a particle in a medium; $V = A\omega$. Since $\omega = ck$, $p_{max} = BV/c$. Also, since $c = \sqrt{B/\rho}$, $p_{max} = V\sqrt{B\rho}$.

4 Intensity or average power per unit area $= I = \frac{1}{2}\omega BkA^2 = \dfrac{p^2_{max}}{2\sqrt{\rho B}} = \dfrac{p^2_{max}}{2\rho c} = \frac{1}{2}p_{max}V$. The largest amplitude tolerable to the human ear is about 30 Pa; its corresponding intensity is 1.07×10^{-4} W $\cdot$ cm^{-2}. The pressure amplitude of the faintest sound that can be heard is about 3×10^{-5} Pa; its corresponding intensity is 1.07×10^{-16} W $\cdot$ cm^{-2}.

5 The speed of sound in air in relation to temperature is given by the expression $c = 331$ m $\cdot$ s^{-1} + 0.60 m $\cdot$ s^{-1} (K)$^{-1}$ (ΔT) where ΔT is the change in temperature from 273 K.

6 The intensity of sound with respect to distance. Consider a source having a power P. Since the power is uniformly distributed over a spherical area, the intensity at a distance r is the power divided by the surface area or $I = \dfrac{P}{4\pi r^2}$. We can compare the intensities at two points from a single source.

Since $I_1 = \dfrac{P}{4\pi r_1^2}$ and $I_2 = \dfrac{P}{4\pi r_2^2}$, it follows that $\dfrac{I_1}{I_2} = \dfrac{r_2^2}{r_1^2}$. Note P is measured in watts.

7 Intensity level $\beta = 10 \log \dfrac{I}{I_0}$ where I is the given intensity and I_0 is an arbitrary reference intensity $= 10^{-12}$ W $\cdot$ m^{-2}. β is measured in decibels (dB), a unitless quantity. If $\beta_1 = 10 \log \dfrac{I_1}{I_0}$ and $\beta_2 = 10 \log \dfrac{I_2}{I_0}$, then $\beta_2 - \beta_1 = 10 \log \dfrac{I_2}{I_1}$. If $I_1 = \dfrac{(p_{max})_1^2}{2\rho c}$ and $I_2 = \dfrac{(p_{max})_2^2}{2\rho c}$, then $\beta_2 - \beta_1 = 20 \log \dfrac{(p_{max})_2}{(p_{max})_1}$. The range of audibility varies with the intensity level. For a tone of 80 dB intensity level, the range of audibility is from 20 to 20,000 Hz. At a level of 20 dB, it is from 200 to 15,000 Hz.

8 Loudness refers to a listener's subjective perception of a sound sensation. Loudness is a function of intensity and frequency. The loudness level (in phons) of any tone is equal to the sound intensity level (in dB) of a 1000 Hz tone having the same perceived loudness as that tone. Thus a loudness level of 40 phons means that the tone appears to be as loud as a 40 dB tone at a frequency of 1000 Hz. The standard unit of perceived loudness is the sone. One sone is the loudness perceived by a listener with normal hearing when a 1000 Hz tone at 40 dB is presented to his ears.

9 Musical tones differ from one another in three ways — intensity, pitch and quality. Intensity is measured by the energy of the sound. Pitch refers to the characteristic of a sound sensation that enables one to classify a note as "high" or "low". For a pure tone of constant intensity, the pitch becomes higher as the frequency is raised. The quality or timbre of a tone is determined in part by the number of overtones present and their corresponding intensity distributions.

10 Beats are the result of the interference of two sound waves of equal amplitude and slightly different frequencies traveling through the same region. On the basis of the principle of superposition, there will be variations of "loudness." The number of beats per second equals the difference in frequencies ($f_{beat} = f_1 - f_2$).

11 The wavelength of the sound from a moving source

$\lambda = \dfrac{c - v_s}{f_s}$ in front of the source and

$\lambda = \dfrac{c + v_s}{f_s}$ in back of the source, where the subscript s refers to the source.

12 Doppler effect refers to the apparent change in the frequency of a sound due to the relative motion of the listener and the source. The mathematical relationship is given by

$\dfrac{f_L}{c + v_L} = \dfrac{f_S}{c + v_S}$, where f_S = frequency of the source, f_L = frequency as heard by the listener, c = speed of sound in medium, v_L = the velocity of the listener relative to the medium and v_S = the velocity of the source relative to the medium. The following sign conventions are used: c is always positive, v_L is positive if the listener is moving toward the source and negative if the listener is moving away from the source, v_S is negative if the source is moving toward the listener and positive if it is moving away from the listener.

Case	Source	Listener	Diagram	Sign	Formula
a	stationary	stationary	ⓛ ⓢ	$v_L = v_S = 0$	$f_L = f_S$
b	stationary	moving toward source	ⓛ→ ⓢ	$v_L = +$	$f_L = f_S \left(\dfrac{c + v_L}{c} \right)$
c	stationary	moving away from source	←ⓛ ⓢ	$v_L = -$	$f_L = f_S \left(\dfrac{c - v_L}{c} \right)$
d	moving toward listener	stationary	ⓛ ←ⓢ	$v_S = -$	$f_L = f_S \left(\dfrac{c}{c - v_S} \right)$
e	moving away from listener	stationary	ⓛ ⓢ→	$v_S = +$	$f_L = f_S \left(\dfrac{c}{c + v_S} \right)$
f	moving in one direction	moving in the same direction behind source	ⓛ→ ⓢ→	$v_L = +, v_S = +$	$f_L = f_S \left(\dfrac{c + v_L}{c + v_S} \right)$
g	moving in one direction	moving in the same direction in front of source	←ⓛ ←ⓢ	$v_L = -, v_S = -$	$f_L = f_S \left(\dfrac{c - v_L}{c - v_S} \right)$
h	moving toward listener	moving toward source	ⓛ→◄←ⓢ	$v_L = +, v_S = -$	$f_L = f_S \left(\dfrac{c + v_L}{c - v_S} \right)$
i	moving away from listener	moving away from source	←ⓛ ⓢ→	$v_L = -, v_S = +$	$f_L = f_S \left(\dfrac{c - v_L}{c + v_S} \right)$

13 The Doppler effect for electromagnetic vibration.

$f_L = f_S \sqrt{\dfrac{c - v}{c + v}}$ where c is the speed of light and v is the relative speed between the source and observer.

When the source moves away from the observer, v is positive; when the source moves toward the observer, v is negative.

14 Problem solving strategy.

a) Understand the basic terms and relationships:

i) Pressure amplitude p_{max} represents the maximum pressure variation:
     $p_{max} = BkA$.

ii) There is a difference between intensity and intensity level. Intensity I is the average power per unit area:
$$I = \tfrac{1}{2}B\omega kA^2 = \dfrac{p^2_{max}}{2\sqrt{\rho B}} = \dfrac{P}{4\pi r^2} .$$

The unit of I is $W \cdot m^{-2}$. The power of the source is P.

iii) The intensity level β of a sound wave

$$\beta = 10 \log \dfrac{I}{I_0} ,$$ where I_0 = reference intensity = 10^{-12} W $\cdot$ m^{-2}. The unit of β is decibel = dB.

b) Review logarithms:

$$\log (ab) = \log a + \log b$$

$$\log \frac{a}{b} = \log a - \log b$$

$$\log a^n = n \log a$$

$\log a = n$ means that $10^n = a$

$\ln a = n$ means that $e^n = a$

PROGRAMMED QUIZ

1 What is the intensity of a sound whose intensity level is 100 dB if the reference intensity is 10^{-12} W $\cdot$ m^{-2}?

1

$$\beta = 10 \log \frac{I}{I_0}$$

$$100 \text{ dB} = 10 \log \frac{I}{10^{-12} \text{ W} \cdot \text{m}^{-2}}$$

$$10 = \log \frac{I}{10^{-12}}$$

$$= \log I - \log 10^{-12}$$

$$= \log I + 12$$

$$-2 = \log I$$

$$I = 10^{-2} \text{ W} \cdot \text{m}^{-2}$$

---

2 What is the acoustic power in watts of this source at a distance of 40 m?

2

$$I = \frac{P}{4\pi r^2}$$

$$P = 4\pi (10^{-2} \text{ W} \cdot \text{m}^{-2}) (40 \text{ m})^2$$

$$= 201 \text{ W}$$

---

3 A 40 dB sound is how many times more intense than a 10 dB sound?

3

$$\beta_2 - \beta_1 = 10 \log \frac{I_2}{I_1}$$

$$40 - 10 = 10 \log \frac{I_2}{I_1}$$

$$3 = \log \frac{I_2}{I_1}$$

$$10^3 = 1000 = \frac{I_2}{I_1}$$

---

4 Two sources of sound 455 and 445 Hz in frequency produce beats. What frequency will you hear?

4

$$\frac{f_1 + f_2}{2} = \frac{455 \text{ Hz} + 445 \text{ Hz}}{2} = 450 \text{ Hz}$$

---

5 How many beats per second will you hear?

5 $f_1 - f_2 = 455 \text{ Hz} - 445 \text{ Hz} = 10 \text{ s}^{-1}$

---

6 What is the new intensity if the pressure amplitude in a sound wave is tripled?

6

$$I = \frac{p^2_{max}}{2\rho c}$$

if $p'_{max} = 3p_{max}$, $p'^2_{max} = 9p^2_{max}$

then $I' = \frac{p'^2_{max}}{2\rho c} = \frac{9p^2_{max}}{2\rho c} = 9I$

---

7 What is the velocity amplitude of a sound wave whose pressure amplitude is 30 Pa and intensity is 1×10^{-4} W · m^{-2}?

7

$$I = \tfrac{1}{2}p_{max} V$$
$$V = \frac{2(1 \times 10^{-4} \text{ W} \cdot \text{m}^{-2})}{30 \text{ Pa}}$$
$$= 6.67 \times 10^{-6} \text{ m} \cdot \text{s}^{-1}$$

---

8 What is the speed of sound in air at 20°C?

8

$$c = [331 \text{ m} \cdot \text{s}^{-1} + (0.60 \text{ m} \cdot \text{s}^{-1}) (\text{C}°)^{-1}] (\Delta T)$$
$$= [331 \text{ m} \cdot \text{s}^{-1} + (0.60 \text{ m} \cdot \text{s}^{-1}) (\text{C}°)^{-1}] (20 \text{ C}°)$$
$$= 343 \text{ m} \cdot \text{s}^{-1}$$

---

9 A latecomer to the opera hurries down the aisle so quickly that the C (264 Hz) seems to be 1 Hz higher in frequency. How fast is he walking?

9

$$f_L = \frac{f_S(c + v_L)}{c}$$
$$265 \text{ Hz} = \frac{264 \text{ Hz}(345 \text{ m} \cdot \text{s}^{-1} + v_L)}{345 \text{ m} \cdot \text{s}^{-1}}$$
$$v_L = 1.31 \text{ m} \cdot \text{s}^{-1}$$

---

10 The intensity 4 m from a loudspeaker is 50×10^{-12} W · m^{-2}. What is the intensity 12 m from the loudspeaker?

10

$$\frac{I_1}{I_2} = \frac{r_2^2}{r_1^2}$$
$$\frac{50 \times 10^{-12} \text{ W} \cdot \text{m}^{-2}}{I_2} = \frac{(12 \text{ m})^2}{(4 \text{ m})^2}$$
$$I_2 = \frac{50 \times 10^{-12} \text{ W} \cdot \text{m}^{-2} (4 \text{ m})^2}{(12 \text{ m})^2}$$
$$= 5.56 \times 10^{-12} \text{ W} \cdot \text{m}^{-2}$$

11 If β_1 and β_2 are the intensity levels in decibels of sounds of intensities I_1 and I_2, respectively, prove that $\beta_2 - \beta_1 = 10 \log \dfrac{I_2}{I_1}$.

Remember that $\log \dfrac{a}{b} = \log a - \log b$.

11

$$\beta_2 = 10 \log \frac{I_2}{I_0}$$

$$\beta_1 = 10 \log \frac{I_1}{I_0}$$

$$\beta_2 - \beta_1 = 10 \log \frac{I_2}{I_0} - 10 \log \frac{I_1}{I_0}$$

$$= 10 \log \left(\frac{\dfrac{I_2}{I_0}}{\dfrac{I_1}{I_0}} \right)$$

$$= 10 \log \frac{I_2}{I_1}$$

---

12 Express the difference in intensity levels of the sounds in terms of their respective distances r_1 and r_2 from a source of power P.

12

$$\beta_2 - \beta_1 = 10 \log \frac{I_2}{I_1}$$

$$= 10 \log \left(\frac{\dfrac{P}{4\pi r_2^2}}{\dfrac{P}{4\pi r_1^2}} \right)$$

$$= 10 \log \left(\frac{r_1^2}{r_2^2} \right)$$

$$= 20 \log \frac{r_1}{r_2}$$

STEP BY STEP SOLUTIONS OF PROBLEMS

Problem 1 Consider two sound waves of the same frequency, one in water and the other in air. a) If the intensities are equal, what is the ratio of the pressure amplitude of the wave in water to that of the wave in air? b) If the pressure amplitudes are equal, what is the ratio of their intensities? c) If the pressure amplitudes are equal, what is the difference between their intensity levels? (Use $c_a = 345$ m $\cdot$ s^{-1}, $c_w = 1490$ m $\cdot$ s^{-1}, $\rho_a = 1.22$ kg $\cdot$ m^{-3} and $\rho_w = 1000$ kg $\cdot$ m^{-3})

1 Write the relationship between pressure amplitude, intensity, density and speed for water and air.

1

$$I_w = \frac{(p_{max})_w^2}{2\rho_w c_w}$$

$$I_a = \frac{(p_{max})_a^2}{2\rho_a c_a}$$

2 Equate I_w and I_a and solve for the ratio $(p_{max})_w/(p_{max})_a$

2

$$\frac{(p_{max})_w{}^2}{2\rho_w c_w} = \frac{(p_{max})_a{}^2}{2\rho_a c_a}$$

$$\frac{(p_{max})_w}{(p_{max})_a} = \sqrt{\frac{\rho_w c_w}{\rho_a c_a}}$$

---

3 Substitute the numerical values and solve.

3

$$\frac{(p_{max})_w}{(p_{max})_a} = \sqrt{\frac{(1000 \text{ kg} \cdot \text{m}^{-3})(1490 \text{ m} \cdot \text{s}^{-1})}{(1.22 \text{ kg} \cdot \text{m}^{-3})(345 \text{ m} \cdot \text{s}^{-1})}}$$

$$= 59.5$$

---

4 If $(p_{max})_w = (p_{max})_a$, what is the ratio of I_a/I_w?

4

$$\frac{I_a}{I_w} = \frac{\rho_w c_w}{\rho_a c_a}$$

$$= \frac{(1000 \text{ kg} \cdot \text{m}^{-3})(1490 \text{ m} \cdot \text{s}^{-1})}{(1.22 \text{ kg} \cdot \text{m}^{-3})(345 \text{ m} \cdot \text{s}^{-1})} = 3540$$

---

5 Find the difference between the intensity levels.

5

$$\beta = 10 \log \frac{I_a}{I_w} = 10 \log (3540) = 35.5$$

Problem 2 A source of sound emits a power of 100 W uniformly in all directions. a) At what distance from the source is the sound level 120 dB? b) What is the algebraic solution?

6 What is the relationship between intensity, power and surface area?

6

$$I = \frac{P}{A} = \frac{P}{4\pi r^2}$$

---

7 Relate this to the difference in intensity level with respect to I_0.

7

$$\beta = 10 \log \frac{I}{I_0}$$

$$= 10 \log \frac{P/4\pi r^2}{I_0}$$

$$= 10 \log \frac{P}{4\pi r^2 I_0}$$

---

8 Substitute the numerical values and solve for the distance. Remember that I_0 is an arbitrary reference intensity, taken as 10^{-12} W $\cdot$ m^{-2}.

8

$$
\begin{aligned}
120 \text{ dB} &= 10 \log \frac{100 \text{ W}}{4\pi r^2 \,(10^{-12} \text{ W} \cdot \text{m}^{-2})} \\
&= 10 \log \frac{7.96 \times 10^{12}}{r^2(\text{m}^{-2})} \\
12 &= \log 7.96 \times 10^{12} - \log r^2(\text{m}^{-2}) \\
&= 12.901 - \log r^2(\text{m}^{-2}) \\
\log r^2(\text{m}^{-2}) &= 0.901 \\
r^2(\text{m}^{-2}) &= 7.96 \\
r &= 2.82 \text{ m}
\end{aligned}
$$

---

9 In order to obtain the algebraic solution, solve frame 7 for r. Write the logarithmic equation in exponential form; $\log a = n$ means $10^n = a$.

9

$$
\frac{\beta}{10} = \log \frac{P}{4\pi r^2 I_0}
$$

$$
10^{\beta/10} = \frac{P}{4\pi r^2 I_0}
$$

$$
r = \sqrt{\frac{P}{4\pi I_0 (10^{\beta/10})}}
$$

Problem 3 Two sources radiate sound uniformly in all directions. Source A has an output of 6×10^{-4} W and B has an output of 9.5×10^{-4} W. Both sources are vibrating in phase at 518 Hz. a) Determine the intensity at point C (5 m from A and 4 m from B along a straight line) from source A if source B is turned off and from source B if A is turned off. b) Determine the difference in phase of the two sources. c) With both sources on, find the intensity and intensity level at C.

10 Draw a sketch.

10

---

11 Find the intensity at C due to A with source B turned off.

11

$$
\begin{aligned}
I_A &= \frac{P}{A} = \frac{P}{4\pi r^2} \\
&= \frac{6 \times 10^{-4} \text{ W}}{4\pi(5 \text{ m})^2} = 1.91 \times 10^{-6} \text{ W} \cdot \text{m}^{-2}
\end{aligned}
$$

---

12 Find the intensity at C due to B with source A turned off.

12

$$
I_B = \frac{9.5 \times 10^{-4} \text{ W}}{4\pi(4 \text{ m})^2} = 4.73 \times 10^{-6} \text{ W} \cdot \text{m}^{-2}
$$

---

13 Before we can find the phase difference, we must find the wavelength of the sound wave.

13

$$
c = f\lambda
$$

$$
\lambda = \frac{345 \text{ m} \cdot \text{s}^{-1}}{518 \text{ s}^{-1}} = 0.666 \text{ m}
$$

14 Find the phase difference from the path difference.

14 The path difference $= 5\text{ m} - 4\text{ m} = 1\text{ m}$.

$$1\text{ m} = \frac{\phi}{k} = \frac{\phi\lambda}{2\pi}$$

$$\phi = \frac{2\pi(\text{m})}{0.666\text{ m}} = 3\pi$$

---

15 What kind of interference do we have at C?

15 A phase difference of 3π results in destructive interference.

---

16 Find the pressure amplitude at C due to A if B is turned off.

16

$$
\begin{aligned}
(p_{\max})_A{}^2 &= 2I_A\rho c \\
&= 2(1.91 \times 10^{-6}\text{ W}\cdot\text{m}^{-2})\,(1.22\text{ kg}\cdot\text{m}^{-3}) \\
&\quad \times (345\text{ m}\cdot\text{s}^{-1}) \\
(p_{\max})_A &= 0.0401\text{ Pa}
\end{aligned}
$$

---

17 Find the pressure amplitude at C due to B if A is turned off.

17

$$
\begin{aligned}
(p_{\max})_B{}^2 &= 2(4.73 \times 10^{-6}\text{ W}\cdot\text{m}^{-2}) \\
&\quad \times (1.22\text{ kg}\cdot\text{m}^{-3})\,(345\text{ m}\cdot\text{s}^{-1}) \\
(p_{\max})_B &= 0.0631\text{ Pa}
\end{aligned}
$$

---

18 Because of the destructive interference of the waves, the pressure amplitude at C is equal to the difference between the pressure amplitudes.

18
$(p_{\max})_B - (p_{\max})_A = 0.0631\text{ Pa} - 0.0401\text{ Pa} = 0.023\text{ Pa}$

---

19 Find the intensity at C due to both sources.

19

$$
\begin{aligned}
I_{A+B} &= \frac{(0.023\text{ Pa})^2}{2(1.22\text{ kg}\cdot\text{m}^{-3})\,(345\text{ m}\cdot\text{s}^{-1})} \\
&= 0.628 \times 10^{-6}\text{ W}\cdot\text{m}^{-2}
\end{aligned}
$$

---

20 What is the intensity level at C?

20

$$
\begin{aligned}
\beta &= 10\log\frac{0.628 \times 10^{-6}\text{ W}\cdot\text{m}^{-2}}{10^{-12}\text{ W}\cdot\text{m}^{-2}} \\
&= 58.0\text{ dB}
\end{aligned}
$$

PROGRAMMED TEST

1 *Problem 1* a) What is the intensity level of a sound wave whose intensity is $4 \times 10^{-8}\text{ W}\cdot\text{m}^{-2}$? b) What is the intensity level of a sound wave in air whose pressure amplitude is 0.3 Pa?

1 *Answer*
46.0 dB, 80.3 dB

If you solved this problem correctly, go to frame 5. If you could not solve this problem, go through frames 2–4.

2 Find the intensity level of the sound wave.

2

$$\beta = 10 \log \frac{I}{I_0}$$
$$= 10 \log \frac{4 \times 10^{-8} \text{ W} \cdot \text{m}^{-2}}{10^{-12} \text{ W} \cdot \text{m}^{-2}}$$
$$= 46.0 \text{ dB}$$

---

3 Find the intensity of the sound wave in air.

3

$$I = \frac{p^2_{\text{max}}}{2\rho c}$$
$$= \frac{(0.3 \text{ Pa})^2}{2(1.22 \text{ kg} \cdot \text{m}^{-3}) (345 \text{ m} \cdot \text{s}^{-1})}$$
$$= 1.07 \times 10^{-4} \text{ W} \cdot \text{m}^{-2}$$

---

4 Find the intensity level.

4

$$\beta = 10 \log \frac{I}{I_0}$$
$$= 10 \log \frac{1.07 \times 10^{-4} \text{ W} \cdot \text{m}^{-2}}{10^{-12} \text{ W} \cdot \text{m}^{-2}}$$
$$= 80.3 \text{ dB}$$

---

5 *Problem 2* A sound source of 880 Hz radiates uniformly in all directions in air. At a distance of 4 m the sound level is 90 dB. Find a) the intensity of the sound at 4 m, b) the pressure amplitude, c) the displacement amplitude at this distance and d) the distance at which the sound level is 70 dB.

5 *Answer*
$10^{-3} \text{ W} \cdot \text{m}^{-2}$, 0.917 Pa, 4.04×10^{-7} m, 40 m

---

If you solved this problem correctly, go to frame 19. If you could not solve this problem, go through frames 6–18.

---

6 Find the intensity from the relationship for the difference in intensity level.

6

$$\beta = 10 \log \frac{I}{I_0}$$
$$90 \text{ dB} = 10 \log \frac{I}{10^{-12} \text{ W} \cdot \text{m}^{-2}}$$
$$9 = \log I(\text{W} \cdot \text{m}^{-2})^{-1} + 12$$
$$\log I(\text{W} \cdot \text{m}^{-2})^{-1} = -3$$
$$I = 10^{-3} \text{ W} \cdot \text{m}^{-2}$$

---

7 Find the pressure amplitude.

7

$$I = \frac{p^2_{\text{max}}}{2\rho c}$$
$$p^2_{\text{max}} = 2(10^{-3} \text{ W} \cdot \text{m}^{-2}) (1.22 \text{ kg} \cdot \text{m}^{-3})$$
$$\times (345 \text{ m} \cdot \text{s}^{-1})$$
$$p_{\text{max}} = 0.917 \text{ Pa}$$

---

8 Find the angular frequency.

8

$$\omega = 2\pi f = 2\pi(880 \text{ s}^{-1}) = 5530 \text{ s}^{-1}$$

---

9 What is the wave number?

9

$$k = \frac{\omega}{c} = \frac{5530 \text{ s}^{-1}}{345 \text{ m} \cdot \text{s}^{-1}} = 16.0 \text{ m}^{-1}$$

---

10 What is the bulk modulus for air?

10

$$B = \gamma p = 1.4(1.013 \times 10^5 \text{ Pa})$$
$$= 1.42 \times 10^5 \text{ Pa}$$

---

11 Find the displacement amplitude.

11

$$A = \frac{p_{max}}{Bk}$$
$$= \frac{0.917 \text{ Pa}}{(1.42 \times 10^5 \text{ Pa})(16.0 \text{ m}^{-1})}$$
$$= 4.04 \times 10^{-7} \text{ m}$$

---

12 Write the relationships for β_1 and β_2 in terms of the pressure amplitudes, distances and reference intensity.

12

$$\beta_1 = 10 \log \frac{p_{max}}{4\pi r_1^2 I_0}$$
$$\beta_2 = 10 \log \frac{p_{max}}{4\pi r_2^2 I_0}$$

---

13 Solve for r_1^2 and r_2^2.

13

$$r_1^2 = \frac{p_{max}}{4\pi I_0 10^{\beta_1/10}}$$

$$r_2^2 = \frac{p_{max}}{4\pi I_0 10^{\beta_2/10}}$$

---

14 Find the ratio of r_1^2/r_2^2.

14

$$\frac{r_1^2}{r_2^2} = \frac{10^{\beta_2/10}}{10^{\beta_1/10}}$$

---

15 Take logarithms of both sides and solve for $\beta_2 - \beta_1$.

15

$$\beta_2 - \beta_1 = 20 \log \frac{r_1}{r_2}$$

---

16 Find the distance for which the sound level is 70 dB.

16

$$70 \text{ dB} - 90 \text{ dB} = 20 \log \frac{4 \text{ m}}{r_2}$$
$$- 1 = \log \frac{4 \text{ m}}{r_2}$$
$$10^{-1} = \frac{4 \text{ m}}{r_2}$$
$$r_2 = 40 \text{ m}$$

17 Check the answer by calculating the intensity I_2 where the sound level is 70 dB.

17

$$\beta = 10 \log \frac{I_2}{I_0}$$

$$70 \text{ dB} = 10 \log \frac{I_2}{10^{-12} \text{ W} \cdot \text{m}^{-2}}$$

$$7 = \log I_2 (\text{W} \cdot \text{m}^{-2})^{-1} + 12$$

$$\log I_2 (\text{W} \cdot \text{m}^{-2})^{-1} = -5$$

$$I_2 = 10^{-5} \text{ W} \cdot \text{m}^{-2}$$

---

18 Check your answer by finding r_2.

18

$$\frac{I_1}{I_2} = \frac{r_2^2}{r_1^2}$$

$$\frac{10^{-3} \text{ W} \cdot \text{m}^{-2}}{10^{-5} \text{ W} \cdot \text{m}^{-2}} = \frac{r_2^2}{(4 \text{ m})^2}$$

$$r_2 = 40 \text{ m}$$

---

19 **Problem 3** A locomotive traveling at $35 \text{ m} \cdot \text{s}^{-1}$ emits a whistle note of 800 Hz. Find the wavelength of the sound waves a) in front of the locomotive and b) behind the locomotive. Find the frequency of the sound heard by a listener under the following conditions: c) the listener is stationary and in front of the locomotive, d) the listener is stationary and behind the locomotive, e) the listener is approaching the locomotive at $20 \text{ m} \cdot \text{s}^{-1}$, f) the listener is receding from the locomotive at $20 \text{ m} \cdot \text{s}^{-1}$ (they are now moving in opposite directions).

19 **Answer**
0.388 m, 0.475 m, 890 Hz, 726 Hz, 942 Hz, 712 Hz.

If you could not solve this problem, go through frames 20–27.

20 Find the wavelength of the sound waves in front of the locomotive.

20 The waves are crowded in front of the source.

$$\lambda_{\text{in front}} = \frac{c - v_S}{f_S}$$

$$= \frac{345 \text{ m} \cdot \text{s}^{-1} - 35 \text{ m} \cdot \text{s}^{-1}}{800 \text{ s}^{-1}}$$

$$= 0.388 \text{ m}$$

---

21 Find the wavelength of the sound waves behind the locomotive.

21 The waves are spread out behind the source.

$$\lambda_{\text{behind}} = \frac{c + v_S}{f_S}$$

$$= \frac{345 \text{ m} \cdot \text{s}^{-1} + 35 \text{ m} \cdot \text{s}^{-1}}{800 \text{ s}^{-1}}$$

$$= 0.475 \text{ m}$$

---

22 What is the expression for the frequency of the sound heard by the listener in terms of the frequency of the sound source, i.e., the Doppler effect?

22

$$\frac{f_L}{c + v_L} = \frac{f_S}{c + v_S}$$

23 What are the sign conventions for v_L and v_S?

23 If the listener is moving toward the source, the sign of v_L is positive. If the listener is moving away from the source, the sign of v_L is negative. The sign of v_S is negative if the source of sound is moving toward the listener and positive if it is moving away.

24 Find the frequency of the sound heard by a listener who is stationary and in front of the locomotive.

24 Since the listener is stationary, $v_L = 0$; since the source is moving toward the listener, v_S is negative (case d).

$$f_L = f_S \left(\frac{c}{c - v_S} \right)$$

$$= \frac{800 \text{ Hz } (345 \text{ m} \cdot \text{s}^{-1})}{345 \text{ m} \cdot \text{s}^{-1} - 35 \text{ m} \cdot \text{s}^{-1}} = 890 \text{ Hz}$$

25 Find the frequency of the sound heard by the listener who is stationary and behind the locomotive.

25 Since the listener is stationary, $v_L = 0$; since the source is moving away from the listener, v_S is positive (case e).

$$f_L = f_S \left(\frac{c}{c + v_S} \right)$$

$$= \frac{800 \text{ Hz } (345 \text{ m} \cdot \text{s}^{-1})}{345 \text{ m} \cdot \text{s}^{-1} + 35 \text{ m} \cdot \text{s}^{-1}} = 726 \text{ Hz}$$

26 Find the frequency of the sound heard by a listener who is approaching the locomotive at $20 \text{ m} \cdot \text{s}^{-1}$.

26 Since the listener is approaching the source of sound, $v_L = +$. Since the source of sound is approaching the listener, v_S is $-$ (case h).

$$f_L = f_S \left(\frac{c + v_L}{c - v_S} \right)$$

$$= \frac{800 \text{ Hz } (345 \text{ m} \cdot \text{s}^{-1} + 20 \text{ m} \cdot \text{s}^{-1})}{345 \text{ m} \cdot \text{s}^{-1} - 35 \text{ m} \cdot \text{s}^{-1}}$$

$$= 942 \text{ Hz}$$

27 Find the frequency of the sound heard by the listener who is receding from the locomotive at $20 \text{ m} \cdot \text{s}^{-1}$.

27 Since the listener is receding from the source of sound, $v_L = -$. Since the source of sound is moving away from the listener, v_S is $+$ (case i).

$$f_L = f_S \left(\frac{c - v_L}{c + v_S} \right)$$

$$= \frac{800 \text{ Hz } (345 \text{ m} \cdot \text{s}^{-1} - 20 \text{ m} \cdot \text{s}^{-1})}{345 \text{ m} \cdot \text{s}^{-1} + 20 \text{ m} \cdot \text{s}^{-1}}$$

$$= 712 \text{ Hz}$$

24

Coulomb's Law

CHAPTER SUMMARY

The next major topic in physics, electricity and magnetism, begins with a discussion of Coulomb's law which describes the interaction between two charged paticles. After a description of the basic constituents of the atom, the differences between conductors and insulators are considered. Electrical interactions and charging by contact and induction are also included.

BASIC TERMS — *Give definitions or meanings for the following:*

electrostatics (24-I)
electric charge (24-1)
electron (24-2)
atom (24-2)
proton (24-2)
neutron (24-2)
ionization (24-2)
positive ion (24-2)
negative ion (24-2)
atomic number (24-2)

conservation of charge (24-2)
nucleus (24-2)
conductor (24-3)
insulator (24-3)
induction (24-4)
induced charge (24-4)
Coulomb's law (24-5)
principle of superposition (24-5)
coulomb (24-5)

PROGRAMMED QUIZ

1 What do we mean when we say that an object has a positive electrical charge?

1 It has a deficiency of electrons.

2 What do we call an atom from which an electron has been removed?

2 Positive ion.

3 Two positive charges are a certain distance apart. One of the charges is replaced with a negative charge of the same magnitude. What happens to the force between them?

3 Remains the same in magnitude but whereas the force was repulsive when the two charges were positive, it is attractive when the charges are opposite.

4 What happens to the magnitude of the force when the distance between two charges is doubled? Let $1/4\pi\epsilon_0 = k$

4

Becomes $\dfrac{1}{4}$.

$$F = \frac{k\,|\,q_1 q_2\,|}{r^2}$$

if $r' = 2r$, then

$$F' = \frac{k\,|\,q_1 q_2\,|}{r^2} = \frac{k\,|\,q_1 q_2\,|}{(2r)^2} = \frac{k\,|\,q_1 q_2\,|}{4r}$$

$$= \frac{F}{4}$$

5 Where is the mass of an atom concentrated? What about the charge?

5 In the nucleus; the positive charge is concentrated in the nucleus and the negative in the electrons surrounding the nucleus.

6 What are some methods of charging objects?

6 By contact, induction.

7 In charging an object by contact, are both the electrons and protons transferred from one object to another?

7 No, only the electrons.

8 Coulomb's law reminds you of what law that you have studied previously? What is the fundamental difference between these two laws?

8 Newton's law of universal gravitation. The electrostatic force may be attractive or repulsive; the gravitational force is always attractive.

9 When we say that a neutral body has no charge, does this mean that it does not contain any electrons nor protons?

9 No, it has no excess charge, i.e. the number of electrons equals the number of protons.

10 If charged particles are in motion, what additional forces are involved?

10 Magnetic force.

11 Compare the magnitudes of the charges of a proton and an electron.

11 Equal in magnitude.

12 Give examples of good conductors; good insulators.

12 Conductors — all metals; insulators — rubber, wood, asbestos, glass.

13 What do we mean by a point charge?

13 One whose size is negligible compared to the other distances involved.

14 What is the principle of conservation of charge?

14 The algebraic sum of all the electric charges in any closed system is constant. Electric charge cannot be created or destroyed; it can be transferred from one body to another.

---

15 In what respect is hydrogen different from all other atoms?

15 It has no neutrons.

---

16 Which force is much stronger than the electrical force? Is it attractive, repulsive or both?

16 Nuclear force; attractive.

MAIN IDEAS

The existence of positive and negative charge manifests itself in the following experiment: If two objects are rubbed together they will subsequently attract or repel each other. If a plastic rod is rubbed with fur, we say that the rod has acquired a negative charge and the fur a positive charge. The amount of negative charge acquired by the rod is exactly equal to the amount of positive charge obtained by the fur. Similarly, if a glass rod is rubbed with silk, the positive charge acquired by the glass will equal the negative charge acquired by the silk. Like charges repel and unlike charges attract each other.

The atom consists of three particles: the negatively charged electron, the positively charged proton and the neutral neutron. (Hydrogen is the only atom without a neutron.) The charges of the proton and electron are equal in magnitude and are equal to 1.60×10^{-19}C. The number of protons is referred to as the atomic number. The Bohr model of the atom is analogous to the model of our solar system. The nucleus corresponds to the sun, the electrons to the planets and the electrical force of the atom to the gravitational attraction of the solar system.

The hydrogen atom consists of one proton and one electron. Next in the hierarchy of atoms is helium, its nucleus is comprised of two protons and two neutrons and it has two orbiting electrons. A helium atom minus two electrons is called an alpha particle.

A conductor is a material in which charges move about freely. A nonconductor is called an insulator or a dielectric.

Charging a conductor by induction: a) When a negatively charged rod is brought near conductor AB (not touching), the free electrons will be repelled toward side B leaving region A positively charged.

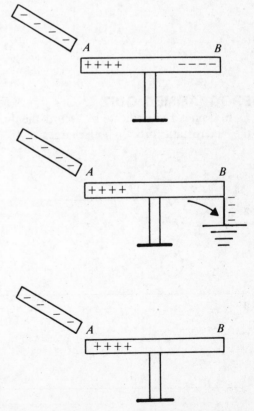

b) With the charged rod still near A the conductor is grounded, giving the electrons the opportunity to escape.

c) With the charged rod remaining in the same position, the ground connection is broken leaving the conductor positively charged.

d) When the charged rod is removed, the positive charge is uniformly distributed at the surface of the conductor. It should be noted that in the entire process the negatively charged rod did not lose any of its charge.

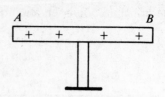

Consider two charges q_1 and q_2 separated by a distance r. The force of attraction or repulsion between the two charges is given by Coulomb's law, $F = \dfrac{1}{4\pi\epsilon_0} \dfrac{|q_1 q_2|}{r^2} = \dfrac{k|q_1 q_2|}{r^2}$, where q_1 and q_2 are measured in coulombs, r in meters, F in newtons and $\epsilon_0 = 8.854188 \times 10^{-12} C^2 \cdot N^{-1} \cdot m^{-2}$. Thus $k = 1/4\pi\epsilon_0 = 8.98755 \times 10^9 N \cdot m^2 \cdot C^{-2} \approx 9 \times 10^9 N \cdot m^2 \cdot C^{-2}$ and we will use this value in solving problems in electrostatics. Since electric charges exert forces on one another, vector addition and the procedure for solving equilibrium problems must be used *here*.

Problem solving strategy:

1 Be consistent with units:

$$F = \frac{1}{4\pi\epsilon_0} \frac{|q_1 q_2|}{r^2}$$

where F is in newtons, q_1 and q_2 are in coulombs, and r is in meters.

$$\frac{1}{4\pi\epsilon_0} = 9.0 \times 10^9 \ N \cdot m^2 \cdot C^{-2}.$$

If the charge is expressed in microcoulombs, remember that $1 \ \mu C = 10^{-6} \ C$.

2 Use k for $\dfrac{1}{4\pi\epsilon_0}$ in problems where all the terms are expressed in symbols.

3 If the forces acting on a single charge are caused by two or more other charges, then the total force on the charge is the resultant of the individual forces. Review the material on vector addition and equilibrium.

PROGRAMMED QUIZ

1 In frames 1–4, indicate by vectors the direction of the electrostatic force on both charges.

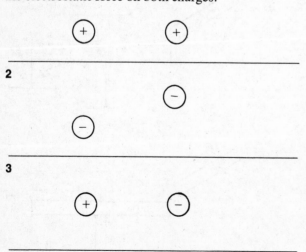

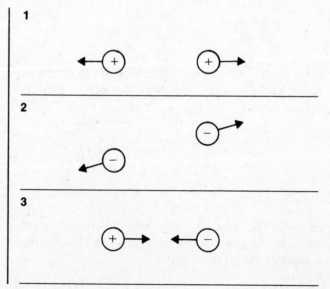

4

4

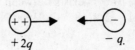

Note that, in accordance with Newton's third law, the forces are equal and opposite.

5 Indicate by vectors the electrostatic forces on q_3. All three charges are equal in magnitude.

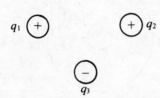

5

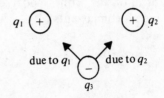

6 Indicate by a vector the resultant of the electrostatic forces on q_3.

6

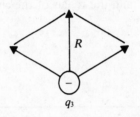

7 Show what happens to the charges when the positively charged rod is brought near the piece of fur.

7

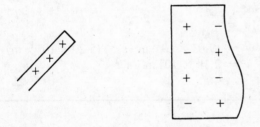

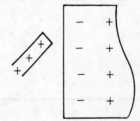

8 Two charges, both $+ 2 \times 10^{-9}$ C, are 5 cm apart. What is the force between them? Is it attractive or repulsive?

$$q_1 = q_2 = q$$

8

$$F = \frac{1}{4\pi\epsilon_0} \frac{q^2}{r^2}$$
$$= \frac{(9.0 \times 10^9 \text{ N} \cdot \text{m}^2 \cdot \text{C}^{-2})\,(2 \times 10^{-9}\text{C})^2}{(0.05 \text{ m})^2}$$
$$= 1.44 \times 10^{-5} \text{ N}$$

Repulsive since both charges are positive.

9 A force of 4×10^{-4} N exists between two charges, $+3 \times 10^{-9}$ C and -2×10^{-9} C. What is the distance separating them?

9

$$F = \frac{1}{4\pi\epsilon_0} \frac{|q_1 q_2|}{r^2}$$

$$r^2 = \frac{(9.0 \times 10^9 \, \text{N} \cdot \text{m}^2 \cdot \text{C}^{-2})(3 \times 10^{-9} \, \text{C})(2 \times 10^{-9} \, \text{C})}{4 \times 10^{-4} \, \text{N}}$$

$$r = 1.16 \times 10^{-2} \, \text{m}$$

10 Draw a sketch of the Bohr model of atomic hydrogen labelling all components.

10

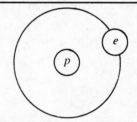

11 Find the force of attraction between the electron and the proton. The charge of the electron is 1.60×10^{-19} C and the radius of the circular orbit is 5.29×10^{-11} m.

11

$$F = \frac{1}{4\pi\epsilon_0} \frac{|q_1 q_2|}{r^2}$$

$$= \frac{(9 \times 10^9 \, \text{N} \cdot \text{m}^2 \cdot \text{C}^{-2}) \, (1.60 \times 10^{-19} \, \text{C})^2}{(5.29 \times 10^{-11} \, \text{m})^2}$$

$$= 8.23 \times 10^{-8} \, \text{N}$$

12 Find the radial acceleration of the electron. Note that the centripetal force is provided by the electrostatic force. The mass of the electron is 9.11×10^{-31} kg.

12

$$F = ma$$

$$a = \frac{8.23 \times 10^{-8} \, \text{N}}{9.11 \times 10^{-31} \, \text{kg}}$$

$$= 9.03 \times 10^{22} \, \text{m} \cdot \text{s}^{-2}$$

13 What is the velocity of the electron?

13

$$a = \frac{v^2}{r}$$

$$v^2 = (9.03 \times 10^{22} \, \text{m} \cdot \text{s}^{-2}) \, (5.29 \times 10^{-11} \, \text{m})$$

$$v = 2.19 \times 10^6 \, \text{m} \cdot \text{s}^{-1}$$

14 Find the net force on the negative charge as shown.

14

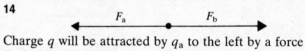

Charge q will be attracted by q_a to the left by a force F_a. It will also be attracted to the right by a force F_b.

$$F = \frac{1}{4\pi\epsilon_0} \frac{|q_1 q_2|}{r^2}$$

$$F_a = \frac{(9 \times 10^9 \, \text{N} \cdot \text{m}^2 \cdot \text{C}^{-2}) \, (3 \times 10^{-6} \, \text{C}) \, (4 \times 10^{-6} \, \text{C})}{(1 \, \text{m})^2}$$

$$= 0.108 \, \text{N} = \text{force on } q \text{ due to } q_a$$

$$F_b = \frac{(9 \times 10^9 \, \text{N} \cdot \text{m}^2 \cdot \text{C}^{-2}) \, (5 \times 10^{-6} \, \text{C}) \, (4 \times 10^{-6} \, \text{C})}{(2 \, \text{m})^2}$$

$$= 0.045 \, \text{N} = \text{force on } q \text{ due to } q_b.$$

The net force on $q = 0.108 \, \text{N} - 0.045 \, \text{N} = 0.063 \, \text{N}$ to the left.

The force diagram for problem 14:

q_a •——1 m——• q ——— 2 m ——— • q_b

STEP BY STEP SOLUTIONS OF PROBLEMS

Problem 1 A positive and a negative point charge are located on the x-axis at $(a, 0)$ and $(-a, 0)$ respectively. What is the force on a positive charge located on the y-axis at $(0, h)$? All three charges have the same magnitude.

1 Draw a sketch. If $h >> a$, the pair of equal and opposite charges is called an electric dipole.

1

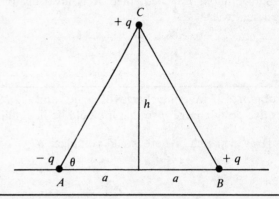

2 Draw a diagram to show the forces acting on the charge at C.

2 F_1 is a force of repulsion and F_2 is a force of attraction. Their magnitudes are equal to each other.

3 Construct a set of rectangular axes and resolve into rectangular components all forces acting on C.

3

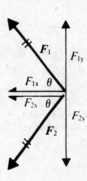

4 Find the resultant force R in terms of F_1. Note $R = \Sigma F_x$.

4

$\Sigma F_y = 0$, since magnitude of F_{1y} = magnitude of F_{2y}.
$\Sigma F_x = F_{1x} + F_{2x} = 2F_{1x}$ (since $F_{1x} = F_{2x}$).

$$R = 2F_1 \cos \theta = 2F_1 \frac{a}{\sqrt{a^2 + h^2}}.$$

5 Use Coulomb's law to find F_1.
$q_1 = q_2 = q$

5

$$F_1 = \frac{k\,q^2}{a^2 + h^2}$$

From the Pythagorean theorem,

$$BC = \sqrt{a^2 + h^2}$$

6 Substitute the value of F_1 in frame 4 and solve for R.	**6** $$R = \frac{2kq^2a}{(a^2 + h^2)^{3/2}}$$
7 Show that if $h \gg a$, then R is inversely proportional to h^3.	**7** $R = \dfrac{2kq^2a}{h^3}$, since a^2 can be neglected if $h \gg a$.

Problem 2 Two point charges of $+ 5\mu C$ and $- 2\mu C$ are fastened to a table 1 m apart. Where should we place a positive point charge q so that it would be in equilibrium?

8 Draw a sketch. Where would you place q?

8

$$q_1 = + 5\,\mu\,C \qquad q_2 = - 2\,\mu\,C$$

We could not place q between q_1 and q_2 because q_2 would attract q and q_1 would repel q in the same direction. Therefore q could not achieve equilibrium in this position. Likewise if q was placed to the left of q_1, the force of repulsion from q_1 would not balance the force of attraction from q_2. Hence q must be placed to the right of q_2.

9 Draw a free-body diagram for q. Let F_{1x} be the force of repulsion on q due to q_1 and F_{2x} be the force of attraction on q due to q_2.

9

10 Using Coulomb's law express F_{1x} and F_{2x} in terms of the given variables.

10

$$F_{1x} = \frac{kqq_1}{x^2} = \frac{kq(5\mu C)}{x^2}$$

$$F_{2x} = \frac{kqq_2}{(x - 1\text{ m})^2} = \frac{kq(2\mu C)}{(x - 1\text{ m})^2}$$

11 Set $\Sigma F_x = 0$.

11 $F_{1x} + F_{2x} = 0$. Note that F_{1x} is positive and F_{2x} is negative.

$$\frac{kq(5\mu C)}{x^2} - \frac{kq(2\mu C)}{(x - 1\text{ m})^2} = 0$$

12 Simplify and obtain the resulting quadratic. Solve for x.

12
$3x^2 - 10x + 5 = 0$
$$x = 2.72 \text{ m}$$
$$x = 0.613 \text{ m}$$
We cannot accept 0.613 m as a solution since q cannot lie between q_1 and q_2.

The student should verify that if he had placed q to the left of q_1, the solution to the resulting quadratic $(3x^2 + 10x + 5 = 0)$ would be $- 2.72$ m and $- 0.613$ m, denoting that q should be to the right of q_1.

Problem 3 Two equally charged spheres, each having a mass of 0.2 kg are suspended from the same point by insulating threads 0.1 m long. If the spheres, which should be considered as point charges, are in equilibrium (due to repulsion) when they are 0.12 m apart, find the charge on each sphere.

13 Draw a sketch.

13

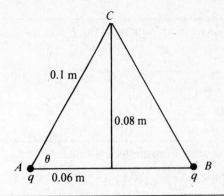

14 Select one of the charges, we will use A and draw a free-body diagram. Identify the forces.

14

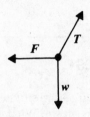

The sphere at A is in equilibrium under the action of three forces: the weight of the sphere w, the tension in the thread T, and the horizontal force F of repulsion due to the charge at B.

15 Choose a coordinate system an resolve all forces into horizontal and vertical components.

15

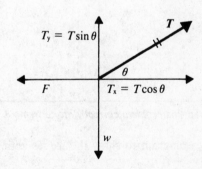

16 Set $\Sigma F_x = 0$ and $\Sigma F_y = 0$.

16

$$T \cos \theta - F = 0$$
$$T \sin \theta - w = 0$$

17 Solve both equations for T and equate them to each other. Solve for F. Note that $w = mg$.

17

$$\frac{F}{\cos \theta} = \frac{w}{\sin \theta}$$
$$\frac{F}{w} = \cot \theta$$
$$F = mg \cot \theta$$

18 What is F from Coulomb's law?
$q_1 = q_2 = q$

18

$$F = \frac{kq^2}{r^2}$$

---

19 Equate both equations for F and solve for q.

19

$$\frac{kq^2}{r^2} = mg \cot \theta$$

$$q = r \sqrt{\frac{mg \cot \theta}{k}}$$

---

20 Substitute the numerical values to find q.
$$\cot \theta = \frac{0.06}{0.08} = 0.75$$

20

$$q = 0.12 \text{ m} \sqrt{\frac{0.2 \text{ kg } (9.8 \text{ m} \cdot \text{s}^{-2}) (0.75)}{9 \times 10^9 \text{ N} \cdot \text{m}^2 \cdot \text{C}^{-2}}}$$
$$= 1.54 \times 10^{-6} \text{ C}$$

PROGRAMMED TEST

Problem 1 Three charges are situated at the corners of a 5–12–13 triangle as shown. What is the magnitude and direction of the force on the charge $q = +6\mu\text{C}$?

1

$q_1 = +8 \, \mu\text{C}$

$r_1 = 0.13$ m

$r_3 = 0.12$ m

$q = +6 \, \mu\text{C}$ α $r_2 = 0.05$ m $q_2 = -1 \, \mu\text{C}$

Answer   26.3 N at 63.6°

If you solved this problem correctly, go to frame 8. If you could not solve this problem, go through frames 2–7.

2 Draw a diagram to show the forces acting on the charge $q = +6 \, \mu\text{C}$.

2

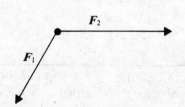

F_1 is the force of repulsion on q due to q_1. F_2 is the force of attraction on q due to q_2.

3 Set up a coordinate system and resolve the forces into horizontal and vertical components.

3

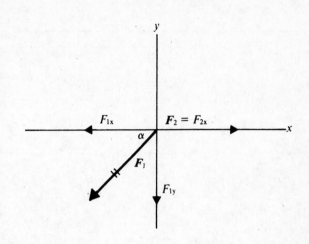

---

4 Find the magnitude of F_1 by Coulomb's law.

4

$$F_1 = \frac{1}{4\pi\epsilon_0} \frac{|qq_1|}{r_1^2}$$

$$= \frac{9 \times 10^9 \, \text{N} \cdot \text{m}^2 \cdot \text{C}^{-2} \, (6 \times 10^{-6} \, \text{C}) \, (8 \times 10^{-6} \, \text{C})}{(13 \times 10^{-2} \, \text{m})^2}$$

$$= 25.6 \, \text{N}$$

---

5 Find the numerical values of F_{1x} and F_{1y}.
$\cos \alpha = 5/13 = 0.385$, $\sin \alpha = 12/13 = 0.923$.

5

$$F_{1x} = -F_1 \cos \alpha = (-25.6 \, \text{N}) \, (0.385) = -9.86 \, \text{N}$$
$$F_{1y} = -F_1 \sin \alpha = (-25.6 \, \text{N}) \, (0.923) = -23.6 \, \text{N}$$

---

6 Find the magnitude of F_2 by Coulomb's law.

6

$$F_2 = \frac{1}{4\pi\epsilon_0} \frac{|qq_2|}{r_2^2}$$

$$= \frac{9 \times 10^9 \, \text{N} \cdot \text{m}^2 \cdot \text{C}^{-2} \, (6 \times 10^{-6} \, \text{C}) \, (1 \times 10^{-6} \, \text{C})}{(5 \times 10^{-2} \, \text{m})^2}$$

$$= 21.6 \, \text{N}$$

7 Find ΣF_x, ΣF_y and the resultant

$$F = \sqrt{\Sigma F_x{}^2 + \Sigma F_y{}^2}$$

7

$\Sigma F_x = -9.86 \text{ N} + 21.6 \text{ N} = +11.7 \text{ N}$
$\Sigma F_y = F_{1y} = -23.6 \text{ N}$
$F = \sqrt{(11.7 \text{ N})^2 + (-23.6 \text{ N})^2} = 26.3 \text{ N}$
$\tan \theta = \dfrac{|F_y|}{|F_x|} = \dfrac{23.6 \text{ N}}{11.7 \text{ N}} = 2.017$
$\theta = 63.6°$

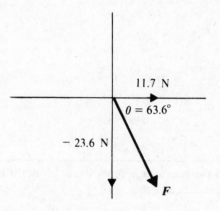

11.7 N

$\theta = 63.6°$

-23.6 N

F

---

8 **Problem 2** Two spheres are positively charged. If the combined charge is 8×10^{-8} C and they repel each other with a force of 5.4×10^{-4} N when placed 0.1 m apart, find the charge on each sphere. (Consider the charges as point charges.)

8 **Answer**
7.16×10^{-8} C, 0.84×10^{-8} C

If you solved this problem correctly, go to frame 13. If you could not solve this problem, go through frames 9–12.

---

9 Let q = the charge on one sphere. What is the charge on the second sphere?

9 8×10^{-8} C $- q$

---

10 Substitute all values in Coulomb's law.

10

$$F = \frac{1}{4\pi\epsilon_0} \frac{|q_1 q_2|}{r^2}$$

5.4×10^{-4} N

$= \dfrac{9 \times 10^9 \text{ N} \cdot \text{m}^2 \cdot \text{C}^{-2} \, (q) \, (8 + 10^{-8} \text{ C} - q)}{(0 \cdot 1 \text{ m})^2}$

---

11 What is the quadratic equation in terms of q?

11 $10^9 q^2 - 80q + 6 \times 10^{-7} = 0$

---

12 Solve for q.

12

$q_1 = 7.16 \times 10^{-8}$ C
$q_2 = 0.84 \times 10^{-8}$ C

---

13 *Problem 3* Two fixed charges, both magnitude $+q$, are separated by a distance $2a$ on a table. A conducting bead of mass m and charge $+q$ slides without friction on a nonconducting rod perpendicular to the table at a point midway between the other two charges. If the bead achieves equilibrium at a height h above the table, find m.

13

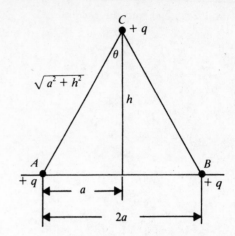

Answer

$$m = \frac{2kq^2 \cos \theta}{g(a^2 + h^2)} = \frac{2 hkq^2}{g (a^2 + h^2)^{3/2}}$$

If you could not solve this problem, go through frames 14–17.

14 Draw a free-body diagram to show all the forces acting on the charge at C. Identify the forces.

14

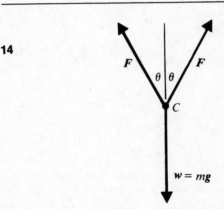

Three forces are acting on the charge at C: the weight of the bead and two forces of repulsion due to A and B.

---

15 Horizontal equilibrium is satisfied by symmetry. Thus we are only interested in vertical equilibrium. Write the condition for vertical equilibrium.

15

$$\Sigma F_y = 0$$
$$2F \cos \theta = w = mg$$

---

16 Find F by Coulomb's law.

16

$$F = \frac{kq^2}{r^2}$$
$$= \frac{kq^2}{a^2 + h^2}$$

---

17 Substitute this value of F in frame 15 and solve for m.

$$\cos \theta = \frac{h}{\sqrt{a^2 + h^2}}$$

17

$$\frac{2kq^2 \cos \theta}{a^2 + h^2} = mg$$

$$m = \frac{2kq^2 \cos \theta}{g(a^2 + h^2)} = \frac{2 hkq^2}{g (a^2 + h^2)^{3/2}}$$

25

The Electric Field

CHAPTER SUMMARY

We continue our discussion of electrical interactions. In the previous chapter we were concerned with the effects charges have on each other; here we are concerned with the effects of charges on the properties of their environment. This concept is termed the electric field. The mathematical relationships for calculating the electric field are presented as well as a technique for visualizing the field by drawing field lines. These are the basis for the formulation of Gauss's law. In addition to a mathematical analysis, many applications of Gauss's law are presented in which the electric field is calculated for closed surfaces with symmetric charge distributions inside. Charges on conductors and electrostatic shielding are also discussed.

BASIC TERMS — *Give definitions or meanings for the following:*

test charge (25-1)
vector field (25-1)
electric field (25-1)
electric dipole (25-2)
field lines (25-3)

electric flux (25-4)
Gauss's law (25-4)
Faraday's ice pail experiment (25-6)
electrostatic shielding (25-6)

PROGRAMMED QUIZ

1 The electric field reminds you of what physical phenomenon that you have studied previously?

1 Gravitational field.

2 How would you determine experimentally if a field is electrical or gravitational?

2 Compare the effects of the field on a charged and an uncharged particle.

3 A rod is positively charged at one end and negatively charged at the other end. What will happen if we place it in an electric field?

3 It will align itself with the field.

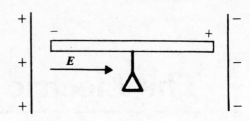

---

4 When is the force on a charge in the same direction as the electric field?

4 If the charge is positive.

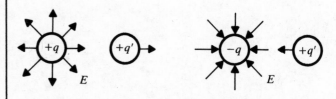

---

5 The electric field exerts a force on a point charge and a _____ on an electric dipole.

5 Torque.

---

6 Do electric field lines actually exist?

6 No, they are a device to aid us in visualizing the electric field.

---

7 Can field lines intersect?

7 No, a field line indicates the direction of acceleration of a charged particle at that point in the field. A particle can be accelerated in only one direction at a given point.

---

8 What is the electric field within a conductor in electrostatic equilibrium?

8 Zero, if the electric field is not zero, the charge would move.

---

9 As you approach an infinite sheet, the electric field increases, decreases or stays the same?

9 Stays the same; $E = \sigma/\epsilon_0$, there is no relationship with distance.

---

10 Is the electric field a vector or a scalar? If it is a vector, what is its direction?

10 A vector; the same as the direction of the force experienced by a positive test charge.

---

11 What do we mean when we say E is a vector field? Give an example of a vector field that you have studied previously.

11 Not one vector but an infinite number of vectors which vary with each point in space. Description of motion of a flowing fluid; the different points in the fluid have different velocities, therefore the velocity is a vector field.

---

12 Why must the test charge be very small?

12 So it does not alter the distribution of charge.

---

13 Can electric field lines ever close on themselves?

13 No, each field line originates on a positive charge and terminates on a negative charge.

---

14 What do we mean by a Gaussian surface?

14 Any surface, real or imaginary in space or within a physical body, to which Gauss's law is applied.

---

15 Why must the electric field just outside a conductor be perpendicular to the surface under equilibrium conditions?

15 Because any component of the electric field parallel to the surface would produce a current, i.e. the charges would move.

MAIN IDEAS

1 Electric field. If a charged body experiences a force of electrical origin at a point in space, we say that an electric field exists at that point. The magnitude of the electric field at the position of a test charge q' is given by $E = F/q'$, where F is the force (due to electric origin) acting on q'. Since the charge q' may affect the electric field, E can be defined more precisely as $E = \lim_{q' \to 0} F/q'$. If an electric field exists within a conductor, a force is exerted on every charge in the conductor. The unit of the electric field is $N \cdot C^{-1}$.

2 The magnitude of the electric field at any point at a distance r from a point charge q is given by $E = \dfrac{1}{4\pi\epsilon_0} \dfrac{q}{r^2}$, where $\dfrac{1}{4\pi\epsilon_0} \sim 9 \times 10^9 \, N \cdot m^2 \cdot C^{-2}$. The direction of the field is away from the charge if it is positive, toward the charge if it is negative.

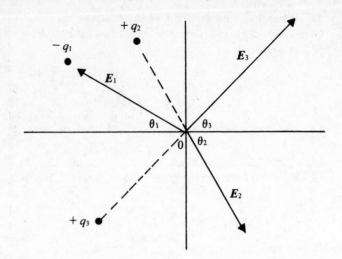

3 To find the magnitude and direction of the electric field at any point due to a number of point charges: Consider the charges $-q_1$, $+q_2$ and $+q_3$ as in the figure. The electric field at O, for example, can be obtained by placing a test charge q' at O, determining the effects on q' due to the charges and obtaining the vector sum.

The resultant electric field may be obtained as follows: a) Find the magnitude of the vectors E_1, E_2 and E_3 by using $E_1 = \dfrac{1}{4\pi\epsilon_0} \dfrac{q_1}{r_1^2}$, $E_2 = \dfrac{1}{4\pi\epsilon_0} \dfrac{q_2}{r_2^2}$ and $E_3 = \dfrac{1}{4\pi\epsilon_0} \dfrac{q_3}{r_3^2}$. The direction of the field is in the same direction as the vector displacement r when q is positive. b) Set up a coordinate system and resolve all vectors into horizontal and vertical components. c) Find ΣE_x and ΣE_y. d) Find the resultant electric field by the Pythagorean relationship $E = \sqrt{(\Sigma E_x)^2 + (\Sigma E_y)^2}$ and the angle that E makes with the x-axis by $\tan \theta_R = \left| \dfrac{\Sigma E_y}{\Sigma E_x} \right|$.

4 A field line, with regard to an electric field, is an imaginary line which indicates the direction of the field. The direction at any point is denoted by the tangent to the line of force through that point. Here are some examples of field lines.

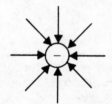

isolated negative charge

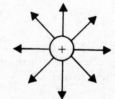

isolated positive charge

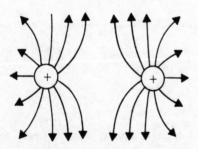

field lines between two
equal and similar charges

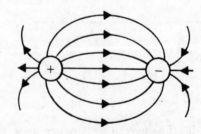

field lines between two
equal and opposite charges

Field lines are so spaced that the number of lines per unit area passing through a surface perpendicular to the direction of the field is proportional to the magnitude of the electric field. In a uniform field, field lines are straight, parallel and uniformly spaced.

5 Fields of various charge distributions:

a) point charge $E = \dfrac{1}{4\pi\epsilon_0}\dfrac{q}{r^2}$

b) uniformly charged spherical shell of radius R

$E = 0$ when $r < R$ (i.e., inside the shell)

$E = \dfrac{1}{4\pi\epsilon_0}\dfrac{q}{r^2}$ when $r \geq R$ (i.e., outside the shell or on the surface)

c) long straight line charge

$E = \dfrac{1}{2\pi\epsilon_0}\dfrac{\lambda}{r}$ where $\lambda = q/l$ and $r = $ distance from the line (wire)

d) cylindrical shell of charge which is distributed uniformly over the surface of a cylindrical shell or pipe of radius R

$E = 0$ when $r < R$

$E = \dfrac{1}{2\pi\epsilon_0}\dfrac{\lambda}{r}$ when $r > R$ and $\lambda = q/l$

e) charge q distributed over a plane of area A; the field near the plane on either side

$E = \dfrac{\sigma}{2\epsilon_0}$ where $\sigma = q/A = $ surface charge density

f) field between two large parallel charged planes if they have surface charges σ and $-\sigma$

$E = \dfrac{\sigma}{\epsilon_0}$.

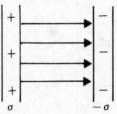

6 Open and closed surfaces. An open surface is one which has an edge or ridge like the surface of a sheet of paper. The surface is not necessarily a plane. A hemisphere, for example, is an open surface. A closed surface is one with no edge or rim. Spheres and cubes are examples of closed surfaces. A closed surface divides space into two regions – an outside volume and an inside volume.

7 Gauss's law describes how to relate the electric field through a closed surface to the charge distribution contained within the surface. Consider a closed surface surrounding a charge q. The following mathematical steps are implied in Gauss's law: a) Divide the surface into infinitesimal areas ΔA. b) Find the magnitude and direction of the electric field $\boldsymbol{E}$ at each point. c) Find the normal component $E_\perp$ of $\boldsymbol{E}$. Let θ be the angle between the normal to the surface and the radial line from q; then $E\cos\theta$ is the component of E perpendicular to the surface at each point, i.e., $E_\perp = E\cos\theta$. d) Form the products $E_\perp \Delta A$ and sum these products over the entire surface. e) Set $\Sigma E_\perp \Delta A = Q/\epsilon_0$, where $Q = \Sigma q$ and $\epsilon_0 = 1/4\pi k$ $= 8.85 \times 10^{-12}$ C$^2\cdot$N$^{-1}\cdot$m^{-2}.

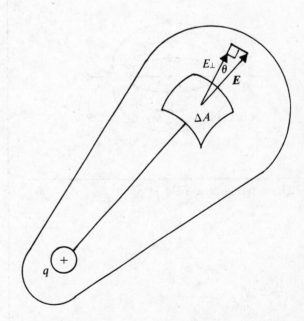

8 Electric flux. The quantity $E_\perp \Delta A$ is defined as the electric flux through the area ΔA. $\Sigma E_\perp \Delta A$ is the total electric flux out of a closed surface and it is proportional to the magnitude of the charge enclosed. The electric flux is denoted by Ψ.

9 Helpful hints in solving problems involving Gauss's law. a) If E is normal to the surface of area A at all points and has the same magnitude at these points, then $E_\perp = E =$ constant. It follows that $\Sigma E_\perp \Delta A = E A$. b) If E is parallel to the surface at all points, then $E_\perp = 0$. It follows that $\Sigma E_\perp \Delta A = 0$. c) If $E = 0$ at all points on the surface, then $\Sigma E_\perp \Delta A = 0$. d) It should be emphasized that in problems involving Gauss's law, the surface is not necessarily a real physical surface. It may be one developed by mathematical imagination. However, Gauss's law applies only to closed surfaces. e) The following steps are recommended for a Gauss's law problem: (i) Write E in terms of a given variable. Determine or assume a direction for E. (ii) Choose a closed surface (referred to as the Gaussian surface). Examine the problem for symmetry. (iii) Since we are not using integral calculus, E must be factored from the summation sign Σ. (iv) Evaluate $Q = \Sigma q$ and set up Gauss's law.

PROGRAMMED QUIZ

1 In frames 1–3, label the charges positive or negative.

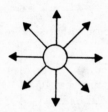

1 Positive. Remember that the direction of the electric field is always the same as the direction of a force experienced by a positive test charge. Here the test charge is repelled. Therefore the charge producing the field must be positive.

2

2 Negative. A positive test charge is attracted to a negative charge.

3

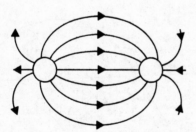

3

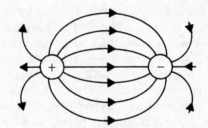

4 Draw the electric field at point *P*.

4

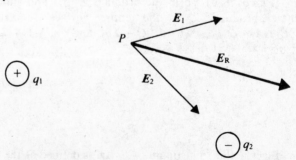

E_R is the resultant electric field due to E_1 and E_2.

5 Draw the field lines in a uniform electric field.

5

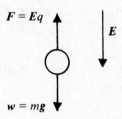

6 What must be the direction of the electric field so that an electron is in equilibrium under the combined influence of the electric field and gravity? Draw a free-body diagram.

6 Since q is negative, E must be directed downward so that $F = Eq$ is upward.

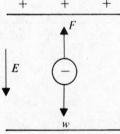

Note: for a proton in equilibrium, the direction of the electric field would be up.

7 What is the magnitude of an electric field in which the Coulomb force on an electron is equal in magnitude to the weight of the electron? Mass of an electron = 9.11×10^{-31} kg; charge of an electron = 1.602×10^{-19} C.

7

$$F = w$$
$$Eq = mg$$
$$E = \frac{(9.11 \times 10^{-31} \text{ kg}) (9.8 \text{ m} \cdot \text{s}^{-2})}{1.602 \times 10^{-19} \text{ C}}$$
$$= 5.57 \times 10^{-11} \text{ N} \cdot \text{C}^{-1}$$

8 If the electric field above was generated by two large oppositely charged parallel plates include them in the diagram.

8

The electron is attracted by the top (positive) plate and repelled by the bottom (negative) plate. Thus $F = Eq$ upward and $w = mg$ downward. The direction of E is from the positive plate to the negative plate.

9 What if the particle was a proton?

9 For a proton in equilibrium, we would reverse the plates.

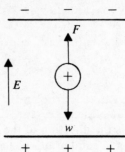

10 What is the magnitude of the force on a test charge due to a charge $q = 3 \times 10^{-9}$ C which is 0.5 m away?

10

$$F = \frac{1}{4\pi\epsilon_0} \frac{|qq'|}{r^2}$$

$$= \frac{(9 \times 10^9 \text{ N} \cdot \text{m}^2 \cdot \text{C}^{-2}) (3 \times 10^{-9} \text{ C}) \, q'}{(0.5 \text{ m})^2}$$

$$= 108 \text{ N} \cdot \text{C}^{-1} \, (q')$$

11 What is the magnitude of the electric field at this point?

11

$$E = \frac{F}{q'}$$

$$= \frac{108 \text{ N} \cdot \text{C}^{-1} \, (q')}{q'} = 108 \text{ N} \cdot \text{C}^{-1}$$

12 At what distance from a charge 4×10^{-9} C is the electric field 300 N $\cdot$ C^{-1}?

12

$$E = \frac{1}{4\pi\epsilon_0} \frac{q}{r^2}$$

$$r^2 = \frac{(9 \times 10^9 \text{ N} \cdot \text{m}^2 \cdot \text{C}^{-2}) (4 \times 10^{-9} \text{ C})}{300 \text{ N} \cdot \text{C}^{-1}}$$

$$r = 0.346 \text{ m}$$

13 Frames 13–16 refer to the following charge distribution.

13

$$E_1 = \frac{1}{4\pi\epsilon_0} \frac{q_1}{r^2}$$

$$= \frac{(9 \times 10^9 \text{ N} \cdot \text{m}^2 \cdot \text{C}^{-2}) (12 \times 10^{-9} \text{ C})}{(0.6 \text{ m})^2}$$

$$= 300 \text{ N} \cdot \text{C}^{-1} \text{ downward}$$

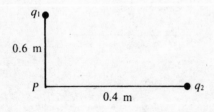

$q_1 = 12 \times 10^{-9}$ C, $\qquad q_2 = -8 \times 10^{-9}$ C.
Find E_1 at the point P due to q_1.

14 Find E_2 at point P due to q_2.

14

$$E_2 = \frac{1}{4\pi\epsilon_0} \frac{q_2}{r^2}$$

$$= \frac{(9 \times 10^9 \text{ N} \cdot \text{m}^2 \cdot \text{C}^{-2}) (8 \times 10^{-9} \text{ C})}{(0.4 \text{ m})^2}$$

$$= 450 \text{ N} \cdot \text{C}^{-1} \text{ to the right}$$

---

15 Find the resultant electric field at point P.

15

$$E = \sqrt{(\Sigma E_x)^2 + (\Sigma E_y)^2}$$

$$= \sqrt{(450 \text{ N} \cdot \text{C}^{-1})^2 + (300 \text{ N} \cdot \text{C}^{-1})^2}$$

$$= 541 \text{ N}$$

$$\tan \theta = \frac{|\Sigma E_y|}{|\Sigma E_x|} = \frac{300 \text{ N} \cdot \text{C}^{-1}}{450 \text{ N} \cdot \text{C}^{-1}}$$

$$\theta = 33.7°$$

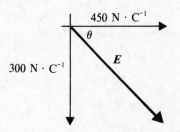

---

16 What is the charge enclosed by a surface 1 m^2 in area at right angles to an electric field of 200 N $\cdot$ C^{-1}?

16 Apply Gauss's law, $\Sigma E_\perp A = \Sigma q/\epsilon_0$. Since E is at right angles to the surface area at all points and has the same magnitude at all points of the surface, then $E_\perp = E$ and $\Sigma E_\perp \Delta A = EA$. Therefore,

$$EA = \frac{Q}{\epsilon_0}$$

$$Q = (200 \text{ N} \cdot \text{C}^{-1}) (1 \text{ m}^2) (8.85 \times 10^{-12} \text{ C}^2 \cdot \text{N}^{-1} \cdot \text{m}^{-2})$$

$$= 1.77 \times 10^{-9} \text{ C}$$

---

17 What is the electric field at point P outside an insulating sphere of radius R? First draw the Gaussian surface. The charge within the surface is Q.

17

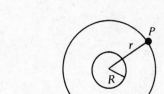

The Gaussian surface is a sphere of radius r, concentric with the insulating sphere.

18 What is the equation for the electric field at P?

18 Apply Gauss's law, $\Sigma E_\perp A = \Sigma q/\epsilon_0$. Since E is at right angles to the surface area at all points and has the same magnitude at all points of the surface, then $E_\perp = E$ and $\Sigma E_\perp \Delta A = EA$. Therefore,

$$EA = \frac{Q}{\epsilon_0} \text{ where } A = 4\pi r^2$$

$$E4\pi r^2 = \frac{Q}{\epsilon_0}$$

$$E = \frac{Q}{4\pi\epsilon_0 r^2}$$

---

19 Consider a charged insulated conductor which has a surface charge density $\sigma = q/A$. What is the electric field a short distance from the surface? In order to use Gauss's law, set up a cylindrical Gaussian surface with one end face within the conductor, while the other lies outside.

19

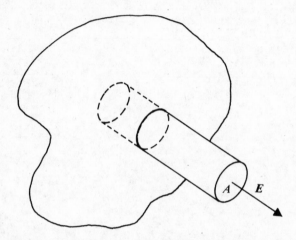

---

20 Why is the direction of E close to the surface normal to the surface?

20 Assume that the direction of E is not perpendicular to the surface. Hence it has a component which lies on the surface. This component would cause electric charges to move along the surface of the conductor, thus producing a current. But there are no such currents because we have assumed electrostatic equilibrium. Hence, E is normal to the surface.

---

21 What is the electric field inside the conductor? through the curved surface of the cylinder? through the outside face of the cylinder?

21 Zero, zero, E.

---

22 Apply Gauss's law to find E.

22

$$\Sigma E_\perp \Delta A = EA = \frac{Q}{\epsilon_0} = \frac{\sigma A}{\epsilon_0};$$

$$E = \frac{Q}{\epsilon_0}.$$

---

23 In frames 23–25 derive Coulomb's law on the basis of Gauss's law by considering the field due to a point charge q. Select as a Gaussian surface a spherical surface of radius r. What is $E_\perp$?

23 $E_\perp = E =$ constant at all points of the surface.

---

24 Write out Gauss's law for this surface and solve for E.

24

$$\Sigma E_{\perp}\Delta A = E\Sigma\Delta A = 4\pi r^2 E = \frac{q}{\epsilon_0}$$

$$E = \frac{1}{4\pi\epsilon_0}\frac{q}{r}$$

---

25 Find the force on a point charge q' at a distance r from the charge q on the basis of the above.

25

$$F = q'E$$

$$= \frac{1}{4\pi\epsilon_0}\frac{qq'}{r^2}$$

which is Coulomb's law.

---

26 A long straight wire has a charge per unit length $\lambda = 4 \times 10^{-12}\ \text{C} \cdot \text{m}^{-1}$. At what distance from the wire is the electric field equal to $0.8\ \text{N} \cdot \text{C}^{-1}$? Use

$$E = \frac{\lambda}{2\pi r\epsilon_0}.$$

26

$$r = \frac{\lambda}{2\pi\epsilon_0 E}$$

$$= \frac{4 \times 10^{-12}\ \text{C} \cdot \text{m}^{-1}}{2\pi(8.85 \times 10^{-12}\ \text{C}^2 \cdot \text{N}^{-1} \cdot \text{m}^{-2})(0.8\ \text{N} \cdot \text{C}^{-1})}$$

$$= 0.0899\ \text{m}$$

STEP BY STEP SOLUTIONS OF PROBLEMS

Problem 1 Point charges q_1 and q_2 of $+ 2 \times 10^{-8}$ C and $- 5 \times 10^{-8}$ C respectively are placed 0.05 m apart, as in the figure. Compute the electric field at C.

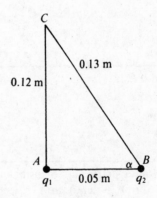

1 Draw a diagram to show the electric field at C due to q_1 and q_2. Identify the respective fields.

1 E_1 is directed along AC away from q_1. E_2 is directed along CB towards q_2.

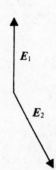

2 Compute the magnitude of the fields at C due to q_1 and q_2.

2

$$E = \frac{1}{4\pi\epsilon_0}\frac{q}{r^2}$$

$$E_1 = \frac{9 \times 10^9 \, \text{N} \cdot \text{m}^2 \cdot \text{C}^{-2} \, (2 \times 10^{-8} \, \text{C})}{(0.12 \, \text{m})^2}$$

$$= 1.25 \times 10^4 \, \text{N} \cdot \text{C}^{-1}$$

$$E_2 = \frac{9 \times 10^9 \, \text{N} \cdot \text{m}^2 \cdot \text{C}^{-2} \, (5 \times 10^{-8} \, \text{C})}{(0.13 \, \text{m})^2}$$

$$= 2.66 \times 10^4 \, \text{N} \cdot \text{C}^{-1}$$

---

3 Set up a coordinate system and resolve the fields into horizontal and vertical components.

3

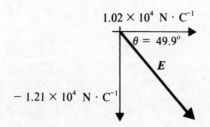

$$\sin \alpha = 0.923$$
$$\cos \alpha = 0.385$$
$$E_{2x} = E_2 \cos \alpha = 0.385 \, E_2$$
$$E_{2y} = E_2 \sin \alpha = -0.923 \, E_2$$

---

4 Find ΣE_x and ΣE_y.

4

$$\Sigma E_x = 2.66 \times 10^4 \, \text{N} \cdot \text{C}^{-1} \, (0.385) = 1.02 \times 10^4 \, \text{N} \cdot \text{C}^{-1}$$
$$\Sigma E_y = 1.25 \times 10^4 \, \text{N} \cdot \text{C}^{-1} - 2.66 \times 10^4 \, \text{N} \cdot \text{C}^{-1} \, (0.923)$$
$$= -1.21 \times 10^4 \, \text{N} \cdot \text{C}^{-1}$$

---

5 Find the resultant electric field by using
$$E = \sqrt{(\Sigma E_x)^2 + (\Sigma E_y)^2} \text{ and}$$

$$\tan \theta_R = \frac{|\Sigma E_y|}{|\Sigma E_x|}.$$

5

$$E = \sqrt{(1.02 \times 10^4 \, \text{N} \cdot \text{C}^{-1})^2 + (-1.21 \times 10^4 \, \text{N} \cdot \text{C}^{-1})^2}$$
$$= 1.58 \times 10^4 \, \text{N} \cdot \text{C}^{-1}$$

$$\tan \theta_R = \frac{|\Sigma E_y|}{|\Sigma E_x|} = \frac{1.21 \times 10^4 \, \text{N} \cdot \text{C}^{-1}}{1.02 \times 10^4 \, \text{N} \cdot \text{C}^{-1}}$$
$$\theta_R = 49.9°$$

Problem 2 An electron is projected into a uniform electric field of 10^4 N $\cdot$ C^{-1} directed vertically upward. The initial velocity of the electron is 10^7 m $\cdot$ s^{-1} and the angle of elevation is 60°. a) Find the maximum elevation of the electron, i.e. the maximum distance the electron rises vertically above its initial position. b) Find the range of the elevation, i.e. the horizontal distance the electron must travel to return to its original elevation.

6 Make a sketch of the trajectory of the electron.

6

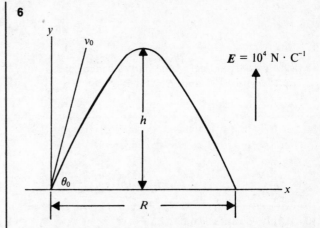

7 The key to this problem is to find the acceleration of the electron. The net force on the electron is primarily due to the electric field. The gravitational influence is negligible. Find a_y.

7 The direction of the field is upward. Therefore the force on the electron is downward. The x-acceleration is zero and the y-acceleration can be obtained from Newton's second law and the definition of the electric field intensity. Thus we have

$$a_y = \frac{F}{m} = \frac{e E}{m}$$

8 Find the maximum elevation by using

$$h = \frac{v_0^2 \sin^2 \theta_0}{2 a_y}.$$

Note that we are substituting the acceleration of the electron for g.

8

$$h = \frac{m v_0^2 \sin^2 \theta_0}{2 e E}$$

9 Substitute the given data and solve.

9
$$h = \frac{9.1 \times 10^{-31} \text{ kg} (10^7 \text{ m} \cdot \text{s}^{-1})^2 \sin^2 60°}{2 (1.60 \times 10^{-19} \text{ C})(10^4 \text{ N} \cdot \text{C}^{-1})}$$
$$= 2.13 \times 10^{-2} \text{ m} = 2.13 \text{ cm}$$

10 Find the range of the electron by using

$$R = \frac{v_0^2 \sin 2\theta_0}{a_y}.$$

10
$$R = \frac{m v_0^2 \sin 2\theta_0}{e E}$$

11 Substitute the given data and solve.

11
$$R = \frac{9.1 \times 10^{-31} \text{ kg} (10^7 \text{ m} \cdot \text{s}^{-1})^2 \sin 120°}{(1.60 \times 10^{-19} \text{ C})(10^4 \text{ N} \cdot \text{C}^{-1})}$$
$$= 4.93 \times 10^{-2} \text{ m} = 4.93 \text{ cm}$$

Problem 3 Consider a sphere of radius R with a uniform positive charge distribution $\rho = q/V$. Using Gauss's law, prove: a) that the magnitude of the electric field outside the spherical volume is $E = q/4\pi\epsilon_0 r^2 = \rho R^3/3\epsilon_0 r^2$, b) that the magnitude of the electric field inside the sphere at a distance r from the center is $E = \rho r/3\epsilon_0$. c) Compare the results of a) and b) when $r = R$.

12 Draw a spherical Gaussian surface of radius $r > R$. Identify r, R and E.	**12**	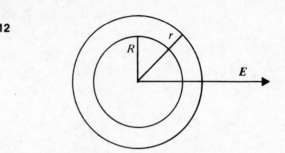	

13 Apply Gauss's law.	**13** $\sum E_\perp \Delta A = \dfrac{Q}{\epsilon_0}$
14 Since $E_\perp = E$, factor E from the summation sign.	**14** $E \sum \Delta A = \dfrac{Q}{\epsilon_0}$
15 What is the value of $\sum \Delta A$? What is Q?	**15** $\sum \Delta A = 4\pi r^2$ $Q = \text{the total charge} = q.$
16 Find E.	**16** $E = \dfrac{q}{4\pi\epsilon_0 r^2}$
17 Express E in terms of ρ, R and r.	**17** $q = \rho V \quad \text{and} \quad V = (4/3)\pi R^3$ $\therefore E = \dfrac{\rho R^3}{3\epsilon_0 r^2}$
18 For part b) draw a spherical Gaussian surface of radius $r < R$. Identify r, R and **E**.	**18**

19 Since q is the charge contained within the volume V, let q' be the charge contained within the volume V' (radius r). Express q' in terms of q.

19 Since $\rho = \dfrac{q}{V} = \dfrac{q'}{V'}$,

$$q' = \frac{qV'}{V} = \frac{q\,(4/3)\,\pi\,r^3}{(4/3)\,\pi\,R^3}$$

$$\therefore \; q' = q\left(\frac{r}{R}\right)^3$$

20 Apply Gauss's law to the surface of radius r. Note that the charge within this surface is q'. However, express E in terms of q.

20

$$E = \frac{q'}{4\,\pi\,\epsilon_0\,r^2} = \frac{q\,r}{4\,\pi\,\epsilon_0\,R^3}$$

21 Express E in terms of ρ and r.

21 Since $\rho = \dfrac{q}{V} = \dfrac{q}{(4/3)\,\pi\,R^3}$,

$$q = (4/3)\,\pi\,R^3\,\rho .$$

$$\therefore \; E = \frac{q\,r}{4\,\pi\,\epsilon_0\,R^3} = \frac{(4/3)\,\pi\,R^3\,\rho\,r}{4\,\pi\,\epsilon_0\,R^3}$$

$$= \frac{\rho\,r}{3\,\epsilon_0}$$

22 Part c. Compare a) and b) when $r = R$.

22 When $r = R$,

for a) $E = \dfrac{\rho\,R^3}{3\,\epsilon_0\,r^2} = \dfrac{\rho\,R^3}{3\,\epsilon_0\,R^2} = \dfrac{\rho\,R}{3\,\epsilon_0}$

for b) $E = \dfrac{\rho\,r}{3\,\epsilon_0} = \dfrac{\rho\,R}{3\,\epsilon_0}$

PROGRAMMED TEST

1 *Problem 1* Calculate the magnitude and direction of the electric field at C (see figure).

1

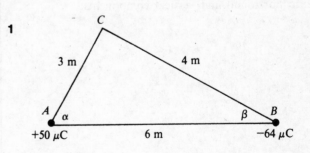

Answer

$7.38 \times 10^4\,\mathrm{N \cdot C^{-1}}$, $10.6°$

If you solved this problem correctly, go to frame 8. If you could not solve the problem, go through frames 2–7.

2 Draw a diagram to indicate the electric field at C due to the charges at A and B.

2

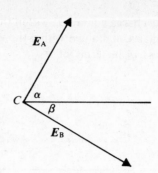

---

3 Compute the magnitude of the electric field at C due to A and B.

3

$$E = \frac{1}{4\pi\epsilon_0} \frac{q}{r^2}$$

$$E_A = \frac{9 \times 10^9 \, \text{N} \cdot \text{m}^2 \cdot \text{C}^{-2} \, (50 \times 10^{-6} \, \text{C})}{(3 \, \text{m})^2}$$

$$= 5 \times 10^4 \, \text{N} \cdot \text{C}^{-1}$$

$$E_B = \frac{9 \times 10^9 \, \text{N} \cdot \text{m}^2 \cdot \text{C}^{-2} \, (64 \times 10^{-6} \, \text{C})}{(4 \, \text{m})^2}$$

$$= 3.6 \times 10^4 \, \text{N} \cdot \text{C}^{-1}$$

---

4 Since α and β are needed to find the components of E_A and E_B, find α and β by the law of cosines.

4 Using the cosine law, $a^2 = b^2 + c^2 - 2bc \cos \alpha$,

$$\cos \alpha = \frac{b^2 + c^2 - a^2}{2bc} = \frac{(3 \, \text{m})^2 + (6 \, \text{m})^2 - (4 \, \text{m})^2}{2(3 \, \text{m})(6 \, \text{m})}$$

$$= 0.806$$
$$\alpha = 36.3°$$

$$\cos \beta = \frac{a^2 + c^2 - b^2}{2ac} = \frac{(4 \, \text{m})^2 + (6 \, \text{m})^2 - (3 \, \text{m})^2}{2(4 \, \text{m})(6 \, \text{m})}$$

$$= 0.896$$
$$\beta = 26.4°$$

---

5 Set up a coordinate system and resolve the fields into horizontal and vertical components.

5

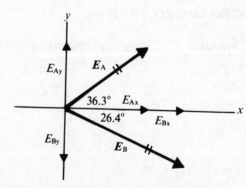

$E_{Ax} = 5 \times 10^4 \, \text{N} \cdot \text{C}^{-1} \cos 36.3° = 4.03 \times 10^4 \, \text{N} \cdot \text{C}^{-1}$
$E_{Ay} = 5 \times 10^4 \, \text{N} \cdot \text{C}^{-1} \sin 36.3° = 2.96 \times 10^4 \, \text{N} \cdot \text{C}^{-1}$
$E_{Bx} = 3.6 \times 10^4 \, \text{N} \cdot \text{C}^{-1} \cos 26.4° = 3.22 \times 10^4 \, \text{N} \cdot \text{C}^{-1}$
$E_{By} = -3.6 \times 10^4 \, \text{N} \cdot \text{C}^{-1} \sin 26.4° = -1.60 \times 10^4 \, \text{N} \cdot \text{C}^{-1}$

6 Find ΣE_x and ΣE_y.

6 $\Sigma E_x = 4.03 \times 10^4 \, \text{N} \cdot \text{C}^{-1} + 3.22 \times 10^4 \, \text{N} \cdot \text{C}^{-1}$
$\qquad = 7.25 \times 10^4 \, \text{N} \cdot \text{C}^{-1}$
$\Sigma E_y = 2.96 \times 10^4 \, \text{N} \cdot \text{C}^{-1} - 1.60 \times 10^4 \, \text{N} \cdot \text{C}^{-1}$
$\qquad = 1.36 \times 10^4 \, \text{N} \cdot \text{C}^{-1}$

---

7 Find the resultant electric field by using
$E = \sqrt{(\Sigma E_x)^2 + (\Sigma E_y)^2}$ and

$\tan \theta_R = \dfrac{|\Sigma E_y|}{|\Sigma E_x|}$.

7

$E = \sqrt{(7.25 \times 10^4 \, \text{N} \cdot \text{C}^{-1})^2 + (1.36 \times 10^4 \, \text{N} \cdot \text{C}^{-1})^2}$
$\quad = 7.38 \times 10^4 \, \text{N} \cdot \text{C}^{-1}$

$\tan \theta_R = \dfrac{1.36 \times 10^4 \, \text{N} \cdot \text{C}^{-1}}{7.25 \times 10^4 \, \text{N} \cdot \text{C}^{-1}} = 0.188$

$\theta_R = 10.6°$

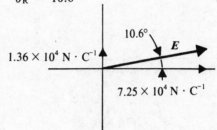

---

8 **Problem 2** An electron is projected into a uniform field of $1.5 \times 10^4 \, \text{N} \cdot \text{C}^{-1}$ between the parallel plates as in the figure. The direction of the field is vertically upward and the field is zero except in the space between the plates. If the electron enters the field as shown (midway between the plates) and misses the bottom plate as it emerges, find the initial velocity of the electron.

8

Answer
$1.09 \times 10^7 \, \text{m} \cdot \text{s}^{-1}$

If you solved the problem correctly, go to frame 15. If you could not solve the problem, go through frames 9–14.

9 Find a_y.

9 The direction of the field is upward, so the force on the electron is downward. The x-acceleration is zero and the y-acceleration can be obtained from

$$a_y = \frac{F}{m} = \frac{-eE}{m}.$$

---

10 What is the expression for x after t seconds of flight?

10 $\qquad x = v_0 t$

---

11 What is the expression for y after t seconds of flight?

11
$$y = v_{0y}t + \tfrac{1}{2}at^2$$
$$= -\tfrac{1}{2}\left(\frac{eE}{m}\right)t^2$$

---

12 Eliminate t from the expressions for x and y.

12
$$y = \frac{-eE}{2mv_0^2}x^2$$

---

13 Solve for v_0.

13
$$v_0 = x\sqrt{\frac{-eE}{2my}}$$

---

14 Substitute given values and solve for v_0.

14
$$v_0 = 0.03\ \text{m}\sqrt{\frac{-1.60\times10^{-19}\,\text{C}\,(1.5\times10^{4}\,\text{N}\cdot\text{C}^{-1})}{2(9.1\times10^{-31}\,\text{kg})(-0.01\ \text{m})}}$$
$$= 1.09\times10^{7}\ \text{m}\cdot\text{s}^{-1}$$

---

15 *Problem 3* a) Find the electric field within a long straight rod with uniform positive charge density $\rho = q/V$ at a distance $r \leqslant R$ from its axis, where R = radius of the rod. b) What is the electric field at a distance $r > R$ from the axis of the rod in terms of the charge per unit length λ? c) Compare the results of a) and b) when $r = R$.

15 *Answer*
$$E = \frac{\rho r}{2\epsilon_0},\ E = \frac{\lambda r}{2\pi R^2 \epsilon_0},$$
$$E = \frac{\lambda}{2\pi \epsilon_0 r}\ \text{in both cases.}$$

If you could not solve this problem, go through frames 16-22.

---

16 Draw a cylindrical Gaussian surface of radius $r < R$ and length L = length of rod.

16

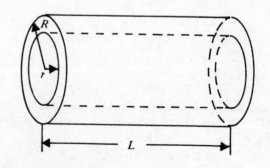

17 Since q is the charge contained within the volume V, let q' be the charge contained within the volume V' (radius r). Express q' in terms of q.

17 Since $\rho = \dfrac{q}{V} = \dfrac{q'}{V'}$,

$$q' = \frac{q V'}{V} = \frac{q \pi r^2 L}{\pi R^2 L} = q\left(\frac{r}{R}\right)^2$$

---

18 Apply Gauss's law to the cylindrical surface of radius r. (Note that there is no flux through the ends of the cylinder.)

18

$$\Sigma E_\perp \Delta A = \frac{Q}{\epsilon_0}$$

$$E(2\pi r L) = \frac{q'}{\epsilon_0} = \frac{q r^2}{\epsilon_0 R^2}$$

since $q = \rho V = \rho(\pi R^2 L)$,

$$E(2\pi r L) = \frac{\pi r^2 \rho L}{\epsilon_0}$$

$$E = \frac{\rho r}{2\epsilon_0}$$

---

19 What is the electric field at a distance $r > R$ from the axis of the rod in terms of the charge per unit length λ? Apply Gauss's law to the cylindrical surface of radius r where $r > R$ and λL is the enclosed charge (λ is the charge per unit length).

19

$$\Sigma E_\perp \Delta A = \frac{Q}{\epsilon_0}$$

$$E(2\pi r L) = \frac{\lambda L}{\epsilon_0}$$

$$E = \frac{\lambda}{2\pi r \epsilon_0}$$

---

20 Express ρ in terms of λ.

20 Since $\lambda = q/L$ and $\rho = q/V$,

$$\lambda = \frac{\rho V}{L} = \frac{\rho(\pi R^2) L}{L} = \pi \rho R^2$$

or $\rho = \dfrac{\lambda}{\pi R^2}$

---

21 Substitute this value for ρ in

$$E = \frac{\rho r}{2\epsilon_0}.$$

21

$$E = \frac{\lambda r}{2\pi R^2 \epsilon_0}$$

---

22 Compare the results of a) and b) when $r = R$.

22 When $R = r$, we obtain

$$E = \frac{\lambda}{2\pi \epsilon_0 r} \text{ in each case.}$$

26

Electrical Potential

CHAPTER SUMMARY

We are introduced to the concepts of electrical potential energy of charged particles in an electric field as well as the work involved in moving them. On the basis of this discussion, electrostatic potential and potential difference are defined. The potential distribution in an electric field may be represented graphically by equipotential surfaces; the potential gradient expresses the magnitude of the electric field. The Millikan oil-drop experiment, in which the charge of a single electron is determined, and the cathode-ray oscilloscope are described.

BASIC TERMS — *Give definitions or meanings for the following:*

potential energy (26-1)
conservative force field (26-1)
potential (26-2)
volt (26-2)
voltmeter (26-2)

equipotential surface (26-3)
potential gradient (26-4)
Millikan oil-drop experiment (26-5)
electron volt (26-6)
cathode-ray tube (26-7)

PROGRAMMED QUIZ

1 Why do potential gradient and the electric field have the same units? What are they?

1 The potential gradient is another way of expressing the magnitude of the electric field in terms of the difference of potential per unit distance; $N \cdot C^{-1}$ and $V \cdot m^{-1}$. ($E = \Delta V / \Delta s$)

2 What is the relationship between the field lines and the equipotential surfaces?

2 At right angles to each other at all points.

3 What is the usual shape for equipotential surfaces? Are they ever planes?

3 Curved surfaces; yes in a uniform electric field. In general, the field lines of a field are curves and the equipotentials are curved surfaces.

4 An irregularly shaped conductor has the greatest charge density at the curved ends and the least at the flat surfaces. What about the potential at the surface?

4 Constant over the entire surface.

5 What other types of potential energy have you studied? Give the formulas.

5 Gravitational potential energy $= mgy$ and elastic potential energy $= \frac{1}{2}kx^2$.

6 In calculating the potential difference between two points, what path should you choose?

6 Any path (because the electric force is conservative).

7 What do we mean by a 5 MeV electron?

7 An electron whose kinetic energy is 5 MeV, i.e. it was accelerated from rest through a potential difference of 5×10^6 volts.

8 To find the work done by an electric force, why can't we multiply the force by the distance?

8 The force is not constant, it changes with distance.

9 Why is there no work done on a test charge displaced inside a charged spherical conductor?

9 Because the field is zero.

10 Why is there a limit as to the maximum potential to which a conductor in air can be raised?

10 The limiting value is due to the electric field at which air molecules become ionized and therefore the air becomes a conductor.

11 What is dielectric strength?

11 The upper limit of the electric field.

12 A test charge $+q'$ is placed in an electric field generated by a fixed charge $+q$. What will happen to q'?

12 It will be accelerated in the direction of the electric field.

13 What two forces are acting on q' to keep it in equilibrium? Indicate by arrows.

13 The electric force and the external force.

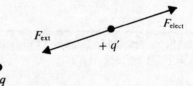

14 What is the relationship between the electric force and the external force?

14 Equal in magnitude, opposite in direction.

15 How much electrical work is required to move a charged body over an equipotential surface?

15 Zero, since the potential energy of the charged body is the same at all points of the equipotential surface.

16 What is the reference position for electrical potential energy (the position at which $U = 0$)?

16 That position at which all the distances are infinite; that is, when the test charge is very far removed from all the charges setting up the field.

17 What did Millikan demonstrate?

17 In his famous oil-drop experiment, Millikan demonstrated the discrete nature of electric charge and actually measured the charge of an individual electron.

MAIN IDEAS

In an earlier chapter we learned that the work done by the gravitational force during the displacement from a to b can be expressed as $W_{grav} = U_a - U_b$ where U_a = initial gravitational potential energy and U_b = final gravitational potential energy. In a similar manner consider a test charge particle moving in a uniform electric field; the field exerts a force on the particle and thus does work on it. The work done by the force is independent of the particle's path and is equal to $W_{a \to b} = U_a - U_b$. Since every electric field caused by electric charges at rest is conservative, the work can be associated with a potential energy function.

Consider the work done on a test charge q' by the electric field due to a single point charge q. Although such a field is not uniform, the work done by the field on the charge q' as it moves from a to b can be expressed in terms of the potential energies at a and b.

If the potential energy is U_a at a and U_b at b, then the work done by a force in a displacement from a to b is $W_{a \to b} = U_a - U_b$. That is, the work done on the body is equal to the change in potential energy. The work done on charge q' by the field produced by q is $W_{a \to b} = \frac{1}{4\pi\epsilon_0} qq' \left(\frac{1}{r_a} - \frac{1}{r_b} \right)$ where r_a and r_b are the distances from q to a and b respectively.

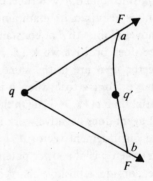

The potential energy U of a test charge q' a distance r from q is given by $U = \frac{1}{4\pi\epsilon_0} \frac{qq'}{r}$. The potential energy of q' due to many charges is given by $U = \frac{1}{4\pi\epsilon_0} q' \left(\frac{q_1}{r_1} + \frac{q_2}{r_2} + \frac{q_3}{r_3} + ... \right) = \frac{1}{4\pi\epsilon_0} q' \Sigma \frac{q_i}{r_i}$. The total electric potential energy of a group of charges is the sum of the energies of each pair. Thus the potential energy of the system comprising q_1, q_2 and q_3 is $U = \frac{1}{4\pi\epsilon_0} \left(\frac{q_1 q_2}{a} + \frac{q_2 q_3}{b} + \frac{q_1 q_3}{c} \right)$.

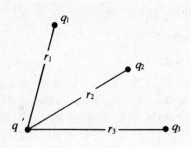

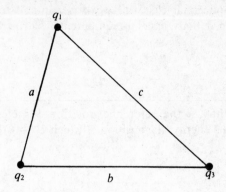

The reference level for electrostatic potential energy is chosen to be infinity. The potential energy at infinity equals zero, that is, the potential energy of the test charge is zero when it is far removed from all the charges setting up the field. The potential energy of a test charge at any point in an electric field is equal to the work done on it by the electric force (due to the field) when the test charge is brought from the point in question to infinity. It is the negative of the work of the electric force when the test charge is brought in from infinity to the point in question by an external force.

The potential at any point in an electrostatic field is defined as the potential energy per unit test charge. The potential due to a single charge q is $V = \dfrac{U}{q'} = \dfrac{1}{4\pi\epsilon_0} \dfrac{qq'}{rq'} = \dfrac{1}{4\pi\epsilon_0} \dfrac{q}{r}$. The potential due to a collection of charges is $V = \dfrac{1}{4\pi\epsilon_0} \left(\dfrac{q_1}{r_1} + \dfrac{q_2}{r_2} + \dfrac{q_3}{r_3} + ... \right) = \dfrac{1}{4\pi\epsilon_0} \Sigma \dfrac{q_i}{r_i}$. The volt is the unit of potential; 1 volt = 1 joule per coulomb ($1V = 1 J \cdot C^{-1}$).

Usually in our discussions on charged particles we are interested in the work done by the electric field, but there may be situations where an external force does work on the particle. Consider a positive charged particle q' in an electric field generated by a fixed positive charge q. Since q and q' will repel each other, an external agent is required to maintain q' in equilibrium as it moves from a to b at constant speed. If an external force does positive work (F_{ext} and the displacement vector $a{\rightarrow}b$ are in the same direction) in moving a charge from a to b, then b is at a higher electric potential than $a(V_b > V_a)$. On the other hand, if an external agent does negative work in going from $a{\rightarrow}b$ (F_{ext} and displacement vector $a{\rightarrow}b$ are in opposite directions), then b is at a lower potential.

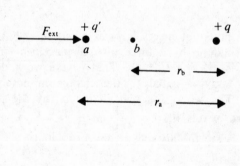

In this case, consider a positive charged particle q' in an electric field generated by a fixed negative charge $-q$. Since $-q$ and q' will attract each other, an external agent opposing the motion is required to maintain q' in equilibrium as it moves from $a{\rightarrow}b$ at constant speed. Remember that, if the external force does positive work, the electric force does negative work and vice versa.

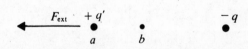

The potential difference between a and b is $V_{ab} = V_a - V_b$. If V_{ab} is positive, then a is at a higher potential than b and work must be done by an external force to move a positive charge from b to a; $V_{ab} = -V_{ba}$. The work done by an external force in moving a charge q from a to b is $W_{a{\rightarrow}b} = qV_{ba}$.

The potential difference between any two points can be obtained by finding the potential at each point or by calculating the work done on a test charge in a known electric field.

Calculations of potential difference:

Solid spherical conductor, radius R, total charge q:

$r < R$	$V = \dfrac{1}{4\pi\epsilon_0}\dfrac{q}{R}$, relative to infinity	$E = 0$
$r = R$	$V = \dfrac{1}{4\pi\epsilon_0}\dfrac{q}{R}$, relative to infinity	$E = \dfrac{1}{4\pi\epsilon_0}\dfrac{q}{R^2}$
$r > R$	$V = \dfrac{1}{4\pi\epsilon_0}\dfrac{q}{r}$, relative to infinity	$E = \dfrac{1}{4\pi\epsilon_0}\dfrac{q}{r^2}$

Parallel plates: $V_a - V_b = Ed$.

Potential can be graphically represented by equipotential surfaces, i.e. surfaces where the potential has the same value at all points. Equipotential surfaces are orthogonal to the field lines.

Electron volt. An electron accelerated through a potential difference of 1 volt acquires an energy of 1 electron volt (1 eV). Since $W = qV$, 1 eV $= (1.602 \times 10^{-19}$ C$) (1.00$ V$) = 1.602 \times 10^{-19}$ J.

Air molecules can be ionized and hence the air becomes a conductor at an electric field $\approx 0.8 \times 10^9$ N $\cdot$ C^{-1}.

Potential gradient $= \Delta V/\Delta s$, where ΔV is the spacing between equipotentials equal to some constant difference and Δs is the perpendicular distance between two equipotentials. $E = \Delta V/\Delta s$ expresses the magnitude of the electric field in terms of the difference in potential per unit distance in a direction perpendicular to the equipotential.

The cathode ray tube: the accelerating anode is maintained at a high positive potential V_1 relative to the cathode, producing an electric field directed from right to left in the region between the anode and the cathode. Electrons evaporate from the heated surface of the cathode and pass through a small hole in the anode, forming a narrow beam. They then travel with constant velocity and pass between horizontal and vertical deflecting plates toward a fluorescent screen.

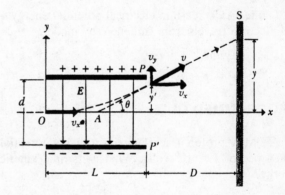

$$v_x = \sqrt{\frac{2eV_1}{m}},$$
$e = 1.60 \times 10^{-19}$ C,
$m = 9.11 \times 10^{-31}$ kg,
$V_1 =$ potential of accelerating anode.

If there is no electric field between the horizontal deflecting plates, and if the potential difference between the vertical plates is V_2 (with the upper plate positive), then

$$E = \frac{V_2}{d} \text{ (downward electric field);}$$

$$a_y = \frac{eE}{m} = \frac{eV_2}{md};$$

$$v_x = \frac{L}{t}, \text{ where } t = \text{time required for the electrons to travel the length } L \text{ of the plates;}$$

$$v_y = \left(\frac{eV_2}{md}\right)\frac{L}{v_x};$$

$$\tan\theta = \frac{v_y}{v_x}.$$

Problem solving strategy:

1 Use $V = \dfrac{U}{q'} = \dfrac{1}{4\pi\epsilon_0} \sum \dfrac{q_i}{r_i}$ to find the potential due to a collection of point charges. Remember that V is a scalar quantity.

2 In order to find the potential due to a continuous charge distribution (such as a circular arc), divide the distribution into small elements Δq that can be considered as point charges and use

$$V = \; = \; \dfrac{1}{4\pi\epsilon_0} \sum \dfrac{\Delta q}{r_i} \, .$$

3 Useful mathematical relationships for specific problems:

a) Charged spherical conductor of radius R:

$$V = \dfrac{1}{4\pi\epsilon_0} \dfrac{q}{R} = \text{potential inside and on surface.}$$

$$V = \dfrac{1}{4\pi\epsilon_0} \dfrac{q}{r} \qquad \text{if } r > R.$$

b) Parallel plates:

$$V_{ab} = V_a - V_b = Ed.$$

c) Conservation of energy:

$$K_A + U_A = K_B + U_B,$$
where $U_A = qV_A$ and $U_B = qV_B$;
$$W_{AB} = q(V_A - V_B).$$

d) Diode: A decrease in electrical potential energy $- e(V_c - V_a) = eV_{ac}$ is equal to a gain in kinetic energy as the electron travels from cathode c to anode a:

$$eV_{ac} = \tfrac{1}{2}mv_a^2 + \tfrac{1}{2}mv_c^2.$$

If $v_c = 0$, $v_a = \sqrt{2eV_{ac}/m}$.

PROGRAMMED QUIZ

1 A 2 MeV proton is accelerated through a potential difference of 4×10^6 volts. What is its final kinetic energy?

1 The gain in kinetic energy = 4 MeV. Therefore, the final kinetic energy = 2 MeV + 4 MeV = 6 MeV.

2 Draw the field lines and equipotential surfaces for an electron.

2

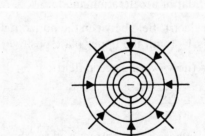

3 Draw the field lines and equipotential surfaces in the vicinity of a positive and a negative point charge.

3

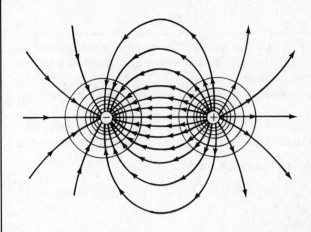

---

4 What is the electric field between two metal plates, 5 cm apart, if a charge of 2×10^{-9} C between them experiences a force of 8×10^{-7} N?

4

$$E = \frac{F}{q}$$
$$= \frac{8 \times 10^{-7} \text{ N}}{2 \times 10^{-9} \text{ C}}$$
$$= 400 \text{ N} \cdot \text{C}^{-1}$$

---

5 What is the potential difference between the plates?

5

$$E = \frac{V}{d}$$
$$V = (400 \text{ N} \cdot \text{C}^{-1}) \, (0.05 \text{ m})$$
$$= 20 \text{ V}$$

Note:
$$1 \text{ N} \cdot \text{m C}^{-1} = 1 \text{ J} \cdot \text{C}^{-1} = 1 \text{ V}$$

---

6 How much work is done by the field on a charge of 2×10^{-9} C as it moves from the higher potential plate to the lower?

6

$$W = qV$$
$$= (2 \times 10^{-9} \text{ C}) \, (20 \text{ V})$$
$$= 4.0 \times 10^{-8} \text{ J}$$

---

7 Use another method to calculate the work.

7

$$W = Fd$$
$$= (8 \times 10^{-7} \text{ N}) \, (0.05 \text{ m}) = 4.0 \times 10^{-8} \text{ J}$$

---

8 Find the electrical potential energy of a hydrogen atom which consists of a proton and an electron 5.28×10^{-11} m apart. Remember that $1/4\pi\epsilon_0 \approx 9 \times 10^9$ N $\cdot$ m$^2 \cdot$ C^{-2}.

8

$$U = \frac{1}{4\pi\epsilon_0} \, \frac{qq'}{r} = \frac{1}{4\pi\epsilon_0} \, \frac{(e)(-e)}{r}$$
$$= - \, \frac{(9 \times 10^9 \text{ N} \cdot \text{m}^2 \cdot \text{C}^{-2}) \, (1.602 \times 10^{-19} \text{ C})^2}{5.28 \times 10^{-11} \text{ m}}$$
$$= - \, 4.37 \times 10^{-18} \text{ J}$$

---

9 What is the electrical potential energy in electron volts?

9

$$\left(-4.37 \times 10^{-18}\,\text{J}\right)\left(\frac{1\,\text{eV}}{1.602 \times 10^{-19}\,\text{J}}\right) = -27.3\,\text{eV}$$

---

10 A charged sphere 5 cm in radius is surrounded by a second sphere 12 cm in radius. The charge on the inner sphere is 8×10^{-9} C. What is the potential difference between these two surfaces? The potential at the surface of the inner sphere is $V_a = \frac{1}{4\pi\epsilon_0} \frac{q}{r_a}$. The potential at the surface of the outer sphere due to the charged inner sphere is $V_b = \frac{1}{4\pi\epsilon_0} \frac{q}{r_b}$.

10

$$
\begin{aligned}
V_{ab} &= V_a - V_b \\
&= \frac{1}{4\pi\epsilon_0} \frac{q}{r_a} - \frac{1}{4\pi\epsilon_0} \frac{q}{r_b} \\
&= \frac{1}{4\pi\epsilon_0} q \left(\frac{1}{r_a} - \frac{1}{r_b}\right) \\
&= (9 \times 10^9\,\text{N} \cdot \text{m}^2 \cdot \text{C}^{-2})\,(8 \times 10^{-9}\,\text{C}) \\
&\quad \times \left(\frac{1}{0.05\,\text{m}} - \frac{1}{0.12\,\text{m}}\right) \\
&= 840\,\text{V}
\end{aligned}
$$

---

11 Draw the electric field lines and the equipotential surfaces for this pair of conductors. Which conductor is at the higher potential?

11

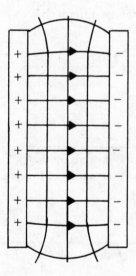

Positive conductor

---

12 In order for the field to move a 2×10^{-8} C charge from one conductor to the other, 8×10^{-6} J of work were required. What is the potential difference between the conductors?

12

$$
\begin{aligned}
W &= U = q'V \\
V &= \frac{8 \times 10^{-6}\,\text{J}}{2 \times 10^{-8}\,\text{C}} \\
&= 400\,\text{V}
\end{aligned}
$$

---

13 Three charges $q_1 = -2 \times 10^{-9}$ C, $q_2 = 3 \times 10^{-9}$ C, and $q_3 = 4 \times 10^{-9}$ C, are arranged at the points of an equilateral triangle whose side is 0.1 m as shown. What is the potential energy of the system?

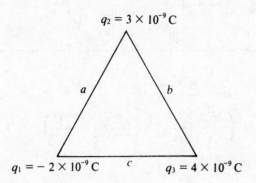

$q_2 = 3 \times 10^{-9}$ C

a b

$q_1 = -2 \times 10^{-9}$ C c $q_3 = 4 \times 10^{-9}$ C

13

$$U = U_{12} + U_{23} + U_{31}$$

$$= \frac{1}{4\pi\epsilon_0} \left(\frac{q_1 q_2}{r_a} + \frac{q_2 q_3}{r_b} + \frac{q_3 q_1}{r_c} \right)$$

$$= \frac{(9 \times 10^9 \, \text{N} \cdot \text{m}^2 \cdot \text{C}^{-2})}{0.1 \, \text{m}}$$

$$\times \left[(-2)(3) + (3)(4) + (4)(-2) \right] \times 10^{-18} \, \text{C}$$

$$= 1.80 \times 10^{-7} \, \text{J}$$

---

14 A particle of charge $+5 \times 10^{-5}$ C is in a uniform electric field directed to the right. It is released from rest and moves a distance of 0.08 m after which its kinetic energy is found to be $+6 \times 10^{-5}$ J. What work was done by the electric force? Use the work-energy theorem,

14

$+$ $E \longrightarrow$ $-$

$+$ $(+)$ $-$

$+$ $-$

a $d = 0.08$ m b

Since $K_a = 0$, $K_b = 6 \times 10^{-5}$ J

$$W_{a \to b} = \Delta K = K_b - K_a$$
$$= 6 \times 10^{-5} \, \text{J} - 0$$
$$= 6 \times 10^{-5} \, \text{J}$$

---

15 What is the magnitude of the electric force?

15

$$W_{a \to b} = Fd$$
$$F = \frac{6 \times 10^{-5} \, \text{J}}{0.08 \, \text{m}} = 7.5 \times 10^{-4} \, \text{N}$$

---

16 What is the magnitude of the electric field?

16

$$E = \frac{F}{q}$$
$$= \frac{7.5 \times 10^{-4} \, \text{N}}{5 \times 10^{-9} \, \text{C}} = 1.5 \times 10^5 \, \text{N} \cdot \text{C}^{-1}$$

---

17 What is the potential difference between a and b? Which point is at the higher potential?

17

$$V_{ab} = V_a - V_b = \frac{W_{a \to b}}{q'}$$
$$= \frac{6 \times 10^{-5} \, \text{J}}{5 \times 10^{-9} \, \text{C}} = 1.2 \times 10^4 \, \text{V}$$

The potential at a is 12,000 volts higher than the potential at b.

18 Two point charges $q_1 = +50 \times 10^{-9}$ C and $q_2 = -25 \times 10^{-9}$ C are 0.20 m apart as shown. Find the potential at point a.

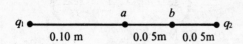

q_1 ●————————————●————————●————————● q_2
　　　　0.10 m　　　　　0.0 5m　　0.0 5m

18 The potential at a is the algebraic sum of the potentials due to q_1 and q_2.

$$V_a = \frac{1}{4\pi\epsilon_0} \sum \frac{q_i}{r_i} = 9.0 \times 10^9 \,\text{N} \cdot \text{m}^2 \cdot \text{C}^{-2}$$
$$\times \left(\frac{50 \times 10^{-9}\text{C}}{0.10 \text{ m}} + \frac{-25 \times 10^{-9}\text{C}}{0.10 \text{ m}} \right) = 2250 \text{ V}$$

---

19 Find the potential at point b.

19

$$V_b = \frac{1}{4\pi\epsilon_0} \sum \frac{q_i}{r_i} = 9 \times 10^9 \,\text{N} \cdot \text{m}^2 \cdot \text{C}^{-2}$$
$$\times \left(\frac{50 \times 10^{-9}\text{ C}}{0.15 \text{ m}} + \frac{-25 \times 10^{-9}\text{ C}}{0.05 \text{ m}} \right)$$
$$= -1500 \text{ V}$$

---

20 Compute the work done by the field (due to q_1 and q_2) on a charge of 4×10^{-9} C as it moves from a to b.

20

$$\begin{aligned} W_{a \to b} &= q' \ (V_a - V_b) \\ &= 4 \times 10^{-9} \text{ C } [2250 \text{ V} - (-1500 \text{ V})] \\ &= 1.5 \times 10^{-5} \text{ J} \end{aligned}$$

STEP BY STEP SOLUTIONS OF PROBLEMS

Problem 1 A 1×10^{-4} kg sphere hangs by a thread between two parallel vertical plates 0.10 m apart. The charge on the sphere (which should be considered as a point particle) is 1.2×10^{-9} C. If the potential difference between the plates is 10,000 V, what angle will the thread make with the vertical?

1 Draw a sketch of the apparatus — include the free-body diagram. Identify the forces acting on the sphere.

1

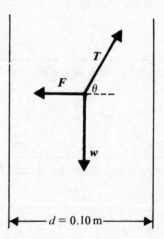

2 Find F and w.

2

Since $F = qE$, $E = V/d$

$$F = \frac{qV}{d} = \frac{1.2 \times 10^{-9} \text{ C } (10,000 \text{ V})}{0.10 \text{ m}}$$
$$= 1.2 \times 10^{-4} \text{ N}$$
$$\begin{aligned} w &= mg \\ &= (1 \times 10^{-4} \text{ kg}) (9.8 \text{ m} \cdot \text{s}^{-2}) \\ &= 9.8 \times 10^{-4} \text{ N} \end{aligned}$$

3 Construct a set of rectangular axes and resolve into rectangular components all forces acting on the sphere.

3

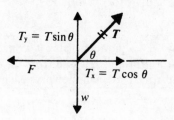

4 Set $\Sigma F_x = 0$ and $\Sigma F_y = 0$.

4

$$T \cos \theta - 1.2 \times 10^{-4}\,\text{N} = 0$$
$$T \sin \theta - 9.8 \times 10^{-4}\,\text{N} = 0$$

5 Eliminate T and solve for θ

5

$$\frac{T \sin \theta}{T \cos \theta} = \frac{9.8 \times 10^{-4}\,\text{N}}{1.2 \times 10^{-4}\,\text{N}}$$
$$\tan \theta = 8.167$$
$$\theta = 83.0°$$

6 What angle will the thread make with the vertical?

6 $90° - 83° = 7°$

Problem 2 A ring shaped conductor of radius a carries a total charge q. Find the electrical potential at a point P distance x from the center of the ring, along the line perpendicular to the plane of the ring through its center.

7 Draw a sketch. Consider a small segment Δs of the ring. Since the circumference of the ring $= 2\pi a$, the charge Δq on the segment is $\Delta q = q\Delta s/2\pi a$.

7

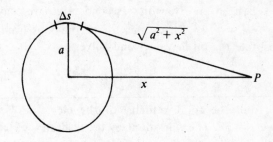

8 What is the distance r from P to the charge Δq?

8 $r = \sqrt{a^2 + x^2}$

9 Find ΔV.

9

$$\Delta V = \frac{1}{4\pi\epsilon_0}\frac{\Delta q}{r} = \frac{1}{4\pi\epsilon_0}\frac{q\Delta s}{2\pi a\sqrt{a^2 + x^2}}$$

10 Find the total potential $V = \Sigma\Delta V$.

10

$$V = \sum \frac{1}{4\pi\epsilon_0}\frac{q\Delta s}{2\pi a\sqrt{a^2 + x^2}}$$

11
Since $\dfrac{1}{4\pi\epsilon_0}\dfrac{q}{2\pi a\sqrt{a^2+x^2}}$ is a constant, it can be factored from the summation sign. Note that $\Sigma\Delta s = 2\pi a$. Solve for V.

11
$$V = \frac{1}{4\pi\epsilon_0}\frac{q}{\sqrt{a^2+x^2}}$$

Problem 3 Two parallel plates 0.05 m apart have a potential difference of 1800 V between them. At the same instant that a proton is released from the positive plate, an electron is released from the negative plate. a) How far from the positive plate will they pass each other? b) What is the velocity of each particle as it strikes the opposite plate?

12 Draw a sketch. Let $x =$ distance from positive plate at which the particles pass each other.

12
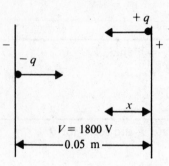

---

13 Since $x = x_0 + v_0 t + 1/2 at^2$ and the time intervals are equal to each other, the distances from the plates for each particle are proportional. Express this relationship.

13
$$\frac{\Delta x_p}{\Delta x_e} = \frac{x}{0.05 - x} = \frac{a_p}{a_e}$$

---

14 Since the force acting on the electron between the plates equals the force acting on the proton ($F = Eq$), from Newton's second law we have $F = m_p a_p = m_e a_e$. Relate this to the previous frame, substitute the given values and solve for x.

14
$$\frac{x}{0.05 - x} = \frac{m_e}{m_p} = \frac{9.11\times 10^{-31}\text{ kg}}{1.673\times 10^{-27}\text{ kg}}$$
$$x = (0.05\text{ m} - x)(5.445\times 10^{-4})$$
$$= 2.72\times 10^{-5}\text{ m}$$

---

15 Find the final velocity of the electron. Use $\frac{1}{2}mv^2 = qV$. The work done by the field on the electron is equal to the change in its kinetic energy.

15 $\frac{1}{2}(9.11\times 10^{-31}\text{ kg})v_e^2 = (1.602\times 10^{-19}\text{ C})(1800\text{ V})$
$$v_e = 2.52\times 10^7\text{m}\cdot\text{s}^{-1}$$

---

16 Find the final velocity of the proton using the same expression.

16 $\qquad\qquad \frac{1}{2}mv_p^2 = qV$
$\frac{1}{2}(1.673\times 10^{-27}\text{ kg})(v_p^2) = (1.602\times 10^{-19}\text{ C})(1800\text{ V})$
$$v_p = 5.87\times 10^5\text{ m}\cdot\text{s}^{-1}$$

---

17 How do the velocities of the electron and the proton compare when they strike the opposite plates?

17
$$\frac{v_e}{v_p} = \frac{2.52\times 10^7\text{ m}\cdot\text{s}^{-1}}{5.87\times 10^5\text{ m}\cdot\text{s}^{-1}} = 42.9$$

Problem 4 A metal sphere of radius r_a is supported on an insulating stand at the center of a hollow metal sphere of inner radius r_b. If there is a charge $+q$ on the inner sphere and a charge $-q$ on the outer sphere, find V_{ab}. Show that V_{ab} would not change if the charge on the outer sphere had a value of $-Q$.

18 Find the potential V_a on the surface of the inner sphere due to the charge of the individual spheres.

18 The potential on the surface of the inner sphere due to its charge is

$$\frac{1}{4\pi\epsilon_0}\,\frac{q}{r_a}.$$

The potential on the surface of the inner sphere due to the charge on the surface of the outer sphere is

$$\frac{1}{4\pi\epsilon_0}\left(\frac{-q}{r_b}\right).$$

Therefore,

$$V_a = \frac{1}{4\pi\epsilon_0}\,\frac{q}{r_a} - \frac{1}{4\pi\epsilon_0}\,\frac{q}{r_b}$$

$$= \frac{q}{4\pi\epsilon_0}\left(\frac{1}{r_a} - \frac{1}{r_b}\right).$$

---

19 Find the potential V_b on the surface of the outer sphere due to the charge of the individual spheres.

19 The potential on the surface of the outer sphere due to its charge is $\frac{1}{4\pi\epsilon_0}\left(\frac{-q}{r_b}\right)$. The potential on the surface of the outer sphere due to the charge on the surface of the inner sphere is $\frac{1}{4\pi\epsilon_0}\,\frac{q}{r_b}$. Therefore,

$$V_b = -\frac{1}{4\pi\epsilon_0}\,\frac{q}{r_b} + \frac{1}{4\pi\epsilon_0}\,\frac{q}{r_b}$$

$$= 0$$

---

20 Find V_{ab}.

20

$$V_{ab} = V_a - V_b$$

$$= \frac{q}{4\pi\epsilon_0}\left(\frac{1}{r_a} - \frac{1}{r_b}\right)$$

---

21 Repeat for a charge $-Q$ on the outer sphere. Find the potential on the inner sphere due to the charges of the individual spheres.

21

$$V_a = \frac{1}{4\pi\epsilon_0}\,\frac{q}{r_a} - \frac{1}{4\pi\epsilon_0}\,\frac{Q}{r_b}$$

---

22 Find the potential on the outer sphere due to the charges of the individual spheres.

22

$$V_b = -\frac{1}{4\pi\epsilon_0}\,\frac{Q}{r_b} + \frac{1}{4\pi\epsilon_0}\,\frac{q}{r_b}$$

23 Find V_{ab}.

23

$$V_{ab} = V_a - V_b$$

$$= \frac{1}{4\pi\epsilon_0} \frac{q}{r_a} - \frac{1}{4\pi\epsilon_0} \frac{Q}{r_b}$$

$$- \left(- \frac{1}{4\pi\epsilon_0} \frac{Q}{r_b} + \frac{1}{4\pi\epsilon_0} \frac{q}{r_b} \right)$$

$$= \frac{q}{4\pi\epsilon_0} \left(\frac{1}{r_a} - \frac{1}{r_b} \right)$$

which is the same result obtained in frame 20.

PROGRAMMED TEST

1 *Problem 1* Two positive charges, each of magnitude q, are fixed on the x-axis at $x = +a$ and $x = -a$. Find the potential at a) any point on the y-axis, b) any point on the x-axis between the two charges.

1 *Answer*

$$V_A = \frac{1}{4\pi\epsilon_0} \frac{2q}{\sqrt{a^2 + y^2}} ,$$

$$V_B = \frac{1}{4\pi\epsilon_0} \frac{2qa}{a^2 - x^2}$$

If you solved this problem correctly, go to frame 5. If you could not solve this problem, go through frames 2-4.

2 Draw a sketch.

2

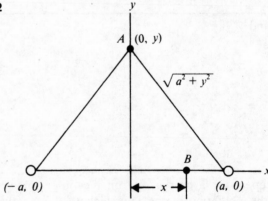

3 Find the potential at A due to both charges.

3

$$V_A = \frac{1}{4\pi\epsilon_0} \sum \frac{q_i}{r_i} = \frac{1}{4\pi\epsilon_0} \frac{2q}{\sqrt{a^2 + y^2}}$$

4 Find the potential at B due to both charges. Note that the distance from $(-a, 0)$ to B is $a + x$ and the distance from B to $(a, 0)$ is $a - x$.

4

$$V_B = \frac{1}{4\pi\epsilon_0} \sum \frac{q_i}{r_i} = \frac{1}{4\pi\epsilon_0}\left(\frac{q}{a+x} + \frac{q}{a-x}\right)$$

$$= \frac{1}{4\pi\epsilon_0} \frac{2qa}{a^2 - x^2}$$

Note that the potential is a minimum at $x = 0$.

$$V_0 = \frac{1}{4\pi\epsilon_0} \frac{2q}{a}.$$

---

5 **Problem 2** Two charges, -60×10^{-9} C and $+144 \times 10^{-9}$ C, are fixed at two vertices of a $5 - 12 - 13$ triangle as in the figure. Point A is midway between the charges and point B is at the right angle. Find the potentials at A and B and the work required by the electric field to carry a 35×10^{-9} C charge from A to B.

5

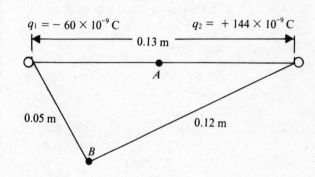

Answer

1.16×10^4 V, 0, 4.06×10^{-4} J

If you solved this problem correctly, go to frame 9. If you could not solve this problem, go through frames 6-8.

6 Find the potential at A due to q_1 and q_2.

6

$$V_1 = \frac{1}{4\pi\epsilon_0} \frac{q_1}{r}$$

$$= \frac{(9 \times 10^9\,\text{N} \cdot \text{m}^2 \cdot \text{C}^{-2})(- 60 \times 10^{-9}\,\text{C})}{0.065\,\text{m}}$$

$$= -8.31 \times 10^3\,\text{V}$$

$$V_2 = \frac{(9 \times 10^9\,\text{N} \cdot \text{m}^2 \cdot \text{C}^{-2})(144 \times 10^{-9}\,\text{C})}{0.065\,\text{m}}$$

$$= 1.99 \times 10^4\,\text{V}$$
$$V_A = V_1 + V_2 = 1.16 \times 10^4\,\text{V}$$

---

7 Find the potential at B due to q_1 and q_2.

7

$$V_1 = \frac{(9 \times 10^9\,\text{N} \cdot \text{m}^2 \cdot \text{C}^{-2})(- 60 \times 10^{-9}\,\text{C})}{0.05\,\text{m}}$$

$$= -1.08 \times 10^4\,\text{V}$$

$$V_2 = \frac{(9 \times 10^9\,\text{N} \cdot \text{m}^2 \cdot \text{C}^{-2})(144 \times 10^{-9}\,\text{C})}{0.12\,\text{m}}$$

$$= 1.08 \times 10^4\,\text{V}$$
$$V_B = V_1 + V_2 = 0$$

---

8 Find the work required by the electric field to carry the charge from A to B.

8

$$W_{AB} = q(V_A - V_B)$$
$$= 35 \times 10^{-9}\,\text{C}(1.16 \times 10^4\,\text{V} - 0)$$
$$= 4.06 \times 10^{-4}\,\text{J}$$

---

9 Problem 3 A particle, $m = 0.002$ kg and $q = 3 \times 10^{-9}$ C starts from rest at point A and moves in a straight line to point B under the influence of the electric field. Find a) the potentials at A and B, b) the velocity of the particle at B and c) the work done by the field on the particle ($q_1 = +8 \times 10^{-9}$ C and $q_2 = -8 \times 10^{-9}$ C).

9

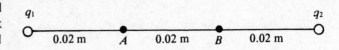

Answer
1800 V, $-$ 1800 V, 0.104 m · s^{-1}, 1.08 J.

If you solved this problem correctly go to frame 18. If you could not solve this problem, go through frames 10-17.

10 Find the potential at A due to q_1 and q_2.

10

$$V_1 = \frac{1}{4\pi\epsilon_0} \frac{q_1}{r_1}$$

$$= \frac{(9 \times 10^9 \text{ N} \cdot \text{m}^2 \cdot \text{C}^{-2})(8 \times 10^{-9} \text{ C})}{0.02 \text{ m}}$$

$$= 3600 \text{ V}$$

$$V_2 = \frac{(9 \times 10^9 \text{ N} \cdot \text{m}^2 \cdot \text{C}^{-2})(- 8 \times 10^{-9} \text{ C})}{0.04 \text{ m}}$$

$$= - 1800 \text{ V}$$

$$V_A = V_1 + V_2 = 1800 \text{ V}$$

---

11 Find the potential at B due to q_1 and q_2.

11

$$V_1 = \frac{(9 \times 10^9 \text{ N} \cdot \text{m}^2 \cdot \text{C}^{-2})(8 \times 10^{-9} \text{ C})}{0.04 \text{ m}}$$

$$= 1800 \text{ V}$$

$$V_2 = \frac{(9 \times 10^9 \text{ N} \cdot \text{m}^2 \cdot \text{C}^{-2})(- 8 \times 10^{-9}\text{C})}{0.02 \text{ m}}$$

$$= - 3600 \text{ V}$$

$$V_B = V_1 + V_2 = - 1800 \text{ V}$$

---

12 What is the kinetic energy of the particle at A?

12 Since the particle has an initial velocity $= 0$, $K_A = 0$.

---

13 Write the expression for the kinetic energy of the particle at B.

13 $\quad K_B = \frac{1}{2}mv^2$

---

14 What is the expression for conservation of energy at A and B? Express the potential energies in terms of the potentials.

14 $\quad K_A + U_A = K_B + U_B$
$\quad\quad 0 + qV_A = \frac{1}{2}mv^2 + qV_B$

---

15 Solve for v and substitute the numerical values.

15
$$v^2 = \frac{2q(V_A - V_B)}{m}$$

$$= \frac{2(3 \times 10^{-9}\ C)[1800\ V - (-1800\ V)]}{0.002\ kg}$$

$$v = 0.104\ m \cdot s^{-1}$$

---

16 Find the work done on the particle by the field.

16
$$\begin{aligned} W_{A \to B} &= q(V_A - V_B) \\ &= (3 \times 10^{-9}\ C)(3600\ V) \\ &= 1.08 \times 10^{-5}\ J \end{aligned}$$

---

17 The work done on the particle by the field can be obtained from $W = Fx$, where $F = ma$ and a is found from $v^2 = 2ax$.

17

$$a = \frac{v^2}{2x}$$

$$= \frac{(0.104\ m \cdot s^{-1})^2}{2(0.02\ m)}$$

$$= 0.270\ m \cdot s^{-2}$$
$$F = ma = (0.002\ kg)(0.270\ m \cdot s^{-2})$$
$$= 5.40 \times 10^{-4}\ N$$
$$W = Fx = (5.40 \times 10^{-4}\ N)(0.02\ m)$$
$$= 1.08 \times 10^{-5}\ J$$

which agrees with frame 16.

---

18 *Problem 4*   What is the final velocity of an electron which is accelerated from rest through a potential difference of 1000 V?

18   *Answer*

$$1.87 \times 10^7\ m \cdot s^{-1}$$

If you could not solve this problem, go through frame 19.

---

19 Use the equation from frame 15 that gives you the final velocity of a particle of constant mass m and charge q that is accelerated from rest in an electric field through a potential difference of V_{AB}.

19 $v = \sqrt{\dfrac{2q(V_A - V_B)}{m}}$

$$= \sqrt{\frac{2(1.60 \times 10^{-19}\ C)(1000\ V)}{9.11 \times 10^{-31}\ kg}}$$

$$= 1.87 \times 10^7\ m \cdot s^{-1}$$

27

Capacitance and Dielectrics

CHAPTER SUMMARY

Capacitors, with special emphasis on the parallel-plate capacitor, are the subject of this chapter. Capacitance is defined and the various relationships for capacitance, charge, potential difference and energy are presented. Series and parallel combinations of capacitors are discussed as well as the effects, due to induced charges, of dielectrics.

BASIC TERMS — *Give definitions or meanings for the following:*

capacitor (27-1)
capacitance (27-1)
farad (27-1)
parallel-plate capacitor (27-1)
equivalent capacitance (27-3)
parallel connection (27-3)

series connection (27-3)
energy density (27-4)
dielectric (27-5)
dielectric constant (27-5)
dielectric strength (27-5)
dielectric breakdown (27-5)

PROGRAMMED QUIZ

1 The induced surface charges set up a(n) _____ in a dielectric inserted between oppositely charged parallel plates. Describe this.

1 Electric field, weaker than the original field between the plates and opposite in direction.

2 What happens to a dielectric body in a nonuniform electric field if the dielectric constant of the body is less than that of the medium in which it is immersed?

2 It experiences a force urging it from the region of a strong field to the region where the field is weaker.

3 What happens to the electric field when a dielectric is placed between the plates of a charged capacitor?

3 It is decreased because the electric field set up in the dielectric is in the opposite direction.

4 What are some practical applications of capacitors?

4 Storing energy, filtering frequencies, tuning radio circuits.

5 What is the net charge on a capacitor?

5 Zero, both plates have charges of equal magnitude and opposite sign.

6 As the charge of the capacitor is increased, what happens to the capacitance?

6 Stays the same; $C = Q/V$, C is independent of Q, V is proportional to Q.

7 What does the capacitance of a parallel-plate capacitor depend on?

7 Geometry of the capacitor and the permittivity of free space, $C = \epsilon_0 A/d$.

8 The equivalent capacitance for a series circuit is always greater than, smaller than, or equal to the individual capacitances?

8 Less than the smallest individual capacitance.

9 For a given charge, what happens to C, Q and V when a dielectric is inserted between the plates?

9 The charge stays the same, the potential difference decreases, therefore the capacitance increases.

10 What is the increase in capacitance due to?

10 Induced charges on the surface of the dielectric, due to the alignment of dipoles within it, result in an electric field which opposes the original electric field. Therefore the potential difference decreases causing the capacitance to increase.

11 What is the difference between the charges in a dielectric and in a conductor?

11 In a conductor they are free; in a dielectric they are bound — they can rotate to align themselves with the applied field but they are not free to move.

12 What occurs when a capacitor is charged?

12 Positive charge is transferred from the plate at lower potential to the plate at higher potential.

13 Why is the charge the same on all plates in capacitors connected in series?

13 The net charge must be zero. If the net charge were not zero the resulting electric field in the conductor connecting the two capacitors would cause a current to flow between the capacitors until the total charge on each would be zero.

14 What must be the numerical values of the dielectric constants?

14 Greater than one; $K = C/C_0$, C is always greater than C_0.

15 What do we mean when we say a capacitor has a charge Q?

15 The conductor at the higher potential has a charge $+Q$; the one at the lower potential $-Q$.

MAIN IDEAS

A capacitor consists of two conductors separated by an insulator. Since the conductors carry equal and opposite charges ($+Q$ and $-Q$), the net charge on the capacitor is zero. If Q is the magnitude of the charge on each plate and V is the potential difference between the conductors, the capacitance $C = Q/V$; the unit of capacitance is the farad, $1\,\mathrm{F} = 1\,\mathrm{C} \cdot \mathrm{V}^{-1}$. Since the farad is a large unit, the microfarad (μF) and the picofarad (pF) are usually used. In charging a capacitor, the work required is given by $W = \frac{1}{2}QV = \frac{1}{2}CV^2 = \frac{1}{2}Q^2/C$.

A parallel-plate capacitor is made from two parallel plates equal in area and separated by a distance which is much smaller than the dimensions of the plates. The capacitance of the parallel-plate capacitor is given by $C = \epsilon_0 A/d$, where A is the area of the plates, d is their separation (in a vacuum) and $\epsilon_0 = 8.85 \times 10^{-12}\,\mathrm{C}^2 \cdot \mathrm{N}^{-1} \cdot \mathrm{m}^{-2}$ is the permittivity of free space.

The equivalent capacitance of any number of capacitors in series is given by

$$\frac{1}{C} = \frac{1}{C_1} + \frac{1}{C_2} + \frac{1}{C_3} + \cdots.$$

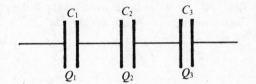

Note: $Q = Q_1 = Q_2 = Q_3 = \cdots$ and $V = V_1 + V_2 + V_3 + \cdots$.

The equivalent capacitance of any number of capacitors in parallel is given by $C = C_1 + C_2 + C_3 + \cdots$. Here $Q = Q_1 + Q_2 + Q_3 + \cdots$ and $V = V_1 = V_2 = V_3 = \cdots$.

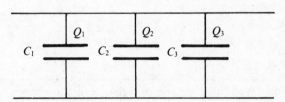

The dielectric constant K of a material is defined as $K = C/C_0$, where C is the capacitance with a dielectric and C_0 the capacitance in a vacuum (no dielectric). The permittivity of a dielectric $\epsilon = K\epsilon_0$. Thus the capacitance of a parallel plate capacitor is given by $C = \epsilon_0 A/d$. The dielectric strength is defined as the maximum electric field a material can withstand without a breakdown. The dielectric strength of dry air $\approx 0.8 \times 10^6\,\mathrm{V} \cdot \mathrm{m}^{-1}$.

Procedure for finding the equivalent capacitance. Consider the circuit shown. How do we find the equivalent capacitance between A and B?

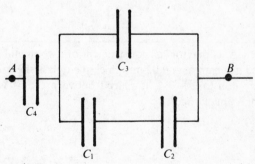

Step 1 Find the equivalent capacitance of C_1 and C_2. Denote it by C'. Since C_1 and C_2 are connected in series, $\dfrac{1}{C'} = \dfrac{1}{C_1} + \dfrac{1}{C_2}$. Thus C' replaces C_1 and C_2 in the circuit.

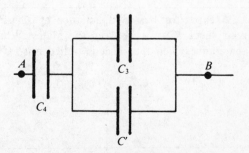

Step 2 We note that C_3 and C' are connected in parallel. Replace them with their equivalent capacitance C'' where $C'' = C_3 + C'$.

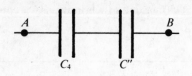

Step 3 Now C_4 and C'' are connected in series and could be replaced by their equivalent capacitance C''' where $\frac{1}{C'''} = \frac{1}{C_4} + \frac{1}{C''}$. Thus C''' is the equivalent capacitance between A and B.

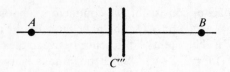

PROGRAMMED QUIZ

1 Two conductors have equal and opposite charges, $Q = 40 \times 10^{-6}$ C. What is the capacitance if the potential difference between them is 200 V?

1
$$C = \frac{Q}{V}$$
$$= \frac{40 \times 10^{-6} \text{ C}}{200 \text{ V}}$$
$$= 0.2 \times 10^{-6} \text{ F} = 0.2 \, \mu\text{F}$$

---

2 How much work is done during the charging process?

2
$$W = \tfrac{1}{2}QV$$
$$= \tfrac{1}{2}(40 \times 10^{-6} \text{ C})(200 \text{ V})$$
$$= 4 \times 10^{-3} \text{ J}$$

---

3 What will be the capacitance if the charge of a parallel plate capacitor is doubled?

3 If the charge is doubled, the voltage will be doubled also. The capacitance will remain the same.
$$C = \frac{Q}{V}$$
$$C' = \frac{2Q}{2V} = C$$

---

4 A capacitor is constructed of two metal sheets 0.5 m² in area. A 0.02 mm thick plexiglass sheet, dielectric constant = 3.4, is placed between them. What is the capacitance?

4
$$C = K\epsilon_0 \frac{A}{d}$$
$$= \frac{3.4(8.85 \times 10^{-12} \text{ C}^2 \cdot \text{N}^{-1} \cdot \text{m}^{-2})(0.5 \text{ m}^2)}{0.02 \times 10^{-3} \text{ m}}$$
$$= 0.752 \, \mu\text{F}$$

---

5 A capacitor has a capacitance of 0.5 μF with a mylar sheet $K = 3.1$ between the plates. What is the capacitance when the sheet is pulled out?

5
$$K = \frac{C}{C_0}$$
$$C_0 = \frac{0.5 \, \mu\text{F}}{3.1}$$
$$= 0.161 \, \mu\text{F}$$

---

6 Are the capacitors in series or in parallel?

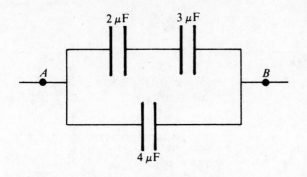

2 μF   3 μF

A   B

4 μF

6 The 2 μF and 3 μF capacitors are in series; together they are in parallel with the 4 μF capacitor.

7 The potential difference between the terminals *AB* is 20 volts. What is the potential difference across the single capacitor? the series combination?

7 20 V; 20 V. In a parallel combination the potential difference is the same.

8 What is the charge on the single capacitor?

8
$$Q_S = C_S V$$
$$= (4 \times 10^{-6} \text{ F})(20 \text{ V})$$
$$= 80 \times 10^{-6} \text{ C}$$

9 Draw a diagram showing an equivalent capacitor for the series combination in parallel with the 4 μF capacitor.

9

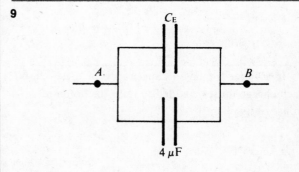

C_E

A   B

4 μF

10 What is the value for the equivalent capacitor for the series combination?

10
$$\frac{1}{C_E} = \frac{1}{C_1} + \frac{1}{C_2}$$
$$= \frac{1}{2 \text{ μF}} + \frac{1}{3 \text{ μF}}$$
$$C_E = 1.2 \text{ μF}$$

11 What is the charge of the equivalent capacitor?

11
$$Q_E = C_E V$$
$$= (1.2 \times 10^{-6} \text{ F})(20 \text{ V})$$
$$= 24 \times 10^{-6} \text{ C}$$

12 What is the charge on each capacitor in the series combination?

12 $Q_E = Q_1 = Q_2 = 24 \times 10^{-6}$ C

13 What is the equivalent capacitance of the entire combination?

13
$$C = C_S + C_E$$
$$= 4 \times 10^{-6} \, F + 1.2 \times 10^{-6} \, F$$
$$= 5.2 \times 10^{-6} \, F$$

---

14 What is the charge of the entire combination?

14
$$Q = CV$$
$$= (5.2 \times 10^{-6} \, F)(20 \, V)$$
$$= 104 \times 10^{-6} \, C$$

---

15 Does this agree with the fact that the total charge of capacitors in parallel equals the sum of the charges of each individual capacitor?

15 Yes, $Q = 80 \times 10^{-6} \, C + 24 \times 10^{-6} \, C$
$$= 104 \times 10^{-6} \, C$$

---

16 Prove that the additional charge that must be added to a capacitor to raise the potential difference of its plates by ΔV is $\Delta Q = C\Delta V$.

16 Since $C = Q/V$, if Q is to be raised by ΔQ there will be a change in the potential difference in order for C to remain constant.

$$\therefore \ C = \frac{Q}{V} = \frac{Q + \Delta Q}{V + \Delta V}$$
$$QV + Q\Delta V = QV + V\Delta Q$$
$$\Delta Q = \frac{Q\Delta V}{V} = C\Delta V$$

---

17 If a capacitor has a capacitance of 6 μF, how much charge must be added to raise the potential difference of its plates by 20 V?

17 $\Delta Q = C\Delta V$

$$= (6 \times 10^{-6} F)\,(20 \, V)$$

$$= 1.2 \times 10^{-4} \, C$$

---

18 A parallel-plate air capacitor has a capacitance of 0.005 μF. What potential difference is required for a charge of 1 μC on each plate?

18 $C = \dfrac{Q}{V}$

$$V = \frac{1 \times 10^{-6} \, C}{0.005 \times 10^{-6} \, F}$$

$$= 200 \, V$$

---

19 If the plates are 1.0 mm apart, what is the area of each plate?

19 $C = \epsilon_0 \dfrac{A}{d}$

$$A = \frac{(0.005 \times 10^{-6} \, F)\,(1 \times 10^{-3} m)}{8.85 \times 10^{-12} \, C^2 \cdot N^{-1} \cdot m^{-2}}$$

$$= 0.565 \, m^2$$

---

20 What potential difference is required for a dielectric breakdown?

20 For a dielectric breakdown,

$$E = 0.8 \times 10^6 \text{ V} \cdot \text{m}^{-1}$$
$$V = Ed$$
$$= (0.8 \times 10^6 \text{ V} \cdot \text{m}^{-1})(1 \times 10^{-3} \text{ m})$$
$$= 800 \text{ V}$$

STEP BY STEP SOLUTIONS OF PROBLEMS

Problem 1 Three capacitors, $C_1 = 6 \mu F$, $C_2 = 12 \mu F$ and $C_3 = 16 \mu F$, are connected across a 60 V supply line as in the figure. Find a) the single capacitance that is equivalent to this combination, b) the charge on the equivalent capacitance, c) the charge on each capacitor, d) the voltage across each capacitor, e) the energy required to charge each capacitor and f) the total energy of the three capacitors.

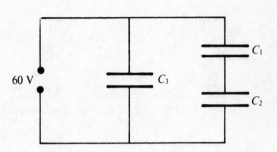

1 In order to find the equivalent capacitance of the combination, first find the equivalent capacitance of C_1 and C_2.

1 C_1 and C_2 are in series. Hence

$$\frac{1}{C} = \frac{1}{C_1} + \frac{1}{C_2}$$
$$= \frac{1}{6 \mu F} + \frac{1}{12 \mu F}$$
$$C = 4 \mu F$$

2 Find the equivalent capacitance of the 4 μF capacitor and C_3. This is the equivalent capacitance of C_1, C_2 and C_3.

2 These are in parallel, so the equivalent capacitance is equal to the sum of the capacitors.
$$C = 4 \mu F + 16 \mu F = 20 \mu F$$

3 Find the charge on the equivalent capacitor using $Q = CV$.

3
$$Q = (20 \times 10^{-6} \text{ F})(60 \text{ V})$$
$$= 1200 \times 10^{-6} \text{ C}$$

4 Find the charge on C_3. The voltage across $C_3 = 60$ V.

4
$$Q_3 = CV$$
$$= (16 \mu F)(60 \text{ V}) = 960 \times 10^{-6} \text{ C}$$

5 Find the charge on C_1 and C_2. Remember that the charges are equal for capacitors in series.

5
$$Q = Q_1 = Q_2 = CV$$
$$= (4 \mu F)(60 \text{ V}) = 240 \times 10^{-6} \text{ C}$$

6 What is the voltage across each capacitor? Use $Q = CV$.

6
$$V_1 = \frac{Q}{C} = \frac{240 \times 10^{-6}\,\text{C}}{6 \times 10^{-6}\,\text{F}} = 40\,\text{V}$$

$$V_2 = \frac{240 \times 10^{-6}\,\text{C}}{12 \times 10^{-6}\,\text{F}} = 20\,\text{V}$$

$$V_3 = 60\,\text{V}$$

---

7 Find the energy required to charge each capacitor using $W = \frac{1}{2}QV$.

7 for C_1: $W = \frac{1}{2}Q_1 V_1$
$= \frac{1}{2}(240 \times 10^{-6}\,\text{C})(40\,\text{V})$
$= 4800 \times 10^{-6}\,\text{J}$
for C_2: $W = \frac{1}{2}(240 \times 10^{-6}\,\text{C})(20\,\text{V})$
$= 2400 \times 10^{-6}\,\text{J}$
for C_3: $W = \frac{1}{2}(960 \times 10^{-6}\,\text{C})(60\,\text{V})$
$= 28{,}800 \times 10^{-6}\,\text{J}$

---

8 Find the total energy of the three capacitors.

8
$$W = \frac{1}{2}(1200 \times 10^{-6}\,\text{C})(60\,\text{V})$$
$$= 36{,}000 \times 10^{-6}\,\text{J}$$

---

9 Check your answer with frame 7.

9
$$36{,}000 \times 10^{-6}\,\text{J} = 4800 \times 10^{-6}\,\text{J} + 2400 \times 10^{-6}\,\text{J}$$
$$+ 28{,}800 \times 10^{-6}\,\text{J}$$

Problem 2 A parallel-plate capacitor is made from two square metal plates 0.25 m on a side. The separation of the plates is 0.01 m and the potential difference is 200 V. Find a) the capacitance, b) the charge on each plate, c) the electric field between the plates and d) the energy stored in the capacitor. e) If the capacitor is disconnected from its voltage source and a material with a dielectric constant $K = 4$ is inserted between the plates, find the new voltage. f) What is the new capacitance? g) What is the new charge on the plates? h) What is the permittivity of the dielectric? i) Find the electric field after the insertion of the dielectric.

10 Find the capacitance using $C_0 = \epsilon_0 A / d$.

10
$$C_0 = \frac{(8.85 \times 10^{-12}\,\text{C}^2 \cdot \text{N}^{-1} \cdot \text{m}^{-2})(0.25\,\text{m})^2}{0.01\,\text{m}}$$
$$= 55.3 \times 10^{-12}\,\text{F} = 55.3\,\text{pF}$$

---

11 What is the charge on each plate? Use $Q = CV$.

11
$Q_0 = C_0 V_0$
$= (55.3 \times 10^{-12}\,\text{F})(200\,\text{V})$
$= 1.106 \times 10^{-8}\,\text{C}$

---

12 What is the electric field between the plates? Use $E = V/d$.

12
$$E_0 = \frac{V_0}{d}$$
$$= \frac{200\,\text{V}}{0.01\,\text{m}} = 2 \times 10^4\,\text{V} \cdot \text{m}^{-1}$$

---

13 Using $W = \frac{1}{2}QV$, find the energy stored in the capacitor.

13
$W = \frac{1}{2}Q_0 V_0$
$= \frac{1}{2}(1.106 \times 10^{-8}\,\text{C})(200\,\text{V})$
$= 1.106 \times 10^{-6}\,\text{J}$

---

14 Find the voltage with a dielectric inserted between the plates. Use $K = V_0/V$.

14
$$V = \frac{V_0}{K} = \frac{200 \text{ V}}{4} = 50 \text{ V}$$

---

15 What is the new capacitance? Note $C = K\epsilon_0 A/d$.

15
$$C = K\epsilon_0 \frac{A}{d} = KC_0$$
$$= 4(55.3 \text{ pF})$$
$$= 221 \text{ pF}$$

---

16 What is the new charge?

16
$$Q = CV = (4\,C_0)\frac{V_0}{4} = C_0 V_0 = Q_0$$
$$= 1.106 \times 10^{-8} \text{ C}$$
The charge on the plates remains the same.

---

17 Find the permittivity of the dielectric, $\epsilon = K\epsilon_0$.

17
$$\epsilon = 4\,(8.85 \times 10^{-12} \text{ C}^2 \cdot \text{N}^{-1} \cdot \text{m}^{-2})$$
$$= 35.4 \times 10^{-12} \text{ C}^2 \cdot \text{N}^{-1} \cdot \text{m}^{-2}$$

---

18 What is the new electric field?

18
$$E = \frac{V}{d} = \frac{50 \text{ V}}{0.01 \text{ m}} = 5000 \text{ V} \cdot \text{m}^{-1}$$

---

19 Check your answer by using $E = E_0/K$ and $E = Q/A\epsilon$.

19
$$E = \frac{E_0}{K} = \frac{20000 \text{ V} \cdot \text{m}^{-1}}{4} = 5000 \text{ V} \cdot \text{m}^{-1}$$
$$E = \frac{Q}{A\epsilon}$$
$$= \frac{1.106 \times 10^{-8} \text{ C}}{(0.25 \text{ m})^2 (35.4 \times 10^{-12} \text{ C}^2 \cdot \text{N}^{-1} \cdot \text{m}^{-2})}$$
$$= 5000 \text{ V} \cdot \text{m}^{-1}$$

Problem 3 A capacitor is charged to a potential difference V_0 and then connected to the terminals of an uncharged capacitor C_2. Find a) the original charge of the system, b) the final potential difference across each capacitor, c) the initial and final energies of the system and d) the decrease in energy when the capacitors are connected.

20 Draw the two sketches.

20

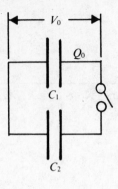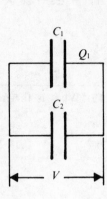

21 Find the original charge Q_0 by using $C = Q/V$.

21 $\quad Q_0 = C_1 V_0$

22 When C_1 is connected to C_2, the original charge Q_0 will be shared by both capacitors. Write the expression for the distribution of charge.

22 $\quad Q_0 = Q_1 + Q_2$

23 Substitute CV for each Q and solve for V.

23 $\quad C_1 V_0 = C_1 V + C_2 V$

$$V = V_0 \frac{C_1}{C_1 + C_2}$$

24 Find the initial stored energy by using $W = \frac{1}{2}QV = \frac{1}{2}CV^2$.

24 $\quad W_0 = \frac{1}{2}C_1 V_0^2$

25 What is the final stored energy? Express this in terms of V_0.

25
$$W = \frac{1}{2}C_1 V^2 + \frac{1}{2}C_2 V^2$$
$$= \frac{1}{2}(C_1 + C_2)V^2$$
$$= \frac{1}{2}(C_1 + C_2)\left(\frac{V_0 C_1}{C_1 + C_2}\right)^2$$
$$= \frac{V_0^2 C_1^2}{2(C_1 + C_2)}$$

26 Express the final stored energy in terms of the initial stored energy.

26
$$W = \frac{C_1}{C_1 + C_2} \cdot \frac{C_1 V_0^2}{2}$$
$$= \frac{C_1}{C_1 + C_2} \cdot W_0$$

It should be noted that W is less than W_0.

27 Find the expression for the decrease in energy when the capacitors are connected.

27
$$\Delta W = \frac{C_1}{C_1 + C_2} W_0 - W_0$$
$$= \frac{-C_2}{C_1 + C_2} W_0$$

Problem 4 A spherical capacitor consists of an inner metal sphere of radius r_a supported on an insulating stand at the center of a hollow metal sphere of inner radius r_b. There is a charge $+Q$ on the inner sphere and a charge $-Q$ on the outer sphere. If the potential difference V_{ab} between the spheres is

$$\frac{Q}{4\pi\epsilon_0} \left(\frac{1}{r_a} - \frac{1}{r_b} \right),$$

what is the capacitance of this spherical capacitor? If $r_b - r_a = d$ and d is very small in comparison to r_a, prove that the capacitance reduces to

$$C = \frac{\epsilon_0 A}{d},$$

where A = surface area of each sphere.

---

28 Find the capacitance by using $C = \dfrac{Q}{V_{ab}}$.

28

$$C = \frac{Q}{\dfrac{Q}{4\pi\epsilon_0} \left(\dfrac{1}{r_a} - \dfrac{1}{r_b} \right)}$$

$$= \frac{4\pi\epsilon_0}{\dfrac{(r_b - r_a)}{(r_a r_b)}}$$

$$= \frac{4\pi\epsilon_0 \, r_a \, r_b}{r_b - r_a}$$

---

29 Let $r_b - r_a = d$. Since d is much less than r_a, then $r_a \approx r_b \approx r$, the radius of the sphere. Simplify the above.

29

$$C = \frac{\epsilon_0 \, (4\pi r^2)}{d}$$

---

30 What is $4\pi r^2$?

30 $4\pi r^2 = A$ = surface area of each sphere, and so

$$C = \frac{\epsilon_0 A}{d}.$$

PROGRAMMED TEST

1 **Problem 1** A parallel plate capacitor has a plate area A and a separation x. a) If the charge on each plate is Q, find the total energy stored in the capacitor. b) A force is now applied to the plates and the new separation is $x + \Delta x$. What is the new total energy? c) Find the force.

1 **Answer**

$$W = \frac{Q^2 x}{2\epsilon_0 A}, \quad (W + \Delta W) = \frac{Q^2 (x + \Delta x)}{2\epsilon_0 A},$$

$$F = \frac{Q^2}{2\epsilon_0 A}$$

If you solved this problem correctly, go to frame 7. If you could not solve this problem, go through frames 2–6.

2 Express the energy stored in the capacitor in terms of Q and x.

2
$$W = \tfrac{1}{2}QV = \frac{Q^2}{2C} \quad \left(\text{since } C = \frac{Q}{V}\right)$$

but $C = \dfrac{\epsilon_0 A}{x}$

$$\therefore \ W = \frac{Q^2 x}{2\epsilon_0 A}$$

---

3 Find the new total energy of the capacitor after the plates have been separated an additional distance Δx.

3
$$W + \Delta W = \frac{Q^2(x + \Delta x)}{2\epsilon_0 A}$$

---

4 What is the change in energy?

4
$$\Delta W = \frac{Q^2 \Delta x}{2\epsilon_0 A}$$

---

5 What is the work done by the force in separating the plates?

5
$$\Delta W = F\Delta x$$

---

6 To find F, equate the work done in separating the plates to the change in the energy.

6
$$F\Delta x = \frac{Q^2 \Delta x}{2\epsilon_0 A}$$
$$F = \frac{Q^2}{2\epsilon_0 A}$$

---

7 **Problem 2** Two capacitors C_1 and C_2 are charged as follows: $Q_1 = 600\,\mu C$, $V_1 = 100$ V; $Q_2 = 150\,\mu C$, $V_2 = 50$ V. Find the potential difference and the charge for each capacitor when the capacitors are connected a) with terminals of like sign together and b) with terminals of unlike sign together (note: no external voltage is applied in either case). c) What is the total energy stored originally and after connections a and b?

7 **Answer**
500 μC, 250 μC, 83.3 V, 83.3 V, 300 μC, 150 μ C, 50 V, 50 V, 3.375×10^{-2} J, 3.12×10^{-2} J, 1.125×10^{-2} J.

If you solved this problem correctly, go to frame 18. If you could not solve this problem, go through frames 8–17.

---

8 Find the capacitance of each capacitor.

8
$$C_1 = \frac{Q}{V} = \frac{600 \times 10^{-6}\,\text{C}}{100\,\text{V}} = 6 \times 10^{-6}\,\text{F}$$

$$C_2 = \frac{150 \times 10^{-6}\,\text{C}}{50\,\text{V}} = 3 \times 10^{-6}\,\text{F}$$

9 Draw a sketch for the connection in part a.

9

---

10 Find the charge on each capacitor.

10 The total charge of $750\,\mu C$ will be redistributed when the capacitors are connected. Let Q = charge on C_1, then $750\,\mu C - Q$ = charge on C_2. The potential drop V is the same for each capacitor.

$$V = \frac{Q_1}{C_1} = \frac{Q_2}{C_2}$$

$$= \frac{Q}{6 \times 10^{-6}\,F} = \frac{750 \times 10^{-6}\,C - Q}{3 \times 10^{-6}\,F}$$

$$Q = 2(750 \times 10^{-6}\,C - Q)$$
$$= 500 \times 10^{-6}\,C = Q_1$$
$$750 \times 10^{-6}\,C - Q = 250 \times 10^{-6}\,C = Q_2$$

---

11 Find the potential difference across each capacitor.

11

$$V_1 = \frac{Q_1}{C_1} = \frac{500 \times 10^{-6}\,C}{6 \times 10^{-6}\,F} = 83.3\,V$$

$$V_2 = \frac{250 \times 10^{-6}\,C}{3 \times 10^{-6}\,F} = 83.3\,V$$

Note $V_1 = V_2$.

---

12 Draw a sketch of the connection for part b.

12

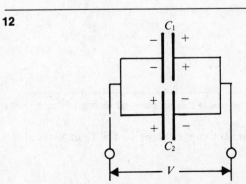

13 Find the charge on each capacitor.

13 The net charge in this case is $+600\ \mu C - 150\ \mu C = 450\ \mu C$. Let $Q =$ charge on C_1, then $450\ \mu C - Q =$ charge on C_2. The potential drop V is the same for both capacitors.

$$V = \frac{Q_1}{C_1} = \frac{Q_2}{C_2}$$

$$= \frac{Q}{6 \times 10^{-6}\ F} = \frac{450 \times 10^{-6}\ C - Q}{3 \times 10^{-6}\ F}$$

$$Q = 300 \times 10^{-6}\ C = Q_1$$
$$450 \times 10^{-6}\ C - Q = 150 \times 10^{-6}\ C = Q_2$$

---

14 Find the potential difference across each capacitor.

14

$$V_1 = \frac{Q_1}{C_1} = \frac{300 \times 10^{-6}\ C}{6 \times 10^{-6}\ F} = 50\ V$$

$$V_2 = \frac{150 \times 10^{-6}\ C}{3 \times 10^{-6}\ F} = 50\ V$$

---

15 Find the total energy of the capacitors before any connections were made.

15
$$W = \tfrac{1}{2}QV$$
$$W_1 = \tfrac{1}{2}(600 \times 10^{-6}\ C)(100\ V) = 3.0 \times 10^{-2}\ J$$
$$W_2 = \tfrac{1}{2}(150 \times 10^{-6}\ C)(50\ V) = 0.375 \times 10^{-2}\ J$$
$$W = W_1 + W_2 = 3.375 \times 10^{-2}\ J$$

---

16 Find the total energy for part a.

16
$$W_1 = \tfrac{1}{2}(500 \times 10^{-6}\ C)(83.3\ V) = 2.08 \times 10^{-2}\ J$$
$$W_2 = \tfrac{1}{2}(250 \times 10^{-6}\ C)(83.3\ V) = 1.04 \times 10^{-2}\ J$$
$$W = 3.12 \times 10^{-2}\ J$$

---

17 Find the total energy for part b.

17
$$W_1 = \tfrac{1}{2}(300 \times 10^{-6}\ C)(50\ V) = 0.75 \times 10^{-2}\ J$$
$$W_2 = \tfrac{1}{2}(150 \times 10^{-6}\ C)(50\ V) = 0.375 \times 10^{-2}\ J$$
$$W = 1.125 \times 10^{-2}\ J$$

---

18 **Problem 3** Two sheets of dielectric with constants K_1 and K_2 and equal thicknesses are inserted between the plates of a parallel plate capacitor. The separation of the plates is d. Find the capacitance by considering this as two capacitors with dielectric constants K_1 and K_2 in series with each other.

18

Answer
$$C = \frac{2\epsilon_0 A}{d} \left(\frac{K_1 K_2}{K_1 + K_2} \right)$$

If you could not solve this problem, go through frames 19–21.

19 What are the capacitances C_1 and C_2 in terms of A and d?

19

$$C_1 = \frac{K_1 \epsilon_0 A}{d/2} = \frac{2K_1 \epsilon_0 A}{d}$$

$$C_2 = \frac{K_2 \epsilon_0 A}{d/2} = \frac{2K_2 \epsilon_0 A}{d}$$

20 What is the equivalent capacitance?

20
$$\frac{1}{C} = \frac{1}{C_1} + \frac{1}{C_2}$$
$$C = \frac{C_1 C_2}{C_1 + C_2}$$

21 Substitute the values in the expression for the equivalent capacitance.

21
$$C = \frac{\left(\dfrac{2K_1\epsilon_0 A}{d}\right)\left(\dfrac{2K_2\epsilon_0 A}{d}\right)}{\dfrac{2\epsilon_0 A}{d}(K_1 + K_2)}$$
$$= \frac{2\epsilon_0 A}{d}\left(\frac{K_1 K_2}{K_1 + K_2}\right)$$

28

Current, Resistance and Electromotive Force

CHAPTER SUMMARY

This chapter deals with charged particles in motion and the relationship for current, voltage and resistance in a conductor as expressed by Ohm's law. Note that resistance is temperature dependent. The energy required to move the charge through the conductor is supplied by the seat of electromotive force; the energy relations also lead to a discussion of work and power in electrical circuits. In addition, physiological effects of current, the electric field of the earth and the theory of metallic conduction are presented.

BASIC TERMS — *Give definitions or meanings for the following:*

current (28-1)
ampere (28-1)
current density (28-1)
resistivity (28-2)
semiconductor (28-2)
temperature coefficient of resistivity (28-2)
superconductor (28-2)
resistance (28-3)
Ohm's law (28-3)
ohm (28-3)

resistor (28-3)
electromotive force (28-4)
complete circuit (28-4)
voltmeter (28-4)
ammeter (28-4)
Kirchhoff's loop rule (28-4)
internal resistance (28-4)
mean free path (28-7)
mean free time (28-7)

PROGRAMMED QUIZ

1 If the diameter of a wire is doubled, what happens to the resistance?

1 Becomes ¼.

$$R = \frac{\rho l}{A} = \frac{\rho l}{\pi d^2/4} = \frac{4\rho l}{\pi d^2}$$

if $d' = 2d$, then

$$R' = \frac{\rho l}{\pi d^2} = \frac{R}{4}$$

2 Why isn't Ohm's law a basic physical law?

2 It is an idealized model that describes the behavior of certain materials, but it is not a general property of all matter.

3 Does the shape of the wire, i.e. whether it is bent in a circle or square, affect its resistance?

3 No, $R = \rho l/A$.

4 Is the current the same at all points in a closed loop? Why?

4 Yes, because of conservation of charge.

5 What do we call the "influence" that makes charge move from a lower to a higher potential?

5 Electromotive force (emf).

6 What is the relationship between the emf and the terminal potential difference of a source when there is no current?

6 The emf of a source equals its potential difference.

7 How do we treat a source of emf which has an internal resistance?

7 As if it were a resistanceless emf of the same value in series with a resistance equal to the internal resistance.

8 Can this internal resistance be measured directly?

8 No, it must be calculated from measurements of the current and terminal voltage, $V = \mathcal{E} - Ir$.

9 What are some sources of emf?

9 Batteries, solar cells, generators.

10 Can a material have a negative temperature coefficient of resistivity?

10 Yes, for certain nonmetals, such as carbon, silicon and germanium, an increase in temperature brings about a decrease in resistivity.

11 The electromotive force has the same units as potential difference. Are these two quantities the same?

11 No, the potential difference is the work of an electrostatic field and the electromotive force is the work of a non-electrostatic field.

12 Does the emf of a source vary with current? What about the voltage?

12 The emf is nearly constant; the voltage depends on the current.

13 Do all the charged particles in a conductor move in the same direction?

13 No, the positively charged particles move in the direction of the electric field and the negatively charged particles move in the opposite direction.

14 Metals are good conductors because of their free electrons. This results in what other property?

14 Good thermal conductivity.

15 Compare the electrostatic and non-electrostatic fields for a source on open circuit.

15 Opposite in direction, equal in magnitude, $E_e = -E_n$.

---

16 How do we know if an emf is positive or negative?

16 An emf is positive if the direction of the non-electrostatic field (from negative to positive terminal) is in the direction that you chose to be positive, it is negative if this field is in the opposite direction.

---

17 Can the electrostatic field in a source be greater than the non-electrostatic? Give an example.

17 Yes, charging a battery.

---

18 Current is the motion of charge from a _____ potential to a _____ potential.

18 Higher; lower.

MAIN IDEAS

A current in a conductor is produced by an electric field which exerts a driving force on its free charge. The current $I = \Delta Q / \Delta t$, where ΔQ is the net charge which flows across a given area in time Δt. One coulomb per second is defined as one ampere. The current density $J = I/A$ is the current per unit cross-sectional area. A charge in a conductor experiences a force $F = qE$ where E is the electric field within the conductor.

The resistivity ρ of a material is defined as $\rho = E/J$, where E is the electric field within the conductor. $E = \rho J$ is referred to as Ohm's law. The resistivity varies with temperature, $\rho_T = \rho_0[1 + \alpha(T - T_0)]$ where ρ_0 is the resistivity at a reference temperature T_0 and ρ_T at the temperature T. The temperature coefficient of resistivity is α.

The resistance R of a conductor is defined as $R = \rho l / A = V/I$, where ρ = resistivity, l = length and A = constant cross-sectional area. The resistance is measured in ohms, where one ohm $(1\ \Omega) = 1\ \mathrm{V \cdot A^{-1}}$. The resistance also varies with temperature, $R_T = R_0[1 + \alpha(T - T_0)]$ where R_T is the resistance at temperature T and R_0 is the resistance at T_0, usually taken as 20°C or 0°C. The relation $V = IR$ is often referred to as Ohm's law.

A source (e.g. dry cell, storage battery, generator) is a device which supplies energy to a circuit. It maintains a potential difference between its two terminals, the higher potential is indicated by + and the lower potential by −. An electrostatic field E_e is associated with the potential difference. It exists at all points between and around the terminals a and b of the source. E_e gives rise to the voltage V_{ab} between the terminals. However, there also exists a field E_n of non-electrostatic origin which gives rise to an electromotive force (emf) which is denoted by $\mathcal{E}$ and remains constant for a given source. The terminal potential difference under closed circuit conditions is given by V_{ab} and related to $\mathcal{E}$ by $V_{ab} = \mathcal{E} - Ir$, where I is the current flowing in the circuit and r is the internal resistance of the source. If R is the external resistance of a circuit, $I = \dfrac{\mathcal{E}}{R + r}$. In charging a battery $V_{ab} = \mathcal{E} + Ir$ and in discharging a battery $V_{ab} = \mathcal{E} - Ir$.

As charge passes through a conductor, an electric field does work on it. In a time Δt, the work ΔW done on charge ΔQ is given by the product of the potential difference and the quantity of charge,

$$\Delta W = V_{ab}\Delta Q = V_{ab}I\Delta t$$
Power $= P = \Delta W / \Delta t = V_{ab}I = I^2 R = V^2/R.$
Power output of a source: $P = \mathcal{E}I - I^2 r.$
Power input to a source (ex: automobile battery being charged by an alternator): $P = \mathcal{E}I + I^2 r.$

A thermocouple consists of two different metals joined to each other at two junctions. When these two junctions are maintained at different temperatures, a thermal emf will be produced. This phenomenon is known as the Seebeck effect. The reverse, that is the evolution or absorption of heat when an electric current crosses the junction of two dissimilar metals is known as the Peltier effect.

The symbol for a battery is 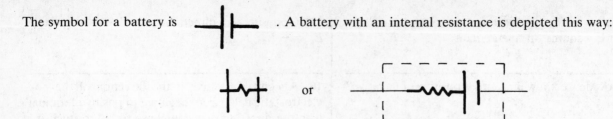 . A battery with an internal resistance is depicted this way:

or

The rule $I = \dfrac{\mathcal{E}}{R + r}$ for finding the current in a single seat circuit can be rewritten for complex circuits which have several seats of emf or several branches. If we traverse a loop and measure potential differences across each circuit element, we will find that when we return to the starting point the algebraic sum of these potential differences is zero in accordance with the law of conservation of energy. This procedure is outlined in Kirchhoff's loop rule $\Sigma (\mathcal{E} + IR) = 0$. To use Kirchhoff's loop rule follow these steps:

1 Label all quantities, known and unknown. Assume that the current is flowing in a particular direction. The selection is arbitrary: if we make the wrong choice, the current I will be negative. Although, strictly speaking, emf is not a vector quantity, it is useful to assign to it a direction (or sense). We shall consider the direction of an emf to be from the − toward the + terminal of the seat within the seat. (Batteries and generators are called seats of electromotive force.) This emf is denoted by an arrow:

2 Designate a direction, clockwise or counter-clockwise, to traverse the loop.

3 Go around the loop in the designated direction, adding emfs and IR products. We will use the following sign conventions: a) An emf is positive when it is traversed in the same direction as the emf arrow (from − to +) and negative when it is traversed in the opposite direction. b) An IR term is negative if the resistance is traversed in the same direction as the assumed current, positive if in the opposite direction.

4 Equate the sum of step 3 to zero, $\Sigma(\mathcal{E} + IR) = 0$.

In this problem, we assume a counter-clockwise direction for the current. Starting at a, we traverse the loop in a counter-clockwise direction adding emf's and IR terms in accordance with our sign convention:

$$\Sigma(\mathcal{E} + IR) = 0$$
$$24\,V - I(2\Omega) - I(4\Omega) - 6V - I(9\Omega) - I(1\Omega)$$
$$- 8V - I(4\Omega) = 0$$
$$10V = I(20\Omega)$$
$$I = 0.5\ A$$

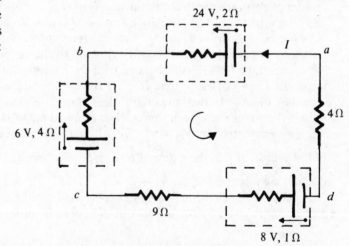

Problem solving strategies: The potential difference between any two points can be obtained by using the same bookkeeping system described in step 3 above. Start at point a; the potential of this point is designated V_a. Traverse the circuit to the second point b, adding algebraically the potential changes including those associated with emf's and the resistances encountered. Then $V_a + \Sigma\limits_{a \to b} (\mathcal{E} + IR) = V_b$, the potential at point b.

Find V_{ab} for the above circuit by traversing the loop in a counterclockwise direction. Remember $I = 0.5\ A$.
$$V_a + \sum_{a \to b} (\mathcal{E} + IR) = V_b$$
$$V_a + 24V - (0.5\ A)(2\Omega) = V_b$$
$$V_a + 23V = V_b$$
$$V_a - V_b = V_{ab} = -23V$$

Find V_{ab} by traversing the loop in a clockwise direction.

$$V_a + (0.5\text{ A})(4\Omega) + 8\text{V} + (0.5\text{ A})(1\Omega) + (0.5\text{ A})(9\Omega) + 6\text{V} + (0.5\text{ A})(4\Omega) = V_b$$

$$V_a + 23\text{V} = V_b$$

$$V_a - V_b = V_{ab} = -23\text{V}.$$

PROGRAMMED QUIZ

1 What net charge flows through an area in 0.02 s if the current is 3 milliamperes?

1

$$I = \frac{Q}{t}$$

$$Q = (3 \times 10^{-3}\text{ A})(0.02\text{ s})$$
$$= 6 \times 10^{-5}\text{ C}$$

2 If the above cross-sectional area is $5 \times 10^{-6}\text{ m}^2$, what is the current density?

2

$$J = \frac{I}{A}$$
$$= \frac{3 \times 10^{-3}\text{ A}}{5 \times 10^{-6}\text{ m}^2} = 6 \times 10^2\text{ A}\cdot\text{m}^{-2}$$

3 At room temperature, the resistivity of copper is $1.72 \times 10^{-8}\,\Omega\cdot\text{m}$. What electric field is needed to establish a current density of $3 \times 10^7\text{ A}\cdot\text{m}^{-2}$?

3

$$\rho = \frac{E}{J}$$

$$E = (1.72 \times 10^{-8}\,\Omega\cdot\text{m})(3 \times 10^7\text{ A}\cdot\text{m}^{-2})$$
$$= 0.516\text{ V}\cdot\text{m}^{-1}$$

Note: $(\Omega\cdot\text{m})(\text{A}\cdot\text{m}^{-2}) = (\text{V}\cdot\text{A}^{-1})(\text{A}\cdot\text{m}^{-1}) = \text{V}\cdot\text{m}^{-1}$

4 At room temperature, what would be the resistance of a copper wire 1 m long and 0.1 mm in radius?

4

$$R = \frac{\rho l}{A} = \frac{\rho l}{\pi r^2}$$

$$= \frac{(1.72 \times 10^{-8}\,\Omega\cdot\text{m})(1\text{ m})}{\pi(0.1 \times 10^{-3}\text{ m})^2}$$

$$= 0.547\,\Omega$$

5 What is the resistance of the copper wire at 5 C° above room temperature? ($\alpha = 0.00393\,(\text{C}^\circ)^{-1}$)

5

$$R_T = R_0[1 + \alpha(T - T_0)]$$
$$= 0.547\,\Omega[1 + (3.93 \times 10^{-3}\,(\text{C}^\circ)^{-1})(5\text{ C}^\circ)]$$
$$= 0.558\,\Omega$$

6 Indicate by an arrow the direction for the current I in this circuit.

6

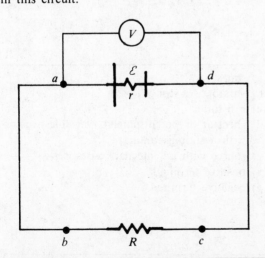

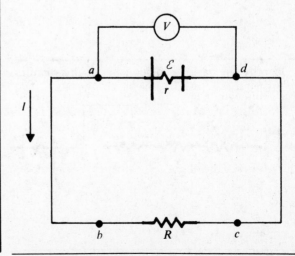

7 Write the expression for V_{ad} traversing the loop in a counterclockwise direction.

7
$$V_a - IR = V_d$$
$$V_{ad} = V_a - V_d = IR$$

8 Write the expression for V_{ad} traversing the loop in a clockwise direction.

8
$$V_a - \mathcal{E} + Ir = V_d$$
$$V_{ad} = V_a - V_d = \mathcal{E} - Ir$$

9 Equate the two expressions for the potential difference and solve for I.

9
$$IR = \mathcal{E} - Ir$$
$$I = \frac{\mathcal{E}}{r + R}$$

10 A source of emf = 4 V has a terminal voltage of 3.2 V. If the current of the source emf is 2 mA, what is the internal resistance of the source?

10
$$V_{ab} = \mathcal{E} - Ir$$
$$r = \frac{4\,V - 3.2\,V}{2 \times 10^{-3}\,A} = 400\,\Omega$$

11 What is the external resistance of this circuit?

11
$$I = \frac{\mathcal{E}}{R + r}$$
$$R = \frac{\mathcal{E}}{I} - r$$
$$= \frac{4\,V}{2 \times 10^{-3}\,A} - 400\,\Omega$$
$$= 2000\,\Omega - 400\,\Omega = 1600\,\Omega$$

12 How much power is dissipated in the external resistor?

12
$$P = VI$$
$$= (3.2\,V)(2 \times 10^{-3}\,A) = 6.4 \times 10^{-3}\,W$$
another method
$$P = I^2R$$
$$= (2 \times 10^{-3}\,A)^2(1600\,\Omega) = 6.4 \times 10^{-3}\,W$$

13 Identify the various components of this circuit.

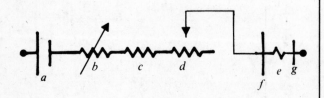

13
a) source
b) variable resistor
c) resistor
d) rheostat or potentiometer (variable resistor with a sliding contact)
e) source with an internal resistance
f) positive terminal
g) negative terminal

14 What is the internal resistance of a dry cell (emf = 1.35 V) if the short-circuit current is 20 A?

14

$$I = \frac{\mathcal{E}}{r}$$

$$r = \frac{1.35 \text{ V}}{20 \text{ A}} = 0.0675 \ \Omega$$

---

15 To derive Ohm's law, consider a conductor with uniform cross section A and length l. Using $E = \rho J$ and $I = JA$ and the definition for R, what is the potential difference between the ends?

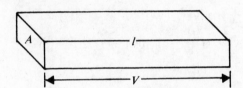

15

$$\begin{aligned} V &= El \\ &= \rho J l \\ &= \frac{\rho l I}{A} \end{aligned}$$

but $\dfrac{\rho l}{A} = R$

$\therefore \ V = IR$ which is Ohm's law.

---

16 Derive the expression for the potential difference between the terminals of a battery that is discharging.

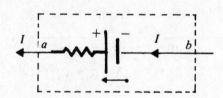

16 When a battery is discharging, there is a current from the negative to the positive terminal within the battery. Starting at a, traverse the battery in a clockwise direction.

$$V_a + Ir - \mathcal{E} = V_b$$
$$V_a - V_b = V_{ab} = \mathcal{E} - Ir$$

We are moving against the current, so I is $+$. We are moving opposite to the direction of $\mathcal{E}$ so $\mathcal{E}$ is $-$.

---

17 Derive the expression for the potential difference between the terminals of a battery that is being charged.

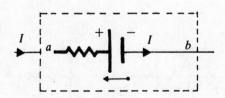

17 When a battery is being charged there is a current from the positive to the negative terminal within the battery. Starting at a, traverse the battery in a clockwise direction.

$$V_a - Ir - \mathcal{E} = V_b$$
$$V_a - V_b = V_{ab} = \mathcal{E} + Ir$$

We are moving with the current, so I is $-$. We are moving opposite to the direction of $\mathcal{E}$ so $\mathcal{E}$ is $-$.

STEP BY STEP SOLUTIONS OF PROBLEMS

Problem 1 a) Find the current in this circuit (assume the counterclockwise direction as positive). b) Find V_{ad} by following two different paths. c) A source of emf = 23 V and internal resistance = 3 Ω is inserted in the circuit at d, its positive terminal connected to the positive terminal of the 10 V battery. What is the potential difference between the terminals of the 6 V battery?

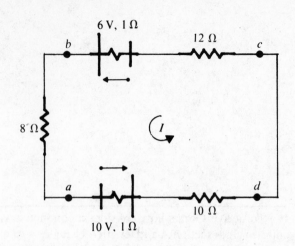

1 Starting at a and going counterclockwise, add the potential changes and set the sum equal to zero. Solve for I.

1
$$\Sigma(\mathcal{E} + IR) = 0$$
$$10V - I(1\Omega) - I(10\Omega) - I(12\Omega) + 6V - I(1\Omega)$$
$$- I(8\Omega) = 0$$
$$16V = I(32\Omega)$$
$$I = 0.5 \text{ A}$$

2 Find V_{ad} from the top part of the loop. Note that we are going against the current.

2
$$V_a + \sum_{a\_d}(\mathcal{E} + IR) = V_d$$
$$V_a + (0.5\,\text{A})(8\,\Omega) - 6V + (0.5\,\text{A})(1\,\Omega) + (0.5\,\text{A})(12\,\Omega) = V_d$$
$$V_{ad} = V_a - V_d = 6\text{ V} - (0.5\,\text{A})(21\,\Omega) = -4.5\text{ V}$$

3 Find V_{ad} from the bottom part of the loop.

3
$$V_a + 10\text{ V} - (0.5\,\text{A})(1\,\Omega) - (0.5\,\text{A})(10\,\Omega) = V_d$$
$$V_{ad} = -10\text{ V} + (0.5\,\text{A})(11\,\Omega) = -4.5\text{ V}$$

4 Redraw the circuit for part c.

4

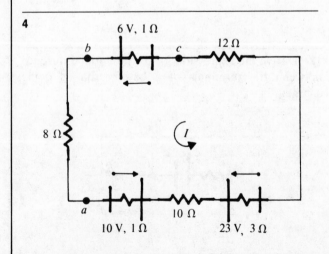

5 Find I; assume the counterclockwise direction as positive.

5

$\Sigma(\mathcal{E} + IR) = 0$
$10 \text{ V} - I(1 \text{ }\Omega) - I(10\Omega) - 23 \text{ V} - I(3\Omega) - I(12\Omega)$
$\qquad + 6\text{V} - I(1\Omega) - I(8\Omega) = 0$
$\qquad - 7\text{V} = I(35\Omega)$
$\qquad I = -0.2 \text{ A}$

The negative sign indicates that the actual direction of the current is opposite to the assumed direction.

---

6 Find V_{bc} from the top part of the circuit. It should be noted that the direction of the current is from b to c.

6

$$V_b + \sum_{b \to c} (\mathcal{E} + IR) = V_c$$
$$V_b - 6 \text{ V} - (0.2 \text{ A}) (1 \text{ }\Omega) = V_c$$
$$V_{bc} = V_b - V_c = 6\text{ }V + 0.2 \text{ V} = 6.2 \text{ V}$$

---

7 To check, find V_{bc} from the lower part of the circuit.

7

$V_b + (0.2 \text{ A}) (8 \text{ }\Omega) + 10 \text{ V} + (0.2 \text{ A}) (1 \text{ }\Omega)$
$+ (0.2 \text{ A}) (10 \text{ }\Omega) - 23 \text{ V} + (0.2 \text{ A}) (3 \text{ }\Omega)$
$+ (0.2 \text{ A}) (12 \text{ }\Omega) = V_c$
$\qquad V_{bc} = 13 \text{ V} - (0.2 \text{ A}) (34 \text{ }\Omega) = 6.2 \text{ V}$

Problem 2 In the circuit, when the switch S is open, the voltmeter reads 1.6 V and when S is closed, the voltmeter reads 1.4 V. Find a) the emf and the internal resistance of the dry cell (it should be noted that $R_v = \infty$ and $R_A = 0$) and b) the current in the circuit when S is closed.

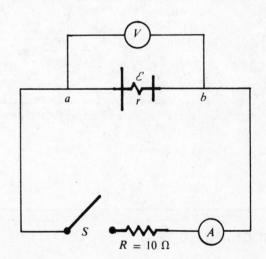

8 What is the emf of the dry cell?

8 Since the emf is the open circuit voltage between the terminals, $\mathcal{E} = 1.6$ V.

---

9 Write the expression relating V_{ab} and $\mathcal{E}$ when the current is being supplied by the battery.

9 $V_{ab} = \mathcal{E} - Ir$

---

10 Express the relationship among I, $\mathcal{E}$ r and R.

10

$$I = \frac{\mathcal{E}}{r + R}$$

11 Substitute this into the equation for V_{ab} and solve for r.

11
$$r = \left(\frac{\mathcal{E} - V_{ab}}{V_{ab}} \right) R$$

---

12 Substitute the given values.

12
$$r = \frac{1.6 \text{ V} - 1.4 \text{ V}}{1.4 \text{ V}} (10 \ \Omega)$$
$$= 1.43 \ \Omega$$

---

13 Find the value of I.

13
$$I = \frac{\mathcal{E}}{r + R}$$
$$= \frac{1.6 \text{ V}}{1.43 \ \Omega + 10 \ \Omega} = 0.140 \text{ A}$$

Problem 3 A copper wire has a temperature coefficient of resistivity of 0.00393 $(C°)^{-1}$ at 20°C. If the resistance is 224 Ω at 50°C, find its resistance at 150°C.

14 First we must find the resistance at $T_0 = 20°C$.

14
$$R_T = R_0[1 + \alpha(T - T_0)]$$
$$224 \ \Omega = R_0[1 + 0.00393 \ (C°)^{-1} \ (30 \ C°)]$$
$$= 200 \ \Omega$$

---

15 Apply the same formula again to find the resistance at $T = 150°C$.

15
$$R_T = 200 \ \Omega[1 + 0.00393 \ (C°)^{-1} \ (130 \ C°)]$$
$$= 302 \ \Omega$$

PROGRAMMED TEST

1 ***Problem 1*** A storage battery, emf = 10 V and internal resistance = 0.12 Ω is to be charged from a 112 V dc supply. a) Which terminal should be connected to the + side of the line? b) What is the charging current if the battery is connected directly across the line? c) What series resistance will limit the current to 10 A? Using this resistor find d) the potential difference across the terminals of the battery, e) the power from the line, f) the power dissipated in the resistor and g) the useful power input to the battery.

1
Answer
+ terminal, 850 A, 10.08 Ω. 11.2 V, 1120 W, 1008 W, 1120 W

If you solved this problem correctly, go to frame 10. If you could not solve this problem, go through frames 2–9.

2 Which terminal should be connected to the + side of the line?

2 The positive terminal.

---

3 What is the current for charging the battery?

3 $V_{ab} = \mathcal{E} + Ir$

$$I = \frac{112\ \text{V} - 10\ \text{V}}{0.12\ \Omega} = 850\ \text{A}$$

---

4 Find the series resistor that will limit the current to 10 A.

4 $V_{ab} = \mathcal{E} + I(R + r)$

$$R = \frac{112\ \text{V} - 10\ \text{V}}{10\ \text{A}} - 0.12\ \Omega = 10.08\ \Omega$$

---

5 Find the potential difference across the battery. Remember that the battery is being charged.

5 $V_{ab} = \mathcal{E} + Ir$
$$= 10\ \text{V} + (10\ \text{A})(0.12\ \Omega)$$
$$= 11.2\ \text{V}$$

---

6 What is the power from the line?

6 $P = V_{ab}I$
$$= (112\ \text{V})(10\ \text{A}) = 1120\ \text{W}$$

---

7 What is the power dissipated in the series resistor?

7 $P = I^2 R$
$$= (10\ \text{A})^2(10.08\ \Omega)$$
$$= 1008\ \text{W}$$

---

8 What is the power dissipated in the internal resistor of the battery?

8 $P = I^2 r$

$$= (10\ \text{A})^2(0.12\ \Omega) = 12\ \text{W}$$

---

9 What is the useful power input to the battery?

9 The useful power input to the battery is the power supplied by the line minus the power dissipated in the series resistor minus the power dissipated in the internal resistor of the battery.
$P = 1120\ \text{W} - 1008\ \text{W} - 12\ \text{W} = 100\ \text{W}$

---

10 **Problem 2** The potential difference across the terminals of a battery is 10 V when there is a current from the negative to the positive terminal. When the current is in the reverse direction, the potential difference is 13 V. A voltmeter connected across the terminals of the battery reads 11 V under open circuit conditions. The internal resistance is 0.4 Ω. What is a) the emf, and the current when the battery is b) discharging and c) charging?

10 **Answer**
11 V, 2.5 A, 5 A

If you solved this problem correctly, go to frame 14. If you could not solve this problem, go through frames 11–13.

11 What is the emf?

11 11 V; under open circuit conditions, the voltmeter connected across the terminals reads the emf.

---

12 What is the current when the battery is discharging, i.e., the direction of the current is from the negative to the positive terminal within the battery and from the positive to the negative terminal in the external circuit?

12

$$V_{ab} = \mathcal{E} - Ir$$
$$I = \frac{11\ V - 10\ V}{0.4\ \Omega} = 2.5\ A$$

---

13 What is the current when the battery is being charged, i.e., the direction of the current is from the positive to the negative terminal within the battery?

13

$$V_{ab} = \mathcal{E} + Ir$$
$$I = \frac{13\ V - 11\ V}{0.4\ \Omega} = 5\ A$$

---

14 **Problem 3** A 720 W heater operates from a 120 V line. Find a) its resistance, b) the current that it draws and c) the rate of dissipation of energy in calories per second. d) If the line voltage drops to 106 V, what power does the heater take? (Assume constant resistance.)

14 **Answer**
20 Ω, 6 A, 172 cal · s^{-1}, 562 W

If you solved this problem correctly, go to frame 19. If you could not solve this problem, go through frames 15–18.

15 Find the resistance using power relationships.

15

$$P = \frac{V^2}{R}$$
$$R = \frac{(120\ V)^2}{720\ W} = 20\ \Omega$$

---

16 Find the current.

16
$$I = \frac{V}{R}$$
$$= \frac{120 \text{ V}}{20 \text{ }\Omega} = 6 \text{ A}$$

---

17 What is the rate of dissipation of energy? (1 W = 1 J · s^{-1} = 0.239 cal · s^{-1}).

17
$$\left(720 \text{ W}\right) \left(\frac{0.239 \text{ cal} \cdot \text{s}^{-1}}{1 \text{ W}}\right) = 172 \text{ cal} \cdot \text{s}^{-1}$$

---

18 What is the power when the line voltage decreases to 106 V?

18
$$P = \frac{V^2}{R}$$
$$= \frac{(106 \text{ V})^2}{20 \text{ }\Omega}$$
$$= 562 \text{ W}$$

---

19 **Problem 4** Calculate the value of $\mathcal{E}$ so that the current will be 1 A in the clockwise direction. Find V_{ab} by considering the top of the circuit and check your result by considering the bottom section.

19

Answer
25 V, 11 V

If you could not solve this problem, go through frames 20–22.

20 Go around the loop in a clockwise direction starting at a. Add emf's and IR terms in accordance with our sign conventions. Compute $\Sigma(\mathcal{E} + IR) = 0$.

20
$$-1 \text{ A} (1 \text{ }\Omega) - 10 \text{ V} + \mathcal{E} - 1 \text{ A} (2 \text{ }\Omega) - 1 \text{ A} (12 \text{ }\Omega) = 0$$
$$-25 \text{ V} + \mathcal{E} = 0$$
$$\mathcal{E} = 25 \text{ V}$$

---

21 Find V_{ab} by considering the top of the circuit.

21
$$V_a - 1 \text{ A} (1 \text{ }\Omega) - 10 \text{ V} = V_b$$
$$V_a - V_b = V_{ab} = 11 \text{ V}$$

---

22 Find V_{ab} by considering the bottom of the circuit.

22
$$V_a + 1 \text{ A} (12 \text{ }\Omega) + 1 \text{ A} (2 \text{ }\Omega) - 25 \text{ V} = V_b$$
$$V_a - V_b = V_{ab} = 11 \text{ V}$$

29

Direct-current Circuits

CHAPTER SUMMARY

The mathematical method for finding the equivalent resistance for resistors in series and parallel is presented as well as Kirchhoff's rules for networks that cannot be reduced to simple combinations. Networks with capacitors in series with resistors are also dealt with. Ammeters, voltmeters, ohmmeters and the relationships among the various electrical quantities in each instrument are described.

BASIC TERMS — *Give definitions or meanings for the following:*

network (29-I)
series (29-1)
parallel (29-1)
equivalent resistance (29-1)
branch point (29-2)
loop (29-2)
Kirchhoff's point rule (29-2)
Kirchhoff's loop rule (29-2)

d'Arsonval galvanometer (29-3)
ammeter (29-3)
voltmeter (29-3)
ohmmeter (29-3)
shunt resistor (29-3)
time constant (relaxation time) (29-4)
short circuit (29-5)
open circuit (29-5)

PROGRAMMED QUIZ

1 Kirchhoff's rules are applications of the conservation principles. The point rule is related to conservation of _____, the loop rule to conservation of _____.

1 Electric charge; energy.

2 Can you apply Kirchhoff's rules if the direction of the current is not known?

2 Yes, choose an arbitrary direction for the current; the answer will be negative if the actual direction is opposite to the one you chose.

3 Should an ammeter have a high or low resistance? Why?

3 The ammeter is connected in series in the circuit so the current that is to be measured passes through the ammeter. The resistance should be as low as possible so insertion of the ammeter does not produce an appreciable change in the current.

4 Should a voltmeter have a high or low resistance? Why?

4 Since it is connected in parallel with the circuit, the resistance should be as large as possible so it does not alter the potential difference between two points; i.e. so it diverts as little current from the original circuit as possible.

5 What instruments would you use to measure the resistance and power in a circuit?

5 A voltmeter together with an ammeter.

6 What is the basic measuring instrument for direct current circuits?

6 Galvanometer; by adding appropriate resistors it can be used as a voltmeter, ammeter or ohmmeter.

7 If two resistors are connected in parallel, what can we say about the potential differences between their ends?

7 Potential differences must be the same.

8 How must resistors be connected so that the current flowing through each resistor is the same?

8 In series.

9 Do the current and potential values depend on time?

9 Only when a capacitor is included in the circuit.

10 Does Kirchhoff's point rule hold for any circuit element?

10 It does not hold for a capacitor that is charging or discharging since charge can flow from a capacitor without any charge entering it (or vice versa).

11 What are the units of the time constant?

11 Seconds; $\tau = RC$; $(1\ \text{V} \cdot \text{A}^{-1})(1\ \text{C} \cdot \text{V}^{-1}) = 1\ \text{s}$.

12 Why can't you take an exact measurement of the emf of a cell with a voltmeter?

12 When the voltmeter is connected to the cell, a circuit is formed. Since $V_{ab} = \mathcal{E} - Ir$, the terminal voltage will be less than the emf.

---

13 What is a device for measuring voltage which does not draw any current?

13 Potentiometer.

---

14 What can we say about the voltage, current and resistance of resistors in series?

14 The current is the same through each resistor, the equivalent resistance is equal to the sum of the individual resistances and the potential difference across the entire network equals the sum of the potential differences across each resistor.

---

15 What can we say about the voltage, current and resistance of resistors in parallel?

15 The line current is equal to the sum of the currents through each resistor, the potential difference across each resistor is the same and the reciprocal of the equivalent resistance equals the sum of the reciprocals of the individual resistances.

---

16 What is the meaning of an equivalent resistance?

16 An equivalent resistance replaces a combination of resistances without changing the potential difference between the terminals of the combination or the current in the rest of the circuit.

---

17 What is a branch point in a network? Identify the branch points in this network.

17 A point where three or more conductors are joined; b, d, e and g.

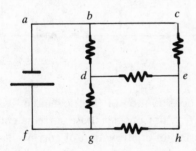

---

18 What is a loop in a network? Identify the loops in the above network.

18 Any closed conducting path;
abdgfa,
bcedb,
bcehgdb,
dehgd,
abcehgfa,
abcedgfa,
abdehgfa.

MAIN IDEAS

1 Resistors in series. R_1, R_2 and R_3 are connected in series; they provide a single path for the current I as it goes from a to d. $V_{ad} = V_{ab} + V_{bc} + V_{cd}$ and $R = R_1 + R_2 + R_3$, where R is the equivalent resistance.

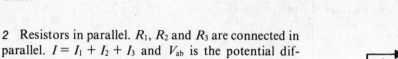

2 Resistors in parallel. R_1, R_2 and R_3 are connected in parallel. $I = I_1 + I_2 + I_3$ and V_{ab} is the potential difference across each resistor. $1/R = 1/R_1 + 1/R_2 + 1/R_3$, where R is the equivalent resistance.

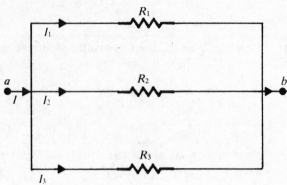

3 A network consists of various electrical components (e.g. sources, resistors, capacitors, inductances). A branch point in a network is a point where three or more conductors are joined. A loop is any closed conducting path.

Identification of branch points and loops: b, d, e and g are branch points; a, c, h and f are not branch points because only two conductors are joined. Possible loops: $abdgfa$, $bcedb$, $bcehgdb$, $dehgd$, $abcehgfa$.

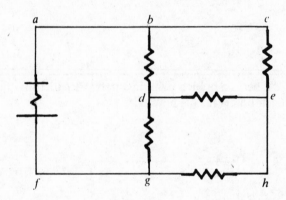

4 Kirchhoff's rules. The point rule is an application of the principle of conservation of electric charge. It states that the algebraic sum of the currents toward any branch point is zero, $\Sigma I = 0$. Consider those currents entering a point as positive; those leaving as negative. The loop rule is an expression of conservation of energy. It states that the algebraic sum of the potential differences in any loop must equal zero, $\Sigma(\mathcal{E} + IR) = 0$. Thus the potential differences associated with emf's and those of resistive elements must be included. The procedure to follow in using the loop rule can be broken down into the following steps: a) Label all quantities, both known and unknown. Include an assumed sense of direction for each unknown current and emf. If a particular direction is chosen incorrectly, the value of the quantity will emerge from the analysis with a negative sign. b) Choose any closed loop in the network and designate a direction, clockwise or counterclockwise, to traverse the loop. c) Go around the loop in the designated direction, adding emf's and IR terms. An emf is considered positive when it is traversed in the same direction as the emf arrow (from $-$ to $+$) and negative when it is traversed in the opposite direction. An IR term is considered negative if the resistor is traversed in the same direction as the assumed current; positive if in the opposite direction. d) Use $\Sigma(\mathcal{E} + IR) = 0$; equate the sum of emf and IR terms from the previous step to zero. e) If necessary, choose another loop to obtain a different relationship between the unknowns and continue until there are as many equations as unknowns or until every circuit element has been included in at least one of the loops.

5 An ammeter is a galvanometer which is shunted (has a resistance in parallel with the coil resistance). $V_{ab} = I_c R_c = I_{sh} R_{sh}$. The equivalent resistance R of the ammeter is given by $1/R = 1/R_c + 1/R_{sh}$. In order to measure current, the ammeter must be placed in series with that part of the circuit whose current we wish to know. Hence an ammeter must have a very low resistance.

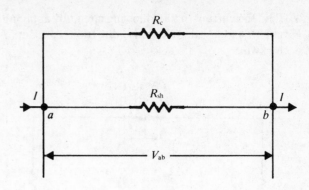

6 A voltmeter is a galvanometer which has a resistance in series with the coil resistance. $V_{ab} = I(R_c + R_s)$. The equivalent resistance R of the voltmeter is given by $R = R_c + R_s$. The voltmeter is connected in parallel with the element whose voltage drop we are measuring.

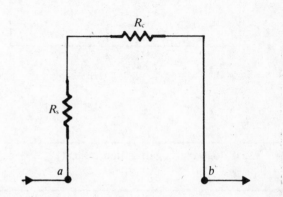

7 The R-C series circuit. The sudden appearance of a voltage V across an uncharged capacitor C in series with a resistance R will produce a current i given by $i = I_0 e^{-t/RC}$ where $I_0 = V/R$ is the initial current. It should be noted that at the instant connections are made, $q = 0$ (or $Q_0 = 0$). In time the charge increases and eventually $q = CV = Q_f$, the final charge on the capacitor. The current, on the other hand, will go from I_0 to zero. After a time $\tau = RC$ (called the time constant), the current will decrease from I_0 to I_0/e. The half-life of the circuit t_h is the time for the current to decrease to half its value: $t_h = RC \ln 2 = 0.693 RC$. Likewise, consider a capacitor with an initial charge Q_0 which is discharged through a resistor until its charge eventually decreases to zero. When $t = 0$ and $q = Q_0$, the initial current $I_0 = Q_0/RC = V_0/R$ where V_0 is the initial potential difference across the capacitor. As the capacitor discharges, q and i decrease in accordance with the relationships $q = Q_0 e^{-t/RC}$ and $i = I_0 e^{-t/RC}$.

PROGRAMMED QUIZ

1 What is the equivalent resistance for the following resistors in series: $R_1 = 4\ \Omega$, $R_2 = 5\ \Omega$, $R_3 = 6\ \Omega$ and $R_4 = 7\ \Omega$?

1

$$
\begin{aligned}
R &= R_1 + R_2 + R_3 + R_4 \\
&= 4\ \Omega + 5\ \Omega + 6\ \Omega + 7\ \Omega \\
&= 22\ \Omega
\end{aligned}
$$

2 What is the equivalent resistor for the following resistors in parallel: $R_1 = 10\ \Omega$, $R_2 = 20\ \Omega$, $R_3 = 25\ \Omega$ and $R_4 = 50\ \Omega$?

2

$$
\begin{aligned}
\frac{1}{R} &= \frac{1}{R_1} + \frac{1}{R_2} + \frac{1}{R_3} + \frac{1}{R_4} \\
&= \frac{1}{10\ \Omega} + \frac{1}{20\ \Omega} + \frac{1}{25\ \Omega} + \frac{1}{50\ \Omega} \\
R &= 4.76\ \Omega
\end{aligned}
$$

3 Find the current in the following circuit by applying Kirchhoff's loop rule (clockwise direction). Assume I is clockwise.

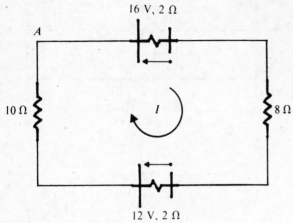

4 What does the negative sign indicate?

5 Apply Kirchhoff's point rule to junction A.

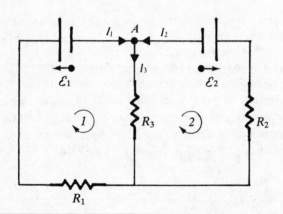

6 Apply Kirchhoff's loop rule to loop 1.

7 Apply Kirchhoff's loop rule to loop 2.

3 Go around the loop in a clockwise direction starting at A. Add emf's and IR terms in accordance with our sign conventions.
$$\Sigma(\mathcal{E} + IR) = 0$$
$$- 16\text{ V} - I(2\text{ }\Omega) - I(8\text{ }\Omega) + 12\text{ V} - I(2\text{ }\Omega)$$
$$- I(10\text{ }\Omega) = 0$$
Solving for I,
$$- 4\text{ V} - I(22\text{ }\Omega) = 0$$
$$I = - 0.182\text{ A}$$

4 That the current is in the opposite direction.

5
$$\Sigma I = 0$$
$$I_1 + I_2 = I_3$$

6 Go around the loop in a clockwise direction starting at A. Add emfs and IR terms in accordance with the sign conventions: An IR product is negative if the resistor is traversed in the same direction as the assumed current, positive if in the opposite direction. An emf is positive when it is traversed in the same direction as the emf arrow (from $-$ to $+$) and negative when it is traversed in the opposite direction.
$$\Sigma(\mathcal{E} + IR) = 0$$
$$-I_3 R_3 - I_1 R_1 - \mathcal{E}_1 = 0$$

7 Go around the loop in a clockwise direction starting at A.
$$\Sigma(\mathcal{E} + IR) = 0$$
$$\mathcal{E}_2 + I_2 R_2 + I_3 R_3 = 0$$

8 Find the unknown current I by applying the point rule to point a in this circuit.

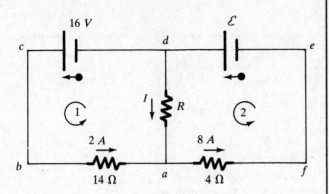

8 At point a,

$$\Sigma I = 0,$$
$$I + 2\,\text{A} - 8\,\text{A} = 0,$$
$$I = 6\,\text{A}.$$

---

9 Determine R by applying the loop rule to loop 1.

9 Start at a and traverse loop 1.
$$\Sigma(\mathcal{E} + IR) = 0$$
$$6\,\text{A}\,(R) + 16\,\text{V} - 2\,\text{A}\,(14\,\Omega) = 0$$
$$R = 2\,\Omega$$

---

10 Find $\mathcal{E}$ by applying the loop rule to loop 2.

10 Start at a and traverse loop 2.
$$\Sigma(\mathcal{E} + IR) = 0$$
$$-8\,\text{A}\,(4\,\Omega) + \mathcal{E} - 6\,\text{A}\,(2\,\Omega) = 0$$
$$\mathcal{E} = 44\,\text{V}$$

---

11 Check your answers by applying the loop rule to the outermost loop.

11 Start at a and traverse the loop.

$$\Sigma(\mathcal{E} + IR) = 0$$
$$-8\,\text{A}\,(4\Omega) + 44\,\text{V} + 16\,\text{V} - 2\,\text{A}\,(14\,\Omega) = 0$$
$$0 = 0$$

---

12 Find the potential difference V_{da} between d and a by going directly from d to a. Which point is at the higher potential?

12
$$V_d - 6\,\text{A}\,(2\,\Omega) = V_a$$
$$V_d - V_a = V_{da} = 12\,\text{V}$$
There is an IR drop of 12 V from d to a. Since the direction of the current is from d to a, this means that d is at a higher potential.

---

13 Find V_{da} by traversing the path $dcba$.

13
$$V_d + 16\,\text{V} - 2\,\text{A}\,(14\,\Omega) = V_a$$
$$V_d - V_a = V_{da} = 12\,\text{V}$$

---

14 Find V_{da} by traversing the path $defa$.

14
$$V_d - 44\,\text{V} + 8\,\text{A}\,(4\,\Omega) = V_a$$
$$V_d - V_a = V_{da} = 12\,\text{V}$$
Regardless of the path taken, the potential difference between two points is the same.

15 A 4×10^6 Ω resistor is connected in series with a 2×10^{-6} F capacitor. What is the time constant?

15

$$\tau = RC$$
$$= (4 \times 10^6 \text{ Ω}) (2 \times 10^{-6} \text{ F})$$
$$= 8 \text{ s}$$

---

16 If the initial current was 10 A, what is the current after one time constant?

16

$$i = I_0 e^{-t/RC}$$
$$\ln i = \ln I_0 - \frac{t}{RC} \ln e$$
if $t = \tau = RC$,
$$\ln i = \ln I_0 - 1$$
$$= \ln 10 - 1 = 2.30 - 1 = 1.30$$
$$i = 3.68 \text{ A}$$
Note: after 1 time constant,
$$I = \frac{I_0}{e} = \frac{10 \text{ A}}{e} = 3.68 \text{ A}$$

---

17 What will be the current after two time constants?

17

$$i = I_0 e^{-t/RC}$$
if $t = 2\tau$
$$\ln i = \ln I_0 - 2$$
$$= \ln 10 - 2 = 2.30 - 2 = 0.30$$
$$i = 1.35 \text{ A}$$
Note: after 2 time constants:
$$I = \frac{I_0}{e^2} = \frac{10 \text{ A}}{e^2} = 1.35 \text{ A}$$

---

18 What is the half-life?

18

$$t_h = RC \ln 2$$
$$= 0.693 \, RC$$
$$= 0.693 \, (8 \text{ s}) = 5.54 \text{ s}$$

STEP BY STEP SOLUTIONS OF PROBLEMS

Problem 1 Calculate the equivalent resistance of the circuit between a and b. If the current in the 4 Ω resistor between d and e is 1.0 A, what is the potential difference between a and c?

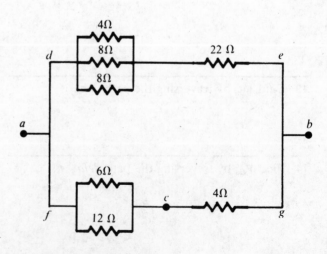

1 Find the equivalent resistance of the three resistors in parallel. Use

$$\frac{1}{R} = \frac{1}{R_1} + \frac{1}{R_2} + \frac{1}{R_3}$$

1

$$\frac{1}{R} = \frac{1}{8\ \Omega} + \frac{1}{8\ \Omega} + \frac{1}{4\ \Omega}$$

$$R = 2\ \Omega$$

2 Find the equivalent resistance of the two resistors in parallel.

2

$$\frac{1}{R} = \frac{1}{6\ \Omega} + \frac{1}{12\ \Omega}$$

$$R = 4\ \Omega$$

3 Redraw the circuit.

3

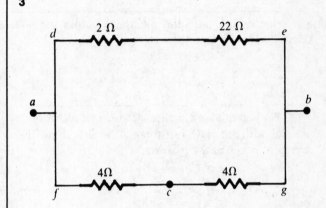

4 Find the equivalent resistance of each pair of resistors in series. Use $R = R_1 + R_2$.

4 $R = 2\ \Omega + 22\ \Omega = 24\ \Omega$
$R' = 4\ \Omega + 4\ \Omega = 8\ \Omega$

5 Redraw the circuit.

5

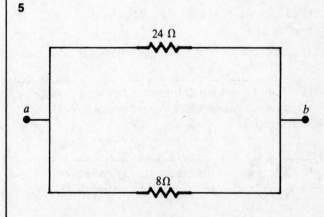

6   What is the equivalent resistance of the two resistors in parallel?

6
$$\frac{1}{R} = \frac{1}{8\ \Omega} + \frac{1}{24\ \Omega}$$
$$R = 6\ \Omega$$

---

7   Draw a sketch for the above.

7

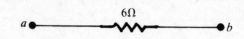

---

8   What is the potential difference across the 4 Ω resistor? The current through it is 1.0 A.

8
$$V = IR$$
$$= (1.0\ \text{A})(4\ \Omega) = 4\ \text{V}$$

---

9   The potential difference across the resistors in parallel with the 4 Ω resistor is 4 V also. Find the current through each resistor.

9
$$I = \frac{V}{R}$$
$$= \frac{4\ \text{V}}{8\ \Omega} = 0.5\ \text{A}$$

---

10   What is the current that enters the 22 Ω resistor?

10 $I = 1.0\ \text{A} + 0.5\ \text{A} + 0.5\ \text{A} = 2.0\ \text{A}$

---

11   Find the potential difference across the 22 Ω resistor.

11
$$V = IR$$
$$= (2\ \text{A})\ (22\ \Omega) = 44\ \text{V}$$

---

12   Find the potential difference between d and e by adding the potential differences across the 2 Ω and 22 Ω resistors.

12 $V_{\text{de}} = 4\ \text{V} + 44\ \text{V} = 48\ \text{V}$

---

13   The potential difference across f and g is also 48 V. Note that fc and cg each include resistors of 4 Ω. What is V_{ac}?

13 $V_{\text{ac}} = 24\ \text{V}$

Problem 2 Calculate the three currents indicated in the circuit. Neglect the internal resistances of the batteries. Find the potential difference V_{EB} by taking three different paths.

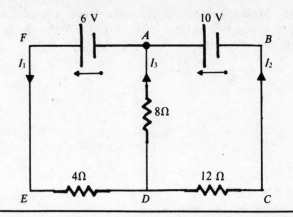

14 Apply Kirchhoff's point rule at point A. Note that I_1 is leaving the junction, hence it is negative. I_2 and I_3 are entering the junction, therefore they are positive.

14

$$I_3 + I_2 - I_1 = 0$$
$$\therefore I_3 = I_1 - I_2$$

15 Since I_3 could be replaced by $I_1 - I_2$, we need two independent equations with I_1 and I_2. This could be accomplished by using Kirchhoff's loop rule. Draw three possible configurations.

15

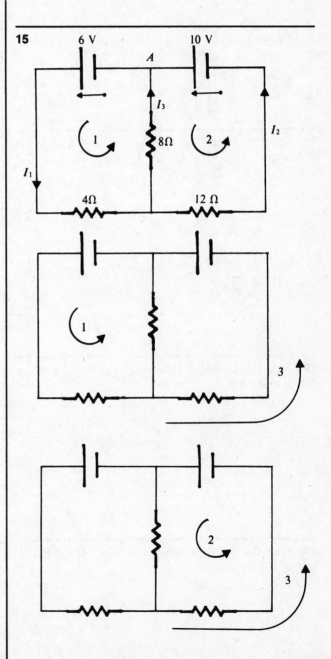

16 Working with the first configuration, apply Kirchhoff's loop rule to loop 1: $\Sigma(\mathcal{E} + IR) = 0$. Remember that $I_3 = I_1 - I_2$.

16

$$6\,V - I_1(4\,\Omega) - (I_1 - I_2)(8\,\Omega) = 0$$
$$6\,V - I_1(4\,\Omega) - I_1(8\,\Omega) + I_2(8\,\Omega) = 0$$
$$6\,V - I_1(12\,\Omega) + I_2(8\,\Omega) = 0$$
$$I_1(6\,\Omega) - I_2(4\,\Omega) = 3\,V$$

17 Apply Kirchhoff's loop rule to loop 2. Note that $(I_1 - I_2)$ is against our assumed direction.

17

$$10\,V + (I_1 - I_2)(8\,\Omega) - I_2(12\,\Omega) = 0$$
$$10\,V + I_1(8\,\Omega) - I_2(8\,\Omega) - I_2(12\,\Omega) = 0$$
$$10\,V + I_1(8\,\Omega) - I_2(20\,\Omega) = 0$$
$$- I_1(4\,\Omega) + I_2(10\,\Omega) = 5\,V$$

18 Frames 16 and 17 give us two equations with two unknowns. Solve for I_1 and I_2, then solve for I_3, noting that $I_3 = I_1 - I_2$.

18

$$I_1(6\,\Omega) - (I_2)(4\,\Omega) = 3\,V$$
$$- I_1(4\,\Omega) + (I_2)(10\,\Omega) = 5\,V$$
$$I_1 = 1.136\,A$$
$$I_2 = 0.955\,A$$
$$I_3 = I_1 - I_2 = 0.181\,A$$

19 Find the potential difference V_{EB} by traversing the path $EFAB$.

19

$$V_E - 6\,V - 10\,V = V_B$$
$$V_{EB} = V_E - V_B = 16\,V$$

20 Find the potential difference V_{EB} by traversing the path $EDCB$.

20

$$V_E - I_1(4\,\Omega) - I_2(12\,\Omega) = V_B$$
$$V_E - 1.136\,A(4\,\Omega) - 0.955\,A(12\,\Omega) = V_B$$
$$V_E - 4.544\,V - 11.46\,V = V_B$$
$$V_{EB} = V_E - V_B = 16\,V$$

21 Find the potential difference V_{EB} by traversing the path *EDAB*.

21

$$V_E - I_1\,(4\ \Omega) - I_3\,(8\ \Omega) - 10\ V = V_B$$
$$V_E - 1.136\ A\,(4\ \Omega) - 0.181\ A\,(8\ \Omega) - 10\ V = V_B$$
$$V_E - 4.544\ V - 1.448\ V - 10\ V = V_B$$
$$V_{EB} = V_E - V_B = 16\ V$$

Regardless of the path taken, the potential difference between two points is the same.

Problem 3 A 4 μF capacitor with an initial stored energy of 4.5 J is discharged through a 2.00 MΩ resistor. Find a) the initial charge Q_0 on the capacitor, b) the initial current I_0, i.e. the current through the resistor when discharge starts, c) the time constant, d) the half-life of the circuit, e) the time required for the charge to decrease to $1/e$ of its initial value, f) the voltage across the capacitor as a function of time, g) the voltage across the resistor as a function of time, and h) the power produced in the resistor as a function of time.

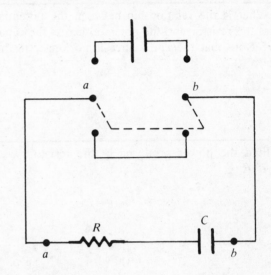

---

22 Find the initial charge from the relationship $W = \frac{1}{2}\dfrac{Q_0^2}{C}$.

22

$$4.5\ J = \frac{Q_0^2}{2(4 \times 10^{-6}\ F)}$$
$$Q_0 = 6 \times 10^{-3}\ C$$

---

23 Find the initial current from
$$I_0 = \frac{V_0}{R} = \frac{Q_0}{RC}.$$

23

$$I_0 = \frac{6 \times 10^{-3}\ C}{(2 \times 10^6\ \Omega)\,(4 \times 10^{-6}\ F)}$$
$$= 7.5 \times 10^{-4}\ A$$

---

24 Find the time constant from $\tau = RC$.

24 $\tau = (2 \times 10^6\ \Omega)\,(4 \times 10^{-6}\ F) = 8\ s$

---

25 What is the half-life of the circuit? Use $\tau_h = RC \ln 2$.

25

$$\tau_h = (8\ s)\,(\ln 2)$$
$$= 5.55\ s$$

---

26 Find the time required for the charge to decrease to $1/e$ of its original value by using $q = Q_0 e^{-t/\tau}$.

26

Since $q = \dfrac{Q_0}{e}$

$$\frac{Q_0}{e} = Q_0 e^{-t/\tau}$$
$$e^{-1} = e^{-t/\tau}$$
$$-t/\tau = -1$$
$$t = \tau = 8\ s$$

27 Find the voltage V_C across the capacitor as a function of time from

$$V_C = \frac{q}{C} = \frac{Q_0}{C} e^{-t/\tau}$$

27

$$V_C = \frac{6 \times 10^{-3} \text{ C}}{4 \times 10^{-6} \text{ F}} e^{-t/8 \text{ s}}$$

$$= 1500 \, e^{-0.125t(s)^{-1}} \text{ V}$$

---

28 What is the relationship between the potential across the resistor and the potential across the capacitor? Note that the emf source is no longer in the circuit.

28 When the capacitor discharges through the resistor, $V_{ab} = V_R + V_C = 0$.
Therefore $V_R = -V_C = -1500 \, e^{-0.125t(s)^{-1}}$ V.

---

29 Find the power produced in the resistor. Use $P = I^2 R$.

29

$$P = (I_0 e^{-t/\tau})^2 \text{ R}$$
$$= (7.5 \times 10^{-4} e^{-0.125t(s)^{-1}})^2 \, (2 \times 10^6 \, \Omega)$$
$$= 1.125 \, e^{-0.25t(s)^{-1}} \text{ W}$$

PROGRAMMED TEST

1 *Problem 1* Neglecting the internal resistances of the batteries, find the currents in the branches of the multiloop circuit.

1

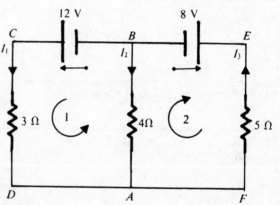

Answer
1.62 A, $-$ 1.79 A, $-$ 0.17 A

If you solved this problem correctly, go to frame 7. If you could not solve this problem, go through frames 2–6.

2 The directions of the currents have been arbitrarily chosen. Apply Kirchhoff's point rule to junction A.

2 $\Sigma I = 0$
$I_1 + I_2 - I_3 = 0$

---

3   Apply Kirchhoff's loop rule to loop 1.

3 $\Sigma(\mathcal{E} + IR) = 0$

$$12 \text{ V} - (I_1)(3\Omega) + (I_2)(4\Omega) = 0$$

---

4   Apply the loop rule to the second loop.

4 $8 \text{ V} + (I_3)(5\Omega) + (I_2)(4\Omega) = 0$

---

5   Substitute $I_3 = I_1 + I_2$ in the above equation. Simplify the two equations for the two loops to get simultaneous equations in terms of I_1 and I_2.

5 $8 \text{ V} = -(I_1)(5\ \Omega) - (I_2)(9\ \Omega)$
$12 \text{ V} = (I_1)(3\ \Omega) - (I_2)(4\ \Omega)$

---

6   Solve the equations.

6 $I_1 = 1.62 \text{ A}$
$I_2 = -1.79 \text{ A}$
$I_3 = -0.17 \text{ A}$

The negative signs indicate that the currents are actually in a direction opposite to our assumed direction.

---

7   **Problem 2**   Find $\mathcal{E}_1$ and $\mathcal{E}_2$ and the potential difference V_{ab}.

7

Answer
23 V, 6 V, 9 V

If you solved this problem correctly, go to frame 14. If you could not solve this problem, go through frames 8-13.

---

8   Apply Kirchhoff's point rule to point a and solve for I.

8 $\Sigma I = 0$
$I + 1 \text{ A} - 3 \text{ A} = 0$
$I = 2 \text{ A}$

---

9   Apply the loop rule to loop 1 and solve for $\mathcal{E}_1$. Start at a. Remember $I = 2$A.

9 $\Sigma(\mathcal{E} + IR) = 0$
$2A(6\Omega) - \mathcal{E}_1 + 2A(1\Omega) - 1A(8\Omega)$
$- 1A(1\Omega) + 18V = 0$
$\mathcal{E}_1 = 23V$

10 Find $\mathcal{E}_2$ by applying the loop rule to loop 2. Start at a.

10
$$\Sigma(\mathcal{E} + IR) = 0$$
$$-\mathcal{E}_2 - 3A(1\Omega) + 23V - 2A(1\Omega) - 2A(6\Omega) = 0$$
$$\mathcal{E}_2 = 6\text{ V}$$

---

11 Find V_{ab}.

11 $V_a + (2\text{ A})(6\ \Omega) - \mathcal{E}_1 + (2\text{ A})(1\ \Omega) = V_b$
$$V_{ab} = V_a - V_b = 9\text{ V}$$

---

12 Check by circling the bottom loop.

12 $V_a - \mathcal{E}_2 - (3\text{ A})(1\ \Omega) = V_b$
$$V_{ab} = 9\text{ V}$$

---

13 We can also check by circling the top loop.

13 $V_a - 18\text{ V} + (1\text{ A})(1\Omega) + (8\text{ A})(1\ \Omega) = V_b$
$$V_{ab} = 9\text{ V}$$

---

14 ***Problem 3*** The Wheatstone bridge is used to measure an unknown resistance X by comparing it with the given resistances M, N and P. At least one of the resistances should be variable (in our case M). When the switches are closed, M is adjusted until the galvanometer registers zero current. If M, N and P are 2000 Ω, 20 Ω and 33.6 Ω respectively, find X.

14

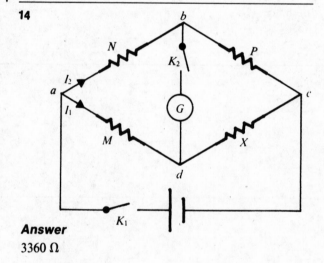

Answer
3360 Ω

If you could not solve this problem, go through frames 15-21.

15 When the galvanometer reads zero (the bridge is balanced), what can you say about the potential at b and d?

15 b and d are at the same potential.

---

16 If b and d are at the same potential, what is the relationship between V_{ab} and V_{ad}?

16
$$V_{ab} = V_{ad}$$
$$I_2 N = I_1 M$$

---

17 If I_1 is the current that passes through M when the bridge is balanced, what is the current that passes through X?

17 I_1

---

18 If I_2 is the current that passes through N when the bridge is balanced, what is the current that passes through P?

18 I_2

---

19 What are the voltage drops across X and P?

19 $I_2 P = I_1 X$

---

20 Divide the two equations in frames 16 and 19 and solve for X.

20

$$\frac{I_2 N}{I_2 P} = \frac{I_1 M}{I_1 X}$$
$$X = \frac{M P}{N}$$

---

21 Substitute the numerical values and solve.

21

$$X = \frac{(2000\ \Omega)(33.6\ \Omega)}{20\ \Omega}$$
$$= 3360\ \Omega$$

30

The Magnetic Field and Magnetic Forces

CHAPTER SUMMARY

We have studied the electric field due to charges at rest; we will now turn our attention to the magnetic field created by a moving charge or current. The mathematical relationships for magnetic field lines, magnetic flux and magnetic force are presented and these are compared to their electrical counterparts, i.e. the electric field lines, electric flux and the electric force. The motion of charged particles in magnetic fields is described as well as two applications — Thomson's measurement of the charge-to-mass ratio of an electron and mass spectroscopy. The magnetic field exerts a force on a moving charge. We are particularly concerned with the effects of the magnetic field on current-carrying conductors and the net force and torque exerted on a complete circuit. The Hall effect gives us the sign of the charge carriers in a conductor and enables us to determine the charge carrier density.

BASIC TERMS — *Give definitions or meanings for the following:*

magnetic monopole (30-1)
magnetism (30-1)
magnetic field (30-2)
tesla (30-2)
gauss (30-2)
weber (30-3)
magnetic flux density (30-3)
magnetic field lines (30-3)
magnetic flux (30-3)

Thomson's measurement of e/m (30-5)
mass number (30-6)
atomic mass unit (30-6)
isotopes (30-6)
mass spectrometer (30-6)
magnetic moment (30-8)
solenoid (30-8)
Hall effect (30-10)

PROGRAMMED QUIZ

1 Where do all magnetic fields originate?

1 In moving electric charges or currents.

2 If you are moving past a stationary electric charge, what fields will you detect?

2 Since there is motion relative to an observer, both electric and magnetic fields.

3 The electric force depends on the electric field and the charge; does the magnetic force depend on the magnetic field and the charge?

3 It depends on the magnetic field, charge and velocity of the particle.

4 What is the direction of the electric force? magnetic force?

4 The electric force is parallel to the electric field; the magnetic force is perpendicular to the magnetic field and velocity of the particle.

5 Can the direction of the force on a negative charge be found by the right-hand rule?

5 Yes, use the right-hand rule but the direction is opposite to the one determined.

6 Does the magnetic field change the speed of a particle? Why?

6 No, only the direction of its velocity because the work done by the magnetic force is always zero since the force is at right angles to the motion.

7 Is the particle accelerated?

7 Yes, from Newton's second law, when a force acts on a particle it is accelerated (direction of velocity changes).

8 What kind of motion will the particle have?

8 Circular if v is perpendicular to B, otherwise it is helical.

9 What is the magnetic force on a charge moving parallel to a magnetic field? When will the force be maximum?

9 $F = qv_\perp B = qvB \sin \phi$, if $\phi = 0$, $F = 0$. At 90°, $F = qvB$.

10 What are the phenomena attributed to Faraday, Henry and Oersted?

10 Faraday and Henry showed that currents can be produced by moving magnets; Oersted demonstrated that moving electric charges have magnetic effects.

11 Are there any other atoms besides iron which exhibit magnetic effects?

11 All atoms; magnetic properties of matter are the result of atomic currents.

12 What are some similarities between electric and magnetic forces?

12 Both are exerted by fields, both have magnitudes proportional to charge and both are proportional to the magnitudes of the respective fields.

13 Do magnetic field lines point in the direction of the force on a charge?

13 No, they are in the same direction as the magnetic field vector B at that point.

14 How can you find the direction of the force on a current-carrying conductor placed in a magnetic field?

14 Use the right-hand screw rule: Rotate the right-hand screw from the direction of I toward B. The direction of F is the direction of advance.

---

15 In the equation $\Gamma = I B A \sin \alpha$, what angle is α?

15 The angle between the normal to the loop and the magnetic field.

---

16 Why does a current loop rotate in a magnetic field if the sum of the magnetic forces on the loop is zero?

16 Because the sum of the torques is not zero.

---

17 When is the force on a wire in a magnetic field maximum?

17 When the field is perpendicular to the wire; $F = IlB \sin \phi$, if $\phi = 90°$, $F = IlB$.

---

18 At what angle will $F = \frac{1}{2} F_{max}$?

18 At 30°, $F = IlB \sin \phi$
if $\phi = 30°$
$F' = (0.5)(IlB) = 0.5\,F$

---

19 Can the force be zero if I, l and B are not zero?

19 Yes, if the wire is parallel to the field, $\phi = 0$, $F = 0$.

---

20 From what equation is the equation $F = IlB$ deduced?

20 $F = qVB$.

---

21 Can there be a situation where the magnetic field would exert no torque on a rectangular current-carrying loop?

21 $\Gamma = I B A \sin \alpha$, when the plane of the loop is perpendicular to the field, $\alpha = 0$, $\Gamma = 0$.

---

22 What is the effect of the torque on a current-carrying loop in a magnetic field?

22 It tends to rotate the loop toward its equilibrium position.

23 Why does a compass needle point north?

23 The earth is a magnet. The north geographic pole is actually a magnetic south pole.

24 Draw a sketch of the earth's magnetic field.

24

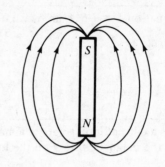

MAIN IDEAS

A magnetic field exerts a force on a moving charge. The electric and magnetic fields are analogous to each other.

Magnetic Field

a) A moving charge or current creates a magnetic field in the space surrounding it.

b) A moving charge or current in a magnetic field will experience a force F which is a function of the magnetic field B and the velocity v of the charge. Its direction is perpendicular to the velocity vector and the direction of the field.

Electric Field

a) A charge sets up an electric field in the space surrounding it.

b) If a charge q is placed in an electric field, it will experience a force $F = qE$. It should be noted that the electric force on a charge does not depend on the velocity of the charge.

The magnitude of the magnetic force F is given by $F = q v_\perp B = q v B \sin \phi$, where q is the magnitude of the charge, v is the velocity, B the magnitude of the magnetic field and ϕ is the angle between the vectors v and B. The magnetic force F is mutually perpendicular to the plane containing B and v. The direction of F is obtained by the right-hand rule: If the curled fingers of the right hand turn vector v towards vector B (using the smaller angle), then the thumb of the right hand will point in the direction of F. The direction of F on a negative charge will be opposite to that of a positive charge. The unit of B is the tesla, $1 \text{ T} = 1 \text{ N} \cdot \text{A}^{-1} \cdot \text{m}^{-1}$. The magnetic field of the earth is of the order of 10^{-4} T.

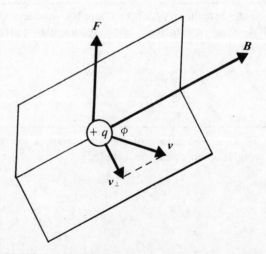

A magnetic field can be represented by lines in the direction of B at every point. The magnetic flux Φ across any area ΔA is defined as $\Phi = B_\perp \Delta A = B \cos \theta \Delta A$. If B is perpendicular to the surface, $\theta = 0°$, $\Phi = BA$. The unit of magnetic flux is the weber, $1 \text{ Wb} = 1 \text{ N} \cdot \text{m} \cdot \text{A}^{-1}$. The magnetic flux per unit area across an area at right angles to the magnetic field is equal to the magnetic field and may be expressed as $B = \Delta\Phi/\Delta A$. The magnetic field B is sometimes called the magnetic flux density.

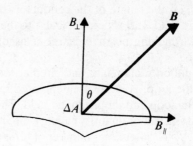

Motion of a charged particle in a magnetic field. Consider a positively charged particle moving in a magnetic field directed away from the reader. (The crosses represent a uniform magnetic field directed into the paper, i.e., away from the reader. Dots would be used to represent a uniform magnetic field coming out of the paper, i.e., toward the reader.) In accordance with the right-hand rule, F will be directed towards the center of the circle. Since the magnetic force will supply the necessary centripetal force, we have

$$F = qvB = \frac{mv^2}{R} \text{ or}$$

$$R = \frac{mv}{Bq}.$$

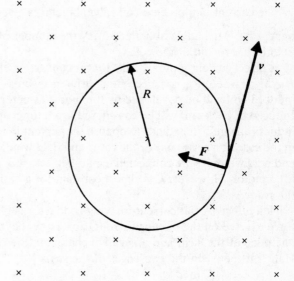

The period T of the rotating charged particle may be obtained from

$$\frac{2\pi}{T} = \frac{v}{r} = \frac{qB}{m} \text{ or } T = \frac{2\pi m}{qB}.$$

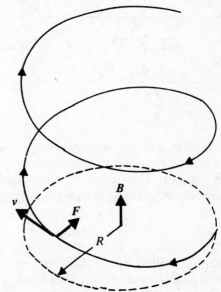

When a particle of mass m and charge q is projected into a magnetic field at an angle ϕ with the direction of the field, the path of the particle will be a helix,

$$R = \frac{mv \sin \phi}{qB} \text{ and}$$

$$T = \frac{2\pi m}{qB}.$$

The helix advances with a velocity $v \cos \phi$.

Thomson's measurement of e/m. Under the simultaneous influence of an electric field E and a magnetic field B, adjusted so that the forces cancel, i.e., $eE = evB$, an electron beam is undeflected. The loss of potential energy eV = gain in kinetic energy $\frac{1}{2}mv^2$, and

$$\frac{e}{m} = \frac{E^2}{2B^2 V} = 1.7588 \times 10^{11} \text{ C} \cdot \text{kg}^{-1}.$$

A current-carrying conductor in a magnetic field will experience a force of magnitude $F = IlB \sin \phi$ where I is the current, l is the length of the conductor, B the magnetic field and ϕ the angle that the conductor makes with the magnetic field. If B is perpendicular to the wire, the equation reduces to $F = IlB$. The right-hand rule used in the case of a moving positive charge is used for a current-carrying conductor. However, v is replaced by the direction of I.

The torque on rectangular and circular loops in a magnetic field $= \Gamma = I B A \sin \alpha$, where I is the current flowing in the loop, A is the area enclosed by the loop, B is the magnetic field and α is the angle between the normal to the loop and the magnetic field. The product $I A$ is called the magnetic moment m of the loop. It may be regarded as a vector quantity having a direction perpendicular to the plane of the loop. In the case of a solenoid, $\Gamma = N I B A \sin \alpha$, where $N = $ number of turns and α is the angle between the axis of the solenoid and the direction of the field. The torque is maximum when the magnetic field is parallel to the planes of the individual turns or perpendicular to the long axis of the solenoid.

The current in a pivoted coil galvanometer is given by $I = \dfrac{k'\theta}{NAB}$, where k' is the torsional constant of the hairspring, θ the angle of deflection, N the number of turns, A the area enclosed by the coil and B the magnetic field in the region of the coil.

A direct current motor is a device for converting electrical energy into mechanical energy. The power input is $P = V_{ab}I$, where V_{ab} is the potential difference across the terminals and I is the current supplied to the motor. An induced emf will be developed by the motor as determined by $V_{ab} = \mathcal{E} + Ir$, where r is the internal resistance. Induced or back emf will be considered in a later chapter (Lenz's law). A running motor acts as a generator and induces an emf which tends to oppose the current in the rotor (armature). Remember in using $V_{ab} = \mathcal{E} + Ir$ that in the case of a series motor the rotor and field windings are connected in series and for a shunt motor the rotor and field windings are connected in parallel. $V_{ab} = \mathcal{E} + Ir$, which was used in charging a battery, can also be used for a motor. However, $\mathcal{E}$ is almost constant for a battery, but for a motor it depends on the speed of rotation of the rotor.

Hall effect. A flat current-carrying conductor is placed in a magnetic field perpendicular to its flat side. The force exerted on the moving current carriers by the magnetic field causes a net positive charge to accumulate at one edge of the strip and a negative charge on the other, thus producing a potential difference, known as the Hall emf, between the two edges of the strip.

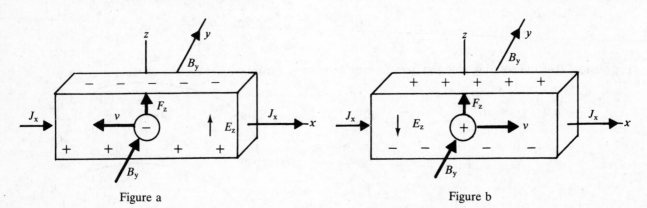

Figure a

Figure b

Negative current carriers (electrons) are pushed toward the top of the conductor, resulting in the charge distribution shown. This is the situation found in metals. The bottom edge is at a higher potential than the top edge.

Positive current carriers are pushed toward the top of the conductor, giving us the charge distribution shown. This occurs in semiconductors. The top edge is at a higher potential than the bottom edge.

In reference to Figure a, since the current is in the positive x-direction, the electrons are moving in the negative x-direction. In accordance with the right-hand rule, the force due to the magnetic field on the electrons is in the positive z-direction. This causes the electrons to accumulate on the top edge of the strip and the positive charges to accumulate on the bottom edge. Since the electric field is directed from positive to negative charges, the direction of the electric field is in the positive z-direction.

When the electrostatic force on the charge is equal to the magnetic force,
$$qE_z = qvB_y$$
$$E_z = vB_y.$$

The current density $J_x = \dfrac{I}{A}$ is given by

$J_x = nqv$, where n is the density of the current-carrying charges in the material. Eliminating v between the above two equations, we obtain

$$nq = \frac{J_x B_y}{E_z}.$$

Problem solving strategy: visualizing three dimensions. If you have trouble visualizing the vectors F, B and v, try drawing them in three dimensions. Use the plane of the table as the x and y components, and hold a paper vertically to represent the z-direction. Or use a corner of the room. The x and y directions will be represented by the lines where the floor meets the walls, the z-direction is where the two walls meet. You can also take a metal coat hanger and construct the three mutually perpendicular axes.

PROGRAMMED QUIZ

1 Find the force on a 2×10^{-9}C charge moving at 0.8×10^7 m $\cdot$ s^{-1} in a magnetic field of magnitude 2 T perpendicular to the velocity.

1
$$
\begin{aligned}
F &= qvB \\
&= (2 \times 10^{-9}\ \text{C})(0.8 \times 10^7\ \text{m} \cdot \text{s}^{-1})(2\ \text{T}) \\
&= 3.2 \times 10^{-2}\ \text{N}
\end{aligned}
$$
Note: $1\ \text{C} \cdot \text{m} \cdot \text{s}^{-1} \cdot \text{T} = 1\ \text{C} \cdot \text{m} \cdot \text{s}^{-1}\ \text{N} \cdot \text{A}^{-1} \cdot \text{m}^{-1}$
$= 1\ \text{N}$

2 What is the direction of the force?

2 Perpendicular to both v and B.

3 When will the force be half of this magnitude?

3 When the angle between v and B is 30°.
$$F = qvB \sin \phi$$
if $\phi' = 30°$, $\sin \phi' = 0.5$,
$$F' = qvB(0.5) = 0.5\ F$$

4 What is the magnetic flux across a surface 1 m^2 if the perpendicular magnetic field has a magnitude of 0.3 T?

4
$$
\begin{aligned}
\Phi &= BA \\
&= 0.3\ \text{T}(1\ \text{m}^2) = 0.3\ \text{Wb}
\end{aligned}
$$
Note: $1\ \text{T} = 1\ \text{Wb} \cdot \text{m}^{-2}$

5 A particle, $m = 2 \times 10^{-12}$ kg and $q = 3 \times 10^{-8}$ C moves in a circular path of radius 50 cm at a speed of 4×10^4 m $\cdot$ s^{-1}. What is the magnitude of the magnetic field?

5
$$R = \frac{mv}{Bq}$$
$$B = \frac{(2 \times 10^{-12}\ \text{kg})(4 \times 10^4\ \text{m} \cdot \text{s}^{-1})}{(0.5\ \text{m})(3 \times 10^{-8}\ \text{C})}$$
$$= 5.33\ \text{T}$$
Note: $1\ \text{T} = 1\ \text{N} \cdot \text{s} \cdot \text{C}^{-1} \cdot \text{m}^{-1}$

6 In a mass spectrometer, the magnetic field in the velocity selector is 1.2 T. A singly charged particle $m = 1.1 \times 10^{-26}$ kg moves in a semicircular path 40 cm in radius. What is the velocity of the particle?

6
$$
\begin{aligned}
v &= \frac{qBR}{m} \\
&= \frac{(1.602 \times 10^{-19}\ \text{C})(1.2\ \text{T})(0.40\ \text{m})}{1.1 \times 10^{-26}\ \text{kg}} \\
&= 6.99 \times 10^6\ \text{m} \cdot \text{s}^{-1}
\end{aligned}
$$

7 A charged particle is traveling in a straight line at 10^7 m $\cdot$ s^{-1} in a region where an electric field and a magnetic field are applied simultaneously. If the magnitude of the magnetic field is 4×10^{-5} T, what is the magnitude of the electric field? Both fields are normal to each other and to the direction of the path of the charged particle.

7
$$v = \frac{E}{B}$$
$$
\begin{aligned}
E &= (10^7\ \text{m} \cdot \text{s}^{-1})(4 \times 10^{-5}\ \text{T}) \\
&= 4 \times 10^2\ \text{N} \cdot \text{C}^{-1}
\end{aligned}
$$

8 A magnetic field of 3 T is directed parallel to the positive *x*-axis. What is the magnetic flux across the surface *abcd*? (Each side = 0.20 m.)

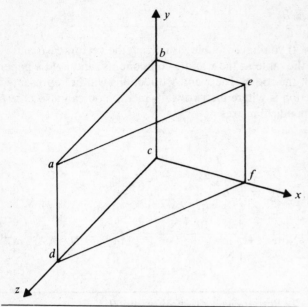

9 What is the magnetic flux across the surface *befc*?

10 A particle, $m = 0.4$ g and $q = 3 \times 10^{-8}$ C, is given an initial horizontal velocity of 8×10^4 m·s⁻¹. What is the minimum magnetic field that will keep the particle moving in a horizontal direction?

11 An electron is accelerated by a potential difference of 1000 V. It then enters a region where the simultaneous influences of an electric field of 5×10^3 V·m⁻¹ and a magnetic field of 0.266×10^{-3} T, both fields normal to each other, produce no deflection. What is e/m?

---

8 $\Phi = BA \cos \theta$, where θ is the angle between $B_\perp$ and B. In this case $\theta = 0$.
$$\Phi = BA$$
$$= 3 \text{ T}(0.20 \text{ m})^2$$
$$= 0.12 \text{ Wb}$$

9 $\theta = 90°$
$$\Phi = BA \cos \theta = 0$$

10

$$F = qvB$$

$$w = mg$$

$$qvB = mg$$

$$B = \frac{(4 \times 10^{-4} \text{ kg})(9.8 \text{ m·s}^{-2})}{(3 \times 10^{-8} \text{ C})(8 \times 10^4 \text{ m·s}^{-1})}$$

$$= 1.63 \text{ T perpendicular to the direction of } v \text{ and } F, \text{ directed away from the reader.}$$

11
$$\frac{e}{m} = \frac{E^2}{2B^2 V}$$
$$= \frac{(5 \times 10^3 \text{ V·m}^{-1})^2}{2(0.266 \times 10^{-3} \text{ T})^2(1000 \text{ V})}$$
$$= 1.77 \times 10^{11} \text{ C·kg}^{-1}$$

12 A force of 50 N is exerted on 2 m of wire in a magnetic field of 1.5 T. What is the current assuming that B is perpendicular to the wire?

12 $F = I l B \sin \phi$, where $\phi = 90°$

$$I = \frac{50 \text{ N}}{(2 \text{ m}) (1.5 \text{ T})} = 16.7 \text{ A}$$

Note $1 \text{ T} = 1 \text{ N} \cdot \text{A}^{-1} \cdot \text{m}^{-1}$

---

13 What would be the force if the angle between the direction of current and the field was 60°?

13 $F = I l B \sin \phi$
   $= (16.7 \text{ A}) (2 \text{ m}) (1.5 \text{ T}) (\sin 60°)$
   $= 43.4 \text{ N}$

The same result can be obtained by using
$$F = 50 \text{ N} \sin 60°.$$

---

14 What is the magnetic moment of a loop, area 0.5 m^2, through which the current is 10 A?

14 $m = I A$
   $= (10 \text{ A}) (0.5 \text{ m}^2)$
   $= 5 \text{ A} \cdot \text{m}^2$

---

15 What is the torque on this loop in a magnetic field of magnitude 2 T at an angle α of 45°?

15
$\Gamma = I A B \sin \alpha$
   $= (10 \text{ A}) (0.5 \text{ m}^2) (2 \text{ T}) \sin 45°$
   $= 7.07 \text{ N} \cdot \text{m}$

---

16 What would be the value of the maximum torque? When would the torque be maximum?

16
$\Gamma = I A B$
   $= (10 \text{ A}) (0.5 \text{ m}^2) (2 \text{ T})$
   $= 10 \text{ N} \cdot \text{m}$

When the plane of the coil is parallel to the field ($\alpha = 90°$).

---

17 The maximum torque on a solenoid, 0.02 m^2 in area, carrying a current of 3 A in a magnetic field of magnitude 1 T is $1.68 \text{ N} \cdot \text{m}$. The solenoid has how many windings?

17

$\Gamma = N I A B$
$$N = \frac{1.68 \text{ N} \cdot \text{m}}{(3 \text{ A}) (0.02 \text{ m}^2) (1 \text{ T})}$$
   $= 28$

---

18 What is the magnetic moment of a coil which experiences a maximum torque of $15 \text{ N} \cdot \text{m}$ in a magnetic field 12 T in magnitude?

18

$\Gamma = m B \sin \alpha$, where $\alpha = 90°$
$$m = \frac{15 \text{ N} \cdot \text{m}}{12 \text{ T}}$$
   $= 1.25 \text{ A} \cdot \text{m}^2$

19 A silver ribbon has the dimensions indicated in the sketch. It is carrying a current of 250 A in the positive x-direction. The ribbon lies in a uniform magnetic field where $B = B_y = 2$ T. If $n = 7.40 \times 10^{28}$ free electrons per m³, find the drift velocity of the electrons in the x-direction.

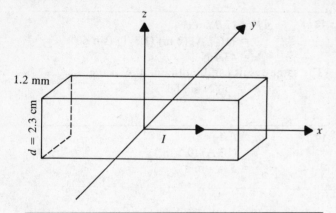

19

$$J_x = \frac{I}{A}$$

$$= \frac{250 \text{ A}}{(0.023 \text{ m}) (0.0012 \text{ m})}$$

$$= 9.06 \times 10^6 \text{ A} \cdot \text{m}^{-2}$$

Since $J_x = nqv$

$$v = \frac{9.06 \times 10^6 \text{ A} \cdot \text{m}^{-2}}{(7.40 \times 10^{28} \text{ m}^{-3}) (1.60 \times 10^{-19} \text{ C})}$$

$$= 7.65 \times 10^{-4} \text{ m} \cdot \text{s}^{-1}$$

20 Find the magnitude and direction of the electric field.

20

$$F_E = F_B$$
$$qE = qvB$$
$$E = vB$$
$$= (7.65 \times 10^{-4} \text{ m} \cdot \text{s}^{-1}) (2 \text{ T})$$
$$= 1.53 \times 10^{-3} \text{ V} \cdot \text{m}^{-1}$$

E is in the +z-direction

21 Find the Hall emf.

21 The Hall emf is the potential difference between the edges of the 2.3 cm strip.

$E_{Hall} = V = Ed$ where d is the width of the strip.

$$E_{Hall} = (1.53 \times 10^{-3} \text{ V} \cdot \text{m}^{-1}) (0.023 \text{ m})$$
$$= 3.52 \times 10^{-5} \text{ V}$$

STEP BY STEP SOLUTIONS OF PROBLEMS

Problem 1 An electron is accelerated through a potential difference of 2.0 kV and enters a region between two parallel plates (a and b) which are 0.01 m apart with a potential difference of $V_{ab} = 150$ V between them. If the path of the electron is perpendicular to the electric field between the plates, what magnetic field (mutually perpendicular to both the path of the electron and the electric field) is required to keep the electron moving in a straight line?

1 Tabulate the given data.

1

$$e = 1.602 \times 10^{-19} \text{ C}$$
$$m = 9.11 \times 10^{-31} \text{ kg}$$
$$V = 2000 \text{ V}$$
$$d = 0.01 \text{ m}$$
$$V_{ab} = 150 \text{ V}$$

2 Equate the kinetic energy of the electron to its loss in potential energy. Obtain an expression for the velocity from the work-energy relation.

2

$$\tfrac{1}{2}mv^2 = eV$$

$$v = \sqrt{\frac{2eV}{m}}$$

3 The electron is traveling at constant speed in a straight line. What is the net force acting on it?

3 Zero.

---

4 What can we say about the two forces due to B and E?

4 They must be equal.

$$evB = eE$$

$$B = \frac{E}{v}$$

---

5 Substitute the value of v from frame 2.

5

$$B = E\sqrt{\frac{m}{2eV}}$$

---

6 Substitute V_{ab}/d for E.

6

$$B = \frac{V_{ab}}{d}\sqrt{\frac{m}{2eV}}$$

---

7 Substitute the numerical values and solve.

7

$$B = \frac{150\ \text{V}}{0.01\ \text{m}}$$

$$\times\sqrt{\frac{9.11 \times 10^{-31}\ \text{kg}}{2(1.602 \times 10^{-19}\ \text{C})\,(2000\ \text{V})}}$$

$$= 5.66 \times 10^{-4}\ \text{T}$$

Problem 2 A beam of protons is accelerated horizontally from rest through a potential difference V to a velocity v. The beam enters a magnetic field B (normal to the plane of the trajectory) which extends from $x = 0$ to $x = L$. a) Find the exit angle α. b) Find the deflection δ. c) Show that the y-coordinate at any time is given by $y = -Bx^2\left(\dfrac{q}{8mV}\right)^{1/2}$, where $y \ll x$, i.e., the deflection is very small compared with the distance the particles have moved into the magnetic field.

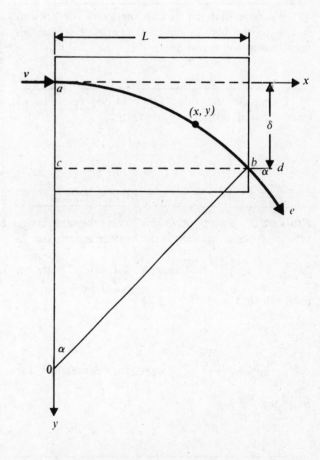

8 Since the protons move in a circular path inside the magnetic field, express the radius of curvature R in terms of m, q, B and v.

8
$$R = \frac{mv}{qB}$$

9 Since be is $\perp$ ob and cd is $\perp$ oc, hence $\alpha = \angle boc$. Find $\sin \alpha$ in right triangle obc and substitute the value of R.

9
$$\sin \alpha = \frac{L}{R} = \frac{qBL}{mv}$$

10 Find δ. Note that $\delta = oa - oc = R(1 - \cos \alpha)$. Find $\cos \alpha$ from the trigonometric identity $\cos \alpha = \sqrt{1 - \sin^2 \alpha}$ and express δ in terms of the given variables.

10
$$\delta = \frac{mv}{qB}\left[1 - \sqrt{1 - \left(\frac{qBL}{mv}\right)^2}\right]$$

11 Consider any point (x, y) on the circular trajectory. Write the equation of the circle, with respect to the origin O, and solve for R.

11
$$x^2 + (R + y)^2 = R^2$$
$$R = -\frac{(x^2 + y^2)}{(2y)}$$
$$R \approx -\frac{x^2}{2y}, \text{ if we consider } y \ll x.$$

12 Eliminate R between frames 8 and 11 and solve for y.

12
$$y = -\frac{qBx^2}{2mv}$$

13 We note that the kinetic energy of the protons is due to the loss in potential energy. Express this relationship for v and solve.

13
$$\tfrac{1}{2}mv^2 = qV$$
$$v = \sqrt{\frac{2qV}{m}}$$

14 Substitute the value for v in the equation of frame 12 and simplify.

14
$$y = \frac{-qBx^2}{2m\left(\dfrac{2qV}{m}\right)^{1/2}}$$
$$= -Bx^2\left(\frac{q}{8mV}\right)^{1/2}$$

Problem 3 Two positive ions having the same charge q and masses m and $m + \Delta m$ strike the photographic plate of a mass spectrometer. If the heavier ion strikes the plate at a distance $d + \Delta d$ from the entry slit, prove that $\Delta m = B\left(\dfrac{mq}{2V}\right)^{1/2}\Delta d$. Calculate Δd for a beam of slightly ionized magnesium atoms ($m = 24$ and 25 u) if $B = 0.60$ T and $V = 8.5$ kV.

15 Using $m = \dfrac{B^2qd^2}{8V}$, write the expression for $m + \Delta m$.

15
$$m + \Delta m = \frac{B^2q(d + \Delta d)^2}{8V}$$
$$= \frac{B^2q(d^2 + 2d\,\overline{\Delta d} + \overline{\Delta d}^2)}{8V}$$

16
Substract $m = \dfrac{B^2 q d^2}{8V}$ from the expression.

16
$$\Delta m = \frac{B^2 q (2d\,\overline{\Delta d} + \overline{\Delta d}^2)}{8V}$$

---

17 Since $\overline{\Delta d}^2 \ll 1$, it can be omitted.

17
$$\Delta m = \frac{d\,\overline{\Delta d}\,B^2 q}{4V}$$

18
Solve $m = \dfrac{B^2 q d^2}{8V}$ for d and substitute in the above.

18
$$d = \frac{1}{B}\sqrt{\frac{8Vm}{q}}$$

$$\Delta m = \frac{B^2 q}{4V}\;\frac{1}{B}\sqrt{\frac{8\,Vm}{q}}\,\Delta d$$

$$= B\left(\frac{mq}{2V}\right)^{1/2}\Delta d$$

---

19 Substitute the numerical values and solve.

19
$$\Delta d = \frac{1.661 \times 10^{-27}\ \text{kg}}{0.60\ \text{T}\left(\dfrac{24(1.661 \times 10^{-27}\ \text{kg})(1.602 \times 10^{-19}\ \text{C})}{2(8500\ \text{V})}\right)^{1/2}}$$

$$= 0.00452\ \text{m} = 4.52\ \text{mm}$$

Problem 4 An irregular shaped wire lies in the yz-plane and carries a current of 20 A in the $+z$ direction. If $a = 0.04$ m, $b = 0.15$ m and $B = 2$ T, find a) the force on sections a and b and b) the torque on sections a and b about the z-axis.

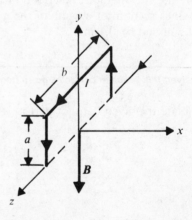

---

20 Find the force on section a; use $F = I\,l\,B \sin\phi$.

20 Since section a is parallel to $\boldsymbol{B}$, $\phi = 0$ and $\sin\phi = 0$. $\therefore\ F = 0$. (Note: we have two sections which have a length a.)

---

21 Find the force on length b. Use $F = I\,l\,B \sin\phi$.

21 Since section b is perpendicular to $\boldsymbol{B}$, $\sin\phi = 1.00$. $F = (20\ \text{A})(0.15\ \text{m})(2\ \text{T}) = 6\ \text{N}$

---

22 Find the direction of the force acting on b. Use the righthand rule.

22

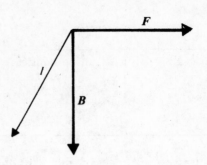

23 Find the torque on the irregular shaped wire about the z-axis. Use $\Gamma = Fl$ and check with $\Gamma = I B A \sin \alpha$.

23

$$\begin{aligned} \Gamma &= Fl = Fa = (6 \text{ N}) (0.04 \text{ m}) \\ &= 0.24 \text{ N} \cdot \text{m} \\ &= I B A \sin \alpha = (20 \text{ A}) (2 \text{ T}) (0.006 \text{ m}^2) \\ &= 0.24 \text{ N} \cdot \text{m} \end{aligned}$$

PROGRAMMED TEST

1 Problem 1 A beam of protons is accelerated horizontally from rest through a potential difference of 4.23×10^7 V to a velocity of 9×10^7 m $\cdot$ s^{-1}. The beam enters a magnetic field of 1 T (normal to the plane of the trajectory). Find the deflection of the beam by the two methods described in Problem 2 in the previous section for a width of the magnetic field of a) 0.5 m and b) 0.1 m.

1 Answer
0.144 m, 0.133 m, 0.00536 m, 0.00532 m

If you solved this problem correctly, go to frame 10. If you could not solve this problem, go through frames 2–9.

2 Tabulate the given data for part a.

2

$$\begin{aligned} B &= 1 \text{ T} \\ V &= 4.23 \times 10^7 \text{ V} \\ L &= 0.5 \text{ m} \\ v &= 9 \times 10^7 \text{ m} \cdot \text{s}^{-1} \\ q &= 1.602 \times 10^{-19} \text{ C} \\ m &= 1.673 \times 10^{-27} \text{ kg} \end{aligned}$$

3 Find the radius of curvature of the beam as it enters the magnetic field, use

$$R = \frac{mv}{qB}.$$

3

$$R = \frac{(1.673 \times 10^{-27} \text{ kg}) (9 \times 10^7 \text{ m} \cdot \text{s}^{-1})}{(1.602 \times 10^{-19} \text{ C}) (1 \text{ T})}$$
$$= 0.940 \text{ m}$$

4 Find the exit angle α from

$$\sin \alpha = \frac{L}{R}.$$

4

$$\sin \alpha = \frac{0.5 \text{ m}}{0.940 \text{ m}} = 0.5319$$
$$\alpha = 32.1°$$

5 Find the deflection δ from
$$\delta = R(1 - \cos \alpha).$$

5

$$\delta = 0.94 \text{ m}(1 - \cos 32.1°) = 0.144 \text{ m}$$

or use $\delta = \dfrac{mv}{qB}\left[1 - \sqrt{1 - \left(\dfrac{qBL}{mv}\right)^2}\right]$

$$= \frac{(1.673 \times 10^{-27} \text{ kg}) (9 \times 10^7 \text{ m} \cdot \text{s}^{-1})}{(1.602 \times 10^{-19} \text{ C}) (1 \text{ T})}$$

$$\times \left[1 - \sqrt{1 - \left(\frac{1.602 \times 10^{-19} \text{ C}) (1 \text{ T}) (0.5 \text{ m})}{(1.673 \times 10^{-27} \text{ kg}) (9 \times 10^7 \text{ m} \cdot \text{s}^{-1})}\right)^2}\right]$$

$$= 0.144 \text{ m}$$

---

6 Find the deflection of the beam by the second method. Use

$$\delta = y = - Bx^2 \left(\frac{q}{8 \, mV}\right)^{1/2}.$$

It should be noted that the deflection is below the x-axis.

6

$$\delta = (1 \text{ T}) (0.5 \text{ m})^2$$

$$\times \left(\frac{1.602 \times 10^{-19} \text{ C}}{8(1.673 \times 10^{-27} \text{ kg}) (4.23 \times 10^7 \text{ V})}\right)^{1/2}$$

$$= 0.133 \text{ m}$$

---

7 Repeat the two methods for $L = 0.1$ m. Note that the radius of curvature is still 0.940 m. Find the exit angle α.

7

$$\sin \alpha = \frac{L}{R} = \frac{0.1 \text{ m}}{0.940 \text{ m}} = 0.1064$$

$$\alpha = 6.11°$$

---

8 Find the deflection.

8

$$\delta = R(1 - \cos \alpha)$$
$$= 0.940 \text{ m}(1 - \cos 6.11°) = 0.00536 \text{ m}$$

or use $\delta = \dfrac{mv}{qB}\left[1 - \sqrt{1 - \left(\dfrac{qBL}{mv}\right)^2}\right]$

$$= \frac{(1.673 \times 10^{-27} \text{ kg}) (9 \times 10^7 \text{ m} \cdot \text{s}^{-1})}{(1.602 \times 10^{-19} \text{ C}) (1 \text{ T})}$$

$$\times \left[1 - \sqrt{1 - \left(\frac{1.602 \times 10^{-19} \text{ C}) (1 \text{ T}) (0.1 \text{ m})}{(1.673 \times 10^{-27} \text{ kg}) (9 \times 10^7 \text{ m} \cdot \text{s}^{-1})}\right)^2}\right]$$

$$= 0.00536 \text{ m}$$

---

9 Find the deflection by the second method.

9

$$\delta = - Bx^2 \left(\frac{q}{8 \, mv}\right)^{1/2}$$

$$= (1 \text{ T}) (0.1 \text{ m})^2 \left(\frac{1.602 \times 10^{-19} \text{ C}}{8(1.673 \times 10^{-27} \text{ kg}) (4.23 \times 10^7 \text{ V})}\right)^{1/2}$$

$$= 0.00532 \text{ m}$$

It is apparent that the second method will approximate the correct solution for small values of $x = L$.

---

10 **Problem 2** An α-particle which is a doubly charged helium ion having a mass of 4 u is accelerated to an energy of 3 MeV and enters a constant magnetic field of 5 T at right angles to the field. a) Find the speed of the particle as it enters the field. b) Compare the kinetic energy of the particle with its rest energy. c) What is the radius of its path? d) What is the angular velocity?

10 **Answer**

1.203×10^7 m $\cdot$ s^{-1}, 1240, 0.0499 m, 2.41×10^8 rad $\cdot$ s^{-1}

If you solved this problem correctly, go to frame 16. If you could not solve this problem, go through frames 11–15.

11 Tabulate the given data.

11

$$B = 5\,\text{T} = 5\,\text{N} \cdot \text{A}^{-1} \cdot \text{m}^{-1}$$
$$K = 3\,\text{MeV} = 3 \times 10^6\,\text{eV}$$
$$= 4.806 \times 10^{-13}\,\text{J}$$
$$q = +\,2e = 3.204 \times 10^{-19}\,\text{C}$$
$$m = 4\,\text{u} = 6.644 \times 10^{-27}\,\text{kg}$$

---

12 Find the speed of the particle from $K = \frac{1}{2}mv^2$.

12

$$v = \sqrt{\frac{2K}{m}}$$
$$= \sqrt{\frac{2(4.806 \times 10^{-13}\,\text{J})}{6.644 \times 10^{-27}\,\text{kg}}}$$
$$= 1.203 \times 10^7\,\text{m} \cdot \text{s}^{-1}$$

---

13 Find the rest energy by using $E = mc^2$ and compare it with the kinetic energy.

13

$$E = (6.644 \times 10^{-27}\,\text{kg})\,(3 \times 10^8\,\text{m} \cdot \text{s}^{-1})^2$$
$$= 5.98 \times 10^{-10}\,\text{J}$$
$$= \left(5.98 \times 10^{-10}\,\text{J}\right)\left(\frac{1\,\text{eV}}{1.602 \times 10^{-19}\,\text{J}}\right)$$
$$= 3.73 \times 10^9\,\text{eV}$$
$$= 3730\,\text{MeV}$$
$$\frac{3730\,\text{MeV}}{3\,\text{MeV}} = 1240 \text{ times as great.}$$

Since the kinetic energy of the particle is much less than its rest energy, we are justified in using Newtonian mechanics.

---

14 Find the radius of the path.

14

$$R = \frac{mv}{Bq}$$
$$= \frac{(6.644 \times 10^{-27}\,\text{kg})\,(1.203 \times 10^7\,\text{m} \cdot \text{s}^{-1})}{(5\,\text{N} \cdot \text{A}^{-1} \cdot \text{m}^{-1})\,(3.204 \times 10^{-19}\,\text{C})}$$
$$= 0.0499\,\text{m}$$

---

15 What is the angular velocity?

15

$$\omega = \frac{V}{R}$$

$$= \frac{1.203 \times 10^7 \, \text{m} \cdot \text{s}^{-1}}{0.0499 \, \text{m}}$$

$$= 2.41 \times 10^8 \, \text{rad} \cdot \text{s}^{-1}$$

Note that since

$$\omega = \frac{v}{R} = \frac{Bq}{m},$$

the angular velocity is independent of the speed of the particle and the radius of its path.

---

16 **Problem 3** In a shunt-wound dc motor the rotor and field windings are connected in parallel. If the resistance R_f of the field coils is 160 Ω, the resistance R_a of the rotor is 1.5 Ω, the potential difference V_{ab} at the brushes is equal to 112 V and the current supplied to the motor is 5 A when it is running at full speed, find a) the current in the field coils, b) the current in the rotor, c) the emf developed by the motor and d) the mechanical power developed.

16

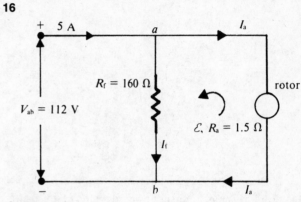

Answer
0.7 A, 4.3 A, 105.6 V, 454 W

If you could not solve this problem, go through frames 17–21.

17 Find the current I_f in the field coils by using
$$I_f = \frac{V_{ab}}{R_f}.$$

17

$$I_f = \frac{112 \, \text{V}}{160 \, \Omega} = 0.7 \, \text{A}$$

---

18 Apply Kirchhoff's point rule to point a to find the current in the rotor.

18

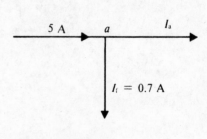

$$\Sigma I = 0$$
$$5 \, \text{A} - 0.7 \, \text{A} - I_a = 0$$
$$I_a = 4.3 \, \text{A}$$

19 Find the emf developed by the rotor by using Kirchhoff's loop rule. The induced emf or back emf has a sense of direction which is opposite to the direction of the current. This situation is analogous to that of a battery being charged.

19 The loop with the rotor can be redrawn thus:

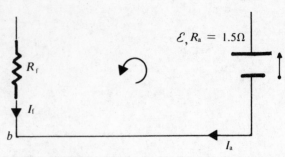

Starting at a

$$- I_f R_f + I_a R_a + \mathcal{E} = 0$$

$$- 0.7\,\text{A}\,(160\,\Omega) + 4.3\,\text{A}\,(1.5\,\Omega) + \mathcal{E} = 0$$

$$- 112\text{V} + 6.45\text{V} + \mathcal{E} = 0$$

$$\mathcal{E} = 105.6\text{V}$$

20 Find the mechanical power developed by using power $= VI = \mathcal{E}I_a$.

20 mechanical power $= (105.6\text{ V})\,(4.3\text{ A})$
$= 454\text{ W}$

21 Check your answer by finding the power delivered to the motor and loss of power in the field coils and in the rotor. Mechanical power = power delivered to the motor − loss of power.

21 Power delivered to motor $= I\,V_{ab}$
$= 5\text{ A}\,(112\text{ V}) = 560\text{ W}$
Loss of power in the field $= I_f^2\,R_f$
$= (0.7\text{ A})^2\,(160\ \Omega) = 78.4\text{ W}$
Loss of power in the rotor $= I_a^2\,R_a$
$= (4.3\text{ A})^2\,(1.5\ \Omega) = 27.7\text{ W}$
Total loss of power $= 78.4\text{ W} + 27.7\text{ W}$
$= 106.1\text{ W}$
Mechanical power $= 560\text{ W} - 106.1\text{ W}$
$= 454\text{ W}$

31

Sources of Magnetic Field

CHAPTER SUMMARY

The previous chapter was devoted to charges moving in an external magnetic field; here we are concerned with the creation of the magnetic field by moving charges. The mathematical relationships between the magnetic field and current for a long straight conductor, parallel conductors and a circular loop are presented. Ampere's law and the law of Biot and Savart are used to calculate the magnetic field caused by current-carrying conductors of various configurations. In addition, ferromagnetic, paramagnetic and diamagnetic effects are discussed in terms of the molecular theory and magnetic permeability, magnetization and magnetic intensity are analyzed.

BASIC TERMS — *Give definitions or meanings for the following:*

ampere (31-2)
solenoid (31-4)
toroidal solenoid (31-4)
source point (31-5)
field point (31-5)
superposition principle (31-5)
law of Biot and Savart (31-5)

Ampere's law (31-6)
ferromagnetic (31-7)
paramagnetic (31-7)
diamagnetic (31-7)
permeability (31-7)
magnetic susceptibility (31-7)
relative permeability (31-7)

PROGRAMMED QUIZ

1 A toroid can be considered as a _____.

1 Solenoid bent into a circle.

2 Describe the magnetic field inside a solenoid.

2 Nearly uniform and parallel to the axis.

3 Ampere's law is similar to what law that you have studied previously? Why?

3 Gauss's law; although it is a general law, it is only useful in symmetrical situations.

4 Ampere's law is useful for problems having sufficient symmetry. What would be a more general law for calculating the magnetic field of a current-carrying conductor?

4 Biot and Savart law.

513

5 What is the shape of the lines of a magnetic field about a current?

5 Loops.

6 In Ampere's law, what is I?

6 The net current passing through the area enclosed by the closed path.

7 What does the field within a solenoid carrying a given current depend on?

7 The current and the number of turns per unit length.

8 What is the field outside a tightly wound toroid?

8 Zero.

9 Are magnetic field lines similar to electric field lines?

9 No, electric field lines begin and end on charges, magnetic field lines form closed loops.

10 When are the forces on current carrying parallel conductors repulsive? attractive?

10 If the currents are in opposite directions; if the currents are in the same direction.

11 How are the two constants, ϵ_0 from Coulomb's law and μ_0 from the law of Biot and Savart, related?

11

$$\frac{1}{\mu_0 \epsilon_0} = c^2 = \text{square of the speed of light.}$$

12 How can we find the direction of the B lines around a straight conductor?

12 Use the righthand rule: grasp the conductor with the thumb extended in the direction of the current; the fingers then curl around the conductor in the direction of the B lines.

13 A diamagnetic substance is attracted, repelled by a magnetic field.

13 Repelled.

14 Which magnetic effect is present in all materials? Which magnetic effect is much larger than the other?

14 Diamagnetic; paramagnetic effects, when they occur, are always much larger than the diamagnetic effects.

15 How can we greatly increase the change in flux within a solenoid, keeping current constant?

15 Wind the solenoid on a solid ferromagnetic rod.

16 What if the rod is paramagnetic? diamagnetic?

16 The change in flux will only be slightly larger than if the core were empty; the change in flux would be slightly smaller.

17 What is the molecular basis for magnetic effects?

17 Each atom consists of one or more current loops which become aligned with the plane of their orbits perpendicular to the applied magnetic field. Within the substance adjacent atoms cause currents to cancel, at the surface there is a net surface current.

18 What is the magnetization of iron due to?

18 The magnetization of iron is due almost entirely to the alignment of the magnetic moments of its two uncompensated electrons. When a sample of iron is magnetically saturated, these unpaired electrons spin with their axes in the direction of the magnetizing field.

19 If a substance is placed in a magnetic field, is the field always strengthened?

19 No, it may be strengthened (if the substance is paramagnetic) or weakened (if the substance is diamagnetic),

20 The magnetic susceptibility has what values for paramagnetic materials? diamagnetic materials?

20 It is positive for paramagnetic materials and negative for diamagnetic ones.

21 Are paramagnetic and diamagnetic susceptibilities temperature dependent?

21 Paramagnetic susceptibility decreases with increasing temperature; diamagnetic susceptibility is not temperature dependent.

22 To what can we compare the earth's magnetic field?

22 To the field of a short bar magnet located near the center of the earth, the S-pole of the magnet pointing toward the north magnetic pole.

23 What does a moving charge create?	**23** A magnetic field.
24 What is the unit of the magnetic field?	**24** Tesla (T) $1 \text{ T} = 1 \text{ N} \cdot \text{A}^{-1} \cdot \text{m}^{-1}$
25 If two parallel conductors carry current in the same direction, will they attract or repel each other?	**25** Attract.

MAIN IDEAS

The magnetic field of a long straight conductor is given by $B = \dfrac{\mu_0 I}{2\pi r}$ where B is the magnitude of the magnetic field, I is the current, r is the distance from the conductor and $\mu_0 = 4\pi \times 10^{-7} \text{ T} \cdot \text{m} \cdot \text{A}^{-1}$.

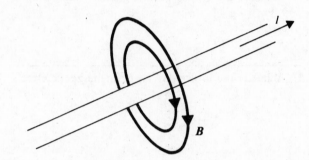

The direction of the magnetic field around a straight conductor can be found by grasping the conductor with the right hand so that the thumb points in the direction of the current. The fingers then curl in the direction of the B lines.

Two parallel conductors carrying current in the same direction attract each other. The two conductors will repel each other if they are carrying currents in opposite directions. The current in each of two parallel infinitely long conductors one meter apart in empty space that will cause the conductors to repel or attract each other with a force of 2×10^{-7} newtons per meter of length is one ampere. The force of attraction or repulsion per length is given by $\dfrac{F}{l} = \dfrac{\mu_0 I I'}{2\pi r}$, where I and I' are the currents in the two wires separated by a distance r.

The magnetic field at the center of a circular loop is found to be $B = \dfrac{\mu_0 I}{2R}$ where $R = $ radius of the loop and

$B = \dfrac{\mu_0 N I}{2R}$ for N circular loops. The direction of the field can be found by the righthand rule.

The magnetic field at any point on the axis of a loop can be obtained from $B = \dfrac{\mu_0 I R^2}{2(x^2 + R^2)^{3/2}}$ where x is the distance from the center of the loop. The magnetic field at the center of the solenoid is given by $B = \mu_0 n I$, where $n = N/L = $ the number of turns per unit length.

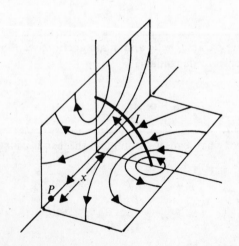

Ampere's law expresses the relationship between the tangential component of the magnetic field at any point on a closed curve and net current through the area bounded by the curve. $\Sigma B_{\parallel} \Delta s = \mu_0 I$.

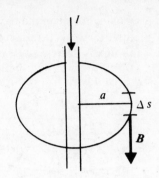

Applications of Ampere's law. Field of a solenoid: $B = \mu_0 n I$, where n is the number of turns per unit length of windings.

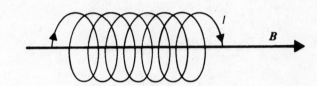

Field of a toroidal solenoid: $B = \dfrac{\mu_0 N I}{2\pi r}$; N = number of windings and r = radius of the toroid. If $n = \dfrac{N}{2\pi r}$, $B = \mu_0 n I$. The field of a toroidal solenoid is confined wholly to the space enclosed by the windings. The toroid may be considered a solenoid that has been bent into the shape of a doughnut. The field at the center of a solenoid with length L and radius R is given by

$$B = \frac{\mu_0 N I}{\sqrt{4R^2 + L^2}}.$$

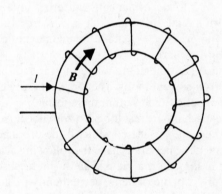

Law of Biot and Savart. Consider a current-carrying conductor. The magnitude of ΔB due to the element Δl of a wire carrying current I is given by

$$\Delta B = \frac{\mu_0 I \Delta l \sin \theta}{4\pi r^2}$$

where r is the distance between Δl and point P and θ is the angle between r and Δl. For $\theta = 0$, it follows that $\Delta B = 0$ at all points on the axis of the element. For $\theta = 90°$, ΔB will be maximum.

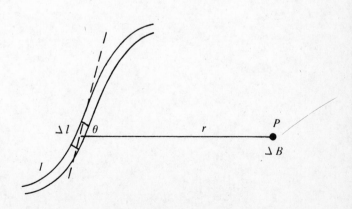

Materials may be categorized on the basis of how they alter the flux of a solenoid. If the material increases the change in flux greatly, it is called ferromagnetic; if it increases the flux by a lesser amount, it is called paramagnetic; and if the flux is decreased, it is called diamagnetic.

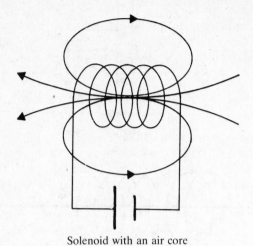

Solenoid with an air core

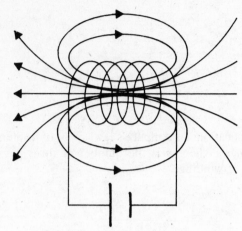

Solenoid with a ferromagnetic core

If the space enclosed by a solenoid is a vacuum, the magnetic field (flux density) is given by $B = \mu_0 nI$, where n = number of turns per unit length of windings. However, if the core contains a given material, the magnetic field B can be found from $K_m = B/B_0$, where K_m is the relative permeability. $K_m = 1$ for vacuum, > 1 for paramagnetic materials, $\gg 1$ for ferromagnetic materials and < 1 for diamagnetic materials.

The permeability of a material $\mu = K_m \mu_0$. In vacuum $\mu = \mu_0$; for paramagnetic materials $\mu > \mu_0$; for ferromagnetic materials $\mu \gg \mu_0$; and for diamagnetic materials $\mu < \mu_0$. The magnetic susceptibility of a material is denoted by χ, where $K_m = 1 + \chi$.

Magnetic phenomena are related to the motion of electrons; each atom within a substance consists of one or more electron current loops. The loops tend to become aligned with the plane of their orbits perpendicular to the applied magnetic field. Within the substance, currents in adjacent loops are moving in opposite directions and thus cancel each other, resulting in a zero net current in the interior. However, at the surface there are no adjacent currents, hence a surface current will be produced.

Ferromagnetic materials have the following distinctive properties: The magnetic field in such materials is much greater than the external field. The magnetic susceptibility, although not constant, is very large. Ferromagnetic materials are capable of being permanently magnetized. Iron, nickel, cobalt and gadolinium are the only ferromagnetic materials at room temperature.

The north geomagnetic pole of the earth is really a south pole and the south geomagnetic pole is a north pole. The angle that the earth's magnetic field makes with the horizontal is called the angle of dip or inclination.

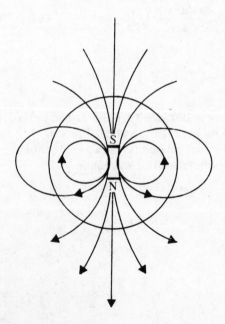

Problem solving strategy:

Step 1   In magnetic field calculations, draw the plane containing a segment Δl of the conductor and the line joining it to the point at which you want to determine the magnetic field. Visualize your diagram in three dimensions. Remember that the field lines are circles with directions determined by the right-hand rule.

Step 2   Examine the problem for symmetry. If the ΔB's at the point in question have the same direction for all the current elements, then the magnitude of B is $\Sigma \Delta B$. On the other hand, if the ΔB's have different directions for different current elements, then you will have to set up a coordinate system and represent each ΔB in terms of its components.

Step 3   Use the Law of Biot and Savart in problems involving current-carrying circular (or any segment of a circle) conductors.

Step 4   Ampere's law. If you are interested in obtaining the magnetic field at a certain point in the region of a current-carrying wire, then you must select a path (usually a circle) that passes through that point. If B is tangent to the path at every point, then $\Sigma B_{\parallel} \, \Delta s = B(2\pi r)$ for a circular path. If B is perpendicular to the path for some portion of the path, then that portion makes no contribution. Remember, $\Sigma B_{\parallel} \, \Delta s = \mu_0 I$.

PROGRAMMED QUIZ

1   What is the magnitude of the magnetic field due to a long straight wire carrying a current of 15 A at a distance of 2 m from the wire?

1

$$B = \frac{\mu_0 I}{2\pi r}$$
$$= \frac{2(10^{-7} \text{ T} \cdot \text{m} \cdot \text{A}^{-1}) \, (15 \text{ A})}{2 \text{ m}}$$
$$= 15 \times 10^{-7} \text{ T}$$

2   Two parallel conductors 1 m apart, each carrying the same current, experience a force of 2×10^{-7} N per meter of length. What is the current?

2

$$\frac{F}{l} = \frac{\mu_0 I I'}{2\pi r} = \frac{\mu_0 I^2}{2\pi r}$$
$$I^2 = \frac{(2) \, (10^{-7} \text{ N} \cdot \text{m}^{-1}) \, (1 \text{ m})}{2(10^{-7} \text{ T} \cdot \text{m} \cdot \text{A}^{-1})}$$
$$I = 1 \text{ A}$$

3   What statement can you make about the previous frame?

3   These values are the basis for the SI definition of the ampere.

4   What must be the radius of a circular loop carrying a current of 5 A if the magnetic field at the center is to have a magnitude of 2×10^{-5} T?

4   From the law of Biot and Savart,

$$B = \frac{\mu_0 I}{2R}$$
$$R = \frac{(4\pi)(10^{-7} \text{T} \cdot \text{m} \cdot \text{A}^{-1})(5\text{A})}{2(2 \times 10^{-5} \text{T})}$$
$$= 0.157 \text{ m}$$

5 What would be the magnitude of the magnetic field at the center of 30 circular loops, 10 cm in radius, each carrying a current of 2 A?

5

$$B = \frac{\mu_0 NI}{2R}$$

$$= \frac{(4\pi)(10^{-7}\text{T} \cdot \text{m} \cdot \text{A}^{-1})(30)(2\text{A})}{2(0.10\text{m})}$$

$$= 3.77 \times 10^{-4}\,\text{T}$$

---

6 What must be the current through a solenoid 30 cm long with 300 turns of wire if the magnetic field near the center is 0.02 T in magnitude?

6

$$B = \mu_0 n I$$

$$= \frac{0.02\,\text{T}}{4\pi \times 10^{-7}\,\text{T} \cdot \text{m} \cdot \text{A}^{-1}(300/0.3\,\text{m})}$$

$$= 15.9\,\text{A}$$

---

7 Find the magnitude of the magnetic field at the center of a toroidal solenoid of 200 windings and 8 cm in radius. The current in the windings is 6 A.

7

$$B = \frac{\mu_0 NI}{2\pi r}$$

$$= \frac{(4\pi \times 10^{-7}\,\text{T} \cdot \text{m} \cdot \text{A}^{-1})(200)(6\,\text{A})}{2\pi(0.08\,\text{m})}$$

$$= 3 \times 10^{-3}\,\text{T}$$

---

8 How many turns must a closely wound coil have for the magnetic field at the center to be 2.52×10^{-4} T? The coil is 0.2 m in radius and carries a current of 5 A.

8

$$B = \frac{\mu_0 NI}{2R}$$

$$N = \frac{2(2.52 \times 10^{-4}\text{T})(0.2\text{m})}{(4\pi)(10^{-7}\text{T} \cdot \text{A}^{-1} \cdot \text{m})(5\text{A})}$$

$$= 16$$

---

9 Find the magnitude of the magnetic field on the axis of a loop 0.1 m from the center. The loop is 0.2 m in radius and the current through the loop is 2.25 A.

9

$$B = \frac{\mu_0 IR^2}{2(x^2 + R^2)^{3/2}}$$

$$= \frac{(4\pi)(10^{-7}\text{T} \cdot \text{A}^{-1} \cdot \text{m})(2.25\text{A})(0.2\text{m})^2}{2\,[\,(0.1\text{m})^2 + (0.2\text{m})^2\,]^{3/2}}$$

$$= 5.06 \times 10^{-6}\,\text{T}$$

---

10 What is the permeability of a material, $K_m = 396$?

10

$$\mu = K_m \mu_0$$
$$= 396(4\pi \times 10^{-7}\,\text{Wb} \cdot \text{A}^{-1} \cdot \text{m}^{-1})$$
$$= 4.98 \times 10^{-4}\,\text{Wb} \cdot \text{A}^{-1} \cdot \text{m}^{-1}$$

---

11 What is the magnetic susceptibility for uranium, $K_m = 41$?

11

$$\chi = K_m - 1$$
$$= 41 - 1 = 40$$

---

12 At a certain location, the magnitude of the earth's magnetic field is 6.0×10^{-5} T. If the angle of dip is 70°, find the horizontal and vertical components.

12

$$B_V = B \sin \theta$$
$$= (6 \times 10^{-5}\,\text{T})(\sin 70°)$$
$$= 56.4\,\text{T}$$
$$B_H = B \cos \theta$$
$$= (6 \times 10^{-5}\,\text{T})(\cos 70°)$$
$$= 20.5\,\text{T}$$

13 What is the angle of dip at the magnetic poles?

13 $90°$

STEP BY STEP SOLUTIONS OF PROBLEMS

Problem 1 A wire of a circular cross section and radius R has a uniform current density. If the wire carries a current I, a) find the current through a circular area of radius r_1 inside the wire. b) Find the magnetic field B inside the wire at a distance r_1 from the axis. c) Find B on the surface of the wire. d) What is B outside the wire at a distance r_2 from the axis?

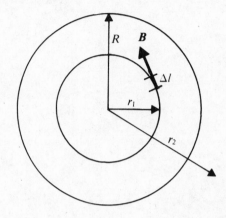

1 Find the current through a circular area of radius r_1 inside the wire. Use current density $= \dfrac{\text{current}}{\text{area}}$.

1

$$\frac{I}{\pi R^2} = \frac{I_1}{\pi r_1^2}$$

$$\therefore \ I_1 = \frac{r_1^2 I}{R^2}$$

---

2 Find the magnetic field B inside the wire at a distance r_1 from the axis by using Ampere's law. $B_{\parallel} = B$ and is constant along the circumference of the circle.

2 $\quad \Sigma B_{\parallel} \Delta l = \mu_0 I$

For the circle of radius r_1,

$$B(2\pi r_1) = \mu_0 I_1$$

$$B 2\pi r_1 = \mu_0 \frac{r_1^2 I}{R^2}$$

$$B = \frac{\mu_0 r_1 I}{2\pi R^2}$$

---

3 Find B on the surface of the wire. Let $r_1 = R$.

3

$$B = \frac{\mu_0 I}{2\pi R}$$

---

4 What is B outside the wire at a distance r_2 from the axis?

4

$$B = \frac{\mu_0 I}{2\pi r_2}$$

Problem 2 Two long (not infinite) parallel wires are hung by cords of length L from a common point as shown. The wires have a mass per unit length of λ and carry equal currents in opposite directions. If the cords make an angle θ with the vertical, find a) the current in each wire in terms of the variables λ, L and θ and b) the current in each wire for $\lambda = 0.06\,\text{kg}\cdot\text{m}^{-1}$, $L = 0.04\,\text{m}$ and $\theta = 5°$.

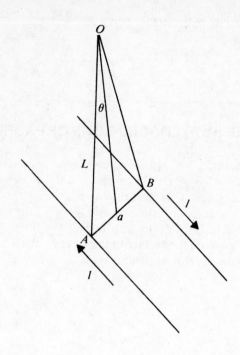

5 Find the weight of a wire of length l.

5 Since λ = mass per unit length, the mass of each wire is λl and the weight of each wire is λlg.

6 Since each wire lies in the magnetic field produced by the other, each experiences a force. Express this force in terms of the given variables and the length l.

6 $F = \dfrac{2k'll^2}{a}$, where a is the separation distance of the wires. Since $\sin \theta = \dfrac{a}{2L}$,

$$F = \frac{\mu_0 ll^2}{4\pi L \sin \theta}$$

7 Let us consider the wires as having their respective masses concentrated at A and B. Draw the free-body diagram for body A. Note that F = force due to the magnetic field.

7

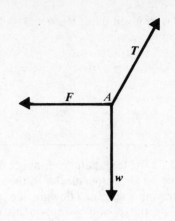

8 Resolve all forces into horizontal and vertical components.

8

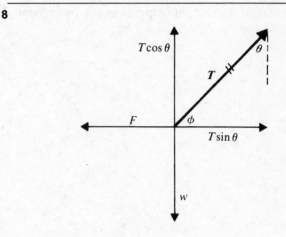

9 Set $\Sigma F_x = 0$ and
$\Sigma F_y = 0$.

9

$$T \sin \theta - \frac{\mu_0 l I^2}{4\pi L \sin \theta} = 0$$

$$T \cos \theta - \lambda l g = 0$$

10 Solve the second equation for T and substitute in the first. Solve for I.

10

$$I = \sqrt{\frac{(4\pi)\lambda L g \sin^2 \theta}{\mu_0 \cos \theta}}$$

11 Substitute given values and solve for I.

11

$$I = \sqrt{\frac{(4\pi)0.06 \text{kg} \cdot \text{m}^{-1}(0.04\text{m})(9.8\text{m} \cdot \text{s}^{-2})(\sin^2 5°)}{(4\pi)(10^{-7}\text{T} \cdot \text{m} \cdot \text{A}^{-1}) \cos 5°}}$$

$$= 42.3 \text{ A}$$

12 Since $\sin \theta \approx \tan \theta \approx \theta$ (in radians) for angles $< 5°$, express I in terms of θ.

12

$$I = \sqrt{\frac{(4\pi)\lambda L g \sin^2 \theta}{\mu_0 \cos \theta}}$$

$$= \sqrt{\frac{(4\pi)\lambda L g (\tan \theta)(\sin \theta)}{\mu_0}}$$

replace $\tan \theta$ and $\sin \theta$ by θ.

$$I = \sqrt{\frac{(4\pi)\lambda L g \theta^2}{\mu_0}} = \theta \sqrt{\frac{(4\pi)\lambda L g}{\mu_0}}$$

13 Check with given data. Use $\theta = 5° = 0.08725$ rad.

13

$$I = 0.08725 \sqrt{\frac{(4\pi)0.06\text{kg} \cdot \text{m}^{-1}(0.04\text{m})(9.8\text{m} \cdot \text{s}^{-2})}{(4\pi)(10^{-7}\text{T} \cdot \text{m} \cdot \text{A}^{-1})}}$$

$= 42.3$ A (which checks with the value obtained previously).

Problem 3 Two long parallel conductors separated by a distance $2a$ are perpendicular to the xy-plane and are each carrying a current I flowing in opposite directions. a) Find the x- and y-components of the magnetic field at any point in the first quadrant of the figure. b) Derive the expression for the magnitude of B at any point on the x-axis.

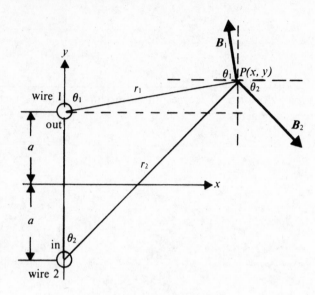

---

14 Select any point $P(x,y)$ in the first quadrant. Note the directions of B_1 due to wire 1 and B_2 due to wire 2.

14 Use the righthand rule. Grasp the wire with your right hand so that your thumb points in the direction of the current, your curled fingers will point in the direction of the encircling field.

---

15 Let B_{1x} be the x-component of the magnetic field at P due to B_1 and B_{2x} be the x-component of the magnetic field at P due to B_2. Find B_x, the x-component of the resultant magnetic field at P.

15
$$B_x = B_{1x} + B_{2x}$$
$$= -B_1 \cos\theta_1 + B_2 \cos\theta_2$$

---

16 What are the values of B_1 and B_2 in terms of I and their respective distances to P?

16
$$B_1 = \frac{\mu_0 I}{2\pi r_1}$$
$$B_2 = \frac{\mu_0 I}{2\pi r_2}$$

---

17 Substitute the values of B_1 and B_2 into the expression for B_x.

17
$$B_x = \frac{\mu_0 I}{2\pi}\left(\frac{-\cos\theta_1}{r_1} + \frac{\cos\theta_2}{r_2}\right)$$

---

18 Express $\cos \theta_1$ and $\cos \theta_2$ in terms of a, x and y and and substitute in the above.

18

$$\cos \theta_1 = \frac{y - a}{r_1}$$

$$\cos \theta_2 = \frac{a + y}{r_2}$$

$$B_x = \frac{\mu_0 I}{2\pi} \left(\frac{a - y}{r_1^2} + \frac{a + y}{r_2^2} \right)$$

---

19 Follow the same procedure for B_y.

19

$$B_y = B_{1y} + B_{2y}$$
$$= B_1 \sin \theta_1 - B_2 \sin \theta_2$$
$$= \frac{\mu_0 I}{2\pi} \left(\frac{\sin \theta_1}{r_1} - \frac{\sin \theta_2}{r_2} \right)$$

But $\sin \theta_1 = \dfrac{x}{r_1}$

$\sin \theta_2 = \dfrac{x}{r_2}$

$$B_y = \frac{\mu_0 I}{2\pi} \left(\frac{x}{r_1^2} - \frac{x}{r_2^2} \right)$$

---

20 Determine B_y at any point on the x-axis. Note that $r_1 = r_2$.

20 When
$$r_1 = r_2$$
$$B_y = 0$$
(as expected)

---

21 $\therefore B = B_x$. Find B_x on the x-axis; $y = 0$ and $r_1^2 = r_2^2 = a^2 + x^2$.

21

$$B = B_x = \frac{\mu_0 I}{2\pi} \left(\frac{a - 0}{a^2 + x^2} + \frac{a + 0}{a^2 + x^2} \right)$$

$$= \frac{\mu_0 I a}{\pi(a^2 + x^2)}$$

Note: at the origin $x = 0$.

$$B = \frac{\mu_0 I}{\pi a}$$

Problem 4 The electron in the Bohr model of the hydrogen atom orbits the nucleus in a circular path thus producing a circular loop. Derive the relationship between the magnetic dipole moment μ of the electron and its orbital angular momentum L.

22 Find the velocity of the electron by equating the coulomb force of attraction to the centripetal force;

$$F = \frac{1}{4\pi\epsilon_0} \frac{q_1 q_2}{r^2} = ma = \frac{mv^2}{r} .$$

22

Let $q_1 = q_2 = e$

$$\frac{1}{4\pi\epsilon_0} \frac{e^2}{r^2} = \frac{mv^2}{r}$$

$$v = \sqrt{\frac{e^2}{4\pi\epsilon_0 mr}}$$

23 Find the angular velocity from $v = \omega r$.

23

$$\omega = \frac{v}{r} = \sqrt{\frac{e^2}{4\pi\epsilon_0 mr^3}}$$

---

24 Find the electron current. The current i is equal to the electron charge multiplied by its orbital frequency. (Note: $\omega = 2\pi f$.)

24

$$i = e\left(\frac{\omega}{2\pi}\right) = \sqrt{\frac{e^4}{16\pi^3 \epsilon_0 mr^3}}$$

---

25 Find the magnetic dipole moment from $\mu = iA$, where $A = \pi r^2$.

25

$$\mu = \sqrt{\frac{e^4}{16\pi^3 \epsilon_0 mr^3}}\,(\pi r^2)$$

$$= \frac{e^2}{4}\sqrt{\frac{r}{\pi\epsilon_0 m}}$$

---

26 The angular momentum of the electron is given by $L = mvr$. Substitute v from frame 22 in this expression for L and simplify.

26

$$L = mr\sqrt{\frac{e^2}{4\pi\epsilon_0 mr}}$$

$$= \sqrt{\frac{mre^2}{4\pi\epsilon_0}}$$

---

27 Express μ in terms of L by eliminating r between the equations in frames 25 and 26.

27 Square both sides of the equations.

$$\mu^2 = \frac{e^4 r}{16\pi\epsilon_0 m}$$

$$L^2 = \frac{mre^2}{4\pi\epsilon_0}$$

Divide one side of each equation by the other.

$$\frac{\mu^2}{L^2} = \frac{e^2}{4m^2}$$

$$\mu = L\left(\frac{e}{2m}\right)$$

PROGRAMMED TEST

1 **Problem 1** Two long straight parallel wires are $2a$ meters apart as in the figure. The upper wire carries a current of I into the figure of the plane and the bottom wire carries an equal current out of the plane. What is the resultant magnetic field at any point P (on the plane) which lies on the perpendicular bisector of the line joining M and N?

1

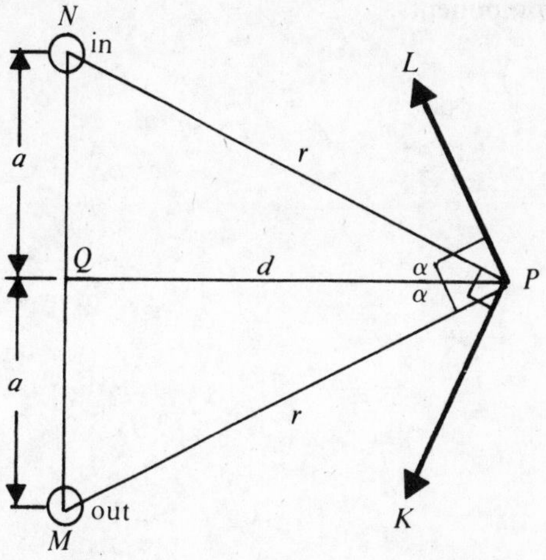

Answer

$$B = -\frac{\mu_0 I a}{\pi(a^2 + d^2)}$$

If you solved this problem correctly, go to frame 8. If you could not solve this problem, go through frames 2–7.

2 Find the magnitude and direction of the field at P due to the current in the wire M.

2 By the righthand rule, the magnetic field at P due to the current in wire M is directed along PL ($PL \perp MP$). Its magnitude is $\frac{\mu_0 I}{2\pi r}$.

---

3 Find the magnitude and direction of the field at P due to the current in wire N.

3 The magnetic field is directed along PK ($PK \perp NP$). Its magnitude is also $\frac{\mu_0 I}{2\pi r}$.

---

4 Resolve the magnetic fields obtained in frame 2 into x- and y-components. Draw a sketch to denote the components.

4 Field due to M:

$$B_x = \frac{-\mu_0 I}{2\pi r} \cos(90° - \alpha) = \frac{-\mu_0 I}{2\pi r} \sin \alpha$$

$$B_y = \frac{+\mu_0 I}{2\pi r} \sin(90° - \alpha) = \frac{+\mu_0 I}{2\pi r} \cos \alpha$$

Field due to N:

$$B_x = \frac{-\mu_0 I}{2\pi r} \sin \alpha$$

$$B_y = \frac{-\mu_0 I}{2\pi r} \cos \alpha$$

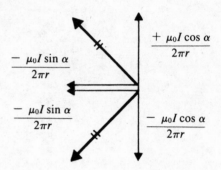

5 Find the resultant magnetic field by obtaining ΣB_x. Note that $\Sigma B_y = 0$. Hence $B = \Sigma B_x$.

5

$$B = \Sigma B_x = \frac{-\mu_0 I}{2\pi r} \sin \alpha$$

6 Express $\sin \alpha$ and r in terms of a and d.

6

$$r = \sqrt{a^2 + d^2}$$

$$\sin \alpha = \frac{a}{r} = \frac{a}{\sqrt{a^2 + d^2}}$$

7 Substitute the values of $\sin \alpha$ and r in the expression for B.

7

$$B = \frac{-\mu_0 I a}{\mu(a^2 + d^2)}$$

Note that the negative sign indicates that the direction of B is to the left (along PQ).

8 **Problem 2** The magnetic field at the center of a circular coil (radius 0.08 m and 300 turns of wire) is 5×10^{-4} T. a) Find the current carried by the coil. b) What is the magnetic field at a point on the axis of the coil 0.12 m from its center?

8

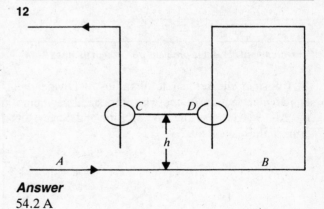

Answer

0.212 A, 8.52×10^{-5} T

If you solved this problem correctly, go to frame 12. If you could not solve this problem, go through frames 9–11.

9 Tabulate the given data.

9

$N = 300$ turns
$B = 5.0 \times 10^{-4}$ T
$R = 0.08$ m
$x = 0.12$ m

---

10 Find I by using

$$B = \frac{\mu_0 NI}{2R}$$

10

$$I = \frac{2BR}{\mu_0 N}$$

$$= \frac{2(5 \times 10^{-4} \text{ T}) (0.08 \text{ m})}{(4\pi) (10^{-7} \text{ T} \cdot \text{m} \cdot \text{A}^{-1}) (300)}$$

$$= 0.212 \text{ A}$$

---

11 Find the magnetic field at a point on the axis of the coil 0.12 m from its center. Use

$$B = \frac{\mu_0 NIR^2}{2(x^2 + R^2)^{3/2}}$$

11

$$B = \frac{(4\pi) (10^{-7} \text{ T} \cdot \text{m} \cdot \text{A}^{-1}) (300) (0.212 \text{ A}) (0.08 \text{ m})^2}{2[(0.12 \text{ m})^2 + (0.08 \text{ m})^2]^{3/2}}$$

$$= 8.52 \times 10^{-5} \text{ T}$$

---

12 **Problem 3** A horizontal wire AB lies on a table. Another wire CD is free to move up and down above AB. What must be the current (same in each wire) for CD to acquire an equilibrium height $h = 0.01$ m assuming the magnetic force on it is due wholly to the current in AB? The mass per unit length of wire CD is $0.006 \text{ kg} \cdot \text{m}^{-1}$.

12

Answer

54.2 A

If you solved this problem correctly, go to frame 18. If you could not solve this problem, go through frames 13–17.

13 What are the forces acting on wire CD?

13 The electrical repulsive force due to AB (upward) and the weight of the wire.

---

14 Write the expression for the electrical repulsive force.

14
$$F_e = \frac{\mu_0 I^2 l}{2\pi h}, \text{ where } l = \text{length of wire.}$$

---

15 Write the expression for the weight of CD.

15 $w = \lambda l g.$

---

16 Use the first condition of equilibrium $\Sigma F_y = 0$ and solve for I.

16
$$\frac{\mu_0 I^2 l}{2\pi h} - \lambda l g = 0$$

$$I = \sqrt{\frac{\lambda g h (2\pi)}{\mu_0}}$$

---

17 Substitute given values and solve for I.

17
$$I = \sqrt{\frac{(0.006 \text{ kg} \cdot \text{m}^{-1})(9.8 \text{ m} \cdot \text{s}^{-2})(0.01 \text{ m})(2\pi)}{4\pi \times 10^{-7} \text{ T} \cdot \text{m} \cdot \text{A}^{-1}}}$$
$$= 54.2 \text{ A}$$

---

18 *Problem 4* Calculate the magnitude and direction of the magnetic field at point P due to the current I in the wire semicircles.

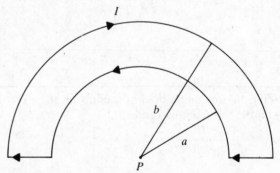

Answer
$$B = \frac{\mu_0 I}{4}\left(\frac{1}{a} - \frac{1}{b}\right) \text{ out of the page}$$

If you could not solve this problem, go through frames 19–24.

---

19 Consider the semicircle of radius a. Divide the semicircular section of the wire into small segments $\Delta l_1, \Delta l_2 \cdots$. Express the law of Biot and Savart in terms of these elements.

19 ΔB is the magnetic field due to each element.
$$\Delta B = \frac{\mu_0 I \sin\theta}{4\pi r^2}\Delta l$$
The resultant magnetic field due to all the elements in semicircle a is
$$B_a = \frac{\mu_0 I \sin\theta}{4\pi a^2}(\Delta l_1 + \Delta l_2 + \cdots)$$

---

20 Since each Δl is perpendicular to the radius, what is the value of $\sin\theta$?

20 $\sin 90° = 1$
$$B_a = \frac{\mu_0 I}{4\pi a^2}(\Delta l_1 + \Delta l_2 + \cdots)$$

---

21 To what is $\Delta l_1 + \Delta l_2 + \cdots$ equal?

21

$$\Delta l_1 + \Delta l_2 + \cdots$$
$$= \Sigma \Delta l = \pi a$$

which is the length of the semicircular arc.

---

22 Substitute this in the equation for B_a and simplify.

22

$$B_a = \frac{\mu_0 I (\pi a)}{4\pi a^2} = \frac{\mu_0 I}{4a}$$

directed out of the plane of the semicircular wire. Remember, the field lines are circles, with directions determined by the right-hand rule.

---

23 Calculate the magnitude and direction of the magnetic field at P due to the current in semicircle b.

23 Following the same procedure, we obtain

$$B_b = \frac{\mu_0 I}{4b}$$

directed into the plane of the semicircular wire.

---

24 What is the resultant of B_a and B_b?

24

$$B = B_a - B_b = \frac{\mu_0 I}{4a} - \frac{\mu_0 I}{4b}$$

$$= \frac{\mu_0 I}{4} \left(\frac{1}{a} - \frac{1}{b} \right)$$

Since $a < b, \dfrac{1}{a} > \dfrac{1}{b}$. Hence B has the direction of B_a, out of the page.

32

Electromagnetic Induction

CHAPTER SUMMARY

An induced electromotive force, due to the magnetic force on the charges, exists in conductors which are in motion in a magnetic field. Stationary conductors may also have an induced emf as a result of the induced electric field brought about by a varying magnetic flux. The emf can be determined by Faraday's law for both cases; Lenz's law gives us the direction of the induced currents. The induced emfs need not be confined to wires; the induced currents in metallic masses are referred to as eddy currents.

BASIC TERMS — *Give definitions or meanings for the following:*

induced current (32-1)
induced electromotive force (32-1)
motional electromotive force (32-2)
Faraday's law of induction (32-3)

non-electrostatic field (32-4)
Lenz's law (32-5)
eddy current (32-6)

PROGRAMMED QUIZ

1 Lenz's law is based on conservation of _____ . Explain.

1 Energy: If Lenz's law were not true, the induced current in this hypothetical situation would produce a flux in the same direction as the original change in flux. This would be followed by a greater change in flux that would produce a larger current followed by a still greater change in flux .... The current would continue to increase indefinitely, producing a vast amount of power I^2R and would violate the law of conservation of energy.

2 How often does the direction of the induced emf of a wire loop rotating in a magnetic field change?

2 Twice in one revolution.

3 What are some examples of induced emf?

3 Alternating generator, transformer.

4 Induced emf is caused by a changing magnetic flux. What are some ways in which the flux through a loop may change?

4 The magnetic field may change in magnitude or direction, the loop may change in size or orientation or the loop may move to a region where the magnetic field is different.

---

5 Does the magnetic field due to the induced current always oppose the flux?

5 No, if the flux is increasing the magnetic field will oppose it but if the flux is decreasing, the magnetic field will aid the flux. The magnetic field created by the induced current always opposes the change in the given flux.

---

6 What happens to the motion of a body because of eddy currents?

6 They impede the motion.

---

7 The charges moving within a conductor move with constant velocity, i.e. they are in equilibrium. What are the forces acting on them?

7 The non-electrostatic force (which may be magnetic) and an electrostatic force. The two forces are equal in magnitude and opposite in direction.

---

8 What is the relationship between Lenz's law and Faraday's law?

8 Lenz's law gives us the same information as the sign convention in Faraday's law.

---

9 What are the sign conventions in Faraday's law?

9 If one faces the circuit, the emf is $+$ if it results in a current in the counterclockwise direction, $-$ if the current is clockwise. $\Delta\Phi/\Delta t$ is $+$ if there is an increase in flux toward the observer or a decrease in flux away from the observer. $\Delta\Phi/\Delta t$ is $-$ if there is a decrease in flux toward the observer or an increase in flux away from the observer. The electromotive force and flux always have opposite signs.

---

10 Can an emf be induced in stationary conductors?

10 Yes, as long as there is a change in flux.

---

11 Can Lenz's law be applied to open circuits?

11 Yes, find the direction of the induced emf by thinking of what would happen if the circuit were closed.

---

12 Using Lenz's law, what is the direction of the current in the wire if the wire is moving toward the right?

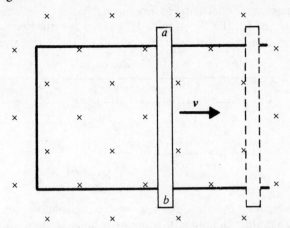

The crosses denote that the field is entering the page.

12 Since $\Phi = BA$ and the area is increasing as the wire is moving to the right, the flux is increasing also. Therefore, the induced emf attempts to decrease the flux by causing current to flow from b to a. This current generates a flux into the paper on the right side of the wire ab, thus bolstering the magnetic field and pushing the wire to the left. On the left side of the wire the field is decreased, thus assisting the motion of the wire to the left. The magnitude of the force is given by $F = IlB$ and the direction by the right-hand screw rule.

13 Use the sign convention to show that $\mathcal{E}$ and $\frac{\Delta\Phi}{\Delta t}$ should have opposite signs.

13 Since the current is counterclockwise, the emf is positive. The flux is directed away from the observer and is increasing so $\frac{\Delta\Phi}{\Delta t}$ is negative. Therefore $\mathcal{E}$ and $\frac{\Delta\Phi}{\Delta t}$ have opposite signs.

14 Using Lenz's law, what is the direction of the current in the wire if the wire is moving toward the left?

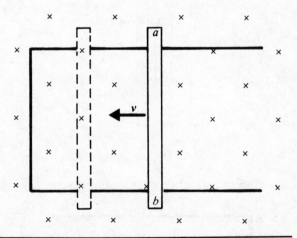

14 Since the flux is decreasing, the induced emf will aid the flux by setting up a field that reinforces the field to the left of the wire; i.e. the current will flow from a to b. This means that on the right side of the wire, part of the field is negated and the wire will be pushed to the right.

15 Show how this is compatible with the right-hand rule.

15 Turn a right-hand screw from v (left direction) toward B (into the paper). The direction of $\mathcal{E}$ is the direction in which the screw advances (downward from a to b). Or point the fingers of your right hand in the direction of v so that you will be able to curl your fingers toward B. Your thumb points in the direction of $\mathcal{E}$.

16 Is it correct to say that the induced emf depends on the flux through the loop?

16 No, it depends on the rate of change of the flux.

17 Using Lenz's law, determine the direction of the current in resistor R_2 when the switch is closed. Indicate on the sketch the directions of I_1, I_2, B_1 and B_2.

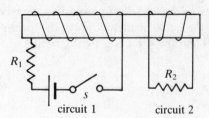

circuit 1   circuit 2

17 When the switch is closed, the current in circuit 1 takes a small amount of time to change from zero to its maximum value. While the current in circuit 1 is increasing, the changing flux through circuit 2 induces current I_2. The flux due to I_2 opposes the increase in flux due to I_1.

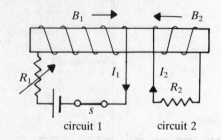

circuit 1   circuit 2

B_1 and B_2 are obtained by the right-hand rule. Grasp the solenoid with your right hand so that your fingers curl around the coil in the direction of the current. Your thumb will point in the direction of the magnetic field within the solenoid.

MAIN IDEAS

1 Motional electromotive force. A charged particle $+ q$ moving within a conductor with a velocity v perpendicular to the length of the conductor and a uniform magnetic field B will experience a magnetic force $F = qvB$. The direction of this force is upward. The upper end of the wire acquires an excess positive charge and the lower end an excess negative charge, creating an electric field from a to b. A downward force qE is exerted on the charge. When $qE = qvB$, the charges are in equilibrium. The potential difference $V_{ab} = El = vBl$. The crosses indicate that the field is perpendicular to the plane of the diagram and directed into the paper.

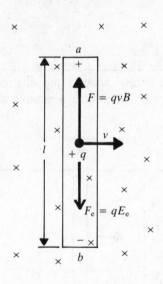

Let a conductor ab slide along a U-shaped conductor with velocity v. Note that no magnetic force acts on charges in the stationary conductor. However, the stationary conductor lies in the electrostatic field produced by the charges accumulated at a and b. A current is established due to this field. The moving rod has become a source of emf called motional electromotive force. Within the rod, charges move from the lower to the higher potential and in the stationary conductor from higher to lower potential. If the resistance of the sliding conductor is negligible, then $\mathcal{E} = vBl$. If the external resistance is R and the internal resistance of the sliding conductor is r, then

$$I = \frac{\mathcal{E}}{(R + r)}.$$

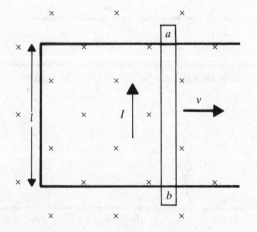

2 The total emf induced in a rectangular loop rotating with a constant angular velocity in a uniform magnetic field $= \mathcal{E} = \omega BA \sin \theta$, where $\omega =$ uniform angular velocity about the y-axis, $A =$ area of the loop ab, $\theta =$ angle between the plane of the loop and the x-axis. If $\theta = 0$ at $t = 0$, i.e. the loop lies in the xy-plane, then $\mathcal{E} = \omega AB \sin \omega t$. The maximum emf $= \mathcal{E}_m = \omega AB$, therefore $\mathcal{E} = \mathcal{E}_m \sin \omega t$.

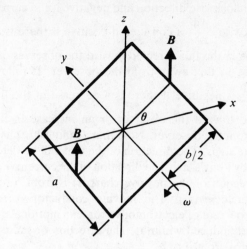

3 Faraday disk dynamo. The induced emf between the center and rim of a disk of radius R rotating about an axis parallel to a constant field B is $\mathcal{E} = \frac{1}{2}\omega BR^2$.

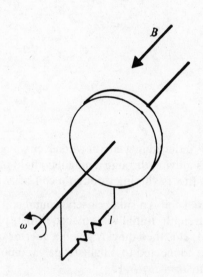

4 Faraday's law. Let conductor ab slide along a U-shaped conductor $abcd$ with a velocity v. The cross-sectional area of the circuit $abcd$ increases by $\Delta A = l\Delta s$ and the change in flux is given by $\Delta \Phi = B\Delta A = B/\Delta s$ or $\frac{\Delta \Phi}{\Delta t} = \frac{\Delta s}{\Delta t} Bl = vBl$. The quantity vBl is the induced emf. Hence it is equal in magnitude to the rate of change of the magnetic flux. $\mathcal{E} = -\Delta \Phi / \Delta t$ is Faraday's law. If one faces the circuit, the emf is positive if it results in a current in the

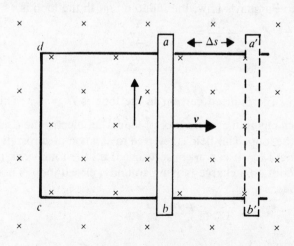

counterclockwise direction and negative if the current is clockwise. $\frac{\Delta\Phi}{\Delta t}$ is considered positive if there is an increase in the flux directed toward the observer or a decrease in flux away from the observer. It follows that $\frac{\Delta\Phi}{\Delta t}$ is negative if there is a decrease in the flux directed toward the observer or an increase in flux away from the observer. Note that $\mathcal{E}$ and $\Delta\Phi/\Delta t$ have opposite signs. The direction of the emf will be determined by Lenz's law. The direction of the current (i.e., the direction of the positive charges) is from b to a (counterclockwise). The moving conductor corresponds to a seat of electromotive force; a motional emf has been induced within it. The direction or sense of the emf is from b to a.

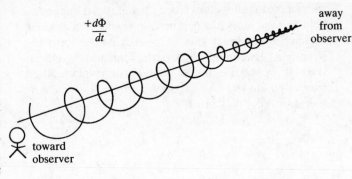

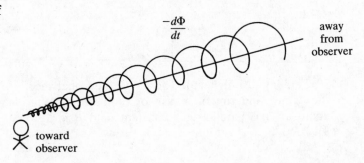

An emf is induced in a circuit whenever we have a change in the enclosed flux. The flux may vary because the conductor is moving through a magnetic field or because the magnetic field is varying through a stationary conductor. If a flux is varying through a coil of N turns, $\mathcal{E} = -N(\Delta\Phi/\Delta t)$.

5 The search coil is a small closely wound coil of an enclosed area A and N turns used for measuring the magnetic field strength. Initially it is placed with its plane perpendicular to a magnetic field; therefore the flux through it is $\Phi = BA$. It is then quickly given a quarter of a turn so that its plane is parallel to the field; therefore $\Phi = 0$. If the coil is connected to a ballistic galvanometer calibrated to measure the charge q which flowed during the quarter turn, $B = Rq/NA$.

6 Induced electric fields. A long, thin solenoid is encircled by a conducting loop. The current I in the coil of the solenoid produces a magnetic field $B = \mu_0 nI$ along the axis of the solenoid. The magnetic flux Φ through the loop is given by $\Phi = BA = \mu_0 nIA$. If I changes with time, Φ will also change, and, according to Faraday's Law, the induced emf in the loop is

$$\mathcal{E} = \frac{-\Delta\Phi}{\Delta t} = -\mu_0 nA\frac{\Delta I}{\Delta t}.$$

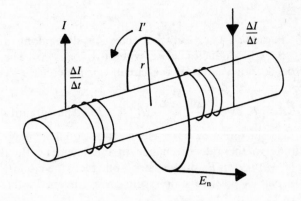

The induced current in the loop is $I' = \frac{\mathcal{E}}{R}$. The changing magnetic flux produces an electric field in the loop. This field is referred to as a non-electrostatic field E_n. It is non-conservative; i.e., the total work it does on a charge moving around a closed loop is not zero.

$$E_n = \frac{\mathcal{E}}{2\pi r} = \frac{\mu_0 nA}{2\pi r}\frac{\Delta I}{\Delta t}$$

7 Lenz's law. The direction of an induced current is such as to oppose the cause producing it, i.e. oppose the change in the magnetic flux through the circuit. Consider a magnet moving toward a stationary coil. The magnetic field of the coil is such as to oppose the motion of the magnet.

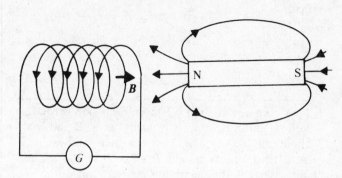

Lenz's law is a consequence of the principle of conservation of energy. For example, in moving the conductor along a U-shaped conductor (see Faraday's law above) against the opposing force produced by the magnetic field created by the induced current, work had to be done by the applied force. The electrical energy $\mathcal{E}It$ supplied to the circuit comes from this outside source.

8 If a conducting disk rotates in a magnetic field, the charges in the conductor will experience forces which give rise to induced currents, called eddy currents, which circulate throughout the volume of the disk.

PROGRAMMED QUIZ

1 A 0.5 m long conductor moves in a magnetic field $B = 1.2$ T at 0.08 m·s^{-1} perpendicular to the field. What is the induced emf?

1
$$\mathcal{E} = v_\perp Bl$$
$$= (0.08 \text{ m·s}^{-1})(1.2 \text{ T})(0.5 \text{ m})$$
$$= 0.048 \text{ V}$$
Note: $1 \text{ T·m}^2·\text{s}^{-1} = (1 \text{ N·A}^{-1}·\text{m}^{-1})(\text{m}^2·\text{s}^{-1})$
$$= 1 \text{ J·C}^{-1} = 1 \text{ V}$$

2 If the magnetic field is directed into the page and v is in the $+x$ direction, what is the direction of the emf?

2 $+y$ direction. Use the righthand screw rule.

3 A coil of 400 turns is placed in a magnetic field perpendicular to the plane of the coil. What is the rate of change of flux if the magnitude of the induced emf is 0.36 V?

3
$$|\mathcal{E}| = N\frac{\Delta\Phi}{\Delta t}$$
$$\frac{\Delta\Phi}{\Delta t} = \frac{0.36 \text{ V}}{400} = 9 \times 10^{-4} \text{ V}$$
$$= 9 \times 10^{-4} \text{ Wb·s}^{-1}$$

4 What would be the induced emf if the coil is tilted so that a line perpendicular to its plane would be at $20°$ with B?

4 $\quad\mathcal{E} = (0.36 \text{ V}) (\cos 20°) = 0.338 \text{ V}$

5 What is the speed of a rod $l = 0.50$ m moving in a perpendicular magnetic field of magnitude $B = 1.5$ T if the induced emf is 3 V?

5
$$\mathcal{E} = v_\perp Bl$$
$$v = \frac{3 \text{ V}}{(1.5 \text{ T})(0.50 \text{ m})}$$
$$= 4 \text{ m·s}^{-1}$$

6 What is the magnitude of the non-electrostatic field?

6
$$E_n = vB$$
$$= (4\ \text{m} \cdot \text{s}^{-1})(1.5\ \text{T})$$
$$= 6\ \text{V} \cdot \text{m}^{-1}$$

---

7 A rectangular loop 0.1 m on each side is rotating with a uniform angular velocity $\omega = 8\ \text{rad} \cdot \text{s}^{-1}$ about the y-axis. The loop lies in a uniform magnetic field of magnitude $B = 0.3$ T in the x-direction. What is the maximum induced emf?

7
$$\mathcal{E}_\text{m} = \omega AB$$
$$= (8\ \text{rad} \cdot \text{s}^{-1})(0.1\ \text{m})^2(0.3\ \text{T})$$
$$= 0.024\ \text{V}$$

---

8 If the loop lies in the yz-plane at $t = 0$, what is the induced emf at $t = 0.05$ s?

8
$$\mathcal{E} = \omega AB\ \sin \omega t$$
$$= (8\ \text{rad} \cdot \text{s}^{-1})(0.1\ \text{m})^2(0.3\ \text{T})$$
$$\times\ \sin\ [(8\ \text{rad} \cdot \text{s}^{-1})(0.05\ \text{s})]$$
$$= 9.35 \times 10^{-3}\ \text{V}$$

or

$$\mathcal{E} = \mathcal{E}_\text{m}\ \sin \omega t$$
$$= (0.024\ \text{V})\ \sin\ [(8\ \text{rad} \cdot \text{s}^{-1})(0.05\ \text{s})]$$
$$= 9.35 \times 10^{-3}\ \text{V}$$

---

9 Find the maximum torque on the loop if the current is 0.2 A.

9
$$\Gamma = IBA\ \sin \alpha \qquad\qquad \alpha = 90°$$
$$= (0.2\ \text{A})(0.3\ \text{T})(0.1\ \text{m})^2$$
$$= 6 \times 10^{-4}\ \text{N} \cdot \text{m}$$

---

10 A 0.25 m conducting rod slides along a U-shaped conductor which is in a uniform magnetic field 0.8 T perpendicular to the plane of the conductor. Find the magnitude and direction of the emf induced in the rod when it is moving to the right at 6 m · s^{-1}.

10
$$\mathcal{E} = v_\perp Bl$$
$$= (6\ \text{m} \cdot \text{s}^{-1})(0.8\ \text{T})(0.25\ \text{m})$$
$$= 1.2\ \text{V up from}\ b\ \text{to}\ a$$

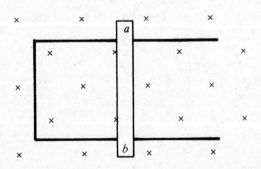

11 If the resistance of the entire circuit is 0.3 Ω, what is the current in the circuit?

11
$$I = \frac{\mathcal{E}}{R}$$
$$= \frac{1.2 \text{ V}}{0.3 \text{ Ω}} = 4 \text{ A}$$

12 What is the force required to maintain the rod in motion (neglect friction)?

12
$$F = IBl$$
$$= (4 \text{ A})(0.8 \text{ T})(0.25 \text{ m}) = 0.8 \text{ N}$$

STEP BY STEP SOLUTIONS OF PROBLEMS

Problem 1 A long rectangular loop of width l, mass m and resistance R is at rest in a uniform magnetic field B, perpendicular to the plane of the loop. It is then acted upon by a constant force F which is pulling the loop out of the magnetic field region. a) Derive the expression for the terminal velocity in terms of F, R, B and l. b) Prove that the electrical power is equal to the power supplied by the external agent.

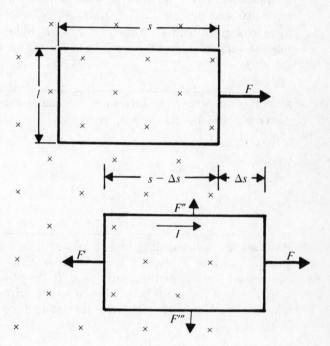

1 What is the magnetic flux Φ through the area enclosed by the loop before it is pulled from the magnetic field?

1 $\Phi_1 = BA_1 = Bls$

2 What is the magnetic flux Φ_2 through the area enclosed by the loop when part (Δs) of the loop emerges from the magnetic field?

2 $\Phi_2 = BA_2 = Bl(s - \Delta s)$

3 Obtain the magnitude of the change in flux $\Delta \Phi$ by subtracting Φ_2 from Φ_1.

3
$$\Delta \Phi = \Phi_1 - \Phi_2$$
$$= Bls - Bl(s - \Delta s)$$
$$= Bl\Delta s$$

4 If Δt is the time for the loop to move through a distance Δs, find the rate of change of the flux by dividing both sides of the equation by Δt.

4
$$\frac{\Delta \Phi}{\Delta t} = Bl \frac{\Delta s}{\Delta t}$$

5 But $\Delta s / \Delta t = v =$ exit speed of the loop from the magnetic field. Substitute v for $\Delta s / \Delta t$ and note that you have obtained the magnitude of the induced emf $\mathcal{E}$ from Faraday's law.

5
$$|\mathcal{E}| = \frac{\Delta \Phi}{\Delta t} = Blv$$

6 Find the current in the circuit. Use Ohm's law. In accordance with Lenz's law, the current in the loop will be clockwise; it opposes the change by setting up its own field. Also, the current in the loop will cause forces F', F'' and F''' to act on the three conductors.

6
$$I = \frac{\mathcal{E}}{R} = \frac{Blv}{R}$$

7 Since the forces on the top and bottom wires are equal and opposite, $\Sigma F_y = 0$ and we only have to be concerned with F'. Thus $F' = F = IlB$. Substitute the value of I from the previous frame and solve for v.

7
$$F = IlB$$
$$= \frac{Blv}{R}(lB)$$
$$v = \frac{FR}{B^2 l^2}$$

8 Prove that the electrical power is equal to the power supplied by the external agent.

8
$$P_{elect} = I^2 R$$
$$= \left(\frac{F}{Bl}\right)^2 R = \frac{F^2 R}{B^2 l^2}$$
$$P_{ext} = Fv = F\frac{FR}{B^2 l^2} = \frac{F^2 R}{B^2 l^2}$$

which is the same as the electrical power.

Problem 2 A 0.4 m long rod rotates with an angular velocity of 5 rev $\cdot$ s^{-1} about an axis through one end of the rod perpendicular to it. If the plane of rotation of the rod is perpendicular to the earth's magnetic field (6×10^{-5} T), find the induced emf in the rod.

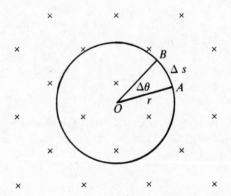

9 Find the area ΔA of the sector OAB.

9
$$\Delta A = \frac{1}{2}r \cdot \Delta s = \frac{1}{2}r \cdot r \, \Delta \theta$$
$$= \frac{1}{2}r^2 \Delta \theta$$

10 Find the change in magnetic flux through this area. Use $\Delta \Phi = B \, \Delta A$.

10
$$\Delta \Phi = B(\frac{1}{2}r^2 \Delta \theta)$$
$$= \frac{1}{2}Br^2 \Delta \theta$$

11 Divide both sides of the equation by Δt. Substitute ω for $\Delta\theta / \Delta t$.

11
$$\frac{\Delta\Phi}{\Delta t} = \tfrac{1}{2}Br^2 \frac{\Delta\theta}{\Delta t} = \tfrac{1}{2}Br^2\omega$$

12 Find the magnitude of the induced emf by substituting given values in $\mathcal{E} = \Delta\Phi / \Delta t$. (Note 1 rev = 2π rad).

12
$$\mathcal{E} = \tfrac{1}{2}(6 \times 10^{-5}\ \text{T})(0.4\ \text{m})^2(5)$$
$$\times (2\pi\ \text{rad} \cdot \text{s}^{-1})$$
$$= 1.51 \times 10^{-4}\ \text{V}$$

Problem 3 A closely wound rectangular coil of 200 turns has dimensions of 0.14 m $\times$ 0.30 m. It is rotating at 600 rpm about the y-axis. The entire loop lies in a uniform magnetic field of 0.4 T, parallel to the z-axis. Calculate a) the maximum induced emf, b) the instantaneous induced emf when the coil makes an angle of 65° with the field, c) the average emf induced in the coil during the period when the plane of the coil rotates from a position where it makes an angle of 40° with the magnetic field to a position of 65°.

13 Convert 600 rpm to rad $\cdot$ s^{-1}.

13
$$600\ \text{rpm} = \left(600\frac{\text{rev}}{\text{min}}\right)\left(\frac{1\ \text{min}}{60\ \text{s}}\right)\left(\frac{2\pi\ \text{rad}}{1\ \text{rev}}\right)$$
$$= 20\pi\ \text{rad} \cdot \text{s}^{-1}$$

14 Find the area of the loop.

14
$$A = (0.14\ \text{m})(0.30\ \text{m}) = 4.2 \times 10^{-2}\ \text{m}^2$$

15 Find the magnitude of the maximum induced emf. Use $\mathcal{E}_m = \omega NAB$.

15
$$\mathcal{E}_m = (20\pi\ \text{rad} \cdot \text{s}^{-1})(200)(4.2 \times 10^{-2}\ \text{m}^2)(0.4\ \text{T})$$
$$= 211\ \text{V}$$

16 Find the magnitude of the instantaneous induced emf when the coil makes an angle of 65° with the field. Use $|\mathcal{E}| = \mathcal{E}_m \sin\theta$.

16
$$|\mathcal{E}| = 211\ \text{V} \sin 65° = 191\ \text{V}$$

17 Find the time required for the coil to rotate through $65° - 40° = 25°$. Use θ (rad) $= \omega t$.
$$(\pi\ \text{rad} = 180°)$$

17
$$25° = 0.436\ \text{rad}$$
$$0.436\ \text{rad} = 20\pi\ \text{rad} \cdot \text{s}^{-1}(t)$$
$$t = 6.94 \times 10^{-3}\text{s}$$

18 Find the magnitude of the average emf induced in the coil from $\theta = 40°$ to $\theta = 65°$; use $|\mathcal{E}_{av}| = N\ \Delta\Phi / \Delta t$, where $\Phi_1 = BA \cos 40°$ and $\Phi_2 = BA \cos 65°$.

18 Since $\Phi = BA \cos\theta$
$$\Delta\Phi = BA(\cos 40° - \cos 65°)$$
$$= 0.343\ BA$$
$$|\mathcal{E}_{av}| = \frac{(200)(0.343)(0.4\ \text{T})(4.2 \times 10^{-2}\ \text{m}^2)}{6.94 \times 10^{-3}\ \text{s}}$$
$$= 166\ \text{V}$$

19 Repeat the problem for a rotation from 64° to 65°. The value of the instantaneous $\mathcal{E}$ will be very close to the average $\mathcal{E}$.

19

$$1° = 0.01745 \text{ rad}$$

$$t = \frac{0.01745 \text{ rad}}{20\pi \text{ rad} \cdot \text{s}^{-1}} = 2.78 \times 10^{-4} \text{ s}$$

$$|\mathcal{E}_{\text{av}}| = \frac{(200)(0.4 \text{ T})(4.2 \times 10^{-2} \text{ m}^2)(\cos 64° - \cos 65°)}{2.78 \times 10^{-4} \text{ s}}$$

$$= 190 \text{ V}$$

PROGRAMMED TEST

1 *Problem 1* A long straight solenoid (radius 0.04 m) has 10^4 turns $\cdot$ m^{-1} and the windings carry a current of 2 amperes. A coil of 50 turns (radius 0.02 m) is placed at the center of the solenoid so that the axis of the solenoid is perpendicular to the coil and passes through its center. When the primary (solenoid) circuit is opened, the magnetic field of the solenoid becomes zero in 0.04 s. What is the magnitude of the average induced emf in the coil?

1

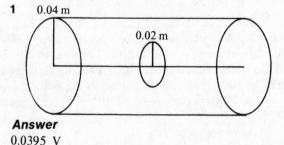

Answer
0.0395 V

If you solved this problem correctly, go to frame 7. If you could not solve this problem, go through frames 2–6.

2 Tabulate the given data.

2

$$R_s = 0.04 \text{ m}$$
$$R_c = 0.02 \text{ m}$$
$$n_s = 10^4 \text{ turns} \cdot \text{m}^{-1}$$
$$N_c = 50 \text{ turns}$$
$$I_s = 2 \text{ A}$$
$$t = 0.04 \text{ s}$$

3 Find the magnetic field at the center of the solenoid.

3

$$B = \mu_0 n I$$
$$= (4\pi \times 10^{-7} \text{ Wb} \cdot \text{A}^{-1} \cdot \text{m}^{-1})(10^4 \text{ turns} \cdot \text{m}^{-1})(2 \text{ A})$$
$$= 0.0251 \text{ T}$$

4 Find the area of the coil.

4

$$A = \pi r^2 = \pi(0.02 \text{ m})^2 = 1.26 \times 10^{-3} \text{ m}^2$$

5 Find the magnetic flux through the coil.

5

$$\Phi_c = BA$$
$$= (0.0251 \text{ T})(1.26 \times 10^{-3} \text{ m}^2)$$
$$= 3.16 \times 10^{-5} \text{ Wb}$$

6 Using Faraday's law, find the magnitude of the average induced emf in the coil.

6

$$|\mathcal{E}| = N\frac{\Delta\Phi_c}{\Delta t}$$
$$= \frac{50(3.16 \times 10^{-5} \text{ Wb})}{0.04 \text{ s}}$$
$$= 0.0395 \text{ V}$$

7 **Problem 2** The betatron is an application of electromagnetic induction whereby orbiting electrons are accelerated to high energies by the action of electric fields induced by a changing magnetic flux. In the simplified version of the betatron, the changing magnetic field may be obtained by the changing current in the electromagnet. The changing magnetic field will guide and accelerate the electrons in a circular path as well as maintain a constant orbit. If a betatron has an orbiting radius of 0.85 m and its magnetic field changes at the rate of 200 T · s⁻¹, how many revolutions must an electron make to acquire 100 MeV?

7

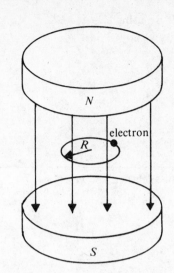

Answer

2.20×10^5

If you solved this problem corretly, go to frame 11. If you could not solve this problem, go through frames 8–10.

8 We can regard the circular path of the electron as a conducting loop in a magnetic field. Find the area enclosed by the orbiting electron.

8

$$A = \pi r^2$$
$$= \pi (0.85 \text{ m})^2 = 2.27 \text{ m}^2$$

---

9 Using Faraday's law, find the magnitude of the average emf gained by the electron in one revolution.

9

$$|\mathcal{E}| = \frac{\Delta \Phi}{\Delta t} = \frac{\Delta (BA)}{\Delta t} = \left(A \frac{\Delta B}{\Delta t} \right)$$
$$= 2.27 \text{ m}^2 (200 \text{ T} \cdot \text{s}^{-1})$$
$$= 454 \text{ V}$$

---

10 Hence an electron acquires 454 eV in one revolution. How many revolutions must the electron make to acquire 100 MeV?

10

$$\frac{100 \times 10^6 \text{ eV}}{454 \text{ eV} \cdot \text{rev}^{-1}} = 2.20 \times 10^5 \text{ rev}$$

---

11 **Problem 3** A Faraday disk dynamo rotating at 1 rev · s⁻¹ and operating in a magnetic field of 2 T supplies a current of 18,000 A at 1.5 V. a) What is the radius of the disk? b) If all the mechanical energy is dissipated as heat in the electromagnet, find the torque required.

11 **Answer**

0.489 m, 4300 N · m

If you could not solve this problem, go through frames 12-15.

12 Convert 1 rev · s⁻¹ to rad · s⁻¹.

12

$$\omega = 1 \text{ rev} \cdot \text{s}^{-1} (2\pi \text{ rad} \cdot \text{rev}^{-1})$$
$$= 2\pi \text{ rad} \cdot \text{s}^{-1}$$

13 Find R by using $\mathcal{E} = \frac{1}{2}\omega BR^2$.

13
$$R = \sqrt{\frac{2\mathcal{E}}{\omega B}}$$

$$= \sqrt{\frac{2(1.5\ \text{V})}{(2\pi\ \text{rad} \cdot \text{s}^{-1})(2\ \text{T})}} = 0.489\ \text{m}$$

---

14 Find the electrical power.

14
$$P = \mathcal{E}I$$
$$= (1.5\ \text{V})(18{,}000\ \text{A}) = 27{,}000\ \text{W}$$

---

15 Find the torque.

15
$$P = \Gamma\omega$$

$$\Gamma = \frac{27{,}000\ \text{V}}{2\pi\ \text{rad} \cdot \text{s}^{-1}}$$

$$= 4300\ \text{N} \cdot \text{m}$$

33

Inductance

CHAPTER SUMMARY

A coil carrying a varying current will not only induce an emf in a nearby coil, but within the coil itself the changing current also induces an emf. The mathematical relationships for mutual and self-inductance are presented as well as the equations for the energy stored in the magnetic field surrounding the inductor. Series circuits with various combinations of resistors, inductors and capacitors are also discussed.

BASIC TERMS — *Give definitions or meanings for the following:*

henry (33-1)
mutual inductance (33-1)
self-inductance (33-2)
inductor (33-2)
self-induced electromotive force (32-2)
energy density (33-3)
time constant (33-4)

electrical oscillation (33-5)
natural frequency (33-5)
L-C circuit (33-5)
damped harmonic motion (33-6)
critical damping (33-6)
overdamping (33-6)
underdamping (33-6)

PROGRAMMED QUIZ

1 Is the inductance of a toroid containing N turns proportional to N?

1 No, it is proportional to N^2.

$$L = \frac{N\Phi}{i} = \frac{\mu_0 N^2 A}{l}$$

2 What is the direction of the self-induced emf in a circuit if the current is decreasing? increasing?

2 Same direction; opposite direction.

3 The above can be found from what law?

3 Lenz's law.

4 What is an example of an inductor?

4 A coil of wire.

5 What can inductors be used for?

5 Storing energy, filtering frequencies.

---

6 Inductance depends on what properties of the device?

6 Geometry (i.e. size, shape, number of turns) and the magnetic properties of the material in which there exists a magnetic field.

---

7 If two coils induce an emf in each other, $M_1 = M_2$. This is analogous to what law?

7 Newton's third law.

---

8 What happens when an inductor is connected to the plates of a charged capacitor (neglect resistance)?

8 Charge flows through the inductor and back to the plates of the capacitor, charging it in the opposite sense. Current then flows through the inductor in the opposite direction until the capacitor is charged as originally and the process repeats indefinitely.

---

9 Does this process occur in an *R-L-C* circuit?

9 The oscillations will die out because energy will be dissipated in the resistor.

---

10 When is an emf induced in a stationary circuit?

10 Whenever the magnetic flux varies with time.

---

11 When a switch in an *R-L* circuit is closed, why doesn't the current rise to its final value immediately?

11 Because of the self-induced emf.

---

12 What is the relationship between the growth of current and the self-inductance in an *R-L* circuit?

12 The greater the self-inductance, the more slowly does the current start to increase.

---

13 In an *R-L* circuit, does the final current depend on the self-inductance?

13 No, it only depends on *R*.

---

14 As the current decays in an *R-L* circuit, where does the energy necessary to maintain the current come from?

14 The magnetic field of the inductor.

---

15 Electrical oscillation is analogous to what system in mechanics? Resistance is analogous to what quantity?

15 An oscillating system where energy is transferred from kinetic to potential and vice-versa; friction, since the effect of resistance is to dissipate the electromagnetic energy and convert it to heat.

MAIN IDEAS

Self-inductance. The variation of current in a conducting circuit will produce a change in the magnetic field around the circuit resulting in an induced counter emf in the circuit. When a current changes in a coil of N turns, an emf will be induced in the coil in accordance with Faraday's law:

$$\mathcal{E} = -L\frac{\Delta i}{\Delta t} = -N\frac{\Delta \Phi}{\Delta t},$$ where L = self-inductance. The unit of inductance is the Henry: $1\ H = 1\ V \cdot s \cdot A^{-1}$.

An inductor is represented by the symbol ⌒⌒⌒ . The direction of the self-induced emf is given by Lenz's law: the change in current is opposed by the induced field. If the current is decreasing, the self-induced emf has a direction which is the same as the direction of the current. If the current is increasing, the self-induced emf has a direction which is opposite to that of the current.

Mutual inductance. Consider two coils that are near each other. A changing current in coil 1 will induce an emf in coil 2 and vice versa.

$$\mathcal{E}_2 = -M\frac{\Delta i_1}{\Delta t} = -N_2\frac{\Delta \Phi_2}{\Delta t};$$
$$\mathcal{E}_1 = -M\frac{\Delta i_2}{\Delta t} = -N_1\frac{\Delta \Phi_1}{\Delta t},$$

where M = mutual inductance for the two coils, Φ_2 = flux through coil 2 due to current change in coil 1, Φ_1 = flux through coil 1 due to current change in coil 2. The mutual inductance may be

rewritten as $$M = \frac{N_2 \Phi_2}{i_1} = \frac{N_1 \Phi_1}{i_2}.$$

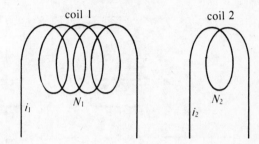

Energy associated with an inductor. Since an inductor opposes a change in current, work must be done to establish a current in it. The energy stored in the magnetic field is given by $U = \frac{1}{2}LI^2$. The energy stored in the

magnetic field of a toroid is $U = \frac{1}{2}\left(\frac{\mu_0 N^2 A}{l}\right) I^2$, where N = total number of turns in the windings, A = cross-

sectional area, l = mean circumferential length = $2\pi r$, I = current. The energy per unit volume (energy density)

of a toroid $= u = \frac{B^2}{2\mu_0}$.

The *R-L* circuit. The potential difference across R and L can be obtained as follows:

$V_a - iR - L\frac{\Delta i}{\Delta t} = V_b.$ Therefore $V_a - V_b = V_{ab} =$

$V = iR + L\frac{\Delta i}{\Delta t}$, where i is the current at any mo-

ment after the switch is closed. The rate of increase of the current is

$\frac{\Delta i}{\Delta t} = \frac{V}{L} - \frac{iR}{L}$. The initial rate of increase of the

current is $\frac{\Delta i}{\Delta t} = \frac{V}{L}$. The current at any instant is

given by $i = \frac{V}{R}(i - e^{-t/\tau})$, where τ = time constant

= L/R. The final steady state value of $i = I = V/R$. When $t = \tau$, the current has increased to $1/e$ of its original value. If there is a steady current I in the circuit and the switch is suddenly opened, the current will decay in accordance with $i = Ie^{-t/\tau}$ where $\tau = L/R$ = time constant. When $t = \tau$, the current will decrease to $1/e$ of its original value ($i = I/e$).

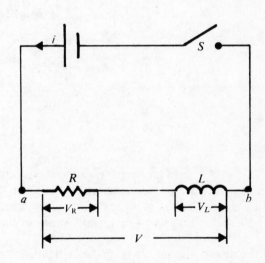

Energy relationships at the various stages of oscillation of an *L-C* circuit.

a) Initially capacitor with charge Q is connected to inductor,

b) capacitor is partially discharged, current produces magnetic field in inductor;

c) capacitor is discharged, all energy is in the magnetic field of the inductor;

d) charge builds up on capacitor plates (reverse polarities) and magnetic field of inductor decreases;

e) capacitor is fully charged, no magnetic field in inductor;

f) capacitor begins to discharge and cycle continues.

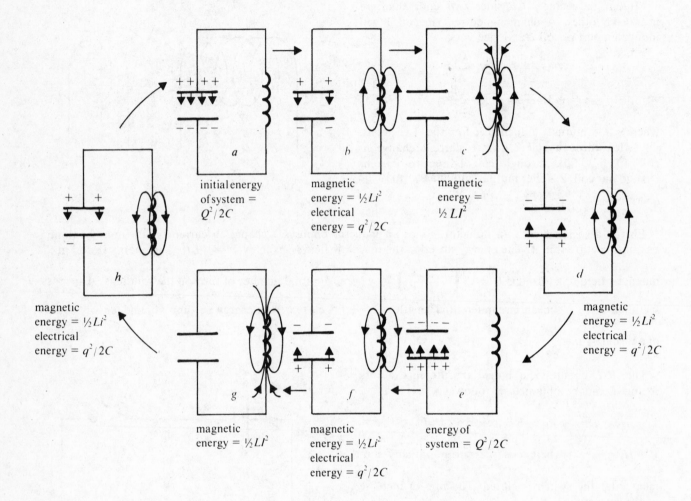

The oscillation of an electric circuit consists of the transfer of energy from the electric field of the capacitor to the magnetic field of the inductor and vice versa. The total energy associated with the circuit remains constant. This system is analogous to the back and forth transfer of energy in an oscillating mechanical system (from kinetic to potential energy and vice versa). At any instant $\frac{1}{2}Li^2 + q^2/2C = Q^2/2C$.

The angular frequency of an *L-C* circuit $\omega = \sqrt{\dfrac{1}{LC}}$. The instantaneous current $i = \sqrt{\dfrac{1}{LC}}\sqrt{Q^2 - q^2}$ and the instantaneous charge $q = Q \cos \omega t$. Remember, $\omega = 2\pi f$ where f is the natural frequency in Hz.

Problem solving strategy:

1 If a problem involves circuit analysis, Kirchhoff's rules can be applied for each instant of time. This is due to the fact that all voltages, currents and capacitor charges are functions of time.

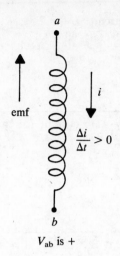

V_{ab} is +

2 Remember that self-induced emf can be treated as though it were a potential difference. If $\frac{\Delta i}{\Delta t} > 0$, then according to Lenz's law, the direction of the emf is opposite to that of the current. Therefore the direction of the emf is from b to a. This situation is similar to a battery with a as the positive terminal and b as the negative terminal.

However, V_{ab} is positive because a is at a higher potential than b. When $\frac{\Delta i}{\Delta t} < 0$, the direction of the emf is from a to b and V_{ab} is negative.

PROGRAMMED QUIZ

1 What is the self-induced emf in a coil, $L = 0.005$ H if the current decreases at a rate $\Delta i/\Delta t = -0.04$ A $\cdot$ s^{-1}?

1

$$\mathcal{E} = -L\frac{\Delta i}{\Delta t}$$
$$= -0.005 \text{ H}(-0.04 \text{ A} \cdot \text{s}^{-1})$$
$$= 2 \times 10^{-4} \text{ V}$$

---

2 Show that the following two expressions for mutual inductance,

$\frac{N\Phi}{i}$ and $\frac{\mathcal{E}}{\Delta i/\Delta t}$, have the same units.

2

$$\frac{N\Phi}{i} = \frac{\text{N} \cdot \text{m} \cdot \text{A}^{-1}}{\text{A}} = \frac{\text{N} \cdot \text{m}}{\text{A}^2}$$

$$\frac{\mathcal{E}}{\Delta i/\Delta t} = \frac{\text{V}}{\text{A} \cdot \text{s}^{-1}} = \frac{\text{N} \cdot \text{m} \cdot \text{C}^{-1}}{\text{A} \cdot \text{s}^{-1}} = \frac{\text{N} \cdot \text{m}}{\text{A}^2}$$

---

3 What is the self-inductance of a coil if the induced emf is 0.1 V and the current decreases at a rate of -0.01 A $\cdot$ s^{-1}?

3

$$\mathcal{E} = -L\frac{\Delta i}{\Delta t}$$
$$L = \frac{0.1 \text{ V}}{0.01 \text{ A} \cdot \text{s}^{-1}}$$
$$= 10 \text{ H}$$

---

4 How much energy must be supplied to increase the current in a 0.02 H inductor from zero to its final value of 0.05 A?

4

$$U = \frac{1}{2}LI^2$$
$$= \frac{1}{2}(0.02 \text{ H})(0.05 \text{ A})^2$$
$$= 2.5 \times 10^{-5} \text{ J}$$

---

5 What is the energy per unit volume stored in the magnetic field of an inductor, $B = 3.5 \times 10^{-4}$ T?

5

$$u = \frac{B^2}{2\mu_0}$$

$$= \frac{(3.5 \times 10^{-4} \text{ T})^2}{2(4\pi \times 10^{-7} \text{ T} \cdot \text{m} \cdot \text{A}^{-1})}$$

$$= 0.0487 \text{ J}$$

6 What is τ for a circuit, $L = 3.2$ H, $R = 1000$ Ω, connected to a cell of emf 100 V?

6
$$\tau = \frac{L}{R}$$
$$= \frac{3.2 \text{ H}}{1000 \text{ } \Omega} = 3.2 \times 10^{-3} \text{ s}$$

---

7 What is the steady state current for this circuit?

7
$$I = \frac{V}{R}$$
$$= \frac{100 \text{ V}}{1000 \text{ } \Omega} = 0.1 \text{ A}$$

---

8 What is the current 2×10^{-3} s after the circuit is closed?

8
$$i = I(1 - e^{-Rt/L})$$
$$= (0.1 \text{ A})(1 - e^{-2 \times 10^{-3} \text{ s}/3.2 \times 10^{-3} \text{ s}})$$
$$= 0.0464 \text{ A}$$

---

9 Find the angular frequency of a circuit, $L = 3$ μH, $C = 0.0075$ μF.

9
$$\omega = \sqrt{\frac{1}{LC}}$$
$$= \sqrt{\frac{1}{(3 \times 10^{-6} \text{ H})(0.0075 \times 10^{-6} \text{ F})}}$$
$$= 6.67 \times 10^{6} \text{ Hz}$$

---

10 What is the number of turns of wire if the self-inductance is 40μH, the flux through each turn is 2×10^{-8} Wb and the current is 0.1 A?

10
$$L = \frac{N\Phi}{i}$$
$$N = \frac{(40 \times 10^{-6} \text{ H}) (0.1 \text{ A})}{2 \times 10^{-8} \text{ Wb}} = 200$$

---

11 An inductor $L = 50$ mH is to be combined with a capacitor to make an L-C circuit with natural frequency $f = 3 \times 10^{6}$ Hz. What capacitance should be used?

11

angular frequency $\omega = \sqrt{\dfrac{1}{LC}}$

$$C = \frac{1}{L\omega^2}$$

But $\omega = 2\pi f$ where f is the natural frequency.
$$C = \frac{1}{L(2\pi f)^2}$$
$$= \frac{1}{(50 \times 10^{-3} \text{ H}) (4\pi^2) (3 \times 10^{6} \text{ s}^{-1})^2}$$
$$= 0.0563 \text{ pF}$$

STEP BY STEP SOLUTIONS OF PROBLEMS

Problem 1 Consider a toroid which has two coils with N_1 and N_2 turns respectively, radius r and cross-sectional area A. a) Derive an expression for the self-inductance L_1 when only the first coil is used and similarly for L_2 when only the second coil is used. b) Derive an expression for the mutual inductance M of the two coils. c) Show that $M^2 = L_1 L_2$.

1 Find the total flux through the central region when only the first coil is used;

$$B = \frac{\mu_0 N I}{2\pi r}.$$

1

$$\Phi = BA = \frac{\mu_0 N_1 i_1 A}{2\pi r}$$

---

2 Since the total flux links with each turn, find the self inductance by using

$$L = \frac{N_1 \Phi}{i}.$$

2

$$L_1 = \frac{N_1}{i_1} \left(\frac{\mu_0 N_1 i_1 A}{2\pi r} \right)$$
$$= \frac{\mu_0 N_1^2 A}{2\pi r}$$

---

3 Following the same procedure, find the expression for L_2 when only the second coil is used.

3

$$L_2 = \frac{\mu_0 N_2^2 A}{2\pi r}$$

---

4 Derive an expression for the mutual inductance M of the two coils. Use

$$M = \frac{N_2 \Phi_2}{i_1}.$$

4 The flux through the central region is equal to $\Phi = \Phi_2 = BA$. This flux links with the second coil.

$$M = \frac{N_2}{i_1} \left(\frac{\mu_0 N_1 i_1 A}{2\pi r} \right)$$
$$= \frac{\mu_0 N_1 N_2 A}{2\pi r}$$

---

5 Show that $M^2 = L_1 L_2$.

5

$$M^2 = \frac{\mu_0^2 N_1^2 N_2^2 A^2}{4\pi^2 r^2}$$

$$L_1 L_2 = \left(\frac{\mu_0 N_1^2 A}{2\pi r} \right) \left(\frac{\mu_0 N_2^2 A}{2\pi r} \right)$$

$$= \frac{\mu_0^2 N_1^2 N_2^2 A^2}{4\pi^2 r^2} \text{ which is equal to } M^2.$$

Problem 2 An inductor has an inductance of 4 H and a resistance of 8 Ω. It is connected to an emf source of 24 V (and negligible internal resistance). Find a) the initial rate of increase in the current, b) the rate of increase at the instant the current is 2 A, c) the time constant of the current, d) the current 0.5 s after the circuit is closed and e) the final steady-state current.

6 Find the initial rate of increase in the current. Use

$$\frac{\Delta i}{\Delta t} = \frac{V}{L} - \frac{Ri}{L}.$$

6 At the instant the circuit is closed, $i = 0$.

$$\therefore \left(\frac{\Delta i}{\Delta t} \right)_{initial} = \frac{V}{L}$$
$$= \frac{24\,\text{V}}{4\,\text{H}} = 6 \text{ A} \cdot \text{s}^{-1}$$

---

7 Find the rate of increase at the instant the current is 2 A. Use

$$\frac{\Delta i}{\Delta t} = \frac{V}{L} - \frac{Ri}{L}.$$

7

$$\left(\frac{\Delta i}{\Delta t} \right)_{i=2A} = \frac{24\,\text{V}}{4\,\text{H}} - \frac{8\,\Omega(2\,\text{A})}{4\,\text{H}} = 2 \text{ A} \cdot \text{s}^{-1}$$

---

8 Find the time constant of the circuit, $\tau = L/R$.

8
$$\tau = \frac{4\text{ H}}{8\,\Omega} = 0.5\text{ s}$$

$$\left(\text{Note } \frac{1}{\tau} = \frac{R}{L} = \frac{1}{0.5\text{ s}} = 2\text{ s}^{-1}\right)$$

---

9 Find the current 0.5 s after the circuit is closed.

Use $i = \dfrac{V}{R}(1 - e^{-Rt/L})$.

9
$$i = \frac{24\text{V}}{8\,\Omega}\,(1 - e^{(-2\text{s}^{-1})(0.5\text{ s})})$$

$$= 3\text{ A}(1 - e^{-1}) = 3\text{ A}(1 - 0.368)$$

$$= 1.90\text{ A}$$

---

10 Find the final steady-state current. Use

$$i = \frac{V}{R}(1 - e^{-t/\tau}).$$

Note that when $t \to \infty$, $i \to \dfrac{V}{R}$.

10
$$i = \frac{V}{R} = \frac{24\text{V}}{8\,\Omega} = 3\text{ A}$$

Problem 3 A circuit consists of an inductor of inductance 6 H and a resistor of resistance 12 Ω connected in series to an emf source of 24 V and of negligible internal resistance. a) What is the power input (i.e. the rate at which the source of emf delivers energy to the circuit) to the inductor at the instant when the current in it is 0.4 A? b) What is the rate of dissipation of energy at this instant (that is the rate at which electrical energy is converted to thermal energy in the resistor)? c) What is the rate at which energy is being stored in the magnetic field of the inductor? d) How much energy is stored in the magnetic field when the current has reached its final steady state value?

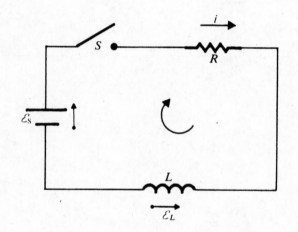

---

11 Apply Kirchhoff's loop rule to the circuit. Note that the loop rule is a statement of the principle of conservation of energy for single loop circuits.

11
$$\Sigma(\mathcal{E} + iR) = 0$$

$$\mathcal{E}_\text{S} - iR - \mathcal{E}_\text{L} = 0$$

---

12 Transpose $-iR$ and $-\mathcal{E}_\text{L}$ to the right side and multiply each term of the equation by i.

12
$$\mathcal{E}_\text{S} = iR + \mathcal{E}_\text{L}$$

$$\mathcal{E}_\text{S}i = i^2R + i\mathcal{E}_\text{L}$$

---

13 Replace $\mathcal{E}_\text{L}$ by

$$L\frac{\Delta i}{\Delta t}.$$

13
$$\mathcal{E}_\text{S}i = i^2R + Li\frac{\Delta i}{\Delta t}$$

---

14 Let $\mathcal{E}_s i = P_S$, $i^2 R = P_R$, and

$Li\dfrac{\Delta i}{\Delta t} = P_B$.   Rewrite the equation.

14 $P_S = P_R + P_B$ which states that the rate at which the source of emf delivers energy to the circuit is equal to the sum of the rates at which the electrical energy is converted to thermal energy and the rate at which energy is being stored in the magnetic field of the inductor.

---

15 Find $P_S = \mathcal{E}_s i$ at the instant the current is 0.4 A.

15 $P_S = 24 \text{ V} (0.4 \text{ A}) = 9.6 \text{ W}$

---

16 Find $P_R = i^2 R$ at the instant the current is 0.4 A.

16 $P_R = (0.4 \text{ A})^2 (12 \ \Omega) = 1.92 \text{ W}$

---

17 Find the rate of increase of current at the instant the current is 0.4 A; use

$\dfrac{\Delta i}{\Delta t} = \dfrac{V}{L} - \dfrac{Ri}{L}$.

17 $\left(\dfrac{\Delta i}{\Delta t}\right)_{i=0.4A} = \dfrac{24 \text{ V}}{6 \text{ H}} - \dfrac{12\Omega(0.4 \text{ A})}{6 \text{ H}}$

$= 3.2 \text{ A} \cdot \text{s}^{-1}$

---

18 Find

$P_B = Li\dfrac{\Delta i}{\Delta t}$ at the instant the current is

0.4 A.

18 $P_B = 6 \text{ H}(0.4 \text{ A})(3.2 \text{ A} \cdot \text{s}^{-1})$
$= 7.68 \text{ W}$

---

19 Verify that $P_S = P_R + P_B$.

19 $9.60 \text{ W} = 1.92 \text{ W} + 7.68 \text{ W}$

---

20 How much energy is stored in the magnetic field when the current has reached its final steady state value? Find

$I = \dfrac{\mathcal{E}_s}{R}$. Then use $U = \frac{1}{2}LI^2$.

20 $I = \dfrac{24 \text{ V}}{12 \ \Omega} = 2 \text{ A}$

$U = \frac{1}{2}(6 \text{ H}) (2 \text{ A})^2 = 12 \text{ W}$

1 ***Problem 1*** Find the equivalent inductance of two inductors connected in a) series b) parallel. The inductors are separated by a great distance.

Use $V = -L\dfrac{\Delta i}{\Delta t}$.

1

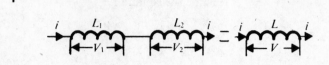

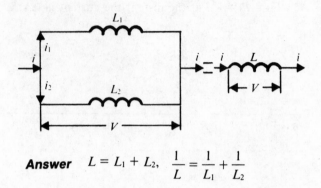

Answer $L = L_1 + L_2$, $\quad \dfrac{1}{L} = \dfrac{1}{L_1} + \dfrac{1}{L_2}$

If you solved this problem correctly, go to frame 9. If you could not solve this problem, go through frames 2–8.

2 What is the relationship among V_1, V_2 and V for the two inductors connected in series?

2 $\qquad V = V_1 + V_2$

---

3 In accordance with Faraday's law, the induced emf =

$V = -L\dfrac{\Delta i}{\Delta t}$. Replace each potential

difference by its equivalent expression.

3 $-L\dfrac{\Delta i}{\Delta t} = -L_1\dfrac{\Delta i}{\Delta t} - L_2\dfrac{\Delta i}{\Delta t}$

---

4 Divide each term by $-\dfrac{\Delta i}{\Delta t}$.

4 $\qquad L = L_1 + L_2$ (where L is the equivalent inductance)
Note: in order to avoid mutual induction, L_1 and L_2 should be separated by a great distance.

---

5 Find the equivalent inductance of two inductors connected in parallel. Using Kirchhoff's junction rule, write the relationship among i_1, i_2, i.

5 $\qquad i = i_1 + i_2$

---

6 Take a Δ increment of both sides of the equation and then divide each term by Δt.

6 $\Delta i = \Delta(i_1 + i_2) = \Delta i_1 + \Delta i_2$
$\dfrac{\Delta i}{\Delta t} = \dfrac{\Delta i_1}{\Delta t} + \dfrac{\Delta i_2}{\Delta t}$

---

7 Replace each term by its equivalent from

$V = -L\dfrac{\Delta i}{\Delta t}$.

7 $-\dfrac{V}{L} = -\dfrac{V}{L_1} - \dfrac{V}{L_2}$

---

8 Divide each term by $-V$.

8

$$\frac{1}{L} = \frac{1}{L_1} + \frac{1}{L_2}$$

(where L is the equivalent inductance)
Note: in order to avoid mutual induction L_1 and L_2 must be separated by a great distance.

---

9 *Problem 2* A toroidal solenoid has a mean radius of 0.18 m and a cross-sectional area of 25×10^{-4} m^2. When the solenoid carries a current of 22 A the energy stored in the magnetic field is 0.15 J. a) How many turns does the winding have? b) Find the inductance of the solenoid. c) Find the energy per unit volume. d) Find the magnitude of the magnetic field B.

9 *Answer*
472, 6.20×10^{-4} H, 53.1 J $\cdot$ m^{-3}, 0.0115 T.

If you solved this problem correctly go to frame 16. If you could not solve this problem, go through frames 10–15.

---

10 Find the mean circumference l.

10

$$l = 2\pi r$$
$$= 2\pi(0.18 \text{ m})$$

---

11 Find the number of turns in the solenoid.

11

$$U = \tfrac{1}{2}\left(\frac{\mu_0 N^2 A}{l}\right) I^2$$

$$N = \sqrt{\frac{2(0.15 \text{ J}) \, 2\pi \,(0.18\text{m})}{(4\pi \times 10^{-7}\text{Wb}\cdot \text{A}^{-1\cdot\text{m}^{-1}}) \, (25 \times 10^{-4} \text{ m}^2) \, (22 \text{ A})^2}}$$

$$= 472 \text{ turns}$$

---

12 Find the inductance of the coil.

12

$$U = \tfrac{1}{2}LI^2$$
$$L = \frac{2(0.15 \text{ J})}{(22 \text{ A})^2}$$
$$= 6.20 \times 10^{-4} \text{ H}$$

---

13 Find the energy per unit volume.

13

$$u = \frac{U}{lA}$$

$$= \frac{0.15 \text{ J}}{2\pi(0.18 \text{ m}) \, (25 \times 10^{-4} \text{ m}^2)}$$

$$= 53.1 \text{ J} \cdot \text{m}^{-3}$$

14 Find the magnitude of the magnetic field.

14

$$u = \frac{B^2}{2\mu_0}$$

$$B = \sqrt{2(4\pi \times 10^{-7} \text{ Wb} \cdot \text{A}^{-1} \cdot \text{m}^{-1})(53.1 \text{ J} \cdot \text{m}^{-3})}$$
$$= 0.0115 \text{ T}$$

---

15 Check on the value of B by using

$$B = \frac{\mu_0 NI}{2\pi r}$$

15

$$B = \frac{(4\pi \times 10^{-7} \text{Wb} \cdot \text{A}^{-1} \cdot \text{m}^{-1})(472 \text{ turns})(22 \text{ A})}{2\pi (0.18 \text{ m})}$$
$$= 0.0115 \text{ T}$$

---

16 *Problem 3* A 9.00×10^{-4} F capacitor is charged by connecting it to a 60 V battery. The capacitor is disconnected from the battery and at $t = 0$ connected across an inductor with $L = 4.00$ H. a) What are the angular frequency ω, the natural frequency f and the period τ of the electrical oscillation? b) What is the initial charge on the capacitor? c) What is the maximum current? d) What is the charge q on the capacitor 0.05 s after the connection to the inductor is made? e) What is the current i in the inductor 0.05 s after the connection to the inductor is made? f) How much electrical energy is stored in the capacitor and how much magnetic energy is stored in the inductor 0.05 s after the connection is made? g) How much energy was initially stored in the capacitor? h) Show that the law of conservation of energy is obeyed.

16 *Answer*
16.7 s^{-1}, 2.65 Hz, 0.377 s, 0.054 C, 0.900 A, 0.0362 C, 0.667 A, 0.728 J, 0.890 J, 1.62 J,

---

If you could not solve this problem correctly, go through frames 17–24.

---

17 What are the angular frequency ω, the natural frequency f and the period τ of the electrical oscillation?

17

$$\omega = \sqrt{\frac{1}{LC}}$$

$$= \sqrt{\frac{1}{(4.00 \text{ H})(9.00 \times 10^{-4} \text{ F})}}$$
$$= 16.7 \text{ s}^{-1}$$

$$\omega = 2\pi f$$
$$f = \frac{16.7 \text{ s}^{-1}}{2\pi} = 2.65 \text{ s}^{-1} = 2.65 \text{ Hz}$$

$$\tau = \frac{1}{f} = \frac{1}{2.65 \text{ s}^{-1}} = 0.377 \text{ s}$$

---

18 What is the initial charge Q on the capacitor?

18

$$Q = CV$$
$$= (9.00 \times 10^{-4} \text{ F})(60 \text{ V})$$
$$= 0.054 \text{ C}$$

---

19 What is the maximum current I?

19

$$I = \omega Q = \frac{Q}{\sqrt{LC}}$$

$$= \frac{0.054\ C}{\sqrt{(4.00\ H)\ (9.00 \times 10^{-4}\ F)}}$$

$$= 0.900\ A$$

---

20 What is the charge q on the capacitor 0.05 s after the connection to the inductor is made?

20

$$\begin{aligned} q &= Q \cos \omega t \\ &= 0.054\ C \cos(16.7\ s^{-1})\ (0.05\ s) \\ &= 0.054\ C \cos(0.835\ rad) \\ &= 0.054\ C(0.671) \\ &= 0.0362\ C \end{aligned}$$

---

21 What is the current i in the inductor 0.05 s after the connection to the inductor is made?

21

$$\begin{aligned} i &= I \sin \omega t \\ &= 0.900\ A \sin(16.7\ s^{-1})\ (0.05\ s) \\ &= 0.900\ A \sin(0.835\ rad) \\ &= 0.900\ A\ (0.741) \\ &= 0.667\ A \end{aligned}$$

---

22 How much electrical energy is stored in the capacitor and how much magnetic energy is stored in the inductor 0.05 s after the connection is made?

22

$$\begin{aligned} U_{cap} &= \frac{q^2}{2C} \\ &= \frac{(0.0362\ C)^2}{2(9.00 \times 10^{-4}\ F)} \\ &= 0.728\ J \\ U_{ind} &= \tfrac{1}{2}Li^2 \\ &= \tfrac{1}{2}(4.00\ H)\ (0.667\ A)^2 \\ &= 0.890\ J \end{aligned}$$

---

23 How much energy was initially stored in the capacitor?

23

$$\begin{aligned} U_{initial} &= \frac{Q^2}{2\ C} \\ &= \frac{(0.054\ C)^2}{2(9.00 \times 10^{-4}\ F)} \\ &= 1.62\ J \end{aligned}$$

---

24 Show that the law of conservation of energy is obeyed by comparing the initial energy with the amounts stored in the capacitor and inductor 0.05 s after the connection is made.

24

$$U_{cap} + U_{ind} = U_{initial}$$
$$0.728\ J + 0.890\ J = 1.62\ J$$

The law of conservation of energy is verified.

34

Alternating Currents

CHAPTER SUMMARY

The subject of this chapter is alternating current circuits. Phasor diagrams and the mathematical relationships for circuits containing resistance, inductance or capacitance as well as R-L-C series and parallel circuits are discussed. The conditions for resonance and applications of ac circuits such as ac instruments, the transformer, power and average and root-mean-square values of currents and voltages are also considered.

BASIC TERMS — *Give definitions or meanings for the following:*

alternating current (34-I)
alternator (34-1)
phasor (34-1)
ac source (34-1)
voltage amplitude (34-1)
phasor diagram (34-1)
average value (34-1)
root-mean-square value (34-1)
current amplitude (34-2)
phase angle (34-2)

capacitive reactance (34-2)
inductive reactance (34-2)
impedance (34-3)
reactance (34-3)
resonance frequency (34-4)
resonance (34-4)
power factor (34-6)
transformer (34-7)
primary (34-7)
secondary (34-7)

PROGRAMMED QUIZ

1 When are current and voltage in phase in an ac circuit?

1 When the reactance is 0; $X = X_L - X_C = 0$.

2 What is the power factor of this circuit?

2 One; since $\phi = 0$, the power factor $= \cos \phi = 1$.

3 Resistance, capacitive reactance and inductive reactance determine which properties of an ac circuit?

3 Resistance determines how much energy will be dissipated as heat; the capacitive reactance determines how much the capacitor will oppose the flow of current without dissipating energy; the inductive reactance determines the same for an inductor.

4 What quantity in ac circuits is analogous to the resistance in dc circuits?

4 The impedance is analogous to the resistance only with respect to current.

---

5 At a frequency higher than the resonant frequency, does the voltage lead or lag the current in an R-L-C series circuit?

5 Voltage leads current, $X_L > X_C$.

---

6 How many times per second is the current equal to the root-mean-square current?

6 Twice each cycle or $2f$ times per second.

---

7 What is the relationship between the phase angle and the voltage and the current?

7 If voltage leads current by ϕ, $\phi > 0$; if voltage lags current by ϕ, $\phi < 0$.

---

8 Describe the phase relationship when a resistance is connected across an ac source. A capacitor. An inductor.

8 Resistance: Current and voltage are in phase. Capacitor: Voltage lags current by 90°. Inductor: Voltage leads current by 90°.

---

9 Do the maximum voltages across each element add up to the emf?

9 No, the voltages across each element of the circuit attain their maximum values at different times.

---

10 Describe what happens in a R-L-C series circuit as the frequency increases.

10 At very low frequencies, X_C is the dominant quantity, Z is large, voltage lags current by almost 90°. As the frequency increases, X_C gets smaller, X_L gets larger until the resonant frequency where $X_L = X_C$. As the frequency increases beyond this frequency, X_L dominates and voltage leads current by almost 90°.

---

11 Describe the current in an R-L-C series circuit.

11 It is the same throughout the circuit at a particular instant, but it varies with time.

---

12 What is the average value of a sinusoidally varying current over a period of time?

12 Zero.

---

13 In an R-L-C parallel circuit, is current maximum at resonant frequency?

13 No, current is minimum; $\omega C = 1/\omega L$, $I = V/R$.

---

14 Why are transformers used?

14 Because power can be more efficiently transmitted at high voltages and small currents ($I^2 R$ heating is reduced).

---

15 What are some sources of alternating emf or voltage that you have studied previously?

15 Coil of wire rotating in a magnetic field, an L-C circuit.

---

16 In ac circuits, why are there two symbols for potential difference, v and V, and two for the current, i and I?

16 I and V are the symbols for maximum current and maximum potential difference; i and v are the instantaneous values.

MAIN IDEAS

An alternator is a coil of wire rotating with constant angular velocity in a magnetic field. This device will develop a sinusoidal alternating emf given by $v = V \cos \omega t$, where V is the voltage amplitude or maximum potential difference, t the time and ω the angular frequency equal to 2π times the frequency f.

The phasor (rotating vector) is used to visualize the phase relationship between voltage and current. If a resistor is connected across the alternator, the instantaneous current through the resistor is given by

$$i = \frac{v_{ab}}{R} = \frac{V}{R} \cos \omega t = I \cos \omega t,$$

where R is the resistance and I denotes the current amplitude. Note: the voltage and current phasors are in phase in the phasor diagram drawn at an arbitrary instant of time t. The current amplitude I or maximum current is given by $I = V/R$.

The average current $I_{av} = \frac{2}{\pi} I = 0.637 \, I$.

The root-mean-square current $I_{rms} = \dfrac{I}{\sqrt{2}}$.

The root-mean-square voltage $V_{rms} = \dfrac{V}{\sqrt{2}}$.

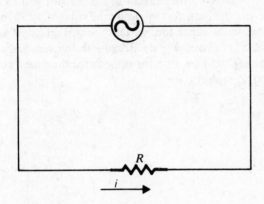
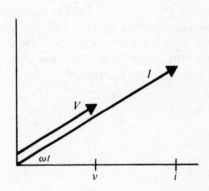

When a capacitor of capacitance C is connected across the alternator, the resulting current i is given by $i = -\omega CV \sin \omega t$. The capacitive reactance X_C is defined as $X_C = 1/\omega C$ and has the dimensions of ohms (Ω). Since $i = \omega CV \cos (\omega t + 90°)$, the current leads the voltage by 90°. The maximum current $I = V/X_C$.

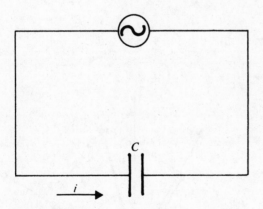
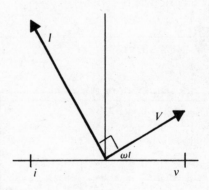

If an inductor is connected across the source, the resulting current is given by $i = \dfrac{V}{\omega L} \sin \omega t$. The inductive reactance $X_L = \omega L$ also has dimensions of ohms. Since $i = \dfrac{V}{\omega L} \cos(\omega t - 90°)$, the current lags the voltage by 90°. The maximum current $I = V/X_L$.

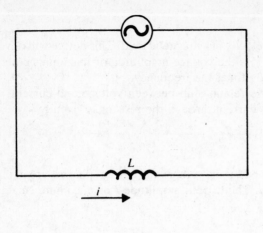

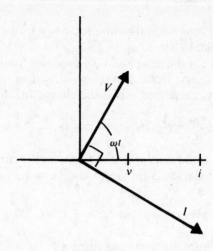

In an R-L-C series circuit, the current is the same in each element (R, L and C), but it varies with time. The instantaneous potential difference across the resistor, v_R, is in phase with the current in the resistor and its maximum value is given by $V_R = IR$. The instantaneous voltage across the inductor, v_L, leads the current by 90° and its maximum value is given by $V_L = IX_L$. The instantaneous voltage in the capacitor, v_c, lags the current by 90° and its maximum value is given by $V_C = IX_C$. The instantaneous current $i = I \cos(\omega t - \phi)$. Because the current is the same throughout the circuit at all times, the phasor diagram can be replaced by a vector impedance diagram, where R replaces V_R, X_L and X_C replace V_L and V_C respectively and Z replaces V.

The instantaneous potential difference between the terminals a and b equals the algebraic sum of the potential differences v_R, v_C and v_L at that instant. Note that v_R is the projection of V_R on the horizontal axis, v_L the projection of V_L and v_C the projection of V_C; v is the projection of V. The phasor diagram is a geometric representation of $V = \sqrt{V_R{}^2 + (V_L - V_C)^2}$.

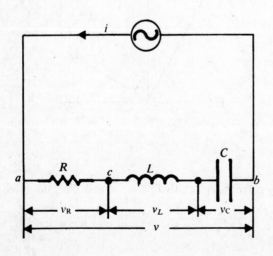

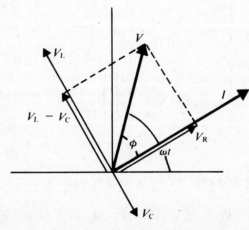

phasor diagram $X_L > X_C$

Remember that the instantaneous potential differences in an ac series circuit add algebraically while the voltage amplitudes add vectorially.

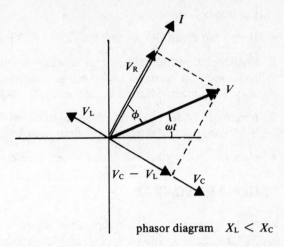

phasor diagram $X_L < X_C$

The quantity $X_L - X_C = X$ is defined as the reactance of the circuit. The impedance of the circuit $Z = \sqrt{R^2 + (X_L - X_C)^2} = \sqrt{R^2 + X^2}$. Hence $V = IZ$. The phase angle ϕ of the source voltage with respect to the current is given by $\tan \phi = \dfrac{X_L - X_C}{R} = \dfrac{X}{R}$. When ϕ is a positive angle, the current lags the voltage and when ϕ is a negative angle, the current leads the voltage. It should be stressed that the instantaneous potential differences in an ac series circuit add algebraically (as in the case of a dc circuit) whereas the voltage amplitudes add vectorially.

The mean square current or average value of $i^2 = (I^2)_{av} = I^2/2$; $I_{rms} = \sqrt{(I^2)_{av}} = I/\sqrt{2}$; $V_{rms} = V/\sqrt{2}$, where I and V are the peak values of the sinusoidally varying current and voltage respectively.

The average power dissipated in a resistor in an ac circuit is $P = \frac{1}{2}IV \cos \phi = V_{rms}I_{rms} \cos \phi$, where ϕ is the phase angle between current and voltage. It should be noted that in a steady state operation, the average energy stored in the electric field of the capacitor and the magnetic field of the inductor remains constant. Hence the net flow of energy is from the generator to the resistor. The factor $\cos \phi$ is called the power factor of the circuit.

The current in an R-L-C series circuit is a maximum when $X_L = X_C$, i.e. the impedance is a minimum. The frequency f_0 for the maximum current is called the resonant frequency, $f_0 = \dfrac{1}{2\pi} \sqrt{\dfrac{1}{LC}}$. The resonant angular frequency $= \omega_0 = 2\pi f_0 = 1/\sqrt{LC}$.

If R, L, and C are connected in parallel across an ac source,

$$I = \sqrt{I_R^2 + (I_C - I_L)^2}$$
$$= V\sqrt{1/R^2 + (\omega C - 1/\omega L)^2}$$

The maximum current I is frequency dependent. It is a minimum at resonant frequency $\omega_0 = 1/\sqrt{LC}$.

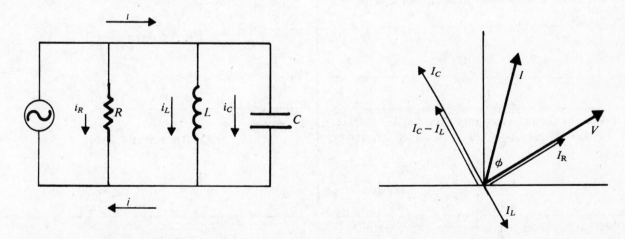

The alternating current transformer transforms electric energy at an alternating voltage and current to another voltage and current. If V_1 and N_1 are the terminal voltage and number of turns in the primary coil and V_2 and N_2 the voltage and number of turns in the secondary, then $V_2/V_1 = N_2/N_1 = I_1/I_2$.

Problem solving strategy:

1 If you are given the natural frequency f, remember to convert it to angular frequency $\omega = 2\pi f$.

2 Phase relationships: When a resistance is connected across an ac source, the current and voltage are in phase. When a capacitor is connected across an ac source, the voltage lags the current by 90° and $\phi = -90°$. When an inductor is connected across an ac source, the voltage leads the current by 90° and $\phi = +90°$.

3 Kirchhoff's rules can be used for ac circuits as for dc, but they should be applied at a particular instant of time since all voltages and currents are sinusoidal functions of time.

4 Reactance $X = (X_L - X_C)$ and impedance $Z = \sqrt{R^2 + X^2}$ and analogous to resistance. The units are ohms.

PROGRAMMED QUIZ

1 A capacitor $C = 2\mu F$ is connected across an ac source of angular frequency = 500 rad · s⁻¹. What is the capacitive reactance?

1
$$X_C = \frac{1}{\omega C}$$
$$= \frac{1}{(500 \text{ rad} \cdot \text{s}^{-1})(2 \times 10^{-6} \text{ F})}$$
$$= 1 \times 10^3 \ \Omega$$

2 If the maximum voltage of this source is 50 V, what is the maximum current?

2
$$I = \frac{V}{X_C}$$
$$= \frac{50 \text{ V}}{1 \times 10^3 \ \Omega}$$
$$= 0.050 \text{ A}$$

3 A 0.5 H inductor is connected to an ac source. What is the inductive reactance if the angular frequency is 800 rad · s⁻¹?

3
$$X_L = \omega L$$
$$= (800 \text{ rad} \cdot \text{s}^{-1})(0.5 \text{ H})$$
$$= 400 \ \Omega$$

4 If the maximum current through the above inductor is 0.04 A, what is the maximum voltage?

4
$$I = \frac{V}{X_L}$$
$$V = (0.04 \text{ A})(400 \ \Omega)$$
$$= 16 \text{ V}$$

5 What is the reactance of a circuit if $X_L = 800 \ \Omega$, $X_C = 600 \ \Omega$ and $R = 120 \ \Omega$ in an R-L-C series circuit?

5
$$X = X_L - X_C$$
$$= 800 \ \Omega - 600 \ \Omega = 200 \ \Omega$$

6 What is the impedance of the above circuit?

6
$$Z = \sqrt{R^2 + X^2}$$
$$= \sqrt{(120 \ \Omega)^2 + (200 \ \Omega)^2}$$
$$= 233 \ \Omega$$

7 Draw an impedance diagram for this circuit.

7

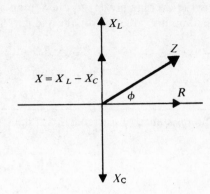

Draw an arrow of magnitude R in the $+x$ direction, an arrow of magnitude X_L in the $+y$ direction and an arrow of magnitude X_C in the $-y$ direction. The "vector" sum of these arrows has magnitude Z. The angle between Z and the x-axis (measured counterclockwise from the $+x$ axis) is ϕ.

---

8 All the above arrows represent quantities which have what units?

8 Ohms.

---

9 Calculate the phase angle for the circuit of frame 5.

9

$$\tan \phi = \frac{X}{R}$$

$$= \frac{200\ \Omega}{120\ \Omega}$$

$$\phi = 59°$$

---

10 Does current lead voltage?

10 No, voltage leads current; $X_L > X_C$.

---

11 If the maximum current through an R-L-C series circuit is 0.5 A, what is the average current?

11

$$I_{av} = \frac{2}{\pi}(I)$$

$$= \frac{2}{\pi}(0.5\ \text{A})$$

$$= 0.318\ \text{A}$$

---

12 What is the root-mean-square current?

12

$$I_{rms} = \frac{I}{\sqrt{2}}$$

$$= \frac{0.318\ \text{A}}{\sqrt{2}}$$

$$= 0.225\ \text{A}$$

---

13 What is the average power supplied to an ac circuit if the maximum values of voltage and current are 100 V and 2 A?

13
$$P = \tfrac{1}{2}VI$$
$$= \tfrac{1}{2}(100\text{ V})(2\text{ A})$$
$$= 100\text{ W}$$

---

14 Find the resistance of a circuit, $I_{rms} = 0.85$ A and $P = 230$ W.

14
$$P = I_{rms}^2\, R$$
$$R = \frac{230\text{ W}}{(0.85\text{ A})^2}$$
$$= 318\ \Omega$$

---

15 Find the power factor for the above if $V_{rms} = 360$ V.

15
$$P = V_{rms} I_{rms} \cos\phi$$
$$\cos\phi = \frac{230\text{ W}}{(0.85\text{ A})(360\text{ V})}$$
$$= 0.752$$

---

16 What is the resonant frequency of a circuit which has a 0.9 H inductance in series with a $2\,\mu$F capacitance?

16
$$\omega_0 = \frac{1}{\sqrt{LC}}$$
$$= \frac{1}{\sqrt{(0.9\text{ H})\,(2 \times 10^{-6}\text{ F})}}$$
$$= 745\text{ rad}\cdot\text{s}^{-1}$$

---

17 If there are twice as many turns in the primary coil as in the secondary, what is the voltage in the primary if the secondary has a voltage of 120 V?

17
$$\frac{V_2}{V_1} = \frac{N_2}{N_1}$$
$$\frac{120\text{ V}}{V_1} = \frac{1}{2}$$
$$V_1 = 240\text{ V}$$

STEP BY STEP SOLUTIONS OF PROBLEMS

Problem 1 A 300 Ω resistor, a 0.8 H inductor and a 1.6×10^{-6} F capacitor are connected in series across a source of constant voltage amplitude of 60 V and an angular frequency of 1000 rad$\cdot$s^{-1}. Find a) the impedance of the circuit, b) the current amplitude, c) the voltage amplitude across each element and d) the phase angle for the following three cases: I) the capacitor is omitted, II) the inductor is omitted, III) the resistor is omitted.

1 Find the inductive and capacitive reactances:
$$X_L = \omega L \quad\text{and}$$
$$X_C = \frac{1}{\omega C}.$$

1
$$X_L = 1000\text{ rad}\cdot\text{s}^{-1}(0.8\text{ H})$$
$$= 800\ \Omega$$
$$X_C = \frac{1}{1000\text{ rad}\cdot\text{s}^{-1}(1.6 \times 10^{-6}\text{ F})}$$
$$= 625\ \Omega$$

---

2 Consider case I (R and L in series). Find the impedance; $Z = \sqrt{R^2 + X_L^2}$.

2 $Z = \sqrt{(300\ \Omega)^2 + (800\ \Omega)^2} = 854\ \Omega$

---

3 Find the current amplitude using $V = IZ$.

3
$$I = \frac{V}{Z} = \frac{60\ \text{V}}{854\ \Omega} = 0.0703\ \text{A}$$

---

4 Find the voltage amplitudes across the resistor and the inductor.

4
$$V_R = IR = (0.0703\ \text{A})(300\ \Omega)$$
$$= 21.1\ \text{V}$$
$$V_L = IX_L = (0.0703\ \text{A})(800\ \Omega)$$
$$= 56.2\ \text{V}$$

5
Find the phase angle; use $\tan \phi = \dfrac{X_L}{R}$.

5
$$\tan \phi = \frac{800\ \Omega}{300\ \Omega} = 2.67$$
$$\phi = 69.5°$$
Note: since ϕ is positive, the current lags the voltage.

---

6 Consider case II (R and C in series). Find the impedance; use $Z = \sqrt{R^2 + X_C^2}$.

6
$$Z = \sqrt{(300\ \Omega)^2 + (625\ \Omega)^2} = 693\ \Omega$$

---

7 Find the current amplitude using $V = IZ$.

7
$$I = \frac{V}{Z} = \frac{60\ \text{V}}{693\ \Omega} = 0.0866\ \text{A}$$

---

8 Find the voltage amplitude across the resistor and the capacitor.

8
$$V_R = IR = (0.0866\ \text{A})(300\ \Omega) = 26.0\ \text{V}$$
$$V_C = IX_C = (0.0866\ \text{A})(625\ \Omega) = 54.1\ \text{V}$$

9
Find the phase angle. Use $\tan \phi = \dfrac{-X_C}{R}$.

9
$$\tan \phi = \frac{-625\ \Omega}{300\ \Omega} = -2.08$$
$$\phi = -64.3°$$
Since ϕ is negative, the current leads the voltage.

---

10 Consider case III (L and C in series). Find the impedance; use $Z = X_L - X_C$.

10 $Z = 800\ \Omega - 625\ \Omega = 175\ \Omega$

---

11 Find the current amplitude using $V = IZ$.

11
$$I = \frac{60\ \text{V}}{175\ \Omega} = 0.343\ \text{A}$$

---

12 Find the voltage amplitudes across the inductor and the capacitor.

12
$$V_L = IX_L = (0.343\ \text{A})(800\ \Omega)$$
$$= 274\ \text{V}$$
$$V_C = IX_C = (0.343\ \text{A})(625\ \Omega)$$
$$= 214\ \text{V}$$

13
Find the phase angle. Use $\tan \phi = \dfrac{X_L - X_C}{R}$.

13 Since $R = 0$ (we have an inductor and a capacitor in series), $\tan \phi \to +\infty$. Therefore, $\phi = 90°$; since ϕ is positive, the current lags the voltage.

Problem 2 An *R-L-C* series circuit has an impedance of 40 Ω and a power factor of 0.8 at 60 Hz; the voltage is lagging the current. What should be the value of an inductor such that when it is placed in series with the circuit, the power factor will be raised to unity?

14 At what phase angle will the power factor = 1?

14 Power factor $= \cos \phi = 1$
$$\phi = 0°$$

---

15 Draw an impedance diagram to indicate the inductance which must be placed in series with the circuit so that $\phi = 0$. Evidently the inductance must have an inductive reactance of X. Since the voltage lags the current, ϕ is negative and $X_L < X_C$.

15

---

16 Write the expressions relating $(X_L - X_C)$, Z and ϕ.

16
$$Z = \sqrt{R^2 + (X_L - X_C)^2}$$
$$\tan \phi = \frac{X_L - X_C}{R}$$

---

17 Square both sides of the two equations and eliminate R^2.

17
$$Z^2 = R^2 + (X_L - X_C)^2$$
$$R^2 = \frac{(X_L - X_C)^2}{\tan^2 \phi}$$
$$Z^2 = (X_L - X_C)^2 \left(\frac{1}{\tan^2 \phi} + 1 \right)$$
$$= (X_L - X_C)^2 \csc^2 \phi$$
$$X_L - X_C = Z \sin \theta$$

---

18 But $X_L - X_C = X$. Substitute the given values and solve for X.

18 If $\cos \phi = 0.8$
$$\sin \phi = 0.6$$
$$X = Z \sin \phi = 40\ \Omega (0.6)$$
$$= 24\ \Omega$$

---

19 In order to achieve a power factor of unity, we must add an inductive reactance of 24 Ω to the circuit. Find the inductance which must be added by using $X = X_L = \omega L$.

19
$$L = \frac{X_L}{\omega} = \frac{24\ \Omega}{2\pi(60\ \text{rad} \cdot \text{s}^{-1})}$$
$$= 0.0637\ \text{H}$$

Problem 3 In the alternating current parallel circuit shown in the figure $R_1 = 70\ \Omega$, $L = 0.17\ \text{H}$, $R_2 = 80\ \Omega$ and $C = 50\ \mu\text{F}$. The alternator supplies a constant voltage amplitude of 220 V at 60 Hz. Find a) the magnitude and phase angle of the current in each branch of the circuit, b) the magnitude and phase angle of the current in the main line and c) the total impedance.

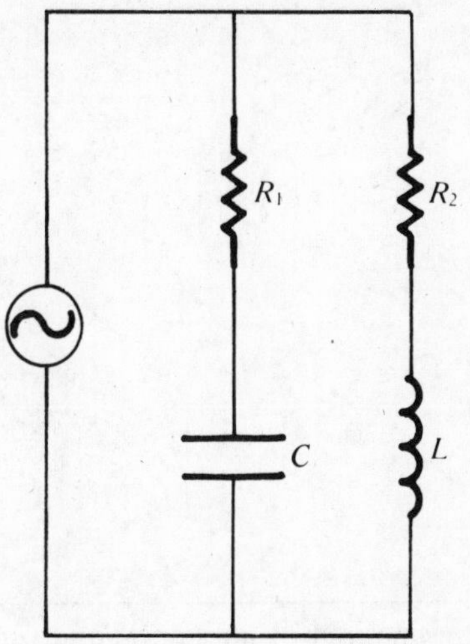

20
$$X_C = \frac{1}{2\pi f C} = \frac{1}{2\pi(60\ \text{s}^{-1})(50 \times 10^{-6}\ \text{F})}$$
$$= 53.1\ \Omega$$
$$X_L = 2\pi f L = 2\pi(60\ \text{s}^{-1})(0.17\ \text{H}) = 64.1\ \Omega$$

20 Find the capacitive and inductive reactances by using $X_C = 1/\omega C$ and $X_L = \omega L$. Remember $\omega = 2\pi f$.

---

21 Find the current in the R_2-L (the inductive) branch by using $I_L = \dfrac{\mathcal{E}}{\sqrt{R_2^2 + X_L^2}}$ and its phase angle by using $\tan \phi_L = X_L / R_2$.

21
$$I_L = \frac{220\ \text{V}}{\sqrt{(80\ \Omega)^2 + (64.1\ \Omega)^2}}$$
$$= 2.14\ \text{A}$$
$$\tan \phi_L = \frac{64.1\ \Omega}{80\ \Omega} = 0.801$$
$$\phi_L \doteq 38.7°$$
Thus I_L lags behind the voltage by 38.7°.

---

22 Find the current in the R_1-C (the capacitive) branch by using $I_C = \dfrac{\mathcal{E}}{\sqrt{R_1^2 + X_C^2}}$ and its phase angle by using $\tan \phi_C = X_C / R_1$.

22
$$I_C = \frac{220\ \text{V}}{\sqrt{(70\ \Omega)^2 + (53.1\ \Omega)^2}} = \frac{220\ \text{V}}{87.9\ \Omega}$$
$$= 2.50\ \text{A}$$
$$\tan \phi_C = \frac{53.1\ \Omega}{70\ \Omega} = 0.759$$
$$\phi_C \doteq 37.2°$$
Thus I_C leads the voltage by 37.2°.

23 Draw a phasor diagram denoting $\mathcal{E}$ (on the x-axis), I_L, ϕ_L, I_C and ϕ_C. Indicate by I the resultant phasor.

23

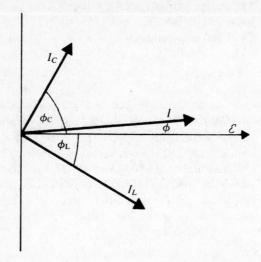

By the parallelogram method I is the resultant of I_L and I_C.

---

24 Using the method of horizontal and vertical components, write the expression for I.
$$I = \sqrt{(\Sigma I_x)^2 + (\Sigma I_y)^2}$$

24 $I = \sqrt{(I_C \cos\phi_C + I_L \cos\phi_L)^2 + (I_C \sin\phi_C - I_L \sin\phi_L)^2}$
$\cos\phi_C = \cos 37.2^\circ = 0.797$
$\cos\phi_L = \cos 38.7^\circ = 0.780$
$\sin\phi_C = \sin 37.2^\circ = 0.605$
$\sin\phi_L = \sin 38.7^\circ = 0.625$

---

25 Substitute the values and find I, the current in the main line.

25
$$I = \left(\begin{array}{l} [(2.50\text{ A})(0.797) + (2.14\text{ A})(0.780)]^2 \\ + [(2.50\text{ A})(0.605\text{ A}) - (2.14\text{ A})(0.625)]^2 \end{array} \right)^{1/2}$$

$$= \sqrt{(3.66\text{ A})^2 + (0.17\text{ A})^2} = 3.67\text{ A}$$

---

26 Find the phase angle of the current in the main line by using

$$\tan\phi = \frac{I_C \sin\phi_C - I_L \sin\phi_L}{I_C \cos\phi_C + I_L \cos\phi_L},$$
i.e. $\tan\phi = \dfrac{I_y}{I_x}$.

26
$$\tan\phi = \frac{0.170\text{ A}}{3.66\text{ A}} = 0.0464$$

$$\phi = 2.66^\circ$$
Thus I leads the voltage by 2.66°.

---

27 Find the magnitude of the total impedance of the circuit. Use $Z = \mathcal{E}/I$.

27
$$Z = \frac{220\text{ V}}{3.67\text{ A}} = 59.9\ \Omega$$

PROGRAMMED TEST

1 *Problem 1* A capacitor of unknown capacitance and an 80 Ω resistor are connected in series to a 60 Hz source whose voltage amplitude is 120 V. a) If the current amplitude is 1.3 A, find the capacitive reactance of the circuit and the value of the capacitance. b) A 0.50 H inductor is connected in series to the same resistor and capacitor. If the voltage applied across this *R-L-C* series circuit is still 120 V, what will be the current amplitude? c) Find the average power of the *R-L-C* series circuit described in b).

1

Answer

46.0 Ω, 57.7 μF, 0.736 A, 21.7 W

If you solved this problem correctly, go to frame 11. If you could not solve this problem, go through frames 2-10.

2 Find the impedance of the circuit.

2

$$Z = \frac{V}{I}$$

$$= \frac{120 \text{ V}}{1.3 \text{ A}} = 92.3 \ \Omega$$

---

3 Solve for the capacitive reactance.

3

$$Z = \sqrt{R^2 + X_C^2}$$

$$92.3 \ \Omega = \sqrt{(80 \ \Omega)^2 + X_C^2}$$
$$(92.3 \ \Omega)^2 = (80 \ \Omega)^2 + X_C^2$$
$$X_C = 46.0 \ \Omega$$

---

4 Find the capacitance.

4

$$X_C = \frac{1}{\omega C}$$

$$C = \frac{1}{\omega X_C} = \frac{1}{2\pi f X_C}$$

$$= \frac{1}{2\pi (60 \text{ s}^{-1})(46.0 \ \Omega)}$$

$$= 57.7 \ \mu\text{F}$$

---

5 Find the inductive reactance.

5

$$X_L = \omega L = 2\pi f L$$
$$= (2\pi)(60 \text{ s}^{-1})(0.50 \text{ H}) = 188 \ \Omega$$

---

6 Find the impedance.

6

$$Z = \sqrt{R^2 + (X_L - X_C)^2}$$

$$= \sqrt{(80 \ \Omega)^2 + (188 \ \Omega - 46.0 \ \Omega)^2} = 163 \ \Omega$$

---

7 Find the current amplitude from $I = V/Z$.

7

$$I = \frac{V}{Z}$$

$$= \frac{120 \text{ V}}{163 \ \Omega} = 0.736 \text{ A}$$

---

8 Before you can find the average power, you must find ϕ.

8
$$\tan \phi = \frac{X_L - X_C}{R}$$
$$= \frac{188\ \Omega - 46.0\ \Omega}{80\ \Omega} = 1.78$$
$$\phi = 60.6°$$

---

9 Find the average power.

9 $P = \frac{1}{2} IV \cos \phi$
$= \frac{1}{2}(0.736\ \text{A})(120\ \text{V})(\cos 60.6°) = 21.7\ \text{W}$

---

10 Check your answer by using $P = \frac{1}{2} I^2 R$.

10 $P = \frac{1}{2}(0.736\ \text{A})^2 (80\ \Omega) = 21.7\ \text{W}$
Note that power is dissipated in the resistor only.

---

11 **Problem 2** A series circuit draws 500 W from a 110 V, 60 Hz ac line. The power factor is 0.5 and the voltage leads the current. What size capacitor placed in series with the circuit is required to raise the power factor to unity? Voltages and currents in power distributions are always referred to in terms of their root-mean-square values. Thus 110 V ac means that the rms voltage is 110 V. The voltage amplitude is

$$V = \sqrt{2}\ V_{\text{rms}} = \sqrt{2}\,(110\ \text{V}) = 156\ \text{V}.$$

11 **Answer**
$253 \mu\text{F}$

If you solved this problem correctly, go to frame 17. If you could not solve this problem, go through frames 12-16.

12 Draw an impedance diagram to indicate the capacitance which must be placed in series with the circuit so that $\phi = 0$. Evidently the capacitance must have a capacitive reactance $= X$. Since the voltage leads the current, ϕ is positive and $X_L > X_C$.

12

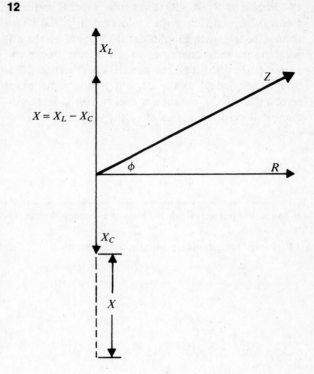

---

13 Express the power of the circuit in terms of V, Z and ϕ.

13
$$P = \tfrac{1}{2} IV \cos \phi = \tfrac{1}{2} \frac{V^2}{Z} \cos \phi,$$
since $I = \dfrac{V}{Z}$.

---

14 From the impedance diagram we note that $Z = X/\sin \phi$. Substitute this value for Z in the above and solve for the reactance X of the circuit.

14
$$P = \tfrac{1}{2} \frac{V^2 \cos \phi}{X/\sin \phi}$$
$$X = \frac{V^2 \sin \phi \cos \phi}{2P}$$

---

15 Substitute the given values and solve for X.

15
$$X = \frac{(156\text{V})^2 (0.866)(0.5)}{2(500\text{ W})}$$
$$= 10.5 \ \Omega$$

Note: if $\cos \phi = 0.5$, $\phi = 60°$; $\sin \phi = 0.866$.

---

16 Find the capacitance which must be added to the circuit.

16
$$C = \frac{1}{\omega X} = \frac{1}{2\pi f X}$$
$$= \frac{1}{2\pi(60\text{ s}^{-1})(10.5 \ \Omega)}$$
$$= 253 \mu\text{F}$$

---

17 Problem 3 A $120\,\Omega$ resistor, a $0.2\,H$ inductor and a $0.2\,\mu F$ capacitor are connected in parallel to a voltage source with amplitude 100 V. Find a) the angular resonant frequency and the resonant frequency, b) the current through the parallel combination at resonant frequency, c) the current in the inductor at resonance, d) the maximum energy stored in the inductor at resonance and e) in the capacitor at resonance.

17

Answer

$5 \times 10^3\,\text{rad} \cdot \text{s}^{-1}$, 769 Hz, 0.833 A, 0.1 A, 1×10^{-3} J, 1×10^{-3} J.

If you could not solve this problem, go through frames 18-24.

18 Find the angular resonant frequency.

18

$$\omega_0 = \frac{1}{\sqrt{LC}}$$

$$= \frac{1}{\sqrt{(0.2\,H)(0.2 \times 10^{-6}\,F)}}$$

$$= 5 \times 10^3\,\text{rad} \cdot \text{s}^{-1}$$

19 Find the resonant frequency.

19

$$\omega_0 = 2\pi f_0$$

$$f_0 = \frac{5 \times 10^3\,\text{rad} \cdot \text{s}^{-1}}{2\pi} = 769\,\text{Hz}$$

20 Find the current through the parallel combination at resonant frequency.

20

$$I = V\sqrt{\frac{1}{R^2} + \left(\omega C - \frac{1}{\omega L}\right)^2};$$

At resonance $\omega C = \dfrac{1}{\omega L} = 0$. Therefore,

$$I = \frac{V}{R} = \frac{100\,V}{120\,\Omega} = 0.833\,A$$

Note that 0.833 A also represents the maximum current in the resistor at resonance. At resonance L and C have equal currents and cancel each other, thus the total current only passes through R.

21 What is the inductive reactance?

21

$$\begin{aligned}X_L &= \omega_0 L \\ &= (5 \times 10^3\,\text{rad} \cdot \text{s}^{-1})(0.2\,H) \\ &= 1 \times 10^3\,\Omega\end{aligned}$$

22 Find the maximum current in the inductor at resonance.

22

$$I_L = \frac{V}{X_L}$$

$$= \frac{100\,V}{1000\,\Omega} = 0.1\,A$$

23 Find the maximum energy stored in the magnetic field of the inductor at resonance.

23

$U = \frac{1}{2}LI^2$
$\quad = \frac{1}{2}(0.2 \text{ H})(0.1 \text{ A})^2 = 1 \times 10^{-3} \text{ J}$

---

24 Find the maximum energy stored in the capacitor at resonance.

24

$U = \frac{1}{2}CV^2$
$\quad = \frac{1}{2}(0.2 \times 10^{-6} \text{ F})(100 \text{ V})^2 = 1 \times 10^{-3} \text{ J}$

35

Electromagnetic Waves

CHAPTER SUMMARY

In his study of the characteristics of electromagnetic waves, Maxwell postulated that a changing electric field gives rise to a magnetic field. On this basis, it was determined that electromagnetic waves exist in free space and are propagated at the speed of light. This chapter deals with a mathematical treatment of sinusoidal electromagnetic waves and the propagation of electromagnetic waves in matter. The energy of electromagnetic waves and radiation from an antenna are also discussed.

BASIC TERMS — *Give definitions or meanings for the following:*

electromagnetic wave (35-1)
displacement current (35-1)
Maxwell's equations (35-1)
transverse wave (35-2)
energy density (35-3)
intensity (35-3)
Poynting vector (35-3)
radiation pressure (35-3)

index of refraction (35-4)
plane wave (35-5)
polarization (35-5)
standing wave (35-6)
nodal plane (35-6)
electromagnetic spectrum (35-7)
oscillating dipole (35-8)

PROGRAMMED QUIZ

1 When can we treat electric and magnetic fields separately? When do we have to treat them together?

1 Electric and magnetic fields can be treated separately when they do not vary with time; when either field is changing with time they have to be treated together.

2 What are some examples of electromagnetic waves?

2 Light, radio waves, x-rays.

3 What were the contributions of Maxwell and Hertz in electromagnetic theory?

3 Maxwell proved theoretically that an electrical disturbance will propagate in space at the speed of light and, on the basis of this, postulated that light waves were electromagnetic. Hertz actually produced electromagnetic waves with the aid of oscillating circuits and detected these waves with other circuits tuned to the same frequency.

---

4 What are the basic features of all electromagnetic waves?

4 They are transverse, the electric field is perpendicular to the magnetic field and both are perpendicular to the direction of propagation of the field, there is a definite ratio between the magnitudes of these two fields, the two fields are in phase with each other, the waves travel in vacuum with a speed c.

---

5 What is the minimum value of the index of refraction of a dielectric?

5 The index of refraction of any material is always greater than 1.

---

6 What is the speed of electromagnetic waves in a dielectric?

6 Always less than the speed in vacuum.

---

7 Can electromagnetic waves propagate in a conducting material?

7 No, the electric field leads to currents which dissipate the energy.

---

8 What is a basic difference between electromagnetic waves and sound waves?

8 Electromagnetic waves may propagate through a vacuum; sound waves cannot.

---

9 What quantity is related to the Poynting vector?

9 The energy transported by the electromagnetic wave.

---

10 What is the direction of the Poynting vector?

10 In the direction of propagation of the wave.

---

11 What happens to the electromagnetic wave when it strikes an ideal conductor with zero resistivity?

11 It is totally reflected.

---

12 How is the energy associated with an electromagnetic wave carried?

12 It is equally divided between the E and B fields.

---

13 Do electromagnetic waves carry momentum?

13 Yes, in electromagnetic waves momentum is a property of the fields and is not associated with a moving mass.

---

14 What is the relationship between the speed of light in vacuum and the permittivity and permeability of free space?

14 The speed of light in vacuum is equal to the inverse of the square root of the product of the permittivity and permeability of free space; $c = 1/\sqrt{\epsilon_0\mu_0}$.

---

15 Are electromagnetic waves transverse or longitudinal?

15 Transverse.

---

16 Which one of Maxwell's equations implies that magnetic monopoles do not exist? Explain.

16 The second equation, $\Sigma B_\perp \Delta A = 0$ concerns itself with the flux of B out of a closed surface. The zero on the right side means that there is no such thing as a magnetic charge creating a magnetic field. Note that the first equation $\Sigma E_\perp \Delta A = \dfrac{Q}{\epsilon_0}$ is concerned with the flux of E, due to charge Q, out of a closed surface.

---

17 Which one of Maxwell's equations is Ampere's law? Faraday's law? What is the significance of each equation?

17 Ampere's law is Maxwell's third equation. It states that both conduction current and displacement current act as sources of magnetic field. Faraday's law is Maxwell's fourth equation. It states that a changing magnetic field or magnetic flux induces an electric field E_n.

MAIN IDEAS

In a parallel plate capacitor the electric field E between the plates is given by

$$E = \frac{\sigma}{\epsilon_0} = \frac{Q}{\epsilon_0 A},$$

where σ = charge density, A = plate area and Q = charge on each plate. The displacement current

$$i_D = \epsilon_0 A \frac{\Delta E}{\Delta t},$$

where $\dfrac{\Delta E}{\Delta t}$ = rate of change of electric field between the plates. The corresponding current density = j_D = $\epsilon_0 \left(\dfrac{\Delta E}{\Delta t}\right)$. When the displacement current is added to the conducting current, the total current obeys Kirchhoff's current rule. If Ψ = total electric flux coming out of the capacitor plate, then $i_D = \epsilon_0 \dfrac{\Delta \Psi}{\Delta t}$.

Maxwell's equations:

1 $\Sigma E_\perp \Delta A = \dfrac{Q}{\epsilon_0}$ (Gauss's law). This equation pertains to the electric flux out of a closed surface.

2 $\Sigma B_\perp \Delta A = 0$. This equation pertains to the magnetic flux out of a closed surface. It implies that there is no such thing as a magnetic charge as a source of magnetic field.

3 $\Sigma B_\parallel \, \Delta s = \epsilon_0 \left(I_c + \epsilon_0 \dfrac{\Delta \Psi}{\Delta t} \right)$ (Ampere's law). Both conduction current I_c and displacement current $\epsilon_0 \dfrac{\Delta \Psi}{\Delta t}$ act as sources of magnetic field.

4 $\Sigma E_\parallel \, \Delta s = \dfrac{-\Delta \Phi}{\Delta t}$ (Faraday's law). A changing magnetic field or magnetic flux Φ induces an electric field E_n.

The total electric field $E_\parallel$ includes both electrostatic and non-electrostatic contributions.

A variable electric field $\Delta E/\Delta t$ will induce a magnetic field B in an adjacent region of space. Similarly, a changing field $\Delta B/\Delta t$ gives rise to an electric field E in an adjacent region of space. Electromagnetic waves can exist in and propagate energy through empty space with the speed of light c after the radiation departs from the generating source. By applying Ampere's law and Faraday's law to an electromagnetic disturbance in free space, it can be shown that $c = 1/\sqrt{\epsilon_0 \mu_0}$, where $\epsilon_0 = 8.85 \times 10^{-12} \text{ C}^2 \cdot \text{N}^{-1} \cdot \text{m}^{-2}$ is the permittivity of free space and $\mu_0 = 4\pi \times 10^{-7} \text{ Wb} \cdot \text{A}^{-1} \cdot \text{m}^{-1}$ is the permeability of free space.

All electromagnetic waves have the following characteristics: a) The wave is transverse; B and E are perpendicular to each other and to the direction of the wave. b) The ratio of the amplitudes of E and B is c, i.e. $c = E/B$. c) The wave travels in a vacuum at constant speed c.

The energy per unit volume (density) of an electromagnetic wave travelling through empty space is given by $u = \frac{1}{2}\epsilon_0 E^2 + \frac{1}{2}\mu_0 B^2 = \epsilon_0 E^2$, where E and B are the magnitudes of the electric field and magnetic field, respectively. Note that $\dfrac{B}{E} = \sqrt{\epsilon_0 \mu_0}$. The energy passing through area A in time Δt is $\Delta U = \epsilon_0 E^2 A c \Delta t$.

The magnitude of the rate of energy flow per unit area is given by $S \; \Delta U/A\Delta t = \epsilon_0 c E^2 = \sqrt{\epsilon_0/\mu_0} \, E^2 = EB/\mu_0$. The unit of S is $1 \text{ J} \cdot \text{s}^{-1} \cdot \text{m}^{-2}$ or $1 \text{ W} \cdot \text{m}^{-2}$. The Poynting vector S is a vector with magnitude S in the direction of propagation of the wave.

Electromagnetic waves can carry momentum p with a corresponding momentum density (momentum per unit volume V) of magnitude $\dfrac{p}{V} = \dfrac{EB}{\mu_0 c^2} = S/c^2$. The momentum flow rate which represents the momentum transferred per unit surface area per unit time is given by $EB/\mu_0 c$. Radiation pressure due to the absorption of an electromagnetic wave by a surface which is perpendicular to the propagation direction is the time rate of change of momentum. It is equal to the force per unit area on the surface and is given by S/c. If the wave is totally reflected, the pressure is $2S/c$.

The wave speed of an electromagnetic wave in a dielectric medium is given by $v = 1/\sqrt{\epsilon\mu} = 1/(KK_m\epsilon_0\mu_0)^{1/2} = \dfrac{c}{\sqrt{KK_m}}$, where ϵ and μ are the permittivity and permeability of the dielectric, respectively. The frequency f, the wavelength λ and the speed of propagation c of an electromagnetic wave are related by $c = f\lambda$. Electromagnetic waves cannot propagate within a conductor; they are totally reflected when they strike a conducting surface.

Sinusoidal electromagnetic waves are analogous to sinusoidal transverse mechanical waves on a stretched string. At any point in space, the E and B fields are sinusoidal functions of time.

$$E = E_{max}\sin(\omega t - kx)$$
$$B = B_{max}\sin(\omega t - kx)$$

where

ω = angular frequency = $2\pi f$,

k = wave number (propagation constant) = $\dfrac{(2\pi)}{\lambda}$.

The Poynting vector S,

$$S = \frac{EB}{\mu_0} = \frac{E_{max} B_{max}}{\mu_0} = \sin^2(\omega t - kx)$$

$$S_{av} = \frac{E_{max} B_{max}}{2\mu_0} = \frac{1}{2} \epsilon_0 c E^2_{max}$$

$S_{av} = I =$ intensity of radiation which is the average power transmitted per unit area.

An oscillating dipole, two charges of equal magnitude and opposite sign, will produce an electromagnetic wave consisting of an electric and magnetic field varying sinusoidally in two mutually perpendicular planes and in phase with one another.

PROGRAMMED QUIZ

1 An electromagnetic wave propagating in vacuum has a wavelength of 0.032 m. What is its frequency?

1

$$c = f\lambda$$
$$f = \frac{3 \times 10^8 \text{ m} \cdot \text{s}^{-1}}{0.032 \text{ m}}$$
$$= 9.38 \times 10^9 \text{ Hz}$$

2 The wave enters a dielectric having $K = 10$ and $K_m = 1000$. What is the frequency?

2 9.38×10^9 Hz; the frequency is independent of the medium.

3 What is the index of refraction of this material?

3

$$n = \sqrt{KK_m}$$
$$= \sqrt{10(1000)} = 100$$

4 What is the speed of the electromagnetic wave in this medium?

4

$$n = \frac{c}{v}$$
$$v = \frac{3 \times 10^8 \text{ m} \cdot \text{s}^{-1}}{100}$$
$$= 3 \times 10^6 \text{ m} \cdot \text{s}^{-1}$$

5 What is the wavelength of a wave having a frequency of 200 MHz in this medium?

5

$$v = f\lambda$$
$$\lambda = \frac{3 \times 10^6 \text{ m} \cdot \text{s}^{-1}}{200 \times 10^6 \text{ s}^{-1}}$$
$$= 0.015 \text{ m} = 1.5 \text{ cm}$$

6 The maximum electric field in the vicinity of a radio transmitter is 1.2×10^{-3} V · m^{-1}. What is the maximum magnitude of the magnetic field?

6

$$B_{max} = \frac{E_{max}}{c}$$
$$= \frac{1.2 \times 10^{-3} \text{ V} \cdot \text{m}^{-1}}{3 \times 10^8 \text{ m} \cdot \text{s}^{-1}}$$
$$= 4.00 \times 10^{-12} \text{ T}$$

7 Compare this to the earth's magnetic field.

7 Much smaller, the earth's magnetic field is approximately 10^{-5} T.

8 What is the energy density?

8

$$u = \epsilon_0 E^2_{max}$$
$$= (8.85 \times 10^{-12} \text{ C}^2 \cdot \text{N}^{-1} \cdot \text{m}^{-2})(1.2 \times 10^{-3} \text{ V} \cdot \text{m}^{-1})^2$$
$$= 1.27 \times 10^{-19} \text{ J} \cdot \text{m}^{-3}$$

9 What is the intensity of the radiation (i.e. the magnitude of the Poynting vector)?

9

$$S = \frac{E_{max} B_{max}}{\mu_0}$$

$$= \frac{(1.2 \times 10^{-3} \text{ V} \cdot \text{m}^{-1}) [4.00 \times 10^{-12} \text{T}]}{4\pi \times 10^{-7} \text{ Wb} \cdot \text{A}^{-1} \cdot \text{m}^{-1}}$$

$$= 3.82 \times 10^{-9} \text{ W} \cdot \text{m}^{-2}$$

---

10 If this wave is completely absorbed, what would be the radiation pressure?

10

$$p = \frac{S}{c}$$

$$= \frac{3.82 \times 10^{-9} \text{ W} \cdot \text{m}^{-2}}{3 \times 10^8 \text{ m} \cdot \text{s}^{-1}}$$

$$= 1.27 \times 10^{-17} \text{ N} \cdot \text{m}^{-2}$$

---

11 What average force does the radiation pressure exert on a totally absorbing surface 0.4 m^2 in area perpendicular to the direction of propagation?

11

$$F = pA$$

$$= (1.27 \times 10^{-17} \text{ N} \cdot \text{m}^{-2}) (0.4 \text{ m}^2)$$

$$= 5.08 \times 10^{-18} \text{ N}$$

---

12 The electric field amplitude $E_{max} = 0.100 \text{ V} \cdot \text{m}^{-1}$ at a distance of 100 km from a radio station antenna. If the antenna radiates equally in all directions, what is the total power output of the transmitter?

12

$$I = S_{av} = \frac{E^2_{max}}{2\mu_0 c}$$

$$= \frac{(0.100 \text{ V} \cdot \text{m}^{-1})^2}{2(4\pi \times 10^{-7} \text{ T} \cdot \text{m} \cdot \text{A}^{-1}) (3.00 \times 10^8 \text{ m} \cdot \text{s}^{-1})}$$

$$= 1.33 \times 10^{-5} \text{ W} \cdot \text{m}^{-2}$$

Since $I =$ power per unit area, the power output of the transmitter is $P = IA$, where A is the surface area of a sphere of radius $r = 100$ km.

$$P = IA = I(4\pi r^2)$$

$$= (1.33 \times 10^{-5} \text{ W} \cdot \text{m}^{-2}) (4\pi) (10^5 \text{ m})^2$$

$$= 1.67 \times 10^6 \text{ W}$$

$$= 1670 \text{ kilowatts}$$

STEP BY STEP SOLUTIONS OF PROBLEMS

Problem 1 The intensity of radiation of sunlight is 1.4 kW $\cdot$ m^{-2}. If a beam of sunlight falls for 1 minute on a perfectly reflecting surface of 1 m^2, find a) the energy that is reflected, b) the momentum delivered to the mirror during this time and c) the force acting on the mirror.

1 Find the energy that is reflected by using $S = \Delta U/A\Delta t$.

1

$$\Delta U = SA\Delta t$$

$$= (1.4 \times 10^3 \text{ W} \cdot \text{m}^{-2}) (1.0 \text{ m}^2) (60 \text{ s})$$

$$= 8.4 \times 10^4 \text{ J}$$

---

2 Find the momentum delivered to the mirror during this time. Since the energy is totally reflected, Δp and ΔU are related by $\Delta p = 2U/c$. (For total absorption $\Delta p = \Delta U/c$.)

2

$$\Delta p = \frac{2(8.4 \times 10^4 \text{ J})}{3 \times 10^8 \text{ m} \cdot \text{s}^{-1}}$$

$$= 5.6 \times 10^{-4} \text{ kg} \cdot \text{m} \cdot \text{s}^{-1}$$

---

3 Check your answer by using the momentum flow rate relationship for total reflection $\Delta p / A \Delta t = 2S/c$.

3

$$\Delta p = \frac{2SA\Delta t}{c}$$

$$= \frac{2(1.4 \times 10^3 \,\text{W} \cdot \text{m}^{-2})\,(1 \,\text{m}^2)\,(60 \,\text{s})}{3 \times 10^8 \,\text{m} \cdot \text{s}^{-1}}$$

$$= 5.6 \times 10^{-4} \,\text{kg} \cdot \text{m} \cdot \text{s}^{-1}$$

4 Find the force acting on the mirror by using $F\Delta t = \Delta p$; i.e., the impulse of the force is equal to the change in momentum.

4

$$F = \frac{\Delta p}{\Delta t} = \frac{5.6 \times 10^{-4} \,\text{kg} \cdot \text{m} \cdot \text{s}^{-1}}{60 \,\text{s}}$$

$$= 9.33 \times 10^{-6} \,\text{N}$$

5 Check your answer by finding the radiation pressure $2S/c$ and multiplying the result by the area.

5

$$\text{radiation pressure} = \frac{2S}{c}$$

$$= \frac{2(1.4 \times 10^3 \,\text{W} \cdot \text{m}^{-2})}{3 \times 10^8 \,\text{m} \cdot \text{s}^{-1}}$$

$$= 9.33 \times 10^{-6} \,\text{N} \cdot \text{m}^{-2}$$

$$F = (\text{radiation pressure})\,(\text{area})$$

$$= (9.33 \times 10^{-6} \,\text{N} \cdot \text{m}^{-2})\,(1 \,\text{m}^2)$$

$$= 9.33 \times 10^{-6} \,\text{N}$$

Problem 2 Prove that for a sinusoidal electromagnetic wave in a vacuum, the average density of energy in the electric field equals the average density of energy stored in the magnetic field.

6 Combine the energy density due to an electric field and the sinusoidal expression for the instantaneous value of the electric field, $u_E = \frac{1}{2}\epsilon_0 E^2$ and $E = E_{max} \sin(\omega t - kx)$, where E denotes the instantaneous value and E_{max} the maximum value or amplitude of the electric field.

6

$$u_E = \frac{1}{2}\epsilon_0 E^2_{max} \sin^2(\omega t - kx)$$

(It should be noted that since the electric and magnetic fields are in phase, there is no need for time-average calculations.)

7 Substitute $E_{max} = B_{max}c$, where B_{max} denotes the maximum value (amplitude) of the magnetic field.

7

$$u_E = \frac{1}{2}\epsilon_0 c^2 \, B^2_{max} \sin^2(\omega t - kx)$$

8 Substitute $B^2 = B^2_{max} \sin^2(\omega t - kx)$, where B denotes the instantaneous value of the magnetic field.

8

$$u_E = \frac{1}{2}\epsilon_0 c^2 \, B^2$$

9 Substitute $c^2 = 1/\epsilon_0\mu_0$ and note that u_B, the energy density due to a magnetic field is equal to $B^2/2\mu_0$.

9

$$u_E = \frac{1}{2}\epsilon_0 \left(\frac{1}{\epsilon_0\mu_0} \right) B^2 = u_B$$

Problem 3 A cylindrical conductor of circular cross section has a radius a and resistivity ρ and carries a constant current I. a) Find the magnitude of the E-vector, B-vector, and the Poynting vector S at a point inside the wire at a distance r from the axis. b) Show that the rate at which energy flows into the conductor through its cylindrical surface is equal to the rate at which thermal energy is produced.

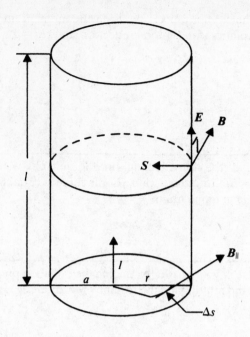

10 Find the magnitude of the electric field at a point just inside the wire at a distance r from the axis of the wire. The electric field E = voltage gradient, $E = V/l$. Use $V = IR$ and the definition of resistivity.

10

$$E = \frac{V}{l} = \frac{IR}{l} = \frac{I\rho l}{lA} = \frac{\rho I}{\pi a^2} \text{ or}$$

$$E = \rho J = \rho \frac{I}{A} = \frac{\rho I}{\pi a^2}$$

11 Find the magnitude of B by using Ampere's law and the expression for resistivity in terms of the current density.

11 In accordance with Ampere's law, $\Sigma B_{\parallel} \Delta s = \mu_0 I_r$, where I_r is the current enclosed by the path of radius r. Thus $B(2\pi r) = \mu_0 I_r$.

12 Express I_r in terms of a and r by using the relationship for current density $J = I/A$.

12

$$I_r = JA_r = \frac{I}{A}(\pi r^2) = \frac{I}{\pi a^2}(\pi r^2)$$
$$= \frac{Ir^2}{a^2}$$

13 Substitute the value obtained for I_r in Ampere's law and solve for B.

13

$$B = \frac{\mu_0 I_r}{2\pi r} = \frac{\mu_0}{2\pi r}\left(\frac{Ir^2}{a^2}\right)$$
$$= \frac{\mu_0 Ir}{2\pi a^2}$$

14 Solve for S, the rate at which energy flows into the conductor through its cylindrical surface by using

$$S = \frac{EB}{\mu_0}.$$

14

$$S = \frac{EB}{\mu_0} = \left(\frac{\rho I}{\pi a^2}\right)\left(\frac{\mu_0 Ir}{2\pi a^2}\right)\frac{1}{\mu_0}$$
$$= \frac{I^2 r\rho}{2\pi^2 a^4}$$

15 Find the power dissipated in a volume of length l and radius r within the wire by using $P_r = I_r V$.

15

$$P_r = I_r V = I_r(I_r R) = I_r^2 R$$
$$= \frac{(JA_r)^2 \, \rho l}{A_r} = J^2 A_r \rho l$$
$$= \left(\frac{I}{\pi a^2}\right)^2 (\pi r^2) \rho l$$
$$= \frac{\rho l I^2 r^2}{\pi a^4}$$

16 Find the power per unit cylindrical surface area. Surface area $= 2\pi r l$.

16

$$\frac{P_r}{\text{surface area}} = \frac{1}{2\pi r l} \frac{(\rho l I^2 r^2)}{\pi a^4}$$
$$= \frac{\rho r I^2}{2\pi^2 a^4} \text{, which is equal to } S. \text{ Thus}$$

we have proven part b).

PROGRAMMED TEST

1 *Problem 1* Find the maximum magnitude of *E* and *B* at a distance of 50 km from the antenna of an 80 kW radio station. Assume that the antenna radiates equally in all directions.

1 *Answer*
4.38×10^{-2} V $\cdot$ m^{-1}, 1.46×10^{-10} T

If you solved this problem correctly, go to frame 7. If you could not solve this problem, go through frames 2–6.

2 Let P_0 denote the power output of the antenna. Express P_0 in terms of the average intensity of radiation S_{av} and the surface area of a sphere of radius r.

2

$$P_0 = S_{av} A$$
$$= S_{av}(4\pi r^2)$$

3 Express S_{av} in terms of μ_0, c and E_{max}.

3 Solve

$$c = \frac{1}{\sqrt{\epsilon_0 \mu_0}} \text{ for } \epsilon_0.$$

$$\epsilon_0 = \frac{1}{c^2 \mu_0}$$

Substituting this value in $S_{av} = \frac{1}{2}\epsilon_0 c E^2_{max}$ we obtain $S_{av} = \frac{E^2_{max}}{2\mu_0 c}$.

4 Substitute the value of S_{av} obtained in frame 3 in the expression in frame 2 and solve for E_{max}.

4

$$P_0 = \frac{E^2_{max}}{2\mu_0 c}(4\pi r^2)$$

$$E_{max} = \frac{1}{r}\sqrt{\frac{P_0 \mu_0 c}{2\pi}}$$

5 Substitute the given values and solve for E_{max}.

5

$$E_{max} = \frac{1}{5 \times 10^4 \, m}$$

$$\times \sqrt{\frac{(8.0 \times 10^4 \, W)\,(4\pi \times 10^{-7} \, Wb \cdot A^{-1} \cdot m^{-1})\,(3.0 \times 10^8 \, m \cdot s^{-1})}{2\pi}}$$

$$= 4.38 \times 10^{-2} \, V \cdot m^{-1}$$

---

6 Find B by using the relationship $E_{max}/B_{max} = c$.

6

$$B_{max} = \frac{E_{max}}{c} = \frac{4.38 \times 10^{-2} \, V \cdot m^{-1}}{3 \times 10^8 \, m \cdot s^{-1}}$$

$$= 1.46 \times 10^{-10} \, T$$

---

7 **Problem 2** The electromagnetic radiation from the sun is $1.4 \, kW \cdot m^{-2}$. Find a) the radiation pressure on a totally absorbing surface, b) the radiation pressure on a totally reflecting surface, c) the maximum values of E and B for a wave of this intensity, d) the total power radiated by the sun (distance from the sun is $1.5 \times 10^{11} \, m$).

7 **Answer**

4.7×10^{-6} Pa, 9.4×10^{-6} Pa, $1.03 \times 10^3 \, V \cdot m^{-1}$, 3.43×10^{-6} T, 3.96×10^{26} W.

If you solved this problem correctly, go to frame 13. If you could not solve this problem, go through frames 8–12.

---

8 Find the radiation pressure on a totally absorbing surface.

8

$$p = \frac{S}{c}$$

$$= \frac{1.4 \times 10^3 \, W \cdot m^{-2}}{3 \times 10^8 \, m \cdot s^{-1}} = 4.7 \times 10^{-6} \, Pa$$

---

9 Find the radiation pressure on a totally reflecting surface.

9

$$p = \frac{2S}{c}$$

$$= 2(4.7 \times 10^{-6} \, Pa) = 9.4 \times 10^{-6} \, Pa$$

---

10 Find the maximum values of E for a wave of this intensity.

10

$$S_{av} = \frac{E^2}{2\mu_0 c}$$

$$E = \sqrt{2\mu_0 c S_{av}}$$

$$= \sqrt{2(4\pi \times 10^{-7} \, Wb \cdot A^{-1} \cdot m^{-1})\,(3 \times 10^8 \, m \cdot s^{-1})\,(1.4 \times 10^3 \, W \cdot m^{-2})}$$

$$= 1.03 \times 10^3 \, V \cdot m^{-1}$$

---

11 Find the maximum value of B for a wave of this intensity.

11

$$B_{max} = \frac{E_{max}}{c} = \frac{1.03 \times 10^3 \, V \cdot m^{-1}}{3 \times 10^8 \, m \cdot s^{-1}}$$

$$= 3.43 \times 10^{-6} \, T$$

---

12 Find the total power P_0 radiated by the sun.

12
$$P_0 = S_{av}A = S_{av}(4\pi r^2)$$
$$= (1.4 \times 10^3 \text{ W} \cdot \text{m}^{-2}) (4\pi) (1.5 \times 10^{11} \text{ m})^2$$
$$= 3.96 \times 10^{26} \text{ W}$$

---

13 *Problem 3* A plane electromagnetic wave has a wavelength of 0.4 m and an *E*-field amplitude of $60 \text{ V} \cdot \text{m}^{-1}$. Find a) the frequency of the wave, b) the magnitude of the *B*-field amplitude, c) the intensity of radiation S, d) the radiation pressure exerted on a totally absorbing surface.

13 *Answer*
$7.5 \times 10^8 \text{ Hz}, 2 \times 10^{-7} \text{ T}, 4.78 \text{ W} \cdot \text{m}^{-2},$
$1.59 \times 10^{-8} \text{ Pa}$

If you could not solve this problem, go through frames 14–17.

14 Find the frequency of the wave.

14
$$c = f\lambda$$
$$f = \frac{3 \times 10^8 \text{ m} \cdot \text{s}^{-1}}{0.4 \text{ m}} = 7.5 \times 10^8 \text{ Hz}$$

---

15 Find the magnitude of the *B*-field.

15
$$B_{max} = \frac{E_{max}}{c}$$
$$= \frac{60 \text{ V} \cdot \text{m}^{-1}}{3 \times 10^8 \text{ m} \cdot \text{s}^{-1}} = 2 \times 10^{-7} \text{ T}$$

---

16 Find the intensity of radiation.

16
$$S_{av} = \frac{E^2_{max}}{2\mu_0 c}$$
$$= \frac{(60 \text{ V} \cdot \text{m}^{-1})^2}{2(4\pi \times 10^{-7} \text{ Wb} \cdot \text{A}^{-1} \cdot \text{m}^{-1}) (3 \times 10^8 \text{ m} \cdot \text{s}^{-1})}$$
$$= 4.78 \text{ W} \cdot \text{m}^{-2}$$

---

17 Find the radiation pressure exerted on a totally absorbing surface.

17
$$p = \frac{S_{av}}{c}$$
$$= \frac{4.78 \text{ W} \cdot \text{m}^{-2}}{3 \times 10^8 \text{ m} \cdot \text{s}^{-1}}$$
$$= 1.59 \times 10^{-8} \text{ Pa}$$

36

The Nature and Propagation of Light

CHAPTER SUMMARY

The wave and corpuscular nature of light is presented on the basis of waves, wave fronts, rays and Huygens' principle. The laws of reflection refraction, total internal reflection and dispersion are derived, and scattering is discussed. The chapter also considers the different ways of polarizing transverse waves and the various effects and applications of polarization, such as photoelasticity.

BASIC TERMS — *Give definitions or meanings for the following:*

ray (36-I)
thermal radiation (36-1)
wave front (36-1)
geometrical optics (36-1)
physical optics (36-1)
reflection (36-2)
refraction (36-2)
Snell's law (36-2)
index of refraction (36-2)
law of refraction (36-2)
law of reflection (36-2)
total internal reflection (36-3)
critical angle (36-3)
fiber optics (36-3)
dispersion (36-4)
quarter-wave plate (36-5)

dichroism (36-5)
polarizing axis (36-5)
analyzer (36-5)
polarizing angle (36-5)
linear polarization (36-5)
polarizing filter (36-5)
Malus' law (36-5)
Brewster's law (36-5)
double refracting (36-5)
birefringence (36-5)
circular polarization (36-5)
elliptical polarization (36-5)
photoelasticity (36-5)
optical activity (36-5)
scattering (36-6)
Huygens' principle (36-7)

PROGRAMMED QUIZ

1 What general phenomena are described by the wave theory? corpuscular theory?

1 The wave theory describes light propagation; the corpuscular theory is concerned with the interaction of light with matter in the processes of emission and absorption.

2 How does the laser differ from other light sources?

2 It is much more intense and more nearly monochromatic than any other light source.

3 Who was the first to determine the speed of light from terrestrial measurements?

3 Fizeau, using the toothed-wheel method.

4 Describe visible light.

4 Electromagnetic waves 4 to 7×10^{-7} m in wavelength that are perceived by the sense of sight.

5 What are some units in which light wavelengths are measured? Compare these to the meter.

5 1 micrometer = 1 μm = 10^{-6} m
    1 nanometer = 1 nm = 10^{-9} m
    1 angstrom = 1 Å = 10^{-10} m

6 What are the colors in the visible spectrum? Start with the shortest wavelength.

6 Violet, blue, green, yellow, orange, red.

7 What is the relationship between rays and wave fronts?

7 Rays are perpendicular to the wave fronts.

8 What happens to the speed, frequency and wavelength of light as it proceeds into a medium of greater n?

8 The speed decreases, the wavelength decreases and the frequency remains the same.

9 What is the angle of refraction relative to the angle of incidence?

9 It may be larger (if the second medium has a smaller n than the first medium), smaller (if the second medium has a larger n) or equal (if both have equal n).

10 If a light ray enters another medium normally, what is the angle of refraction?

10 Zero, $n_a \sin \phi_a = n_b \sin \phi_b$. If the light ray enters normally, $\phi_a = 0$.

11 Light is incident on a second medium of lower n at the critical angle. What is the angle of refraction?

11 90°

12 How are the directions of the incident, reflected and refracted rays specified?

12 In terms of the angles that the rays make with the normal to the surface at the point of incidence.

---

13 A light ray diverging from a point source in medium a of index n_a strikes the interface of a second medium n_b, where $n_b < n_a$. What happens if the angle of incidence is greater than the critical angle?

13 Total internal reflection occurs; all the incident light is reflected back into the first medium.

---

14 If a ray is incident to this page, in what plane do the reflected and refracted rays lie?

14 The incident, reflected and refracted rays (and the normal to the surface) all lie in the same plane which is perpendicular to this page.

---

15 What is the relationship between the angle of incidence and the intensity of the ray reflected from a glass surface?

15 At normal incidence about 4% of the intensity of a beam of light is reflected from a single glass surface (96% of the intensity is transmitted). If I_0 denotes the intensity of the incident beam and I denotes the intensity of the reflected beam, then I/I_0 increases with the angle of incidence until at 90°, when the incident ray is grazing the surface, all light is reflected. It can be shown that

$$\frac{I}{I_0} = \left(\frac{n \cos \phi_b - \cos \phi_a}{n \cos \phi_b + \cos \phi_a} \right)^2 ,$$

where n = index of reflecting surface, ϕ_a = angle of incidence and ϕ_b = angle of refraction.
In the case of normal incidence, $\phi_a = \phi_b = 0°$, $\cos 0° = 1$,

$$\frac{I}{I_0} = \left(\frac{n \cos 0° - \cos 0°}{n \cos 0° + \cos 0°} \right)^2 = \left(\frac{n - 1}{n + 1} \right)^2 .$$

---

16 Do we see objects because of the light they absorb?

16 No, we see objects by means of the light they emit or reflect.

---

17 Which is most efficient — a fluorescent or an incandescent lamp?

17 A fluorescent lamp has an overall luminous efficiency of about five times greater than that of an incandescent lamp.

---

18 Do all waves exhibit polarization effects?

18 No, only transverse waves.

---

19 When we talk about the direction of polarization of an electromagnetic wave, what direction are we referring to?

19 An electromagnetic wave consists of electric and magnetic fields which are perpendicular to each other and to the direction of propagation. The direction of polarization is, by convention, taken to be the direction of the electric field vector.

---

20 What is the intensity of light passing through an ideal polarizer, assuming that the incident light is a random mixture of all states of polarization?

20 Half of the incident intensity, corresponding to the component parallel to the polarizer axis.

---

21 How would we arrange two polarizers so that no light would be transmitted?

21 With the two polarizing axes perpendicular to each other.

22 When natural light strikes a reflecting surface, are all waves reflected equally?

22 Only at normal incidence; at other angles there is a preferential reflection for waves in which the electric field vector is perpendicular to the plane of incidence. At the polarizing angle only these waves are reflected.

23 When light is incident at the polarizing angle, what happens to the component in which the electric field is parallel to the plane of incidence?

23 It is 100% transmitted in the refracted beam.

24 When light is incident at the polarizing angle, what is the relationship between the directions of the reflected and refracted rays?

24 They are perpendicular to each other.

25 Does Snell's law hold for the extraordinary ray?

25 No, since the velocity is different in different directions.

26 In a doubly refracting crystal, are the waves polarized? What are the directions of polarization of the ordinary and extraordinary rays?

26 Yes, the ordinary and the extraordinary rays are linearly polarized in mutually perpendicular directions. The ordinary ray is polarized perpendicular to the optic axis; the extraordinary ray is polarized parallel to it.

27 What are the deficiencies of Polaroid sheets?

27 They do not polarize all wavelengths equally; when two such disks are crossed, small amounts of red and violet are transmitted.

28 How is a Polaroid sheet used in sunglasses (in terms of its polarizing properties)?

28 When sunlight is reflected from a horizontal surface, the reflected light is preponderantly polarized in the horizontal direction. (This is perceived as glare). In sunglasses, the transmission direction of the Polaroid sheet is vertical so the horizontally polarized light is blocked out.

29 What color would the sky appear to be if the earth had no atmosphere? What phenomenon accounts for the blue sky?

29 Black, scattering.

30 What substances exhibit optical activity?

30 Sugar solutions; plastics under stress.

31 If light is incident at the polarizing angle, part will be reflected, part transmitted. Will both rays be completely polarized?

31 No, only the reflected ray.

32 If all light is scattered, why does the sky appear blue? Why does the sun appear red at sunrise and sunset?

32 Blue and violet light is scattered much more than the other colors. Blue and colors other than red are scattered in directions other than the line of sight.

MAIN IDEAS

Light consists of electromagnetic waves with a speed $c = 2.99792458 \times 10^8$ m $\cdot$ s^{-1}. The theory of light includes both wave and particle properties.

A wave front is the locus of all points on the wave train which have the same phase. A light ray is an imaginary line drawn in the direction in which the wave is traveling. Light waves are always perpendicular to wave fronts.

When a ray of light is incident upon the interface of two media, for example air and glass, it is partly reflected and partly refracted. The normal is a line drawn perpendicular to the interface at the point of incidence. All angles are measured with respect to the normal. In the figure, ray 1 is the incident ray, ray 2 the reflected ray and ray 3 the refracted ray.

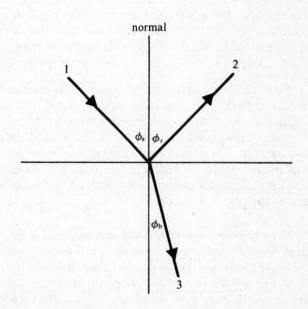

Laws of reflection and refraction. a) The incident, reflected, refracted rays and the normal to the surface all lie in the same plane. b) For reflection $\phi_a = \phi_r$. This relationship is independent of the wavelength of the light and the nature of the two media. c) For monochromatic light and any two media a and b, $n_a \sin \phi_a = n_b \sin \phi_b$, where n_a and n_b are the indices of refraction of the two media with respect to a vacuum. This relationship is known as Snell's law. The indices of refraction are also related by $n_a v_a = n_b v_b$, where v_a and v_b are the speeds of light in media a and b. Note, when light enters a medium of larger refractive index than the first ($n_b > n_a$), the refracted ray is bent toward the normal ($\phi_b < \phi_a$).

When a light wave passes from one medium to another, the wavelength changes but not the frequency: $\lambda_a n_a = \lambda_b n_b = \lambda_o$, where the subscripts a and b represent any two media and the subscript 0 represents a vacuum. Since frequency is constant, $\lambda_a / v_a = \lambda_b / v_b$.

The critical angle is a particular angle of incidence for which the angle of refraction is 90°. This can occur only when the second material has a lower refractive index than the first. If the angle of incidence is greater than the critical angle, the light ray is totally internally reflected back into the first medium.

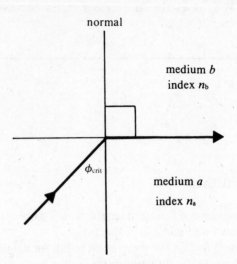

$$\sin \phi_{\text{crit}} = n_{\text{b}}/n_{\text{a}}$$

A wave is linearly polarized in the y-direction if it has only y-displacements. Similarly, a wave which only has z-displacements is linearly polarized in the z-direction. By convention, the direction of the electric field vector gives the direction of polarization. Polarization is possible only with transverse waves.

A polarizer (polarizing filter) transmits 100% of the incident light which is polarized in the direction of its polarizing axis. When unpolarized light (a random mixture of waves linearly polarized in all possible directions) is incident on a polarizer, one-half of the incident intensity is transmitted. This is polarization by absorption.

A polarizer that is used to determine the plane of polarization of plane polarized light is called an analyzer. Consider polarized light incident upon an analyzer which has been oriented so that θ is the angle between the transmission directions of the polarizer and analyzer. The transmission intensity is given by Malus' law, $I = I_{\text{max}} \cos^2 \theta$, where I_{max} is the maximum amount of light transmitted and I is the amount transmitted at angle θ.

Light can be polarized by reflection. If unpolarized light is incident upon a reflecting surface between two media, the reflected light is partially polarized. In the case where the reflected and refracted rays are perpendicular to each other, the reflected ray is completely plane polarized. The polarizing angle ϕ_{p} is given by Brewster's law, $\tan \phi_{\text{p}} = n'/n$, where light in medium of index n is reflected by a surface, the medium of which has index n'. The plane of polarization is $\perp$ to the plane of incidence (i.e. the plane containing the incident ray and the normal to the surface). Polarization by scattering is the phenomenon of absorption and reradiation. In the atmosphere, for example, clusters of air molecules will scatter short wavelengths more than long wavelengths, giving the sky its blue color.

In an anisotropic material, the speed of light is not the same in all directions. These substances are birefringent — doubly refracting. If the optic axis of the substance is parallel to the surface, a ray incident normally will be broken into two rays as it enters the substance: the ordinary ray will be plane polarized perpendicular to the optic axis and the extraordinary ray will be plane polarized parallel to the optic axis. (The optic axis is the direction in which there is no distinction between the O- and E- rays.) The ordinary ray travels through the material with a speed c/n_O and obey's Snell's law when it strikes the surface between two media. Snell's law does not hold for the extraordinary ray since its velocity depends upon its direction in the substance.

However, if the two rays do not separate in a doubly refracting material but travel together at different speeds, the resulting waves will be circularly or elliptically polarized. The type of polarization depends on the phase difference between the two rays. Consider plane polarized light incident upon a crystal plate which is split into an O- and an E- ray in the plate, where the O-ray travels with a speed c/n_O and the E-ray with speed c/n_E. Although the waves were in phase at the incident interface, due to the difference in speeds, they will emerge from the crystal out of phase. The wave difference between $\phi_E - \phi_O = \dfrac{2\pi t}{\lambda}(n_E - n_O)$. It should be noted that if $n_E < n_O$, then $\phi_E < \phi_O$. If the thickness of the plate is such that the phase difference is $\pi/2$, the crystal plate is called a quarterwave plate.

Huygens' principle. Every point of a wave front may be considered as the source of secondary wavelets, which spread out in all directions with a speed equal to the speed of propagation of the wave. The envelope, i.e. the surface tangent to the wavelets is the new wave.

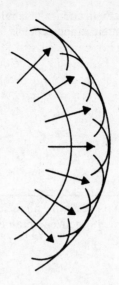

Problem solving strategy:

1 Refraction of light:

$$n_a \sin \phi_a = n_b \sin \phi_b \text{ (Snell's law)},$$
$$n_a v_a = n_b v_b,$$
$$\lambda_a n_a = \lambda_b n_b,$$
$$n = \frac{c}{v},$$

where v = speed of light in a material,

$$\lambda = \frac{\lambda_0}{n},$$

where λ = wavelength of light in a material, λ_0 = wavelength of light in a vacuum,

$$\sin \phi_{crit} = \frac{n_b}{n_a}.$$

When a light wave passes from one medium to another, the wavelength changes but not the frequency.

2 Polarization of light: When polarized light is incident upon an analyzer, the transmission intensity is given by $I = I_{max} \cos^2\theta$, where I_{max} is the maximum amount of light transmitted and I is the amount transmitted at angle θ. Remember the special case of polarization by reflection. In the case when the reflected and refracted rays are perpendicular to each other, $\tan \phi_p = \frac{n'}{n}$, where light is medium of index n is reflected by a surface of index n' and ϕ_p = polarizing angle.

PROGRAMMED QUIZ

1 The wavelength of green light is 525 nm. What is this in angstroms? in meters?

1

$$(525 \text{ nm}) \left(\frac{10^{-9} \text{ m}}{1 \text{ nm}} \right) = 5.25 \times 10^{-7} \text{ m}$$

$$(5.25 \times 10^{-7} \text{ m}) \left(\frac{1 \text{ Å}}{10^{-10} \text{ m}} \right) = 5250 \text{ Å}$$

---

2 What is the frequency of this light?

2

$$c = f\lambda$$
$$f = \frac{3 \times 10^8 \text{ m}}{5.25 \times 10^{-7} \text{ m} \cdot \text{s}^{-1}}$$
$$= 5.71 \times 10^{14} \text{ Hz}$$

---

3 A ray of light strikes a mirror at an angle of 40° with the surface. What is the angle of reflection?

3 The angle of incidence is 50° (remember that it is always measured with the normal). Since $\phi_r = \phi_a$, the angle of reflection is also 50°.

---

4 Light goes from benzene ($n = 1.50$) into diamond ($n = 2.42$). If the angle of incidence is 65°, what is the angle of refraction?

4

$$n_a \sin \phi_a = n_b \sin \phi_b$$
$$(1.5) \sin 65° = (2.42) \sin \phi_b$$
$$\phi_b = 34.2°$$

---

5 Draw a diagram representing an incident, reflected and refracted ray at the benzene-diamond interface.

5

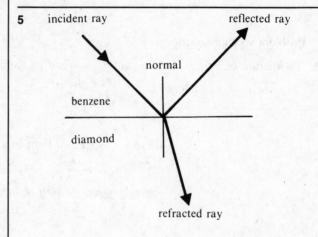

---

6 What is the speed of light in diamond?

6

$$n = \frac{c}{v}$$
$$v = \frac{3 \times 10^8 \ \mathrm{m \cdot s^{-1}}}{2.42}$$
$$= 1.24 \times 10^8 \ \mathrm{m \cdot s^{-1}}$$

---

7 What is the critical angle for a quartz ($n = 1.54$) − water ($n = 1.33$) interface?

7

$$\sin \phi_{\mathrm{crit}} = \frac{n_b}{n_a}$$
$$= \frac{1.33}{1.54}$$
$$\phi_{\mathrm{crit}} = 59.7°$$

---

8 What happens if light is incident on the water at an angle of 62°?

8 Since the angle of incidence is greater than the critical angle, the ray gets totally reflected back into the quartz.

---

9 What should be the angle of incidence ϕ for glass ($n = 1.6$) for the angle of refraction to be $\phi/2$? Remember that

$$\sin \phi/2 = \sqrt{\frac{1 - \cos \phi}{2}} \text{ and}$$
$$\sin^2 \phi + \cos^2 \phi = 1.$$

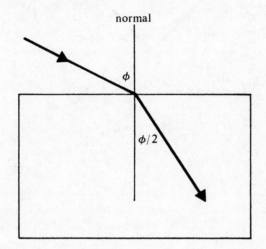

10 What is the wavelength of light in ice ($n = 1.31$) if the wavelength is 455 nm in vacuum?

11 Find the critical angle for a water-air surface.

9

$$n_a \sin \phi_a = n_b \sin \phi_b$$
$$(1) \sin \phi = (1.6) \sin \phi/2$$
$$\sin \phi = (1.6) \sqrt{\frac{1 - \cos \phi}{2}}$$
$$\sin^2 \phi = 2.56 \frac{(1 - \cos \phi)}{2}$$
$$1 - \cos^2 \phi = 1.28(1 - \cos \phi)$$
$$(1 + \cos \phi)(1 - \cos \phi) = 1.28(1 - \cos \phi)$$
$$1 + \cos \phi = 1.28$$
$$\cos \phi = 0.28$$
$$\phi = 73.7°$$

10

$$\lambda_a = \frac{\lambda_0}{n_a}$$
$$= \frac{455 \text{ nm}}{1.31}$$
$$= 347 \text{ nm}$$

11

$$\sin \phi_{crit} = \frac{n_a}{n_b}$$
$$= \frac{1}{1.333}$$
$$\phi_{crit} = 48.6°$$

12 A point source of light is 0.25 m below the surface of a lake. What is the radius of the largest circle at the surface through which light can emerge from the water?

12

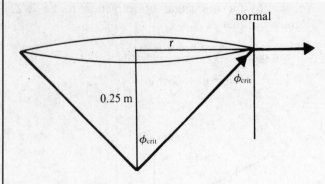

$$\tan 48.6° = \frac{r}{0.25 \text{ m}}$$
$$r = 0.284 \text{ m}$$

13 The critical angle for a glass-air surface is 42°. Trace the path of the light ray in the glass prism.

13

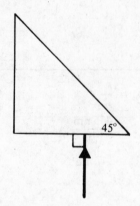

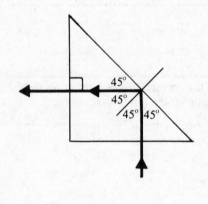

14 Trace the path of a light ray through a window pane ($n = 1.50$). The angle of incidence is 50°.

14

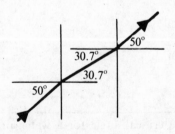

$$n_a \sin \phi_a = n_b \sin \phi_b$$
$$(1) \sin 50° = (1.50) \sin \phi_b$$
$$\phi_b = 30.7°$$

Note: the emerging ray is parallel to the incident ray.

15 Light is incident upon a reflecting surface with the angle of incidence equal to the polarizing angle ϕ_p. Prove that the reflected and refracted rays are perpendicular to each other, $\phi_1 + \phi_2 = 90°$.

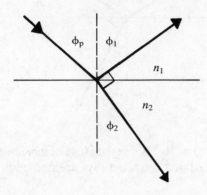

15 From Brewster's law,

$$\tan \phi_p = \frac{n_2}{n_1}$$

$$\frac{\sin \phi_p}{\cos \phi_p} = \frac{n_2}{n_1}$$

$$n_1 \sin \phi_p = n_2 \cos \phi_p$$

From Snell's law,

$$n_1 \sin \phi_p = n_2 \sin \phi_2$$

Therefore,

$$n_2 \sin \phi_2 = n_2 \cos \phi_p$$

$$\sin \phi_2 = \cos \phi_p$$

But $\phi_p = \phi_1$ from the law of reflection; therefore $\sin \phi_2 = \cos \phi_1$.

This means that ϕ_2 and ϕ_1 are complementary angles.

$$\phi_1 + \phi_2 = 90°$$

16 Unpolarized light of intensity I_0 is incident on a polarizing filter. With what intensity does it emerge from the polarizer?

16 $I_0/2$

17 What is the intensity of the beam if it passes through a second polarizer with its axis at 35° to that of the first? Remember when unpolarized light is incident on a polarizer, one-half of the incident intensity is transmitted.

17

$$I = I_{max} \cos^2 \theta$$

$$= \frac{I_0}{2} \cos^2 35°$$

$$= 0.336 \, I_0$$

18 Light is incident from air on water ($n = 1.33$). What must be the angle of incidence for the reflected rays to be completely polarized?

18 For light to be completely polarized, the incident angle must equal the polarizing angle.

$$\tan \phi_p = \frac{n'}{n} = \frac{1.33}{1}$$

$$\phi_p = 53.1°$$

19 What must be the angle of refraction for the above?

19

$$n \sin \phi = n' \sin \phi'$$

$$(1) \sin 53.1° = 1.33 \sin \phi'$$

$$\phi' = 36.9°$$

Note: 53.1° + 36.9° = 90.0°.

If the reflected ray is completely polarized, the reflected and refracted rays are perpendicular to each other.

20 A beam of light is incident at an angle of 60° on a plane glass surface. If the reflected beam is completely polarized, what is the angle of refraction of the transmitted beam? Draw a diagram.

20

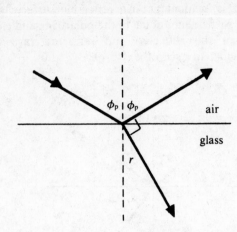

If $\phi_p = 60°$, $r = 30°$. When the angle of incidence $= \phi_p$, the reflected and refracted rays are perpendicular to each other.

---

21 For what incident angle is light reflected from a plane glass surface ($n = 1.60$) completely polarized if the glass is immersed in water?

21

$$\tan \phi_p = \frac{n'}{n}$$
$$= \frac{1.60}{1.33}$$
$$\phi_p = 50.3°$$

---

22 Depending on the way a stack of polarizing filters is arranged, the intensity of the emerging beam may vary from 50% to 20%. What is the percent polarization?

22

$$\% \text{ polarization} = \frac{I_{max} - I_{min}}{I_{max} + I_{min}} \times 100\%$$
$$= \frac{0.50 \, I_0 - 0.20 \, I_0}{0.50 \, I_0 + 0.20 \, I_0} \times 100\%$$
$$= 42.9\%$$

---

23 What is the angle between two polarizers if the intensity of light emerging from the second is 80% of the intensity of light emerging from the first filter?

23

$$I = I_{max} \cos^2 \theta$$
$$0.80 \, I = I \cos^2 \theta$$
$$\cos^2 \theta = 0.80$$
$$\cos \theta = 0.894$$
$$\theta = 26.6°$$

---

24 The polarizing angle for light incident on glass ($n = 1.65$) is 50°. What is the index of refraction of the incident medium?

24

$$\tan \phi_p = \frac{n'}{n}$$
$$n = \frac{1.65}{\tan 50°}$$
$$= 1.38$$

---

25 A parallel beam of linearly polarized light of wavelength 589 nm is incident on a quartz crystal. What are the wavelengths of the ordinary and extra-ordinary waves in the crystal?

$n_E = 1.553$
$n_0 = 1.544$

25

$$\lambda_E = \frac{\lambda}{n_E} = \frac{589 \text{ nm}}{1.553} = 379 \text{ nm}$$

$$\lambda_O = \frac{\lambda}{n_O} = \frac{589 \text{ nm}}{1.544} = 381 \text{ nm}$$

STEP BY STEP SOLUTIONS OF PROBLEMS

Problem 1 A ray of light is incident on a surface of a 90° prism and emerges at the second surface such that the angle of refraction is 90°. Derive the expression for the index of refraction of the prism in terms of the angle of incidence.

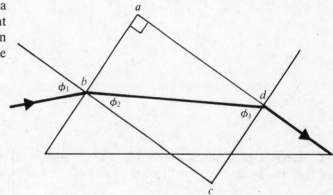

1 Apply Snell's law at d.

1

$$n = \frac{\sin 90°}{\sin \phi_3}$$
$$= \frac{1}{\sin \phi_3}$$

2 Express ϕ_3 in terms of ϕ_2 (triangle bcd is a right triangle).

2

$$\phi_3 = 90° - \phi_2$$
$$\sin \phi_3 = \cos \phi_2$$
$$n \cos \phi_2 = 1$$

3 Express $\cos \phi_2$ in terms of $\sin \phi_2$. Use the identity $\sin^2 \phi_2 + \cos^2 \phi_2 = 1$.

3 $n\sqrt{1 - \sin^2 \phi_2} = 1$

4 Apply Snell's law at b. What is the value of $\sin \phi_2$?

4

$$\frac{\sin \phi_1}{\sin \phi_2} = n$$
$$\sin \phi_2 = \frac{\sin \phi_1}{n}$$

5 Eliminate $\sin \phi_2$ from frames 3 and 4 and solve for n.

5

$$n\sqrt{1 - \frac{\sin^2 \phi_1}{n^2}} = 1$$

$$n\sqrt{\frac{n^2 - \sin^2 \phi_1}{n^2}} = 1$$

$$n = (1 + \sin^2 \phi_1)^{1/2}$$

Problem 2 Light passes through a transparent plate as in the figure. If the surfaces of the plate are plane and parallel to each other, a) derive an expression for the lateral displacement d of the emergent beam. b) If $t = 4$ cm, $\phi_a = 55°$ and the index of refraction $n = 1.6$, find d. c) Prove that for small angles of incidence,

$$d = t\phi_a \left(\frac{n-1}{n} \right).$$

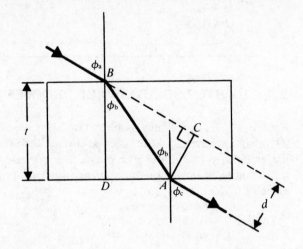

6 Draw a perpendicular line AC to the extension BC of the incident ray and find the value of $\angle ABC$.

6 $\angle ABC = \phi_a - \phi_b$, since $\phi_a = \phi_b + \angle ABC$ (vertical angles are equal to each other).

7 Solve right triangle ABC for AC (which is equal to d).

7 $$d = AB \sin (\phi_a - \phi_b)$$

8 Solve right triangle ABD for BD (which is equal to t) and substitute in the above.

8
$$BD = AB \cos \phi_b$$
$$AB = t/\cos \phi_b$$
$$d = \frac{t \sin (\phi_a - \phi_b)}{\cos \phi_b}$$

9 In order to find d for the given set of data, we must first obtain ϕ_b by using Snell's law.

9
$$\frac{\sin 55°}{\sin \phi_b} = 1.6$$
$$\phi_b = 30.8°$$

10 Substitute the given data and $\phi_b = 30.8°$ in the expression for d.

10
$$d = \frac{(4 \text{ cm}) \sin (60° - 30.8°)}{\cos 30.8°}$$
$$= 2.27 \text{ cm}$$

11 For small angles, $\sin \phi \approx \phi$, where ϕ is expressed in radians. Rewrite Snell's law in terms of small angles.

11
$$\frac{\sin \phi_a}{\sin \phi_b} = n; \quad \frac{\phi_a}{\phi_b} = n$$
Solve for ϕ_b
$$\phi_b = \frac{\phi_a}{n}$$

12 Rewrite the expression for d in terms of angular equivalents. Note, if ϕ_a is small, so is ϕ_b. Therefore $\cos \phi_b \approx 1$. Also,
$$\sin (\phi_a - \phi_b) = \sin \phi_a \cos \phi_b - \cos \phi_a \sin \phi_b$$
$$= (\phi_a) (1) - (1) (\phi_b) = \phi_a - \phi_b.$$

12
$$d = \frac{t \sin (\phi_a - \phi_b)}{\cos \phi_b} = \frac{t(\phi_a - \phi_b)}{1}$$
Substitute $\phi_b = \frac{\phi_a}{n}$
$$d = t\left(\phi_a - \frac{\phi_a}{n} \right)$$
$$= t\phi_a \left(\frac{n - 1}{n} \right)$$

Problem 3 A light ray is incident at an angle ϕ on one side of a prism with apex angle A and is parallel to the base as it passes through the prism. If it emerges at an angle of refraction ϕ, derive an expression for the index of refraction of the prism in terms of the apex angle and the angle of deviation δ. (Note that the light ray passes symmetrically through the prism.)

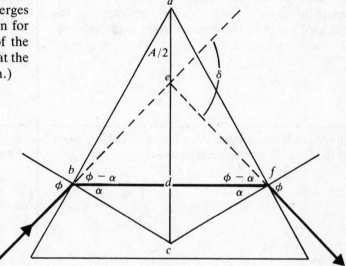

13 Find the value of the angle of refraction α in terms of A.

13 Since $\angle bad$ and $\angle cbd$ are complementary to $\angle dba$, $\alpha = A/2$.

14 Express the angle of deviation δ in terms of ϕ and α.

14 $\delta = 2(\phi - \alpha)$. The exterior angle of a triangle is equal to the sum of the two remote interior angles.

15 Substitute $\alpha = A/2$ in the expression for δ and solve for ϕ.

15
$$\delta = 2(\phi - A/2) = 2\phi - A$$
$$\phi = \tfrac{1}{2}(A + \delta)$$

16 Use Snell's law to relate ϕ and α.

16
$$n = \frac{\sin \phi}{\sin \alpha}$$

17 Combine frames 14, 15 and 16 to express n in terms of A and δ.

17

$$n = \frac{\sin\left(\dfrac{A + \delta}{2}\right)}{\sin\dfrac{A}{2}}$$

Problem 4 a) Show that the phase difference $\delta = \phi_O - \phi_E$ between the O- and E- rays emerging from a birefringent crystal is given by $\delta = \dfrac{2\pi t}{\lambda}(n_O - n_E)$, where t = crystal thickness in the direction of propagation, n_O the index for the ordinary ray, n_E the index for the extraordinary ray and λ the wavelength in vacuum. b) Show that the minimum thickness for a quarter-wave plate is given by $t = \lambda/4|n_O - n_E|$. c) Compute the minimum thickness for a quarter-wave quartz plate, $n_O = 1.544$, $n_E = 1.553$, $\lambda = 600$ nm.

---

18 What is the relationship between λ, the wavelength in vacuum, and λ_O, the wavelength of the ordinary waves in the crystal? What is the relationship between λ_O and λ_E?

18

$$\lambda_O = \frac{\lambda}{n_O}$$

$$\lambda_E = \frac{\lambda}{n_E}$$

---

19 What is the number of ordinary waves in a plate of thickness t? extraordinary waves?

19 Number of ordinary waves:

$$\frac{t}{\lambda_O} = \frac{tn_O}{\lambda}$$

number of extraordinary waves:

$$\frac{t}{\lambda_E} = \frac{tn_E}{\lambda}$$

---

20 The difference between tn_O/λ and tn_E/λ represents the difference in the number of waves between the two rays as they emerge from the plate (the wavetrains were in phase prior to entering the crystal).

20

$$\delta = \phi_O - \phi_E = \frac{2\pi t}{\lambda}(n_O - n_E)$$

$$\text{or } \delta = \phi_E - \phi_O = \frac{2\pi t}{\lambda}(n_E - n_O).$$

---

21 Since each wave indicates a phase angle of 2π radians, what is the phase difference between the emergent waves?

21

$$\phi_O - \phi_E = \frac{\pi}{2}$$

---

22 Determine the minimum thickness for the quarter-wave plate.

22

$$\frac{\pi}{2} = \frac{2\pi t}{\lambda}(n_O - n_E)$$

$$t = \frac{\lambda}{4(n_O - n_E)}$$

Note: since $(\phi_O - \phi_E)$ and $(n_O - n_E)$ have the same algebraic sign, the thickness should be represented by

$$t = \frac{\lambda}{4|\,n_O - n_E\,|}$$

23 Compute the minimum thickness for a quarter-wave quartz plate.

23

$$t = \frac{600 \text{ nm}}{4|\,1.544 - 1.553\,|}$$
$$= 0.0167 \times 10^{-3} \text{ m} = 0.0167 \text{ mm}$$

PROGRAMMED TEST

1 *Problem 1* A light ray is transmitted through parallel plates of two different media having indices of refraction $n_a = 1.7$ and $n_b = 1.3$. a) If the angle of incidence on the first plate is 60°, what is ϕ_b? b) Find the angle at which the light emerges from the second plate into air.

1

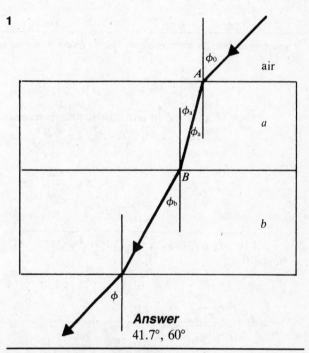

Answer
41.7°, 60°

If you solved this problem correctly, go to frame 5. If you could not solve this problem, go through frames 2–4.

2 Apply Snell's law at point A.

2
$$n_0 \sin \phi_0 = n_a \sin \phi_a$$
$$(1) \sin 60° = 1.7 \sin \phi_a$$
$$\phi_a = 30.6°$$

3 Apply Snell's law at point B.

3
$$n_a \sin \phi_a = n_b \sin \phi_b$$
$$1.7 \sin 30.6° = 1.3 \sin \phi_b$$
$$\phi_b = 41.7°$$

4 What is the angle of refraction ϕ as the light ray emerges from the second plate into air?

4 Reversing our steps we have:
$$(1) \sin \phi = 1.3 \sin \phi_b = 1.7 \sin \phi_a = (1) \sin 60°.$$
$$\therefore \phi = 60°$$

5 **Problem 2** Derive an expression for the time required for a light ray to go from a point A in a medium where the velocity of light is v_a to a point B where the velocity of light is v_b.

5

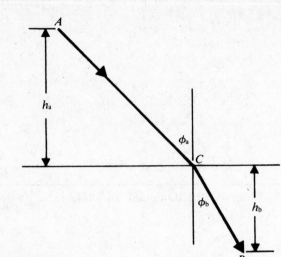

Answer

$$t = \frac{h_a}{v_a \cos \phi_a} + \frac{h_b}{v_b \cos \phi_b}$$

If you solved this problem correctly, go to frame 9. If you could not solve this problem, go through frames 6-8.

---

6 Express AC and CB in terms of h_a and h_b respectively.

6

$$h_a = AC \cos \phi_a, \quad AC = \frac{h_a}{\cos \phi_a}$$

$$h_b = BC \cos \phi_b, \quad BC = \frac{h_b}{\cos \phi_b}$$

---

7 Find the time t_a for the ray to travel distance AC. Repeat for t_b.

7

$$t_a = \frac{h_a}{v_a \cos \phi_a}$$

$$t_b = \frac{h_b}{v_b \cos \phi_b}$$

---

8 Find the total time t by adding t_a and t_b.

8

$$t = \frac{h_a}{v_a \cos \phi_a} + \frac{h_b}{v_b \cos \phi_b}$$

---

9 Interesting note: How many paths can a light ray take in order to go from A to B?

9 In accordance with Fermat's principle of minimum time there is only one path, and this results in Snell's law.

$$v_a n_a = v_b n_b;$$

$$n_a \sin \phi_a = n_b \sin \phi_b$$

10 **Problem 3** The reflecting surfaces of two plane mirrors make an angle θ. A light ray is incident on one of the surfaces at an angle α, traverses the paths $EDBC$ and is reflected on itself. What is α in terms of θ?

10

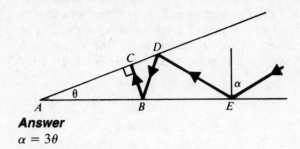

Answer
$\alpha = 3\theta$

If you solved this problem correctly, go to frame 19. If you could not solve this problem, go through frames 11–18.

---

11 Since the light ray is reflected on itself at C, $BC \perp AD$. What is $\angle ABC$?

11 $90° - \theta$

---

12 Therefore, what are the angles of incidence and reflection at B?

12 θ, θ

---

13 What is $\angle DBE$?

13 $90° - \theta$

---

14 BCD is a right triangle; $\angle CBD$ is 2θ, what is $\angle CDB$?

14 $90° - 2\theta$

---

15 What are the angles of incidence and reflection at D?

15 $2\theta, 2\theta$

---

16 What is $\angle DEB$?

16 $90° - \alpha$

---

17 What is the sum of the angles of triangle BDE?

17 $90° - \theta + 2\theta + 2\theta + 90° - \alpha = 180°$

---

18 Solve for α.

18

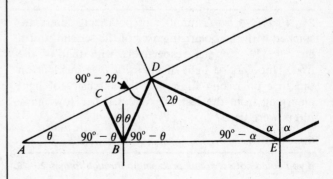

$\alpha = 3\theta$

---

19 **Problem 4** A light ray is incident on a glycerine surface of 1.473 refractive index. The reflected ray A is completely linearly polarized. a) What is the angle of incidence (polarizing angle) ϕ_p? b) A block of glass 1.65 refractive index having a flat upper surface is immersed in the glycerine as in the figure such that ray B is also completely linearly polarized. Find angle α.

19

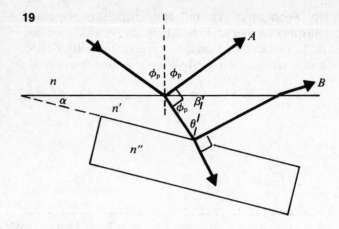

Answer
55.8°, 14°

If you solved this problem correctly, go to frame 21. If you could not solve this problem, go through frames 20–23.

20 Denote the indices of air, glycerine and glass as n, n' and n'' respectively. Find ϕ_p by Brewster's law.

20
$$\tan \phi_p = \frac{n'}{n} = \frac{1.473}{1}$$
$$\phi_p = 55.8°$$
Note that the angle between the refracted ray and the surface of the glycerine is $\phi_p = 55.8°$.

---

21 Since ray B is polarized, find θ by Brewster's law.

21
$$\tan \theta = \frac{n''}{n'} = \frac{1.65}{1.473}$$
$$\theta = 48.2°$$

---

22 Find β.

22
Since $\phi_p + \theta + \beta = 180°$
$$\beta = 180° - 55.8° - 48.2° = 76°$$

---

23 Find α.

23 Since α is the complement of β,
$\alpha = 90° - 76° = 14°$.

---

24 **Problem 5** A number of polarizing filters are stacked with the polarizing axes of the second, third, etc. at 15°, 30° etc. respectively with that of the first. Unpolarized light of intensity I_0 is incident on the first polarizing filter and the intensity of light emerging from the last one is 0.330 I_0. How many filters were used?

24 **Answer**
7

If you could not solve this problem go through frames 25–29.

25 What is the intensity of light transmitted by the first polarizer?

25 $\frac{1}{2}I_0$

26 What is the intensity transmitted by the second polarizer?

26

$$\tfrac{1}{2}I_0 \cos^2 15° = \tfrac{1}{2}I_0(0.9330)$$

---

27 What is the intensity transmitted by the third polarizer?

27

$$\tfrac{1}{2}I_0(\cos^2 15°)(\cos^2 15°)$$
$$= \tfrac{1}{2}I_0(\cos^2 15°)^2$$

---

28 Generalize. What is the intensity transmitted by n polarizers?

28 $\tfrac{1}{2}I_0(\cos^2 15°)^{n-1}$

---

29 Equate this intensity to $0.330\ I_0$ and solve for n. Take logarithms of both sides.

29

$$\tfrac{1}{2}I_0(\cos^2 15°)^{n-1} = 0.330\ I_0$$
$$\tfrac{1}{2}I_0(0.9330)^{n-1} = 0.330\ I_0$$
$$0.933^{n-1} = 0.660$$
$$(n-1)\ln 0.933 = \ln 0.660$$
$$(n-1)(-0.0694) = -0.415$$
$$n - 1 = 5.99$$
$$n = 6.99 \approx 7$$

37

Images Formed by a Single Surface

CHAPTER SUMMARY

The mathematical expressions for reflection and refraction from plane and spherical surfaces are developed in this chapter, as well as the relationships for lateral and longitudinal magnification. Real and virtual images are defined and the graphical methods of finding them using the principal ray diagrams are described.

BASIC TERMS — *Give definitions or meanings for the following:*

object (37-1)
image (37-1)
real image (37-1)
virtual image (37-1)
mirror (37-1)
lateral magnification (37-1)
erect image (37-1)
inverted image (37-1)
reversed image (37-1)

paraxial rays (37-2)
center of curvature (37-2)
spherical aberration (37-2)
optic axis (37-2)
paraxial approximation (37-2)
vertex (37-2)
focal length (37-3)
focus (37-3)
principal ray (37-4)

PROGRAMMED QUIZ

1 When is the object distance positive?

1 When the direction from the object to the reflecting or refracting surface is the same as that of the incident light.

2 When is the image distance positive?

2 When the direction from the reflecting or refracting surface to the image point is the same as that of the reflected or refracted light.

3 Is the image distance for a real image formed by mirrors positive or negative?

3 Positive; the direction from the mirror to the real image point is the same as the direction of the reflected light.

4 Label all distances. Be sure to include the signs. P is the object point, P' the image point and C the center of curvature of the mirror.

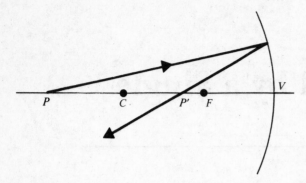

4

$$PV = +s \quad \text{object distance}$$
$$P'V = +s' \quad \text{image distance}$$
$$CV = +R \quad \text{radius of curvature}$$
$$FV = +f \quad \text{focal length}$$

---

5 What happens as incident rays become less paraxial?

5 The image point moves closer to the vertex and there is no longer a point image of a point object.

---

6 Describe the image when the height of an object is comparable to the object distance. What is this aberration called?

6 The image will be curved; curvature of field.

---

7 What does the negative sign in the equation of lateral magnification indicate?

7 A negative value of magnification indicates that the image is inverted relative to the object.

---

8 Does magnification mean that the image is always larger than the object? Does a positive magnification mean that the image is larger than the object?

8 Not necessarily; if $m < 1$, the image is smaller. No, it means that the image is erect.

---

9 What are the two ways in which the focal point of a mirror may be considered?

9 As the image point of an infinitely distant object point on the axis or as the object point of an infinitely distant image point.

---

10 You are looking at an object submerged in a medium of $n > 1$. How does the object appear to you?

10 Same size but closer than it actually is.

---

11 How can we find the focus of a refracting surface?

11 There are two focal points: One is the object point when the image is at infinity ($s' = \infty$), the other is the image point when the object is at infinity ($s = \infty$).

---

12 The plane mirror is a special case of a spherical mirror. Explain this.

12 The plane mirror can be considered a spherical mirror with a radius $r = \infty$.

---

13 Describe the image in a plane mirror.

13 Virtual, same size, erect, perverted (left-right reversed).

---

14 Real images formed by a single surface are erect or inverted? virtual images?

14 Inverted; erect.

---

15 Indicate whether the quantity is + or −.

	concave mirror	convex mirror
object distance s		
image distance s'		
lateral magnification m		
focal length f		

15

	concave mirror	convex mirror
object distance s	+	+
image distance s'	+ for real, − for virtual images	−
lateral magnification m	+ for virtual, − for real images	+
focal length f	+	−

MAIN IDEAS

This chapter is concerned with the analysis of the paths of two or more rays that diverge from a common point and are either reflected or refracted by a plane or spherical surface.

Rays 1 and 2 diverge from P. Ray 1 is normal to the plane reflecting surface and rebounds on itself. Ray 2 strikes the surface at an angle ϕ and is reflected as ray 3. When the reflected rays are extended backwards, they intersect at point P', denoted as the image of P. Thus P' is a virtual image. Plane mirrors produce virtual images. Whereas light rays actually pass through real image points, light rays seem to diverge from virtual image points. The distance s is called the object distance, s' the image distance. An object distance s is considered to be + if the distance from the object to the reflecting or refracting surface is the same as the direction of the incident rays. Thus all real objects have a positive object distance. An image distance s' is considered to be + if the direction from the re-

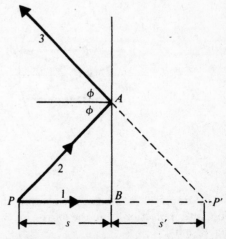

IMAGES FORMED BY A SINGLE SURFACE 615

flecting or refracting surface to the image point is the
same direction as that of the rays which are reflected or
refracted from the surface. Thus a real image has a
positive image distance and a virtual image has a negative image distance.

Lateral magnification is defined as $m = y'/y$ where y and y' represent the lengths of the object and image respectively. For a plane mirror, $m = 1$. Since $s' = -s$ for a plane mirror, $m' = -1$, which means that the plane mirror
forms a perverted image (left-right reversed).

In the spherical surfaces depicted, C is the center of curvature, R is the radius of curvature, V the vertex, PCV the
principal axis for the concave mirror, PVC the principal axis for the convex mirror and P' is the image of P. The
radius of curvature is $+$ if the direction from a reflecting or refracting surface to the center of curvature is the same
as that of the reflected or refracted ray. Therefore R is $+$ for a concave spherical mirror and $-$ for a convex spherical
mirror. The distances s and s' are $+$ for real objects and images and $-$ for virtual objects and images. Rays that are
nearly parallel with the principal axis are called paraxial rays. For paraxial rays, R, s and s' are related by
$1/s + 1/s' = 2/R$.

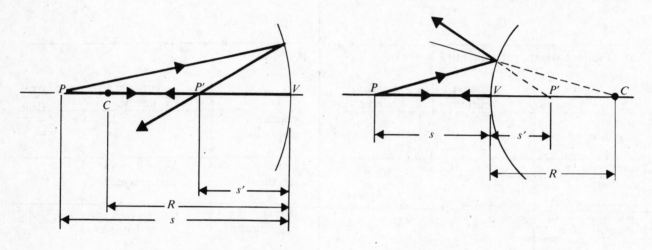

The lateral magnification of a spherical mirror is $m = y'/y = -s'/s$. The significance of the negative sign is
that the object and image are on opposite sides of the optic axis. A negative value of m indicates that the image is
inverted relative to the object.

Incident rays which are parallel to the axis converge to the focus F of a concave mirror and diverge as though
coming from the focus F of a convex mirror.

The graphical method of determining the position and size of the image consists of finding the point of intersection, after reflection from the mirror, of two particular rays diverging from the same point on the object (not on the
mirror axis):

A ray parallel to the axis strikes the surface and is reflected through the focus of a concave mirror, or it diverges as though coming from the focus of a convex mirror.

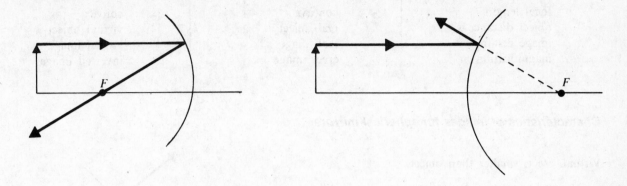

A ray passing through the focus of a concave mirror is reflected parallel to the axis. A ray proceeding toward the focus (the incident ray is extended) of a convex mirror is reflected parallel to the axis.

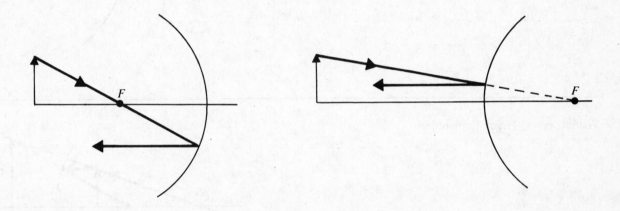

A ray passing through the center of curvature (normal to the surface) of a concave mirror is reflected back on itself. For a convex mirror, the ray is normal to the surface and the extended incident ray passes through the center of curvature.

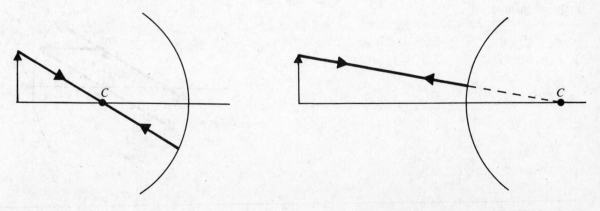

QUANTITY	POSITIVE	NEGATIVE
focal length f	concave	convex
object distance s	real object	virtual object
image distance s'	real image	virtual image
magnification m	erect image	inverted image

Characteristics of images for spherical mirrors

Virtual, erect, smaller than object.

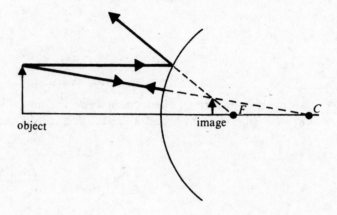

Virtual, erect, larger than object.

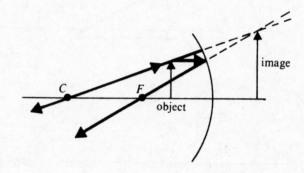

Image at infinity.

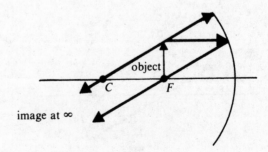

Real, inverted, larger than object.

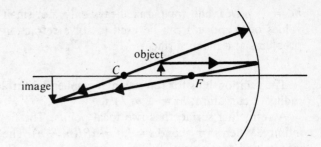

Real, inverted, same size as object.

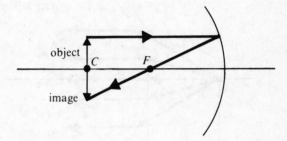

Real, inverted, smaller than object.

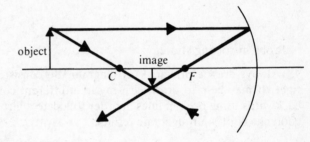

Real, inverted, smaller than object.

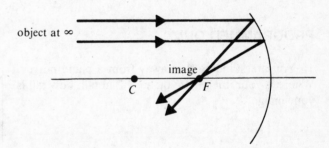

The procedure for finding the image of a point object formed by rays refracted at a plane surface is the same as for reflection — except that we use Snell's law instead of the law of reflection. Rays 1 and 2 diverge from P. Ray 1 is incident normally and passes through the second medium without deviation. Ray 2 is refracted towards the normal and its extension passes through P'. The two rays appear to diverge from P' after refraction. The image distance s' is negative because the distance from the refracting surface to the image point is opposite to the direction of the rays which were refracted from the surface. Snell's law, $n \sin \phi = n' \sin \phi'$ and $s'/s = -n'/n$, $m = 1$ and

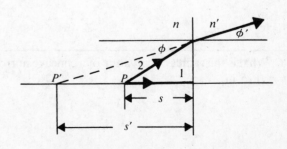

$m' = -n'/n$ (valid for paraxial rays only, i.e. small values of ϕ and ϕ') can be used to solve refraction problems at a plane surface.

The relationships for refraction at a spherical surface are given by $n/s + n'/s' = (n' - n)/R$, where R is the radius of curvature; $m = -ns'/n's$.

A refracting surface has two focal points. The first denoted by F is the object point when the image is at infinity. When $s' = \infty$ and $s = f$, $f = nR/(n' - n)$. The second focal point denoted by F' is the image point of an infinitely distant object. When $s = \infty$ and $s' = f'$, $f' = n'R/(n' - n)$.

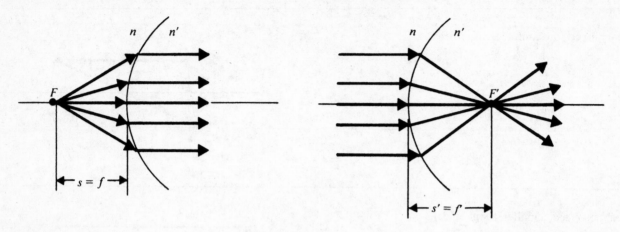

Problem solving strategy:

1 Always draw a principal ray diagram. Be consistent: Always have the incoming ray traveling from left to right. It may help to draw each ray in a different color. If your principal rays do not converge, extend them backwards using broken lines in order to locate a virtual image point. A diagram drawn to scale will serve as a good check of your algebraic results.

2 Follow the sign rules for reflection and refraction. Remember that a negative value of m indicates that the image is inverted relative to the object.

PROGRAMMED QUIZ

1 You are standing 2 m away from a plane mirror. Where is your image? If you are 1.7 m tall, how tall is your image?

1

$s = -s'$, 2 m behind the mirror.

$m = \dfrac{y'}{y}$. For a plane mirror, $m = +1$.

$y' = 1.7$ m

2 You are walking to the right — toward the mirror. What about your image?

2 The image is moving to the left — toward the mirror.

3 What is the radius of curvature of a concave mirror, $f = 0.25$ m?

3

$f = \dfrac{R}{2}$

$R = 2(0.25 \text{ m}) = 0.50 \text{ m}$

4 An object 0.05 m high is located 0.10 m from a concave spherical mirror, $R = 0.50$ m. Where is the image located?

4

$$\frac{2}{R} = \frac{1}{s} + \frac{1}{s'}$$

$$\frac{1}{s'} = \frac{2}{0.50 \text{ m}} - \frac{1}{0.10 \text{ m}}$$

$$s' = -0.167 \text{ m}$$

---

5 What is the lateral magnification?

5

$$m = \frac{-s'}{s}$$

$$= -\frac{-0.167 \text{ m}}{0.1 \text{ m}}$$

$$= 1.67$$

---

6 What is the image size?

6

$$m = \frac{y'}{y}$$

$$y = 1.67(0.05 \text{ m})$$

$$= 0.0835 \text{ m}$$

---

7 Draw a ray diagram for frame 4.

7

---

8 Find the focal length of a convex mirror if an object 0.30 m from the mirror forms an image 0.10 m behind the mirror.

8 The image formed by a convex mirror is always virtual; therefore s' is negative.

$$\frac{1}{f} = \frac{1}{s} + \frac{1}{s'} = \frac{1}{0.30 \text{ m}} - \frac{1}{0.10 \text{ m}}$$

$$f = -0.15 \text{ m}$$

Note: the focal length of a convex mirror is always negative.

9 You are looking straight down at a fish in a lake ($n = 1.333$). The fish is 1.2 m below the surface. Where does the fish appear to be?

9

$$\frac{s'}{s} = \frac{-n'}{n}$$

$$s' = -\frac{1}{1.333} \, (1.2 \text{ m})$$

$$= -0.90 \text{ m}$$

The fish appears to be closer to the surface than it actually is.

---

10 The end of a long solid glass ($n = 1.5$) rod is ground and polished to a hemispherical surface of radius 2 cm. A small object is placed on the axis 8 cm to the left of the vertex. Find the position of the image.

10

$$\frac{n}{s} + \frac{n'}{s'} = \frac{n' - n}{R}$$

$$\frac{1}{8 \text{ cm}} + \frac{1.5}{s'} = \frac{1.5 - 1}{2 \text{ cm}}$$

$$s' = 12 \text{ cm}$$

A real image is formed in the glass rod 12 cm to the right of the vertex.

---

11 The rod is immersed in a liquid and the image of the same object appears 24 cm to the right of the vertex. What is the index of refraction of the liquid?

11

$$\frac{n}{s} + \frac{n'}{s'} = \frac{n' - n}{R}$$

$$\frac{n}{8 \text{ cm}} + \frac{1.5}{24 \text{ cm}} = \frac{1.5 - n}{2 \text{ cm}}$$

Multiply each term by 24 cm.

$$3n + 1.5 = 12(1.5 - n)$$

$$n = 1.1$$

---

12 Paraxial light rays from an infinitely distant object are brought to a focus at the vertex of a surface of a sphere opposite from the point of incidence. What is the index of refraction n' of the sphere? Note: $s = \infty$, $s' = 2R$, $n = 1$.

12

$$\frac{n}{s} + \frac{n'}{s'} = \frac{n' - n}{R}$$

$$\frac{1}{\infty} + \frac{n'}{2R} = \frac{n' - 1}{R}$$

$$n' = 2$$

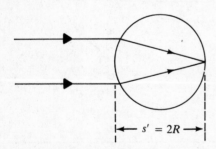

---

13 Find the first focal length of a solid glass hemisphere which has a radius of 5 cm and $n = 1.5$.

13 The first focal length $f = s$ where $s' = \infty$.

$$\frac{n}{s} + \frac{n'}{s'} = \frac{n' - n}{R}$$

$$\frac{1}{f} + \frac{1.5}{\infty} = \frac{1.5 - 1}{5 \text{ cm}}$$

$$f = 10 \text{ cm}$$

14 Find the second focal length of the same rod.

14 The second focal length $f' = s'$ when $s = \infty$.

$$\frac{n}{s} + \frac{n'}{s'} = \frac{n' - n}{R}$$

$$\frac{1}{\infty} + \frac{1.5}{f'} = \frac{1.5 - 1}{5 \text{ cm}}$$

$$f' = 15 \text{ cm}$$

STEP BY STEP SOLUTIONS OF PROBLEMS

Problem 1 One end of a transparent 48 cm long rod is flat and the other end has a hemispherical surface of 15 cm radius. A small pellet is imbedded midway within the rod along its axis. When viewed from the flat end the apparent depth of the pellet is 16 cm. a) What is the index of refraction of the rod? b) What is the apparent depth when viewed from the hemispherical end?

1 Draw a sketch of the rod. Indicate all dimensions.

1

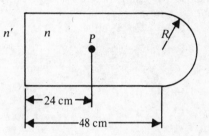

2 The index of refraction n' of the rod can be obtained from the relationship $n/s + n'/s' = 0$ when the pellet is viewed from the flat end (note $n' = 1$).

2

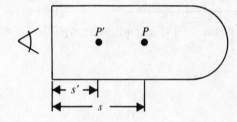

$$n = -\frac{sn'}{s'} = -\frac{24 \text{ cm} (1)}{-16 \text{ cm}}$$

$$= 1.5$$

3 Find the apparent depth when viewed from the curved end by using $n/s + n'/s' = (n' - n)/R$. Note that R is $-$, why? Draw a sketch and explain how we obtained the image P'.

3

$$\frac{1.5}{24 \text{ cm}} + \frac{1}{s'} = \frac{1 - 1.5}{-15 \text{ cm}}$$

$$s' = -34.2 \text{ cm}$$

The radius of curvature is $-$ if the direction from a refracting surface to the center of curvature is opposite to the direction of the refracted ray.

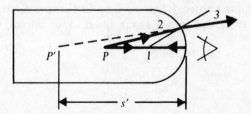

Two rays, 1 and 2 diverge from P. Ray 1 is normal to the surface and rebounds on itself. Ray 2 is refracted at the surface as ray 3 (away from the normal) and its extension intersects the axis at P'.

Problem 2 Assuming that the surface of the earth is a perfectly reflecting surface, find a) the location of the image of the moon, b) the lateral magnification, and c) the displacement of the image. (Radius of the moon = 1740 km, radius of earth R_e = 6380 km, mean distance from the center of the earth to the center of the moon = 386,000 km. Assume that object distance $s = 60\,R_e$.)

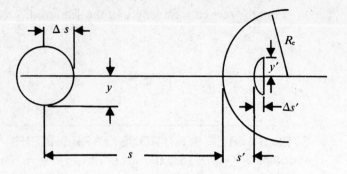

4 Find s' by using $1/s + 1/s' = 2/R$. Note that $R = -R_e$.

4

$$\frac{1}{60\,R_e} + \frac{1}{s'} = -\frac{2}{R_e}$$

$$\frac{1}{s'} = \frac{1}{R_e}\left(-2 - \frac{1}{60}\right) = -\frac{121}{60\,R_e}$$

$$s' = -\frac{60\,R_e}{121} = \frac{-60\,(6.38 \times 10^6 \text{ m})}{121}$$

$$= -3.164 \times 10^6 \text{ m} = -3164 \text{ km}$$

Note that the image of the moon is inside the earth.

---

5 Find the lateral magnification by using $m = y'/y = -s'/s$.

5

$$m = -\frac{-60\,R_e/121}{60\,R_e} = \frac{1}{121}$$

---

6 What is the radius y' of the moon's image?

6

$$y' = my = \frac{1740 \text{ km}}{121} = 14.4 \text{ km}$$

Problem 3 A real image is formed when an object is placed 10 cm from a concave spherical mirror. When the object is moved 2 cm farther from the mirror, the image moves 16 cm closer to the mirror. Find f.

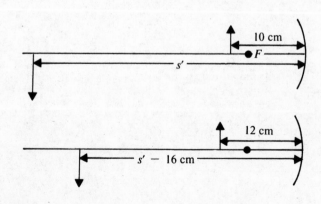

7 Substitute the given values in the mirror equation for the first situation.

7

$$\frac{1}{f} = \frac{1}{s} + \frac{1}{s'}$$

$$\frac{1}{f} = \frac{1}{10 \text{ cm}} + \frac{1}{s'}$$

---

8 Substitute the given values in the mirror equation when the object is moved 2 cm farther from the mirror.

8 $\dfrac{1}{f} = \dfrac{1}{12 \text{ cm}} + \dfrac{1}{s' - 16 \text{ cm}}$

---

9 Equate the above and solve for s'.

9

$$\frac{1}{10 \text{ cm}} + \frac{1}{s'} = \frac{1}{12 \text{ cm}} + \frac{1}{s' - 16 \text{ cm}}$$

$$\frac{1}{s'} + \frac{1}{60} = \frac{1}{s' - 16}$$

$$60 (s' - 16) + s'(s' - 16) = s'(60)$$

$$s'^2 - 16s' - 960 = 0$$

$$(s' - 40)(s' + 24) = 0$$

$$s' = 40 \text{ cm}$$

$$s' = -24 \text{ cm}$$

---

10 Note that $s' = -24$ cm is extraneous because we know that the image is real. Substitute $s' = 40$ cm in the equation in frame 7 and solve for f.

10

$$\frac{1}{f} = \frac{1}{10 \text{ cm}} + \frac{1}{40 \text{ cm}}$$

$$f = 8 \text{ cm}$$

PROGRAMMED TEST

1 *Problem 1* A concave mirror has a radius of curvature of 27 cm. What two object distances will give us images $3 \times$ the size of the object?

1 *Answer*
9 cm, 18 cm

If you solved this problem correctly, go to frame 7. If you could not solve this problem, go through frames 2–6.

---

2 We have two cases: When the object is between the mirror and F, we will have an erect virtual image and $m = +3$ (+ because it is erect and 3 because it is $3 \times$ the object size). When the object is between F and C, we will have an inverted real image and $m = -3$. We will use $m = +3$ first.

2

$$m = \frac{y'}{y} = -\frac{s'}{s} = 3$$

$$\therefore \quad s' = -3s$$

3 Substitute the above in the mirror equation. Note $R = +27$ cm. Find s.

3
$$\frac{1}{s} + \frac{1}{s'} = \frac{2}{R}$$
$$\frac{1}{s} - \frac{1}{3s} = \frac{2}{27 \text{ cm}}$$
$$s = 9 \text{ cm}$$

---

4 Describe the image.

4 The image is erect (since $m > 0$) and virtual. The object is within the focal length of the mirror.

---

5 Find s for the second case, $m = -3$.

5
$$m = -3 = -\frac{s'}{s}$$
$$\therefore \quad s' = 3s$$
$$\frac{1}{s} + \frac{1}{3s} = \frac{2}{27 \text{ cm}}$$
$$s = 18 \text{ cm}$$

---

6 Describe the image.

6 The image is inverted (since $m < 0$) and real. The object is located between the focal point and the center of curvature.

---

7 **Problem 2** If f is the first focal length and f' the second focal length, prove that a) $n/n' = f/f'$ and

b) $\dfrac{f}{s} + \dfrac{f'}{s'} = 1$.

7

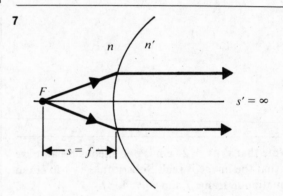

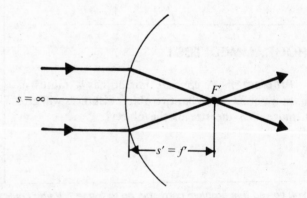

If you solved this problem correctly, go to frame 13. If you could not solve this problem, go through frames 8–12.

8 Using $\dfrac{n}{s} + \dfrac{n'}{s'} = \dfrac{n' - n}{R}$,

find the value of n/f for the first focus.

8 For the first focus, $s = f$ and $s' = f'$.
$$\frac{n}{f} + \frac{n'}{\infty} = \frac{n' - n}{R}$$
$$\frac{n}{f} = \frac{n' - n}{R}$$

9 Find the value of n/f for the second focus.

9 For the second focus, $s = \infty$, $s' = f'$.

$$\frac{n}{\infty} + \frac{n'}{f'} = \frac{n' - n}{R}$$

$$\frac{n'}{f'} = \frac{n' - n}{R}$$

---

10 Equate the results of the two previous frames and solve for the ratio n/n'.

10

$$\frac{n}{f} = \frac{n'}{f'}$$

$$\therefore \frac{n}{n'} = \frac{f}{f'}$$

---

11 Prove part b) by dividing each term of

$$\frac{n}{s} + \frac{n'}{s'} = \frac{n' - n}{R}$$

by n' and using the results of frames 8 and 10.

11

$$\frac{n}{n's} + \frac{n'}{n's'} = \frac{1}{n'}\left(\frac{n' - n}{R}\right)$$

$$\frac{n}{n's} + \frac{1}{s'} = \frac{n}{fn'}$$

$$\frac{f}{f's} + \frac{1}{s'} = \frac{1}{f'}$$

---

12 Multiply each term by f'.

12

$$\frac{f}{s} + \frac{f'}{s'} = 1$$

---

13 *Problem 3* A spherical mirror produces an erect image ¼ the size of the object. The radius of curvature of the mirror is 20 cm. a) Is the mirror convex or concave? b) Find the image and object distances.

13 *Answer*
Convex, $- 7.5$ cm, 30 cm.

If you could not solve this problem, go through frames 14–17.

14 What kind of mirror produces an erect image which is smaller than the object?

14 The convex mirror produces a virtual image that is erect and smaller than the object.

---

15 What is the expression for magnification in terms of object and image distances? Find the object distance in terms of the image distance.

15

$$m = \frac{y'}{y} = -\frac{s'}{s} = +\frac{1}{4}$$

$$s = - 4s'$$

---

16 Substitute the above in the mirror equation and solve for s'.

16

$$\frac{1}{s} + \frac{1}{s'} = \frac{2}{R}$$

$$\frac{1}{- 4s'} + \frac{1}{s'} = \frac{2}{-20 \text{ cm}}$$

$$s' = - 7.5 \text{ cm}$$

17 Solve for *s*.

17
$$s = -4s'$$
$$= -4(-7.5 \text{ cm})$$
$$= 30 \text{ cm}$$

38

Lenses and Optical Instruments

CHAPTER SUMMARY

Thin lenses (converging and diverging), the eye, magnifiers, cameras, projectors, compound microscopes and telescopes are discussed in this chapter. The lensmaker's equation and the graphical methods for finding the position and size of images formed by thin lenses are presented. Various types of lens aberrations and defects of vision are described, including corrective procedures.

BASIC TERMS — *Give definitions or meanings for the following:*

thin lens (38-1)
converging lens (38-1)
positive lens (38-1)
diverging lens (38-1)
negative lens (38-1)
focus (38-1)
focal length (38-1)
optic axis (38-1)
principal ray (38-2)
lensmaker's equation (38-3)
virtual object (38-3)
aberration (38-4)

monochromatic aberration (38-4)
chromatic aberration (38-4)
astigmatism (38-4)
power (38-5)
diopter (38-5)
angular magnification (38-8)
angular size (38-8)
magnifier (38-8)
microscope (38-9)
objective (38-9)
eyepiece (38-9)
telescope (38-10)

PROGRAMMED QUIZ

1 How do we deal with optical systems consisting of many surfaces?

2 What is another name for a converging lens?

3 What is a thin lens?

4 In astigmatism, how does the image of a point off the axis appear?

1 After the first surface, the object for each surface is the image formed by the preceding surface.

2 Positive lens since the focal length is positive.

3 A lens whose thickness is negligible in comparison with the object and image distances.

4 As a line.

5 How are lens aberrations eliminated?

5 By the use of compound lenses of several elements.

---

6 Can the eye focus on objects at any point?

6 No, the eye cannot focus on objects closer than the near point.

---

7 How can we increase the depth of field in a camera?

7 By "stopping down" the lens to a smaller aperture and larger f-number (focal length of lens divided by the diameter of the aperture).

---

8 Can diverging lenses form real images?

8 No, a diverging lens always forms a virtual image.

---

9 What kind of images can be used as objects for a second lens?

9 Both real and virtual.

---

10 How is the eye similar to a camera?

10 In the eye, a variable focal length lens forms an image on the retina; in a camera, a lens or lenses of fixed focal length form images on film.

---

11 Can virtual images be formed on a screen?

11 No, the light rays do not actually meet at the virtual image; they only appear to do so.

---

12 What happens if a converging lens is immersed in a fluid of higher n?

12 It acts as a diverging lens.

---

13 Can a converging lens ever have a virtual image?

13 Yes, if the object is between the lens and the focal point.

---

14 What does the focal length of a thin lens depend on?

14 The radius of curvature and the index of refraction;

$$\frac{1}{f} = (n - 1) \left(\frac{1}{R_1} - \frac{1}{R_2} \right).$$

---

15 All lenses are made of the same material. Which lenses are converging?

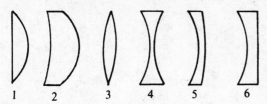

15 1, 2, 3 since they are thicker at the center than at the edges.

MAIN IDEAS

An optical system has two or more reflecting or refracting surfaces. A single lens has two surfaces. Whether the image of the first surface is real or virtual, it will serve as an object for the second surface. Since objects and images may be on either side of the refracting surface, we should make note of the sign conventions which were adopted in the previous chapter. a) An object distance is considered to be + if the direction from the object to the refracting surface is the same as the direction of the incident rays. b) An image distance is considered to be + if the direction from the refracting surface to the image point is the same direction as that of the rays which are refracted from the surface. c) The radius of curvature is + if the direction from a refracting surface to the center of curvature is the same as that of the refracted ray.

Consider a single lens whose thickness is very small relative to the object and image distances. Then $1/s + 1/s' = (n - 1)(1/R_1 - 1/R_2)$, where s and s' are the object and image distances, n the index of refraction of the lens, and R_1 and R_2 the radii of curvature of the first and second surfaces through which the light rays pass. Since the focal length of a thin lens may be defined as the image distance of a point which is infinitely far from the lens, we have $1/f = (n - 1)(1/R_1 - 1/R_2)$, the lensmaker's equation. It should be noted that if the lens were in water or another medium, we would be required to use a relative index in the lensmaker's equation $1/f' = (n_2/n_1 - 1)(1/R_1 - 1/R_2)$, where n_1 is the index of the medium and n_2 the index of the lens.

A converging lens has a positive focal length. Therefore it is called a positive lens. The focal length of a diverging lens is negative and it is called a negative lens. Since a lens has two surfaces, it has two focal points: The first focal point F of a lens is the object point for which the image is at infinity. The second focal point F' is the image point of an infinitely distant object.

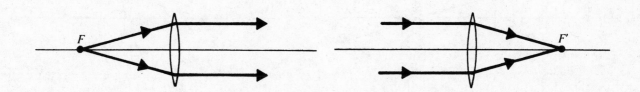

In a diverging lens, incident rays converging toward the first focal point F emerge parallel to its axis. Incident parallel rays diverge after refraction and seem to come from the second focal point F'.

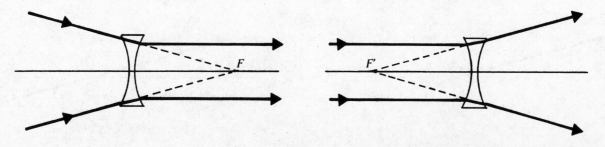

For a thin lens the focal points lie on opposite sides of the lens at a distance f from the vertex. The Gaussian form of the thin lens equation is given by $1/s + 1/s' = 1/f$. The lateral magnification of a thin lens is $m = -s'/s$. The negative sign indicates that when s and s' are both positive, the image is inverted.

The Newtonian form of the thin lens equation: Let x denote the distance from F to the object and x' the distance from F' to the image, then $s = x + f$, $s' = x' + f$ and $xx' = f^2$. The sign convention for the Newtonian form is as follows: x is positive if the object lies to the left of F, negative if it lies to the right; x' is positive if the image lies to the right of F', negative if it lies to the left.

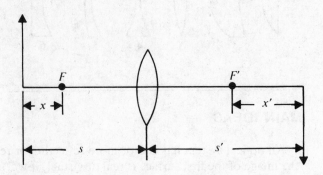

The position and size of the image may be obtained by a graphical method. The method consists of finding the point of intersection, after refraction by the lens, of two principal rays which diverge from the same point on the object (not on the axis).

A ray parallel to the axis, after refraction by the lens, passes through the second focal point of a converging lens. For a diverging lens it appears to come from the second focal point.

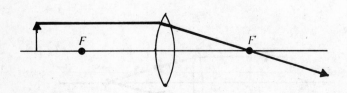
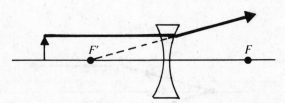

A ray through the center of a converging or diverging lens has a negligible deviation. Therefore we assume that the ray passes through the center without any displacement.

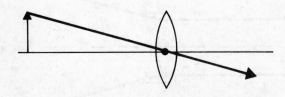
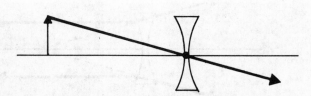

For a converging lens, a ray through the first focus emerges parallel to the axis. For a diverging lens, a ray proceeding toward the first focal point emerges parallel to the axis.

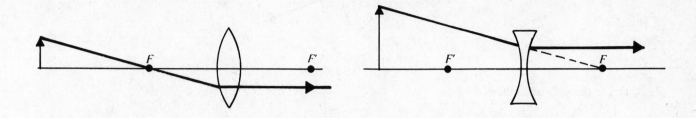

SIGN CONVENTIONS FOR LENSES

QUANTITY	POSITIVE	NEGATIVE
focal length f	converging lens	diverging lens
object distance s	real object	virtual object
image distance s'	real image	virtual image
lateral magnification m	erect image	inverted image

Characteristics of images for thin lenses:

Virtual, erect, smaller than object.

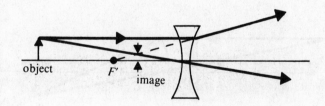

Virtual, erect, larger than object.

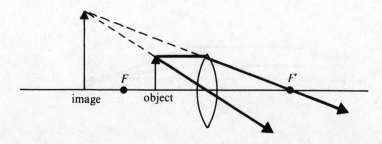

No image (image at infinity).

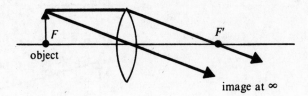

Real, larger than object, inverted.

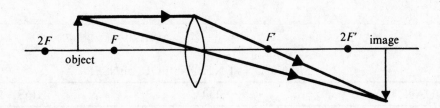

Real, same size as object, inverted.

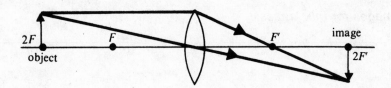

Real, smaller than object, inverted.

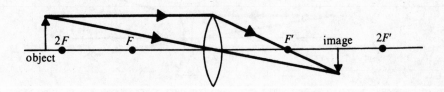

Real, smaller than object, inverted.

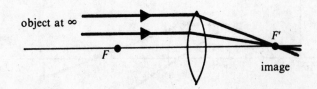

Consider three media separated by two surfaces (thick lens). Ray AB diverges from source A. At B, ray AB is refracted by surface 1 (which has a radius of curvature R_1) to C according to $n/s_1 + n'/s_1' = (n' - n)/R_1$. Arriving at D, ray BD is refracted in the direction DE. For the second surface (which has a radius of curvature R_2) the object distance is $s_2' = s_1' - t$. The final image distance s_2'' is determined by $n'/s_2' + n''/s_2'' = (n'' - n')/R_2$. (Note: C is a virtual object for surface 2, hence s_2' will have a negative value. Also, $R_2 = -$ because the direction from the second surface to its center of curvature is opposite to that of the refracted light.)

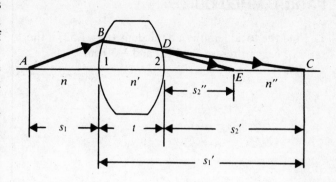

The angular magnification of three basic optical systems:

i) The magnifier: $M = u'/u = 25/f$, where u' is the angle subtended at the eye by the image and u is the angle subtended at the eye by an object at the near point (25 cm).

ii) The compound microscope: $M = 25$ cm $s_1'/f_1 f_2$, where s_1' is the image distance for the objective lens, f_1 the focal length of the objective and f_2 the focal length of the eyepiece. (s', f_1 and f_2 are measured in centimeters.)

iii) The telescope: $M = -f_1/f_2$, where f_1 is the focal length of the objective and f_2 the focal length of the eyepiece. The negative sign denotes an inverted image.

Problem solving strategy:

1 Image formation by a thin lens. Always draw a principal ray diagram. Orient your diagram so that light travels from left to right. A diagram drawn to scale will serve as a good check on the thin lens equation:

$$\frac{1}{f} = \frac{1}{s} + \frac{1}{s'}.$$

2 If a thin lens has two radii, use the lensmaker's equation and the sign conventions:

$$\frac{1}{f} = (n - 1)\left(\frac{1}{R_1} - \frac{1}{R_2}\right).$$

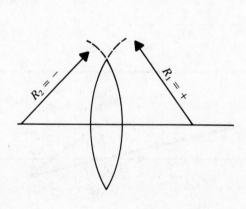

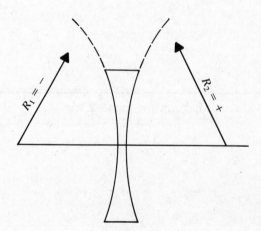

3 For greater accuracy and algebraic problems (derivation of formulas), use the single surface equation

$$\frac{n}{s_1} + \frac{n'}{s_1'} = \frac{n' - n}{R},$$

where
  n = index of refraction of first medium (usually air),
  n' = index of refraction of second medium,
  R = radius of curvature.

PROGRAMMED QUIZ

1 Find the focal length of a thin lens ($n = 1.52$) if the radii of curvature are $+15$ cm and -30 cm.

1

$$\frac{1}{f} = (n - 1)\left(\frac{1}{R_1} - \frac{1}{R_2}\right)$$
$$= (1.52 - 1)\left(\frac{1}{15 \text{ cm}} - \frac{1}{-30 \text{ cm}}\right)$$
$$f = 19.2 \text{ cm}$$

---

2 Where is the image of an object 50 cm from a thin lens, $f = +10$ cm? Is the image real or virtual?

2

$$\frac{1}{s} + \frac{1}{s'} = \frac{1}{f}$$
$$\frac{1}{s'} = \frac{1}{10 \text{ cm}} - \frac{1}{50 \text{ cm}}$$
$$s' = 12.5 \text{ cm}$$

The image distance is positive, so the image is real.

---

3 Find the lateral magnification. Describe the image.

3

$$m = -\frac{s'}{s}$$
$$= -\frac{12.5 \text{ cm}}{50 \text{ cm}}$$
$$= -0.25$$

The image is smaller and inverted.

---

4 The far point of a certain myopic eye is 2 m in front of the eye. What lens should be used to see an object at infinity clearly?

4 If the image is to be formed at the far point then $s = \infty$ and $s' = -200$ cm.

$$\frac{1}{s} + \frac{1}{s'} = \frac{1}{f}$$
$$\frac{1}{\infty} + \frac{1}{-200 \text{ cm}} = \frac{1}{f}$$
$$f = -200 \text{ cm}$$

---

5 Draw a ray diagram for frame 2.

5

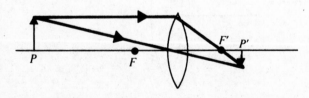

---

6 A person wears corrective lenses, $f = +50$ cm to see an object 25 cm in front of his eye. What is his near point?

6

$$\frac{1}{s} + \frac{1}{s'} = \frac{1}{f}$$
$$\frac{1}{s'} = \frac{1}{50 \text{ cm}} - \frac{1}{25 \text{ cm}}$$
$$s' = -50 \text{ cm}$$

7 What is the power of his lenses?

7

$$\text{power} = \frac{1}{f}$$

$$= \frac{1}{0.50 \text{ m}}$$

$$= +2 \text{ diopters}$$

---

8 What is the focal length of a magnifying glass that gives a magnification of 2?

8

$$M = \frac{25}{f}$$

$$f = \frac{25}{2} = 12.5 \text{ cm}$$

Note: in this equation, f is in centimeters.

---

9 What is the aperture of a lens having $f = 100$ mm and an aperture diameter of 25 mm?

9 $f/4$, the aperture size is the f-number, which is the focal length of the lens divided by the diameter of the aperture.

---

10 What is the angular magnification of a telescope? The lenses have focal lengths of 2.00 m and 0.20 m respectively.

10

$$M = \frac{-f_1}{f_2}$$

$$= -\frac{2.00 \text{ m}}{0.20 \text{ m}}$$

$$= -10 \times$$

The negative sign denotes an inverted image.

---

11 An object is placed at a distance $4R$ from a solid glass sphere of radius R. If we are to consider the sphere as having two surfaces of radii R_1 and R_2, what would be the algebraic signs of R_1 and R_2?

11

$$R_1 = +R$$
$$R_2 = -R$$

The radius of curvature is $+$ if the direction from the refracting surface to the center of curvature is the same as that of the refracted ray.

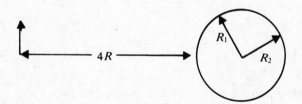

---

12 Determine the position of the image produced by the first surface (air to glass).

   $n = 1.0$ (air)
   $n' = 1.5$ (glass)
   $s_1 = 4R$
   $R_1 = R$

12

$$\frac{n}{s_1} + \frac{n'}{s_1{}'} = \frac{n' - n}{R_1}$$

$$\frac{1}{4R} + \frac{1.5}{s_1{}'} = \frac{1.5 - 1.0}{R}$$

$$\frac{1.5}{s_1{}'} = \frac{0.5}{R} - \frac{1}{4R}$$

$$s_1{}' = 6R$$

13 Determine the position of the image produced by the second surface (glass to air), i.e., the final image. The real image of the first surface serves as a virtual object for the second surface. Therefore, the object distance for the second surface is negative. The real image (or virtual object) is $6R$ from the first surface, or $4R$ from the second surface. Therefore,

$$s_2 = -4R$$
$$n = 1.5 \text{ (glass)}$$
$$n' = 1.0 \text{ (air)}$$
$$R_2 = -R$$

13

$$\frac{n}{s_2} + \frac{n'}{s_2{'}} = \frac{n' - n}{R_2}$$
$$\frac{1.5}{-4R} + \frac{1}{s_2{'}} = \frac{1 - 1.5}{-R}$$
$$\frac{1}{s_2{'}} = \frac{-0.5}{-R} + \frac{1.5}{4R}$$
$$s_2{'} = 1.14R$$

The final image is $1.14R$ from the second surface, or $2.14R$ from the center of the sphere.

---

14 What is the power of the combination of two thin lenses of 40 cm and 50 cm focal lengths which are in contact with each other?

14

$$\frac{1}{0.40 \text{ m}} + \frac{1}{0.50 \text{ m}} = 4.5 \text{ diopters}$$

---

15 When a camera lens is focused on a distant point source of light, the image is formed on a screen at A. When the screen is moved back 5 cm, the circle of light has a diameter of 10 mm. What is the f-number of the lens?

15

$$\triangle ABC \sim \triangle ADE$$

If two triangles are similar, their corresponding parts are proportional.

$$f\text{-number} = \frac{f}{d} = \frac{5 \text{ cm}}{1.0 \text{ cm}} = f/5$$

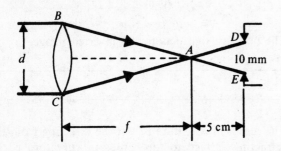

---

16 The distance between an object and a screen is 36 cm. At what points between the object and screen can a lens of focal length 8 cm be placed in order to produce an image on the screen?

16

$$s + s' = 36 \text{ cm}$$
$$s' = 36 \text{ cm} - s$$
$$\frac{1}{s} + \frac{1}{s'} = \frac{1}{f}$$
$$\frac{1}{s} + \frac{1}{36 \text{ cm} - s} = \frac{1}{8 \text{ cm}}$$
$$8 \text{ cm}(36 \text{ cm} - s) + s(8 \text{ cm}) = s(36 \text{ cm} - s)$$
$$(s - 12 \text{ cm})(s - 24 \text{ cm}) = 0$$
$$s = 12 \text{ cm}$$
$$s = 24 \text{ cm}$$

---

17 What is the focal length of a magnifying glass whose power is $+20$ D?

17

$$\text{power} = \frac{1}{f}$$
$$f = \frac{1}{20 \text{ D}} = 0.05 \text{ m}$$

---

18 What is the angular magnification of this magnifying glass?

18

$$M = \frac{25 \text{ cm}}{f}$$
$$= \frac{25 \text{ cm}}{5 \text{ cm}} = 5 \times$$

---

19 A person has a near point of 100 cm and a far point of 200 cm. What is the focal point of the component of his bifocals which will bring the near point to 25 cm?

20 What is the focal point of the component of his bifocals which will shift the far point to a great distance?

19

$$\frac{1}{f} = \frac{1}{s} + \frac{1}{s'}$$

$$= \frac{1}{25 \text{ cm}} - \frac{1}{100 \text{ cm}}$$

$$f = +33.3 \text{ cm}$$

20

$$\frac{1}{f} = \frac{1}{s} + \frac{1}{s'}$$

$$= \frac{1}{\infty} - \frac{1}{200 \text{ cm}}$$

$$f = -200 \text{ cm}$$

STEP BY STEP SOLUTIONS OF PROBLEMS

Problem 1 A thin converging meniscus lens has index n and radii of curvature R_1 and R_2. Show that if the thickness is small relative to the diameter, the magnitude of the focal length is given by $f = d^2/8(n-1)t$, where d and t are the diameter and thickness of the lens respectively.

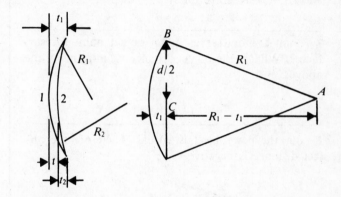

1 Consider surface 1. Apply the Pythagorean theorem to triangle ABC.

1

$$\left(\frac{d}{2}\right)^2 + (R_1 - t_1)^2 = R_1^2$$

$$\frac{d^2}{4} + R_1^2 - 2R_1 t_1 + t_1^2 = R_1^2$$

2 If $t_1 \ll d$, $t_1^2 \approx 0$. Solve the equation for $1/R_1$.

2

$$\frac{1}{R_1} \approx \frac{8t_1}{d^2}$$

3 Go through the same procedure for surface 2 and solve for $1/R_2$.

3

$$\frac{1}{R_2} \approx \frac{8t_2}{d^2}$$

4 Substitute the values of $1/R_1$ and $1/R_2$ in the lensmaker's equation $1/f = (n-1)(1/R_1 - 1/R_2)$.

4

$$\frac{1}{f} = (n-1)\left(\frac{8t_1}{d^2} - \frac{8t_2}{d^2}\right)$$

$$= \frac{8(n-1)(t_1 - t_2)}{d^2}$$

5 But $t_1 - t_2 = t$. Solve the equation for f.

5

$$f = \frac{d^2}{8(n-1)t}$$

Note: This approximation is also applicable for a double convex lens where t is the thickness of the lens.

Problem 2 Parallel light rays are incident on a solid glass sphere of radius R. Locate the image in terms of n and R.

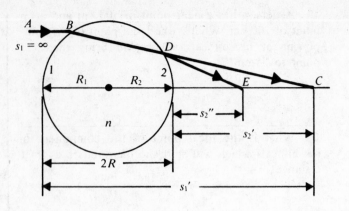

6 What is the relationship between the object distance s_1 and the image distance s_1' for surface 1? Note that the first surface produces an image at C, beyond the second surface. Substituting $s_1 = \infty$ and $R_1 = + R$, solve for s_1'.

6
$$\frac{1}{s_1} + \frac{n}{s_1'} = \frac{n-1}{R_1}$$
$$s_1' = \frac{nR}{n-1}$$

7 Point C now serves as an object point for surface 2. What is the object distance s_2' in terms of the above.

7
$$|s_2'| = |s_1' - 2R|$$
$$= \left| \frac{nR}{n-1} - 2R \right| = \left| \frac{R(2-n)}{n-1} \right|$$

8 But the new object is virtual. Therefore the object distance is negative.

8
$$s_2' = -\frac{R(2-n)}{n-1}$$

9 What is the relationship between the object distance s_2' and the image distance s_2'' for the second surface?

9
$$\frac{n}{s_2'} + \frac{1}{s_2''} = \frac{1-n}{R_2}$$

10 Substitute the value of s_2' in the above and solve for s_2''. Note that $R_2 = -R$. (The radius of curvature is $-$ if the direction from a refracting surface to the center of curvature is opposite to that of the refracted ray.)

10
$$\frac{n}{\dfrac{-R(2-n)}{n-1}} + \frac{1}{s_2''} = \frac{1-n}{-R}$$
$$\frac{-n(n-1)}{R(2-n)} + \frac{1}{s_2''} = \frac{n-1}{R}$$
$$\frac{1}{s_2''} = \frac{2(n-1)}{R(2-n)}$$
$$s_2'' = \frac{R(2-n)}{2(n-1)}$$

Therefore the final image is
$$s_2'' + R = \frac{Rn}{2(n-1)}$$
from the center of the sphere.

Problem 3 A double convex lens 3 cm thick and having radii of curvature 2 cm is mounted at the end of a water tank. An object is placed in air 6 cm from the vertex of the lens. Find the position of the final image. Assume indices of $n = 1.00$, $n' = 1.50$ and $n'' = 1.33$ for air, glass and water respectively. (Mount the lens on the left side of the tank and let the light be incident from the left.)

11 Apply the equation $n/s_1 + n'/s_1' = (n' - n)/R$ to the first surface and solve for s_1'.

11

$$\frac{1.00}{6} + \frac{1.5}{s_1'} = \frac{1.50 - 1.00}{2}$$

$$s_1' = + 18 \text{ cm}$$

Note: $R_1 = +$ because the direction from the first surface to the center of curvature is the same as that of the refracted light.

---

12 Before proceeding with the second surface, find the object distance s_2' for this surface. Draw a sketch. Note that the magnitude of $s_2' = s_1' - t$.

12

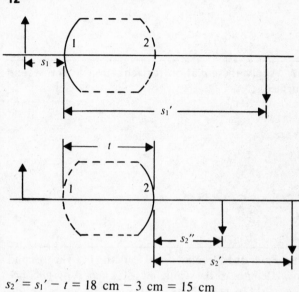

$$s_2' = s_1' - t = 18 \text{ cm} - 3 \text{ cm} = 15 \text{ cm}$$

---

13 Since we are dealing with a virtual object, $s_2' = - 15$ cm. Also, $R_2 = -$ because the direction from the second surface to its center of curvature is opposite to that of the refracted light. Substitute these values in $n'/s_2' + n''/s_2'' = (n'' - n')/R_2$ and solve for s_2''.

13

$$\frac{1.50}{- 15 \text{ cm}} + \frac{1.33}{s_2''} = \frac{1.33 - 1.50}{- 2 \text{ cm}}$$

$$- 0.10 + \frac{1.33}{s_2''} = 0.085 \text{ cm}^{-1}$$

$$s_2'' = 7.19 \text{ cm}$$

The final image is in the water 7.19 cm from the vertex of the second surface.

Problem 4 A plano-convex lens is 3 cm thick along its axis. The radius of curvature of the spherical surface is 12 cm and the refractive index is 1.60. Find the first and second focal points. Assume that light is incident from the left.

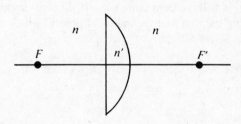

---

14 The first focal point is the value of s corresponding to $s' = \infty$. Find the image distance produced by the plane surface if $f = s_1$ is the distance of the first focal point from the vertex of the plane surface. Note that $n = 1.0$, $n' = 1.6$.

14 From the equation for plane surface refraction,

$$\frac{n}{s_1} + \frac{n'}{s_1'} = 0$$

$$\frac{1}{s_1} + \frac{1.6}{s_1'} = 0$$

$$s_1' = - 1.6 \, s_1$$

15 The plane surface produces a virtual image at infinity which is perceived by the spherical surface as a real object. What is the object distance s_2 for the second surface?

15
$$s_2 = -s_1' + 3 \text{ cm}$$
$$= +1.6 \, s_1 + 3 \text{ cm}$$

---

16 What is the image distance s_2' corresponding to the object distance s_2?

16
$$s_2' = \infty$$
$$\therefore \frac{1}{s_2'} = 0$$

---

17 Apply the equation for refraction at the second surface.

17
$$\frac{n'}{s_2} + \frac{n}{s_2'} = \frac{n - n'}{R}$$
$$\frac{1.6}{1.6 \, s_1 + 3 \text{ cm}} = \frac{1 - 1.6}{-12 \text{ cm}} = \frac{0.6}{12}$$

$s_1 = 18.1$ cm from the vertex of the plane surface.

---

18 Find the second focal length f'. The second focal length is the value of s_2' when $s_2 = \infty$. Since $s_2 = \infty$, $1/s_2 = 0$. Note that $r = -$ because the direction from the refracting surface to the center of curvature is opposite to that of the refracted ray.

18 Apply the equation for refraction at the second surface.
$$\frac{n'}{s_2} + \frac{n}{s_2'} = \frac{n - n'}{R}$$
$$\frac{1}{s_2} = \frac{1 - 1.6}{-12}$$

$s_2 = 20$ cm from the vertex of the convex surface.
     Thus $f = 18.1$ cm and
          $f' = 20$ cm

---

19 Repeat the problem if the lens is reversed and the light is still incident from the left. Sketch the lens, indicating the first and second focal points.

19

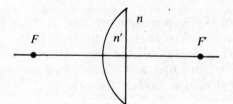

---

20 Using the equation for refraction for the spherical surface, express s' in terms of s_1. Note that $n = 1.0$, $n' = 1.6$ and $R = 12$ cm.

20 For the spherical surface,
$$\frac{n}{s_1} + \frac{n'}{s_1'} = \frac{n' - n}{R}$$
$$\frac{1}{s_1} + \frac{1.6}{s_1'} = \frac{1.6 - 1}{12}$$
$$s_1' = \frac{s_1}{0.03125 \, s_1 - 0.625}$$

---

21 We note that the image produced by the spherical surface is perceived as a virtual object by the plane surface. Express the object distance s_2 for the plane surface in terms of s_1' and the thickness of the lens t. Then substitute the value of s_1' obtained in the previous frame.

21

$$s_2 = s_1' - t = \frac{s_1}{0.03125\, s_1 - 0.625} - 3$$

---

22 The first focal point is the value of s_1 corresponding to an image distance of ∞. Therefore $s_2' = \infty$. Using the equation for refraction for a plane surface, substitute $s_2' = \infty$ and the value of s_2 from the previous frame and solve for s_1.

22

$$\frac{n'}{s_2} + \frac{n}{s_2'} = 0$$

$$\frac{1.6}{\dfrac{s_1}{0.03125\, s_1 - 0.625} - 3} + \frac{n}{\infty} = 0$$

$$1.6\,(0.03125\, s_1 - 0.625) = 0$$

$$s_1 = 20 \text{ cm}$$

$$\therefore f = s_1 = 20 \text{ cm}$$

---

23 The second focal length f' is the value of s_2' when $s_1 = \infty$. First find the image produced by the spherical surface when $s_1 = \infty$.

23

$$\frac{n}{s_1} + \frac{n'}{s_1'} = \frac{n' - n}{R}$$

$$\frac{1}{\infty} + \frac{1.6}{s_1'} = \frac{1.6 - 1}{12}$$

$$s_1' = 32 \text{ cm}$$

---

24 The plane surface perceives this image as a virtual object, hence $s_2' = -(32 - 3)$ cm. Substitute this value in the equation for a plane surface.

24

$$\frac{n'}{s_2} + \frac{n'}{s_2'} = 0$$

$$\frac{1.6}{-(32 - 3)} + \frac{1}{s_2'} = 0$$

$$f' = s_2' = 18.1 \text{ cm}$$

PROGRAMMED TEST

Problem 1   Prove that when two thin lenses are placed in contact as shown in the figure, the focal length of the combination is given by $\dfrac{1}{f} = \dfrac{1}{f_1} + \dfrac{1}{f_2}$.

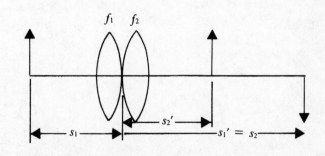

If you solved this problem correctly, go to frame 6. If you could not solve this problem, go through frames 2-5.

1 Consider lens 1. If s_1 = object distance and s_1' = image distance, express s_1' in terms of f_1 and s_1.

1

$$\frac{1}{s_1} + \frac{1}{s_1'} = \frac{1}{f_1}$$

$$\frac{1}{s_1'} = \frac{1}{f_1} - \frac{1}{s_1} \qquad (1)$$

---

2 Let s_2 = the object distance and s_2' = image distance for lens 2. Express s_2 in terms of f_2 and s_2.

2

$$\frac{1}{s_2} + \frac{1}{s_2'} = \frac{1}{f_2}$$

$$\frac{1}{s_2} = \frac{1}{f_2} - \frac{1}{s_2'} \qquad (2)$$

---

3 Lens 2 perceives the image of lens 1 as a virtual object; therefore $s_2 = -s_1'$. Substitute this value in equation 2 and eliminate s_1' from equations 1 and 2.

3

$$-\frac{1}{s_1'} = \frac{1}{f_2} - \frac{1}{s_2'}$$

$$-\left(\frac{1}{f_1} - \frac{1}{s_1} \right) = \frac{1}{f_2} - \frac{1}{s_2'}$$

$$-\frac{1}{f_1} + \frac{1}{s_1} = \frac{1}{f_2} - \frac{1}{s_2'}$$

$$\frac{1}{f_1} + \frac{1}{f_2} = \frac{1}{s_1} + \frac{1}{s_2'}$$

---

4 What does the right side of this equation tell us?

4 That if the two lenses are considered as a compound lens, then

$$\frac{1}{\text{object distance}} + \frac{1}{\text{image distance}} = \frac{1}{f}$$

---

5 What does $1/f$ equal?

5

$$\frac{1}{f} = \frac{1}{f_1} + \frac{1}{f_2}$$

It should be noted that this relationship can be obtained for any value of the object distance and for two diverging lenses.

---

6 **Problem 2** A real image is formed when an object is placed 12 cm from a thin lens. When the object is moved 3 cm closer to the lens, the image moves 18 cm farther from the lens. Find f of the lens.

6

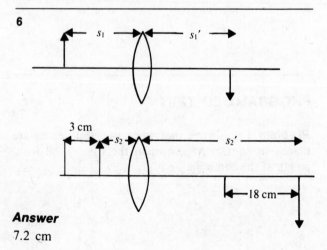

Answer

7.2 cm

If you solved this problem correctly, go to frame 11. If you could not solve this problem, go through frames 7-10.

7 Substitute the given values in the thin lens equation.

7

$$\frac{1}{s_1} + \frac{1}{s_1'} = \frac{1}{f}$$

$$\frac{1}{12 \text{ cm}} + \frac{1}{s_1'} = \frac{1}{f}$$

---

8 When the object is moved 3 cm closer, the new object distance is 12 cm − 3 cm = 9 cm, and the new image distance is $s_1' + 18$ cm. Substitute these values in the thin lens equation.

8

$$\frac{1}{9 \text{ cm}} + \frac{1}{s_1' + 18 \text{ cm}} = \frac{1}{f}$$

---

9 Equate the above and solve for s_1'.

9

$$\frac{1}{12 \text{ cm}} + \frac{1}{s_1'} = \frac{1}{9 \text{ cm}} + \frac{1}{s_1' + 18 \text{ cm}}$$

$$\frac{1}{s_1'} = \frac{1}{s_1' + 18} + \frac{1}{36}$$

$$36(s_1' + 18) = 36 \, s_1' + s_1'(s_1' + 18)$$

$$s_1'^2 + 18 \, s_1' - 648 = 0$$

$$(s_1' + 36)(s_1' - 18) = 0$$

$$s_1' = 18 \text{ cm}$$

$$s_1' = -36 \text{ cm}$$

---

10 Disregard $s_1' = -36$ cm because we know that the image is real. Substitute $s_1' = 18$ cm in the equation in frame 7 and solve for f.

10

$$\frac{1}{12 \text{ cm}} + \frac{1}{18 \text{ cm}} = \frac{1}{f}$$

$$f = 7.2 \text{ cm}$$

---

11 *Problem 3* An illuminated object is placed 60 cm from a screen. a) At what points between the object and the screen should a converging lens of 10 cm focal length be placed to obtain an image on the screen? b) What is the magnification of the image for these positions?

11

Answer
47.32 cm, 12.68 cm, − 3.73, − 0.268

If you could not solve this problem, go through frames 12-15.

12 Draw a sketch. Express the image distance in terms of s.

12

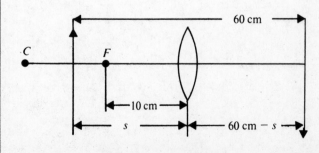

13 Apply the thin lens equation to the given data: $s' = 60 - s$ and $f = 10$ cm.

13

$$\frac{1}{s} + \frac{1}{s'} = \frac{1}{f}$$

$$\frac{1}{s} + \frac{1}{60 - s} = \frac{1}{10}$$

$$s^2 - 60\,s + 600 = 0$$

14 Solve by the quadratic formula.

14

$$s = \frac{60 \pm \sqrt{3600 - 2400}}{2}$$

$$= 47.32 \text{ cm}, \ 12.68 \text{ cm}$$

15 When $s = 12.68$ cm, $s' = 47.32$ cm; when $s = 47.32$ cm, $s' = 12.68$ cm. Find the magnification.

15

$$m_1 = \frac{-s'}{s} = \frac{-47.32 \text{ cm}}{12.68 \text{ cm}} = -3.73$$

$$m_2 = \frac{-s'}{s} = \frac{-12.68 \text{ cm}}{47.32 \text{ cm}} = -0.268$$

39

Interference and Diffraction

CHAPTER SUMMARY

In the study of interference and diffraction we consider light as a wave motion; therefore the principles of geometrical optics which we have used previously cannot be applied. Examples of interference are: the colored patterns of light reflected from thin films, Newton's rings, the nonreflectivity of thin coatings on glass and holography. The interference of light is analyzed on the basis of Young's experiment and the Michelson interferometer, and the mathematical relationships for interference are presented. Fresnel and Fraunhofer diffraction is also included in this chapter. Diffraction by a plane grating and the diffraction of x-rays by a crystal are considered as well as the resolving power of optical instruments.

BASIC TERMS — *Give definitions or meanings for the following:*

monochromatic light (39-1)
interference (39-1)
coherent light (39-1)
principle of linear superposition (39-1)
constructive interference (39-1)
destructive interference (39-1)
Young's two-slit interference (39-2)
Newton's rings (39-3)
Michelson interferometer (39-4)
ether (39-4)
Michelson-Morley experiment (39-4)
diffraction (39-5)

Fresnel diffraction (39-5)
Fraunhofer diffraction (39-5)
single-slit diffraction pattern (39-6)
diffraction grating (39-7)
x-ray diffraction (39-8)
Bragg reflection (39-9)
Bragg condition (39-9)
Airy disk (39-9)
Rayleigh's criterion (39-9)
unit of resolution (39-9)
resolving power (39-9)
holography (39-10)

PROGRAMMED QUIZ

1 When does constructive interference occur?

1 When the path difference for two sources is an integer multiple of the wavelength; when waves from two or more sources arrive at a point in phase.

2 When does destructive interference or cancellation occur?

2 When waves arrive at a point a half-cycle out of phase.

3 Under what conditions can two sources of light have a definite and constant phase relation?

3 When they both emit light coming from a single primary source.

4 How are the colors produced when light is reflected from a soap bubble?

4 By interference effects between the two light waves reflected at opposite surfaces of the thin films of a soap solution.

5 A light ray is incident upon the interface of two media. Explain what happens to the reflected ray in terms of phase.

5 Reflected waves undergo a phase shift of 180° when the initial medium has a smaller n than the second medium. If the second medium has a smaller n, no phase change occurs.

6 Two specimens in contact produce no Newton's interference fringes. What can we say about the two specimens?

6 Newton's rings are a result of the variable thickness of the air film between the two surfaces. Since no Newton's rings are produced, this indicates that the air film is uniform; thus the curvature of the two surfaces must be the same.

7 What is the historical significance of the Michelson interferometer? What is its significance in modern physics?

7 It was used in an attempt to detect the existence of ether (the result was negative). It provides experimental evidence for the special theory of relativity.

8 Diffraction patterns are produced by what kind of light?

8 Point sources of monochromatic light.

9 What is the difference between Fresnel and Fraunhofer diffraction?

9 In Fresnel diffraction, the point source and the screen are at finite (small) distances from the obstacle forming the diffraction pattern; no lenses are used. In Fraunhofer diffraction, a lens is placed just beyond the slit and a reduced image of the pattern is formed in its focal plane.

10 Describe the diffraction pattern of light passing through one slit.

10 A broad central fringe with narrower and weaker fringes symmetrically spaced on both sides.

11 Can any other type of wave motion besides light exhibit interference effects?

11 All wave motions exhibit interference effects.

12 What happens as the number of slits is increased?

12 The fringes become narrower and the resolving power is increased.

13 What does a resolving power of 1000 mean?

13 One can resolve two wavelengths which differ by one part in 1000; $R = \lambda/\Delta\lambda$.

14 For what purpose is x-ray diffraction used in crystallography?

14 To measure x-ray wavelengths and to study the structure of crystals.

15 How would you compare x-ray diffraction by crystals to other types of diffraction?

15 In a crystal, the regularly spaced atoms produce interference effects similar to those produced by a diffraction grating.

16 What must be the grating spacing in order to produce an appreciable deviation of the light?

16 Of the same order of magnitude as the wavelength of the light.

---

17 How can the phenomenon of interference be utilized in non-reflective coatings on glass?

17 If the thickness of the film is ¼ of the wavelength of light, the light reflected from the first surface will be 180° out of phase with the light reflected from the second surface and complete destructive interference will result.

MAIN IDEAS

Interference refers to the overlapping of waves in space. The total displacement at any point at any time is determined by the principle of linear superposition: The resultant displacement of any two overlapping waves is found by adding the instantaneous displacements that would be produced at a given point by each individual wave if each were acting alone; i.e. the total displacement is the algebraic sum of the individual waves. Interference patterns can be exhibited only by coherent light sources (derived from a single source and having a definite phase relation).

In Young's experiment, monochromatic light from a single source is incident upon two slits which serve as coherent sources. A pattern of interference fringes symmetrical about a central bright fringe is observed on a screen placed behind the slits. Slit widths and separation are much smaller than the distances from the source to the slits and from the slits to the screen.

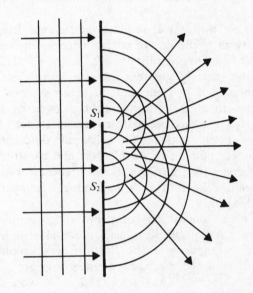

In accordance with Huygens' principle, cylindrical wavelets spread out from S_1 and S_2. Reinforcement at any point P (i.e. P is at the center of a bright fringe) takes place only when $d \sin \theta$ (the path difference $PS_1 - PS_2$) is an integral number of wavelengths. Hence, $d \sin \theta = m\lambda$, where d is the separation of the slits, λ the wavelength of monochromatic light, m the fringe number ($m = 0, \pm1, \pm2, \pm3$, etc.) where the central fringe is denoted the zeroth fringe and θ is the angle made by a line from a point between the two slits to the zeroth fringe and a line from the slits to the mth fringe. The wavelength of the light can be determined from $\lambda = y_m d/mR$, where R is the perpendicular distance from the slits to the screen and y_m the distance from the zeroth to the mth bright fringe. For dark fringes, $\lambda = y\, d/(m + \frac{1}{2})R$, where

    $m = 0$ for the first dark line,
    $m = \pm1$ for the second dark line,
    $m = \pm2$ for the third dark line.

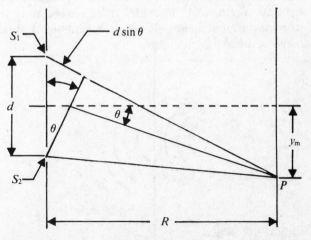

The intensity of light at any distance y from the zeroth fringe is given by $I = I_0 \cos^2 \left(\dfrac{\pi d}{\lambda} \sin \theta \right)$, where I_0 is the intensity of light at the zeroth fringe. When $y \ll R$ and θ is small, $y/R = \sin \theta$ and $I = I_0 \cos^2 (\pi dy/\lambda R)$.

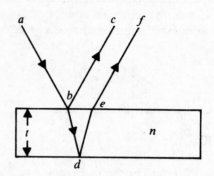

Interference in thin films (soap solution, oil, etc): An incident ray ab of monochromatic light is partly reflected, bc, and partly transmitted, bd, from the top surface to the bottom surface. The reflected ray, bc, will undergo a phase shift of 180°. However part of the transmitted ray will be reflected, de, and emerges as ef. The reflection from the second interface occurs without a change in phase. (A half cycle phase change occurs whenever the material in which the wave is initially traveling before reflection has a smaller index than the second material forming the interface.) For near normal incidence the path difference will approximate $2t$.

The wavelength and the thickness of the film are related by $2t = (m + \frac{1}{2}) \lambda_n$, $m = 0, 1, 2, 3$, etc. where λ_n is the wavelength of the light in the film. Since $\lambda_n = \lambda/n$, where λ is the wavelength of light in air and n the index of refraction of the film, we have $2nt = (m + \frac{1}{2})\lambda$; $m = 0, 1, 2...$ for maximum intensity (bright fringes) and $2nt = m\lambda$; $m = 0, 1, 2...$ for minimum intensity (dark fringes).

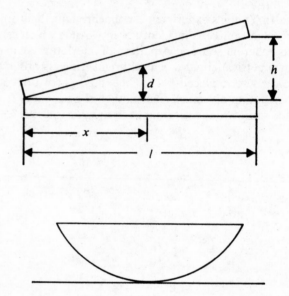

An air wedge will produce interference fringes. The fringe at the line of contact is dark. Successive dark fringes are given by $x = m l\lambda/2h$; $(m = 0, 1, 2...)$ It is immediately apparent that if d_1 and d_2 are the thicknesses of two adjacent bright areas, then the wavelength of the reflected light is given by $\lambda = 2(d_2 - d_1)$. In this case destructive interference (dark fringes) occurs at points for which path difference is an integer number of wavelengths and constructive interference (bright fringes) occurs at points for which the path difference is a half integer number of wavelengths.

A plano-convex lens of radius of curvature R resting on a plane glass plate is illuminated from above by monochromatic light of wavelength λ. The radii of the bright interference rings are given by $r = \sqrt{(m + \frac{1}{2})\lambda R}$; $(m = 0, 1, 2, 3...)$. Note that for the first bright ring $m = 0$. Also, the center of the pattern is dark. When viewed by transmitted light, the center of the pattern is bright.

Diffraction refers to phenomena concerned with the resultant effect produced by a limited portion of a wave front. Fresnel diffraction is the diffraction produced by a source which is too close for a plane wave approximation. No lenses are used. If the source is far enough away so that the light waves may be considered to be plane waves, then the diffraction pattern is called Fraunhofer diffraction. A lens is used to obtain the pattern in the second focal plane of the lens.

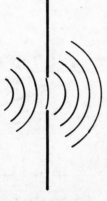

Fresnel diffraction   Fraunhofer diffraction

If a converging lens is placed near a single slit, then dark fringes are observed at $\sin \theta = n\lambda/a$, where θ is the angle between the lens axis and a line from the midpoint of the slit to the dark fringe, λ is the wavelength of light, a the width of the slit and n is the number ($n = 1, 2, 3, ...$) of the dark fringe.

Consider a diffraction grating which consists of a large number of parallel slits separated by a distance d. Bright lines will be obtained in the pattern at angles given by $\sin \theta = m\lambda/d$, where m is the number of the bright line counting from the zeroth-order bright line at $\theta = 0$.

The resolving power of an optical system refers to its ability to form distinct images of two closely spaced objects: i.e. diffraction patterns produced by the objects are sufficiently separated to be distinguished. According to the Rayleigh criterion, two point sources are just resolvable if the central maximum of the diffraction pattern of one source just coincides with the first minimum of the other. Since the first minimum for the diffraction pattern of a circular aperture is given by $\sin \theta = 1.22 \lambda/d$, where d is the diameter of the aperture, the Rayleigh criterion can be expressed by $\theta_R = 1.22 \lambda/d$ (when $\sin \theta \approx \theta$).

The resolving power of a grating is given by $R = \lambda/\Delta\lambda$, where λ is the mean wavelength of two spectral lines that can barely be distinguished and $\Delta\lambda$ is the wavelength difference. It can be shown that $R = Nm$, where N is the total number of rulings in the grating and m is the order of the diffraction. The dispersion D of a grating is a measure of the angular separation between two incident monochromatic waves and is given by $D = \Delta\theta/\Delta\lambda = m/d \cos \theta$.

Problem solving strategy:

1 The equations for a two-source or diffraction grating pattern (bright lines) are similar to the equations for the single-slit pattern (dark lines).

Constructive interference (bright lines) from two sources:
$$d \sin \theta = m\lambda, \text{ where } m = 0, \pm 1, \pm 2, \cdots$$
Destructive interference (dark lines) from two sources:
$$d \sin \theta = (m + \tfrac{1}{2})\lambda, \text{ where } m = 0, \pm 1, \pm 2, \cdots$$
When θ is very small, the position of the mth bright fringe is given by
$$\lambda = \frac{y_m d}{mR}.$$
The position of the dark lines is given by
$$\lambda = \frac{yd}{(m + \tfrac{1}{2})R},$$
where
   $m = 0$ for the first dark line,
   $m = \pm 1$ for the second dark line,
   $m = \pm 2$ for the third dark line.
The spacing between the lines of a diffraction grating is d.

2 The equations for the single-slit pattern (dark lines):
   $a \sin \theta = n\lambda$, where $n = 0, \pm 1, \pm 2, \cdots$,
$$\lambda = \frac{y_n a}{nR}.$$
The single-slit spacing is denoted by a.

PROGRAMMED QUIZ

1 Two slits 0.4 mm apart are placed 70 cm from a screen and illuminated with light of 620 nm wavelength. What is the distance between the second and third bright lines of the interference pattern?

1

$$\lambda = \frac{y_m d}{mR}$$

$$y_3 - y_2 = \frac{3\lambda R}{d} - \frac{2\lambda R}{d} = \frac{\lambda R}{d}$$

$$= \frac{(620 \times 10^{-9} \text{ m})(0.70 \text{ m})}{(4 \times 10^{-4} \text{ m})}$$

$$= 0.00109 \text{ m} = 1.09 \text{ mm}$$

2 What is the separation of the two slits in Young's experiment if the center of the 18th fringe is 10.6 mm from the center of the zeroth fringe? The screen is 60 cm from the double slit and light of 600 nm wavelength is used.

2
$$\lambda = \frac{y_m d}{mR}$$

$$d = \frac{(600 \times 10^{-9} \text{ m})(18)(0.60 \text{ m})}{10.6 \times 10^{-3} \text{ m}}$$

$$= 6.11 \times 10^{-4} \text{ m} = 0.611 \text{ mm}$$

---

3 A radio station has a frequency of 60 MHz. What is the wavelength of the radiation?

3
$$c = f\lambda$$

$$\lambda = \frac{3 \times 10^8 \text{ m} \cdot \text{s}^{-1}}{60 \times 10^6 \text{ s}^{-1}}$$

$$= 5 \text{ m}$$

---

4 If the station uses two identical antennas 12 m apart, what is the intensity of the radiation in the direction $\theta = 30°$? The intensity at $\theta = 0°$ is 0.025 W · m^{-2}

4
$$I = I_0 \cos^2\left(\frac{\pi d}{\lambda}\sin\theta\right)$$

$$= 0.025 \text{ W} \cdot \text{m}^{-2} \cos^2\left[\frac{\pi(12 \text{ m})}{5 \text{ m}}\sin 30°\right]$$

$$= 0.0164 \text{ W} \cdot \text{m}^{-2}$$
Note: the term in the parentheses is in radians.

---

5 Light of wavelength 600 nm is incident perpendicularly from air on a thin film ($n = 1.40$). Part of the light is reflected from the first surface of the film, part enters the film and is reflected back at the second face. What is the wavelength of the light in the film?

5
$$\lambda = \frac{\lambda_0}{n}$$

$$= \frac{600 \text{ nm}}{1.40}$$

$$= 429 \text{ nm}$$

---

6 If the film is 10^{-4} cm thick, how many waves are contained along the path of this light in the film?

6 Note: the path length
$$= 2t = 2(10^{-4} \text{ cm})$$
$$\text{number of waves} = \frac{2 \times 10^{-6} \text{ m}}{429 \times 10^{-9} \text{ m}} = 4.66$$

---

7 What is the phase difference between these waves as they leave the film?

7 180°

---

8 What is the intensity at a point of maximum constructive interference of two coherent sources as compared to the intensity of either source alone? Assume $E_1 = E_2$.
   $E_1 = E_2 = E$ = amplitude of sources
   E_p = resultant amplitude

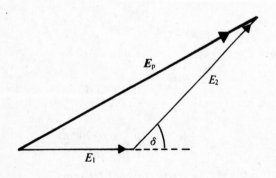

8 Four times as intense. The intensity is proportional to the square of the amplitude of the wave; thus at a point of maximum constructive interference,

$$E_p^2 = E_1^2 + E_2^2 + 2E_1E_2\cos\delta$$
$$= 2E^2 + 2E^2\cos\delta = 2E^2(1 + \cos\delta)$$

$$\text{but } \cos\frac{\delta}{2} = \sqrt{\frac{1 + \cos\delta}{2}}$$

$$\cos^2\frac{\delta}{2} = \frac{1 + \cos\delta}{2}$$

$$\therefore E_p^2 = 2E^2\left(2\cos^2\frac{\delta}{2}\right)$$

$$= 4E^2\cos^2\frac{\delta}{2}$$

9 A plano-convex lens has a radius of curvature of the convex surface = 150 cm. The lens is placed convex side down and illuminated with light of wavelength 680 nm. What is the diameter of the fourth bright ring in the interference pattern?

9 Note, for the fourth ring,
$m = 3$.
$$r = \sqrt{(m + \frac{1}{2})\lambda R}$$
$$= \sqrt{(3 + \frac{1}{2})(680 \times 10^{-9}\text{ m})(1.50\text{ m})}$$
$$= 18.9 \times 10^{-4}\text{ m} = 1.89\text{ mm}$$
diameter $= 2r = 2(1.89\text{ mm}) = 3.78\text{ mm}$

---

10 What is the thinnest film for which destructive interference of light of wavelength 600 nm can take place by reflection? Assume $n = 1.375$.

10 The thickness should be $\frac{1}{4}\lambda$ of the light in the film.

$$t = \frac{1}{4}\frac{\lambda_0}{n} = \frac{600\text{ nm}}{4(1.375)} = 109\text{ nm},$$
where $\lambda_0 = $ wavelength in vacuum.

---

11 Light of 600 nm wavelength from a distant source is incident on a slit 0.8 mm wide. At what angle will the first dark fringe appear?
$n = 1$

11
$$\sin \theta = n\frac{\lambda}{a}$$
$$= \frac{(1)(600 \times 10^{-9}\text{ m})}{0.8 \times 10^{-3}\text{ m}}$$
$$\theta = 7.5 \times 10^{-4}\text{ radians}$$
$$= 0.043°$$
Note: For small angles
$\sin \theta = \theta$ (radians).

---

12 A transmission grating has 6000 lines · cm^{-1}. What is the grating spacing?

12
$$d = \frac{1}{6000\text{ cm}^{-1}} = 1.67 \times 10^{-4}\text{ cm}$$

---

13 What is the longest wavelength that can be observed in the third order for this grating?
$m = 3$

13 The maximum angular deviation = 90°,
$\sin \theta = 1$.
$$\sin \theta = \frac{m\lambda}{d}$$
$$\lambda = \frac{(1)(1.67 \times 10^{-6}\text{ m})}{3} = 557\text{ nm}$$

---

14 How far apart must two objects be on the moon for the unaided eye to recognize them as distinct objects? Use 4 mm as the diameter of the eye pupil and 520 nm as the wavelength of light. The moon is 3.84×10^8 m away.

14
$$\theta_R = \frac{1.22\ \lambda}{d}$$
$$= \frac{1.22(520 \times 10^{-9}\text{ m})}{4 \times 10^{-3}\text{ m}}$$
$$= 1.59 \times 10^{-4}\text{ rad}$$
$$1.59 \times 10^{-4} = \frac{l}{3.84 \times 10^8\text{ m}}$$
$$l = 61.1\text{ km}$$

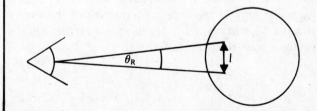

15 A converging lens 25 mm in diameter has a focal length of 15 cm. What angular separation must two distinct objects have to satisfy Rayleigh's criterion? (Use $\lambda = 600$ nm.)

15
$$\theta_R = \frac{1.22\,\lambda}{d}$$
$$= \frac{(1.22)(600 \times 10^{-9}\text{ m})}{25 \times 10^{-3}\text{ m}}$$
$$= 2.93 \times 10^{-5}\text{ rad}$$

---

16 What is the distance between the centers of the diffraction patterns in the focal plane of the lens?

16
$$x = f\theta$$
$$= (15\text{ cm})(2.93 \times 10^{-5}\text{ rad})$$
$$= 4.40\ \mu\text{m}$$

---

17 Two spectral lines have wavelengths λ and $\lambda + \Delta\lambda$, where $\Delta\lambda \ll \lambda$. Show that their angular separation

$$\Delta\theta = \frac{\Delta\lambda}{\sqrt{(d/m)^2 - \lambda^2}}$$

(Hint: start with the equation for the plane diffraction grating and use the dispersion relationship.)

17
$$d\sin\theta = m\lambda$$
$$D = \frac{\Delta\theta}{\Delta\lambda} = \frac{m}{d\cos\theta}$$
$$\Delta\theta = \frac{m\Delta\lambda}{d\cos\theta}$$
$$= \frac{\Delta\lambda}{d/m\cos\theta}$$
But $\sin\theta = \dfrac{m\lambda}{d}$ and
$$\cos\theta = \sqrt{1 - \sin^2\theta} = \sqrt{1 - (m\lambda/d)^2}$$
$$\therefore \Delta\theta = \frac{\Delta\lambda}{d/m\sqrt{1 - (m\lambda/d)^2}}$$
$$= \frac{\Delta\lambda}{\sqrt{(d/m)^2 - \lambda^2}}$$

---

18 Show that the dispersion of a diffraction grating can be expressed by
$$D = \frac{\tan\theta}{\lambda}.$$

18

$$D = \frac{m}{d\cos\theta}$$
but $\sin\theta = \dfrac{m\lambda}{d}$
$$m = \frac{d\sin\theta}{\lambda}$$
$$D = \frac{d\sin\theta}{d\lambda\cos\theta} = \frac{\tan\theta}{\lambda}$$

---

19 A soap bubble is illuminated with violet light ($\lambda = 400$ nm). If the index of refraction of the soap film is 1.42, what would be the thinnest film that could produce constructive interference?

19 For constructive interference,
$$2nt = (m + \tfrac{1}{2})\lambda.$$
For minimum thickness of film, $m = 0$,
$$2nt = \frac{\lambda}{2}$$
$$t = \frac{400\text{ nm}}{2(1.42)\,(2)}$$
$$= 70.4\text{ nm}.$$

STEP BY STEP SOLUTIONS OF PROBLEMS

Problem 1 Plane monochromatic waves of wavelength 550 nm are incident normally on two slits separated by 0.12×10^{-3} m. The resultant interference pattern is observed on a screen 1.5 m away. Find the linear and angular separation of a) the third bright and b) the sixth dark line (Young's experiment).

1 Find the linear separation of the third bright line using

$$\lambda = \frac{y_m d}{mR}, \text{ where } m = 0, 1, 2, 3 \cdots$$

1

$$y_3 = \frac{3\lambda R}{d}$$
$$= \frac{3(550 \times 10^{-9} \text{ m}) (1.5 \text{ m})}{0.12 \times 10^{-3} \text{ m}}$$
$$= 0.0206 \text{ m}$$

2 Find the angular separation of the third bright line.

2

$$\sin \theta_m = \frac{m\lambda}{d} \approx \theta_m$$
$$\text{(for small values of } \theta)$$
$$\theta_3 = \frac{3\lambda}{d}$$
$$= \frac{3(550 \times 10^{-9} \text{ m})}{0.12 \times 10^{-3} \text{ m}}$$
$$= 0.0138 \text{ rad} = 0.79°$$

3 Find the linear separation of the sixth dark line using

$$y = \frac{(m + \frac{1}{2})\lambda R}{d}.$$

$m = 5$ for the sixth dark line.

3

$$y = \frac{(5 + \frac{1}{2}) (550 \times 10^{-9} \text{ m}) (1.5 \text{ m})}{0.12 \times 10^{-3} \text{ m}}$$
$$= 0.0378 \text{ m}$$

4 Find the angular separation of the sixth dark line.

4

$$\sin \theta = \frac{(m + \frac{1}{2})\lambda}{d} \approx \theta$$
$$\theta = \frac{(5 + \frac{1}{2}) (550 \times 10^{-9} \text{ m})}{0.12 \times 10^{-3} \text{ m}} = 0.0252 \text{ rad}$$
$$= 1.44°$$

Problem 2 The radius of curvature of the convex surface of a plano-convex lens is $R = 140$ cm. The lens is placed on a plane glass plate (convex side down) and illuminated from above with green mercury light of wavelength 546 nm. a) Show that the radii of the bright rings are given by

$$r = \sqrt{(m + \frac{1}{2})\lambda R},$$
where $m = 0$, first bright,
$\quad = 1$, second bright,
$\quad = 2$, third bright.

b) Find the diameter of the fourth bright ring.

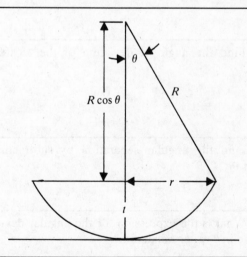

5 Consider a thin film of air wedged between the lens and the plane surface. What is the expression for the maximum intensity of light reflected from the top and bottom surfaces of the film?

5 $$2nt = (m + \frac{1}{2})\lambda,$$
n = index of refraction of the film and t is the thickness of the film for a ring of maximum intensity of radius r.

6 Express t in terms of R and θ.

6 $$t = R - R \cos \theta = R(1 - \cos \theta)$$

7 From the cosine expansion,
$\cos\theta = 1 - \theta^2/2$; substitute in the above.

7
$$t = \frac{R\theta^2}{2}$$

---

8 For small values of θ, $\theta \approx r/R$ (in radians).

8
$$t = \frac{R}{2}\frac{r^2}{R^2} = \frac{r^2}{2R}$$

---

9 Eliminate t between the equations in frames 5 and 8 and solve for r. Since the film is in air, $n = 1$.

9
$$\frac{r^2}{2R} = \frac{(m + \frac{1}{2})\lambda}{2n}$$

$$r = \sqrt{(m + \tfrac{1}{2})\lambda R}$$

---

10 Substitute the given data and find the diameter of the fourth bright ring ($m = 3$).

10
$$r = \sqrt{(3.5)(546 \times 10^{-9}\text{ m})(1.4\text{ m})}$$

$$= 1.64 \times 10^{-3}\text{ m} = 1.64\text{ mm}$$
$$\text{diameter} = 3.28\text{ mm}$$

Problem 3 The yellow light from a sodium vapor lamp is incident normally on a plane transmission grating having 1300 lines $\cdot$ mm^{-1}. The diffraction pattern observed on a screen consists of the sodium doublet of wavelengths 589.00 nm and 589.59 nm. a) Find the angle of deviation of the first order maximum for each of these wavelengths. b) Show that the difference in the angular separation of two spectral lines separated by $\Delta\lambda$ is given by $\Delta\theta = m\Delta\lambda/d \cos\theta$. c) Verify the result obtained in part a) by substituting in the expression of part b).

---

11 Find the grating spacing d.

11
$$d = \frac{1}{1300\text{ mm}^{-1}} = 7.69 \times 10^{-4}\text{ mm}$$
$$= 7.69 \times 10^{-7}\text{ m}$$
$$= 769\text{ nm}$$

---

12 Find the angle of deviation of the 589.59 nm line from $\sin\theta = m\lambda/d$. Note $m = 1$.

12
$$\sin\theta_1 = \frac{589.59\text{ nm}}{769\text{ nm}}$$
$$\theta_1 = 50.06°$$

---

13 Find the angle of deviation of the 589.00 nm line.

13
$$\sin\theta_2 = \frac{589.00\text{ nm}}{769\text{ nm}}$$
$$\theta_2 = 49.99°$$

---

14 Find the angular separation by subtracting θ_2 from θ_1.

14
$$\theta_1 - \theta_2 = 50.06° - 49.99°$$
$$= 0.07°$$

---

15 What is the expression for the angular deviation of the mth order maximum?

15
$$\sin\theta = \frac{m\lambda}{d}$$

---

16 What is the angular deviation of the spectral line $\lambda + \Delta\lambda$?

16
$$\sin(\theta + \Delta\theta) = \frac{m(\lambda + \Delta\lambda)}{d}$$

---

17 Expand. Use
$$\sin(A + B) = \sin A \cos B + \cos A \sin B.$$

17 $\sin \theta \cos \Delta\theta + \cos \theta \sin \Delta\theta$

$$= \frac{m\lambda}{d} + \frac{m\Delta\lambda}{d}$$

---

18 For small values of $\Delta\theta$, $\sin \Delta\theta \approx \Delta\theta$ and $\cos \Delta\theta \approx 1$. Simplify the above.

18 $\sin \theta + \Delta\theta(\cos \theta)$

$$= \frac{m\lambda}{d} + \frac{m\Delta\lambda}{d}$$

---

19 Subtract the expression in frame 15 from the above.

19

$$\Delta\theta(\cos \theta) = \frac{m\Delta\lambda}{d}$$

$$\Delta\theta = \frac{m\Delta\lambda}{d \cos \theta}$$

---

20 Substitute the given data. Use θ_{av}.

$$\theta_{av} = \frac{\theta_1 + \theta_2}{2}$$

$$= \frac{50.06° + 49.99°}{2} = 50.025°$$

20

$$\Delta\theta = \frac{589.59 \text{ nm} - 589 \text{ nm}}{769 \text{ nm} \cos 50.025°}$$
$$= 1.20 \times 10^{-3} \text{ rad} = 0.07°$$

PROGRAMMED TEST

1 *Problem 1* Fraunhofer diffraction from a single slit to determine the wavelength of light from a distant source: Monochromatic light falls on a single slit 0.4 mm wide. A lens with a 60 cm focal length is placed behind the slit to form a diffraction pattern in the focal plane of the lens. If the linear separation between the first and third dark lines is 1.97 mm, what is the wavelength of the light?

1

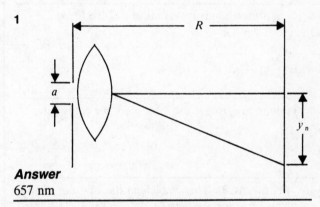

Answer
657 nm

If you solved this problem correctly, go to frame 6. If you could not solve this problem, go through frames 2–5.

---

2 Tabulate the given data.

2
$$a = 0.4 \text{ mm} = 4.0 \times 10^{-4} \text{ m}$$
$$f = R = 60 \text{ cm} = 0.6 \text{ m}$$
$$y_3 - y_1 = 1.97 \text{ mm} = 1.97 \times 10^{-3} \text{ m}$$

---

3 What is the expression for the linear separation of the nth dark line?

3

$$\sin \theta_n = \frac{n\lambda}{a} = \frac{y_n}{R}$$

$$y_n = \frac{n\lambda R}{a}$$

---

4 What is the expression for the linear separation between the first and third dark lines? Solve for λ.

4

$$y_3 - y_1 = \frac{3\lambda R}{a} - \frac{\lambda R}{a} = \frac{2\lambda R}{a}$$

$$\lambda = \frac{a(y_3 - y_1)}{2R}$$

5 Substitute the given data and solve for λ.

5

$$\lambda = \frac{(4.0 \times 10^{-4} \text{ m}) (1.97 \times 10^{-3} \text{ m})}{2(0.6 \text{ m})}$$

$$= 657 \text{ nm}$$

---

6 **Problem 2** Two rectangular glass plates 14 cm long are laid one upon the other on a table and are separated at one end by a metal strip 0.055 mm thick forming a wedge of air. The glass is illuminated normally from above with light of 650 nm wavelength. How many interference fringes are observed per centimeter in the reflected light?

6

14 cm

Answer
12.1 cm^{-1}

If you solved this problem correctly, go to frame 10. If you could not solve this problem, go through frames 7–9.

7 What is the condition for constructive interference at $y = t$?

7 $2t = (m + \frac{1}{2})\lambda$

---

8 Substitute the given values and solve for m.

8

$$2(5.5 \times 10^4 \text{ nm}) = (m + \frac{1}{2}) (650 \text{ nm})$$
$$169.2 = m + 0.5$$
$$m = 168.7$$

---

9 How many fringes are observed per centimeter?

9

$$\frac{168.7}{14 \text{ cm}} = 12.1 \text{ fringes} \cdot \text{cm}^{-1}$$

---

10 **Problem 3** The wavelengths of the visible spectrum are approximately 380–760 nm. The third order spectrum overlaps the second order spectrum regardless of the grating spacing. Find the overlap region (wavelengths and color) by calculating the angular deviation for each of the following wavelengths: violet (380–440 nm), blue (440–470 nm), green (470–550 nm), yellow (550–570 nm), orange (570–620 nm), red (620–760 nm). The spectral lines are produced by a plane grating having 6000 lines · cm^{-1}.

10
Answer
Overlap region: 570 nm (yellow-orange) second order to 507 nm (green) third order.

If you could not solve this problem, go through frames 11–15.

11 Find the grating spacing d.

11

$$d = \frac{1}{6000 \text{ lines} \cdot \text{cm}^{-1}} = 1.67 \times 10^{-6} \text{ m}$$
$$= 1670 \text{ nm}$$

---

12 Find the angular deviation for each of the given wavelengths for each order. Use $\sin \theta = m\lambda/d$. Note, since the angular deviation cannot be greater than 90°, wavelengths beyond 556.7 nm do not produce spectral lines for the third order.

12

λ(nm)	second order	θ
380	$\sin \theta = \dfrac{2(380 \text{ nm})}{1670 \text{ nm}}$	27.1°
440	$\sin \theta = \dfrac{2(440 \text{ nm})}{1670 \text{ nm}}$	31.8°
470	$\sin \theta = \dfrac{2(470 \text{ nm})}{1670 \text{ nm}}$	34.3°
550	$\sin \theta = \dfrac{2(550 \text{ nm})}{1670 \text{ nm}}$	41.2°
570	$\sin \theta = \dfrac{2(570 \text{ nm})}{1670 \text{ nm}}$	43.0°
620	$\sin \theta = \dfrac{2(620 \text{ nm})}{1670 \text{ nm}}$	47.9°
760	$\sin \theta = \dfrac{2(760 \text{ nm})}{1670 \text{ nm}}$	65.5°

λ(nm)	third order	θ
380	$\sin \theta = \dfrac{3(380 \text{ nm})}{1670 \text{ nm}}$	43.0°
440	$\sin \theta = \dfrac{3(440 \text{ nm})}{1670 \text{ nm}}$	52.2°
470	$\sin \theta = \dfrac{3(470 \text{ nm})}{1670 \text{ nm}}$	57.6°
550	$\sin \theta = \dfrac{3(550 \text{ nm})}{1670 \text{ nm}}$	81.1°
556.7	$\sin \theta = \dfrac{3(556.7 \text{ nm})}{1670 \text{ nm}}$	90°

13 Determine the overlap region by comparing angular deviations.

13 The overlap region is from 43° corresponding to 570 nm second order to 65.5° which corresponds to

$$\sin \theta = \frac{m\lambda}{d}$$
$$\lambda = \frac{\sin 65.5°(1670 \text{ nm})}{3}$$
$$= 507 \text{ nm third order}$$

14 How could we determine the overlap region if we knew that all spectral lines of the second order are visible but we are only certain of the first line (380 nm) of the third order?

14 Since d is a constant and the angular deviations of the third order are equal to the angular deviations of the second order (for the boundaries of the overlap region), $m_3\lambda_3 = m_2\lambda_2$. Let λ'' denote the wavelength for which the angular deviation in the second order corresponds to the angular deviation in the third order. Similarly let λ''' denote the wavelength for which the angular deviation in the third order corresponds to the angular deviation in the second. Then

$$3(380 \text{ nm}) = 2\lambda''$$
$$\lambda'' = 570 \text{ nm}$$
$$\text{and } 3\lambda''' = 2(760 \text{ nm})$$
$$\lambda''' = 507 \text{ nm}$$

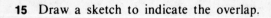
15 Draw a sketch to indicate the overlap.

15

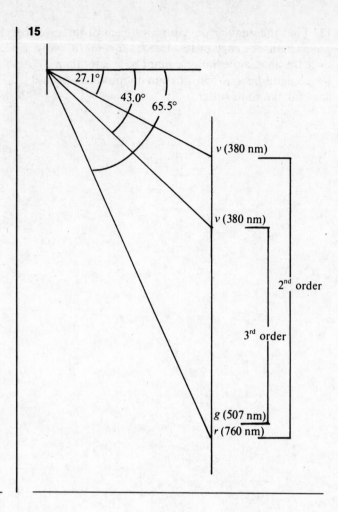

40

Relativistic Mechanics

CHAPTER SUMMARY

Relativistic mechanics is concerned with reference frames moving at speeds comparable to the speed of light. Einstein's principle of relativity states that the laws of physics are the same in every inertial frame of reference. On the basis of this principle in conjunction with his second principle on the constancy of the speed of light in every inertial frame, the Lorentz transformation equations are developed. Among other things, they reveal the phenomena of length contraction and the dilation of time. In accordance with the correspondance principle, the Lorentz transformation reduces to the galilean transformation in newtonian mechanics.

BASIC TERMS — *Give definitions or meanings for the following:*

special theory of relativity (40-I)
principle of relativity (40-1)
galilean coordinate transformation (40-1)
simultaneity (40-2)
time dilation (40-3)
twin paradox (40-3)
length contraction (40-4)

Lorentz transformation (40-5)
relativistic momentum (40-6)
rest mass (40-6)
rest energy (40-7)
correspondence principle (40-8)
general theory of relativity (40-8)

PROGRAMMED QUIZ

1 Can a material body travel with a speed greater than c relative to any frame of reference?

1 No, a body moving with a speed less than c in one frame of reference also has a speed less than c in any other frame of reference.

2 How are the Lorentz transformations related to the galilean transformations?

2 When $u \ll c$, the Lorentz transformations reduce to the galilean transformations.

3 Can we use $F = ma$ in relativistic mechanics?

3 No, the acceleration is not constant but decreases as the particles' speed increases, assuming the force is constant.

4 What is the relativistic generalization of Newton's second law?

4 $F = \Delta p / \Delta t$, where p is the relativistic momentum.

5 What is the rest energy of a particle?

5 It is the energy associated with mass rather than motion, $E = mc^2$.

6 What are some situations in which newtonian mechanics is inadequate?

6 All situations where the speed of the particle approaches c or where there is direct conversion of mass to energy (or energy to mass).

7 What are some situations in which newtonian mechanics is adequate?

7 When dealing with the behavior of macroscopic bodies in mechanical systems.

8 Should the general theory of relativity be applied to the behavior of macroscopic bodies in mechanical systems?

8 No, it only has relevance in cosmology and in problems of astronomical dimensions.

9 What are the two basic principles of the (special) theory of relativity?

9 The laws of physics are the same in every inertial frame of reference, and the speed of light is independent of the frame of reference, i.e., it is the same for all inertial frames.

10 What does the general theory of relativity deal with?

10 Frames of reference which are accelerated with respect to one another.

11 Is the time interval which separates two events occurring at the same point in the frame of reference S' the same as the time interval between these two events as observed in S?

11 No, the time interval depends on the relative motion of the two frames and the speed of light.

12 Are there any particles that actually move at speeds near the speed of light?

12 Yes, elementary particles such as muons move at about $0.998\,c$; massless particles such as photons travel with speed c.

13 The principles of conservation of mass and conservation of energy are independent in newtonian mechanics. Are they also independent in relativistic mechanics?

13 No, they are two special cases of a broader principle — the principle of conservation of mass and energy.

14 A spaceship is approaching the earth at a speed close to *c*. Two identical clocks, one on earth and one on the spaceship, are ticking once per second. At what intervals will the earth observer "hear" the ticks from the spaceship clock?

14 Longer than 1 second due to time dilation.

15 At what intervals will the spaceship hear the earth clock?

15 Longer than 1 second. Note: the earth has a velocity relative to the spacecraft.

16 Can a particle which has no rest mass have energy and momentum?

16 Yes, a photon which has no mass has energy and momentum.

17 Does light require a mechanical medium in which to travel?

17 No; light travels in a vacuum with speed $c \approx 3 \times 10^8 \text{ m} \cdot \text{s}^{-1}$.

18 Is simultaneity an absolute concept?

18 No; two events may seem simultaneous to one observer but not to another.

19 What is proper time?

19 A time interval between two events at the same space point in a frame of reference.

20 What is proper length?

20 The length measured in the rest frame of the body.

21 What about the length of a meter stick measured perpendicular to the direction of motion? Does an observer in another frame of reference note any change in length?

21 No, the contraction formula is for lengths measured parallel to the relative motion of the two frames of reference.

22 How does time dilation explain the twin paradox?

22 Twin 1 remains on earth while twin 2 leaves for outer space at a speed close to *c*. In accordance with time dilation, twin 1 observes twin 2's heartbeat and all other life processes (which can be considered clocks) proceeding more slowly than his own. Therefore, twin 1 concludes that twin 2 is aging at a slower rate and will return to earth younger than twin 1.

MAIN IDEAS

Relativistic mechanics is based upon two principles formulated by Albert Einstein: 1) All laws of physics are valid in every inertial frame of reference. 2) The speed of light *c* in a vacuum is constant regardless of the relative motion of the observer and the light source, i.e. it is the same in all frames of reference.

Galilean coordinate system. Let the coordinate of a point P be x, y, z in inertial frame S and x', y', z' in S' and let u denote the speed with which the origin O' of S' moves relative to O of S along the common x, x' direction. Then $x = x' + ut$, $y = y'$, $z = z'$ and $v = v' + u$. Note that the galilean transformation assumes that time intervals are the same in both reference frames. Also, regardless of the relative velocity between the two frames of reference, a meter stick will always be 1 m in length.

The Lorentz transformation, which is based on the principle of relativity, states that $x' = \dfrac{x - ut}{\sqrt{1 - u^2/c^2}}$, $y' = y$,

$z' = z$, $t' = \dfrac{t - ux/c^2}{\sqrt{1 - u^2/c^2}}$, where x, y, z, t are the space and time coordinates of an event in S and x', y', z', t' are

the space and time coordinates of the same event in S' and u has the same meaning as in the galilean system.

The relationship between intervals to space and/or time between two frames is given by

$$\Delta x' = \frac{\Delta x - u\Delta t}{\sqrt{1 - u^2/c^2}}, \qquad \Delta t' = \frac{\Delta t - u\Delta x/c^2}{\sqrt{1 - u^2/c^2}}.$$

The time interval between two events at different points in space depends on the state of motion of the observer. If two events occur at the same point in S' during a time interval $\Delta t'$, then the time interval Δt measured in reference frame S is given by $\Delta t = \dfrac{\Delta t'}{\sqrt{1 - u^2/c^2}}$ where u is the relative speed between S and S'. Thus t' is

referred to as a proper time — it denotes an interval between two events occurring at the same space point. Note that in this case Δt is not a proper time. However, if Δt is proper in S, then the transformation equation can be written as

$$\Delta t' = \frac{\Delta t}{\sqrt{1 - u^2/c^2}}.$$

Consider the following situations in two frames of reference S and S' with a uniform relative velocity u: A rod at rest in frame S' has a length l', but when measured by an observer in S, it has a length $l = l'\sqrt{1 - u^2/c^2}$. The length measured in the rest frame is denoted as the proper length. Thus l' is a proper length.

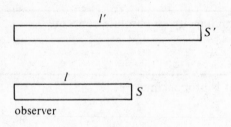

Similarly, a rod at rest in the S frame has a length l, but when observed by S', it has a length $l' = l\sqrt{1 - u^2/c^2}$.

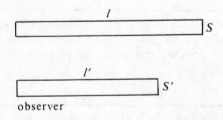

The speed v measured by an observer in S is related to a speed v' measured by an observer in S' by $v' = \dfrac{v - u}{1 - uv/c^2}$ for motion along the x, x' axis only. An outcome of this relationship is that an observer in any

reference frame will measure the same speed of light. The equation may also be written as $v = \dfrac{v' + u}{1 + uv'/c^2}$.

The law of conservation of momentum is valid in relativistic mechanics provided that momentum is defined as $p = \dfrac{mv}{\sqrt{1 - v^2/c^2}}$. Newton's second law is stated as $\boldsymbol{F} = \dfrac{\Delta \boldsymbol{p}}{\Delta t}$.

The work done to accelerate a body from v_1 to v_2 is given by $W = \dfrac{mc^2}{\sqrt{1 - v_2^2/c^2}} - \dfrac{mc^2}{\sqrt{1 - v_1^2/c^2}}$. The rela-

tivistic generalization of kinetic energy is given by $K = \dfrac{mc^2}{\sqrt{1 - v^2/c^2}} - mc^2$, where mc^2 denotes rest energy.

It should be noted that the term mass in our discussion of relativity refers to the rest mass of a particle. The inertial mass is measured by means of $p = \dfrac{mv}{\sqrt{1 - v^2/c^2}}$. Velocity-dependent relativistic mass ($m_{\text{rel}} = \dfrac{m}{\sqrt{1 - v^2/c^2}}$, where m is the rest mass) is not used in our discussion. The total energy of a particle is related to its momentum by $E^2 = (mc^2)^2 + (pc)^2$, where p is the particle's momentum and m is the rest mass. It is interesting to note that even if a particle has no mass (e.g. photon), it will have energy. If $m = 0$ in the above equation, $E = pc$. Also, for a particle at rest ($p = 0$), $E = mc^2$.

The Doppler effect: A light source in frame S' emits light pulses of frequency f' as measured by an observer in that frame. If the source is moving away from S with speed u, then the observed frequency f in S will be given by $f = \sqrt{\dfrac{c - u}{c + u}} f'$. If the source is moving toward the observer, there will be an apparent increase in frequency given by $f = \sqrt{\dfrac{c + u}{c - u}} f'$.

Problem solving strategy:

1 The key to the solution of many problems involving the Lorentz transformation is the understanding of the concepts of proper time and proper length. Proper time in one frame — i.e., a time interval between two events that happen at the same space point — implies that the time interval between the same two events is longer in any other frame.

2 The equation $\Delta t = \dfrac{\Delta t'}{\sqrt{1 - u^2/c^2}}$ may be used only when $\Delta t'$ is a proper time interval in frame S'. Note that Δt is not a proper time interval in S. If Δt is proper in S, use $\Delta t' = \dfrac{\Delta t}{\sqrt{1 - u^2/c^2}}$.

3 Proper length is the length of a body measured in a frame in which it is at rest. In the equation $l = l'\sqrt{1 - u^2/c^2}$, the length l' is a proper length in S' and the length l measured in S is less than l'. Again, if l is a proper length, use $l' = l\sqrt{1 - u^2/c^2}$.

4 The invariant quantity $(\Delta x')^2 - c^2(\Delta t')^2 = (\Delta x)^2 - c^2(\Delta t)^2$ is very useful in many problems. If two events in frame S occurred simultaneously, then $\Delta t = 0$ in the above equation. If two events in frame S occurred at the same space point, then $\Delta x = 0$.

PROGRAMMED QUIZ

1 An unstable particle has a lifetime of 2.6×10^{-8} s (measured in its own frame of reference). If this particle is moving with a speed of $0.8\,c$ with respect to a laboratory, what is the lifetime as measured in the laboratory?

1

$$\begin{aligned}
\Delta t &= \frac{\Delta t'}{\sqrt{1 - u^2/c^2}} \\
&= \frac{2.6 \times 10^{-8} \text{ s}}{\sqrt{1 - (0.8\,c/c)^2}} \\
&= \frac{2.6 \times 10^{-8} \text{ s}}{\sqrt{1 - 0.64}} \\
&= 4.33 \times 10^{-8} \text{ s}
\end{aligned}$$

2 Through what distance, measured in the laboratory, does the particle travel during its lifetime?

2

$$\begin{aligned}
\text{distance} &= u\Delta t \\
&= (0.8)\,(3 \times 10^8 \text{ m} \cdot \text{s}^{-1})\,(4.33 \times 10^{-8}\,\text{s}) \\
&= 10.4 \text{ m}
\end{aligned}$$

3 Two events are observed in a frame of reference S to occur simultaneously at points separated by a distance of 2 m. In a second frame S' moving relative to S, the two events appear to be separated by 4 m. With what velocity does the frame of reference S' move relative to frame S?

3

$$\Delta x' = \frac{\Delta x - u\Delta t}{\sqrt{1 - u^2/c^2}}$$

since $\Delta t = 0$,

$$\Delta x = \Delta x' \sqrt{1 - u^2/c^2}$$
$$2\,\text{m} = 4\,\text{m} \sqrt{1 - u^2/c^2}$$
$$4\,\text{m}^2 = 16\,\text{m}^2\,(1 - u^2/c^2)$$
$$\tfrac{1}{4} = 1 - u^2/c^2$$
$$\tfrac{1}{4}c^2 = c^2 - u^2$$
$$u^2 = 0.75\,c^2$$
$$u = 0.866\,c$$
$$= 2.60 \times 10^8\,\text{m}\cdot\text{s}^{-1}$$

4 What is the time interval between the events as measured in S'? (Note $\Delta t = 0$.) A negative value for $\Delta t'$ denotes that, although the events were simultaneous in the S frame, for a positive value of u the x_2' event occurred before the x_1' event. $\Delta t'$ will be positive for a negative value of u.

4

$$\Delta t' = \frac{\Delta t - u\Delta x/c^2}{\sqrt{1 - u^2/c^2}}$$

$$= \frac{(-2.6 \times 10^8\,\text{m}\cdot\text{s}^{-1})(2\,\text{m})/(3 \times 10^8\,\text{m}\cdot\text{s}^{-1})^2}{\sqrt{1 - (2.6 \times 10^8\,\text{m}\cdot\text{s}^{-1})^2/(3 \times 10^8\,\text{m}\cdot\text{s}^{-1})^2}}$$

$$= \frac{-0.578 \times 10^{-8}\,\text{s}}{\sqrt{1 - 0.751}}$$

$$|\Delta t'| = 1.16 \times 10^{-8}\,\text{s}$$

5 Two particles emerge from a high-energy accelerator in opposite directions, each with a speed $0.5\,c$ as measured by a laboratory observer. What is the relative velocity of the particles?
(Hint: Consider one particle, P_1, as the S frame and the laboratory, containing particle P_2 as the S' frame. What is the speed of P_2 relative to P_1?)

5 Since the particles emerge in opposite directions, we can say that the laboratory is moving away from P_1 with a speed $u = 0.5\,c$. However, the second particle has a speed $v' = 0.5\,c$ relative to the S' frame. But we are interested in the speed of P_2 as observed in the S frame. Therefore,

$$v = \frac{v' + u}{1 + uv'/c^2}$$
$$= \frac{0.5\,c + 0.5\,c}{1 + 0.5\,c(0.5\,c)/c^2}$$
$$= 0.8\,c$$

It should be noted that the above equation is equivalent to

$$v' = \frac{v - u}{1 - u\,v/c^2}$$

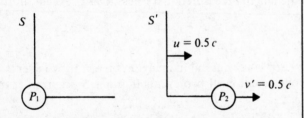

6 What is the speed of a particle whose kinetic energy is equal to its rest energy?

6

$$K = mc^2$$
$$\frac{mc^2}{\sqrt{1 - v^2/c^2}} - mc^2 = mc^2$$
$$\frac{1}{\sqrt{1 - v^2/c^2}} = 2$$
$$1 - v^2/c^2 = \tfrac{1}{4}$$
$$v^2/c^2 = 0.75$$
$$v^2 = 0.75(3 \times 10^8\,\text{m}\cdot\text{s}^{-1})^2$$
$$v = 2.60 \times 10^8\,\text{m}\cdot\text{s}^{-1}$$

7 What is the momentum of an electron moving at a speed of $2 \times 10^8\,\text{m}\cdot\text{s}^{-1}$?

7

$$p = \frac{mv}{\sqrt{1 - v^2/c^2}}$$

$$= \frac{(9.11 \times 10^{-31}\,\text{kg})(2 \times 10^8\,\text{m}\cdot\text{s}^{-1})}{\sqrt{1 - (2 \times 10^8\,\text{m}\cdot\text{s}^{-1})^2/(3 \times 10^8\,\text{m}\cdot\text{s}^{-1})^2}}$$

$$= \frac{18.2 \times 10^{-23}\,\text{kg}\cdot\text{m}\cdot\text{s}^{-1}}{0.745}$$

$$= 24.4 \times 10^{-23}\,\text{kg}\cdot\text{m}\cdot\text{s}^{-1}$$

8 What is the kinetic energy of the electron? Use the relativistic expression.

8

$$K = \frac{mc^2}{\sqrt{1 - v^2/c^2}} - mc^2$$

$$= \left(\frac{1}{\sqrt{1 - v^2/c^2}} - 1 \right) mc^2$$

$$= \left(\frac{1}{\sqrt{1 - (2 \times 10^8 \text{ m} \cdot \text{s}^{-1})^2/(3 \times 10^8 \text{ m} \cdot \text{s}^{-1})^2}} - 1 \right)$$
$$\times (9.11 \times 10^{-31} \text{ kg})(3 \times 10^8 \text{ m} \cdot \text{s}^{-1})^2$$

$$= \left(\frac{1}{0.745} - 1 \right) (82.0 \times 10^{-15} \text{ J})$$

$$= 2.81 \times 10^{-14} \text{ J}$$

---

9 What is the kinetic energy of the electron? Use the nonrelativistic expression.

9

$$K = \frac{1}{2}mv^2$$
$$= \frac{1}{2}(9.11 \times 10^{-31} \text{ kg})(2 \times 10^8 \text{ m} \cdot \text{s}^{-1})^2$$
$$= 1.82 \times 10^{-14} \text{ J}$$

---

10 At what speed is the kinetic energy of a particle equal to $8\,mc^2$?

10

$$K = 8\,mc^2$$

$$\frac{mc^2}{\sqrt{1 - v^2/c^2}} - mc^2 = 8\,mc^2$$

$$\frac{1}{\sqrt{1 - v^2/c^2}} = 9$$

$$\frac{1}{81} = 1 - v^2/c^2$$

$$v^2/c^2 = 0.988$$

$$v = 0.994\,c$$
$$= 2.98 \times 10^8 \text{ m} \cdot \text{s}^{-1}$$

---

11 How much work must be done to accelerate a particle from rest to a speed of $0.5\,c$? Use the work-energy relation $W = \Delta K = K_2 - K_1 =$

$$\left(\sqrt{\frac{mc^2}{1 - v_2^2/c^2}} - mc^2 \right) - \left(\sqrt{\frac{mc^2}{1 - v_1^2/c^2}} - mc^2 \right)$$

11

$$W = \frac{mc^2}{\sqrt{1 - v_2^2/c^2}} - \frac{mc^2}{\sqrt{1 - v_1^2/c^2}}$$

Since $v_1 = 0$

$$W = \frac{mc^2}{\sqrt{1 - (0.5\,c)^2/c^2}} - mc^2$$

$$= \frac{mc^2}{0.866} - mc^2$$

$$= 1.15\,mc^2 - mc^2 = 0.15\,mc^2$$

---

12 An electron and a positron (a positively charged electron), initially at rest, collide and disappear producing electromagnetic radiation. Find the total energy of the radiation. Each particle has a mass of 9.11×10^{-31} kg.

12

$$E = mc^2$$
$$= 2(9.11 \times 10^{-31} \text{ kg}) (3 \times 10^8 \text{ m} \cdot \text{s}^{-1})^2$$
$$= 1.64 \times 10^{-13} \text{ J}$$

13 A spacecraft is approaching the red ($\lambda' = 675$ nm) planet Mars. How fast should it travel in order for the planet to appear violet ($\lambda = 400$ nm)?

13 Use the Doppler equation

$$f = \sqrt{\frac{c+u}{c-u}} f'.$$

Since $c = f\lambda$,

$$f = \frac{c}{\lambda} \text{ and } f' = \frac{c}{\lambda'}$$

Substituting in the Doppler equation, we have

$$\frac{c}{\lambda} = \sqrt{\frac{c+u}{c-u}} \left(\frac{c}{\lambda'}\right)$$

$$\lambda = \sqrt{\frac{c-u}{c+u}} \lambda'$$

$$400 \text{ nm} = \sqrt{\frac{c-u}{c+u}} (675 \text{ nm})$$

$$0.593 = \sqrt{\frac{c-u}{c+u}}.$$

Square both sides and solve for u:

$$0.351 = \frac{c-u}{c+u}$$

$$u = 0.480\, c$$
$$= 0.480\,(3 \times 10^8 \text{ m} \cdot \text{s}^{-1})$$
$$= 1.44 \times 10^8 \text{ m} \cdot \text{s}^{-1}.$$

STEP BY STEP SOLUTIONS OF PROBLEMS

Problem 1   A spaceship moving away from the earth with a speed of $0.6\,c$ fires a 5 m missile in the same direction as its motion with a speed of $0.2\,c$ relative to the spaceship. An astronaut on the ship observes that the firing event takes 10 s. a) What is the missile speed relative to the earth? b) What is the length of the missile (prior to firing), as observed on earth? c) What is the time interval of the firing event as measured on earth?

1 Find v by using $v = \dfrac{v' + u}{1 + uv'/c^2}$, where S is the earth's frame of reference and S' the spaceship's frame of reference.

1

$$u = 0.6\, c$$
$$v' = 0.2\, c$$
$$v = \frac{0.2\, c + 0.6\, c}{1 + (0.6\, c)\,(0.2\, c)/c^2}$$
$$= 0.714\, c$$

---

2 Find the length of the missile (prior to firing), as observed on earth, use $l = l' \sqrt{1 - u^2/c^2}$. Note that it is assumed that the ends of the missile, in its rest frame, were observed simultaneously (i.e. $\Delta t' = 0$). The length l' is denoted as the proper length and the effect of observing a smaller length is called the Lorentz contraction.

2

$$l = 5 \text{ m} \sqrt{1 - \left(\frac{0.6\, c}{c}\right)^2}$$
$$= 4 \text{ m}$$

---

3 Find the time interval of the firing event as measured on earth. Use $\Delta t = \dfrac{\Delta t'}{\sqrt{1 - u^2/c^2}}$. It should be noted that this transformation can only be used when $\Delta t'$ is a proper time interval in S', i.e. the firing event occurred at the same space point in S', $\Delta x' = 0$.

3

$$\Delta t = \frac{10 \text{ s}}{\sqrt{1 - \left(\frac{0.6\, c}{c}\right)^2}}$$
$$= 12.5 \text{ s}$$

Thus 12.5 s on earth seems to be equivalent to 10 s as observed on the spaceship. This phenomenon is called "time dilation".

Problem 2 Two events observed in a frame S occur at points x_1 and x_2 at times t_1 and t_2, respectively. The same events are observed in frame S' at x_1', x_2', t_1' and t_2'. Frame S' is moving relative to S along the x-axis with velocity u. If $(x_2 - x_1) = \Delta x$, $(t_2 - t_1) = \Delta t$, $(x_2' - x_1') = \Delta x'$ and $(t_2' - t_1') = \Delta t'$, prove that the quantity $(\Delta x)^2 = c^2(\Delta t)^2$ is invariant under the Lorentz transformation, $(\Delta x')^2 - c^2(\Delta t')^2 = (\Delta x)^2 - c^2(\Delta t)^2$.

4 Using the transformation equation for length from S to S', express the relationship between change in length in one frame with the other.

4

$$x' = \frac{x - ut}{\sqrt{1 - u^2/c^2}}$$

where u = relative speed between the frames.

$$\therefore x_2' - x_1' = \frac{x_2 - x_1 - u(t_2 - t_1)}{\sqrt{1 - u^2/c^2}}$$

$$\Delta x' = \frac{\Delta x - u\Delta t}{\sqrt{1 - u^2/c^2}}$$

5 Repeat for the time interval relationship between the two frames.

5

$$t' = \frac{t - ux/c^2}{\sqrt{1 - u^2/c^2}}$$

$$t_2' - t_1' = \frac{t_2 - t_1 - u(x_2 - x_1)/c^2}{\sqrt{1 - u^2/c^2}}$$

$$\Delta t' = \frac{\Delta t - u\Delta x/c^2}{\sqrt{1 - u^2/c^2}}$$

6 Square both sides of the equations in frames 4 and 5.

6

$$(\Delta x')^2 = \frac{(\Delta x)^2 - 2u(\Delta x)\,(\Delta t) + u^2(\Delta t)^2}{1 - u^2/c^2}$$

$$(\Delta t')^2 = \frac{(\Delta t)^2 - 2u(\Delta x)\,(\Delta t)/c^2 + u^2(\Delta x)^2/c^4}{1 - u^2/c^2}$$

7 Multiply both sides of this equation by c^2.

7

$$c^2(\Delta t')^2 = \frac{c^2(\Delta t)^2 - 2u(\Delta x)\,(\Delta t) + u^2(\Delta x)^2/c^2}{1 - u^2/c^2}$$

8 Subtract this equation from the equation for $(\Delta x')^2$.

8

$$(\Delta x')^2 - c^2(\Delta t')^2 =$$

$$\frac{[(\Delta x)^2 - c^2(\Delta t)^2] + u^2[(\Delta t)^2 - (\Delta x)^2/c^2]}{1 - u^2/c^2}$$

$$= \frac{[(\Delta x)^2 - c^2(\Delta t)^2] - u^2/c^2\,[(\Delta x)^2 - c^2(\Delta t)^2]}{1 - u^2/c^2}$$

$$= \frac{[(\Delta x)^2 - c^2(\Delta t)^2]\,[1 - u^2/c^2]}{1 - u^2/c^2}$$

$$= (\Delta x)^2 - c^2(\Delta t)^2$$

Problem 3 Two events are observed in a frame of reference S to occur simultaneously at points separated by a distance Δx. In a second frame S' moving relative to S along the line joining the two points in S, the two events appear to be separated by $\Delta x'$. a) Show that the time interval between the events as measured in S' is $\Delta t' = \frac{1}{c}\sqrt{(\Delta x')^2 - (\Delta x)^2}$. b) What is the time interval between the events as measured in S' if $\Delta x = 3$ m and $\Delta x' = 5$ m? c) What is the relative velocity u of the frames S and S'?

9 Since the two events in frames S occurred simultaneously, $\Delta t = 0$. Substitute $\Delta t = 0$ in the relativistic invariant equation
$$(\Delta x')^2 - c^2(\Delta t')^2 = (\Delta x)^2 - c^2(\Delta t)^2$$
and solve for $\Delta t'$.

9
$$(\Delta x')^2 - c^2(\Delta t')^2 = (\Delta x)^2$$
$$c^2(\Delta t')^2 = (\Delta x')^2 - (\Delta x)^2$$
$$\Delta t' = \frac{1}{c}\sqrt{(\Delta x')^2 - (\Delta x)^2}$$

10 What is the time interval between the events as measured in S' if $\Delta x = 3$ m and $\Delta x' = 5$ m.

10
$$\Delta t' = \frac{1}{3\times 10^8 \text{ m}\cdot\text{s}^{-1}}\sqrt{(5\text{ m})^2 - (3\text{ m})^2}$$
$$= 1.33\times 10^{-8}\text{ s}$$

11 The relative velocity u of the two frames can be obtained from the equation in frame 4. Let $\Delta t = 0$ and solve for u.

11
$$\Delta x' = \frac{\Delta x}{\sqrt{1 - u^2/c^2}}$$
Square both sides:
$$(\Delta x')^2 = \frac{(\Delta x)^2}{1 - u^2/c^2}$$
$$\frac{u^2}{c^2} = 1 - \left(\frac{\Delta x}{\Delta x'}\right)^2$$
$$u = c\sqrt{1 - \left(\frac{\Delta x}{\Delta x'}\right)^2}$$

12 Substitute $\Delta x = 3$ m and $\Delta x' = 5$ m in the above equation and solve for u.

12
$$u = 3\times 10^8 \text{ m}\cdot\text{s}^{-1}\sqrt{1 - \left(\frac{3\text{ m}}{5\text{ m}}\right)^2}$$
$$= 3\times 10^8 \text{ m}\cdot\text{s}^{-1}(0.80)$$
$$= 2.4\times 10^8 \text{ m}\cdot\text{s}^{-1}$$

Problem 4 In order to simplify computations involving the Lorentz transformation, it is often desirable to use the following trigonometric transformation: consider a right triangle in which $\sin\theta = v/c$, where θ is the angle adjacent to the base, v the speed of the body and c the speed of light. Let the base of the triangle denote the rest energy mc^2. Show that a) the hypotenuse of the triangle represents the total energy and b) the side opposite θ represents pc, where $p = $ relativistic momentum. c) Verify the relationship $E^2 = (mc^2)^2 + (pc)^2$.

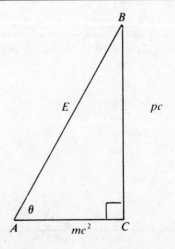

13 Find the expressions for $\cos \theta$ and $\tan \theta$ by using $\cos \theta = \sqrt{1 - \sin^2 \theta}$ and $\tan \theta = \sin \theta / \cos \theta$.

13

$$\cos \theta = \sqrt{1 - \sin^2 \theta}$$
$$= \sqrt{1 - v^2/c^2}$$
$$\tan \theta = \frac{v/c}{\sqrt{1 - v^2/c^2}}$$
$$= \frac{v}{c\sqrt{1 - v^2/c^2}}$$

---

14 Find the expression for AB and thus show that the hypotenuse represents the total energy.

14

$$\cos \theta = \frac{AC}{AB}$$
$$AB = \frac{AC}{\cos \theta}$$
$$= \frac{mc^2}{\sqrt{1 - v^2/c^2}}$$

(which represents the total energy).

---

15 Find the expression for BC and thus show that the side opposite θ represents the product of relativistic momentum and the speed of light.

15

$$\tan \theta = \frac{BC}{AC}$$
$$BC = mc^2 \tan \theta$$
$$= mc^2 \frac{v}{c\sqrt{1 - v^2/c^2}}$$
$$= \left(\frac{mv}{\sqrt{1 - v^2/c^2}} \right) c = pc$$

---

16 Use the Pythagorean theorem to show that the triangle represents the relationship $E^2 = (mc^2)^2 + (pc)^2$. The kinetic energy K is given by the difference in the lengths of the hypotenuse and of the base of the triangle.

16

$$\overline{AB}^2 = \overline{AC}^2 + \overline{BC}^2$$
$$\left(\frac{mc^2}{\sqrt{1 - v^2/c^2}} \right)^2 = (mc^2)^2 + (pc)^2$$
$$K = \frac{mc^2}{\sqrt{1 - v^2/c^2}} - mc^2$$

PROGRAMMED TEST

1 **Problem 1** A constant force of 1 N acts upon a 0.68 kg mass which was originally at rest with respect to earth. a) Over what interstellar distance must the force act to impart a speed of 0.5 c to the mass? b) What is the ratio of the kinetic energy the mass to the rest mass at 0.5 c? c) Compute the relativistic momentum and the non-relativistic momentum, d) compute the kinetic energy and the rest energy and thus find the total kinetic energy.

1

Answer

1 light year, 0.1547, 1.18×10^8 kg $\cdot$ m $\cdot$ s^{-1}, 1.02×10^8 kg $\cdot$ m $\cdot$ s^{-1}, 7.07×10^{16} J

If you solved this problem correctly, go to frame 11. If you could not solve this problem, go through frames 2–10.

2 Find the work done by the force through a distance Δx. This work is equal to the kinetic energy acquired by the mass.	**2** $\qquad K = F\Delta x$
3 What is the relativistic generalization of kinetic energy?	**3** $\qquad K = \dfrac{mc^2}{\sqrt{1 - v^2/c^2}} - mc^2$
4 Equate the two equations and solve for Δx.	**4** $\begin{aligned} \Delta x &= \dfrac{K}{F} = \dfrac{1}{F}\left(\dfrac{mc^2}{\sqrt{1 - v^2/c^2}} - mc^2\right) \\ &= \dfrac{mc^2}{F}\left(\dfrac{1}{\sqrt{1 - v^2/c^2}} - 1\right) \end{aligned}$
5 Substitute the given data and solve for Δx in terms of light years.	**5** $\dfrac{1}{\sqrt{1 - (0.5\,c/c)^2}} - 1 = \dfrac{1}{\sqrt{0.75}} - 1 = 0.1547$ $\Delta x = \dfrac{0.68\text{ kg }(3 \times 10^8\text{ m} \cdot \text{s}^{-1})^2}{1\text{ N}}\,(0.1547)$ $= 9.47 \times 10^{15}\text{ m}$ $= \left(9.47 \times 10^{15}\text{ m}\right)\left(\dfrac{1\text{ light year}}{9.47 \times 10^{15}\text{ m}}\right)$ $= 1.00\text{ light year}$
6 What is the ratio of the kinetic energy of the mass to its rest mass?	**6** $\dfrac{E}{mc^2} = \left(\dfrac{mc^2}{\sqrt{1 - v^2/c^2}} - mc^2\right)/mc^2$ $= \dfrac{1}{\sqrt{1 - v^2/c^2}} - 1$ $= 0.1547\text{ (from the previous frame)}$
7 Compute the relativistic momentum.	**7** $\begin{aligned} \text{relativistic } p &= \dfrac{mv}{\sqrt{1 - v^2/c^2}} \\ &= \dfrac{0.68\text{ kg }(0.5)\,(3 \times 10^8\text{ m} \cdot \text{s}^{-1})}{\sqrt{1 - (0.5\,c/c)^2}} \\ &= 1.18 \times 10^8\text{ kg} \cdot \text{m} \cdot \text{s}^{-1} \end{aligned}$
8 Compute the nonrelativistic momentum.	**8** $\begin{aligned} \text{nonrelativistic } p &= mv \\ &= (0.68\text{ kg})\,(0.5)\,(3 \times 10^8\text{ m} \cdot \text{s}^{-1}) \\ &= 1.02 \times 10^8\text{ kg} \cdot \text{m} \cdot \text{s}^{-1} \end{aligned}$

9 Find the total kinetic energy E by adding the kinetic energy of the mass and its rest energy.

9

$$
\begin{aligned}
K &= F\Delta x \\
&= 1\ \text{N}(9.47 \times 10^{15}\ \text{m}) \\
&= 9.47 \times 10^{15}\ \text{J} \\
&= 0.947 \times 10^{16}\ \text{J}
\end{aligned}
$$

$$
\begin{aligned}
\text{rest energy} &= mc^2 \\
&= 0.68\ \text{kg}\ (3 \times 10^8\ \text{m} \cdot \text{s}^{-1})^2 \\
&= 6.12 \times 10^{16}\ \text{J}
\end{aligned}
$$

$$
\begin{aligned}
E &= K + \text{rest energy} \\
&= 0.947 \times 10^{16}\ \text{J} + 6.12 \times 10^{16}\ \text{J} \\
&= 7.07 \times 10^{16}\ \text{J}
\end{aligned}
$$

---

10 Check your result with the relationship $E^2 = (mc^2)^2 + (pc)^2$.

10

$$
\begin{aligned}
E &= \sqrt{(mc^2)^2 + (pc)^2} \\
&= \sqrt{(6.12 \times 10^{16}\ \text{J})^2 + [(1.18 \times 10^8\ \text{kg} \cdot \text{m} \cdot \text{s}^{-1})\,(3 \times 10^8\ \text{m} \cdot \text{s}^{-1})]^2} \\
&= 7.07 \times 10^{16}\ \text{J}
\end{aligned}
$$

---

11 ***Problem 2*** Two events are observed in a frame of reference S to occur at the same space point with a time interval of Δt. In a second frame S' moving relative to S, the time interval between the events is observed to be $\Delta t'$. a) Show that the distance between the two positions of the two events as measured in S' is $|\Delta x'| = c\sqrt{(\Delta t')^2 - (\Delta t)^2}$. b) Find $\Delta x'$ if $\Delta t' = 4$ s and $\Delta t = 3$ s. c) What is the relative velocity u of the frames S and S'?

11
Answer
7.94×10^8 m, 1.98×10^8 m $\cdot$ s^{-1}

If you solved this problem correctly, go to frame 16. If you could not solve this problem, go through frames 12–15.

12 Since the two events in frame S occurred at the same space point, $\Delta x = 0$. Substitute $\Delta x = 0$ in the relativistic invariant equation
$$(\Delta x')^2 - c^2(\Delta t')^2 = (\Delta x)^2 - c^2(\Delta t)^2$$
and solve for $\Delta x'$.

12

$$
\begin{aligned}
(\Delta x')^2 - c^2(\Delta t')^2 &= -\,c^2(\Delta t)^2 \\
(\Delta x')^2 &= c^2(\Delta t')^2 - c^2(\Delta t)^2 \\
\Delta x' &= c\sqrt{(\Delta t')^2 - (\Delta t)^2}
\end{aligned}
$$

---

13 Find $\Delta x'$ if $\Delta t' = 4$ s and $\Delta t = 3$ s.

13

$$
\begin{aligned}
\Delta x' &= 3 \times 10^8\ \text{m} \cdot \text{s}^{-1}\ \sqrt{(4\ \text{s})^2 - (3\ \text{s})^2} \\
&= 7.94 \times 10^8\ \text{m}
\end{aligned}
$$

---

14 The relative velocity u of the two frames can be obtained from
$$\Delta t' = \frac{\Delta t - u\Delta x/c^2}{\sqrt{1 - u^2/c^2}}.$$
Let $\Delta x = 0$ and solve for u.

14

$$\Delta t' = \frac{\Delta t}{\sqrt{1 - u^2/c^2}}$$

Square both sides:

$$(\Delta t')^2 = \frac{(\Delta t)^2}{1 - u^2/c^2}$$

$$\frac{u^2}{c^2} = 1 - \left(\frac{\Delta t}{\Delta t'}\right)^2$$

$$u = c\sqrt{1 - \left(\frac{\Delta t}{\Delta t'}\right)^2}$$

15 Substitute $\Delta t = 3$ s and $\Delta t' = 4$ s and solve for u.

15

$$u = 3 \times 10^8 \text{ m} \cdot \text{s}^{-1} \sqrt{1 - \left(\frac{3 \text{ s}}{4 \text{ s}}\right)^2}$$

$$= 3 \times 10^8 \text{ m} \cdot \text{s}^{-1} (0.661)$$
$$= 1.98 \times 10^8 \text{ m} \cdot \text{s}^{-1}$$

---

16 **Problem 3** A nucleus, initially at rest with a rest mass M, spontaneously disintegrates into two lighter nuclei of equal mass m. During the process there is a mass loss ΔM and the two lighter nuclei emerge in opposite directions; find their approximate speed if $\Delta M/M \ll 1$.

16
Answer

$$v \approx c \sqrt{\frac{2\Delta M}{M}}$$

If you could not solve this problem, go through frames 17–20.

17 Express the mass m of each lighter nucleus in terms of M and ΔM.

17 $m = \frac{1}{2}(M - \Delta M)$

---

18 In accordance with the principle of conservation of energy, the total energy before the disintegration is equal to the total energy after disintegration. Express this principle in terms of the given variables and K, the kinetic energy of each lighter nucleus.

18 Rest energy of M = rest energy of $2m$ + kinetic energy of $2m$.

$$\therefore Mc^2 = (2m)c^2 + 2K$$

$$\text{where } K = \frac{mc^2}{\sqrt{1 - v^2/c^2}} - mc^2$$

$$Mc^2 = (2m)c^2 + \frac{2mc^2}{\sqrt{1 - v^2/c^2}} - 2mc^2$$

$$= \frac{2mc^2}{\sqrt{1 - v^2/c^2}}$$

$$\sqrt{1 - v^2/c^2} = \frac{2mc^2}{Mc^2} = \frac{2m}{M}$$

Square both sides

$$1 - v^2/c^2 = 4\left(\frac{m}{M}\right)^2$$

---

19 Substitute $m = \frac{1}{2}(M - \Delta M)$ and simplify the expression for $1 - v^2/c^2$.

19

$$1 - v^2/c^2 = 4\left(\frac{\frac{1}{2}(M - \Delta M)}{M}\right)^2$$

$$= \left(1 - \frac{\Delta M}{M}\right)^2$$

$$= 1 - \frac{2\Delta M}{M} + \left(\frac{\Delta M}{M}\right)^2$$

---

20 Since $\Delta M/M \ll 1$, $(\Delta M/M)^2$ could be ignored. Solve for v.

20

$$1 - \frac{v^2}{c^2} \approx 1 - \frac{2\Delta M}{M}$$

$$v \approx c \sqrt{\frac{2\Delta M}{M}}$$

41

Protons, Electrons, and Atoms

CHAPTER SUMMARY

Although the electromagnetic theory adequately explains various phenomena associated with the propagation of light (classical optics), it fails to account for such phenomena as the emission and absorption of light, the photoelectric effect, line spectra of elements and the production and scattering of x-rays. To understand the emission of electrons from metal surfaces we must postulate that light, in addition to its wave properties, also possesses particle characteristics — photons carry the energy of the electromagnetic wave. Furthermore, particles such as electrons and protons also have a wave nature. These quantum concepts are used to describe continuous as well as line spectra. In addition to a discussion of atomic spectra, energy levels are analyzed, and the laser and x-ray production and scattering are presented.

BASIC TERMS — *Give definitions or meanings for the following:*

photons (41-2)
quanta (41-2)
photoelectric effect (41-2)
Planck's constant (41-2)
thermionic emission (41-2)
work function (41-2)
threshold frequency (41-2)
stopping potential (41-2)
Balmer series (41-3)
Rydberg constant (41-3)
ground state (41-3)
excited state (41-3)
resonance radiation (41-3)
line spectrum (41-3)
continuous spectrum (41-3)

absorption spectrum (41-3)
energy level (41-3)
atomic spectrum (41-3)
Rutherford scattering (41-4)
nucleus (41-4)
Bohr model (41-5)
stable orbit (41-5)
quantum number (41-5)
stimulated emission (41-6)
population inversion (41-6)
metastable state (41-6)
laser (41-6)
x-ray (41-7)
Compton scattering (41-7)

PROGRAMMED QUIZ

1 What phenomena are adequately explained by classical optics? What phenomena cannot be explained by classical optics?

1 Adequately explained: interference, diffraction, polarization, reflection and refraction. Not explained: line spectra, the photoelectric effect, emission and absorption of light, the production and scattering of x-rays.

2 How does an electron acquire sufficient energy to escape from the metal surface in thermionic emission? in the photoelectric effect?

2 By the energy of thermal agitation; if the metal is illuminated by light of sufficiently short wavelength.

3 What is the threshold frequency?

3 The minimum frequency below which, for a given emitter, no photoelectrons will be emitted. For most metals it is in the ultraviolet.

4 Which substances produce a continuous spectrum? Which substances produce line spectra?

4 Continuous spectra are produced by incandescent solids or liquids; line spectra by gases through which an electrical discharge is passing or by flames containing volatile salts.

5 Do atoms emit electromagnetic radiation?

5 Atoms radiate by emitting a photon only when a transition is made from one energy level to a lower level. This determines the characteristic line spectrum of the element.

6 What do we mean by the ground state and excited states of an atom?

6 The ground state is the lowest energy level (minimum energy) that an atom can have. All higher levels are called excited states.

7 How can an atom be raised from a ground state to an excited state?

7 With the aid of an electric discharge or by the absorption of radiant energy.

8 How does the sun's spectrum appear?

8 As a continuous spectrum (due to the main body of the sun) crossed by many faint dark lines (the absorption spectrum of the cooler vapors in the atmosphere). The dark lines are called Fraunhofer lines.

9 What is the difference between spontaneous emission and stimulated emission?

9 In spontaneous emission, an excited atom becomes normal by emitting a photon in a random direction with a random phase. In stimulated emission, a photon encounters an excited atom and forces it to emit another photon of the same frequency, in the same direction and in the same phase.

10 Describe the radiation beam produced by a laser.

10 Very intense, almost perfectly parallel, almost monochromatic and spatially coherent at all points within a given cross section.

11 Why can the emission of x-rays be described as an inverse photoelectric effect?

11 In photoelectric emission, the energy of a photon is transformed into kinetic energy of an electron; in x-ray emission, kinetic energy of an electron is transformed into that of a photon.

12 Compare the photograph of the emission spectrum of a certain gas to the photograph of a continuous spectrum source placed behind the gas.

12 The resulting absorption spectrum will look like the photographic negative of the emission spectrum.

---

13 Both optical spectra and x-rays result from the excitation of electrons. How do they differ?

13 Optical spectra arise from the excitation of outer electrons; x-rays result from the excitation of the inner electrons in atoms.

---

14 What was Einstein's explanation of the photoelectric effect?

14 The incident light exists in small bundles (photons). When a photon strikes a metal surface it is completely absorbed. Part of the energy (work function) is used to remove the electron from the metal; the remaining energy is the kinetic energy of the electron.

---

15 In the photoelectric effect, what does the maximum kinetic energy of the photoelectrons depend on?

15 The frequency of the incident light and the work function of the metal.

---

16 In the photoelectric effect, when the intensity of the incident light increases, does the maximum kinetic energy of a photoelectron increase also?

16 No, the maximum kinetic energy does not depend on the intensity of the incident light but on the wavelength. As the light intensity increases, the photoelectric current increases but only in the number of emitted electrons, not in the energy of the individual electron.

---

17 In Compton scattering, a photon collides with an electron initially at rest. What happens?

17 The photon gives up some of its energy and momentum to the electron, which recoils upon impact. The final photon has less energy, smaller frequency and longer wavelength than the initial one.

MAIN IDEAS

Electromagnetic radiation has a dual nature; it can be described in terms of wave and particle properties. Einstein postulated that the energy of radiation is concentrated in discrete units called photons or quanta.

In the photoelectric effect, electrons are liberated from the surface of a conductor by light incident on the surface. The electrons absorb energy from the incident radiation and are thus able to escape the surface by climbing over the potential energy barrier that normally confines them in the material. Consider a phototube as shown in the sketch. The metallic surface (called an emitter) and a metal plate (called a collector) are in an evacuated tube. The negative terminal of a source of potential difference is connected to the emitter and the positive terminal to the collector. If the emitter is illuminated by a frequency of light higher than some threshold frequency, a current will flow through the galvanometer.

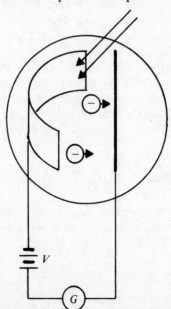

The maximum velocity of the emitted electrons depends only on the frequency of the light illuminating the surface and is given by $\frac{1}{2}mv_{max}^2 = hf - \phi$, where hf is the energy of the photon, f is the frequency of the light and h is Planck's constant $= 6.63 \times 10^{-34}$ J $\cdot$ s; the work function ϕ is the energy the electron needs to escape the surface. This equation states that when a photon delivers energy hf into the surface, it is absorbed by a single electron. Part of the energy, ϕ, is used in the electron's escape from the surface, the remainder, $hf - \phi$, is the electron's kinetic energy.

The electron flow can be made to stop when the reversed potential V is made large enough so that the potential energy eV is greater than the kinetic energy $\frac{1}{2}mv_{max}^2$. This reversed potential is called the stopping potential V_0 and can be calculated from $eV_0 = \frac{1}{2}mv_{max}^2$. Thus $V_0 = mv_{max}^2/2e$, where e is the electron charge $= 1.60 \times 10^{-19}$ C. The stopping potential can also be obtained from $V_0 = hf/e - \phi/e$.

Incandescent solids or liquids produce continuous spectra, i.e. light of all wavelengths is present. However, gases through which an electrical discharge is passing, or a flame into which a volatile salt has been introduced, produce a line spectrum characteristic of the element emitting the light.

The wavelengths of the spectral lines of hydrogen can be obtained from the following series: $1/\lambda = R(1/m^2 - 1/n^2)$, where λ is the wavelength of the emitted line, $R =$ Rydberg constant $= 1.097 \times 10^7$ m^{-1}, and m and n are integers, $n > m$. The series spectra for hydrogen:

for $m = 1$, $n = 2, 3, 4, ...,$	Lyman (ultraviolet)
$m = 2$, $n = 3, 4, 5, ...,$	Balmer (visible light)
$m = 3$, $n = 4, 5, 6, ...,$	Paschen (infrared)
$m = 4$, $n = 5, 6, 7, ...,$	Bracket (infrared)
$m = 5$, $n = 6, 7, 8, ...,$	Pfund (infrared)

According to Bohr, each atom has a series of discrete energy levels. The atom cannot have an energy intermediate between two levels. When an atom makes a transition from one energy level to a lower level, it emits a photon whose energy is equal to the energy difference between the initial and final states. Thus when an electron goes from a higher state E_i to a lower state E_f, the energy difference is emitted as electromagnetic radiation in accordance with $hf = E_i - E_f$. The total energy of an electron in the Bohr atom is given by $E = 1/\epsilon_0^2 \cdot me^4/8n^2h^2$, where e is the electron charge, m is the electron mass, h is Planck's constant, ϵ_0 is the permittivity of vacuum and n is an integer ≥ 1. The lowest energy level is referred to as the ground state and levels of higher energy are called excited states. A spectral line is emitted when an atom goes from an excited state to a lower one.

An atom can absorb only those photons which it has the capability of emitting . Consider the sun's atmosphere which contains vapors consisting of the same elements found in the main body of the sun. When the intense light of the sun passes through its comparatively cooler atmosphere, the lines of the common elements are absorbed. The dark lines in the sun's spectrum are called Fraunhofer lines.

The electrons in an atom are arranged in spherical shells: K, L, M, N, etc. (the K shell being the closest to the nucleus). Each shell can accomodate a maximum number of electrons: the maximum for K is 2 electrons, for L eight, M 18, N 32. The outer electrons of an atom are responsible for optical spectra. Relatively small amounts of energy are required to remove those electrons to excited states and on their return to their normal states wavelengths in or near the visible region are emitted. Since the inner electrons are more tightly bound, much more energy is required to displace them from their normal state. Hence, when an inner electron is displaced and then returns to its normal level, a photon of larger energy and higher frequency is emitted. The high-energy and short-wavelength radiation is called x-rays.

When x-rays strike matter some of the radiation is scattered by the electrons. This phenomenon is called Compton scattering. If λ' is the wavelength of the scattered and λ the wavelength of the incident x-rays, then $\lambda' - \lambda = h/mc (1 - \cos \phi)$, where ϕ is the angle through which the incident x-ray is scattered, m is the electron mass, h is Planck's constant and c is the speed of light in vaccum.

PROGRAMMED QUIZ

1 What is the relation between the threshold frequency f_0 and the work function ϕ in the photoelectric effect?

1 $\phi = hf_0$

2 What is the work function of a photoelectric surface if light of frequency 3×10^{15} Hz will eject photoelectrons with a maximum velocity of 1.76×10^6 m·s^{-1}?

2 $\frac{1}{2}mv_{max}^2 = hf - \phi$

$\phi = (6.63 \times 10^{-34} \text{ J} \cdot \text{s})(3 \times 10^{15} \text{ s}^{-1})$
$\quad - \frac{1}{2}(9.11 \times 10^{-31} \text{ kg})(1.76 \times 10^6 \text{ m} \cdot \text{s}^{-1})^2$

$\quad = 19.9 \times 10^{-19} \text{ J} - 14.1 \times 10^{-19} \text{ J}$

$\quad = 5.8 \times 10^{-19} \text{ J}$

---

3 Convert the work function to eV.

3 $\left(5.8 \times 10^{-19} \text{ J} \right) \left(\dfrac{1 \text{ eV}}{1.60 \times 10^{-19} \text{ J}} \right) = 3.63 \text{ eV}$

---

4 What is the threshold wavelength of a metal whose work function is 2.5 eV?

4 Note: the work function must be expressed in joules.

$\left(2.5 \text{ eV} \right) \left(\dfrac{1.6 \times 10^{-19} \text{ J}}{1 \text{ eV}} \right) = 4 \times 10^{-19} \text{ J}$

$\phi_0 = hf_0 = h\dfrac{c}{\lambda_0}$

$\lambda_0 = \dfrac{(6.63 \times 10^{-34} \text{ J} \cdot \text{s})(3 \times 10^8 \text{ m} \cdot \text{s}^{-1})}{4 \times 10^{-19} \text{ J}}$

$\quad = 4.97 \times 10^{-7} \text{ m} = 497 \text{ nm}, \quad$ which is visible light

---

5 Compute the frequency of a photon whose energy equals the rest energy of the electron.

5 $E = mc^2 = hf$

$f = \dfrac{(9.11 \times 10^{-31} \text{ kg})(3 \times 10^8 \text{ m} \cdot \text{s}^{-1})^2}{6.63 \times 10^{-34} \text{ J} \cdot \text{s}}$

$\quad = 1.24 \times 10^{20} \text{ Hz}$

---

6 What is the wavelength?

6 $c = f\lambda$

$\lambda = \dfrac{3 \times 10^8 \text{ m} \cdot \text{s}^{-1}}{1.24 \times 10^{20} \text{ s}^{-1}}$

$\quad = 2.42 \times 10^{-12} \text{ m}$

---

7 What is the momentum of this photon?

7 $p = \dfrac{E}{c} = \dfrac{mc^2}{c} = mc$

$\quad = (9.11 \times 10^{-31} \text{ kg})(3 \times 10^8 \text{ m} \cdot \text{s}^{-1})$

$\quad = 2.73 \times 10^{-22} \text{ kg} \cdot \text{m} \cdot \text{s}^{-1}$

---

8 A photon has the same momentum as an electron moving at 2×10^6 m·s^{-1}. What is the wavelength of the photon?

8 $(mv)_{electron} = (h/\lambda)_{photon}$

$\lambda = \dfrac{6.63 \times 10^{-34} \text{ J} \cdot \text{s}}{(9.11 \times 10^{-31} \text{ kg})(2 \times 10^6 \text{ m} \cdot \text{s}^{-1})}$

$\quad = 3.64 \times 10^{-10} \text{ m}$

---

9 A photon of $\lambda = 0.420$ nm strikes an electron originally at rest. Afer the collision, the photon is scattered through an angle of 120° to its original direction. What is the wavelength of the photon after collision? Note that cos 120° = − 0.5.

9

$$\lambda' - \lambda = \frac{h}{mc}(1 - \cos \phi)$$
$$\lambda' = 4.20 \times 10^{-10} \text{ m}$$
$$+ \left[\frac{6.63 \times 10^{-34} \text{ J} \cdot \text{s}}{(9.11 \times 10^{-31} \text{ kg}) (3 \times 10^8 \text{ m} \cdot \text{s}^{-1})} \right]$$
$$\times (1 - \cos 120°)$$
$$= 4.20 \times 10^{-10} \text{ m} + (0.0243 \times 10^{-10} \text{ m}) (1.5)$$
$$= 4.24 \times 10^{-10} \text{ m} = 0.424 \text{ nm}$$

10 What is the speed of the photon before and after the collision?

10 The speed of a photon is always c.

11 A photon has a frequency of 6×10^{14} Hz. What is the corresponding photon energy?

11

$$E = hf$$
$$= (6.63 \times 10^{-34} \text{ J} \cdot \text{s}) (6 \times 10^{-4} \text{ s}^{-1})$$
$$= 3.98 \times 10^{-19} \text{ J}$$

12 What must be the difference in energy (in eV) between two states of an atom for this photon to be emitted?

12

$$E = (3.97 \times 10^{-19} \text{ J}) \left(\frac{1 \text{ eV}}{1.6 \times 10^{-19} \text{ J}} \right)$$
$$= 2.48 \text{ eV}$$

13 What is the wavelength of the spectral line emitted as the hydrogen atom goes from the $n = \infty$ to the $n = 2$ state?

13

$$\frac{1}{\lambda} = R \left[\frac{1}{2^2} - \frac{1}{n^2} \right]$$
$$= 1.097 \times 10^7 \text{ m}^{-1} \left[\frac{1}{4} - \frac{1}{\infty^2} \right]$$
$$= 0.274 \times 10^7 \text{ m}^{-1}$$
$$\lambda = 365 \text{ nm}$$

14 What is the maximum increase in x-ray wavelength that can occur during Compton scattering?

14

$$\lambda' - \lambda = \frac{h}{mc}(1 - \cos \phi)$$

$(\lambda' - \lambda)$ has its maximum value when $\phi = 180°$ and $\cos \phi = -1$.

$$\lambda' - \lambda = \frac{2h}{mc}$$
$$= \frac{2(6.63 \times 10^{-34} \text{ J} \cdot \text{s})}{(9.11 \times 10^{-31} \text{ kg}) (3 \times 10^8 \text{ m} \cdot \text{s}^{-1})}$$
$$= 4.85 \times 10^{-12} \text{ m} = 0.00485 \text{ nm}$$

STEP BY STEP SOLUTIONS OF PROBLEMS

Problem 1 The photoelectric work function of potassium is 2.25 eV. If light having a wavelength of 420 nm falls on potassium, find a) the stopping potential, b) the kinetic energy in eV of the most energetic electrons ejected and c) the velocities of these electrons.

1 Find the frequency of the light by using $c = f\lambda$.

1

$$f = \frac{c}{\lambda} = \frac{3 \times 10^8 \text{ m} \cdot \text{s}^{-1}}{420 \times 10^{-9} \text{ m}}$$
$$= 7.14 \times 10^{14} \text{ Hz}$$

---

2 Express $\phi = 2.25$ eV in terms of joules. $1 \text{ eV} = 1.60 \times 10^{-19}$ J.

2

$$\phi = (2.25 \text{ eV}) \left(\frac{1.60 \times 10^{-19} \text{ J}}{1 \text{ eV}} \right)$$
$$= 3.60 \times 10^{-19} \text{ J}$$

---

3 Find the stopping potential by using $eV_0 = hf - \phi$, where $V_0 = $ stopping potential.

3

$$V_0 = \frac{hf - \phi}{e}$$

$$= \frac{6.63 \times 10^{-34} \text{ J} \cdot \text{s}(7.14 \times 10^{14} \text{ s}^{-1}) - 3.60 \times 10^{-19} \text{ J}}{1.6 \times 10^{-19} \text{ C}}$$

$$= \frac{4.73 \times 10^{-19} \text{ J} - 3.60 \times 10^{-19} \text{ J}}{1.60 \times 10^{-19} \text{ C}}$$

$$= 0.706 \text{ V}$$

---

4 Find the kinetic energy in eV of the most energetic electrons ejected. Use kinetic energy $= eV_0$.

4 Since $(1.60 \times 10^{-19} \text{ C})(1 \text{ V}) = 1.60 \times 10^{-19} \text{ J} = 1 \text{ eV}$,
$$eV_0 = e(0.706 \text{ V}) = 0.706 \text{ eV}$$

---

5 Find the velocities of these electrons by using $\frac{1}{2}mv_{max}^2 = eV_0$.

5

$$v_{max} = \sqrt{\frac{2eV_0}{m}}$$

$$= \sqrt{\frac{2(1.60 \times 10^{-19} \text{ J})(0.706 \text{ V})}{9.11 \times 10^{-31} \text{ kg}}}$$

$$= 4.98 \times 10^5 \text{ m} \cdot \text{s}^{-1}$$

Problem 2 When x-rays impinge on matter, some of the radiation is scattered. If the scattered radiation emerges at an angle ϕ with respect to the incident direction and if λ and λ' are the wavelengths of the incident and scattered radiation respectively, show that

$$\lambda' - \lambda = \frac{h}{mc} (1 - \cos \phi),$$ where m is the electron mass.

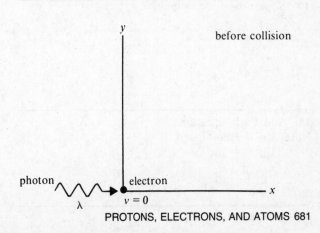

Summary of Symbols

	incident photon	scattered photon	electron at rest	recoiling electron
wavelength	λ	λ'		
frequency	f	f'		
momentum	p	p'		P
energy	pc	$p'c$	mc^2	E

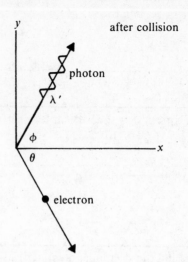

---

6 Consider a photon colliding with an electron at rest. What are the energy and momentum of the photon before collision?

6 $\text{Energy} = hf$

$$\text{momentum} = \frac{hf}{c} = p$$

---

7 Apply the principle of conservation of momentum for each axis. Let f' denote the frequency of the photon and P the momentum of the electron after collision. The speed of the photon before and after the collision is c.

7 For x-axis

$$\frac{hf}{c} = \frac{hf'}{c} \cos \phi + P \cos \theta$$

For y-axis

$$0 = \frac{hf'}{c} \sin \phi - P \sin \theta$$

---

8 Apply the principle of conservation of energy. Let E denote the energy of the electron after collision.

8 $hf + mc^2 = hf' + E$

The initial energy of the electron is mc^2.

---

9 Solve the first equation in frame 7 for $P \cos \theta$ and the second equation for $P \sin \theta$.

9

$$P \cos \theta = \frac{hf}{c} - \frac{hf'}{c} \cos \phi$$

$$P \sin \theta = \frac{hf'}{c} \sin \phi$$

---

10 Square both equations.

10

$$P^2 \cos^2 \theta = \frac{h^2 f^2}{c^2} - \frac{2h^2 ff'}{c^2} \cos \phi + \frac{h^2 f'^2}{c^2} \cos^2 \phi$$

$$P^2 \sin^2 \theta = \frac{h^2 f'^2}{c^2} \sin^2 \phi$$

---

11 Add both equations.
Note: $\sin^2 \theta + \cos^2 \theta = 1$
        $\sin^2 \phi + \cos^2 \phi = 1$

11

$$P^2 = \frac{h^2 f^2}{c^2} + \frac{h^2 f'^2}{c^2} - \frac{2h^2 ff'}{c^2} \cos \phi$$

$$P^2 c^2 = (hf)^2 + (hf')^2 - 2(hf)(hf') \cos \phi$$

---

12 Solve the equation in frame 8 for E and square both sides.

12
$$E = hf - hf' + mc^2$$
$$E^2 = (hf - hf')^2 + 2(hf - hf')mc^2 + (mc^2)^2$$

---

13 Subtract the equation in frame 12 from the one in frame 11.

13
$$P^2c^2 - E^2 = 2(hf)(hf') - 2(hf)(hf')\cos\phi$$
$$- 2hfmc^2 + 2hf'mc^2 - (mc^2)^2$$

---

14 Substitute $E^2 = (mc^2)^2 + (Pc)^2$ and simplify.

14
$$f - f' = \frac{hff'}{mc^2}(1 - \cos\phi)$$
divide both sides by ff'
$$\frac{1}{f'} - \frac{1}{f} = \frac{h\cdot}{mc^2}(1 - \cos\phi)$$

---

15 Multiply both sides by c. Substitute $\lambda' = c/f'$, $\lambda = c/f$.

15
$$\frac{c}{f'} - \frac{c}{f} = \frac{h}{mc}(1 - \cos\phi)$$
$$\lambda' - \lambda = \frac{h}{mc}(1 - \cos\phi)$$

Note: The photon gave up some of its energy and momentum to the electron, which recoiled as a result of the collision. The resulting photon has a smaller frequency, longer wavelength and less energy than the initial one.

Problem 3 The photoelectric threshold wavelength of zinc is 349 nm. Calculate the maximum kinetic energy, in electron volts, of the electrons ejected from a zinc surface by ultraviolet radiation of wavelength 290 nm.

16 What is the relationship between the frequency, wavelength and speed for any wave?

16
$$c = f\lambda$$

---

17 Substitute the above in the relation for kinetic energy, $\frac{1}{2}mv_{max}^2 = eV_0 = hf - \phi$.

17
$$eV_0 = hf - \phi = hf - hf_0$$
$$= hc\left(\frac{1}{\lambda} - \frac{1}{\lambda_0}\right)$$

The threshold frequencies f_0 is the value of f when eV_0 approaches 0. Thus, $hf_0 - \phi = 0$ or $\phi = hf_0$.

---

18 Solve for the stopping potential V_0 and substitute the given values.

18
$$V_0 = \frac{hc}{e}\left(\frac{1}{\lambda} - \frac{1}{\lambda_0}\right)$$
$$= \frac{(6.63 \times 10^{-34}\ \text{J}\cdot\text{s})(3 \times 10^8\ \text{m}\cdot\text{s}^{-1})}{1.60 \times 10^{-19}\ \text{C}}$$
$$\times \left(\frac{1}{290 \times 10^{-9}\ \text{m}} - \frac{1}{349 \times 10^{-9}\ \text{m}}\right)$$
$$= 0.719\ \text{V}$$

19 What is the kinetic energy in electron volts?
Note: $K = eV_0$.

19

$$K = e(0.719) \text{ J}$$

$$= \left(e(0.719) \text{ J} \right) \left(\frac{1 \text{ eV}}{e\text{J}} \right)$$

$$= 0.719 \text{ eV}$$

Note: $1 \text{ eV} = 1.60 \times 10^{-19} \text{ J} = e\text{J}$

PROGRAMMED TEST

1 **Problem 1** When light of wavelength 200 nm falls upon a clean aluminum surface, the retarding potential necessary to stop the emission of photoelectrons is 2.0 V. What is the photoelectric threshold wavelength for aluminum?

1 **Answer**

295 nm

If you solved this problem correctly, go to frame 6. If you could not solve this problem, go through frames 2-5.

2 What is the expression for the stopping potential V_0?

2 $eV_0 = hf - \phi$

3 Express the stopping potential equation in terms of wavelength. Let f_0 and λ_0 denote the threshold frequency and wavelength respectively.

3 Since $hf_0 = \phi$ and
$$c = f_0\lambda_0,$$

$$\phi = \frac{hc}{\lambda_0}$$

$$\therefore eV_0 = \frac{hc}{\lambda} - \frac{hc}{\lambda_0}$$

4 Solve the equation for stopping potential for λ_0.

4
$$\frac{hc}{\lambda_0} = \frac{hc}{\lambda} - eV_0$$

$$= \frac{hc - eV_0\lambda}{\lambda}$$

$$\lambda_0 = \frac{hc\lambda}{hc - eV_0\lambda}$$

5 Substitute the given values.

5

$$\lambda_0 = \frac{6.63 \times 10^{-34} \text{J} \cdot \text{s}(3 \times 10^8 \text{m} \cdot \text{s}^{-1})(2 \times 10^{-7} \text{m})}{6.63 \times 10^{-34} \text{J} \cdot \text{s}(3 \times 10^8 \text{m} \cdot \text{s}^{-1}) - 1.6 \times 10^{-19} \text{C}(2\text{V})(2 \times 10^{-7} \text{m})}$$

$$= 295 \text{ nm}$$

6 **Problem 2** What is the shortest wavelength produced in an x-ray tube by a rapidly moving electron which has been accelerated through a potential difference of 2.5×10^6 V?

6 **Answer**

0.000498 nm

If you solved this problem correctly, go to frame 10. If you could not solve this problem, go through frames 7-9.

7 Find the kinetic energy of the electron.

7
$$K = eV$$
$$= 1.60 \times 10^{-19} \, C(2.5 \times 10^6 \, V)$$
$$= 4.0 \times 10^{-13} \, J$$

---

8 Find the frequency of the photon.

8
$$E = hf$$
$$f = \frac{4.0 \times 10^{-13} \, J}{6.63 \times 10^{-34} \, J \cdot s} = 6.03 \times 10^{20} \, Hz$$

---

9 Find the wavelength.

9
$$c = f\lambda$$
$$\lambda = \frac{3 \times 10^8 \, m \cdot s^{-1}}{6.03 \times 10^{20} \, Hz}$$
$$= 4.98 \times 10^{-13} \, m$$
$$= 0.000498 \, nm$$

---

10 *Problem 3* What is the maximum velocity of the photoelectrons emitted by light of frequency 3×10^{15} Hz from a photoelectric surface whose work function is 2.25 eV?

10 *Answer*
$$1.89 \times 10^6 \, m \cdot s^{-1}$$

If you could not solve this problem, go through frames 11-13.

11 Convert the work function to joules.

11
$$\left(2.25 \, eV \right) \left(\frac{1.60 \times 10^{-19} \, J}{1 \, eV} \right) = 3.6 \times 10^{-19} \, J$$

---

12 What is the maximum kinetic energy of photoelectrons ejected by light of frequency f?

12 $\tfrac{1}{2}mv_{max}^2 = hf - \phi$

---

13 Solve for the maximum velocity and substitute the given values.

13
$$v_{max}^2 = \frac{2(hf - \phi)}{m}$$
$$= \frac{2[(6.63 \times 10^{-34} \, J \cdot s)(3 \times 10^{15} \, s^{-1}) - 3.6 \times 10^{-19} \, J]}{9.11 \times 10^{-31} \, kg}$$
$$v_{max} = 1.89 \times 10^6 \, m \cdot s^{-1}$$

42

Quantum Mechanics

CHAPTER SUMMARY

Although the Bohr atom was successful in predicting the energy levels of a hydrogen atom, it could not be applied to atoms with two or more electrons. This could only be accomplished by the quantum mechanics developed by Schrödinger on the basis of de Broglie's postulate that matter may, under certain circumstances behave like waves. In studying quantum mechanics, we must abandon our usual experiences and what we call common sense and think in terms of probabilities and uncertainties. Thus familiar particles e.g. electrons and protons are described by wave functions. The wave function can be used to calculate the average position of a particle, its average velocity and dynamic quantities such as energy, momentum and angular momentum.

BASIC TERMS — *Give definitions or meanings for the following:*

de Broglie wavelength (42-1)
Davisson-Germer experiment (42-1)
electron diffraction (42-1)
quantum mechanics (42-2)
electron microscope (42-2)
Heisenberg uncertainty principle (42-3)
principal quantum number (42-4)
angular momentum quantum number (42-4)

magnetic quantum number (42-4)
wave function (42-4)
Shcrödinger equation (42-4)
gyromagnetic ratio (42-5)
Zeeman effect (42-5)
electron spin (42-6)
spin-orbit coupling (42-6)

PROGRAMMED QUIZ

1 In what respect is the Bohr atom inconsistent with classical electromagnetic theory?

1 Classically, as the electrons circled the nucleus they would be accelerated toward the center of the circle, radiate energy and emit a continuous spectrum. Observation shows that an atom is stable and radiates only when it makes a transition from one permitted orbit to another.

2 In the Bohr model, what is the significance of the negative sign in the equation for the total energy of an electron in any orbit?

2 It all depends on the way we define potential energy. If a free electron has $E = 0$, an electron which is bound to an atom must have $E < 0$. In its lowest state, the hydrogen electron has an energy of -13.6e V. Thus 13.6 e V (the ionization energy) is required to free the electron from the atom.

3 What is the normal or ground state of the hydrogen atom?

3 The ground state is that of lowest energy, with the electron revolving in the orbit of smallest radius.

4 Can an atom be in an excited state for a long period of time?

4 No, the excited state is unstable. The electron quickly falls back to a state of lower energy, emitting a photon in the process.

5 What did de Broglie postulate?

5 That electrons and protons may in some circumstances behave like waves. A particle of mass m moving with a speed v should have a wavelength given by $\lambda = h/mv$.

6 In quantum mechanics, how do we regard material particles?

6 Not as geometrical points but as intrinsically spreadout entities.

7 According to quantum mechanics, do electrons in an atom move in definite orbits as predicted by the Bohr model?

7 No, the electrons in atoms are visualized as diffuse clouds surrounding the nucleus. However, energy states corresponding to the orbits are still assigned.

8 How can the limit of resolution of a microscope be made smaller? In what device is this applied?

8 By decreasing the wavelength, e.g. using electrons rather than light waves to form an image of the object; electron microscope.

9 What is the meaning of the wave function for a particle?

9 The wave function describes the distribution of the particle in space. If the particle has charge, the wave function can be used to find the charge density at any point in space. It can also be used to calculate the average position, average velocity, momentum, energy and angular momentum of the particle.

10 What are the four quantum numbers in a model of an atom?

10 The principal quantum number n, angular momentum quantum number l, magnetic quantum number m and spin quantum number s.

11 What is Heisenberg's uncertainty principle as applied to the position and momentum of a particle?

11 The product of the uncertainties in the measurement of momentum and position must satisfy the inequality $\Delta x \, \Delta p_x \geqq h/2\pi$.

12 Do only position and momentum have uncertainty?

12 No, there is also uncertainty in the energy of a system, $\Delta E \Delta t \geq h/2\pi$, where Δt is the time interval during which the system remains in a given state. state.

13 In measuring the momentum and positions of a particle simultaneously, can the uncertainty be circumvented by using more sophisticated experimental techniques?

13 No, to detect a particle the detector must interact with it and this unavoidably changes the state of motion of the particle.

14 What was the basic deficiency of the Bohr atom?

14 Although the Bohr model predicted the energy levels of the hydrogen atom it could not be applied to more complex atoms. In addition, it did not predict the relative intensities of spectral lines.

15 What basic principles are used in the mathematical development of the Bohr atom?

15 The electrostatic force of attraction between the nucleus and the electron provides the centripetal force between the charges; the angular momentum of the electron mvr is an integral multiple of $h/2\pi$.

16 Illustrate Bohr's correspondence principle.

16 For large values of n the differences between quantum and classical calculations are not significant.

MAIN IDEAS

The Bohr model of the atom is based on the following into postulates: 1) The only allowable electron orbits are those for which the angular momentum of the electron is an integral multiple of $h/2\pi$, where h is Planck's constant. While in orbit, the atom does not radiate any energy. 2) An atom radiates or absorbs energy when an electron makes a transition from one orbit to another in accordance with $E_i - E_f = hf$, where E_i is the initial energy associated with an orbit and E_f its final energy. If an electron moves from an outer orbit to an inner orbit, energy is radiated. If an electron moves from an inner to an outer orbit, energy is absorbed.

The hydrogen atom is composed of a single electron (mass m and charge $-e$) circling a positively charged nucleus (mass M and charge Ze). For hydrogen, the atomic number $Z = 1$. Since the electrostatic force of attraction between the nucleus and the electron provides the centripetal force between the charges, $1/4\pi\epsilon_0 \cdot Ze^2/r^2 = mv^2/r$. According to Bohr's first postulate, $mvr = nh/2\pi$, where $n = 1, 2, 3$, etc. Thus the radius of the orbit is given by $r = n^2\epsilon_0 h^2/\pi me^2 = n^2(0.529 \times 10^{-10}$ m$)$ and the velocity of the electron is given by $v = 1/n(e^2/2\epsilon_0 h) = 1/n(2.19 \times 10^6$ m $\cdot$ s$^{-1})$. The quantum number n denotes the stable orbit of the electron.

The kinetic energy of the electron in the nth orbit is given by $K = 1/\epsilon_0^2 \cdot me^4/8n^2h^2$ and the potential energy $U = -1/\epsilon_0^2 \cdot me^4/4n^2h^2$. The total energy is $K + U = -1/\epsilon_0^2 \cdot me^4/8n^2h^2$. The total energy has a negative sign because the reference level of the potential energy is taken with the electron at an infinite distance from the nucleus. The energy levels of the hydrogen atom are given by $E_n = E_1/n^2$, $n = 1, 2, 3, ...$ where $E_1 = -13.6$ eV $= -2.18 \times 10^{-18}$ J is the energy of the innermost orbit. The reference level of the potential energy of the electron is taken with the electron at an infinite distance from the nucleus, the minus sign indicates that the electron is bound to the atom. The ionization energy is the work required to remove an electron from an atom in its ground state. Thus the ionization energy of hydrogen is 13.6 eV.

The frequency of a photon during an emission process is given by $f = Rc(1/n_1^2 - 1/n_2^2)$, where $R = $ Rydberg constant $= me^4/8\epsilon_0^2 h^3 = 1.097 \times 10^7$ m^{-1}, $c = $ speed of light, $n_2 = $ the quantum number of the excited state and $n_1 = $ the quantum number of the lower state to which the electron returns after the emission process. The magnetic moment of the current loop associated with an electron in its first orbit is given by $\mu = he/4\pi m = 9.27 \times 10^{-24}$ A $\cdot$ m^2.

Consider a free electron of mass m moving with a speed v; de Broglie postulated that it should have a wavelength given by $\lambda = h/mv$, where h is Planck's constant. Thus not only is electromagnetic radiation dualistic in nature, i.e. behaving in some aspects like waves and in others like particles, but the same is true of matter. Electrons and protons also exhibit wave-like characteristics. The de Broglie concept indicates that the wave seems to be "wrapped" around the orbit. In the figure, $2\pi r = 5\lambda$.

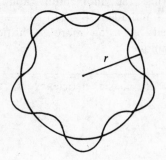

Comparison of massless photons and massive particles, e.g., electrons, protons, neutrons.

Photon	Material particle
travels at speed of light	can never acquire a speed c
rest mass = 0	possesses a rest mass at $v = 0$
possesses no electric charge	may carry a charge; electron −
	neutron (no charge)
	proton +
exists only in flight	exists in motion or at rest
in a collision — when it is brought to rest it transfers all of its energy to another particle and vanishes	in a collision — it transfers its motional energy to another body and remains as a material particle

An electron which passes through a slit of width a has an uncertainty in position and momentum. If Δp_y denotes the uncertainty in the y-component of the momentum of the electron, then $\Delta p_y a \geq h$ where $h =$ Planck's constant and width a represents the uncertainty in the position of the electron with respect to the slit.

The Heisenberg uncertainty principle states that it is not possible to simultaneously specify the position and momentum of a particle with unlimited accuracy. If Δx and Δp denote the uncertainty in position and momentum respectively, then their product must satisfy the inequality $\Delta x \Delta p_x \geq h/2\pi$. The uncertainty principle can also involve energy. The uncertainty in energy ΔE depends on the time interval Δt during which a system remains in a given state. The relation is $\Delta E \Delta t \geq h/2\pi$. On the basis of quantum mechanics, the magnitude L of the angular momentum of an electron in the hydrogen atom in a state with energy E_n and principal quantum number n is given by $L = \hbar \sqrt{l(l + 1)}$, $l = 0, 1, 2, \cdots, (n - 1)$ and $L_z = m\hbar$ ($m = 0, \pm 1, \pm 2, \cdots, \pm l$) where $\hbar = h/2\pi$.

PROGRAMMED QUIZ

1 Determine the kinetic energy, in joules, for a hydrogen atom in the $n = 2$ state.

1

$$K = \frac{1}{\epsilon_0^2} \frac{me^4}{8n^2h^2}$$

$$= \frac{(9.11 \times 10^{-31} \text{ kg}) (1.6 \times 10^{-19} \text{ C})^4}{(8.85 \times 10^{-12} \text{ C}^2 \cdot \text{N}^{-1} \cdot \text{m}^{-2})^2 (8) (2)^2 (6.63 \times 10^{-34} \text{ J} \cdot \text{s})^2}$$
$$= 5.42 \times 10^{-19} \text{ J}$$

2 What is the energy in electron volts?

2

$$(5.42 \times 10^{-19} \text{ J}) \left(\frac{1 \text{ eV}}{1.60 \times 10^{-19} \text{ J}} \right)$$

$$= 3.39 \text{ eV}$$

Another method of finding the energy:

Since $|E_n| = \dfrac{13.6 \text{ eV}}{n^2}$ and $n = 2$, then

$$E_2 = \frac{13.6 \text{ eV}}{2^2} = 3.4 \text{ eV}$$

3 What is the potential energy of this atom in electron volts?

3
$$U = \frac{-1}{\epsilon_0^2} \frac{me^4}{4n^2h^2} = -2K \text{ (from frame 1)}$$
$$= -2(3.39 \text{ eV}) = -6.78 \text{ eV}$$

---

4 What is the total energy?

4
$$E = K + U$$
$$= 3.39 \text{ eV} - 6.78 \text{ eV} = -3.39 \text{ eV}$$

---

5 What is the magnitude of the momentum of the electron in the $n = 2$ Bohr orbit?

5
$$p = mv = m\left(\frac{e^2}{\epsilon_0 2nh}\right)$$
$$= \frac{(9.11 \times 10^{-31} \text{ kg})(1.60 \times 10^{-19} \text{ C})^2}{(8.85 \times 10^{-12} \text{ C}^2 \cdot \text{N}^{-1} \cdot \text{m}^{-2})(2)(2)(6.63 \times 10^{-34} \text{ J} \cdot \text{s})}$$
$$= 9.94 \times 10^{-25} \text{ kg} \cdot \text{m} \cdot \text{s}^{-1}$$

---

6 What is the de Broglie wavelength of an electron if $v = 2 \times 10^7$ m $\cdot$ s^{-1}?

6
$$\lambda = \frac{h}{mv}$$
$$= \frac{6.63 \times 10^{-34} \text{ J} \cdot \text{s}}{(9.11 \times 10^{-31} \text{ kg})(2 \times 10^7 \text{ m} \cdot \text{s}^{-1})}$$
$$= 3.64 \times 10^{-11} \text{ m} = 36.4 \text{ pm}$$

---

7 The uncertainty in an electron's position as it passes through a slit is 1 nm. What is the uncertainty in its momentum? Use $\Delta p_y a = h$, where a is the width of the slit and Δp_y is the y-component of the momentum.

7
$$\Delta p_y a \geq h$$
$$\Delta p_y \geq \frac{6.63 \times 10^{-34} \text{ J} \cdot \text{s}}{1 \times 10^{-9} \text{ m}}$$
$$\geq 6.63 \times 10^{-25} \text{ kg} \cdot \text{m} \cdot \text{s}^{-1}$$

---

8 What is the uncertainty in its velocity?

8
$$\Delta p_y a \geq h$$
$$a(m\Delta v) \geq h$$
$$\Delta v \geq \frac{6.63 \times 10^{-34} \text{ J} \cdot \text{s}}{(9.11 \times 10^{-31} \text{ kg})(1 \times 10^{-9} \text{ m})}$$
$$\geq 7.28 \times 10^5 \text{ m} \cdot \text{s}^{-1}$$

---

9 An unstable particle has a lifetime of $\sim 0.8 \times 10^{-16}$ s. What is the uncertainty in the energy of the particle?

9
$$\Delta E \Delta t \geq \frac{h}{2\pi}$$
$$\Delta E \geq \frac{6.63 \times 10^{-34} \text{ J} \cdot \text{s}}{2\pi(0.8 \times 10^{-16} \text{ s})}$$
$$\geq 1.32 \times 10^{-18} \text{ J}$$

---

10 Assuming that the mass and energy of the particle are related by $E = mc^2$, what is the uncertainty in the mass?

10
$$\Delta mc^2 \Delta t \geq \frac{h}{2\pi}$$
$$\Delta m \geq \frac{6.63 \times 10^{-34} \text{ J} \cdot \text{s}}{2\pi(3 \times 10^8 \text{ m} \cdot \text{s}^{-1})^2(0.8 \times 10^{-16} \text{ s})}$$
$$\geq 1.47 \times 10^{-35} \text{ kg}$$

---

11 The radius of the $n = 1$ Bohr orbit is about 0.53×10^{-10} m. What is the velocity of an electron moving in this orbit?

$$mvr = \frac{nh}{2\pi}$$

$$v = \frac{(1)\,(6.63 \times 10^{-34} \text{ J} \cdot \text{s})}{2\pi(9.11 \times 10^{-31} \text{ kg})\,(0.53 \times 10^{-10} \text{ m})}$$
$$= 2.19 \times 10^6 \text{ m} \cdot \text{s}^{-1}$$

STEP BY STEP SOLUTIONS OF PROBLEMS

Problem 1   a) Show that the frequency of revolution of an electron in its circular orbit in the Bohr model of the hydrogen atom is $f = me^4/4\epsilon_0^2 h^3 n^3$ · b) Illustrate Bohr's correspondence principle by showing that for large n, the frequency of revolution equals the radiated frequency calculated from $f = me^4/8\epsilon_0^2 h^3\,[1/n^2 - 1/(n+1)^2]$.

1   What is the relationship between the frequency of revolution f of the electron and its angular frequency ω?

1

$$\omega = 2\pi f$$

2   Since $v = \omega r$, write the expression for f in terms of v and r.

2

$$f = \frac{\omega}{2\pi} = \frac{v}{2\pi r}$$

3   The electrostatic force of attraction between the nucleus and the electron provides the centripetal force between the charges. Express this statement as an equation. Coulomb force
$$F = \frac{1}{4\pi\epsilon_0}\frac{|e \cdot e|}{r^2}.$$

3

$$\frac{e^2}{4\pi\epsilon_0 r^2} = \frac{mv^2}{r}$$

4   Apply Bohr's first postulate.

4

$$\frac{nh}{2\pi} = mvr$$

5   Solve the previous two equations for v.

5

$$\frac{e^2}{4\pi\epsilon_0} = (mvr)v$$

$$\frac{nh}{2\pi} = mvr$$

combine,

$$v = \frac{e^2}{2\epsilon_0 nh}$$

6   Solve for r by substituting the expression for v in the equation in frame 4.

6

$$r = \frac{nh}{2\pi mv} = \frac{nh}{2\pi m(e^2/2\epsilon_0 nh)}$$
$$= \frac{\epsilon_0 n^2 h^2}{\pi me^2}$$

7 Substitute the expression for v and r in the equation in frame 2.

7
$$f = \frac{e^2/2\epsilon_0 nh}{2\pi\epsilon_0 n^2 h^2/\pi me^2}$$

$$= \frac{me^4}{4\epsilon_0^2 h^3 n^3}$$

---

8 To prove part b, factor $1/n^2$ from the quantum expression for radiated frequency

$$f = \frac{me^4}{8\epsilon_0^2 h^3}\left[\frac{1}{n^2} - \frac{1}{(n+1)^2}\right]$$

8
$$f = \frac{me^4}{8\epsilon_0^2 h^3}\frac{1}{n^2}\left[1 - \frac{1}{(1+1/n)^2}\right]$$

---

9 Expand $\dfrac{1}{(1+1/n)^2}$. Let $1/n = x$ and expand

$$\frac{1}{(1+x)^2} = \frac{1}{1+2x+x^2}$$

by algebraic division.

9
$$\frac{1}{(1+x)^2} = 1 - 2x + 3x^2 - 4x^3 + \dots$$
$$\frac{1}{(1+1/n)^2} = 1 - \frac{2}{n} + \frac{3}{n^2} - \frac{4}{n^3} + \dots$$

---

10 Substitute the expansion for $\dfrac{1}{(1+1/n)^2}$ in the equation in frame 8.

10
$$f = \frac{me^4}{8\epsilon_0^2 h^3 n^2}\left[1 - 1 + \frac{2}{n} - \frac{3}{n^2} + \frac{4}{n^3} - \dots\right]$$

---

11 Simplify the expression for f when n becomes very large and thus show that for large values of n, the differences between quantum calculations and those of classical physics are not significant.

11
If n is large, $\dfrac{1}{n^2} \to 0$, $\dfrac{1}{n^3} \to 0$ etc.

$$\therefore f = \frac{me^4}{8\epsilon_0^2 h^3 n^2}\left(\frac{2}{n}\right)$$

$$= \frac{me^4}{4\epsilon_0^2 h^3 n^3}$$

Problem 2   a) What is the de Broglie wavelength of an electron that has been accelerated through a potential difference of 400 V? b) If the uncertainty in position of this electron is equal to its de Broglie wavelength, show that the uncertainty in its momentum is equal to its momentum. c) Find the uncertainty in the momentum of this electron.

---

12 Find the velocity of the electron. The gain in kinetic energy $\frac{1}{2}mv^2$ is equal to its loss in potential energy eV.

12
$$\frac{mv^2}{2} = eV$$

$$v^2 = \frac{2eV}{m}$$

$$v = \sqrt{\frac{2eV}{m}}$$

13 Substitute the value of v in the expression for the de Broglie wavelength.

13

$$\lambda = \frac{h}{mv}$$

$$= \frac{h}{\sqrt{2meV}}$$

---

14 Subtitute the given data and solve for λ.

14
$$\lambda = \frac{6.63 \times 10^{-34} \text{ J} \cdot \text{s}}{\sqrt{2(9.11 \times 10^{-31} \text{ kg})(1.60 \times 10^{-19} \text{ C})(400 \text{ V})}}$$

$$= 0.0614 \text{ nm}$$

---

15 If the electron passed through a slit of width a with an uncertainty of Δp_y as the y-component of its momentum, express the uncertainty of position and momentum in terms of Δp_y and a.

15 $\Delta p_y a \geqslant h$

---

16 But the uncertainty in the position of the electron is equal to its de Broglie wavelength. Substitute $a = h/mv$ in the above and solve for Δp_y.

16

$$\left(\frac{h}{mv}\right) \Delta p_y \geqslant h$$

$$\Delta p_y \geqslant mv$$

Thus the uncertainty in momentum of the electron is equal to its momentum.

---

17 Find the uncertainty in the momentum of this electron by computing its momentum from the value of λ obtained in frame 14.

17

$$\Delta p_y = mv = \frac{h}{\lambda}$$

$$= \frac{6.63 \times 10^{-34} \text{ J} \cdot \text{s}}{0.0614 \times 10^{-9} \text{ m}}$$

$$= 1.08 \times 10^{-23} \text{ kg} \cdot \text{m} \cdot \text{s}^{-1}$$

Problem 3 An act of observation imposes a limitation on the accuracy with which simultaneous measurement of momentum and position can be made. Consider the single slit diffraction experiment, but instead of a beam of monochromatic light we are using a beam of electrons where the accelerating voltage is 5×10^4 V. If the beam passes through an aperture 0.3 mm in diameter, what is the uncertainty in position of the point where the beam strikes a screen 0.6 m away?

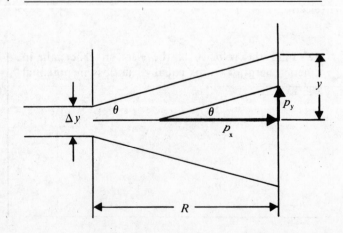

18 An electron passing through the slit has a vertical component of momentum that is zero at the entrance of the slit. However, the de Broglie waves cause the beam to be broadened and the electron acquires a vertical component of momentum. What is the relationship between p_x and p_y, the horizontal and vertical components of the momentum respectively?

18

$$\tan \theta = \frac{p_y}{p_x}$$

If θ is small,

$$p_y = p_x \theta.$$

---

19 What is the expression for θ, the angle between the central peak and the minimum on either side? (We are assuming that all the electrons fall in this region.)

19

$$\sin \theta = \frac{\lambda}{\Delta y}$$

If θ is small,

$$\theta = \frac{\lambda}{\Delta y} \, .$$

---

20 Substitute $\theta = \lambda/\Delta y$ in the equation in frame 18.

20

$$p_y = p_x \left(\frac{\lambda}{\Delta y} \right)$$

---

21 Replace p_x by h/λ and solve for $p_y \Delta y$. The de Broglie expression for wavelength $\lambda = h/p_x = h/mv_x$.

21

$$p_y = \frac{h}{\lambda} \left(\frac{\lambda}{\Delta y} \right) = \frac{h}{\Delta y}$$

$$p_y \Delta y = h$$

Note that this expression is one form of the Heisenberg uncertainty principle; Δy represents the uncertainty in position of an electron as it passes through the slit. The uncertainty in momentum is represented by p_y.

---

22 Find the momentum of an electron in the x-direction by using $p_x = mv = m \sqrt{2eV/m} = \sqrt{2meV}$.

22

$$p_x = \sqrt{2(9.11 \times 10^{-31} \text{ kg})(1.60 \times 10^{-19} \text{ C})(5 \times 10^4 \text{ V})}$$

$$= 1.21 \times 10^{-22} \text{ kg} \cdot \text{m} \cdot \text{s}^{-1}$$

---

23 Substitute this value for p_x and $\theta = y/0.6$ m in the expression for p_y, frame 18.

23

$$p_y = p_x \theta$$

$$= 1.21 \times 10^{-22} \text{ kg} \cdot \text{m} \cdot \text{s}^{-1} \left(\frac{y}{0.6 \text{ m}} \right)$$

Note that y represents the uncertainty in the y-direction.

---

24 Substitute this expression and $\Delta y = 0.3$ mm in the expression for the Heisenberg principle, frame 21 and solve for y.

24

$$p_y \Delta y = h$$

$$\left(1.21 \times 10^{-22} \text{ kg} \cdot \text{m} \cdot \text{s}^{-1} \right) \left(\frac{y}{0.6 \text{ m}} \right) \left(3.0 \times 10^{-4} \text{ m} \right)$$

$$= 6.63 \times 10^{-34} \text{ J} \cdot \text{s}$$

$$y = 1.10 \times 10^{-8} \text{ m}$$

25 What is the uncertainty in position of the point where the electron strikes the screen?

25 Uncertainty = $2y = 2.20 \times 10^{-8}$ m.

To interpret this result, we note that, based on a slit width of 0.3 mm, the electron will strike the screen within a distance of 1.10×10^{-8} m above or below the central maximum.

PROGRAMMED TEST

1 ***Problem 1*** Compute the de Broglie wavelength of a) an electron which has a kinetic energy of 10^4 eV and b) a proton which has the same kinetic energy.

1 ***Answer***

12.3 pm, 0.287 pm

If you solved this problem correctly, go to frame 9. If you could not solve this problem, go through frames 2-8.

2 Convert the kinetic energy to joules.

2
$$10^4 \text{ eV} = \left(10^4 \text{ eV} \right) \left(\frac{1.6 \times 10^{-19} \text{ J}}{1 \text{ eV}} \right)$$
$$= 1.6 \times 10^{-15} \text{ J}$$

---

3 Compute the velocity of the electron by using the expression for kinetic energy.

3
$$\tfrac{1}{2}mv^2 = 1.6 \times 10^{-15} \text{ J}$$
$$v^2 = \frac{2(1.6 \times 10^{-15} \text{ J})}{9.11 \times 10^{-31} \text{ kg}}$$
$$v = 5.92 \times 10^7 \text{ m} \cdot \text{s}^{-1}$$

---

4 Compute the momentum of the electron. Note, there is no need to use relativistic mechanics since the speed of the electron $\approx 0.2\ c$.

4
$$p = mv$$
$$= 9.11 \times 10^{-31} \text{ kg}(5.92 \times 10^7 \text{ m} \cdot \text{s}^{-1})$$
$$= 5.39 \times 10^{-23} \text{ kg} \cdot \text{m} \cdot \text{s}^{-1}$$

---

5 Find the de Broglie wavelength.

5
$$\lambda = \frac{h}{p} = \frac{6.63 \times 10^{-34} \text{ J} \cdot \text{s}}{5.39 \times 10^{-23} \text{ kg} \cdot \text{m} \cdot \text{s}^{-1}}$$
$$= 1.23 \times 10^{-11} \text{ m}$$
$$= 12.3 \text{ pm}$$

---

6 We note that the proton has the same kinetic energy (10^4 eV = 1.6×10^{-15} J). However, the mass of the proton is 1.673×10^{-27} kg. Find the velocity of the proton by using the kinetic energy relationship.

6 $\frac{1}{2}mv^2 = 1.6 \times 10^{-15}$ J

$$v^2 = \frac{2(1.6 \times 10^{-15} \text{ J})}{1.673 \times 10^{-27} \text{ kg}}$$

$$v = 1.38 \times 10^6 \text{ m} \cdot \text{s}^{-1}$$

Another method:

$$K_e = K_p$$

$$\frac{v_e}{v_p} = \sqrt{\frac{m_e}{m_p}}$$

$\therefore v_p = (1840)^{-1/2}(5.92 \times 10^7 \text{ m} \cdot \text{s}^{-1}) = 1.38 \times 10^6 \text{ m} \cdot \text{s}^{-1}$

---

7 Compute the momentum of the proton.

7 $p = mv$
$= (1.673 \times 10^{-27} \text{ kg})(1.38 \times 10^6 \text{ m} \cdot \text{s}^{-1})$
$= 2.31 \times 10^{-21} \text{ kg} \cdot \text{m} \cdot \text{s}^{-1}$

---

8 Find the de Broglie wavelength.

8
$$\lambda = \frac{h}{p} = \frac{6.63 \times 10^{-34} \text{ J} \cdot \text{s}}{2.31 \times 10^{-21} \text{ kg} \cdot \text{m} \cdot \text{s}^{-1}}$$

$$= 2.87 \times 10^{-13} \text{ m}$$

$$= 0.287 \text{ pm}$$

Another method:

$$\frac{\lambda_p}{\lambda_e} = \frac{m_e v_e}{m_p v_p} = \sqrt{\frac{m_e}{m_p}} \quad \text{(from kinetic energy relationship)}$$

$\therefore \lambda_p = (1840)^{-1/2}(12.3 \text{ pm}) = 0.287 \text{ pm}$

---

9 Problem 2 A 1000 kg satellite circles the earth once every 3 hr in an orbit having a radius of 10,000 km. a) Assuming that the angular momentum is quantized in accordance with Bohr's postulate, i.e. it applies to satellites just as it does to an orbiting electron in the hydrogen atom, find the quantum number of the orbit of the satellite. b) On the basis of Newton's law of gravitation and Bohr's first postulate, show that the radius of an earth-satellite orbit is directly proportional to the square of the quantum number, i.e., $r = kn^2$, where k is the constant of proportionality.

9 Answer
5.51×10^{47}

If you solved this problem correctly, go to frame 18. If you could not solve this problem, go through frames 10-17.

---

10 What is the angular momentum of the satellite?

10 $L = mvr$

11 Since Bohr's first postulate states that the only allowable orbits are those for which the angular momentum of the "body" is an integral multiple of $nh/2\pi$, equate this value to the expression for L in the above.

11 $mvr = nh/2\pi$

---

12 Solve for n. Substitute $v = 2\pi r/t$, where $t =$ time to complete one orbit.

12
$$n = \frac{2\pi mvr}{h} = \frac{4\pi^2 mr^2}{ht}$$

---

13 Substitute the given values and solve for n.

13
$$n = \frac{4\pi^2(10^3 \text{ kg})(10^7 \text{ m})^2}{6.63 \times 10^{-34} \text{ J} \cdot \text{s}(1.08 \times 10^4 \text{ s})}$$
$$= 5.51 \times 10^{47}$$

---

14 The force that provides the necessary centripetal acceleration for the satellite is the gravitational attraction of the earth. Let m and m_E denote the masses of the satellite and earth respectively. Express this relationship in mathematical form and simplify.

14
$$\frac{Gm_Em}{r^2} = \frac{mv^2}{r}$$
$$\frac{Gm_E}{r} = v^2$$

---

15 Solve the equation in frame 11 for v and substitute in the above.

15
$$v = \frac{nh}{2\pi mr}$$
$$\frac{Gm_E}{r} = \frac{n^2h^2}{4\pi^2m^2r^2}$$

---

16 Solve for r.

16
$$r = \left(\frac{h^2}{4\pi^2m^2Gm_E}\right)n^2$$

---

17 Let $k = \dfrac{h^2}{4\pi^2m^2Gm_E}$

17 $r = kn^2$

---

18 *Problem 3* Suppose an unstable particle produced in a high energy collision has a mass two times that of the proton and an uncertainty in mass that is 1.5% of the particle's mass. Assuming that the mass and energy of the particle are related by $E = mc^2$, find the lifetime of the particle.

If you could not solve this problem, go through frames 19-23.

18 *Answer*
2.34×10^{-23} s

---

19 State the uncertainty principle involving energy.

19 $\Delta E \Delta t \geqslant \dfrac{h}{2\pi}$

---

20 Since $E = mc^2$, $\Delta E = \Delta mc^2$. Substitute this value for ΔE and solve for Δt.

20 $\Delta mc^2 \Delta t \geqslant \dfrac{h}{2\pi}$

$\Delta t \geqslant \dfrac{h}{2\pi c^2 \Delta m}$

---

21 What is the mass of the particle?

21
Mass of particle $= 2(1.673 \times 10^{-27}$ kg$)$
$= 3.346 \times 10^{-27}$ kg

---

22 What is the uncertainty in mass Δm?

22 $\Delta m \geqslant 0.015(3.346 \times 10^{-27}$ kg$)$
$\geqslant 5.02 \times 10^{-29}$ kg

---

23 Substitute this value in frame 20 and solve for Δt.

23

$\Delta t \geqslant \dfrac{6.63 \times 10^{-34} \text{ J} \cdot \text{s}}{2\pi(3 \times 10^8 \text{ m} \cdot \text{s}^{-1})^2(5.02 \times 10^{-29} \text{ kg})}$

$\geqslant 2.34 \times 10^{-23}$ s

43

Atoms, Molecules, and Solids

CHAPTER SUMMARY

The Pauli exclusion principle enables us to "build" atoms of increasing complexity by arranging the electrons into appropriate shells and subshells. A study of the electron configurations also provides the insight into the nature of chemical bonds, the interaction which holds atoms together to form molecules and solids. Molecular bonds and the structure of complex molecules can be determined from an analysis of the molecular spectra. In studying the microscopic structures of materials, we find that they are related to many macroscopic properties such as specific heat, electrical conductivity, thermal conductivity and optical properties. Semiconductors and super-conductivity are discussed on the basis of the band theory of solids and several applications of these are described.

BASIC TERMS — *Give definitions or meanings for the following:*

central-field approximation (43-1)
exclusion (Pauli) principle (43-1)
periodic table of elements (43-2)
x-ray energy level (43-2)
atomic number (43-2)
diatomic molecule (43-3)
ionic bond (43-3)
electrovalent bond (43-3)
ionization potential (43-3)
covalent bond (43-3)
electron affinity (43-3)
van der Waals bond (43-3)
hydrogen bond (43-3)
rotational energy level (43-4)
vibrational energy level (43-4)
band spectrum (43-4)
molecular spectrum (43-4)
crystalline solid (43-5)

amorphous solid (43-5)
ionic crystal (43-5)
covalent crystal (43-5)
metallic crystal (43-5)
close packing (43-5)
valence band (43-7)
conduction band (43-7)
energy band (43-7)
semiconductor (43-8)
n-type semiconductor (43-8)
p-type semiconductor (43-8)
hole (43-8)
p-n junction (43-9)
diode (43-9)
transistor (43-9)
integrated circuit (43-9)
superconductor (43-10)
critical temperature (43-10)

PROGRAMMED QUIZ

1 What mathematical relationship governs the motion of electrons?

1 The Schrödinger equation.

2 Compare the electron as depicted by the Bohr model and the Schrödinger equation.

2 In the Bohr atom, the electron is a point mass, and in the view that emerges from solving the Schrödinger equation, it is smeared out like a wave.

3 What is the difference between the 2s and 2p states in terms of the nomenclature?

3 Both are in the L shell since $n = 2$ for both. For the 2s state, $l = 0$ and for the 2p state, $l = 1$. Therefore the two states form subshells.

4 The chemical properties of an atom are determined principally by _____.

4 The interactions involving the outermost electrons.

5 What is the characteristic behavior of alkali metals? Name some.

5 Since they have "filled shells plus one" configurations, they form electrovalent (or ionic) bonds with valence $+ 1$. Lithium, sodium, potassium, rubidium.

6 What is the characteristic behavior of halogens? Name some.

6 Since they have "filled shells minus one" structure, they form ionic bonds with valence $- 1$. Fluorine, chlorine, bromine, iodine, astatine.

7 What is the characteristic behavior of the inert gases? Name some.

7 Since all the shells are filled, they have little tendency to gain or lose electrons. Helium, neon, argon, krypton, xenon, radon.

8 What is the characteristic behavior of the alkaline-earth metals? Name some.

8 Since they have "filled shells plus two" configurations, they form ionic compounds with valence $+ 2$. Beryllium, magnesium, calcium, strontium, barium, radium.

9 The two electrons in the helium atom occupy the same shell. Isn't this contrary to the Pauli exclusion principle?

9 No it isn't. The Pauli exclusion principle states that in any atom only one electron can occupy any given state. Since the two electrons have opposite spins, all their quantum numbers are not the same.

10 Two atoms join to form a stable molecule. Compare the energies of the individual atoms to the energy of the final bound state of the molecule.

10 The final bound state of the molecule has a lower total energy than the original state of the atoms.

11 Describe a typical molecular spectrum.

11 It has the appearance of a series of bands, each band corresponding to a particular vibrational transition. The individual lines in a band correspond to a particular rotational transition.

12 What is the separation of adjacent atoms in a solid?

12 Of about the same order of magnitude as the diameter of the electron cloud around the atom.

13 What is the difference between amorphous and crystalline solids? What about liquids?

13 Crystalline solids have a long-range order (a recurring pattern in the arrangement of atoms); in amorphous solids, the atoms are arranged in a short-range rather than a long-range order. Liquids also have a short-range order similar to that of amorphous solids.

14 Which properties of metallic crystals are influenced by the presence of dislocations?

14 Mechanical properties; the ductility and malleability of some metals depends on the presence of dislocations that move through the lattice during plastic deformations.

15 What microscopic properties of solids can be related to the microscopic structure of the material?

15 Specific heat, electrical conductivity and resistivity, thermal conductivity, optical reflectivity and transparency.

16 What is the difference between n-type and p-type semiconductors?

16 In n-type semiconductors, additional electrons, due to the addition of impurity atoms having one valence electron more than the pure conductors, are responsible for the increased conductivity. In p-type semiconductors, the impurity atoms have one less valence electron than the pure semiconductor and the increased conductivity is a result of the movement of holes which can be considered positively charged electrons.

17 How is an electrovalent (ionic) bond formed?

17 An electron which is further from the nucleus than the others will be rather loosely bound. Therefore, the atom will tend to lose this electron to another, converting the neutral atom into a charged ion. It will then form an electrovalent bond with another ion which is oppositely charged.

18 What is the electron charge distribution in the ground state of beryllium ($1s^2 \, 2s^2$)?

18 Beryllium has four electrons, two in the $1s$ state ($n = 1$, $l = 0$) and two in the $2s$ state ($n = 2$, $l = 0$).

19 If the principle quantum number is 4, what values can l have? This corresponds to which shell?

19 $l = 0$, 1, 2, 3; N shell.

MAIN IDEAS

The energy state of an atom may be described by a set of quantum numbers: The principal quantum number n characterizes the energy level in which the electron is found; n can be any positive integer, i.e. 1, 2, 3 .... Although n was associated with a particular orbit in the Bohr atom, here it refers to a shell. The quantum number l determines the magnitude of the angular momentum and can be any integer from 0 to $n - 1$. It is called the orbital quantum number. The magnetic quantum number m can have any of these values: $0, \pm 1, ... \pm l$. The spin quantum number $s = \pm \frac{1}{2}$. The electron acts like a small magnet and can assume two orientations relative to an external magnetic field; $s = + \frac{1}{2}$ for an alignment parallel with an external magnetic field and $s = - \frac{1}{2}$ for an anti-parallel alignment. A particular set of four quantum numbers n, l, m, s constitutes a quantum. The Pauli exclusion principle states that in an atom no two electrons can occupy the same quantum state, i.e. two electrons can occupy the same region of space only when they have opposite spin orientations. It should be noted that each value of n corresponds to a region of space around the nucleus in the form of a spherical shell. States with the same n but different l are said to form subshells.

The atomic states are labelled by a number and letter system. The number indicates the value of n and the letter indicates the value of l. In accordance with Pauli's exclusion principle the orbital electrons are arranged in a series of concentric spheres called shells. In the order of increasing distance from the nucleus, the shells are designated as K, L, M, N, O, P and Q. All electrons in the same shell have the same principal quantum number. The electrons in the same shell are grouped into subshells. The following is a list of a few possible atomic states: $l = 0$ is called an s state, $l = 1$, a p state, $l = 2$, a d state and $l = 3$, an f state. After f the designation of the states continues alphabetically except for the omission of j.

The l quantum number has the effect of subdividing the principal quantum level into subshells (orbitals). An orbital cannot contain more than two electrons. Although both electrons have the same value of n, l and m, they may have opposite values of the spin quantum number ($s = \pm \frac{1}{2}$). Thus, for any given value of n, there can be only one s orbital (2 electrons), no more than three p orbitals (6 electrons), no more than five d orbitals (10 electrons) and no more than seven f orbitals (14 electrons). For a given n, the maximum number of all orbitals is n^2 and the maximum number of electrons is $2n^2$. Consider sodium, which has eleven electrons. Its ground state can be described by the following table:

	n	l	m	s	
K shell	1	0	0	$+\frac{1}{2}$	$1s^2$
	1	0	0	$-\frac{1}{2}$	
	2	0	0	$+\frac{1}{2}$	$2s^2$
	2	0	0	$-\frac{1}{2}$	
	2	1	-1	$+\frac{1}{2}$	
L shell	2	1	-1	$-\frac{1}{2}$	
	2	1	0	$+\frac{1}{2}$	$2p^6$
	2	1	0	$-\frac{1}{2}$	
	2	1	1	$+\frac{1}{2}$	
	2	1	1	$-\frac{1}{2}$	
M shell	3	0	0	$+\frac{1}{2}$	$3s$

The subshell is described as follows: Write the principal quantum number first, followed by s, p, d or f (to specify the value of l). A superscript denotes the number of electrons in the state. Thus $2p^6$ refers to six electrons with values of $n = 2$ and $l = 1$. The data for sodium can be summarized by the electronic configuration of the atom: $1s^2\ 2s^2\ 2p^6\ 3s$. The superscript one is usually omitted.

The atomic number Z is the number of electrons in a neutral atom. The nucleus contains Z protons. Since the charge of a proton and of an electron is of the same magnitude but opposite sign, the net charge of an atom in its neutral state is zero.

The chemical properties of an atom are determined primarily by interactions involving the outermost electrons. If an electron is loosely bound, i.e., it is considerably further from the nucleus than the other electrons, the atom will have a tendency to lose this electron and form an electrovalent or ionic bond with valence $+ 1$. Alkali metals, e.g. sodium and potassium, have a valence of $+ 1$. On the other hand, fluorine ($Z = 9$) has a vacancy in the L shell and thus has an affinity for an electron, forming ionic compounds with a valence of $- 1$.

Two atoms are said to have a covalent bond when they share the same electron. A hydrogen molecule is an example of a covalent bond. However, in this case the molecule consists of two protons and an electron-pair bond.

Diatomic molecules may have ionic or covalent bonds. These molecules possess rotational and vibrational energy. The energy of rotational motion is given by $E = l(l + 1)(\hbar^2/2I)$, where $l = 0, 1, 2, 3, \ldots$, and I is the moment of inertia of the molecule about an axis through the center of mass and perpendicular to the line joining the two nuclei. The energy associated with the vibrational motion is given by $E = (n + \frac{1}{2})hf$, where $n = 0, 1, 2, 3 \ldots$ and f is the frequency of vibration. Since the rotational energy levels are much closer together than the vibrational energy levels, band spectra will be produced where each band corresponds to a vibrational transition and within which there are more closely spaced lines corresponding to a transition between rotational energy levels.

A crystalline solid is one where the component atoms are arranged in a regular geometric array called the crystal or lattice structure. If there is no regular array, the solid is said to be amorphous. In addition to being ionic or covalent, a crystal may be metallic. In this structure, the outermost electrons are not localized at individual lattice points but are detached from their individual atoms and are free to move throughout the crystal. Since metallic crystals have a large number of very loosely bound electrons, they are good conductors. On the other hand, covalent crystals, with tightly bound electrons, are poor conductors.

We have seen that each atom has an associated energy-level diagram denoting the particular quantum states for the electrons and their corresponding energy levels. What if we have a large number of identical atoms separated from each other so that their interactions are negligible? The energy-level diagram for this system would be identical to the diagram for a single atom except that we now have each state occupied by N electrons instead of just one. If the atoms are pushed close together, instead of a sharp energy level accomodating N electrons, we will have a band containing N closely spaced levels. Between adjacent bands there are forbidden regions where there are no possible energy levels. The valence electrons are altered much more by interactions with neighboring atoms than the inside electrons. In insulators and semiconductors the valence electrons completely fill the highest occupied band, the valence band, and the next highest band, the conduction band, is completely empty.

Semiconductors are materials, such as silicon and germanium, whose electrical resistivity is intermediate between that of good conductors and good insulators. Because only a small amount of energy is necessary to set an electron free from the rest of the molecule, these materials have a substantial number of electrons which are roaming around the lattice. Where the electron is removed, it leaves a vacancy — a hole — into which another electron may drop, leaving a vacancy in a neighboring atom. Thus the holes travel through the lattice. If small amounts of certain impurities, such as arsenic, phosphorus or antimony are added to the semiconductor, the conductivity is greatly increased. If the impurity atoms have one valence electron more than the pure material, the additional electrons are responsible for the increased conductivity. Since the conductivity is due to negative charge motion, this material is called an n-type semiconductor. If the impurity atoms have one less valence electron than the pure substance, the conductivity is due to the motion of the holes. Since these correspond to positively charged electrons, this material is called a p-type semiconductor.

Semiconductors are of tremendous importance in electronics. A p-type and n-type semiconductor joined together (p-n junction) acts as a diode, a device which conducts much more readily in one direction than the other. A transistor is a "sandwich" of p-n-p or n-p-n material in which the potential of the central material controls the current, thus amplifying and controlling various electrical signals. The functions of several transistors, capacitors and resistors combined on a square of semiconductor material a few millimeters on a side is called an integrated circuit. This is the basis of calculators and microprocessers.

A material which shows a complete disappearance of all electrical resistance at very low temperatures is called a superconductor. Mercury, for example, has an electrical resistivity of zero at 4.16 K. When a current is magnetically induced in a superconducting ring, the current continues without measurable decrease for months, even though there is no battery or other source of emf in the circuit.

PROGRAMMED QUIZ

1 What is the lowest value for the principle quantum number n? What are the corresponding values of the other quantum numbers?

1 $n = 1$; $l = 0$, $m = 0$, $s = +\frac{1}{2}$ or $-\frac{1}{2}$.

2 When $n = 1$, an electron can occupy how many energy states?

2 Two.

---

3 Which element has one electron? What are its quantum numbers in the ground state?

3 Hydrogen; $n = 1$, $l = 0$, $m = 0$, $s = -\frac{1}{2}$. Note that $s = -\frac{1}{2}$ because this is the lowest energy state and all physical systems tend to be in the lowest possible state. The electron configuration is $1s$.

---

4 Which element has 2 electrons? What are the quantum numbers?

4 Helium. For one electron, $n = 1$, $l = 0$, $m = 0$, $s = -\frac{1}{2}$. For the other electrons, $n = 1$, $l = 0$, $m = 0$, $s = +\frac{1}{2}$. The electron configuration is $1s^2$.

---

5 Can more electrons be added to the $n = 1$ shell?

5 No, for helium, the $n = 1$ shell is filled.

---

6 What is the element with three electrons? What are its quantum numbers?

6 Lithium. Two electrons have the same states as those of helium. For the third electron, $n = 2$, $l = 0$, $m = 0$, $s = -\frac{1}{2}$. The electron configuration is $1s^2\,2s$.

---

7 We can continue in this way to find the quantum numbers of all the other elements. With which element is the $n = 2$ shell filled? How many electrons does it have? What is its electron configuration?

7 Neon; 10; $1s^2\,2s^2\,2p^6$.

---

8 What happens with the next element? What is its electron configuration?

8 The next element, sodium, has 11 electrons; two in the $n = 1$ state, eight in the $n = 2$ state and one in the $n = 3$ state. The electron configuration is $1s^2\,2s^2\,2p^6\,3s$.

---

9 Make a list of the number of electrons in each state for copper ($Z = 29$). What is its electron configuration?

9

	K	L	M	N
n	1	2	3	4
l	s	s, p	s, p, d	s, p, d, f
no. of electrons	2	2, 6	2, 6, 10	1

$1s^2\,2s^2\,2p^6\,3s^2\,3p^6\,3d^{10}\,4s$

---

10 What is the lattice spacing of a crystal if the magnitude of the potential energy of interaction of a charge $+e$ with a charge $-e$ is 1×10^{-18} J?

10

$$U = \frac{e^2}{4\pi\epsilon_0 r}$$

$$r = \frac{(1.60 \times 10^{-19}\,\text{C})^2}{4\pi(8.85 \times 10^{-12}\,\text{C}^2 \cdot \text{N}^{-1} \cdot \text{m}^{-2})(1 \times 10^{-18}\,\text{J})}$$

$$= 2.3 \times 10^{-10}\,\text{m}$$

11 If the moment of inertia of a diatomic oxygen molecule about an axis through the center of mass perpendicular to the line joining the atoms is 5×10^{-46} kg·m^2, find the distance between the two oxygen atoms. The mass of oxygen is 16 u.

11
$$I = \frac{ml^2}{2}$$

$$l^2 = \frac{2(5 \times 10^{-46}\,\text{kg}\cdot\text{m}^2)}{16(1.66 \times 10^{-27}\,\text{kg})}$$

$$l = 1.94 \times 10^{-10}\,\text{m}$$

12 What is the energy of rotational motion of the oxygen molecule for $l = 1$? Note

$$\hbar = \frac{h}{2\pi}.$$

12
$$E = l(l+1)\frac{\hbar^2}{2I}$$
$$= \frac{2(6.63 \times 10^{-34}\,\text{J}\cdot\text{s})^2}{8\pi^2(5 \times 10^{-46}\,\text{kg}\cdot\text{m}^2)}$$
$$= 2.23 \times 10^{-23}\,\text{J}$$

13 What is the spacing of adjacent vibrational energy levels for a typical diatomic molecule ($f = 10^{13}$ Hz) for $n = 0$, 1 and 2?

13
$$E = (n + \tfrac{1}{2})hf$$
for $n = 0$:
$$E = \tfrac{1}{2}(6.63 \times 10^{-34}\,\text{J}\cdot\text{s})(10^{13}\,\text{s}^{-1})$$
$$= 3.32 \times 10^{-21}\,\text{J}$$
for $n = 1$
$$E = 3/2\,(6.63 \times 10^{-34}\,\text{J}\cdot\text{s})(10^{13}\,\text{s}^{-1})$$
$$= 9.95 \times 10^{-21}\,\text{J}$$
for $n = 2$:
$$E = 5/2\,(6.63 \times 10^{-34}\,\text{J}\cdot\text{s})(10^{13}\,\text{s}^{-1})$$
$$= 16.6 \times 10^{-21}\,\text{J}$$

STEP BY STEP SOLUTIONS OF PROBLEMS

Problem 1 a) Show that the frequencies in a pure rotation spectrum (disregard vibrational levels) are proportional to the quantum number l. b) Given the following rotation spectrum of the HCl molecule: $\lambda = 60.4 \times 10^{-6}$ m, 69×10^{-6} m, 80.4×10^{-6} m, 96.4×10^{-6} m and 120.4×10^{-6} m, find the moment of inertia of the molecule.

1 Consider the emission of a photon in the transition from the l state to the $(l - 1)$ state.

Use $E = l(l + 1)\left(\dfrac{\hbar^2}{2I}\right)$.

1
$$hf = E_l - E_{l-1} = \frac{\hbar^2}{2I}\Big[\, l(l+1) - (l-1)l \,\Big]$$
$$= \frac{\hbar^2 l}{I}$$

2 Substitute $\hbar = h/2\pi$ and solve for f.

2
$$f = \frac{h^2}{4\pi^2 h I} \cdot l$$
$$= \frac{h}{4\pi^2 I} \cdot l$$

Thus f is proportional to l.

3 Since f is proportional to l, the frequency difference between adjacent spectral lines is given by

$$\Delta f_l = f_l - f_{l-1} = \frac{h}{4\pi^2 I}.$$

Show this on the basis of the given data and find Δf.

3

$\lambda(\times 10^{-6}\,\text{m})$	$f = c/\lambda\,(\times 10^{12}\,\text{Hz})$	$\Delta f(\times 10^{12}\,\text{Hz})$
60.4	4.97	
		0.62
69	4.35	
		0.62
80.4	3.73	
		0.62
96.4	3.11	
		0.62
120.4	2.49	

4   Find I by using $I = \dfrac{h}{4\pi^2 \Delta f_l}$. Note $\Delta f_l = 0.62$ Hz.

4

$$I = \frac{6.63 \times 10^{-34}\,\text{J}\cdot\text{s}}{4\pi^2 (0.62 \times 10^{12}\,\text{Hz})}$$

$$= 2.72 \times 10^{-47}\,\text{kg}\cdot\text{m}^2$$

Problem 2   a) Find the moment of inertia of the HCl molecule. b) Find the energy of the rotational motion of the HCl molecule in its first excited state ($l = 1$). c) Calculate the wavelength of the photon emitted when the l quantum number changes from $l = 3$ to $l = 1$. (Mass of H atom is 1 u, mass of Cl atom is 35.5 u, the interatomic separation of the two atoms is 1.17×10^{-10} m.)

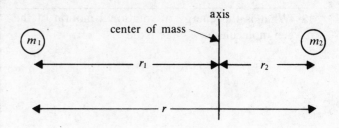

---

5   Calculate the moment of inertia about the axis through the center of mass $\perp$ to the line joining the atoms in terms of m_1, m_2 and r. Take moments of m_1 and m_2 about the axis which passes through the center of mass and express r_2 in terms of m_1, m_2 and r_1.

5

$$m_1 r_1 = m_2 r_2$$

$$r_2 = \frac{m_1 r_1}{m_2}$$

---

6   Substitute this expression in $r_1 + r_2 = r$ and simplify.

6

$$r = r_1 + \frac{m_1 r_1}{m_2}$$

$$= \frac{(m_1 + m_2) r_1}{m_2}$$

---

7   The moment of inertia of m_1 and m_2 about the axis is $I = m_1 r_1^2 + m_2 r_2^2$. Multiply the second term by r_1^2 / r_1^2 and factor r_1^2 from each term.

7

$$I = m_1 r_1^2 + m_2 r_2^2$$

$$= m_1 r_1^2 + m_2 \frac{r_2^2 r_1^2}{r_1^2}$$

$$= \left(m_1 + \frac{m_2 r_2^2}{r_1^2} \right) r_1^2$$

---

8   But $m_1 / m_2 = r_2 / r_1$ from frame 5. Substitute and simplify.

8

$$I = \left(m_1 + m_2 \frac{m_1^2}{m_2^2} \right) r_1^2$$

$$= \left(m_1 + \frac{m_1^2}{m_2} \right) r_1^2$$

$$= \left(\frac{m_1 m_2 + m_1^2}{m_2} \right) r_1^2$$

$$= m_1 \left(\frac{m_1 + m_2}{m_2} \right) r_1^2$$

---

9 Substitute the expression from frame 6 for r_1 and simplify.

9

$$I = m_1 \left(\frac{m_1 + m_2}{m_2} \right) \left(\frac{m_2}{m_1 + m_2} \right)^2 r^2$$

$$= \left(\frac{m_1 m_2}{m_1 + m_2} \right) r^2$$

---

10 Substitute given values.

10
$$I = \frac{(1.67 \times 10^{-27} \text{kg})(35.5 \times 1.67 \times 10^{-27} \text{kg})(1.17 \times 10^{-10} \text{m})^2}{(1 + 35.5)(1.67 \times 10^{-27} \text{kg})}$$

$$= 2.22 \times 10^{-47} \text{ kg} \cdot \text{m}^2$$

---

11 It should be noted that, since the mass of the chlorine atom $\gg$ mass of the hydrogen atom, the moment of inertia could be found by considering the H atom to be rotating about the chlorine atom in a circle of radius 1.17×10^{-10} m. Thus I could be found from $I = mR^2$.

11
$$I = mR^2$$
$$= (1.67 \times 10^{-27} \text{ kg})(1.17 \times 10^{-10} \text{ m})^2$$

$$= 2.29 \times 10^{-47} \text{ kg} \cdot \text{m}^2, \quad \text{which differs}$$
from $2.22 \times 10^{-47} \text{ kg} \cdot \text{m}^2$ by 3%

---

12 Find the energy of the rotational motion of the HCl molecule ($l = 1$) by using $E = l(l + 1)\hbar^2/2I$, where $\hbar = h/2\pi$ and I = moment of inertia, $l = 1$.

12

$$E = l(l + 1)\frac{h^2}{8\pi^2 I}$$

$$= \frac{1(2)(6.63 \times 10^{-34} \text{ J} \cdot \text{s})^2}{8\pi^2 (2.22 \times 10^{-47} \text{ kg} \cdot \text{m}^2)}$$

$$= 5.02 \times 10^{-22} \text{ J}$$

$$= \left(5.02 \times 10^{-22} \text{ J} \right) \left(\frac{1 \text{ eV}}{1.60 \times 10^{-19} \text{J}} \right)$$

$$= 3.14 \times 10^{-3} \text{ eV}$$

---

13 Calculate the wavelength of the photon emitted when the l quantum number changes from $l = 3$ to $l = 1$. Calculate $\Delta E = E_3 - E_1$ and use the expression $\lambda = 1240 \text{ eV} \cdot \text{nm}/\Delta E(\text{eV})$.

13

$$E_1 = 1(1 + 1)\frac{\hbar^2}{2I} = \frac{\hbar^2}{I}$$
$$E_3 = 3(3 + 1)\frac{\hbar^2}{2I} = \frac{6\hbar^2}{I}$$

$$\therefore \ E_3 = 6E_1$$
$$\Delta E = E_3 - E_1 = 6E_1 - E_1 = 5E_1$$
$$= 5(3.14 \times 10^{-3} \text{ eV})$$
$$= 1.57 \times 10^{-2} \text{ eV}$$

$$\lambda = \frac{1240 \text{ eV} \cdot \text{nm}}{1.57 \times 10^{-2} \text{ eV}}$$

$$= 79,000 \text{ nm}$$

PROGRAMMED TEST

1 Problem 1 The mass of a hydrogen atom is 1.66×10^{-27} kg and the distance between atoms in a hydrogen molecule is 0.074 nm. a) Find the moment of inertia of the hydrogen molecule about the perpendicular bisector of the line joining the nuclei. b) Find the energies of the $l = 0$, $l = 1$, $l = 2$ and $l = 3$ rotational states. c) Find the frequency and wavelength of the photon emitted in the transition from $l = 3$ to $l = 0$.

1
Answer
4.55×10^{-48} kg $\cdot$ m^2, 0, 2.44×10^{-21} J, 7.32×10^{-21} J, 14.6×10^{-21} J, 2.20×10^{13} Hz, 13.6 μm.

If you solved this problem correctly, go to frame 5. If you could not solve this problem, go through frames 2–4.

---

2 Find the moment of inertia by using $I = mr^2/2$, where m is the atomic mass of a hydrogen atom and r is the separation of the two atoms.

2 Note that the equation

$$I = \left(\frac{m_1 m_2}{m_1 + m_2} \right) r^2,$$

reduces to $I = \dfrac{m^2}{2m} r^2 = \dfrac{mr^2}{2}$

if $m_1 = m_2 = m$.

$$I = \frac{1.66 \times 10^{-27}\,\text{kg}(0.074 \times 10^{-9}\,\text{m})^2}{2}$$

$$= 4.55 \times 10^{-48}\,\text{kg} \cdot \text{m}^2$$

---

3 Find the energies of the $l = 0, 1, 2$ and 3 rotational states.

3

$$E = l(l + 1) \frac{\hbar^2}{2I}, \text{ where}$$

$$\hbar = \frac{h}{2\pi} = 1.05 \times 10^{-34}\,\text{J} \cdot \text{s}$$

For $l = 0$, $E_0 = 0$

For $l = 1$, $E_1 = \dfrac{2\hbar^2}{2I} = \dfrac{\hbar^2}{I}$

$$= \frac{(1.054 \times 10^{-34}\,\text{J} \cdot \text{s})^2}{4.55 \times 10^{-48}\,\text{kg} \cdot \text{m}^2}$$

$$= 2.44 \times 10^{-21}\,\text{J}$$

For $l = 2$, $E_2 = 2(2 + 1) \dfrac{\hbar^2}{2I}$

$$= \frac{3\hbar^2}{I} = 7.32 \times 10^{-21}\,\text{J}$$

For $l = 3$, $E_3 = 3(3 + 1) \dfrac{\hbar^2}{2I}$

$$= \frac{6\hbar^2}{I} = 14.6 \times 10^{-21}\,\text{J}$$

---

4 Find the frequency and wavelength of the photon emitted in the transition from $l = 3$ to $l = 0$.

4 $E_3 - E_0 = hf = 14.6 \times 10^{-21}$ J

$$f = \frac{14.6 \times 10^{-21} \text{ J}}{6.63 \times 10^{-34} \text{ J} \cdot \text{s}}$$

$$= 2.20 \times 10^{13} \text{ Hz}$$

$$\lambda = \frac{c}{f} = \frac{3 \times 10^8 \text{ m} \cdot \text{s}^{-1}}{2.2 \times 10^{13} \text{ Hz}}$$

$$= 1.36 \times 10^{-5} \text{ m}$$

$$= 13.6 \ \mu\text{m}$$

---

5   **Problem 2**   If the vibrational frequency of the hydrogen molecule is 1.29×10^{14} Hz, find a) the spacing of the vibrational energy levels in electron volts, b) the wavelength of radiation emitted in the transition from the $n = 3$ to $n = 2$ vibrational state of the hydrogen molecule and c) the initial values of n for which transitions to the ground state of vibrational motion will yield radiation in the visible spectrum.

5
Answer
0.535 eV, 2320 nm, 4, 5.

If you could not solve this problem, go through frames 6–10.

6   Find the spacing of adjacent vibrational energy levels in eV.

6 $E = (n + \frac{1}{2})hf_{vib}$
$\Delta E = E_n - E_{n-1} = hf_{vib}$
$\qquad = 6.63 \times 10^{-34} \text{ J} \cdot \text{s}(1.29 \times 10^{14} \text{ Hz})$

$$= \left(8.55 \times 10^{-20} \text{ J} \right) \left(\frac{1 \text{ eV}}{1.60 \times 10^{-19} \text{ J}} \right)$$

$$= 0.534 \ \text{eV}$$

---

7   Find the wavelength emitted in the transition from the $n = 3$ to the $n = 2$ vibrational state.

7
$$\lambda = \frac{1240 \text{ eV} \cdot \text{nm}}{\Delta E (\text{eV})}$$

$$= \frac{1240 \text{ eV} \cdot \text{nm}}{0.534 \ \text{eV}}$$

$$= 2320 \text{ nm}$$

---

8   Find the difference in the energy levels from the nth to the ground state and equate it to hf.

8 $E = (n + \frac{1}{2})hf_{vib}$
$\Delta E = E_n - E_0 = [(n + \frac{1}{2}) - \frac{1}{2}]hf_{vib}$
$\qquad = n(hf_{vib}) = hf$

---

9   Substitute $f = c/\lambda$ and solve for n.

9 $nf_{vib} = f = \dfrac{c}{\lambda}$

$$n = \frac{c}{f_{vib} \cdot \lambda}$$

---

10 The visible spectrum ranges approximately from $\lambda = 400$ nm to $\lambda = 700$ nm. Substitute both these values in the above.

For $\lambda = 400$ nm

$$n = \frac{3 \times 10^8 \text{ m} \cdot \text{s}^{-1}}{(1.29 \times 10^{14} \text{ Hz})(400 \times 10^{-9} \text{ m})}$$
$$= 5.81$$

For $\lambda = 700$ nm

$$n = \frac{3 \times 10^8 \text{ m} \cdot \text{s}^{-1}}{(1.29 \times 10^{14} \text{ Hz})(700 \times 10^{-9} \text{ m})}$$
$$= 3.32$$

In order to obtain visible radiation, the transitions would have to be from $n = 5$ to the ground state and $n = 4$ to the ground state.

$n = 6$ would yield 388 nm and

$n = 7$ would yield 332 nm (not in the visible spectrum)

$n = 5$ yields 465 nm

$n = 4$ yields 581 nm

44

Nuclear and High-energy Physics

CHAPTER SUMMARY

The development of nuclear physics is presented in a historical perspective, from the work of Thomson and Rutherford up to the discovery of fundamental particles in high-energy physics. After reviewing the structure and properties of nuclei, radioactivity and nuclear stability are discussed. Radioactive transformation may be naturally occurring or the result of nuclear reactions, made possible by the invention of particle accelerators, in which nuclei are bombarded with alpha particles, protons and deuterons. Some nuclear reactions produce light mass particles, such as alpha or beta particles; nuclear fission, on the other hand, results in several different heavier elements. Radiation and the life sciences is also discussed.

BASIC TERMS — *Give definitions or meanings for the following:*

nucleus (44-I)
nuclear spin (44-1)
proton (44-1)
neutron (44-1)
nucleon (44-1)
mass defect (44-1)
atomic mass unit (44-1)
nuclear force (44-1)
atomic number (44-1)
mass number (44-1)
neutron number (44-1)
isotope (44-1)
nuclide (44-1)
binding energy (44-1)
radioactivity (44-2)
neutrino (44-3)
beta particle (44-3)
gamma ray (44-3)
decay constant (44-3)
half-life (44-3)
activity (44-3)
alpha particle (44-3)
lifetime (44-3)
becquerel (44-3)
curie (44-3)
relative biological effectiveness (RBE) (44-4)

nuclear reaction (44-5)
reaction energy (44-5)
threshold energy (44-5)
chain reaction (44-6)
nuclear fission (44-6)
nuclear reactor (44-6)
nuclear fusion (44-7)
particle accelerator (44-8)
cyclotron (44-8)
synchrotron (44-8)
pair production (44-9)
muon (44-9)
pion (44-9)
neutron (44-9)
positron (44-9)
meson (44-9)
hyperon (44-10)
boson (44-10)
fermion (44-10)
quantum chromodynamics (44-10)
lepton (44-10)
baryon (44-10)
hadron (44-10)
quark (44-10)
high energy physics (44-10)

PROGRAMMED QUIZ

1 What component of the atom is each associated with: Thomson, Rutherford and Chadwick?

1 Thomson "discovered" the electron, Rutherford concluded that the positive charge of the atom is concentrated in a small volume which he called the nucleus, and Chadwick "discovered" the neutron.

2 Compare the diameter of the nucleus to that of the atom.

2 The diameter of the nucleus is about 100,000 times smaller than the diameter of the atom.

3 Do the nuclei of all atoms have the same radius?

3 No, the radius depends on the mass number, $r = r_0 A^{1/3}$, where $r_0 = 1.2 \times 10^{-15}$ m. Note, the surface of a nucleus is not a sharp boundary, and these values correspond to the approximate radii.

4 What about the density of all nuclei?

4 All nuclei have approximately the same density.

5 Are the particles in the nucleus in motion? What is the experimental verification for this?

5 The particles are in motion; this can be determined from the hyperfine structure — the splitting of spectrum lines into a series of very closely spaced lines.

6 What do A, N and Z represent? How are they related?

6 A is the total number of nucleons (protons and neutrons), N the neutron number (number of neutrons) and Z the atomic number (total number of protons); $A = Z + N$.

7 What is the binding energy? How can it be determined?

7 The energy needed to pull apart a nucleus into its separate nucleons. Since the nuclei of all elements have less mass than the separated protons and neutrons would have, we can find the mass defect by comparing the mass of the nucleus with the masses of its constituents and then determine the equivalent energy. This is the binding energy.

8 What do the numbers in $^{200}_{80}$Hg represent?

8
$A = 200$ (mass number)
$Z = 80$ (atomic number)
$N = A - Z = 120$ (neutron number)

9 What are some features of the nuclear force?

9 Does not depend on charge, is of short range, is stronger than the electrical forces, prevents a nucleon from interacting simultaneously with all other nucleons but only with those in its immediate vicinity and favors the binding of pairs.

10 Since a beta particle is an electron, how can it be emitted from a nucleus which is composed of protons and neutrons?

10 A neutron in the nucleus is transformed into a proton, an electron and a neutrino. Note: A beta particle does not come into existence until it leaves the nucleus.

11 What is the technique of carbon dating?

11 Plants or animals take ^{14}C (an unstable isotope) from the atmosphere. When the organism dies, it stops taking in carbon and the ^{14}C in the remains decays. By measuring the proportion of ^{14}C left, one can determine how long ago the organism died.

12 How can positively charged particles penetrate the nucleus which is positively charged?

12 They must be accelerated to high energies and then travel with very high speeds in order to avoid being repelled or deflected by the nucleus.

13 In high energy physics, how are particles classified according to their properties?

13 On the basis of mass, charge and spin as electrons, mesons (particles having mass intermediate between that of electrons and nucleons) and baryons (nucleons and particles more massive than nucleons).

14 How can we detect radioactive isotopes in a body?

14 The location and concentration can be detected by measuring the radiation emitted.

15 Is exposure to any amount of radiation harmful?

15 No one knows what a safe level of radiation exposure is, but we are constantly exposed to radiation from sunlight, cosmic rays and natural radioactivity. Available evidence indicates that exposure to the extent of 10 to 100 times that from natural sources is rarely harmful.

16 How are the isotopes of an element similar? How do they differ?

16 Isotopes have the same atomic number, therefore they have the same electron structure which means that they have the same chemical behavior. They have different numbers of neutrons, therefore, they have different mass numbers.

17
Fill in the chart.

Radiation	Symbol	Mass	Charge
alpha particles			
beta particles			
gamma rays			

17

Radiation	Symbol	Mass	Charge
alpha particles	α or ^4_2He	4 H or 6.62×10^{-27} kg	$+2e$
beta particles	β or $^0_{-1}e$	m_e	$-1e$
gamma rays	γ	0	0

18 What are the four classes of interaction in order from weakest to strongest?

18 Gravitational, weak, electromagnetic and strong.

MAIN IDEAS

The nucleus, composed of protons and neutrons (except for hydrogen which has one proton and no neutrons), contains most of the total mass of an atom. Protons and neutrons, referred to as nucleons, have approximately the same mass. The atomic number Z denotes the total number of protons and, in a neutral atom, it is equal to the number of electrons. The neutron number N denotes the number of neutrons. The mass number A denotes the total number of nucleons. Thus in any nucleus, $A = Z + N$.

Although the "surface" of a nucleus is not a sharp boundary, the radii of nuclei are given by $r = r_0 A^{1/3}$, where r_0 is an empirical constant equal to 1.2×10^{-15} m and A is the mass number. Thus, the volume of a nucleus is given by $4/3\pi(1.2 \times 10^{-15} \text{ m})^3 A$. It follows that all nuclei have approximately the same density. Nucleons conform to a shell model, exhibit spin and angular momentum and obey the Pauli exclusion principle.

The symbol $^A_Z X$ denotes a nucleus, where X is the chemical symbol for the element or particle, Z the number of protons and A the mass number. Thus, $^{23}_{11}\text{Na}$ refers to sodium which has an atomic number of 11 (number of protons), a mass number A of 23 and a neutron number N of 12. A nuclide refers to a nucleus which has a particular value of Z and N. Nuclei which have the same atomic number but different numbers of neutrons are called isotopes. There are three known isotopes of hydrogen. Hydrogen ^1_1H is denoted as protium, it contains one proton and no neutrons. Deuterium ^2_1H contains one proton and one neutron. Tritium ^3_1H is a radioactive isotope produced by a nuclear reaction. It contains one proton and two neutrons. The nuclei of hydrogen, deuterium and tritium are referred to as proton p, deuteron d and triton t.

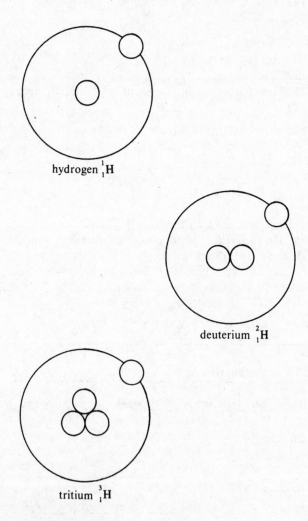

hydrogen ^1_1H

deuterium ^2_1H

tritium ^3_1H

One atomic mass unit u is defined as 1/12 the mass of a neutral carbon atom.

$$1 \text{ u} = 1.660566 \times 10^{-27} \text{ kg}$$
$$\text{mass of a proton} = m_p = 1.007276 \text{ u}$$
$$\text{mass of a neutron} = m_n = 1.008665 \text{ u}$$
$$\text{mass of an electron} = m_e = 0.000549 \text{ u}$$

On the basis of $E = mc^2$, the energy equivalent of 1 u = 931.5 MeV. The binding energy of a nucleus is the energy required to pull the nucleus completely apart into its separate nucleons. For nucleus $_Z^A X$ with atomic mass m_x, the binding energy is given by $(Zm_p + Nm_n + Zm_e - m_x)$ (931.5 meV), where m_p, m_n, m_e and m_x are given in atomic mass units u.

An alpha particle α is a helium atom stripped of its two electrons and is denoted as $_2^4$He. A beta particle β has the same charge and mass as an electron and is emitted from a nucleus with speeds approaching the speed of light. It is denoted as $_{-1}^0$e or β^{-1}. (It should be noted that β particles are created at the instant of emission. They have no independent existence in the nucleus.) Gamma rays γ are electromagnetic waves of extremely short wavelength. The notation for some of the basic particles in this chapter is as follows: electron $_{-1}^0$e, proton $_1^1$H, neutron $_0^1$n, deuterium $_1^2$H, tritium $_1^3$H, positron $_{+1}^0$e, alpha particle $_2^4$He.

A radioactive substance decays according to $N = N_0 e^{-\lambda t}$, where N_0 is the number of nuclei at an initial time $t = 0$, N is the number of nuclei remaining at time t and λ is called the decay constant. The half-life of a sample, denoted by $T_{1/2}$, is the time it takes for one-half the sample to decay; $T_{1/2} = \ln 2/\lambda = 0.693/\lambda$. The activity of a sample is the number of disintegrations per unit time. Activity $= \Delta N/\Delta t = -\lambda N$. The minus sign indicates that the population is decreasing with time. The unit of radioactivity is the curie; 1 Ci $= 3.70 \times 10^{10}$ decays $\cdot$ s^{-1}. The SI unit of activity is the becquerel (Bq); 1 Ci $= 3.70 \times 10^{10}$ Bq. The mean lifetime (or average lifetime) of a nucleus or of an unstable particle is related to the half-life $T_{1/2}$ as follows: $T_{mean} = 1/\lambda = T_{1/2}/\ln 2 = T_{1/2}/0.693$.

Since the number of atoms in a sample is required for problems involving disintegration, it should be noted that one mole of atoms is the number of atoms required to make an amount of material whose mass in grams is equal to the mass of a single atom in atomic mass units. The number of atoms or molecules in a mole is denoted by Avogadro's number $N_0 = 6.022 \times 10^{23}$ molecules $\cdot$ mol^{-1}.

Nuclear reactions may be initiated by the bombardment of a nucleus by energetic particles. The reaction may be described by reaction equations. For example, the bombardment of nitrogen with alpha particles results in an oxygen nucleus plus a proton, $_2^4$He $+ {}_7^{14}$N $\rightarrow {}_8^{17}$O $+ {}_1^1$H. Note that the sum of the atomic numbers on the left side is equal to the sum on the right side, i.e. $2 + 7 = 8 + 1$. Similarly, the mass number is conserved, $4 + 14 = 17 + 1$.

The total mass on each side of a nuclear reaction is not the same. The difference, called the nuclear reaction energy, is given by $\Delta E = (\Delta m)c^2$ where Δm is the difference in total mass before and after the reaction. If the sum of the final rest masses exceeds the sum of the initial rest masses, energy is absorbed in the reaction. If the final sum is less than the initial sum, energy is released. ΔE is referred to as the binding energy of the nucleus.

If an ion of charge $+q$ and mass m is accelerated by the electric field in the gap between the dees of a cyclotron, the angular velocity, maximum velocity and kinetic energy will be given by $\omega = Bq/m$, $v_{max} = BRq/m$ and $K = \frac{1}{2}m(q/m)^2 B^2 R^2$, where R = outside radius of the dees and B = magnetic field. Note: The electric field should reverse at regular intervals, each equal to the time required for the ion to make one revolution.

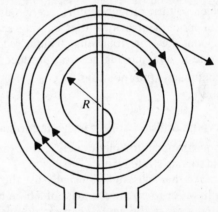

Fundamental particles. Cosmic rays consist largely of high speed protons. A positron was first observed during an investigation of cosmic rays. It has a mass equal to that of an electron. Its charge is equal in magnitude but opposite in sign. An electron and a positron are produced simultaneously by the high energy collision of charged particles or gamma protons with matter in a process called pair production. The inverse process is called positron annihilation — a positron collides with an electron producing two or three gamma photons: $e^{+1} + e^{-1} \rightarrow 2h\nu$; the photons have a total energy of $2mc^2$, where m is the electron rest mass.

Not only can the positron be produced by the collision of two particles as when 2 protons combine to form a deuteron and a position, $_1^1$H $+ {}_1^1$H $\rightarrow {}_1^2$H $+ {}_1^0$e, it can also be produced in the decay of some unstable nuclei. For example, $_{11}^{22}$Na is unstable, it has one less neutron than the stable $_{11}^{23}$Na isotope. Thus, $_{11}^{22}$Na $\rightarrow {}_{10}^{22}$Ne $+ {}_1^0$e.

High energy physics has uncovered fundamental particles which could be categorized in terms of the interactions in which they participate: strong, electromagnetic, weak and gravitational. Particles that experience strong interactions are called hadrons. These include the baryons (which includes protons and neutrons) and mesons. The baryons are composed of three quarks, and the mesons are quark–antiquark pairs. There are six different quarks having electric charges of magnitude $\frac{1}{3}$ and $\frac{2}{3}$ the electron charge. The hadrons are responsible for the nuclear force. Particles that experience weak interactions are called leptons. It is currently believed that there are six leptons and their anti-particles:

    electron

    neutrino

    muon

    neutrino

    tauon

    neutrino

The indivisible elementary particles are:

    six quarks,

    six leptons and their anti-particles,

    three guage bosons (which include the photon).

The transitory nature of fundamental particles can be illustrated by these two examples: The μ meson (muon) has a magnitude of charge equal to that of the electron. However, it could be + or −, and it has a mass 207 × electron mass. The muons have a short existence, and each decays into an electron of the same sign plus two neutrinos. The π meson (pion) could be positive, negative or neutral. The charged pions have a mass 273 × electron mass. The charged pions decay into muons with the same sign plus a neutrino. The neutral pion decays into two gamma ray photons.

Fission is a process by which heavy nuclei which have been bombarded by neutrons split into two lighter elements accompanied by the emission of neutrons. The resulting mass decrement is transformed into kinetic energy, $\Delta E = (\Delta m)c^2$. Although $^{235}_{92}U$ and $^{238}_{92}U$ may be split by the fast neutron, only $^{235}_{92}U$ can be split by a slow neutron.

A chain reaction in $^{235}_{92}U$ may be initiated by a single slow neutron which causes one uranium atom to undergo fission. During this process a large amount of energy and several neutrons are emitted. The emitted neutrons produce fission in neighboring uranium nuclei, which in turn produces more energy and the emission of more neutrons — thus causing a chain reaction. Consider the following fission reaction. Uranium and a slow moving neutron produce tellerium, zirconium and four neutrons, $^{235}_{92}U + ^{1}_{0}n \rightarrow ^{135}_{52}Te + ^{97}_{40}Zr + 4^{1}_{0}n$.

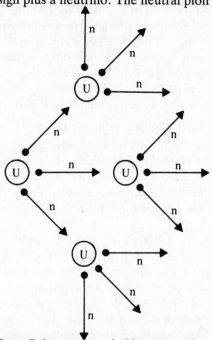

Fusion is the collision of light nuclei to form a more massive nucleus. It is accompanied by a mass decrement which is transformed into kinetic energy. An example is the fusion of two deuterons: $^{2}_{1}H + ^{2}_{1}H \rightarrow ^{4}_{2}He + energy$.

Problem solving strategy:

1 Remember that mass tables usually list the masses of neutral atoms including their full complements of electrons. In order to obtain the mass of a bare nucleus, you have to subtract the masses of these electrons. For example, the mass of the neutral carbon atom is 12.00000 u. The mass of an electron is 0.000549 u. Therefore, the mass of the bare nucleus is

$$m = 12.00000\ u - 6(0.000549\ u)$$
$$= 11.996706\ u.$$

2 Mass defect. The total mass of a nucleus is always less than the total mass of its constituent parts. The difference is the mass defect. For example, the total mass of the six protons and six neutrons in the carbon nucleus is

$$6(1.007276\ u) + 6\ (1.008665\ u) = 12.095646\ u.$$

The mass defect is

$$12.095646\ u - 11.996706\ u = 0.09894\ u.$$

3 Binding energy. The energy equivalent of the mass defect is the binding energy:

$$(0.09894\ u)\left(\frac{931.5\ MeV}{u}\right) = 92.16\ MeV.$$

4 Useful conversions:

$$1\ eV = 1.6 \times 10^{-19}\ J$$
$$1\ curie = 3.7 \times 10^{10}\ decays \cdot seconds^{-1}.$$

PROGRAMMED QUIZ

1 Compare the electrical and gravitational forces between two protons. Assume a separation of 2×10^{-15} m.

1

$$F_g = G \frac{m^2}{r^2}$$

$$= \frac{6.673 \times 10^{-11} \, \text{N} \cdot \text{m}^2 \cdot \text{kg}^{-2} \, (1.673 \times 10^{-27} \, \text{kg})^2}{(2 \times 10^{-15} \, \text{m})^2}$$

$$= 4.67 \times 10^{-35} \, \text{N}$$

$$F_e = \frac{1}{4\pi\epsilon_0} \frac{q^2}{r^2}$$

$$= \frac{9 \times 10^9 \, \text{N} \cdot \text{m}^2 \cdot \text{C}^{-2} (1.602 \times 10^{-19} \, \text{C})^2}{(2 \times 10^{-15} \, \text{m})^2}$$

$$= 57.7 \, \text{N}$$

Thus gravitational forces are negligible.

---

2 Calculate the energy equivalence of 1 u of matter (in MeV). Use

$$1 \, \text{u} = 1.660566 \times 10^{-27} \, \text{kg}$$
$$c = 2.998 \times 10^8 \, \text{m} \cdot \text{s}^{-1}$$
$$1 \, \text{eV} = 1.602 \times 10^{-19} \, \text{J}$$

2

$$E = mc^2$$

$$= (1.660566 \times 10^{-27} \, \text{kg})(2.998 \times 10^8 \, \text{m} \cdot \text{s}^{-1})^2$$

$$= 1.492 \times 10^{-10} \, \text{J}$$

$$\left(1.492 \times 10^{-10} \, \text{J} \right) \left(\frac{1 \, \text{eV}}{1.602 \times 10^{-19} \, \text{J}} \right)$$

$$= 9.315 \times 10^8 \, \text{eV}$$

$$= 931.5 \, \text{MeV}$$

---

3 What is the rest energy of an electron in MeV? of the proton?

3

$$m_e = 0.000549 \, \text{u}$$

This is equivalent to

$$0.000549 \, \text{u} \left(\frac{931.5 \, \text{MeV}}{1 \, \text{u}} \right)$$

$$= 0.511 \, \text{MeV}$$

$$m_p = 1.007276 \, \text{u}$$

This is equivalent to

$$1.007276 \, \text{u} \left(\frac{931.5 \, \text{MeV}}{1 \, \text{u}} \right)$$

$$= 938 \, \text{MeV}$$

---

4 Find the potential energy of an alpha particle 10^{-13} m away from a gold nucleus ($Z = 79$). Express the results in electron volts.

4 An alpha particle is a helium atom consisting of 2 protons and 2 neutrons.

$$U = \frac{1}{4\pi\epsilon_0} \cdot \frac{q_1 q_2}{r}$$

$$= \frac{9 \times 10^9 \, \text{N} \cdot \text{m}^2 \cdot \text{C}^{-2} (2 \times 1.602 \times 10^{-19} \, \text{C})(79 \times 1.602 \times 10^{-19} \, \text{C})}{10^{-13} \, \text{m}}$$

$$= 3.64 \times 10^{-13} \, \text{J}$$

$$= \left(3.64 \times 10^{-13} \, \text{J} \right) \left(\frac{1 \, \text{eV}}{1.602 \times 10^{-19} \, \text{J}} \right)$$

$$= 2.27 \, \text{MeV}$$

5 What is the radius of a $^{238}_{92}$U nucleus?

5
$$r = r_0 A^{1/3}$$
$$= 1.2 \times 10^{-15} \text{ m}(238)^{1/3}$$
$$= 7.44 \times 10^{-15} \text{ m}$$

---

6 Find the energy required to push an alpha particle to the "surface" of the $^{238}_{92}$U nucleus.

6
$$E = \frac{1}{4\pi\epsilon_0} \cdot \frac{q_1 q_2}{r}$$
$$= \frac{9 \times 10^9 \text{ N} \cdot \text{m}^2 \cdot \text{C}^{-2}(2 \times 1.602 \times 10^{-19} \text{ C})(92 \times 1.602 \times 10^{-19} \text{ C})}{(7.44 \times 10^{-15} \text{ m})}$$
$$= 5.71 \times 10^{-12} \text{ J}$$
$$= \left(5.71 \times 10^{-12} \text{ J} \right) \left(\frac{1 \text{eV}}{1.602 \times 10^{-19} \text{ J}} \right)$$
$$= 35.6 \text{ MeV}$$

---

7 Compute the density of a hydrogen nucleus. (All nuclei have approximately the same density. Mass of a proton = 1.673×10^{-27} kg.)

7
$$r = r_0 A^{1/3}$$
$$= 1.2 \times 10^{-15} \text{ m}(1)^{1/3}$$
$$= 1.2 \times 10^{-15} \text{ m}$$
$$\rho = \frac{m}{V} = \frac{m}{4/3 \, \pi r^3}$$
$$= \frac{1.673 \times 10^{-27} \text{ kg}}{4/3 \, \pi (1.2 \times 10^{-15} \text{ m})^3}$$
$$= 2.31 \times 10^{17} \text{ kg} \cdot \text{m}^{-3}$$

---

8 Calculate the mass defect and the binding energy of oxygen $^{16}_{8}$O.

8 mass defect
$$= (Zm_p + Nm_n + Zm_e - m_x), \text{ where}$$
m_p, m_n, m_e and m_x are the masses of the proton, neutron, electron and the atom, respectively,

$Zm_p =$	8.058208 u
$Nm_n =$	8.069320 u
$Zm_e =$	0.004392 u

16.131920 u

$- m_x = -$ 15.994910 u

mass defect = 0.137010 u

binding energy $= \left(0.137010 \text{ u} \right) \left(\frac{931.5 \text{ MeV}}{1 \text{ u}} \right)$

$= 127.6$ MeV

---

9 The half-life of radioactive carbon ^{14}C is 5568 yr. Find its decay constant.

9
$$T_{1/2} = \frac{0.693}{\lambda}$$
$$\lambda = \frac{0.693}{5568 \text{ yr}}$$
$$= 1.245 \times 10^{-4} \text{ yr}^{-1}$$

10 A prehistoric carbon specimen contains 0.1 as much ^{14}C as an equal amount of carbon in living matter. Find the approximate age of the specimen.

10
$$N = N_0 e^{-\lambda t}$$

$$(0.1 N_0) = N_0 e^{-\lambda t}$$

$$0.1 = e^{-1.245 \times 10^{-4} \, yr^{-1}(t)}$$

Take ln of each side.

$$-2.303 = -1.245 \times 10^{-4} \, yr^{-1}(t)$$
$$t = 18,500 \, yr$$

---

11 $^{24}_{11}Na$ undergoes β^{-1} decay. What is the daughter nuclide?

11
$$^{24}_{11}Na \rightarrow \, ^{0}_{-1}e + \, ^{n}_{m}X$$
$$11 = -1 + m$$
$$\therefore m = 12$$
$$24 = 0 + n$$
$$\therefore n = 24$$

$$^{24}_{12}X \equiv \, ^{24}_{12}Mg$$

---

12 In frames 12-16, complete the following nuclear equations: $^{14}_{7}N + \, ^{4}_{2}He \rightarrow \, ^{17}_{8}O + \, ^{n}_{m}X$

12
$$7 + 2 = 8 + m$$
$$\therefore m = 1$$
$$14 + 4 = 17 + n$$
$$\therefore n = 1$$

$$^{n}_{m}X \equiv \, ^{1}_{1}H \, (proton)$$

13
$$^{30}_{15}P \rightarrow \, ^{30}_{14}Si + \, ^{n}_{m}X$$

13
$$15 = 14 + m$$
$$\therefore m = 1$$
$$30 = 30 + n$$
$$\therefore n = 0$$

$$^{0}_{1}X \equiv \, ^{0}_{+1}e \, (positron)$$

14
$$^{14}_{7}N + \, ^{1}_{0}n \rightarrow \, ^{12}_{6}C + \, ^{n}_{m}X$$

14
$$7 + 0 = 6 + m$$
$$\therefore m = 1$$
$$14 + 1 = 12 + n$$
$$\therefore n = 3$$

$$^{3}_{1}X \equiv \, ^{3}_{1}H \, (tritium)$$

15
$$^{9}_{4}Be + \, ^{4}_{2}He \rightarrow \, ^{12}_{6}C + \, ^{n}_{m}X$$

15
$$4 + 2 = 6 + m$$
$$\therefore m = 0$$
$$9 + 4 = 12 + n$$
$$\therefore n = 1$$

$$^{1}_{0}X \equiv \, ^{1}_{0}n \, (neutron)$$

16
$$^{3}_{1}H \rightarrow \, ^{3}_{2}He + \, ^{n}_{m}X$$

16
$$1 = 2 + m$$
$$\therefore m = -1$$
$$3 = 3 + n$$
$$\therefore n = 0$$

$$^{0}_{-1}X \equiv \, ^{0}_{-1}e \, (beta \, particle)$$

17 Two gamma-ray photons are produced in positron annihilation. Find the energy of each photon.

17 In positron annihilation, the total energy of the gamma-ray photons is $2mc^2$, where m is the electron rest mass. $\therefore$ The energy of each photon is mc^2.

$$E = mc^2$$

$$= (9.11 \times 10^{-31} \text{ kg})(3 \times 10^8 \text{ m} \cdot \text{s}^{-1})^2$$

$$= 8.2 \times 10^{-14} \text{ J}$$

---

18 Find its frequency.

18 $E = hf$

$$f = \frac{8.20 \times 10^{-14} \text{ J}}{6.63 \times 10^{-34} \text{ J} \cdot \text{s}} = 1.24 \times 10^{20} \text{ Hz}$$

---

19 Find its wavelength.

19

$$\lambda = \frac{c}{f} = \frac{3 \times 10^8 \text{ m} \cdot \text{s}^{-1}}{1.24 \times 10^{20} \text{ s}^{-1}} = 2.42 \times 10^{-12} \text{ m}$$

---

20 Compute the energy liberated in the following fusion reaction:

$$^2_1\text{H} + ^2_1\text{H} \rightarrow ^4_2\text{He} + E$$

20 mass defect

$$\Delta m = [\text{mass of } (^2_1\text{H} + ^2_1\text{H}) - \text{mass } ^4_2\text{He}]$$

$$\text{mass of } 2\ (^2_1\text{H}) = 4.02820 \text{ u}$$

$$- \text{ mass of } ^4_2\text{He} = -\ 4.00260 \text{ u}$$

$$\Delta m = 0.0256 \text{ u}$$

$$E = 0.0256 \text{ u}\left(\frac{931.5 \text{ MeV}}{1 \text{ u}}\right)$$

$$= 23.8 \text{ MeV}$$

---

21 Identify the unknown particle (and number) in the following nuclear reaction:

$$^{235}_{92}\text{U} + ^1_0\text{n} \rightarrow ^{141}_{56}\text{Ba} + ^{92}_{36}\text{Kr} + ^n_m\text{X}$$

21

$$92 + 0 = 56 + 36 + m$$
$$\therefore m = 0$$
$$235 + 1 = 141 + 92 + n$$
$$\therefore n = 3$$

Since a neutron struck a heavy nucleus and broke it into two heavy fragments with the release of more neutrons, the answer is $3^1_0\text{X} \equiv 3^1_0\text{n}$, a typical fission reaction.

---

22 The magnetic field in a cyclotron that is accelerating protons is 1.4 T. What is the frequency of the applied alternating voltage?

22

$$r_1 = \frac{mv_1}{Bq} = \frac{m(2\pi r_1 f)}{Bq}$$

$$f = \frac{Bq}{2\pi m}$$

$$= \frac{(1.4 \text{ T})\ (1.602 \times 10^{-19} \text{ C})}{2\pi(1.673 \times 10^{-27} \text{ kg})}$$

$$= 2.13 \times 10^7 \text{ Hz}$$

23 What is the maximum velocity of the proton if the maximum radius is 0.3 m?

23

$$v_{max} = BR\left(\frac{q}{m}\right)$$

$$= \frac{(1.4\ T)\ (0.3\ m)\ (1.602 \times 10^{-19}\ C)}{1.673 \times 10^{-27}\ kg}$$

$$= 4.02 \times 10^7\ m \cdot s^{-1}$$

---

24 Consider the nuclear reaction represented by $^2_1H + ^9_4Be \rightarrow ^7_3Li + ^4_2He$.
Find the rest mass of
$^2_1H + ^9_4Be$.
Atomic mass of deuterium H = 2.01410 u.
Atomic mass of beryllium Be = 9.01218 u.
Mass of electron = 0.000549 u.

24

^2_1H has a mass of
    2.01410 u + 0.000549 u
    = 2.014649 u.
^9_4Be has a mass of
    9.01218 u + 4(0.000549 u)
    = 9.014376 u.
Total mass = 2.014649 u + 9.014376 u
             = 11.029025 u

---

25 Find the rest mass of
$^7_3Li + ^4_2He$.
Atomic mass of lithium Li = 7.017647 u.
Atomic mass of helium He = 4.00260 u.

25

^7_3Li has a mass of
    7.01600 u + 3 (0.000549 u)
    = 7.017647 u.
^4_2He has a mass of
    4.00260 u + 2 (0.000549 u)
    = 4.003698 u.
Total mass = 7.017647 u + 4.003698 u
             = 11.021345 u.

---

26 Find the mass decrease in the nuclear reaction and its corresponding energy release in eV.

26 The mass decrease is
    11.029025 u − 11.021345 u
= 0.00768 u;

$$0.00768\ u \left(\frac{931.5\ MeV}{1\ u}\right)$$

= 7.15 MeV.

---

27 What is the minimum or threshold energy of the reaction? This can be obtained by calculating the Coulomb potential energy U when the proton is at a radius r of ^9_4Be. Calculate r.

27

$$r = r_0 A^{1/3}$$

$$= 1.2 \times 10^{-15}\ m\ (9)^{1/3}$$

$$= 2.50 \times 10^{-15}\ m$$

---

28 Calculate the Coulomb potential at this radius.

28

$$U = \frac{1}{4\pi\epsilon_0}\ \frac{q_1 q_2}{r} = \frac{1}{4\pi\epsilon_0} \cdot \frac{(e)\ (4e)}{r}$$

$$= \frac{(9 \times 10^9\ N - m^2 \cdot C^{-2})\ (4)\ (1.60 \times 10^{-19}\ C)^2}{2.50 \times 10^{-15}\ m}$$

$$= 3.69 \times 10^{-13}\ J$$

$$= 3.69 \times 10^{-13}\ J \left(\frac{1\ eV}{1.60 \times 10^{-19}\ J}\right)$$

$$= 2.31\ MeV$$

STEP BY STEP SOLUTIONS OF PROBLEMS

Problem 1 Calculate the binding energy of deuterium. The atomic mass = 2.01410 u, m_p = 1.007276 u, m_n = 1.008665 u, m_e = 0.000549 u, 1 u = 1.660566×10^{-27} kg.

1 The total mass of the nucleus is less than the total mass of its constituent parts. This difference is denoted as the mass defect. The energy equivalent of the mass defect is called the binding energy. First find the mass of the bare nucleus by subtracting the mass of one electron from the atomic mass.

1

$$
\begin{array}{r}
\text{mass of deuterium atom} = 2.01410 \ \text{u} \\
\text{mass of one electron} = 0.000549 \ \text{u} \\
\hline
\text{mass of deuterium nucleus} = 2.013551 \ \text{u}
\end{array}
$$

2 Find the combined mass of 1 proton and 1 neutron.

2

$$
\begin{array}{r}
\text{mass of one proton} = 1.007276 \ \text{u} \\
\text{mass of one neutron} = 1.008665 \ \text{u} \\
\hline
\text{mass of nucleons} = 2.015941 \ \text{u}
\end{array}
$$

3 Find the mass defect by subtracting the mass of the deuterium nucleus from the mass of the nucleons.

3

$$
\begin{array}{r}
\text{mass of nucleons} = 2.015941 \ \text{u} \\
\text{mass of deuterium nucleus} = 2.013551 \ \text{u} \\
\hline
\text{mass defect} = 0.002390 \ \text{u}
\end{array}
$$

4 Find the energy equivalent of the mass defect, i.e. the binding energy of deuterium, by using the energy equivalent of 1 u = 931.5 MeV.

4

$$0.002390 \ \text{u} \left(\frac{931.5 \ \text{MeV}}{1 \ \text{u}} \right)$$

$$= 2.23 \ \text{MeV}$$

Thus, 2.23 MeV would be required to pull the deuterium nucleus apart into two separate nucleons.

Problem 2 Consider the nuclear reaction of deuterium and tritium. $^2_1\text{H} + {}^3_1\text{H} \rightarrow {}^4_2\text{He} + {}^1_0\text{n} + (\Delta E)$, where $\Delta E = (\Delta m)c^2$ and Δm denotes the difference in the mass before and after the reaction. Find ΔE, the energy liberated in this reaction in MeV and in joules.

5 Check on the conservation of charge and mass number.

5 The sum of the atomic numbers before the reaction (1 + 1) is equal to the sum of the atomic numbers after the reaction (2 + 0). Similarly for mass number: 2 + 3 = 4 + 1.

6 Write the expression for ΔE in terms of the mass of the particles. Use $\Delta E = (\Delta m)c^2$.

6
$\Delta E = [\text{atomic mass } ({}^2_1\text{H} + {}^1_1\text{H}) - \text{atomic mass } ({}^4_2\text{He} + {}^1_0\text{n})]c^2$, where c = speed of light.

7 Find the atomic mass of $^2_1\text{H} + {}^3_1\text{H}$.

7

$$
\begin{array}{r}
\text{atomic mass of } {}^2_1\text{H} = 2.01410 \ \text{u} \\
\text{atomic mass of } {}^3_1\text{H} = 3.01605 \ \text{u} \\
\hline
\text{atomic mass of } {}^2_1\text{H} + {}^3_1\text{H} = 5.03015 \ \text{u}
\end{array}
$$

8 Find the atomic mass of $_2^4\text{He} + _0^1\text{n}$.

8
$$\text{atomic mass of } _2^4\text{He} = 4.00260 \text{ u}$$
$$\text{atomic mass of } _0^1\text{n} = 1.00867 \text{ u}$$
$$\text{atomic mass of } _2^4\text{He} + _0^1\text{n} = \overline{5.01127 \text{ u}}$$

---

9 Find the mass differential between $_1^2\text{H} + _1^3\text{H}$ and $_2^4\text{He} + _0^1\text{n}$ and convert to MeV.

9
$$\text{atomic mass of } _1^2\text{H} + _1^3\text{H} = 5.03015 \text{ u}$$
$$\text{atomic mass of } _2^4\text{He} + _0^1\text{n} = \underline{5.01127 \text{ u}}$$
$$(\Delta m) = 0.01888 \text{ u}$$
$$= 0.01888 \text{ u} \left(\frac{931.5 \text{ MeV}}{1 \text{ u}} \right)$$
$$= 17.6 \text{ MeV}$$

---

10 Convert to joules.

10
$$17.6 \times 10^6 \text{ eV} \left(\frac{1.602 \times 10^{-19} \text{ J}}{1 \text{ eV}} \right)$$
$$= 2.82 \times 10^{-12} \text{ J}$$

Problem 3 A certain radioactive sample gives 5 counts (i.e. disintegrations) per second. After a 24 hour period the count rate falls to 2 per second. Calculate the half-life of the radioactive substance.

---

11 Express the activity at $t = 0$ in terms of λ and N_0.

11
$$\text{activity} = \frac{\Delta N}{\Delta t} = -5 \text{ count} \cdot \text{s}^{-1} = \lambda N_0$$

---

12 Express the activity 24 hours later in terms of λ and N_{24}.

12
$$\text{activity} = -2 \text{ count} \cdot \text{s}^{-1} = \lambda N_{24}$$

---

13 Divide the equation in frame 12 by the equation in frame 11.

13
$$\frac{-2 \text{ count} \cdot \text{s}^{-1}}{-5 \text{ count} \cdot \text{s}^{-1}} = \frac{\lambda N_{24}}{\lambda N_0}$$
$$\frac{N_{24}}{N_0} = 0.4$$

---

14 Find the decay constant by using $N = N_0 e^{-\lambda t}$.

14
$$N_{24} = N_0 e^{-\lambda(24 \text{ hr})}$$
$$\frac{N_{24}}{N_0} = e^{-\lambda(24 \text{ hr})}$$
$$0.4 = e^{-\lambda(24 \text{ hr})}$$
$$\ln 0.4 = -\lambda(24 \text{ hr}) \ln e$$
$$-0.916 = -(24 \text{ hr}) \lambda$$
$$\lambda = 0.0382 \text{ hr}^{-1}$$

---

15 Find the half-life by using $T_{1/2} = 0.693/\lambda$.

15
$$T_{1/2} = \frac{0.693}{0.0382 \text{ hr}^{-1}} = 18.1 \text{ hr}$$

PROGRAMMED TEST

1 **Problem 1** Radium $^{226}_{88}$Ra has a half-life of 1620 years. a) What is the decay constant? b) How many atoms are there in a source of 1.0 g? c) What is the activity of the source in curies?

1 **Answer**

1.35×10^{-11} s^{-1}, 2.66×10^{21}, 0.971 Ci.

If you solved this problem correctly, go to frame 5. If you could not solve this problem, go through frames 2–4.

2 Find the decay constant. Note: 1 yr $= 3.16 \times 10^7$ s.

2

$$T_{1/2} = \frac{0.693}{\lambda}$$

$$\lambda = \frac{0.693}{1620 \text{ yr } (3.16 \times 10^7 \text{ s} \cdot \text{yr}^{-1})}$$

$$= 1.35 \times 10^{-11} \text{ s}^{-1}$$

---

3 Find the number of radium atoms in a source of 1 g. One mole of radium is the number of radium atoms in 226 g of radium. One mole of any substance contains 6.02×10^{23} molecules (Avogadro's number).

3

$$N_0 = N_A \left(\frac{1 \text{ mol}}{226 \text{ g}} \right)$$

$$= 6.02 \times 10^{23} \frac{\text{atoms}}{\text{mol}} \left(\frac{1 \text{ mol}}{226 \text{ g}} \right)$$

$$= 2.66 \times 10^{21} \text{ atom} \cdot \text{g}^{-1}$$

N_0 denotes the number of atom $\cdot$ g^{-1} at initial time $t = 0$.

---

4 Find the activity.

4

Activity $= -\lambda N_0$
$= -1.35 \times 10^{-11}$ s^{-1} $(2.66 \times 10^{21}$ atom $\cdot$ g$^{-1})$
$= -3.59 \times 10^{10}$ atom $\cdot$ s^{-1} $\cdot$ g^{-1}

$$= (3.59 \times 10^{10} \text{ atom} \cdot \text{s}^{-1} \cdot \text{g}^{-1}) \left(\frac{1 \text{ Ci}}{3.7 \times 10^{10} \text{ atoms} \cdot \text{s}^{-1} \cdot \text{g}^{-1}} \right)$$

$= -0.971$ Ci

The minus sign indicates that the population is decreasing with time.

---

5 **Problem 2** How much energy would be required to add a proton to a nucleus with $Z = 91$ and $A = 234$? Express your results in joules and in MeV.

5 **Answer**

2.84×10^{-12} J, 17.7 MeV

If you solved this problem correctly, go to frame 9. If you could not solve this problem, go through frames 6–8.

6 Find the radius of the nucleus.

6

$$r = r_0 A^{1/3}$$
$$= 1.2 \times 10^{-15} \text{ m} (234)^{1/3}$$
$$= 7.39 \times 10^{-15} \text{ m}$$

---

7 As a proton moves towards a nucleus, it experiences a retarding force due to the inverse-square field of the positive charge. In order to enter the nucleus, the proton must have sufficient energy to overcome the potential barrier given by $U = q_1 q_2 / 4\pi\epsilon_0 r$, where ϵ_0 is the permittivity of free space $= 8.85 \times 10^{-12}$ C$^2 \cdot$ N$^{-1} \cdot$ m^{-2} and r is the radius of the nucleus. Note: $q_1 = 1.602 \times 10^{-19}$ C and $q_2 = 91(1.602 \times 10^{-19}$ C).

7

$$U = \frac{(1.602 \times 10^{-19} \text{ C}) (91 \times 1.602 \times 10^{-19} \text{ C})}{4\pi(8.85 \times 10^{-12} \text{ C}^2 \cdot \text{N}^{-1} \cdot \text{m}^{-2}) (7.39 \times 10^{-15} \text{ m})}$$

$$= 2.84 \times 10^{-12} \text{ J}$$